Recent Discoveries in Psychology

READINGS FOR THE INTRODUCTORY COURSE

KLINCK MEMORIAL LIBRARY
Concordia Teachers College
River Forest, Illinois 60305

Edited by **JAMES O. WHITTAKER**

The Pennsylvania State University

W. B. Saunders Company · Philadelphia · London · Toronto

1972

W. B. Saunders Company: West Washington Square
                          Philadelphia, Pa. 19105

                          12 Dyott Street
                          London, WC1A 1DB

                          1835 Yonge Street
                          Toronto 7, Ontario

Recent Discoveries in Psychology   ISBN 0-7216-9325-3

© 1972 by W. B. Saunders Company. Copyright under the International Copyright Union. All rights reserved. This book is protected by copyright. No part of it may be reproduced, stored in a retrieval system, or transmitted in any form or by any means, electronic, mechanical, photocopying, recording, or otherwise, without written permission from the publisher. Made in the United States of America. Press of W. B. Saunders Company. Library of Congress catalog card number 78-168602.

Print No: 9   8   7   6   5   4   3   2   1

TO THE PROFESSOR

Why another reader to add to the proliferation of such books designed for the introductory course? First, we wanted to present recent research, and preferably significant studies that have not yet been discussed in the major textbooks in the field. Second, we felt a need for articles of general rather than very limited interest. And third, the topics presented needed to be those likely to involve and stimulate the beginning student.

How well we have succeeded in meeting these objectives will be determined largely by those using this book. Nevertheless, only one of the articles which appear here was published prior to 1960, and nearly half of the articles have been published or presented at meetings within the past three years. In addition, most of the articles are of general content rather than concerned with isolated esoteric bits of information. Finally, on the basis of our own contact with beginning students over the past fifteen years, we feel that the majority of the articles should be of considerable interest to the student.

The selections are distributed over the major content areas of introductory psychology, and essentially the volume was compiled to correlate with the organization of Whittaker's Introduction to Psychology, 2nd Edition (W. B. Saunders Co., Philadelphia, 1970). Of course, it could easily be used as a supplement to any of the major texts in the field, or even without a textbook. However, regardless of how it is used, our feeling is that any reader should supplement and extend the textbook and lectures for a course rather than repeat material usually presented in class or the text (i.e., "classic" studies). Consequently, we have avoided including many of the well-known and widely quoted articles usually seen in readers for the beginning course.

Probably the best use of this book would be to assign the majority of the readings toward the end of the course. Occasional articles can be assigned as the course progresses, but most of these can be profitably read only after the student has developed a basic background in the particular areas involved. Thus our idea is to give the student a picture of some of the significant recent research in the field, and to stimulate "where do we go from here" discussions toward the end of the course.

Because of space limitations, we have not been able to include many of the excellent articles we came across in our literature search, and undoubtedly we have overlooked some articles which should have been included. From those who notice such shortcomings we would most appreciate suggestions for contributions to the next edition. Keeping up with a field as vast as psychology is no easy task. Hence, any editor of a reader such as this must rely at least in part on the good judgment of colleagues.

To those colleagues who made suggestions for the articles included in this volume, we extend our thanks. We are also grateful to the authors of articles we have included and to the journals and other sources for granting permission to reproduce them here. In addition, we are indebted to Rosemary Anderson who typed much of the manuscript, and to James Snyder of North Dakota State University who assisted with many of the chores that go into the preparation of such a book. Finally, our thanks are extended to Sandra J. Whittaker who read most of the articles and made thoughtful comments about their content and quality.

JAMES O. WHITTAKER

TO THE STUDENT

This book contains some of the newest and most exciting research in psychology. In it we will examine such topics as what happens when the living brain is split in half, how behavior is affected by chemicals injected directly into the brain, the basis for the "generation gap," and the effect of depriving a person of dreams. We will also look at recent studies concerning how people in preliterate cultures react to facial expressions in emotion, how learning may be chemically transferred from one organism to another, and some psychological alternatives to war.

All the articles which appear here, except one, have been published within the last ten years and almost half have appeared within the last three years. They are for the most part general in orientation rather than highly specific and technical. All of the research methods currently in use by psychologists are represented, but most of the studies are based on objective, rigorously controlled laboratory studies.

Before reading the articles you will need a brief background or introduction to the area under discussion. This you can secure from your textbook and/or the lectures in your course. You will also need to know something about how to read a scientific or technical article, and in addition you will need a very basic understanding of how psychologists quantify and assess the results of their research. This we propose to give you here.

HOW TO READ A SCIENTIFIC ARTICLE

To read a scientific article you must first understand what the scientist tries to do when he prepares the report, and second, you need to know something about the different ways of presenting scientific information. In this volume we have included review articles, theoretical papers, and research reports of individual studies. For the most part you will have little difficulty in reading the review articles or theoretical papers. On occasion you may have to look up the definition of an unfamiliar technical term, and for this purpose the glossary of your textbook can be used or you can refer to a good dictionary of psychology, which can be found in almost every college library.

Review articles, such as Grossman's "Exploring the Brain with Chemicals," are designed to summarize the work that has been done on a particular topic. Usually they do not contain the detailed information on procedure and results found in research reports of individual studies. Theoretical papers, on the other hand, such as Coons' "Psychology and Society," differ in that they sometimes set forth hypotheses for testing, present theories which tie together existing knowledge and suggest directions for further research, or discuss some problem of a more practical or professional nature facing psychologists.

The research report usually presents the results of only one or two experiments. It is typically quite brief and very precise in the terminology and facts reported. Like the other kinds of papers mentioned above, it is not intended as a source of entertainment. It is intended to convey to the reader the complete and accurate details of a particular study or group of studies. Unlike the theoretical or review paper, a research report sometimes does not enable the reader to have recourse to other papers in order to clarify his understanding of the work. The research report must stand on its own two feet, so to speak, since it is often the sole source of information about procedures followed or results obtained.

Ideally information in a research report should be presented so that a reader has enough facts to replicate the study, should he so desire. Most research reports are quite conventional in terms of their organization, and it would be well to keep this organization in mind when reading papers of this type. Almost always the reader is presented first with a brief abstract of the paper. In the papers included here the editor has written an abstract for each paper and these are grouped together at the beginning of the individual sections. These abstracts should be read by the students before they start to read the individual papers. They summarize succinctly the major findings or points, and will tend to give some direction to the student's thinking as he goes through the actual report.

Research reports usually begin with a statement of the problem. Typically the problem section starts broad and ends narrow, and there is almost always a discussion of related studies which tend to place the current one in proper context. These related studies form the "rationale" for the study. That is, they constitute the basis out of which the idea for the current study emerged. Somewhere toward the end of the problem section the reader will typically find a statement of the hypothesis or hypotheses to be investigated. The hypothesis is simply an idea, supposition, or tentative conclusion stated in a very precise way so that it can be quantitatively evaluated in the study.

Next, the methods or procedures used in the study are reported. Here the investigator tells the reader precisely what he did and why. Ideally, as noted above, enough information should be given so that someone else could repeat the experiment exactly, if he wished to do so. The method section usually describes the subjects involved—their age, sex, educational background, and so on. Any details about the subjects which conceivably could have influenced the results of the experiment must be reported. Also described is any apparatus used in the experiment. Again, sufficient details are provided so that the reader knows exactly the type, size, dimensions, and other pertinent characteristics of the materials employed.

The procedures used in the experiment are set forth step-by-step from the time the subject walks in the door until he leaves. What he is told about the experiment must be reported as well as any instructions given to him.

The methods or procedures section is followed by a section in which the results of the experiment are presented. Here the reader finds descriptions of the statistics involved in analyzing the data, and a summary of the data, usually with confidence or significance levels indicated. The reader does not have to be a statistician to understand these but he does need a basic understanding of how we evaluate the results of such studies. We will take this up briefly in the following section.

After the results are presented, the reader is provided with a discussion of the results which typically refers back to the problem and hypotheses discussed at the beginning of the report. Limitations of the study are usually presented here, as well as implications of the study for further research. Finally, at the end, the reader is presented with a list of references referred to in the body of the report.

This then is the typical organization of a research report in psychology: (1) Abstract, (2) Statement of the Problem and Hypotheses, (3) Methods or Procedures, (4) Results, (5) Discussion, and (6) References. As the reader goes through papers of this type he should keep this outline in mind so that after reading the report he can answer the following questions: What was the problem being investigated? What was the specific hypothesis (or hypotheses) under study? What kinds of subjects were used? How many? With what characteristics? What apparatus was employed? Exactly what procedures were followed? What were subjects told about the nature of the experiment and what were they instructed to do? What were the main results of the experiment? Was the hypothesis substantiated? What were the significance levels reported? What did the author conclude from the study? Did he suggest any further research that should be done?

STATISTICS IN PSYCHOLOGICAL REPORTS

In the papers that follow, the student will find a number of references to statistics. Actually, the statistical methods employed in these papers fall into two broad categories—descriptive and inferential. It is not important for the beginning student to know how to calculate these but it is important to know enough to become an intelligent consumer of statistics. We cannot, of course, in the short space of this section, do a comprehensive job of making the student a statistician or even a very good consumer, but at least we should be able to offer a few guidelines which will be of help in interpreting and evaluating the data presented.

Descriptive statistics are used to summarize data so that we need not review all the raw data in any experiment. In many cases we need to have some idea of the average performance of a group or groups. In other cases, we need something which will allow us to compare the typical performance of two or more groups of subjects. Sometimes we also need a precise idea of the spread or variability in performance among subjects. For such purposes, descriptive statistics are typically used.

One such statistic, with which almost every student is familiar, is the mean or average. If we add together all the scores on a particular test, for example, and divide by the total number of scores, we obtain the mean. Another such statistic which gives us an idea about the central tendency of a distribution of scores is the median. The median is simply that score which exactly divides a distribution of scores in half. For example, if we arrange or rank all the scores on a test from high to low and count down to the score exactly in the middle, we have the median.

The standard deviation (σ) is a statistic which tells us something about the degree of variability in a set of scores. Mathematically the standard deviation is computed so that about 68 percent of the scores in *any* distribution lie from one standard deviation *below* the mean to one standard deviation *above*. Ninety-five percent of the scores lie from minus two standard deviations to plus two, and about 98 percent of the scores lie within the confines of three standard deviations. If a standard deviation is small, then, this means that the spread of scores must be small, while a large standard deviation means there is considerably more variability among the scores. For example, if the standard deviation on one test is 3 and the mean is 100, we find 68 percent of the scores between 97 and 103. However, if the standard deviation is 20, 68 percent of the scores would lie between 80 and 120. Clearly, there is more variability among the scores in the second case.

Inferential statistics are used mainly to give us an idea of the reliability of our data or, to put it another way, how confident we can be that our findings result from something other than chance. Many different kinds of inferential statistics are used by the authors of the papers in this volume. Some refer to a "t-test," others to "chi-square" and so on. The important thing for the beginning student to understand is not the particular statistic used but what the results of using that statistic mean.

For example, after reporting results an author will often indicate the confidence limits for these results as: ($p = <.01$), or ($p = <.05$). These figures are what the student needs to look at and be able to interpret. They refer to the degree of confidence we can place in the data reported. If, for example, it is reported that "one group was more active than that other ($p = <.01$)," this means that if we repeated the experiment in exactly the same way 100 times, it would come out roughly the same way in about 99 cases. In other words, we could be confident that our results were highly reliable and that they were not simply a chance occurrence. When ($p = <.05$) is reported, this means that in about 19 times out of 20 (or 95 out of 100) we would obtain similar results. Thus, although we cannot be quite as confident in our findings, the odds that chance is not responsible for our findings are still favorable.

When the arrow points *toward* the number, i.e., ($p = >.05$), this means that in *more* than five cases out of 100 we would obtain different results. Thus, the odds are less in favor of obtaining similar results than in the example reported above. Usually we do not accept probabilities of more than 5 out of 100 as significant in psychological research. The data, in other words, are not reliable enough at such probability levels.

When we see the probability level reported as ($p = >.01$) this means that if we repeated the study we would get roughly the same results anywhere from 95 out of 100 cases to about 99 out of 100 cases. Our confidence, in other words, would be *less* than if the probability level were ($p = <.01$), but greater than if it were ($p = <.05$). In addition, when probability levels are reported as ($p = <.001$) this means that we would secure about the same results in 999 cases out of 1000. Thus, the data are *highly* reliable. A summary of this information is presented on the facing page and can be referred to as one reads the research reports.

TO THE STUDENT

CONFIDENCE OR PROBABILITY LEVELS REPORTED IN THE RESEARCH REPORTS

Probability Level	Interpretation
(P = <.05)	*Reliable Data.* Experiment would turn out roughly the same way in 95 out of 100 cases.
(p = <.01)	*Very Reliable Data.* Experiment would turn out roughly the same way in 99 out of 100 cases.
(p = <.001)	*Extremely Reliable Data.* Experiment would turn out roughly the same way in 999 out of 1000 cases.
(p = >.05)	*Unreliable Data.* Experiment would turn out in roughly the same way in *less* than 95 out of 100 cases.

CONTENTS

Section One · The Science of Psychology

1 PSYCHOLOGY AND SOCIETY 3
   W. H. Coons

2 A RESTATEMENT OF THE PHILOSOPHY OF BEHAVIORISM 14
   B. F. Skinner

3 THE INVASION OF PRIVACY IN THE
   INVESTIGATION OF HUMAN BEHAVIOR.. 27
   Kenneth E. Clark

Section Two · Biological Foundations of Behavior

4 INTRODUCTION TO DOVER EDITION OF BRAIN MECHANISMS
   AND INTELLIGENCE, by K. S. Lashley... 37
   D. O. Hebb

5 CEREBRAL ORGANIZATION AND BEHAVIOR 45
   R. W. Sperry

6 EXPLORING THE BRAIN WITH CHEMICALS... 55
   Sebastian P. Grossman

7 LEARNING OF VISCERAL AND GLANDULAR RESPONSES........................ 61
   Neal E. Miller

Section Three · Motivation and Emotion

8 OBESITY AND EATING.. 75
   Stanley Schachter

9 THE EFFECT OF DREAM DEPRIVATION 81
William Dement

10 THE EPIGENESIS OF INTRINSIC MOTIVATION AND EARLY COGNITIVE LEARNING 84
J. McV. Hunt

11 COGNITIVE, SOCIAL, AND PHYSIOLOGICAL DETERMINANTS OF EMOTIONAL STATE 98
Stanley Schachter
Jerome E. Singer

12 PAN-CULTURAL ELEMENTS IN FACIAL DISPLAYS OF EMOTION 116
Paul Ekman
E. Richard Sorenson
Wallace V. Friesen

Section Four · Sensation and Perception

13 SEEING WITH THE SKIN 121
Benjamin W. White
Frank A. Saunders
Lawrence Scadden
Paul Bach-Y-Rita
Carter C. Collins

14 WHAT THE FROG'S EYE TELLS THE FROG'S BRAIN 126
J. W. Lettvin
H. R. Maturana
W. S. McCulloch
W. H. Pitts

15 PAIN AS A PUZZLE FOR PSYCHOLOGY AND PHYSIOLOGY 138
Ernest R. Hilgard

16 EFFECT ON BRAIN ENZYME AND BEHAVIOUR IN THE RAT OF VISUAL PATTERN RESTRICTION IN EARLY LIFE 149
Devendra Singh
Richard J. Johnston
Harold J. Klosterman

17 AUTHORITARIANISM AND RESPONSE TO POWER CUES 152
Edward J. Wilkins
Richard deCharms

18 PERCEPTION AND JUDGMENT IN THE POLITICAL EXTREMIST 168
James O. Whittaker

CONTENTS

Section Five · Learning and Retention

19 TECHNIQUES FOR THE STUDY OF LEARNING IN ANIMALS: ANALYSIS AND CLASSIFICATION 177

M. E. Bitterman

20 LEARNING WITHOUT SWIMMING IN A WATER MAZE 188

P. C. Dodwell
D. E. Bessant

21 PERMANENT EFFECTS OF PUNISHMENT DURING EXTINCTION 191

Erling E. Boe
Russell M. Church

22 PROGRAMED INSTRUCTION: INSIGHT vs. CONDITIONING 198

H. A. Thelen

23 THE EFFECTS OF FIVE PRESCHOOL INTERVENTIONS 202

Merle B. Karnes

24 CHEMICAL TRANSFER OF LEARNING 214

A. L. Jacobson

Section Six · The Development of Behavior

25 EFFECTS OF LIMITED PRACTICE ON THE MATURATION OF MOTOR SKILLS 277

Wayne Dennis

26 THE DETERMINANTS OF ATTENTION IN THE INFANT 237

Jerome Kagan

27 THE ADOLESCENT "HIPPIE" AND THE EMERGENCE OF A MATRISTIC CULTURE 246

Luther S. Distler

Section Seven · Thinking and Creativity

28 "WHAT IS HONORED IN A COUNTRY WILL BE CULTIVATED THERE" 253

E. Paul Torrance

29 CREATIVITY AND CONFORMITY 258

Vernon L. Allen
John M. Levine

30 FAMILY ENVIRONMENT AND COGNITIVE STYLE: A Study
of the Sources of Highly Intelligent and
of Highly Creative Adolescents 271
Jacob W. Getzels
Philip W. Jackson

Section Eight · Measurement and Individual Differences

31 PARLEZ-VOUS STATISTICS? 283
Darrell Huff

32 THE STANDARDIZATION OF EDUCATION
AND PSYCHOLOGICAL TESTS 287
William H. Angoff
Scarvia B. Anderson

33 IS TESTING A MENACE TO EDUCATION? 292
Henry S. Dyer

34 BEHAVIOR GENETICS AND INDIVIDUALITY UNDERSTOOD 297
Jerry Hirsch

Section Nine · Personality, Adjustment, and Mental Health

35 INDIVIDUALITY AND GENERALIZATION
IN THE PSYCHOLOGY OF PERSONALITY 307
R. R. Holt

36 THE DEFENSE MECHANISMS RE-EXAMINED:
A LOGICAL AND PHENOMENAL ANALYSIS 330
Raymond J. McCall

37 STRESS AND DISTRESS AND IDENTITY FORMATION
IN COLLEGE AND HIGH SCHOOL 346
Graham B. Blaine, Jr.

38 INTRODUCTION TO BEHAVIOUR THERAPY 353
S. Rachman

39 THE CRIME OF PUNISHMENT 365
Karl Menninger

Section Ten · Social Behavior

40 SOCIAL FACILITATION 373
Robert B. Zajonc

41 THE PSYCHOLOGIST LOOKS AT POVERTY 379
   Warren C. Haggstrom

42 STEREOTYPES 394
   H. Tajfel

43 PROBLEMS IN RESEARCH ON PSYCHOLOGICAL WARFARE 402
   James O. Whittaker

44 SOME PSYCHOLOGICAL PERSPECTIVES ON LEGITIMACY 410
   Richard Flacks

45 PSYCHOLOGICAL ALTERNATIVES TO WAR 430
   Morton Deutsch

Section One

The Science of Psychology

This section of three papers focuses our attention on the goals and objectives of psychology, its research methods, and some of the problems which the field will likely face in the future. In the first paper, "Psychology and Society," Dr. W. H. Coons, formerly President of the Canadian Psychological Association, is concerned with the goals and responsibilities of psychology. He argues that, among other things, the field should be contributing more to the serious social problems faced by modern societies. In this paper he advocates a more "free swinging" and innovative approach to research, and he chides the field for clinging to academic ivory towers, purity, and detached passivity. It is interesting to note in this connection, that undergraduate students are often critical of the field for the very same reasons.

B. F. Skinner, in the second paper, re-emphasizes the need for objective studies of behavior, not only in psychology but in economics, political science, and biology as well. As the strongest modern proponent of behaviorism, he is essentially restating the case presented originally by John B. Watson in the early part of this century. The student will remember that Watson founded behaviorism largely as a protest against what he considered to be the unscientific nature of the psychology that preceded it. Consciousness, the subject matter of much earlier psychology, could never be objectively studied, Watson believed, and therefore he felt that the proper subject matter of psychology should be behavior.

In the third paper, Kenneth E. Clark takes up the controversy over invasions of privacy in the investigation of human behavior. The problem here is mainly ethical in character and it has become increasingly troublesome to psychologists in recent years. Essentially the question is whether or not behavioral scientists are justified in the study of an individual's behavior without his awareness. As Dr. Clark notes, simply ignoring the problem will not cause it to disappear. We need guidelines to help us determine under what conditions and circumstances deception in behavioral research is justifiable.

PSYCHOLOGY AND SOCIETY

W. H. COONS

York University and Ontario Hospital, Whitby, Ontario, Canada

It can be argued, with some justification, that psychology is a young science and must be allowed time to develop its techniques and a core of basic knowledge. During its neo-natal period it should be free of obligation to provide a tangible return to its supporting society. Eventually, however, there must come a time when the supporting society may reasonably expect some kind of pay-off on its investment. Surely, after 30 years of experimentation in the area of learning, it is reasonable to expect psychologists to have added a good deal to the understanding of the learning process in homes, classrooms and industries. The unpleasant fact is, that, since Thorndike, the mainstream of psychology has added very little. After 50 years of rejecting the theories of Freud as unscientific, scientific psychology should have reasonable explanations of the phenomena which Freud labelled as defence mechanisms. We have made only a promising start. Similarly, it seems inconceivable that it could take us 70 years to get around to documenting the flagrant inadequacies of the Kraepelinian system of classifying behaviour disorders, let alone replacing it with a system more in accord with the intricacies of disturbed behaviour. The list could be extended to a distressing length in illustration of my contention. In matters central to human functioning, we know much less than we could reasonably be expected to know in view of the energy and talent which have been at the disposal of psychology over the years. Hebb (1960) puts it charitably when he says, " . . . my thesis . . . is that an outstanding contribution was made in the establishment of a thoroughgoing behaviouristic mode of thinking. But this has been achieved, too frequently, only by excluding the chief problem of human behaviour (p. 736)." The chief problem of human behaviour which Hebb contends has been excluded, is the thought process.

Deficiencies of this magnitude raise serious questions about our basic philosophy and about our priorities. Today I would like to pose some of these questions for your consideration.

SCIENTIFIC DETACHMENT AND SOCIAL PURPOSE

There is a wide range of literature which indicates that these, and similar problems, have caused disquiet to a large number of people of diverse orientations. Psychologists, social critics, newspaper columnists, and politicians (mostly American) have expressed concern about the relationship of psychology and other social and behavioural sciences to society. The consensus seems to be that we psychologists are contributing less than we could. The contention is that we can and should do much more as our part in the evolution of the "Just Society;" much more in the areas of immigration, international relations, drugs, traffic safety, native populations, bicultural relations and other aspects of Canadian and world society. The contention is that we now have information which is relevant to the solution of many of these social problems and we have the techniques for acquiring information relevant to the solution of others. Martin Luther King (1968), writing in the *American Psychologist*, has accused American psychologists, along with other social scientists, of abdicating their responsibilities in the civil rights difficulties in the United States:

> "Negroes want the social scientist to address the white community and 'tell it like it is.' White America has an appalling lack of knowledge concerning the reality of Negro life. One reason some advances were made in the South during the past decade was the discovery by northern whites of the brutal facts of southern segregated life. It was the negro who educated the nation by dramatizing the evils through non-violent protest. The social scientist played little or no role in disclosing the truth (p. 180)."

Canada, too, has social cancers about which we psychologists remain silent.

In opposition to the concept of direct social involvement of scientists are those who contend that this would weaken, if not kill, unfettered scientific enquiry. In essence, they argue for a division of labour based on the notion that out of "basic" or "fundamental" research will come the knowledge which someone else, not the scientists themselves, will have the responsibility of applying. Whether the knowledge is used well, or not used at all, is not the concern of the scientists. It is this argument of "the ethical neutrality of science" which C. P. Snow (1964) describes as a moral trap designed to enable scientists to create a comfortable, irresponsible niche for themselves.

When Snow talks about "Science," he means primarily physics and chemistry. While his basic premise applies to psychology, there are ramifications to the relationship of psychology to society which appear to make his argument even more overwhelming. After all, the subject of psychology is *human* behaviour — even most psychologists who study animal behaviour exclusively concede that, ultimately, their experiments will elucidate the nature of human behaviour. And, we know that human behaviour cannot be understood apart from a clear appreciation of the situation in which the individual is behaving, be that situation the family, the classroom, or the job site. Thus, morality aside, the psychologist, unlike the physicist or the chemist, can't retreat to an ivory tower and carry on his research undisturbed by the outside world. Whatever is done in the psychological laboratory must be a simulation of some aspect of society and whatever conclusions are derived from laboratory research must be validated in the non-laboratory world. A thoroughgoing psychology, even an "ethically neutral" psychology can't exclude society from its activities.

Why have so many of us apparently tried so hard to do so?

SCIENCE OR SCIENTISM

The answer, I think, is inextricably interwoven with our concepts of methodology, rigour, and science, and the meanings we attach to these terms have their roots in our early and continuing identification with a largely mythical conception of the science of physics. We have been led into making distinctions between "pure" and "applied" research which even the physicists can't define operationally (see Kidd, 1959) and have placed "pure" research at the top of our psychological totem pole. As though to compound the error, we have equated purity with methodological precision, the achievement of which automatically excludes, at this stage of our development, much of the central subject-matter of psychology.

If you will permit an illustrative anecdote, I recall a young colleague of a few years ago who was interested in the study of problem solving. His doctoral research had been a study which involved the reactions of monkeys to the Wisconsin General Test Apparatus. Unfortunately, the University at which he had taken his first job refused to provide him with monkeys and he was forced to substitute undergraduate students as subjects for his research. He was depressed for a period of several weeks because his student subjects weren't playing the game. "Those rotten kids are using words to conceptualize the problems," he complained, "and my learning curves are shot all to hell." Finally, when we met one morning, he greeted me with an excited waving of a graph and ecstatic cries about how he had finally solved his problem. "I have modified the task so that it is impossible to conceptualize it verbally and look at these learning curves. They're as smooth as any Harlow has ever obtained with his monkeys." My protestations that he had thrown out the baby with the bath water fell on deaf ears. He had his beautiful curves and the fact that they bore no relationship to the characteristic method of *human* problem-solving was not going to mar his scientific triumph.

In the same vein, Burd (1959) in his celebrated paper in the *O.P.A. Quarterly* of a few years ago, includes a quotation from R. S. Woodworth's (1959) obituary of J. B. Watson in which Woodworth remarks: "Watson's preference for animal experiments and his reliance on them for investigation of the fundamental curves of learning find plenty of support in recent work. Such laws, it is often felt, should be established in the animal laboratory; otherwise they may only reveal human ingenuity and use of language." To which Burd remarks, "Chew upon that 'only' for a while and consider how much of the subject matter of psychology it represents, or *should* represent (p. 55)."

I accept that these may be extreme cases but they do reflect our enthusiasm for a subject-matter and a methodology which produce the neat data we hold to be the essence of science.

Bakan (1965) playfully chides us by commenting: "One is tempted to think that psychologists are like children playing cowboys. When children play cowboys they emulate them in everything but their main work which is taking care of cows. The main work of the scientist is thinking and making discoveries of what was not thought of beforehand. Psychologists often attempt to play scientist by avoiding the main work (p. 189)."

It appears that there is a substantial sentiment amongst many psychologists to the effect that we have developed strong tendencies towards putting ourselves in methodological strait jackets at the expense of studying problems of relevance to either a theory of human behaviour *or* to the welfare of humanity. Yet almost all the really distinguished psychologists of the past 80 years or so (the ones honoured by posterity) have refused to conform to the common mould. They have worked on problems which they felt had genuine significance for them personally, for psychological theory, or for society. Most often their research has been guided more by curiosity than by methodology. In fact, most of their experiments wouldn't pass muster in a modern undergraduate class on research design.

That methodology is the essence of science, is a position which is difficult to maintain. You may recall Boring's (1959) proposition that there is an inverse relationship between the amount of knowledge behind a discipline, and the insistence on rigour in scientific method by members of that discipline. Thus, Boring's proposition would have it, physicists and chemists are least exercised about rigour in the methodology of science, physiologists exercised more than zoologists and psychologists exercised more than physiologists. If it is any consolation to psychologists, Boring claims that sociologists get more excited about scientific methodology than we do. Despite Boring's levitous treatment of the matter, there is an unpleasant lingering doubt that too many of us have over-conformed to a suspect image of what a scientist is.

Our fetish is causing uneasiness in circles outside psychology. In 1962, the Behavioural Sciences Subpanel of the (American) President's Science Advisory Committee released a report on the need for strengthening the Behavioural Sciences (Wiesner, 1962). The Report was (and is) an excellent summary of what has been done, and what needs to be done. John Lear

(1962), Science Editor of *Saturday Review,* saw the report as a call to behavioural scientists to . . . "unleash their courage and their imaginations together, and to design research experiments on a scale worthy of the problems of modern democracy." "There was an implicit recognition," Lear said, "that good minds have been hobbled up to now by fear of disapproval of the larger body of science, which is made up of physical scientists whose traditional belief denies the possibility of applying scientific rigour to the study of human behaviour (p. 35)." The point is made again by Dror (1967) in another U.S. Government publication: "The unique characteristics of the subject-matter of the social sciences becomes an insurmountable barrier to policy-knowledge when their study is encumbered with unsuitable tools and misleading expectations. This is largely the case with most modern trends in the social sciences, which suffer from a physical-science-fixation. Influenced by an incorrect image of the physical sciences and their methods, many of the more behaviourally-oriented students of society tend to a narrow view of knowledge-seeking (p. 245)." United States Senator Fred R. Harris (1967) expresses confidence that, "Social Science does not need the cover of the natural-science umbrella; it must stand or fall on its merit." He goes on to quote a U.S. State Department official as saying, "Perhaps the time has come for the social sciences to be willing and confident enough to run the risks of being appraised in terms of their own contribution to knowledge and society (pp. 508-509)."

However, as you know, it is not necessary to go outside our own ranks to find this kind of criticism of the assumption that scientific respectability is conferred by sophisticated methodology. My predecessor as President of this Association, Dr. Bélanger (1961), has said: " . . . the fact remains that there is today a great deal of intolerance for any kind of cognitive endeavour departing from strictly limited classical fields, or not relying completely on the most rigid use of the experimental method. Thus, some of the most important psychological problems are constantly by-passed because psychologists do not dare venture into these ill-reputed and forbidden regions (p. 97)." George Ferguson (1961) arguing for research as a "creative expressive activity" which should be aided by a methodology which is free of compulsive adherence to the formalities of statistical technology, has said: "The attempt to impose more rationalism on research and a well-balanced perspective, may destroy in some individuals the essence of that which is truly creative in that research (p. 109)." Donald Hebb (1958) has said: "Our current sophistication with respect to the design of experiments, statistically speaking, is a brilliant development of method without which we would be much better off (p. 463)." And all 37 voting delegates to the Opinicon Conference (Bernhardt, 1961) endorsed a resolution which held that the essential nature of research consists of doing one's best to add to knowledge by any means.

There it is. It all seems very clear. An outside observer, unafflicted by psychology's special brand of thought disorder, could be forgiven for assuming that psychologists in Canada are fearlessly wrestling with the real guts of human behaviour, undeterred by its resistance to elegant methodology — but he would be wrong in far too many instances. He would be surprised at the infrequency with which graduate thesis data were collected in schools, in hospitals, in factories, or even in service clubs and churches. He would be surprised to learn that it wasn't until 1967 that the Canadian Psychological Association felt impelled to publish a journal which would accept reports of research in settings of this sort. He would be surprised to learn that, in the recent past, the agency providing by far the greatest amount of money for psychological research had officially deterred applications for support of social psychological research. He would be surprised to learn that (in 1966) studies of animal learning receive twice as much financial support as do studies of human learning and that "basic" research receives over $1,500,000 in financial support while the area of Social Problems (Criminology, poverty and dependence, social conflict and "other") receives $41,200 (Appley & Rickwood, 1967).

It is interesting to observe that, as we strive to exorcize the methodological impurity which sometimes is a part of socially significant research, the physical sciences are becoming increasingly worried about their social responsibilities and their involvement in society. Albert Crewe (1967), Head of the Argonne National Laboratory in the U.S., insists that "science is important to society principally because it is relevant (p. 25)." R. Hobart Ellis, Jr., (1967) in an editorial in *Physics Today*, reminds us that traditionally the best physicists have cared about practical everyday matters, and he suggests that the more applied problems scientists solve, the more support they will have for basic research. He goes on to say, "Part of the conventional wisdom holds that anything practical is impure, that what is not pure is not basic, and if your work is not basic, you belong on a lower social level . . . but the scientist who believes in long term goals and research that is motivated primarily by curiosity should show his concern also for the pressing problems (of society). Dollars for accelerators will come more easily to him who has shown how to eliminate rats and pollution (p. 144)." (It will come as a disappointment to some of you, but the context of this last remark suggests that he didn't have in mind the elimination of white and hooded laboratory rats, so that you can expect no direct action from the physicists in "purifying" psychology). In the same vein, Eugene Rabinovitch (1966), long-time Editor of *The Bulletin of the Atomic Scientists*, argues that, "Scientists must be urged to help formulate the questions, to think about the great political and social problems of our times . . . (p. 22)." Audrieth (1965) assumes participation by scientists in public affairs and moves on from there: ". . . The real issues go beyond the place of the scientist in public affairs. It is much more important to determine in what way science and technology, both now and in the future, can contribute to our goals and objectives as a nation and to the welfare of mankind as a whole (p. 24)."

And biologist Barry Commoner (Spurgeon, 1968) believes " . . . that scientists have a responsibility in relation to the technological uses which are made of scientific developments." In recognition of these sentiments among many physicists, the American Institute of Physics has recently established a new Committee on Physics and Society which is concerned with looking objectively at the relationship of physics to society, at the demands which society should properly place upon physics, and seeing how these needs are being met.

Closer to home, the Chairman of the Science Council of Canada, Dr. Omond Solandt, (MacDonald, 1968) has referred to the "necessity of mobilizing Canadian scientific research to increase the nation's efficiency in fields ranging from industrial production to education and health" and suggests that, "The way to guide the evolution of science in Canada is to initiate a series of major programs aimed at solving national problems. Later, in testifying before the Senate's Special Committee on Science policy, Solandt (Smith, 1968) stressed that research must be followed through to production and use. "We have a particularly bad record of continuity in this regard," he is reported to have said.

Another Canadian with an important role in guiding research priorities in Canada apparently is thinking along similar lines. Dr. W. G. Schneider, President of the National Research Council, in a recent address to the Chemical Institute of Canada, expressed the view that " . . . the public interest and the affairs of science are no longer separable."

There seems no doubt that the winds of change blow everywhere about us. They originate with our fellow scientists, with politicians and with public servants. How are we going to respond — as we have in the past, by chinking the cracks in our old log shack with even more automated Skinner boxes and throwing another clinician on the fire? Or will we heed their message, spelled out for us by Line (1945), Bernhardt (1947 and 1961), Ketchum (1955), MacLeod (1955), Webster (1967), and build a new structure capable of meeting both the needs of theory and the needs of society.

If we opt for change (and I suspect our only alternatives are to engineer the change ourselves or have it imposed on us by others), how can we proceed?

PLOTTING THE FUTURE

Our goals have been reasonably well articulated on many occasions and with a surprising degree of agreement considering the diversity of individuals and groups who have put them forward. In fact, many of us have been amazed at the levels of agreement on the basic issue of psychology's goals which were displayed at Opinicon (Bernhardt, 1961), at Couchiching (Webster, 1967) and by Sydiaha's (1966) survey. Given the premise that psychology's purpose is the furtherance of our understanding of human behaviour, questions of priority in the assignment of resources may be determined by a rational assessment of what constitute the significant areas of activity for the achievement of our ultimate goal. Where are the biggest gaps in our knowledge? In what areas is our need for information greatest if we are to move most expeditiously towards the building of a thoroughgoing theory of human behaviour? It is on *means* of assigning priorities that we tend to separate. Each of us is afflicted with a strong tendency to assume that his own way is the royal road to psychological truth and his own activities the only ones really worthy of support. Thus, one, or a few, individuals cannot be charged with the task. All segments of psychology must be considered when priorities are established, and the groups responsible for executing plans must be capable of being held accountable to their constituents. Then, as Beach (1967) has put it, "Steps must be taken to *manage* the social factors which maintain and satisfy, or frustrate, the kinds of behaviour and values we want to produce and promote (p. 59)."

I have indicated elsewhere (Coons, 1961a, 1961b, 1967) the sorts of areas on which, in my view, it is necessary to focus. They include the policies of our research granting bodies, especially the National Research Council, the various Research Committees of the Department of National Health & Welfare, Canada Council, the Defence Research Board, and their support of more broadly conceived research. They include ways of financing longitudinal and long-term studies. They include ways of ensuring that graduate students and faculty members are able to move into new and difficult areas of research without sacrificing money and status, and that requires attention to our graduate programs and to our university promotion and tenure procedures. They include the development of well-financed centres for field research and recognition of research as being a desirable service activity in our schools, hospitals and industries.

I would hope that planning for the future would make it easier for young psychologists to move into "frontier research." As Bakan (1965) has reminded us " . . . by the time the investigatory enterprise has reached the stage of testing hypotheses, most of the important work, if there has been any, has already been done (p. 189)." We need to create an environment which encourages work in the "hunch" or "I-wonder-what-would-happen-if" stages of research and this requires an assessment of the criteria to be invoked in evaluating thesis research.

I trust that this makes it clear that I am not advocating restrictions on scientific freedom. Quite the contrary. My contention is that we have deprived ourselves of true scientific freedom by the reward system we have built into almost every level of our training and research. After all, it is a commonplace that students now entering university programs in psychology are, as Ketchum (1955) told us he was, impelled toward it by an absorbing interest in human beings, in their thoughts, feelings, and actions, and in the problems of human relations which perplex the world. However, the value systems of our graduate schools, of our granting agencies and of our journals systematically (in the guise of science) deny reward for the student's pursuit of his curiosity about these compelling problems of man-in-society. This constitutes the real threat to free enquiry.

There is another aspect of our planning which is seldom mentioned but which should be dealt with, contentious though it will be. It is the matter raised for science generally by Solandt (1968) who argues that, "Canada's major (science) programs should concentrate on specifically Canadian aspects and complement other nations' programs." Remember, Solandt believes that scientific goals should be closely related to national goals and the national goals which he, personally, supports include ". . . achieving national unity, full employment, a rising Gross National Product, improved educational and health services, aid to Indians and Eskimos, and major contributions to peace through national defence and foreign aid."

MacLeod (1955) raised the matter of national interests for Canadian psychology back in 1955, but this aspect of his report appears to have been consigned to limbo. On the subject, MacLeod said, in part, "The problems of a growing country are an obvious challenge to the scientist who is concerned with natural resources and their development. They should also be a challenge to the student of human behaviour; for the most important thing about the growth of a country is the growth of its people . . . Canadian social scientists have tended, one feels, to follow the beaten track rather than to explore new territory . . . the peculiarly Canadian phenomena that invite psychological investigation have been barely touched (p. 55)." These "peculiarly Canadian phenomena" included bilingualism, assimilation of new groups of immigrants, isolated communities such as the outports of Newfoundland, and the living conditions in the far north. If MacLeod were preparing his report now, I am sure he would have included in his list the Canada Newstart Program (Dept. of Manpower & Immigration, 1967) which is dedicated to the development through research and experimentation, of ways and means of providing new skills to an ever-increasing segment of our society, the unemployed and the underemployed.

I grant you that, since 1955, some Canadian psychologists have studied some aspects of all of these phenomena. But generally, they have been denied the attention they deserve by our amazing facility for turning up boojums (see Beach, 1950). It is high time that we rationally decide what role they (Take your choice about whether the referent is "boojums" or "phenomena") should play in our discipline. Should the views of Solandt and MacLeod influence our hierarchy of priorities?

Solandt's very likely will, whether we wish them to or not —unless we continue to evade attention by virtue of the insignificant proportion of Canada's research budget which is made available to psychologists (After all, the total Canadian contribution of research funds to psychologists in 1966, was only slightly over $2,000,000). However, the delineation of a rational plan which specifies priorities and their relationship to the national welfare might well be expected to bring about dramatic increases in levels of support for Canadian psychological research which would make us more worthy objects of attention in a budgetary sense and as social agents as well.

Certainly, if we are to meet our obligations to science as well as to society, we must renounce our pristine ivory-tower, purity, and detached passivity. Change must be the order of the day, in psychology as in other things. The question is not whether but whither.

References

Appley, M. H. and Rickwood, Jean. *Canada's Psychologists*. Committee on Research Financing, Canadian Psychological Association, 1967. (Mimeo.)

Audrieth, L. F. Scientists on tap or on top? We are missing the real issues. *Bulletin of the Atomic Scientists*, 1965, *21:* 24-25.

Bakan, D. The mystery-mastery complex in contemporary psychology. *American Psychologist*, 1965, *20:* 186-191.

Beach, F. A. The snark was a boojum. *American Psychologist*, 1950, *5:* 115-124.

Beach, H. D. In Webster, E. C. (Ed.), *The Couchiching Conference on Professional Psychology*. Montreal: Industrial Relations Centre, McGill University, 1967, pp. 59-60.

Bélanger, D. The nature of research and the training of psychologists. In Bernhardt, K. S. (Ed.), *Training for Research in Psychology*. Toronto: University of Toronto Press, 1961, pp. 97-98.

Bernhardt, K. S. Canadian psychology—past, present and future. *Canadian Journal of Psychology*, 1947, *1:* 49-60.

Bernhardt, K. S. *Training for Research in Psychology*. Toronto: University of Toronto Press, 1961.

Boring, E. G. CP speaks. *Contemporary Psychology*, 1959, *4:* 45-46.

Burd, F. W. Clinical psychology and the true psychologist. *O.P.A. Quarterly*, 1959, *12:* 47-58.

Canadian Psychological Association. *1967 Directory*. Ottawa, 1967.

Coons, W. H. Training for clinical research. In Bernhardt, K. S. (Ed.), *Training for Research in Psychology*. Toronto: University of Toronto Press, 1961, p. 99. (a)

Coons, W. H. Training for clinical psychology. In Bernhardt, K. S. (Ed.), *Training for Research in Psychology*. Toronto: University of Toronto Press, 1961, pp. 115-117. (b)

Coons, W. H. Keynote address to the Couchiching Conference on professional psychology. In Webster, E. C. (Ed.), *The Couchiching Conference on Professional Psychology*. Montreal: Industrial Relations Centre, McGill University, 1967, pp. 7-13.

Crewe, A. V. Science and the war on . . . *Physics Today*, 1967, *20:* 25-30.

Department of Manpower and Immigration. The *Canada Newstart Program*, 1967. (Mimeo)

Dror, Y. The barriers facing policy science. *The Use of Social Research in Federal Domestic Programs, Part III*. Washington: U.S. Government Printing Office, 1967.

Ellis, R. H. Basic and applied research. *Physics Today*, October 1967: 144.

Ferguson, G. A. On statistics in research in psychology. In Bernhardt, K. S. (Ed.), *Training for Research in Psychology*. Toronto: University of Toronto Press, 1961, pp. 108-109.

Harris, F. R. The case for a national social science foundation. *Science*, 1967, 157: 507-509.

Hebb, D. O. Alice in wonderland or psychology among the biological sciences. In Harlow, H. F. & Woolsey, C. N. (Eds.), *Biological and Biochemical Bases of Behavior*. Madison: University of Wisconsin Press, 1958, pp. 451-467.

Hebb, D. O. The American revolution. *American Psychologist,* 1960, *15:* 735-745.

Ketchum, J. D. Psychology versus man. *Canadian Journal of Psychology,* 1955, *9:* 91-102.

Kidd, C. V. Basic research: Description versus definition. *Science,* 1959 (Feb.), *129:* 368-371.

King, M. L. The role of the behavioral scientist in the civil rights movement. *American Psychologist, 1968, 23:* 180-186.

Lear, J. Summons to science: Apply the human equation. *Saturday Review,* 1962, May 5: 35-39.

Line, W. Psychology and social purpose. *Canadian Psychological Association Bulletin,* 1945, 5: 57-67.

MacDonald, B. Solandt underlines use of research as productivity, education aid. *Globe & Mail,* 25 Jan. 1968.

MacLeod, R. B. *Psychology in Canadian Universities and Colleges: A Report to the Canadian Social Science Research Council.* Ottawa: Canadian Social Science Research Council, 1955.

Northway, Mary L. (Letter to the President of C.P.A.). *Canadian Psychologist,* 1968, *9:* 87-90.

Rabinovitch, E. Open season on scientists. *The New Republic,* 1 Jan. 1966: 20-22.

Smith, C. Solandt says research spending may rise to 4% of G.N.P. *Globe and Mail,* 14 March 1968.

Snow, C. P. The moral un-neutrality of science. *Science,* 1961 (Jan.), *133:* 255-262.

Solandt, O. Reported in the *Globe and Mail,* 22 March 1968.

Spurgeon, D. Should scientists speak out in public? *Globe and Mail,* 27 Jan. 1968.

Sydiaha, D. A survey of psychologists in Canada. *Canadian Psychologist,* 1966, *7a:* 413-485.

Webster, E. C. *The Couchiching Conference on Professional Psychology.* Montreal: Industrial Relations Centre, McGill University, 1967.

Wiesner, J. B. Strengthening the behavioral sciences. *Science,* 1962, *136:* 233-241.

Woodworth, R. S. John Broadus Watson: 1878-1958. *American Journal of Psychology,* 1959, *72:* 301-310.

2

A RESTATEMENT OF THE PHILOSOPHY OF BEHAVIORISM

The rapid growth of a scientific analysis of behavior calls for a restatement of the philosophy of psychology.

B. F. SKINNER

Harvard University

Behaviorism, with an accent on the last syllable, is not the scientific study of behavior but a philosophy of science concerned with the subject matter and methods of psychology. If psychology is a science of mental life—of the mind, of conscious experience—then it must develop and defend a special methodology, which it has not yet done successfully. If it is, on the other hand, a science of the behavior of organisms, human or otherwise, then it is part of biology, a natural science for which tested and highly successful methods are available. The basic issue is not the nature of the stuff of which the world is made, or whether it is made of one stuff or two, but rather the dimensions of the things studied by psychology and the methods relevant to them.

Mentalistic or psychic explanations of human behavior almost certainly originated in primitive animism. When a man dreamed of being at a distant place in spite of incontrovertible evidence that he had stayed in his bed, it was easy to conclude that some part of him had actually left his body. A particularly vivid memory or a hallucination could be explained in the same way. The theory of an invisible, detachable self eventually proved useful for other purposes. It seemed to explain unexpected or abnormal episodes, even to the person behaving in an exceptional way because he was thus "possessed." It also served to explain the inexplicable. An organism as complex as man often seems to behave capriciously. It is tempting to attribute the visible behavior to another organism inside—to a little man or homunculus. The wishes of the little man become the acts of the man observed by his fellows. The inner idea is put into outer words. Inner feelings find outward expression. The explanation is satisfying, of course, only so long as the behavior of the homunculus can be neglected.

Primitive origins are not necessarily to be held against an explanatory principle, but the little man is still with us in relatively primitive form. He was recently the hero of a television program called "Gateways to the Mind," one of a series of educational films sponsored by Bell Telephone Laboratories and written with the help of a distinguished panel of scientists. The viewer learned, from animated cartoons, that when a man's finger is pricked, electrical impulses resembling flashes of lightning run up the afferent nerves and appear on a television screen in the brain. The little man wakes up, sees the flashing screen, reaches out, and pulls a lever. More flashes of lightning go down the nerves to the muscles, which then contract, as the finger is pulled away from the threatening stimulus. The behavior of the homunculus was, of course, not explained. An explanation would presumably require another film. And it, in turn, another.

The same pattern of explanation is invoked when we are told that the behavior of a delinquent is the result of a disordered personality, or that the vagaries of a man under analysis are due to conflicts among his superego, ego, and id. Nor can we escape from primitive features by breaking the little man into pieces and dealing with his wishes, cognitions, motives, and so on, bit by bit. The objection is not that these things are mental but that they **offer no real explanation and stand in the way of a more effective analysis.**

It has been about 50 years since the behavioristic objection to this practice was first clearly stated, and it has been about 30 years since it has been very much discussed. A whole generation of psychologists has grown up without really coming into contact with the issue. Almost all current textbooks compromise: rather than risk a loss of adoptions, they define psychology as the science of behavior *and* mental life. Meanwhile the older view has continued to receive strong support from areas in which there has been no comparable attempt at methodological reform. During this period, however, an effective experimental science of behavior has emerged. Much of what it has discovered bears on the basic issue. A restatement of radical behaviorism would therefore seem to be in order.

Explaining the Mind

A rough history of the idea is not hard to trace. An occasional phrase in classic Greek authors which seemed to foreshadow the point of view need not be taken seriously. We may also pass over the early bravado of a La Mettrie who could shock the philosophical bourgeoisie by asserting that man was only a machine. Nor were those who, for practical reasons, simply preferred to deal with behavior rather than with less accessible, but nevertheless acknowledged, mental activities close to what is meant by behaviorism today.

The entering wedge appears to have been Darwin's preoccupation with the continuity of species. In supporting the theory of evolution, it was important to show that man was not essentially different from the lower animals—that every human characteristic, including consciousness and reasoning powers, could be found in other species. Naturalists like Romanes began to collect stories which seemed to show that dogs, cats, elephants, and many other species were conscious and showed signs of reasoning. It was Lloyd Morgan, of course, who questioned this evidence with his Canon of Parsimony. Were there not other ways of accounting for what looked like signs of consciousness or rational powers? Thorndike's experiments, at the end of the 19th century, were in this vein. They showed that the behavior of a cat in escaping from a puzzle box might seem to show reasoning but could be explained instead as the result of simpler processes. Thorndike remained a mentalist, but he greatly advanced the objective study of behavior which had been attributed to mental processes.

The next step was inevitable: if evidence of consciousness and reasoning could be explained in other ways in animals, why not also in man? And in that case, what became of psychology as a science of mental life? It was John B. Watson who made the first clear, if rather noisy, proposal that psychology be regarded simply as a science of behavior. He was not in a very good position to defend the proposal. He had little scientific material to use in his reconstruction. He was forced to pad his textbook with discussions of the physiology of receptor systems and muscles, and with physiological theories which were at the time no more susceptible to proof than the mentalistic theories they were intended to replace. A need for "mediators" of behavior which might serve as objective alternatives to thought processes led him to emphasize subaudible speech. The notion was intriguing because one can usually observe oneself thinking in this way, but it was by no means an adequate or comprehensive explanation. He tangled with introspective psychologists by denying the existence of images. He may well have been acting in good faith, for it has been said that he himself did not have visual imagery, but his arguments caused unnecessary trouble. The relative importance of a genetic endowment in explaining behavior proved to be another disturbing digression.

All this made it easy to lose sight of the central argument—that behavior which seemed to be the product of mental activity could be explained in other ways. In any case, the introspectionists were prepared to challenge it. As late as 1883 Francis Galton could write (1): "Many persons, especially women and intelligent children, take pleasure in introspection, and strive their very best to explain their mental processes." But introspection was already being taken seriously. The concept of a science of mind in which mental events obeyed mental laws had led to the development of psychophysical methods and to the accumulation of facts which seemed to bar the extension of the principle of parsimony. What might hold for animals did not hold for men, because men could *see* their mental processes.

Curiously enough, part of the answer was supplied by the psychoanalysts, who insisted that although a man might be able to see some of his mental life, he could not see all of it. The kind of thoughts Freud called unconscious took place without the knowledge of the thinker. From an association, verbal slip, or dream it could be shown that a person must have responded to a passing stimulus although he could not tell you that he had done so. More complex thought processes, including problem solving and verbal play, could also go on without the thinker's knowledge. Freud had devised, and he never abandoned faith in, one of the most elaborate mental apparatuses of all time. He nevertheless contributed to the behavioristic argument by showing that mental activity did not, at least, *require* consciousness. His proofs that thinking had occurred without introspective recognition were, indeed, clearly in the spirit of Lloyd Morgan. They were operational analyses of mental life— even though, for Freud, only the unconscious part of it. Experimental evidence pointing in the same direction soon began to accumulate.

But that was not the whole answer. What about the part of mental life which a man can see? It is a difficult question, no matter what one's point of view, partly because it raises the question of what "seeing" means and partly because the events seen are private. The fact of privacy cannot, of course, be questioned. Each person is in special contact with a small part of the universe enclosed within his own skin. To take a noncontroversial example, he is uniquely subject to certain kinds of proprioceptive and interoceptive stimulation. Though two people may in some sense be said to see the same light or hear the same sound, they cannot feel the same distension of a bile duct or the same bruised muscle. (When privacy is invaded with scientific instruments, the form of stimulation is changed; the scales read by the scientist are not the private events themselves.)

Mentalistic psychologists insist that there are other kinds of events uniquely accessible to the owner of the skin within which they occur which lack the physical dimensions of proprioceptive or interoceptive stimuli. They are as different from physical events as colors are from wavelengths of light. There are even better reasons, therefore, why two people cannot suffer each other's toothaches, recall each other's memories, or share each other's happiness. The importance assigned to this kind of world varies. For some, it is the only world there is. For others, it is the only part of the world which can be directly known. For still others, it is a special part of what can be known. In any case, the problem of how one knows about the subjective world of another must be faced. Apart from the question of what "knowing" means, the problem is one of accessibility.

Public and Private Events

One solution, often regarded as behavioristic, is to grant the distinction between public and private events and rule the latter out of scientific consideration. This is a congenial solution for those to whom scientific truth is a matter of convention or agreement among observers. It is essentially the line taken by logical positivism and physical operationism. Hogben (2) has recently redefined "behaviorist" in this spirit. The subtitle of his *Statistical Theory* is, "an examination of the contemporary crises in statistical theory from a behaviorist viewpoint," and this is amplified in the following way: "The behaviorist, as I here use the term, does not deny the convenience of classifying *processes* as mental or material. He recognizes the distinction between personality and corpse: but he has not yet had the privilege of attending an identity parade in which human minds without bodies are by common recognition distinguishable from living human bodies without minds. Till then, he is content to discuss probability in the vocabulary of *events,* including audible or visibly recorded assertions of human beings as such. . . ." The behavioristic position, so defined, is simply that of the publicist and "has no concern with structure and mechanism."

The point of view is often called operational, and it is significant that P. W. Bridgman's physical operationism could not save him from an extreme solipsism even within physical science itself. Though he insisted that he was not a solipsist, he was never able to reconcile seemingly public physical knowledge with the private world of the scientist (3). Applied to psychological problems, operationism has been no more successful. We may recognize the restrictions imposed by the operations through which we can know of the existence of properties of subjective events, but the operations cannot be identified with the events themselves. S. S. Stevens has applied Bridgman's principle to psychology, not to decide whether subjective events exist, but to determine the extent to which we can deal with them scientifically (4).

Behaviorists have from time to time examined the problem of privacy, and some of them have excluded so-called sensations, images, thought processes, and so on, from their deliberations. When they have done so not because such things do not exist but because they are out of reach of their methods, the charge is justified that they have neglected the facts of consciousness. The strategy is, however, quite unwise. It is particularly important that a science of behavior face the problem of privacy. It may do so without abandoning the basic position of behaviorism. Science often talks about things it cannot see or measure. When a man tosses a penny into the air, it must be assumed that he tosses the earth beneath him downward. It is quite out of the question to see or measure the effect on the earth, but an effect must be assumed for the sake of a consistent account. An adequate science of behavior must consider events taking place within the skin of the organism, not as physiological mediators of behavior but as part of behavior itself.

It can deal with these events without assuming that they have any special nature or must be known in any special way. The skin is not that important as a boundary. Private and public events have the same kinds of physical dimensions.

Self-Descriptive Behavior

In the 50 years which have passed since a behavioristic philosophy was first stated, facts and principles bearing on the basic issues have steadily accumulated. For one thing, a scientific analysis of behavior has yielded a sort of empirical epistemology. The subject matter of a science of behavior includes the behavior of scientists and other knowers. The techniques available to such a science give an empirical theory of knowledge certain advantages over theories derived from philosophy and logic. The problem of privacy may be approached in a fresh direction by starting with behavior rather than with immediate experience. The strategy is certainly no more arbitrary or circular than the earlier practice, and it has a surprising result. Instead of concluding that man can know only his subjective experiences—that he is bound forever to his private world and that the external world is only a construct—a behavioral theory of knowledge suggests that it is the private world which, if not entirely unknowable, is at least not likely to be known well. The relations between organism and environment involved in knowing are of such a sort that the privacy of the world within the skin imposes more serious limitations on personal knowledge than on scientific accessibility.

An organism learns to react discriminatively to the world around it under certain contingencies of reinforcement. Thus, a child learns to name a color correctly when a given response is reinforced in the presence of the color and extinguished in its absence. The verbal community may make the reinforcement of an extensive repertoire of responses contingent on subtle properties of colored stimuli. We have reason to believe that the child will not discriminate among colors—that he will not see two colors as different—until exposed to such contingencies. So far as we know, the same process of differential reinforcement is required if a child is to distinguish among the events occurring within his own skin.

Many contingencies involving private stimuli need not be arranged by a verbal community, for they follow from simple mechanical relations among stimuli, responses, and reinforcing consequences. The various motions which comprise turning a handspring, for example, are under the control of external and internal stimuli and are subject to external and internal reinforcing consequences. But the performer is not necessarily "aware" of the stimuli controlling his behavior, no matter how appropriate and skillful it may be. "Knowing" or "being aware of" what is happening in turning a handspring involves discriminative responses, such as naming or describing, which arise from contingencies necessarily arranged by a verbal environment. Such environments are common. The community is generally interested in what a man is doing, has done, or is planning to do, **and why, and it arranges contingencies which generate verbal responses which name and describe the external and internal stimuli associated with these** events. It challenges his verbal behavior by asking, "How do you know?" and the speaker answers, if at all, by describing some of the variables of which his verbal behavior was a function. The "awareness" resulting from all this is a social product.

In attempting to set up such a repertoire, however, the verbal community works under a severe handicap. It cannot always arrange the contingencies required for subtle discriminations. It cannot teach a child to call one pattern of private stimuli "diffidence" and another "embarrassment" as effectively as it teaches him to call one stimulus "red" and another "orange," for it cannot be sure of the presence or absence of the private patterns of stimuli appropriate to reinforcement or lack of reinforcement. Privacy thus causes trouble first of all for the verbal community. The individual suffers in turn. Because the community cannot reinforce self-descriptive responses consistently, a person cannot describe or otherwise "know" events occurring within his own skin as subtly and precisely as he knows events in the world at large.

There are, of course, differences between external and internal stimuli which are not mere differences in location. Proprioceptive and interoceptive stimuli may have a certain intimacy. They are likely to be especially familiar. They are very much with us: we cannot escape from a toothache as easily as from a deafening noise. They may well be of a special kind: the stimuli we feel in pride or sorrow may not closely resemble those we feel in sandpaper or satin. But this does not mean that they differ in physical status. In particular, it does not mean that they can be more easily or more directly known. What is particularly clear and familiar to the potential knower may be strange and distant to the verbal community responsible for his knowing.

Conscious Content

What *are* the private events which, at least in a limited way, a man may come to respond to in ways we call knowing? Let us begin with the oldest and in many ways the most difficult kind, represented by "the stubborn fact of consciousness." What is happening when a person observes the conscious content of his mind, when he looks at his sensations or images? Western philosophy and science have been handicapped in answering these questions by an unfortunate metaphor. The Greeks could not explain how a man could have knowledge of something with which he was not in immediate contact. How could he know an object on the other side of the room, for example? Did he reach out and touch it with some sort of invisible probe? Or did he never actually come into contact with the object at all but only with a copy of it inside his body? Plato supported the copy theory with his metaphor of the cave. Perhaps a man never sees the real world at all but only shadows of it on the wall of the cave in which he is imprisoned. (The "shadows" may well have been the much more accurate copies of the outside world in a camera obscura. Did Plato know of a cave at the entrance of which a happy superposition of objects admitted only the thin pencils of light needed for a camera obscura?) Copies of the real world projected into the body could compose the experience which a man directly knows. A similar theory could also explain how one can see objects which are "not really there," as in hallucinations, after-images, and memories. Neither explanation is, of course, satisfactory. How a copy may arise at a distance is at least as puzzling as how a man may know an object at a distance. Seeing things which are not really there is no harder to explain than the occurrence of copies of things not there to be copied.

The search for copies of the world within the body, particularly in the nervous system, still goes on, but with discouraging results. If the retina could suddenly be developed, like a photographic plate, it would yield a poor picture. The nerve impulses in the optic tract must have an even more tenuous resemblance to "what is seen." The patterns of vibrations which strike our ear when we listen to music are quickly lost in transmission. The bodily reactions to substances tasted, smelled, and touched would scarcely qualify as faithful reproductions. These facts are discouraging for those who are looking for copies of the real world within the body, but they are fortunate for psychophysiology as a whole. At some point the organism must do more than create duplicates. It must see, hear, smell, and so on, and the seeing, hearing, and smelling must be forms of action rather than of reproduction. It must do some of the things it is differentially reinforced for doing when it learns to respond discriminatively. The sooner the pattern of the external world disappears after impinging on the organism, the sooner the organism may get on with these other functions.

The need for something beyond, and quite different from, copying is not widely understood. Suppose someone were to coat the occipital lobes of the brain with a special photographic emulsion which, when developed, yielded a reasonable copy of a current visual stimulus. In many quarters this would be regarded as a triumph in the physiology of vision. Yet nothing could be more disastrous, for we should have to start all over again and ask how the organism sees a picture in its occipital cortex, and we should now have much less of the brain available in which to seek an answer. It adds nothing to an explanation of how an organism reacts to a stimulus to trace the pattern of the stimulus into the body. It is most convenient for both organism and psychophysiologist, if the external world is never copied—if the world we know is simply the world around us. The same may be said of theories according to which the brain interprets signals sent to it and in some sense reconstructs external stimuli. If the real world is, indeed, scrambled in transmission but later reconstructed in the brain, we must then start all over again and explain how the organism sees the reconstruction.

An adequate treatment of this point would require a thorough analysis of the behavior of seeing and of the conditions under which we see (to continue with vision as a convenient modality). It would be unwise to exaggerate our success to date. Discriminative visual behavior arises from contingencies involving external stimuli and overt responses, but possible private accompaniments must not be overlooked. Some of the consequences of such contingencies seem well established. It is usually easiest for us to see a friend when we are looking at him, because visual stimuli similar to those present when the behavior was acquired exert maximal control over the response. But mere visual stimulation is not enough; even after having been exposed to the necessary reinforcement, we may not see a friend who is present unless we have reason to do so. On the other hand, if the reasons are strong enough, we may see him in someone bearing only a superficial resemblance to him, or when no one like him is present at all. If conditions favor seeing something else, we may behave accordingly. If, on a hunting trip, it is important to see a deer, we may glance toward our friend at a distance, see him as a deer, and shoot.

It is not, however, seeing our friend which raises the question of conscious content but "seeing that we are seeing him." There are no natural contingencies for such behavior. We learn to see that we are seeing only because a verbal community arranges for us to do so. We usually acquire the behavior when we are under appropriate visual stimulation, but it does not follow that the thing seen must be present when we see that we are seeing it. The contingencies arranged by the verbal environment may set up self-descriptive responses describing the *behavior* of seeing even when the thing seen is not present.

If seeing does not require the presence of things seen, we need not be concerned about certain mental processes said to be involved in the construction of such things—images, memories, and dreams, for example. We may regard a dream not as a display of things seen by the dreamer but simply as the behavior of seeing. At no time during a day-dream, for example, should we expect to find within the organism anything which corresponds to the external stimuli present when the dreamer first acquired the behavior in which he is now engaged. In simple recall we need not suppose that we wander through some storehouse of memory until we find an object which we then contemplate. Instead of assuming that we begin with a tendency to *recognize* such an object once it is found, it is simpler to assume that we begin with a tendency to *see* it. Techniques of self-management which facilitate recall—for example, the use of mnemonic devices—can be formulated as ways of strengthening behavior rather than of creating objects to be seen. Freud dramatized the issue with respect to dreaming when asleep in his concept of dreamwork—an activity in which some part of the dreamer played the role of a theatrical producer while another part sat in the audience. If a dream is, indeed, something seen, then we must suppose that it is wrought as such, but if it is simply the behavior of seeing, the dreamwork may be dropped from the analysis. It took man a long time to understand that when he dreamed of a wolf, no wolf was actually there. It has taken him much longer to understand that not even a representation of a wolf is there.

Eye movements which appear to be associated with dreaming are in accord with this interpretation, since it is not likely that the dreamer is actually watching a dream on the undersides of his eyelids. When memories are aroused by electrical stimulation of the brain, as in the work of Wilder Penfield, it is also simpler to assume that it is the behavior of seeing, hearing, and so on which is aroused than that it is some copy of early environmental events which the subject then looks at or listens to. Behavior similar to the responses to the original events must be assumed in both cases—the subject sees or hears—but the reproduction of the events seen or heard is a needless complication. The familiar process of response chaining is available to account for the serial character of the behavior of remembering, but the serial linkage of stored experiences (suggesting engrams in the form of sound films) demands a new mechanism.

The heart of the behavioristic position on conscious experience may be summed up in this way: seeing does not imply something seen. We acquire the behavior of seeing under stimulation from actual objects, but it may occur in the absence of these objects under the control of other variables. (So far as the world within the skin is concerned, it always occurs in the absence of such objects.) We also acquire the behavior of seeing-that-we-are-seeing when we are seeing actual objects, but it may also occur in their absence.

To question the reality or the nature of the things seen in conscious experience is not to question the value of introspective psychology or its methods. Current problems in sensation are mainly concerned with the physiological function of receptors and associated neural mechanisms. Problems in perception are, at the moment, less intimately related to specific mechanisms, but the trend appears to be in the same direction. So far as behavior is concerned, both sensation and perception may be analyzed as forms of stimulus control. The subject need not be regarded as observing or evaluating conscious experiences. Apparent anomalies of stimulus control which are now explained by appealing to a psychophysical relation or to the laws of perception may be studied in their own right. It is, after all, no real solution to attribute them to the slippage inherent in converting a physical stimulus into a subjective experience.

The experimental analysis of behavior has a little more to say on this subject. Its techniques have recently been extended to what might be called the psychophysics of lower organisms. Blough's adaptation of the Békésy technique—for example, in determining the spectral sensitivity of pigeons and monkeys—yields sensory data comparable with the reports of a trained observer (5). Herrnstein and van Sommers have recently developed a procedure in which pigeons "bisect sensory intervals" (6). It is tempting to describe these procedures by saying that investigators have found ways to get nonverbal organisms to describe their sensations. The fact is that a form of stimulus control has been investigated without using a repertoire of self-observation or, rather, by constructing a special repertoire the nature and origin of which are clearly understood. Rather than describe such experiments with the terminology of introspection, we may formulate them in their proper place in an experimental analysis. The behavior of the observer in the traditional psychophysical experiment may then be reinterpreted accordingly.

Mental Way Stations

So much for "conscious content," the classical problem in mentalistic philosophies. There are other mental states or processes to be taken into account. Moods, cognitions, and expectancies, for example, are also examined introspectively, and descriptions are used in psychological formulations. The conditions under which descriptive repertoires are set up are much less successfully controlled. Terms describing sensations and images are taught by manipulating discriminative stimuli—a relatively amenable class of variables. The remaining kinds of mental events are related to such operations as deprivation and satiation, emotional stimulation, and various schedules of reinforcement. The difficulties they present to the verbal community are suggested by the fact that there is no psychophysics of mental states of this sort. That fact has not inhibited their use in explanatory systems.

In an experimental analysis, the relation between a property of behavior and an operation performed upon the organism is studied directly. Traditional mentalistic formulations, however, emphasize certain way stations. Where an experimental analysis might examine the effect of punishment on behavior, a mentalistic psychology will be concerned first with the effect of punishment in generating feelings of anxiety and then with the effect of anxiety on behavior. The mental state seems to bridge the gap between dependent and independent variables, and a mentalistic interpretation is particularly attractive when these are separated by long periods of time—when, for example, the punishment occurs in childhood and the effect appears in the behavior of the adult.

Mentalistic way stations are popular. In a demonstration experiment, a hungry pigeon was conditioned to turn around in a clockwise direction. A final, smoothly executed pattern of behavior was shaped by reinforcing successive approximations with food. Students who had watched the demonstration were asked to write an account of what they had seen. Their responses included the following: (i) the organism was conditioned to *expect* reinforcement for the right kind of behavior; (ii) the pigeon walked around, *hoping* that something would bring the food back again; (iii) the pigeon *observed* that a certain behavior seemed to produce a particular result; (iv) the pigeon *felt* that food would be given it because of its action; and (v) the bird came to *associate* his action with the click of the food-dispenser. The observed facts could be stated, respectively, as follows: (i) the organism was reinforced *when* its behavior was of a given kind; (ii) the pigeon walked around *until* the food container again appeared; (iii) a certain behavior *produced* a particular result; (iv) food was given to the pigeon *when* it acted in a given way; and (v) the click of the food-dispenser *was temporally related* to the bird's action. These statements describe the contingencies of reinforcement. The expressions "expect," "hope," "observe," "feel," and "associate" go beyond them to identify effects on the pigeon. The effect actually observed was clear enough: the pigeon turned more skillfully and more frequently. But that was not the effect reported by the students. (If pressed, they would doubtless have said that the pigeon turned more skillfully and more frequently *because* it expected, hoped, and felt that if it did so food would appear.)

The events reported by the students were observed, if at all, in their own behavior. They were describing what *they* would have expected, felt, and hoped for under similar circumstances. But they were able to do so only because a verbal community had brought relevant terms under the control of certain stimuli, and this had been done when the community had access only to the kinds of public information available to the students in the demonstration. Whatever the students knew about themselves which permitted them to infer comparable events in the pigeon must have been learned from a verbal community which saw no more of their behavior than they had seen of the pigeon's. Private stimuli may have entered into the control of their self-descriptive repertoires, but the readiness with which they applied these repertoires to the pigeon indicates that external stimuli had remained important. The extraordinary strength of a mentalistic interpretation is really a sort of proof that, in describing a private way station, one is to a considerable extent making use of public information.

The mental way station is often accepted as a terminal datum, however. When a man must be trained to discriminate between different planes, ships, and so on, it is tempting to stop at the point at which he can be said to *identify* such objects. It is implied that if he can identify an object he can name it, label it, describe it, or act appropriately in some other way. In the training process he always behaves in one of these ways; no way station called "identification" appears in practice or need appear in theory. (Any discussion of the discriminative behavior generated by the verbal environment to permit a person to examine the content of his consciousness must be qualified accordingly.)

Cognitive theories stop at way stations where the mental action is usually somewhat more complex than identification. For example, a subject is said to *know* who and where he is, what something is, or what has happened or is going to happen, regardless of the forms of behavior through which this knowledge was set up or which may now testify to its existence. Similarly, in accounting for verbal behavior, a listener or reader is said to understand the *meaning* of a passage although the actual changes brought about by listening to or reading the passage are not specified. In the same way, schedules of reinforcement are sometimes studied simply for their effects on the *expectations* of the organism exposed to them, without discussion of the implied relation between expectation and action. Recall, inference, and reasoning may be formulated only to the point at which an experience is remembered or a conclusion is reached, behavioral manifestations being ignored. In practice the investigator always carries through to some response, if only a response of self-description.

On the other hand, mental states are often studied as causes of action. A speaker thinks of something to say before saying it, and this explains what he says, although the sources of his thoughts may not be examined. An unusual act is called "impulsive," without further inquiry into the origin of the unusual impulse. A behavioral maladjustment shows anxiety, but the source of the anxiety is neglected. One salivates upon seeing a lemon because it reminds one of a sour taste, but why it does so is not specified. The formulation leads directly to a technology based on the manipulation of mental states. To change a man's voting behavior we change his opinions, to induce him to act we strengthen his beliefs, to make him eat we make him feel hungry, to prevent wars we reduce warlike tensions in the minds of men, to effect psychotherapy we alter troublesome mental states, and so on. In practice, all these ways of changing a man's mind reduce to manipulating his environment, verbal or otherwise.

In many cases we can reconstruct a complete causal chain by indentifying the mental state which is the effect of an environmental variable with the mental state which is the cause of action. But this is not always enough. In traditional mentalistic philosophies various things happen at the way station which alter the relation between the terminal events. The effect of the psychophysical function and the laws of perception in distorting the physical stimulus before it reaches the way station has already been mentioned. Once the mental stage is reached, other effects are said to occur. Mental states alter each other. A painful memory may never affect behavior, or it may affect it an unexpected way if another mental state succeeds in repressing it. Conflicting variables may be reconciled before they have an effect on behavior if the subject engages in mental action called "making a decision." Dissonant cognitions generated by conflicting conditions of reinforcement will not be reflected in behavior if the subject can "persuade himself" that one condition was actually of a different magnitude or kind. These disturbances in simple causal linkages between environment and behavior can be formulated and studied experimentally as interactions among variables, but the possibility has not been fully exploited, and the effects still provide a formidable stronghold for mentalistic theories designed to bridge the gap between dependent and independent variables.

Methodological Objections

The behavioristic argument is nevertheless still valid. We may object, first, to the predilection for unfinished causal sequences. A disturbance in behavior is not explained by relating it to felt anxiety until the anxiety has in turn been explained. An action is not explained by attributing it to expectations until the expectations have in turn been accounted for. Complete causal sequences might, of course, include references to way stations, but the fact is that the way station generally interrupts the account in one direction or the other. For example, there must be thousands of instances in the psychoanalytic literature in which a thought or memory is said to have been relegated to the unconscious because it was painful or intolerable, but the percentage of instances in which even the most casual suggestion is offered as to why it was painful or intolerable must be very small. Perhaps explanations *could* have been offered, but the practice has discouraged the completion of the causal sequence.

A second objection is that a preoccupation with mental way stations burdens a science of behavior with all the problems raised by the limitations and inaccuracies of self-descriptive repertoires. We need not take the extreme position that mediating events or any data about them obtained through introspection must be ruled out of consideration, but we should certainly welcome other ways of treating the data more satisfactorily. Independent variables change the behaving organism, often in ways which persist for many years, and such changes affect subsequent behavior. The subject may be able to describe some of these intervening states in useful ways, either before or after they have affected behavior. On the other hand, behavior may be extensively modified by variables of which, and of the effect of which, the subject is never aware. So far as we know, self-descriptive responses do not alter controlling relationships. If a severe punishment is less effective than a mild one, this is not because it cannot be "kept in mind." (Certain behaviors involved in self-management, such as reviewing a history of punishment, may alter behavior, but they do so by introducing other variables rather than by changing a given relation.)

Perhaps the most serious objection concerns the order of events. Observation of one's own behavior necessarily follows the behavior. Responses which seem to be describing intervening states alone may embrace behavioral effects. "I am hungry" may describe, in part, the strength of the speaker's ongoing ingestive behavior. "I was hungrier than I thought" seems particularly to describe behavior rather than an intervening, possibly causal, state. More serious examples of a possibly mistaken order are to be found in theories of psychotherapy. Before asserting that the release of a repressed wish has a therapeutic effect on behavior, or that when one knows why he is neurotically ill he will recover, we should consider the plausible alternative that a change in behavior resulting from therapy has made it possible for the subject to recall a repressed wish or to understand his illness.

A final objection is that way stations are so often simply invented. It is too easy to say that someone does something "because he likes to do it," or that he does one thing rather than another "because he has made a choice."

The importance of behaviorism as a philosophy of science naturally declines as a scientific analysis becomes more powerful because there is then less need to use data in the form of self-description. The mentalism which survives in the fields of sensation and perception will disappear as alternative techniques prove their value in analyzing stimulus control, and similar changes may be anticipated elsewhere. Cognitive psychologists and others still try to circumvent the explicit control of variables by describing contingencies of reinforcement to their subjects in "instructions." They also try to dispense with recording behavior in a form from which probability of response can be estimated by asking their subjects to evaluate their tendencies to respond. But a person rarely responds to a description of contingencies as he would respond under direct exposure to them, nor can he accurately predict his rate of responding, particularly the course of the subtle changes in rate which are a commonplace in the experimental analysis of behavior. These attempts to short-circuit an experimental analysis can no longer be justified on grounds of expedience, and there are many reasons for abandoning them. Much remains to be done, however, before the facts to which they are currently applied can be said to be adequately understood.

Behaviorism and Biology

Elsewhere, the scientific study of man has scarcely recognized the need for reform. The biologist, for example, begins with a certain advantage in studying the behaving organism, for the structures he analyzes have an evident physical status. The nervous system is somehow earthier than the behavior for which it is largely responsible. Philosophers and psychologists alike have from time to time sought escape from mentalism in physiology. When a man sees red, he may be seeing the physiological effect of a red stimulus; when he merely imagines red, he may be seeing the same effect re-aroused. Psychophysical and perceptual distortions may be wrought by physiological processes. What a man feels as anxiety may be autonomic reactions to threatening stimuli. And so on. This may solve the minor problem of the nature of subjective experience, but it does not solve any of the methodological problems with which behaviorism is most seriously concerned. A physiological translation of mentalistic terms may reassure those who want to avoid dualism, but inadequacies in the formulation survive translation.

When writing about the behavior of organisms, biologists tend to be more mentalistic then psychologists. Adrian could not understand how a nerve impulse could cause a thought. The author of a recent article on the visual space sense in *Science (7)* asserts that "the final event in the chain from the retina to the brain is a psychic experience." Another investigator reports research on "the brain and its contained mind." Pharmacologists study the "psychotropic" drugs. Psychosomatic medicine insists on the influence of mind over matter. And psychologists join their physiological colleagues in looking for feelings, emotions, drives, and the pleasurable aspects of positive reinforcement in the brain.

The facts uncovered in such research are important, both for their own sake and for their bearing on behavior. The physiologist studies structures and processes without which behavior could not occur. He is in a position to supply a "reductionist" explanation beyond the reach of an analysis which confines itself to terminal variables. He cannot do this well, however, so long as he accepts traditional mentalistic formulations. Only an experimental analysis of behavior will define his task in optimal terms. The point is demonstrated by recent research in psychopharmacology. When the behavioral drugs first began to attract attention, they were studied with impromptu techniques based on self-observation, usually designed to quantify subjective reports. Eventually the methods of an experimental analysis proved their value in generating reproducible segments of behavior upon which the effects of drugs could be observed and in terms of which they could be effectively defined and classified. For the same reasons, brain physiology will move forward more rapidly when it recognizes that its role is to account for the mediation of behavior rather than of mind.

Behaviorism in the Social Sciences

There is also still a need for behaviorism in the social sciences, where psychology has long been used for purposes of explanation. Economics has had its economic man. Political science has considered man as a political animal. Parts of anthropology and sociology have found a place for psychoanalysis. The relevance of psychology in linguistics has been debated for more than half a century. Studies of scientific method have oscillated between logical and empirical analyses. In all these fields, "psychologizing" has often had disappointing results and has frequently been rejected in favor of an extreme formalism which emphasizes objective facts. Economics confines itself to its own abundant data. Political scientists limit themselves to whatever may be studied with a few empirical tools and techniques, and confine themselves, when they deal with theory, to formalistic analyses of political structures. A strong structuralist movement is evident in sociology. Linguistics emphasizes formal analyses of semantics and grammar.

Straight-laced commitments to pure description and formal analysis appear to leave no place for explanatory principles, and the shortcoming is often blamed on the exclusion of mental activities. For example, participants at a recent symposium on "The Limits of Behavioralism in Political Science" (*8*) complained of a neglect of subjective experience, ideas, motives, feelings, attitudes, values, and so on. This is reminiscent of attacks on behaviorism. In any case, it shows the same misunderstanding of the scope of a behaviorial analysis. In its extension to the social sciences, as in psychology proper, behaviorism means more than a commitment to objective measurement. No entity or process which has any useful explanatory force is to be rejected on the ground that it is subjective or mental. The data which have made it important must, however, be studied and formulated in effective ways. The assignment is well within the scope of an experimental analysis of behavior, which thus offers a promising alternative to a commitment to pure description on the one hand and an appeal to mentalistic theories on the other. To **extend behaviorism as a philosophy of science to the study of political and economic behavior, of the behavior of people in groups, of people speaking and listening, teaching and learning—this is not "psychologizing" in the traditional sense. It is simply the application of a tested formula to important parts of the field of human behavior.**

References and Notes

1. F. Galton, *Inquiries into Human Faculty* (London, 1883), Everyman ed., p. 60.
2. L. Hogben, *Statistical Theory* (Allen and Unwin, London, 1957).
3. P. W. Bridgman, *The Way Things Are* (Harvard Univ. Press, Cambridge, Mass., 1959).
4. S. S. Stevens, *Am. J. Psychol.* **47**, 323 (1935).
5. D. S. Blough, *J. Comp. Physiol. Psychol.* **49**, 425 (1956); ——— and A. M. Schrier, *Science* **139**, 493 (1963).
6. R. J. Herrnstein and P. van Sommers, *Science* **135**, 40 (1962).
7. K. N. Ogle, *ibid.*, p. 763.
8. *The Limits of Behavioralism in Political Science* (Am. Acad. Political and Social Sci., Philadelphia, 1962).

THE INVASION OF PRIVACY IN THE INVESTIGATION OF HUMAN BEHAVIOR

KENNETH E. CLARK
University of Rochester

"With the growth in our population, the complexity of our society, and the dependence of individuals upon one another for service and support, there is increasing need for people to live in the presence of others. Yet the fundamental human claim to personal freedom and dignity remains. Privacy is the right to live one's life in one's own way, to formulate and hold one's own beliefs, and to express thoughts and share feelings without fear of observation or publicity beyond that which one seeks or acquiesces in."

"The claim to privacy is fragile, but persistent; it is as subtle and powerful as the need for personal dignity; it is a fundamental aspect of individual freedom and worth. The claim to privacy is supported by our society, subject to limitations only when there is risk of injury to others or to society as a whole."

"What is private varies for each person and varies from day to day and setting to setting. Indeed, the very core of the concept is the right of each individual to determine for himself in each particular setting or compartment of his life how much of his many-faceted beliefs, attitudes and behavior he chooses to disclose. Every person lives in several different worlds, and in each his mode of response may—indeed must—be different. The roles of father, husband, clerk, good neighbor, union leader, school board chairman, candidate for office, solicitor of funds for the local church, call for different responses. The right to privacy includes the freedom to live in each of these different roles without having his performance and aspirations in one context placed in another without permission."

These words sound like those of congressmen who have attacked psychological testing and behavioral research for its intrusions upon privacy, or as though they were written by persons concerned about the invasion of privacy through the use of electronic devices. Actually these words were agreed to by the members of the Panel on Privacy and Behavioral Research of the Office of Science and Technology. One of the persons who concurred in those words is your speaker. Another was Robert R. Sears, a psychologist well known for his studies in child development and learning. I think it fair to say that both Dr. Sears and I would not have predicted one year ago that we would have written a statement of this sort.

In my paper this evening I want to discuss some of the ways in which the panel to which I have already referred developed its thinking with regard to problems of privacy, and then to discuss with you the unfinished busi-

---

This is a reprint of a paper given at the Eastern Psychological Association, April 6, 1967.

ness which psychology and the other behavioral sciences have before them as we deal with this important problem.

Let me provide another quotation. The April 1 [1967] issue of the *Saturday Review* carries a review, by James J. Kilpatrick, of the recent book by Senator Edward Long entitled *The Intruders: The Invasion of Privacy by Government and Industry*. In that review Justice Douglas is quoted in his dissenting opinion in Osborn *vs.* United States. Osborn is a lawyer who allegedly attempted to bribe a juror in the James Hoffa trials. The evidence against him was obtained by wire-recording with the authorization of two Federal judges. Justice Douglas commented about this procedure as follows. He said, "Such practices can only have a damaging effect on our society. Once sanctioned, there is every indication that their use will indiscriminately spread. The time may come when no one can be sure whether his words are being recorded for use at some future time; when everyone will feel that his most secret thoughts are no longer his own, but belong to the government; when the most confidential and intimate conversations are always open to eager, prying ears. When that time comes, privacy, and with it liberty, will be gone. If a man's privacy can be invaded at will, who can say he is free? If his every word is taken down and evaluated, or if he is afraid they may be, who can say he enjoys freedom of speech? If his every association is known and recorded, if the conversations with his associates are purloined, who can say he enjoys freedom of association? When such conditions obtain, our citizens will be afraid to utter any but the safest and most orthodox thoughts; afraid to associate with any but the most acceptable people. Freedom as the Constitution envisages it will have vanished."

It was in the climate of concern about matters of wiretapping and other such invasions of privacy that issues with regard to the more subtle aspects of the invasion of privacy by behavioral researchers came to the fore as a problem to concern government and industry. You may remember several years ago a considerable degree of outrage about the use of personality tests in industry. The electronic invasion of privacy provided a simple means for transferring this problem from discussion in the published literature to discussion in the halls of Congress. That discussion led to evidence of a number of abuses. These abuses led in turn to campaigns by members of Congress to reduce the abuses and to establish certain procedures as common throughout the Federal government. Lest the Congressional action lead to a wide variety of differing procedures that might seriously damage behavioral research, the President's Science Adviser established within the Office of Science and Technology a Panel to examine this question.

I think it is fair to say that most of the members of the Panel came together with the general belief that the outcry on intrusions of privacy by behavioral scientists was grossly overstated. The first several meetings of our Panel aimed to try to determine whether or not we could agree on a concept of privacy that would not be offensive to the psychologist, and that would not be too diluted for the lawyers on our panel. We were most fortunate in having two very able lawyers very much concerned with this problem: Oscar Ruebhausen of New York City and Edward Bloustein, President of Bennington College. They served to educate the rest of us well. I trust that we also improved their understanding of the problems of the behavioral scientist. We concluded our report with a unanimity of expression. However, our report did change as a result of the study of the problem, and I wish to review several points in which our beliefs and concepts did change.

Let me go back to the quotation of Justice Douglas. He said, "If his every word is taken down and evaluated or if he is afraid"—and I emphasize the word afraid—"they may be, who can say he enjoys freedom of speech?"

Psychologists tend to be rather empirical types. We tend to ask what really motivates persons to behave as they do, and we stand back and observe what goes on under varying conditions. All of us have noted the substantial amount of activity by college students to protest against Viet Nam, or to burn draft cards, or to use marijuana or LSD even against certain threats, or to engage in sit-downs when they believe that the wrong administrator was fired, or to rock police cars, or to lie in the streets when it suits their fancy. Who is to say that these persons are afraid of having someone record their activities? In a recent episode in my own home city, the news that CBS was sending a television crew to the city increased the turnout of persons for a given demonstration. Thus one rather gets the belief that our populace is not as easily intimidated as is suggested, and one also begins to wonder who these persons are who are so concerned about having their privacy violated.

This is my second point. When we raise questions about the violation of the privacy of an individual, we tend to ask ourselves who is the type of person who would be threatened or damaged by such violations. Who are the persons who work to maintain their inviolacy? Were we to develop a personality inventory with a variety of scales on it, and one of those scales measured need for inviolacy, we would consider that a person who had received a very high score on that scale would be somewhat neurotic. We would immediately try to help him become desensitized so that he is not so concerned about having others learn something about him. We would point out to him that everyone hates, that everyone has sex desires, that everyone is dependent, that everyone is rebellious, that everyone is ambitious, etc.

We gain some support for this belief by the sorts of responses obtained when any publicity about matters of invasion of privacy occurs. As a result of the publication of the Panel's report, I have received a number of letters, and several long distance telephone calls from persons concerned with the problem. Let me quote a few sections.

"Our letter to you is prompted by what in our lives is a most unusual happening; namely, the admitted tapping of the business telephone where my husband was an employee, the apparent tapping of residence telephones and the photographing of personal records, bank records, and the like."

"What I would like to know is, if a bug is placed inside a room, is it considered trespassing and therefore illegal but if the bug is planted outside one's room is this considered legal and therefore can be used to criminally prosecute someone? Or is any electronic device, inside or outside one's room illegal?"

"Glad to hear that a committee, under your direction, has become concerned with the preservation of our 'privacy.' It is hard to preserve what we have already lost, but perhaps we can regain some of it.

"Take only the matter of income tax imposed on all of us. Is there any privacy here? This is so much in our minds just now. Investment houses and banks have to squeal on us. For even a ten-dollar interest payment, we have to be reported. And think of the work and expense this is for these busy institutions."

"As I am a victim of FBI wiretapping, electronic eavesdropping (I believe there is a camera in my kitchen) walking bugs (people asked by the FBI to intimidate me by repeating messages, especially confidential statements on sex said to my husband, or by sitting and standing in obscene, pornographic ways in hope of blackmailing me), open inspection of my letters which are then given to AP and UPI news agencies to blackmail me."

"Well, did you include the Secret Service Research Bureau, too and the FBI's techniques of surveillance (or terrorpsychic voodoo). And also I will propose the entire political intent of research by the United Fund Disease Research Associations and their teams of doctors of the AMA."

"As I sit with my skull on fire from electronic heat, from a laboratory that I discovered alone in the world, knowing so many years later, that it is also known by the US government, and knowing that today I am being misled into believing. . ."

Such evidences as these do lead one to feel that a substantial part of the motivation for the protection of privacy is neurotic, or else that it is misguided, or else that it might be applied in such a way as to impede important investigations of the nature of human beings. Yet I believe that such a generalization leads us to overlook some very important aspects of this problem with which we are faced today.

It is also very easy to argue that a substantial amount of the support for campaigns to reduce invasion of privacy comes from those persons who oppose the enterprises which employ the allegedly invasive techniques rather than from persons who are concerned about the invasion itself. It is easy to generalize that persons who complain about the use of personality tests under certain conditions are persons who actually oppose studies in the behavioral sciences in general, rather than to conclude that they are calling attention to legitimate abuses of various psychological devices. I believe that we must not fall into the trap of disregarding legitimate criticism with this form of rationalization. We do need to recognize the fact that the discovery of abuses lends support to those persons who would rather see less Federal money spent on any form of research and lends support to those persons who are tremendously threatened by thoughts of investigations within the general domains of the behavioral sciences, either because of misunderstanding or because of strongly held political or religious beliefs.

It is also easy to conclude that persons who speak of the invasion of privacy are talking about the very problems of mysticism and metaphysics which impeded the development of psychology for so many years. In a sense we are dealing with the old mind-body problem again and we are finding many persons who object to our procedures because they conceive of a human being as at least dualistic, with a secret inner self which he must protect at all costs from exhibition to the world at large. Some of our critics may have that view, but the fact that they do, does not make it impossible for us to discuss with them the rational consequences of improper procedures by behavioral scientists which we would call invasive and which they would call invasive even though both of us generate different models of the human being whose privacy is being invaded.

I think it is fair to say that the members of our panel changed in our beliefs about the problems of privacy on all of these three issues. First, we decided that there was a serious problem and that it required our attention. Secondly, we believe that the persons who are raising questions about the problem were persons who were concerned about important values of our society and whose values regarding that society we can accept and admire. Third, we believe that it is not necessary for all men to have a monistic or a deterministic view about human behavior in order for us to have an honest and legitimate confrontation on the issues of privacy.

One of the members of our committee, Oscar Ruebhausen, had written an article with Orville Brim, entitled "Privacy and Behavioral Research." Let me quote one section from that. "Although the claim to private personality has yet to reach its destined stature in our law, it has become a moral imperative of our times. Reflecting the ethical values of our civilization, it flows as do most of our values from our concept of the essential dignity and worth of the individual. In discussing this concept in 1958, Pope Pius XII made the following perceptive observations: 'There is a large portion of his inner world which the person discloses to a few confidential friends and shields against the intrusion of others. Certain other matters are kept secret at any price and in regard to anyone. Finally, there are other matters which the person is unable to consider.' Pope Pius then concludes, 'And just as it is illicit to appropriate another's goods or to make an attempt on his bodily integrity without his consent, so it is not permissible to enter into his inner domain against his will whatever is the technique or method used.'"

Phrases of this sort are not in the normal language of American psychology. They are not in the language of American sociology or political science either, and so posed problems with members of our Panel as we came to an understanding with our friends of the legal profession. But we found little problem in joining forces with them in the analysis of issues with regard to the protection of privacy as we came to the discussion of matters of consent. For it became clear that we had no fundamental disagreement about the operational definitions of consent nor about the manner in which consent should be obtained.

In order to be as precise as possible, let me quote again from our Panel report.

"If the subject is fully informed and freely consents, without coercion, to participation in an experiment, the issue of privacy evaporates because it arises not through threatened violation of absolute rules for any particular area of behavior but through threatened frustration of the claim of a specific individual to make his own choice of whether to withhold or disclose and to disclose, if at all, at a time and place and to an extent of his own choosing. Consent is the exercise of that choice and satisfies the claim to privacy."

The Panel had no problem with the identification of that definition for consent, but it began in its deliberations with great concern about the impediments to psychological research which would be presented if such a requirement for consent were universal, and if "fully informed" were defined in a rigorous fashion. But here again our lawyer friends came to our aid, for they pointed out that the problems that we were concerned with in the protection of privacy were precisely the same as the problems encountered in the protection of property rights, that property rights were not sacrosanct against every invasion, and that our society has generated devices for handling conflicts which arise when there is one right which conflicts with another.

When a society is faced with a judgment about the usurpation of an individual's property, obviously undesirable in any event, and the need to build a new thruway, obviously also undesirable I assume, a choice must be made. Some sort of judgmental process must be established by the community so that the right of the individual to the property, and the right of the larger society to come to grips with and solve its major transportation problems can somehow or other be accommodated. Just so, there must be a balancing process between our need to know more about the nature of man in order that we may deal with his manifold problems, his neuroses, his psychoses, the development of adequate human resources, the mobilization of manpower for maintenance of our technology, etc. All of these socially desired outcomes need to be balanced against the cost imposed by intrusions on the privacy of individuals. This balancing process must take into account the fact that upon occasion the privacy of an individual must be intruded upon. There are times when an individual will need to be studied even without his consent. There will be times when a group needs to be carefully examined without the consent of any individual or of the group as a whole. Under these circumstances society must generate some process for the balancing of these desirable features of our society, and decide what costs are proper in terms of the expected benefits.

It is not my intent to review the conclusions of our panel report in detail except to say that we strongly support the development of appropriate techniques to make sure that this balancing process occurs. We are concerned that the enthusiasm of the individual investigator be moderated so that he will not in his search for truth be blinded to the rights and privileges of the subjects with whom he works. We recognize that scientific research is total war, and that the investigator is going to work as hard as he can to find the truth. We therefore believe that there must be individuals in his surround who will review what he is doing to assure that improprieties do not occur.

Our panel did make one recommendation which I want to emphasize. We did not believe that at the present status of our knowledge in the behavioral sciences it is appropriate or desirable or even possible to define any single area, no matter how small or restricted, that is off limits for behavioral research. We think that there is no question which might not be properly asked under certain conditions and for certain purposes. We think there is no facet of the human personality that ought not to be examined at some time under proper circumstances. In other words, we propose that there be no categorical denials of areas for investigation. Our report is directly contrary to the current practices of the Office of Education which does have programs of review of content of items in questionnaires with such review occurring in Washington. We believe that this is improper, that no protection to the subjects is provided thereby, and that the only protection that is provided is protection to the governmental agencies against unfavorable publicity. This sort of review does service to no one, not even to the Federal government itself.

Let me illustrate the point. In any investigation, one cannot necessarily predict what it is that will be considered offensive to the respondent. We heard the report of an investigation of the use of contraceptive devices by housewives. A survey of their use was made by doorstep interviews in a carefully planned schedule. Housewives turned out to be quite willing to discuss with a perfect stranger a wide variety of the details of their use of such devices. One of the last questions in the schedule asked about family income. The housewives were indignant that such a question would be asked and frequently refused to give any indication of family income. The point is simple. The issue is not the content of the item, but rather what it was that the housewives consented to do when the interview began. They had an opportunity at any time to terminate the interview. They terminated the interview when they believed that the items asked did not fall within the domain of questions which they had consented to provide answers for.

I believe that there is an important principle which grows out of this illustration. This is that in general subjects are willing to cooperative in psychological investigations and in investigations in any of the other behavioral sciences. They freely give their consent. They do not ask for a great amount of prior information about what the experiment is about. What they do demand is that their use be somehow or other productive and that the expenditure of time and energy, and whatever distaste or discomfort they may have during the experiment be warranted in terms of providing the proper sort of useful information. When the subject believes that he is being exploited, or when he believes that the nature of the experience somehow or other includes items irrelevant to the major purpose of the experiment as he understands it, he then has a growing distrust of the investigator. Let us hope that we do not continue to generate the impression that we are the ones on campus who say they are doing one thing when they are actually doing something else. The perception of psychologists as the great deceivers is not a perception that makes me feel comfortable.

The discussion of privacy turns out to be a fruitful and profitable activity. As one considers problems of privacy a wide variety of matters of ethics and good conduct come to one's attention which might otherwise never even be thought about. I believe that psychology has ahead of it during the next ten or twenty years the problem of understanding better what our proper behavior is, and also getting a better understanding of what we mean by privacy. Personally, I do not like the word; I would much sooner speak of matters of propriety in behavioral research, of good standards of conduct and the like. For there are more issues involved than just those of privacy. The matter of the deception experiment, for example, is one which requires a considerable amount of attention. It does involve an invasion of privacy, because the subject does not give fully informed consent to participation in the experiment, since he does not know what the experiment is, or else believes it is something entirely different from its true nature.

The deception experiment, however, is only one of a variety of the problems with which we must deal, and about which we must have more explicitly stated principles. If there is any one generalization I would make about our Panel's investigation of this problem, it would be that we discovered that there is no obvious pattern of proper behavior, that there are no clearly established principles that give guidance about what to do in each situation, and that the differences in behavior by various investigators reflect much less a matter of careful analysis of standards of proper behavior than a general non-awareness of the fact that there even was an ethical problem involved.

During the next twenty years psychology must resolve these problems. We had better do it before this time, but it will take many years for us to work out some of the detailed problems involved.

Let me illustrate with a few examples the problems that we have. I shall do this by asking a series of questions.

Who needs protection? We speak of invasion of privacy, in such a way as to suggest that somehow or other it is the individual subject who suffers if his privacy is invaded. Yet many times he suffers not at all, and often does not know that his privacy is invaded. If we run a pure detection experiment, run so perfectly that he never knows that he was deceived, has his privacy been invaded? Suppose our study is a study of persons who are entering a gambling house. We watch them go in and watch them leave and study something of their behaviors. We have observed them under circumstances in which they would prefer not to have been observed. Who has suffered damage if they never know that they were observed?

My suggestion is that it is often the psychologist himself who needs protection, for the generally intrusive and inquisitive nature of the psychologist leads to a gradual erosion of his own values and this erosion is likely to continue. Psychologists ought not ultimately to become known as peeping toms or curiosity seekers.

Likewise our way of life becomes eroded by such procedures, for as our research becomes published, it becomes generally known that there are persons making studies of this sort so all of us feel a certain loss and may feel that this is not the sort of world in which we want to live.

There is protection required not just for subjects, and for our way of life, and for psychologists, but for the data themselves. Let me make my meaning fully clear to you. I read to you earlier in my paper some quotations from letters that I received. I ask you—did I invade the privacy of these letter writers in quoting the contents of their letters? Who owns such letters? Suppose that the literary value of these letters was so great that to have them published would produce income of very substantial amounts from the sale of the books. Who owns the royalties? Who decides whether the letters can be published? Does it make any difference that I gave no names? What difference does that make?

It's much more enjoyable not to answer such questions, and I intend not to answer such questions, although there are legal principles which do apply to the points that I have raised. But let me ask the same question about another class of data.

Suppose you administer in the fall to all of the entering freshmen in your college a set of tests and accumulate on each student a set of test scores. Who owns the test scores? Who gives authorization for the release of the test scores? Suppose the test scores indicate that your freshman class is very poor by national standards. Who decides that those data may be released? Suppose that the data show that those students who moved into fraternity houses had lower scores than students who did not. What right do the fraternities have to prevent the publication of information that might be damaging to their future status? Who owns the individual test score assigned to the individuals named? Under what circumstances can that score be released, and who decides that?

If we collected data on a section of a city, and determine that a particular area of the city has a higher crime rate than some other part of the city, what rights do the persons in that part of the city have to protect their property values from the undesirable effects of the publication of such data? What right does a foreign country have to forbid us to study them, especially if the study of that culture relates to the general instability of the country and the likelihood of revolution? And particularly, if the study is sponsored with federal funds? Do we have the right to make studies of that sort? If the answer is no, then all of a sudden anthropologists may no longer have federal support for any of their field work in places outside the United States.

Let us be grateful that the problems we face as a result of the general outcry about privacy are problems that come from success. The psychologist is able to provide information about an individual that that individual himself did not previously know. It is possible for the psychologist to gain information about the individual's personal characteristics, his capabilities for achievement, and something about his particular frailties. And the psychologist could continue to obtain information of this sort and to study the way in which social processes among human beings occur, even if it were necessary for him to operate according to the most rigid codes to avoid the invasion of privacy. In this I have great confidence, for it is clear that psychologists are most ingenious souls, and that they are able to overcome very serious obstacles in their search for the truth. What concerns me is that we shall direct our attention to finding ways over the obstacles presented to us as a result of the discussion of privacy, rather than our responding to the outcry by a concerted effort to learn more about the nature of privacy and about the degree to which human rights are eroded when privacy is reduced. I am not convinced that the best world is the world in which each man can remain alone, can choose the times when he is unaffected by the presence of others. The outcry about privacy reflects a certain medieval attitude on the part of many persons. It is not a general outcry, as all of you who have been attempting to recruit subjects know. Most persons feel no threat at all by such invasions. We need to understand better the motivations of those who are threatened.

Yet at the same time, we must accommodate to the needs of the individual to retain a certain amount of self-esteem which comes from the defenses against self-revelation. We must help the individual investigator to devise techniques which reduce to a minimum the necessity for his intruding on those aspects of the individual which are irrelevant to his ultimate research objectives.

Thus, discussions of issues of privacy do not deal with a current temporary problem that one of these days will go away, but rather deal with an additional important variable which must be taken into account in the education of our graduate students, in the design of experiments, in the reporting of those experiments in psychological journals, with methods that are used to obtain consent, with techniques for debriefing after deception is included as a part of the procedures in the experiment, and as a part of our growing code of ethics. The issues with which we deal are issues that are not going to be resolved simply by our saying that we are going to be good citizens, but rather require careful study in order that we may determine what being a good citizen requires of us in each of a wide variety of specific situations.

Section Two

Biological Foundations of Behavior

One of the first psychologists to grasp the importance of the study of the brain and nervous system was Karl S. Lashley. His book, "Brain Mechanisms and Intelligence," published in 1929, was a real landmark in the field. In the introduction to a recent reprinting of this work, Professor D. O. Hebb reviews the developments that led up to the publication of this important work. In addition, he places Lashley's contributions in the perspective of time, and then relates some events in psychology since the book's publication which led to a diminished interest in physiological psychology. In conclusion, he states that the passage of time has confirmed the importance of Lashley's approach to the problem of behavior. As we will see in this section, much of the most exciting research in psychology in the last ten years has in fact been in physiological psychology. New techniques have been developed, and new findings have accumulated at a tremendous pace.

In the second paper of this section, Dr. Sperry discusses the effects of splitting the brain into two parts by cutting the corpus callosum—the structure that connects the two hemispheres. For a long time, as he points out, physiological psychologists were uncertain about the exact function of the corpus callosum since sectioning it in human beings did not seem to produce any discernible effect. More recent studies with animals, however, have increased our understanding not only of the functions of the structure itself but of the entire brain. As Dr. Sperry notes, future research with split brain animals, involving permanently implanted electrodes and localized lesions, should substantially increase our understanding of sleep, emotion, learning, problem-solving, and a number of other areas of interest to psychologists.

In the third paper of this section, Sebastian Grossman takes up another type of technique being used today to explore brain functions. This involves the implantation of chemicals in various brain parts. As he points out, recorded electrical events and the electrical stimulation of various brain areas has been invaluable in increasing our understanding of the brain. However, the activity of nerve cells is dependent upon not only electrical activity but chemical processes as well. Therefore, we need to know a great deal more about brain chemistry before we will be able to understand many things about brain functions. Grossman goes on to describe his own research and that of others, particularly in regard to the chemical activation of brain regions regulating the drives of thirst, hunger, and sexual behavior. In addition, he discusses other recent studies of this nature which deal with emotion and arousal.

In the final paper of this section, Dr. Neal Miller describes recent studies dealing with the autonomic nervous system which have important implications for our understanding of learning, psychosomatic illnesses, and homeostasis. Traditionally, he points out, there has been a belief in the inferiority of the autonomic nervous system in contrast to the central nervous system, at least in terms of learning. Most investigators believed the central nervous system to be capable of instrumental conditioning while the autonomic nervous system was believed to be modifiable only through classical conditioning. Recent research by Miller and others, however, has shown this to be untrue. Among other functions, heart rate, vasomotor responses, and galvanic skin responses—all regulated by the autonomic nervous system—can be modified through instrumental conditioning.

4

INTRODUCTION TO DOVER EDITION OF: BRAIN MECHANISMS AND INTELLIGENCE, BY K. S. LASHLEY

D. O. HEBB
McGill University, Montreal, Canada

It is not far-fetched to date the beginning of the modern period in psychology from the publication of this book in 1929. Its importance for physiological psychology, of course, is obvious. In it Lashley developed methods, formulated problems, and established critical standards of analysis that have affected all subsequent studies using brain operation as a method. But the influence extended through a much wider field, unacknowledged and perhaps unrealized by psychologists who nevertheless spoke and experimented differently from what they would have if it had not been written. The student who wants to understand the course of psychology in the past thirty years, and certain peculiarities of psychology today, should have some knowledge of this book and the circumstances in which it appeared.

The behavior theory that existed before its publication was mostly cast in neurological terms, and concerned ideas that could never be the same again. Lashley's critique had been building up in a brilliant series of studies begun about 1920, but examination of the contemporary literature suggests that the full weight of the critique was not felt until the appearance of his book (together with his presidential address to the American Psychological Association in the same year). In the preceding decades it was possible to debate the question seriously, whether consciousness was due to an impulse passing high

---

Reprinted from *Brain Mechanisms and Intelligence*, by K. S. Lashley, published 1963 by Dover Publications, Inc., New York.

resistance at the synapse, or low resistance. It was still possible to put single memories into single brain cells, like little jewel cases, each with its own jewel. It was possible to take as an axiom that "conscious" means 'cortical" and "cortical" means "conscious" (so if a habit becomes automatic and needs no thought, a cortical pathway has been short-circuited and is now subcortical). None of this carefree neurologizing was possible after 1930, at least not for a psychologist.

Instead there was a conspicuous avoidance. In the perspective of time one can see an extraordinary change of theoretical climate between, say, 1928 and 1938. From Wundt onward psychology had been predominantly physiological psychology, however fanciful. Now psychology became anti-physiological or a-physiological, a theme most effectively presented in the work of B. F. Skinner and E. C. Tolman. Both these men argued that talking about the nervous system is unnecessary, even a positive hindrance, in behavioral analysis. C. L. Hull seems to have taken a less extreme position, but the fact that his highly influential theorizing made no real use of neurological conceptions was a vote cast on the same side. (It is said that Hull was rather inclined to take cognizance of the nervous system except after a visit from K. W. Spence, who was opposed, and that Spence visited Yale often enough to keep him on the strait and narrow.)

Now the positivistic views of Skinner and Tolman are really extreme—they go much farther than merely saying that physiology is not essential for a psychologist—and they represent a sharp break from the main tradition of psychological thought. Persuasive as the supporting arguments were, it is astonishing that they could have been so successful in so short a period of time, allowing for the conservativeness of scientific thought—except for one thing.

The traditionalist, the man who might have argued the opposing case, found himself all at once without arguments. The stock-in-trade of physiological behavior theory had been synaptic resistances, detailed localizations of cortical function, and new paths from point to point in the cortex for new habits. Now, suddenly, it appeared from Lashley's work that such ideas were fantasy, not science. In these circumstances the positivistic *coup d'état* becomes more intelligible. Neither of the main movers, Tolman and Skinner, adopted his position because of Lashley, but one hardly doubts that their success in carrying others along with them owed much to work that made the ideas of physiological theory more than slightly ridiculous.

The literature of the day does not directly reveal the impact made by this book and the research papers that led up to it, evident as the impact was in the bars and hotel corridors at the time. It can be seen however in what was *not* said after 1930, what people *stopped* writing. The last major formulation of the pre-Lashley type, with synaptic resistances and receptor-effector connections all complete to account for all behavior, is to be found in E. B. Holt's *Animal Drive and the Learning Process*. Its publication was as late as 1931, but the writing must have been done earlier, and the book was an anachronism before it was published. Tolman's *Purposive Behavior in Animals and Men* took over in 1932, to be followed by Skinner's *The Behavior of Organisms* in 1938, with hardly a murmur from the defenders of physiological psychology. The defenders had in fact become few in number. Positivism is still with us in the 1960's and if the student is (as he might well be) puzzled by some of its manifestations he should look to the historical background of which this book is such a significant part.

It is of some interest to see how the book came to be written. Karl Spencer Lashley (1890–1958) was born in Davis, West Virginia. At the University of West Virginia at the age of 15 he meant to major in Latin or English, but an accidental encounter with John Black Johnston, the neurologist, discovered for him the world of biological science, with which he promptly fell in love; and, by his own account, another accidental encounter the next year with a set of Golgi slides of the frog brain determined that this love would take the form of the study of behavior.

His conversion to neurological problems and psychology seems not to have really been so complete and immediate, for he took his M.S. at Pittsburgh in bacteriology and then went on to zoology at Johns Hopkins, where he took his Ph.D. with H. S. Jennings in 1914. It seems clear, however, that he was deeply involved with psychology by this time, and the earlier contact with the frog brain, in his sophomore year, had something to do with it. Finding the abandoned set of slides, he went to his instructor and proposed, in his innocence (he was only 16 or 17 years old), to work out all the connections: "Then we should know how the frog worked." It was a sharp disappointment to learn that not even the Golgi stain allows one to work out all the connections of the brain, but as Lashley himself said, he spent the rest of his life trying to find out "how the frog worked": frog, rat, monkey or man.

At Johns Hopkins he came into contact with John B. Watson in the period when Watson was preparing the Behaviorist manifesto, in 1912, and collaborated closely with him in a number of studies over the next six years. One collaboration is of special interest here: Lashley wrote a chapter on learning for Watson's *Behavior: an Introduction to Comparative Psychology* (1914), developing in it just those "Watsonian" notions that, later, he spent most of his professional life refuting.

It was during the period at Johns Hopkins that Lashley also encountered Shepherd Ivory Franz and made his first use of the brain-operation method. Franz at this time was working on psychiatric problems at St. Elizabeths Hospital in Washington, D.C., and apparently had his own methods for selecting a junior collaborator. At any rate, Lashley's story was that Franz first set him to photographing naked female patients. This was to find out whether he was a reliable worker. Satisfied on that point, or else concluding that a young man would do better with other material, he undertook with Lashley two studies of the effect of cortical extirpations on habit in the rat. Thus began the line of work that was the chief basis of the present book.

It was at the University of Minnesota that Lashley followed up in earnest the work begun with Franz. He has told us (cf. p. 14) that he began with the simple aim of demonstrating the soundness of Watson's ideas of synaptic modification and the formation of stimulus-response connections through the cortex. But every experiment he did came out wrong, and at some time during this period (1920–1926) it is evident that he abandoned the theory, though he never abandoned Watson's real aim of achieving a completely monistic and objective explanation of behavior. For the rest of his life Lashley was proud of a remark Watson made to him once, that he was the only thoroughgoing behaviorist that Watson knew.

Then in 1926 Lashley moved to the Institute for Juvenile Research, Chicago, where he undertook the experiments that are reported in this book. It is important for the student of behavior, in reading it, to observe that it is not merely a report of brain operations in the rat. Brain operation was a method, and the rat a convenient subject; what Lashley was interested in was understanding behavior, especially (but not exclusively) human behavior. Unlike some other behaviorists, he was not afraid to use the word *mind*, and it was the problem of mind that he wanted to solve. The rat was a convenient subject for the investigation because a more accurate measurement of the size of brain lesions can be made with a smooth-brained animal, adequate methods of testing were available, and such methods could be applied to large groups of subjects. All these considerations make for reliable results, in marked contrast to the clinical data of human brain damage. It can be seen from his discussion that his results are nevertheless relevant to problems of the clinic, and in fact this book has had a continuing influence on neurological thought.

It should also be observed that Lashley's incidental observations were almost as important as his formal data. There was a good deal of talk in the twenties about random behavior, unguided "trial and error," followed by "accidental success." When Lashley observed that

> one does not realize the meaning of "random" behavior until he has compared a normal animal with one having extensive cerebral destruction. The normal animal almost never re-enters a cul-de-sac [immediately]. An animal with severe lesions may repeat a single error as many as two hundred times before passing to other parts of the maze (p. 138),

he was telling us that there is a kind of order and system in the *normal* animal's behavior that is missed in making facile assumptions about randomness. In the same context—discussion of the qualitative changes in the rat's behavior following brain damage—he made the radical suggestion (radical indeed for a behavioristically minded psychologist in 1929) that in learning a light-darkness discrimination the rat shows order and *purpose* in the pre-solution period, and that his *attention* is a factor in learning:

> . . . responses to position, to alternation, or to cues from the experimenter's movements usually precede the reactions to the light and represent attempted solutions which are within the rat's customary range of activity (p. 135).

And again, in problem-box learning:

> . . . the animal which has run across the platform many times without pause, stops and explores the platform thoroughly. The door is opened during this exploration, and thereafter all activity . . . centers about the platform and door (p. 135).

This was a level of analysis that had mostly been absent in experiments on rat behavior. The discussion led directly to I. Krechevsky's studies of "hypotheses" in the rat, and thus to the continuity-noncontinuity controversy of the thirties and forties—another example of the influence the book has had upon psychological theory and experiment.

The general plan of the work is as follows. Lashley first set out to examine the effect of brain damage on the ability to acquire habits, the rats being operated on before training was begun. Tests of continued retention and habit reversal make a total of ten measures, reported on in Chapters III, IV and V.

Chapter VI presents a second main experiment, in which the rats were trained before operation. Here Lashley used one test situation only (Maze III) but with a larger number of animals in the experimental group. The question is whether brain damage affects the retention of habits already established in the same way as it affects the acquisition of a new one. One might say, roughly, that the question is whether *memory* is affected in the same way as learning ability, and the answer is yes for this test.

Chapter VII then raises the special question of the extent to which the impairment of acquisition and retention can be explained by interference with sensory or motor processes rather than learning ability and memory *per se*. Here Lashley first made the brilliant observation that cortical blindness produces a greater deterioration of performance than peripheral blinding by removal of the eyes (pp. 110-112). Even in blind animals, loss of visual cortex produces a disturbance of maze learning. From this it must be concluded that visual cortex has some further function in addition to a sensory one. It is not a mere transmitter of sensory information. Subsequently Lashley's interpretation of the data, or the adequacy of the data, was challenged, and he returned to the topic in a later paper[1] in which the point was established beyond dispute.

On the motor side, similarly, the animal with an intact cortex but a gross disturbance of normal motor control, because of a spinal or cerebellar lesion, can out-perform the cortically-injured rat with normal coordination of the limbs,

although the manner of progression may be almost completely altered. One drags himself through with his forepaws; another falls at every step but gets through by a series of lunges; a third rolls over completely in making each turn, yet manages to avoid rolling into a cul-de-sac and makes an errorless run (p. 137).

This, with the observation that what the normal rat learns first is a general orientation in the maze rather than specific movements, struck directly at the chained-reflex conception of serial learning in the maze. In fact, simple-minded chaining theory soon disappeared, whether because of Lashley or not, replaced by "cognitive maps" on the one hand and modern "learning theory" on the other. Neither of these more or less positivistic formulations acknowledges any great debt to physiological psychology or, more specifically, to brain-operation experiments, but it hardly seems that the fundamental relevance of Lashley's analysis to their problems can be doubted by the impartial reader.

The fact seems to be that Lashley's data were so overwhelming, both in complexity and in their detailed, extensive denial of the central tenets of the learning theory of the twenties, that they were largely forgotten, simplified in memory to a point at which they no longer represented any problem for the theorist. Skinner has pointed out, rightly, that "CNS" often stands for "conceptual nervous system," rather than the complexities of the real central nervous system. To this, however, it must be added that psychological theory, and especially learning theory, mostly deals with a very conceptual animal, shorn of much of the trouble-making complexity of real behavior. Lashley's book, similarly, is remembered only

---

[1] "Studies of cerebral function in learning. XII. Loss of the maze habit after occipital lesions in blind rats," *J. comp. Neurol.*, 1943, *79*, 431–462.

as reporting that there is no localization of function in the rat's cortex, and that large lesions affect learning more than small lesions. "Equipotentiality," and "mass action." Full stop. If this were a true picture, the positivistic learning theorist obviously need not consult the book, and the clinical neurologist who knows that there *is* localization of function in the human brain can say, That's all very well for the rat, but it doesn't apply to man.

But this, of course, is not a true picture of Lashley's research. The qualitative analysis, so relevant to any theory of rat behavior, has already been stressed in the preceding pages. It remains to consider what Lashley did say about brain function and equipotentiality and mass action. In the first place, he did not deny, but rather emphasized, the existence of cortical localizations of function, in rat as well as in man. What he did deny was that localization is all that it has been thought to be. When the double-latch box has been learned by normal animals, lesions in the frontal region produce a loss of retention, but not other lesions. When a brightness discrimination has been acquired, lesions in posterior cortex disrupt it, but not anterior lesions.[2] This is localization of function, if in broad terms. But in either case, if the *same* lesions are made first, the rate of learning is unaffected: a result that is still hard to understand. One result clearly shows localization, the other seems to rule it out.

Lashley concluded, in general, that equipotentiality and mass action may both hold over the whole cortex for one function, such as learning a complex alley maze; but that in another situation, such as the elevated maze, vision becomes more important and equipotentiality disappears or is diminished. When he reports that large lesions, up to 50 per cent of neocortex in extent, do not retard learning in the double-latch-box problem, he is saying that mass is not a factor in such learning. For different situations, different relations. In general, his opinion was that mass action and equipotentiality are most evident in complex problems—in Maze III, for example, as compared with Maze I.

As for man, Lashley's view was that specialization of cortical function has increased with phylogenesis (p. 154), but that the principles of brain function that are evident in the rat, where adequate experimental controls can be made, may still be applied with profit. The effects of functional differentiation of the speech area, for example, mean that the principle

---

[2] It is repeatedly stated in the book that the loss of the brightness habit obeys the law of mass action, being proportional to the size of the lesion. Lashley later discovered that this was an artefact, and reported the correction in his paper, "The mechanism of vision. XII. Nervous structures concerned in habits based on reactions to light," *Comp. Psychol. Monog.*, 1935, *11*, 43–79.

of mass action cannot be applied to cortex in general, when one is considering the effects of brain damage on speech; but it can be applied within the limits of speech-area cortex.

The thirty-odd years that have elapsed since the publication of this book have taken away some of its impact—its argument is no longer new—and subsequent research (by Lashley himself as well as others) has qualified its conclusions in some respects. On the other hand, that passage of time has confirmed the importance of Lashley's approach to the problems of behavior. In the perspective of time it can be seen that this is indeed one of the important books of psychology. It brought psychological theory down to earth in a way that had not been done before, with lasting effect; and the quality of its analyses of behavior, quite apart from its neurological and physiological data, gives it a continuing relevance and importance today.

CEREBRAL ORGANIZATION AND BEHAVIOR

The split brain behaves in many respects like two separate brains, providing new research possibilities.

R. W. SPERRY

California Institute of Technology

The control centers of the brain, including the cortical areas, come in matched pairs, right and left mirror mates, with a complete set to each side. Normally, right and left brain halves are in direct communication through a series of commissures, which are defined as fiber systems that cross the midline to form reciprocal cross-connections between corresponding structures on the right and left sides. The largest of these is the great commissure of the cerebral hemispheres, the corpus callosum, the general proportions of which are indicated in Fig. 1, with reference to the rhesus monkey, its relative size in man being somewhat larger.

The corpus callosum is the most massive by far of any single fiber tract in the brain. It was, therefore, cause for some concern that complete surgical section of the corpus callosum in human patients failed to produce any clear-cut functional impairments detectable even with extensive neurological and psychological testing. The discrepancy between the large size, strategic position, and apparent importance of the corpus callosum on the one hand, and the lack of functional disturbance after its section on the other, posed for many years one of the more intriguing and challenging enigmas of brain function.

During the past seven years or so the old "riddle of the corpus callosum" has been largely resolved, in animal studies in which it has been possible at last to demonstrate definite high-level integrating functions for this structure. More important, perhaps, the results have also opened some promising new approaches to the study of cerebral organization, significantly extending the general scope and analytic possibilities of the brain lesion method and related techniques. The following is a generalized survey of some of these developments.

The animal studies from the beginning have confirmed the earlier clinical observations that complete section of the corpus callosum produces surprisingly little disturbance of ordinary behavior. Callosum-sectioned cats and monkeys are virtually indistinguishable from their normal cagemates under most testing and training conditions. This tends to be the case also with further midline sections added, even to the extent of including all the structures labeled in Fig. 1, plus the cerebellum.

Except for causing partial loss of vision, these midline cuts leave nearly all the sensory inflow, motor outflow, and other brain-stem relations intact, and they leave most of the internal organization of each hemisphere undisturbed. Aside from manifesting an initial tremor and unsteadiness when the cerebellum is bisected, monkeys recovered from such midline surgery show no disabling paralysis, ataxia, or spasticity. There is no forced circling, nor are there other asymmetries. The animals are not overly hyperactive or lethargic. Visceral and other homeostatic functions continue as before. The monkeys remain alert and curious and retain fair-to-good muscular coordination. They perceive, learn, and remember much as normal animals do.

However, if one studies such a "split-brain" monkey more carefully, under special training and testing conditions where the inflow of sensory information to the divided hemispheres can be separately restricted and controlled, one finds that each of the divided hemispheres now has its independent mental sphere or cognitive system—that is,

---

Reprinted from *Science*, Vol. 133, No. 3466, June 2, 1961. Copyright 1961 by the American Association for the Advancement of Science.

its own independent perceptual, learning, memory, and other mental processes. It is as if each of the separated hemispheres is unaware of what is experienced in the other, as if neither has any direct memory of anything that has gone on in the other subsequent to the midline surgery. In these respects it is as if the animals had two separate brains.

Functions of the Corpus callosum

Although there were indications in the earlier literature on the corpus callosum that this might be the case—indications that now can be picked out, in retrospect—the first convincing demonstration came from the experiments of Ronald Myers on the role of the corpus callosum in interocular transfer in the cat (1, 2). In brief, he found that with both the optic chiasm and the corpus callosum sectioned (see Fig. 2), a cat is unable to perform with one eye visual pattern discriminations learned with the other eye. When obliged to use the second eye such a cat behaved normally except that it appeared to have a complete amnesia for the visual training experienced with the first eye. It learned to respond, with the second eye, to a given stimulus in a manner exactly the reverse of that in which it had been trained to respond with the first eye, and learned the two responses with equal ease.

In controls in which only the chiasm is cut and the callosum is left intact, discriminations learned with the first eye are readily performed with the second. If the corpus callosum is not cut until after training with the first eye is completed, the learning again transfers, and thereafter the learned discrimination can be performed with either eye (2). If, after training with the corpus callosum intact, the cortex on the directly trained side is ablated; one still gets transfer of the habit to the second eye (3). In other words, the corpus callosum is shown to be instrumental in laying down a second set of memory traces, or engrams, in the contralateral hemisphere—a mirror-image duplicate or weak carbon copy of the engram on the directly trained side, perhaps, to judge from the symmetry of reciprocal cross-connections in the callosal fiber pattern. These experiments were carried out in apparatus of the type shown in Fig. 3, developed earlier for testing and quantifying refined pattern discrimination in the cat.

Because the memory trace or engram has always been extremely elusive and difficult to pin down or localize by the brain-lesion method, this evidence that it could be confined to one hemisphere by cutting the corpus callosum was not to be accepted without question. Might it merely be, for example, that with chiasm and callosum both sectioned, the hemisphere on the seeing side is more dominant than usual and drains the attention and learning processes off to that side? In partial answer, we find that very large cortical ablations, such as that shown in Fig. 4, that markedly depress pattern vision on the same side, still do not force into the contralateral hemisphere the learning and memory of pattern discriminations performed through the homolateral eye (4, 5). Also, when we compared the learning curves for the first and second eye on a statistical basis, there was no evidence that learning with the second eye was benefited by the previous experience with the first (6).

In a pedal-pressing apparatus, developed largely by Stamm (see Fig. 5), we were able to demonstrate that the same kind of functional independence prevails in the separated hemispheres with respect to somesthetic learning and memory involving touch and pressure on the surface of the forepaw (7). Not only sensory discriminations of the kind illustrated in Fig. 5 but also the simple motor patterns acquired in learning to operate the pedals smoothly were transferred to the second paw in normal cats but were not transferred in the callosum-sectioned subjects. Again, statistical comparison of the learning curves for the first and second paws indicated complete absence of any transfer of learning from one to the other hemisphere. Learning a reverse response with the second paw proceeded as easily in these subjects as relearning the original response. Further, the learning of reversed or diametrically opposed discriminations by right and left paws was carried out simultaneously by the split-brain cats when right and left limbs were alternated every few trials during the training, and still with no apparent interference between the conflicting habits (8).

The findings with respect to visual learning and memory have been confirmed in the main for the monkey as well, with extension to discrimination of colored and three-dimensional objects (9–11). Because the monkey is much less inclined than the cat to be cooperative about wearing an eye patch, a training box was devised like that sketched roughly in Fig. 6, which has one viewing slot accessible only to the left eye and another accessible only to the right eye, each of which can be opened or closed from trial to trial. A sliding arm panel controls the use of the arms and permits the pairing of either eye with either hand from trial to trial.

This has the advantage over the use of an eye patch for monocular testing and training in that one can easily switch from one eye to the other, giving a few trials to the right eye, then a few to the left, and so on. If this is done while the monkey is learning reversed discriminations with the separate eyes, one can show that while one hemisphere is in the process of learning, for example, to avoid crosses and select circles, the other hemisphere can be learning to do exactly the reverse. The learning curves for the two conflicting habits then rise concurrently in parallel in the two hemispheres with no apparent interference. The normal brain does not of course operate in this way—nor does that of controls with only the optic chiasm cut, nor even that of controls with section of chiasm plus anterior commissure plus the anterior half of the corpus callosum.

Without going further into studies dealing with the properties of the callosum, it may be said that several different functions for this structure are now recognized. First, and perhaps most significant, is that of the laying down of duplicate engrams in the contralateral hemisphere, as outlined above. In this the callosum serves to keep each hemisphere up to date on what's new in the other; it tends to equate the two hemispheres for those new organizational properties added through learning. It can also be shown that where learning has been deliberately restricted by experimental procedure to one hemisphere, with the corpus callosum left intact, the callosum can then be utilized by the uneducated hemisphere to tap the engram systems of the trained side (3). The callosum also aids in certain types of bilateral sensory-sensory and sensory-motor integration, as for example in visual use of either hand across the vertical midline of the visual field (8, 12, 13). A general excitatory tonic effect can also be demonstrated in the unilateral blindness of one or two weeks' duration produced by section of the callosum in animals with a surgically isolated visual cortex (8). Qualifications of the above properties and special problems relate to the development of language and its lateralized dominance in the human brain, about which little can be said at present. With further analysis it may

CEREBRAL ORGANIZATION AND BEHAVIOR

prove that some of these diverse functions derive from basically the same mechanism.

Simultaneous Learning Processes

After it had been found that the split-brain monkey is able to learn reverse discriminations concurrently with the separated hemispheres (*10, 11*), the question arose as to whether the two hemispheres could learn their reverse tasks simultaneously. Instead of alternating between right and left eye during the training, what happens if both eyes are left open and each trial feeds conflicting information back through the two eyes at the same time? In other words, does the split-brain animal, in order to learn, have to attend to the information entering one hemisphere at a time? Or does it have two separate attention processes, both able to operate simultaneously, handling the diverse sets of information and filing them in two separate memory systems capable of independent recall?

The question has been answered in part by Trevarthen (*13*), with an apparatus incorporating polarized light filters to make the two stimulus objects to be discriminated appear simultaneously different to the two eyes. As explained in Fig. 7, what looks to one hemisphere, for example, to be a circle on the left and a cross on the right is made to look the reverse to the other hemisphere. While one hemisphere observes that the pushing of circles but not crosses is rewarded, the other eye and brain discover, by the same process, the converse—that is, that the pushing of crosses is rewarded and not circles. Any kind of projectable two-dimensional figure, design, or picture may be used, with or without color. Learning is allowed to proceed with both eyes open until the learning curve reaches the 90-percent level. The eyes are then tested individually to find out if the learning has occurred in one or in both hemispheres, and to what degree.

Although the results vary, as expected, Trevarthen finds that during the time required for the dominant hemisphere to learn its problem, the other also, in the majority of cases, has been learning its own reverse problem in

Fig. 1 (top). Midline structures divided in surgical bisection of mammalian brain. Fig. 2 (bottom). Effect of sectioning crossed fibers in optic chiasm. Half-field overlap from contralateral eye is eliminated; this restricts visual inflow to the homolateral hemisphere.

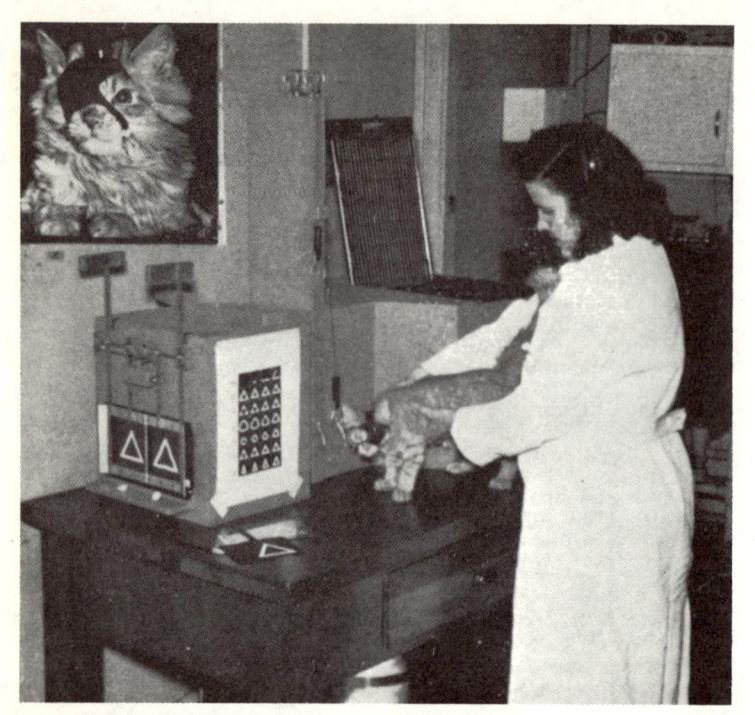

Fig. 3. Visual training apparatus. The cat, placed in the darkened box, obtains a food reward by pushing on the correct one of two translucent patterns interchanged in doors at the end of the box. Inset shows enlargement of the cat wearing the eye patch devised by Myers. Made of rubber, it is simply turned inside out to cover the other eye.

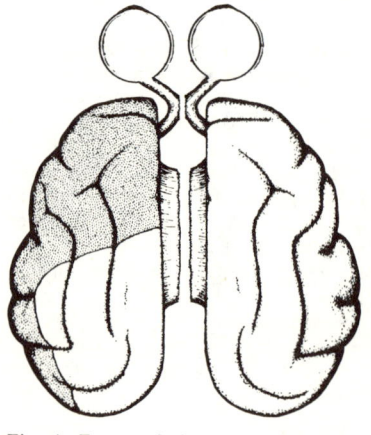

Fig. 4. Extent of the extravisual cortex ablated from the seeing hemisphere of a split-brain cat (4).

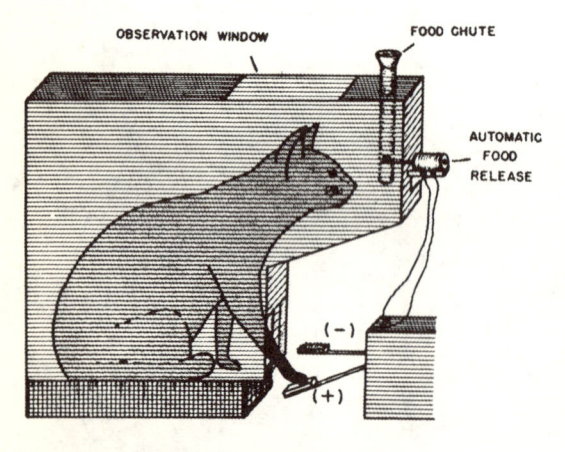

Fig. 5. Simplified diagram of the pedal-pressing apparatus for training in tactile discrimination. Pairs of interchangeable pedal mountings are shown at bottom (7, 15).

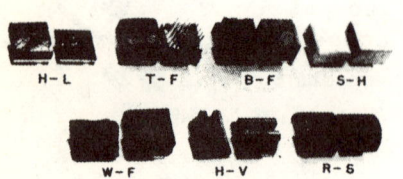

part or in full. In some instances, both hemispheres fully learn their separate problems simultaneously. In other words, in approximately the length of time and number of trials required by an ordinary-brained monkey to learn one discrimination problem, these altered, twin-brain monkeys are able to master two such problems. This raises some questions with regard to learning theory and the role in learning of attention, motivation, mental and motor set, and the like. Are all such components of the learning mechanism doubled in these brains, or are some perhaps bifurcate in form, with a common brain-stem element and qualitatively different cerebral prongs? The implications are intriguing and suggest further variations on the initial experiment.

The question of mental conflict is frequently raised in this connection: What happens when one hemisphere has been trained to do one thing and the other trained to do just the opposite, and the animal is given a free choice to perform either or both? With two separate volitional systems inside the same skull, each wanting its own way and each, by training, wanting the opposite of the other, does each of these thinking entities try to decide for itself?

When such a test is run—by rotating one of the eye filters 90° for example—one sees little evidence of internal conflict, apart from, perhaps, a little hesitance (*14*). By and large, the monkey starts selecting circles consistently or crosses consistently, and it may shift from one to a series of the other, thereby telling us which hemisphere is being used at the moment. These shifts are controllable in part by forcing the use of one or the other hand, which then tends to bring into play the contralateral hemisphere, though this latter correlation is not fixed or rigorous. Apparently when a hemisphere once gains the ascendancy, the lower centers tend to throw their full allegiance to this side. Anything coming down from the other hemisphere that is incompatible or out of line with the going activity of the dominant control is automatically inhibited. This is just another example of the general rule that the patterning of excitation in the central nervous system is an either-or kind of thing. Either one unified pattern or another prevails; seldom is there a confused mixture.

The split-brain cat or monkey is thus in many respects an animal with two separate brains that may be used either together or in alternation. With all pairs of major suprasegmental controls bisected, there is no way for the higher-level integration of one hemisphere to reach and influence that of the other except indirectly through the lower brain stem outflow (Fig. 8). By the time the data processing has reached this stage it already is in such form that any recurrent feedback into the opposite hemisphere carries little of the original content.

Bilateral Hegemony

Each of the twin half brains with its full complement of control centers has much bilateral hegemony over the brain stem and spinal cord and is thus capable, to a large extent, of taking over and governing the total behavior of the body. The cat especially, but also the monkey and even man, with one hemisphere gone manages to get along fairly well, and most central nervous functions are retained. With both hemispheres present, in the split condition, even though one be strongly dominant or in exclusive control of the going higher-level activities, the other presumably continues to contribute much to generalized, background function. Under most ordinary conditions the higher activities also are bound to have much in common. Only in special training and testing circumstances does the double mental control become apparent. The simultaneous use of the two divided hemispheres presents little problem so long as there is unity in the lower centers. Given lower-level harmony, it doesn't matter, as seen above, whether the higher centers function similarly or in direct contradiction.

There is much yet to be learned in following up studies, like the foregoing, that deal directly with the functional properties of the bisected brain, split to different levels and with various incomplete patterns and combinations of commissurotomy. The split brain may also be used to advantage as a basic preparation for attacking other kinds of questions not directly related to problems of commissure function. With the brain bisected, it becomes possible to direct one's ablations, tests, and other analytic procedures to a single one of the hemispheres, leaving the "spare" hemisphere for the use of the animal. In addition to the obvious benefit to the animal over the usual bilateral invasion, there are a number of significant technical advantages in working on the half brain instead of the whole brain. It is important to remember in this connection that the half brain is, in a sense, pretty much a whole brain in that it contains a complete set of cerebral integrating centers and all their interrelations. That is, practically the entire pattern and most of the problems of cerebral organization are there for the unraveling within the half brain.

Advantages for Experimentation

One obvious advantage of the split-brain preparation lies in the factor of built-in controls within the spare hemisphere, controls for all sorts of experiments ranging from short-term studies on innate organization to studies on the long-term effects of early experience on adult behavior. These controls are not only of the homozygous, identical-twin, type but are equated also for almost all experientially derived organization implanted up to the time of splitting. The control hemisphere is fairly well balanced for additions thereafter, also, except for performances that have been deliberately lateralized. These contralateral cerebral controls are thus of a quality almost impossible to obtain by using different animals.

More important is the possibility of extending the surgical analysis within the experimental hemisphere of the split brain far beyond what was possible when the lesions had to be made bilaterally. It has been a long-standing rule in brain-lesion studies of learning and memory that the cortical lesions must be made on both sides to obtain a genuine loss. Unilateral removals are not critical, ordinarily because the functions involved can be handled by the remaining integrating center on the opposite side.

With the split-brain approach it becomes possible to investigate structures like the caudate nucleus, the primary motor cortex, and others, the bilateral ablation of which produces incapacitating or other secondary undesirable effects that act to obscure or confuse possible contributions in other activities. Each brain center tends to be involved in a whole spectrum of different functions. In many cases only the basic impairments can be inferred after bilateral removals, the others being hidden or untestable in the presence of the former.

For the same reasons, with the split-brain approach much larger cortical ablations can be made, even to the extreme of removing most of the cortex

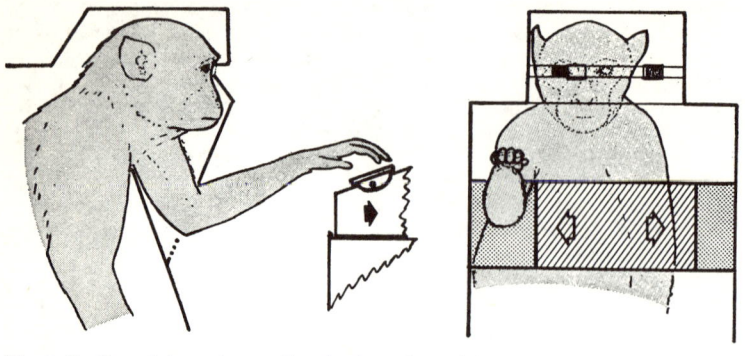

Fig. 6. Profile and front-view outline sketches of a training box for controlling eye-use and eye-hand associations in a monkey.

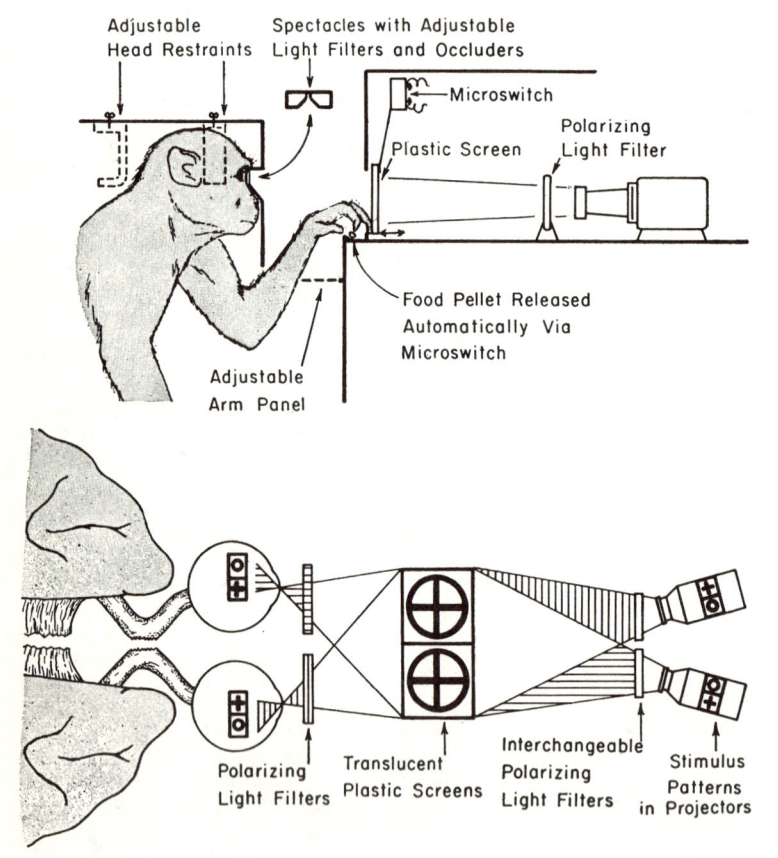

Fig. 7. Profile and schematic diagram of apparatus for testing perceptual conflict in a split-brain monkey (13).

and saving only isolated functional remnants—the converse of the usual procedure. We isolated the visual cortex of the cat in this way (see Fig. 9) and found that the primary visual cortex, without aid from other cortical areas, is incapable of sustaining visual functions beyond a bare minimum. A next step is to go back and restore in other animals different portions of the cortex removed in these subjects to determine the respective contributions of each portion to visual learning and memory.

A very different result followed similar surgical isolation of the frontal cortex that includes the somatic sensory and motor areas. In this case the isolated remnant was found to be capable of mediating excellent learning and memory of new somesthetic discrimination habits performed in the pedal-pressing apparatus shown in Fig. 5 (15). The ever-elusive engrams or memory traces for these new habits would seem to have been at least cornered within the local cortical area illustrated in Fig. 10. It should be possible to further localize the engram by paring away additional parts of the remaining cortical remnant and also by adding deep electrolytic lesions to test the functional contributions of various subcortical centers that remain undegenerated. This somatic island preparation thus furnishes a promising means of determining the critical minimum cerebral apparatus essential for discrimination learning and memory in the mammalian brain. With one hemisphere preserved intact to maintain background and lower-level activity, it becomes feasible, in the experimental hemisphere, to undertake almost complete surgical dissection and analysis as far as function is concerned. About the only limitations that remain are those imposed by surgical technique, particularly that relating to the preservation of circulation.

To further assure, in these studies of somesthetic discrimination habits, that the habits were not being learned and mediated by the contralateral somatic cortex, a complementary removal of the corresponding area was made on the opposite side. The feasibility of thus adding complementary lesion patterns in the intact hemisphere of the split brain offers further possibilities for the analysis of functional relationships—possibilities not available, of course, where the removals have to be made bilaterally.

There are other promising angles in investigations of this "somatic island preparation." For example, it is possible to test the proven pedal-pressing learning capacity of this cortical area with visual or auditory instead of tactile stimuli—in other words, to answer the questions: Could such a cat learn to press a pedal that activates the correct one of two different tone patterns, or the correct one of two different visual patterns? If not, could it then do so if an isolated patch of auditory or visual cortex were left on the same side as the somatic island? If not, again,˙ what kind of inter- and intrahemispheric bridges and˙ connections are needed to satisfy the learning and memory requirements?

Visuomotor Coordination

Figure 11 illustrates a type of complementary lesion preparation we have

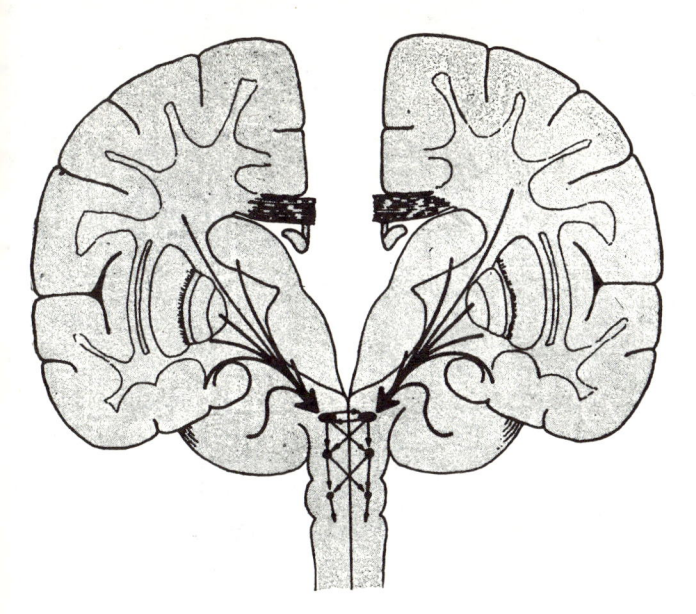

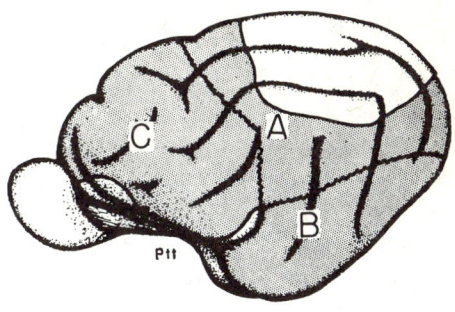

Fig. 8 (left). Schematic diagram to aid in visualizing hegemony of the hemispheres of the split brain over lower centers. Fig. 9 (above). Surgical isolation of central visual cortex in test hemisphere: extravisual cortex removed in three successive operations, *A*, *B*, and *C*, to determine separate functional contributions (*4*).

been using, with a number of variations, to determine the neural pathways used in visuomotor coordination. The experimental question here was: Can visual information that is processed in one hemisphere serve as a guide for limb responses for which the cortical centers lie in the opposite hemisphere and are surgically separated from the visual inflow?

Cats, so prepared, and also monkeys that have undergone similar surgery, are able to use vision to direct the homolateral forelimb and to aim it with near-normal accuracy at both stationary and moving objects (*16*). Presumably the speed and accuracy might be shown to be somewhat below that in control animals using the other limb, governed from the same hemisphere, if sufficiently delicate tests were available. However, the performance is still there and not markedly impaired. Where the visuomotor guidance depends on unilaterally learned visual discriminations in split-brain cats and monkeys, either forelimb can still be used without difficulty both during learning and in retention tests (*11, 17*). The neural pathways for these volitional eye-hand coordinations have yet to be determined.

Somewhat in contradiction to the observations that the split-brain monkey or cat readily pairs either eye with either "hand" is a more recent report (*12*) that visuomotor coordination is markedly disrupted under these conditions, to the extent even that prolonged relearning is required, much like that demanded after unilateral removal of the precentral motor cortex. This observation, though yet unexplained, may be a reflection of particular testing conditions that unduly facilitate the use of the visuomotor system for the contralateral limb.

In any case, the expected preference for the favored arm—that is, for the arm governed from the hemisphere that receives the visual inflow—is found and can be demonstrated in more delicate testing conditions such as those obtainable in the training apparatus described above (Figs. 6 and 7), where the monkey is able to use either arm with either eye. This arm preference is easily overcome, however, in a matter of hours in most cases, and may be lacking from the start in animals in which the homolateral arm is strongly dominant, either naturally or as a result of experience in a given testing situation. Trevarthen (*13*) describes distinct differences in the learning curves obtained in pairing the homolateral and contralateral arms with a given eye that indicate basic differences in the neural mechanisms for the two combinations. With the homolateral arm, the reaction time tends to be longer, and the learning slower and more erratic and unstable. The effect is enhanced in monkeys with deeper splits that include the cerebellum.

Surgical preparations similar to that illustrated in Fig. 11 have been used for study of the old and still puzzling problem of the neural pathways involved in the conditioned response. In this case a visual signal is used as the con-

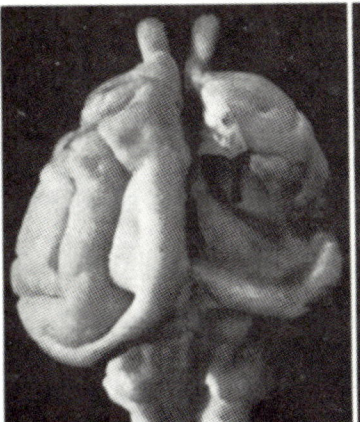

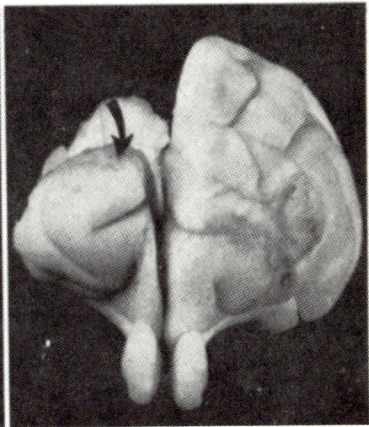

Fig. 10. Top and front views of somatic island preparation with a small complementary ablation in the control hemisphere. Engrams for tactile-discrimination learning appear to be localized within the cortical remnant of the right hemisphere (*15*).

ditioning stimulus to establish a conditioned flexion of the forelimb, the cortical centers for which have been left in the opposite hemisphere. Efforts are now under way to eliminate successively the remaining undegenerated thalamic, midbrain, and other subcortical centers until the critical associations and pathways for the conditioned reflex are delineated (18). At the present stage of this program the conditioned forelimb flexion in response to a flashing light signal has been found to survive the following: section of left optic tract; ablation of left occipital (visual) cortex; near-total removal of neocortex from the right hemisphere; midline section of corpus callosum plus the anterior, posterior, hippocampal, and habenular commissures; and midline section of the massa intermedia and the quadrigeminal plate—produced stepwise in the same animal.

Another application of the split-brain approach is indicated in Fig. 12. The behavior under analysis in this case is a kind of sensory-sensory association in which the monkey is trained to perform a discrimination problem that requires in each trial an association of visual plus tactile stimuli. By controlling the hand and the eye used, and thereby the cortical receptor centers involved, it is possible to test intra- and interhemispheric integration with and without different parts of the corpus callosum and then with various types of separating cuts and ablations, to analyze the kind of neural mechanism and associations that mediate this type of perceptual integration.

It was something of a surprise to find that the split-brain monkey was still able to perform the visuotactile integration with the tactile stimuli presumably restricted to the hemisphere opposite that of the visual inflow. In addition to making the animal use the proper hand, the somesthetic cortex was ablated on the side of the visual inflow. We first used color-plus-weight (largely proprioceptive) discriminations (10, 11) and are now repeating the study with black-and-white patterns and cutaneous rough-smooth stimuli. In the latter study the monkey is required to pull the rougher of two levers when they are presented behind one visual pattern, and the smoother of the two when they are similarly presented in back of another visual pattern, the two visual patterns being black and white and equated for brightness. This latter performance ability is retained even after additional midline sections have been made (see Fig. 12) that include the habenular and posterior commissures, the massa intermedia, and the quadrigeminal plate, in addition to the corpus callosum and the anterior and hippocampal commissures. The removal of the arm area of the tactile cortex on the side of the visual input (Fig. 12) abolishes performance with the affected hand for several weeks but fails to disrupt performance with the hand governed from the opposite hemisphere. This puzzling result is under further investigation, along with similar cross-integration effects that have appeared recently in studies of visuo-visual conditional discriminations. The surgical analysis promises to be easier in the latter because the input pathways for vision are less diffuse and more easily confined than are those for touch.

Application to Old Problems

A simple application of the split-brain approach to an old problem is illustrated in Fig. 13. It has been known for many years that bilateral but not unilateral removal of the prefrontal lobes impairs the performance of delayed response in the rhesus monkey. Whether this impairment is indicative of a genuine function of this portion of the brain has been uncertain, in part because the bilateral removals tend to produce also hypermotility and distractibility. It has been found that the impairment, unaccompanied by hyperactivity and distractibility is produced by unilateral lesion in the split-brain animal (5, 19). The unilateral approach thus yields new information regarding the nature of the syndrome and its intrahemispheric involvement; also it permits further analysis through partial removals of the corpus callosum in combination with complementary lesion patterns—procedures not feasible with bilateral ablation.

The split-brain approach has been applied also to the classic Klüver-Bucy temporal lobe syndrome and some of its subsequent fractionations (20). Bilateral ablation of the temporal lobes in monkeys produces impairments in visual perception, a change in temperament in the direction of tameness, hypersexuality, and certain oral and "stimulus bound" tendencies. Observations to date show that most features of the syndrome are demonstrable after

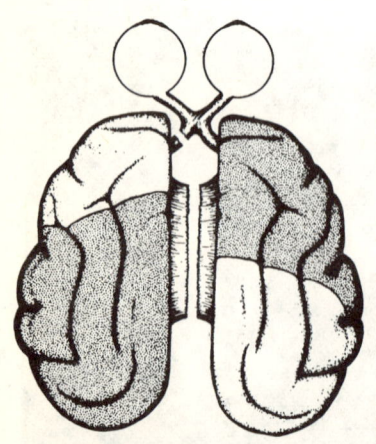

Fig. 11. Basic complementary lesion pattern used with variations for analyzing conditioned response learning and visuo-motor coordination.

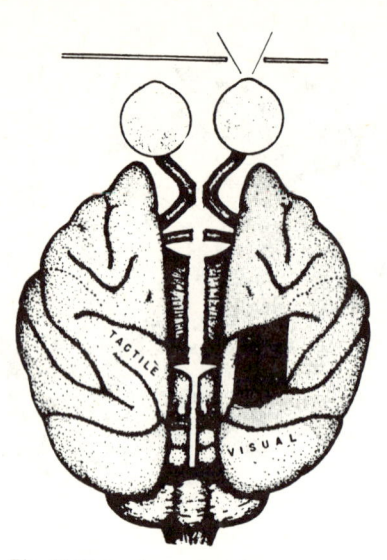

Fig. 12 Stylized representation of monkey-brain hemispheres and underlying midline structures, split through the quadrigeminal plate to the level of the trochlear nerve (11), as prepared for a study of visuo-tactile integration.

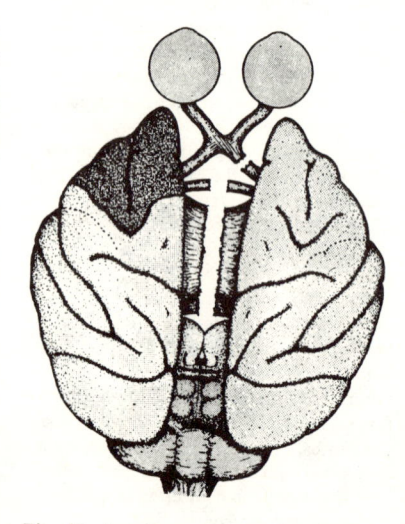

Fig. 13. A split brain, as prepared for a study of prefrontal lobe syndrome (18).

unilateral ablation in split preparations (*21–23*), and the results bring additional insight regarding the underlying neural mechanism. Similarly, a great many of the older brain-lesion studies can be repeated to advantage in the bisected brain, with a gain in information and the possibility of advancing the analysis.

Transfer across the Midplane

With the growing application of brain bisection to a wide variety of problems, it becomes increasingly important to have background information about the functional properties of the split brain in all its various forms—that is, with the midline sections carried to different levels and with different patterns of commissurotomy and ablation. Particularly critical are questions relating to the leakage or transfer of various functions across the midplane. In this connection, observations bearing on the intermanual transfer of learning (*10, 24*) have not been entirely consistent in primates. In our own experience, section of the cerebral commissures may lead to failure of intermanual transfer, but this is not true in all cases nor under all conditions. We have seen intermanual transfer of tactile discriminations in chiasm-callosum-sectioned monkeys that were already experienced in using either hand with either eye and had been trained with pairs of objects that were left in sight because they were distinguishable only by touch, not by vision, the one being harder or heavier or looser than its mate, and this being discernible only upon palpation. Also, we find that an ablation of the somatosensory arm cortex roughly like that shown in Fig. 12 will induce transfer in split-brain monkeys that had failed to exhibit transfer prior to the cortical ablation (*25*). The interpretation of this latter finding is complicated at present by the fact that when the monkeys are trained to reverse the discrimination response with the second hand, this reversal training consistently fails to transfer back again to the first hand.

Certain types of visual discrimination learning also have been found to be subject to interocular transfer after section of all forebrain commissures plus the optic chiasm. This has been shown for obvious brightness discriminations in cats, whereas the more difficult near-threshold discriminations fail to transfer (*26*). Interocular transfer of easy color and brightness discriminations and possibility of very simple pattern discriminations occurs similarly in the monkey, according to Trevarthen (*14*). All of these transferable aspects of visual learning may be elements of visual inflow or learning that cross at the midbrain level. Extension of the tests for color, brightness, and simple pattern to several monkeys having deeper midline sections that include the posterior commissure and rostral half of the quadrigeminal plate (see Fig. 1), plus the cerebellum in one case, show so far a lack of memory transfer for all except simple intensity discriminations.

Evidence is still sketchy regarding the extent to which the divided hemispheres can function independently with respect to emotion. Incidental observations made in the course of training and testing suggest that milder aspects of emotional attitude and temperament, like stubbornness and sulkiness, can be confined to one side (*10, 11*). By employing deliberate procedures for inducing experimental neurosis, it might thus be possible to make one of the separated hemispheres "neurotic" and leave the other normal. The "taming effect" of unilateral deep temporal lobe ablation is much enhanced and lateralized in the split-brain monkey, according to Downer (*21*) and others (*23*). Such animals act normally fearful, or ferocious when using the eye connected to the intact hemisphere, but promptly become more tame, placid, and generally less "touchy" when the lesion hemisphere is made dominant by switching the visual occluder to the other eye. The placement of complementary lesions in right and left hemispheres that produce opposed emotional effects has yet to be explored.

Experimental Possibilities

By the use of positive and negative reinforcement through implanted electrodes under remote control, the development of different or opposed preferences in right and left brain could presumably be extended to animate objects and social relationships, with some interesting consequences. The so-called *encephale isolée* and *cerveau isolé* preparations of Bremer and others (*27*) have found considerable use in physiology, and it should not be too difficult to go further and, by adding hemisections of the brain stem to the midline surgery, prepare isolated half brains of different forms and with different kinds and degrees of isolation that would offer significant advantages over the separated whole brain. The isolated half brain could be studied over a long period in the animal in vivo, in the brain's natural habitat, under normal biochemical conditions, and after recovery from the prolonged depression of surgical cerebral shock. To what extent might such long-isolated (or partially isolated) half brains regain wake-sleep states and consciousness and be capable of learning, remembering, feeling emotion, and the like? Where behavioral output is excluded, electrophysiological indications of some of these capabilities could be obtained with implanted electrodes and conditioning techniques.

By combining various ablations and transections like those described above with more localized lesions produced in subcortical nuclei with the stereotaxic apparatus, it is possible today, with methods now available, to attain a fairly extensive surgical dissection of the mammalian brain and to set up a large variety of combinations and permutations of cerebral centers and connecting pathways in animal subjects for long-term functional testing and analysis. Combine with this the analytic potentialities of the chronically implanted electrode for recording, stimulating, and self-stimulating in free-moving, unanesthetized animals, plus the new automated training and programming techniques, along with other technological advances, and those of us working in brain research find ourselves today, as never before, surrounded by seemingly endless possibilities just waiting to be explored (*28*).

References and Notes

1. R. E. Myers, *J. Comp. and Physiol. Psychol.* **48**, 470 (1955); ———, *Brain* **79**, 358 (1956); ——— and R. W. Sperry, *Anat. Record* **115**, 351 (1953).
2. R. E. Myers, "CIOMS Conference on Brain Mechanisms and Learning," in press.
3. ——— and R. W. Sperry, *A.M.A. Arch. Neurol. Psychiat.* **80**, 298 (1958).
4. R. W. Sperry, R. E. Myers, A. M. Schrier, *Quart. J. Exptl. Psychiat.* **12**, 65 (1960).
5. R. W. Sperry, in *Biological and Biochemical Bases of Behavior*, H. R. Harlow and C. N. Woolsey, Eds. (Univ. of Wisconsin Press, Madison, 1958).
6. R. W. Sperry, J. S. Stamm, N. Miner, *J. Comp. and Physiol. Psychol.* **49**, 529 (1956).
7. J. S. Stamm and R. W. Sperry, *ibid.* **50**, 138 (1957).
8. R. W. Sperry, unpublished.
9. J. L. C. Downer, *Federation Proc.* **17**, 37 (1958).
10. R. W. Sperry, *Anat. Record* **131**, 297 (1958).
11. ———, *Transactions of the Macy Conference on Central Nervous System and Behavior* (1958).
12. J. L. C. Downer, *Brain* **82**, 251 (1959).
13. C. B. Trevarthen, *Am. Psychologist* **15**, 485 (1960).
14. ———, unpublished.
15. R. W. Sperry, *J. Neurophysiol.* **22**, 78 (1959).
16. R. E. Myers, R. W. Sperry, N. Miner, *J. Comp. and Physiol. Psychol.* **48**, 50 (1955).
17. A. M. Schrier and R. W. Sperry, *Science* **129**, 1275 (1959).
18. T. Voneida, unpublished.

19. M. Glickstein, H. Arora, R. W. Sperry, *Physiologist* **3**, 66 (1960).
20. H. Klüver, in *Ciba Foundation Symposium on the Neurological Basis of Behavior* (1958), p. 175.
21. J. L. C Downer, unpublished.
22. G. Ettlinger, *Brain* **82**, 232 (1959); M. Mishkin, *Am. Psychologist* **13**, 414 (1958).
23. J. Steiner and J. S. Bossom, unpublished.
24. F. Ebner and R. E. Myers, *Federation Proc.* **19**, 292 (1960); M. Glickstein and R. W. Sperry, *Am. Psychologist* **14**, 385 (1959); R. E. Myers, *Federation Proc.* **19**, 289 (1960); M. Glickstein and R. W. Sperry, *J. Comp. and Physiol. Psychol.* **53**, 322 (1960).
25. M. Glickstein and R. W. Sperry, *Am. Psychologist* **15**, 485 (1960).
26. T. Meikle, Jr., and J. A. Sechzer, *Science* **132**, 734 (1960); T. Meikle, Jr., *ibid.* **132**, 1496 (1960).
27. F. Bremer, J. Brihaye, G. André-Balisaux, *Arch. suisses neurol. et psychiat.* **78**, 31 (1956).
28. This article is based on a talk given at the Federation Meetings in Chicago for the C. J. Herrick symposium on the physiology of learning, 19 April 1960. A more specialized version is being published in *Federation Proceedings*. Original work discussed has been supported by the National Science Foundation, the National Institutes of Health, and the F. P. Hixon Fund of the California Institute of Technology. Special acknowledgement is made to Harbans Arora, who has performed nearly all our monkey-brain surgery during the past 18 months, and to Lois MacBird who has carried the major responsibility for training, medication, and general laboratory assistance.

EXPLORING THE BRAIN WITH CHEMICALS

The success of electrical methods for studying the brain has led to an overemphasis on the brain's similarity to a giant electronic computer. In reality the activity of the brain cells depends upon complex chemical processes — processes it is just becoming possible to study.

SEBASTIAN P. GROSSMAN
University of Chicago

Before we can hope to gain any understanding of man's behaviour, the nature of the extremely complex interactions between the millions of individual nerve cells which make up his brain must be unravelled. During the past thirty years a great deal of progress has been made. The methods of investigation have all relied on the fact that nerve cells generate small quantities of electricity whenever they are active; sensitive electronic devices have been constructed which can record the electrical activity of a single cell or the cumulative activity of large populations of cells in the brain. In addition, specific portions of the central nervous system can be activated or stimulated by the passage of small electric currents.

Invaluable though these methods of investigation undoubtedly are, they have led to the implicit assumption that the brain and its functions may be completely described in terms of electrical events and that the complex interaction of its parts can be understood by drawing direct analogies with electronic computers. A cell's activity, however, and, just as important, its influence on neighbouring cells, depends on *chemical* processes; the recorded electrical events only reflect these processes in a very gross and non-specific way. Although this has been superficially recognized for some time, and indeed is the basis of our present attempts to treat mental illness with drugs such as tranquillizers, energizers, or other mood-altering agents, we do not yet fully understand how brain chemistry influences behaviour.

However, experimental techniques have recently become available which permit a *direct* investigation of the complex chemical processes which are responsible for the activity of the nerve cells. Through a series of refinements in surgical and recording procedures, we can now observe the behavioural and electrophysiological changes which take place as chemicals are injected directly into the brain. Although the technology is still crude and the questions which we have been able to ask and answer as yet unsophisticated, many important results have already been obtained.

Injecting the brain

The basic procedure is simple. A thin metal tube is inserted into the brain of

---

Reprinted from *Discovery*, Vol. XXVII, No. 5, May, 1966.

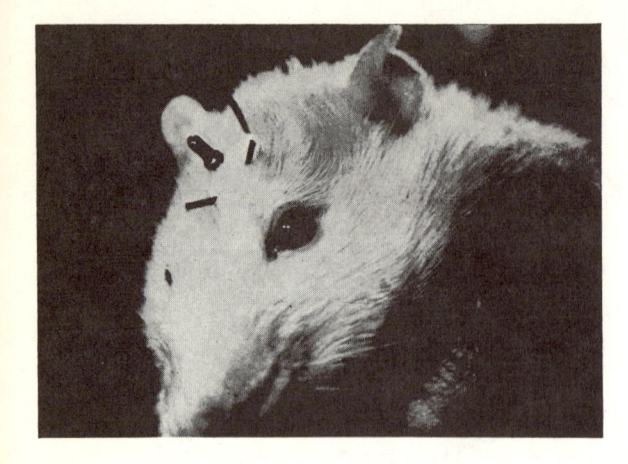

Fig 1 ALBINO RAT after thin metal tubes have been inserted into the brain through small holes drilled in the skull. Through these tubes chemicals may be injected accurately to any part of the brain without causing the animal any discomfort

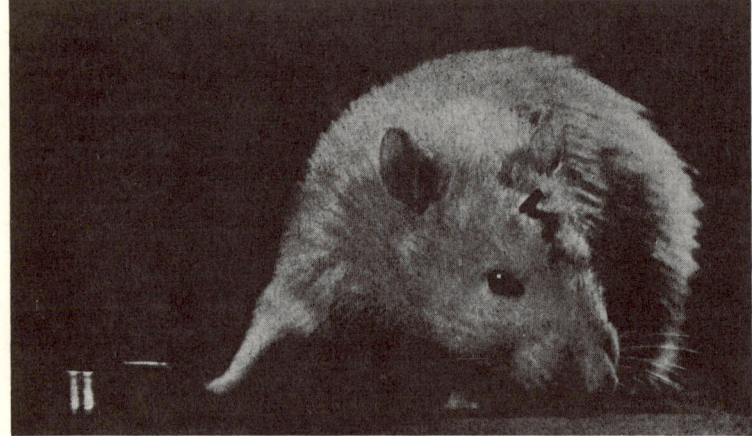

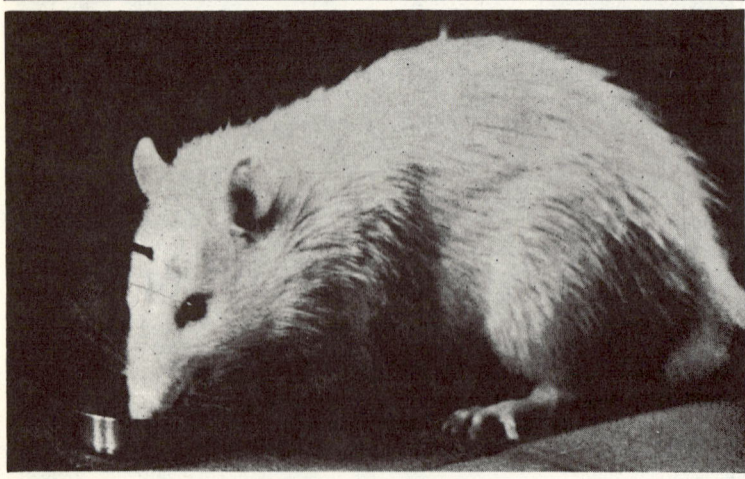

Fig 2 DESPITE BEING GORGED with food and water, the rat in the top photograph can be made to consume still more by injecting noradrenaline into the hypothalamus (bottom). Experimental work so far, indicates that the hunger and thirst 'circuits' in the brain each have their own chemical 'code' to separate the two functions

an animal, such as a rat, through a small hole which has been drilled into the skull. The tubes are positioned by a machine which uses coordinates from a standard map of the brain, and are fastened to the skull by a bit of dental cement. A small cap is placed on the top of the implant to keep dirt from entering the brain. For the experiment itself these caps are removed and small quantities of drugs are injected into the brain without causing the animal any discomfort *(see Fig. 1)*.

The behavioural changes which occur when a particular chemical is injected may either reflect a change in the activity of cells which are *directly* affected by the drug, or a chain reaction resulting in a change in the activity of distant parts of the brain. To check on this, the electrical activity of cells in parts of the brain which are functionally or geographically related to the segment receiving the chemical injections is recorded by wire electrodes inserted into the brain. These reveal the small electrical potentials generated by active nerve cells.

Some recent findings of this new technique suggest that the brain may obtain essential information about the state of the organism or its environment via *chemical* rather than neural routes. The chemical composition of the blood depends on a number of basic metabolic processes, which in turn reflect the state of important homeostatic mechanisms such as the organism's energy and fluid balance. To maintain these processes within the narrow limits which the organism can tolerate immediate corrective action is essential. The quickest and most efficient way of initiating such action is for the regulatory centres in the brain to respond directly to changes in the composition of their blood supply.

Chemical feedback

a) Regulation of thirst

A nice example of just such a direct feedback system has been discovered by Professor Bengt Andersson of Sweden. The body continually loses water through urinary excretion, perspiration and respiration, resulting in a gradual increase in the concentration of salts in the blood stream. If the organism is to survive it must reverse this process by drinking an amount of water exactly proportional to the loss and which will restore the normal concentrations of body fluid. The organism must become aware of the deficit and a specific motivational mechanism in the brain must be activated.

About fifteen years ago, Dr E. B. Verney discovered that an increase in the salt concentration of the blood reaching the hypothalamic region of the brain resulted in the release of an antidiuretic hormone (ADH), which decreases the rate of urine formation. This is a most important water conservation mechanism which operates whenever the organism is losing more water than it is taking in. Verney's observations suggested that this portion of the brain might also contain the regulatory mechanisms which cause the sensation of thirst and set in motion the corrective actions.

To investigate this possibility, Professor Andersson implanted tubes into the hypothalamic region and injected very small amounts of concentrated salt water. In most parts of the hypothalamus, this produced no effect. However, injections into one specific region (about two millimetres square) caused animals already sated with water to seek out and consume further huge quantities—in spite of the fact that this behaviour upset the organism's fluid balance still further. Professor Neal Miller of Yale University later demonstrated that such injections not only cause drinking but also the performance of behaviour sequences which are rewarded with water—an important demonstration of the motivational nature of the effect of chemical stimulation. Miller also found that injections of pure water into this part of the brain produced directly opposite effects, as one would expect if the mechanism indeed regulates thirst in accordance with the body's need.

b) Regulating sexual behaviour

Another approach to the study of the complex relationship between chemical changes in the body and behavioural events is demonstrated in the work of Professor Allan Fisher of Pittsburgh University. The injection of tiny amounts of a male sex hormone into an area of the brain just in front of the hypothalamus was found to elicit male sexual behaviour in female as well as male rats. Males and females treated in this fashion attempted copulation with unreceptive females, males, or even infants. When the same hormone was injected just one or two millimetres from the reactive region, no sexual responses occurred, but both male and female animals displayed maternal behaviours such as nest construction or retrieving of young.

Similar observations have recently been reported following the implantation of a synthetic female hormone into the hypothalamus of female cats. These animals had previously been rendered sexually unresponsive by the surgical removal of the ovaries, but seemed thoroughly hypersexual after treatment with the hormone. They copulated repeatedly with a number of different males and did not display the reluctance normally seen after one or two successive matings. These experiments suggest that nerve cells in this region just in front of the hypothalamus, the preoptic area, may be specifically sensitive to male and female hormones and regulate sexual behaviour in accordance with the level of these hormones in the blood.

c) The rôle of blood-sugar in hunger

Chemical stimulation experiments have also provided important negative evidence which has helped to redirect research effort which might otherwise have been wasted. For instance, fasting produces a fall in the concentration of sugar in the blood and eating almost immediately restores it to normal levels. Since this is the only known metabolic system which responds rapidly and precisely to changes in the organism's energy balance, some cells in the brain were assumed to respond directly to changes in blood glucose and initiate hunger and feeding behaviour when this concentration falls below some critical level. Despite the appeal of such an interpretation, recent observations have suggested that matters may not be quite so simple.

If the blood sugar level carries essential information for regulating feeding, then glucose injections into the centres in the hypothalamic region of the brain which control feeding should curb the appetite of a fasted animal. Our experiments, as well as similar work in Dr Fisher's laboratory, have failed to support this prediction. Thus, it seems that the concentration of glucose cannot be the signal to which the brain responds when it initiates or stops feeding behaviour, although it is still possible that the relationship between blood sugar and appetite is more than a mere coincidence.

Chemical transfer of information

One of the most fascinating problems in neurophysiology has been the question of how the individual nerve cells which make up all neural circuits interact and pass on bits of complex information. The interaction takes place via chemical transmitter substances which are liberated by the active neuron and cross the small gap which separates it from adjacent cells. Here the transmitter substance induces chemical reactions which either allow electrical signals to 'fire' a previously inactive cell, or which prevent the cell from being excited for some period of time and thus prevent its response to signals from other cells.

Only one chemical substance, *acetylcholine,* has been definitely identified as a transmitter of nervous activity in the brain. However, another drug, *noradrenaline,* acts in a similar fashion at some nerve-muscle junctions and is suspected of mediating neural transmission in some portions of the brain, while analysis of the chemical composition of the brain shows non-random distributions of a number of other substances which may also act as selective and specific transmitters in some neural circuits.

The brain is capable of a remarkable specificity of function, despite the fact that it is not geographically divided into compartments, each functionally autonomous. Specific transmitter substances may provide a form of chemical 'coding', separating the neural circuits. For instance, the neural circuits which regulate basic motivational processes such as hunger, thirst, and sexual arousal overlap so extensively, at least in some portions of the brain, that it is impossible to stimulate or inhibit any one of them selectively with conventional procedures. Nevertheless, the brain still manages to attain a specificity of action, and recent experiments have indicated that this may, at least in part, be the result of a chemical coding of the individual circuits such that transmitter X only activates circuit A at a particular junction in the brain and transmitter Y activates only circuit B. Transmitter X may, in fact, exercise some degree of inhibitory influence in circuit B, thereby assuring completely undistorted transmission of information in circuit A.

The chemical code

The mechanisms which control hunger and thirst overlap extensively in the

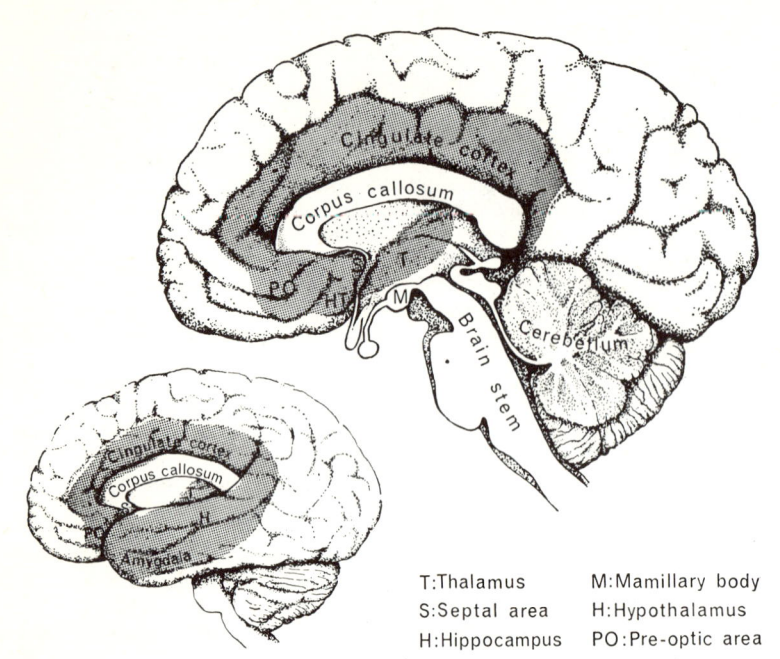

T: Thalamus   M: Mamillary body
S: Septal area H: Hypothalamus
H: Hippocampus PO: Pre-optic area

Fig 3 MEDIAL VIEW OF THE HUMAN BRAIN. The large drawing shows a true medial view with the temporal lobe obscured by the brain stem and cerebellum. In the smaller drawing the temporal lobe is superimposed to show the complete neural circuit (lightly stippled in green) which regulates not only emotional behaviour but also the basic motivational processes such as hunger and thirst

lateral hypothalamus. Damage to this region causes a complete lack of hunger and thirst, and results in death from starvation and dehydration in the midst of plenty. Conversely, electrical stimulation of the lateral hypothalamus causes feeding and drinking in sated animals. Most attempts to study the operation of the two regulatory systems independently failed until chemical stimulation techniques were applied to the problem.

The initial series of experiments in our laboratory showed that local injections of acetylcholine selectively activated the *thirst* mechanism and evoked drinking in sated animals, whereas noradrenaline elicited *feeding* behaviour. Drugs which interfere with the action of these transmitter substances selectively blocked feeding or drinking in hungry and thirsty animals and reversed the effects of the transmitter substances. Electrical recordings from the site of chemical stimulation showed no sign of any gross disturbance to the normal pattern of neural activity. A series of control tests with other drugs and other regions of the brain resulted in no change in the feeding and drinking behaviour of the experimental animals and demonstrated the specificity of the effects.

Whenever a certain behaviour is caused by direct stimulation of the brain, we must ask whether the observed response occurs because a related drive-state has been stimulated or merely because the response has been evoked directly. In other words, does the animal eat because it is actually hungry or simply because we have caused it to chew, lick and swallow? We found that sated animals would not only drink or eat following the application of the transmitter substances, but would also learn to operate a lever in order to gain access to food or water—a behaviour reaction which requires very different motor responses.

Professor Neal Miller has since shown that the local injection of these drugs affects the organism's energy and fluid balance in other and less direct ways. For instance, injections of an acetylcholine-like substance stimulated the secretion of antidiuretic hormone, thus conservating body fluids through an increase in the concentration of urine and reduction of its formation. These injections also produced a sharp rise in blood sugar which may be related to the known inhibitory effect of the drug on food intake. Injections of noradrenaline produced a smaller and apparently paradoxical increase in blood sugar which persisted, in the absence of food, throughout the period during which the animal would have been expected to eat.

Later chemical explorations of the brain have demonstrated that hunger and thirst do not seem to be controlled exclusively by the hypothalamic centres as had been believed in the past. In our laboratory, as well as Dr Fisher's laboratory at Pittsburgh, it has been shown that the injection of acetylcholine-like substances into a number of other areas of the brain (the dorsal hippocampus, the septal and preoptic areas, cingulate cortex, and mamillary region) evokes drinking, whereas injections of noradrenaline into many of the same areas elicits feeding *(see Fig. 3)*.

Yet other areas seem to contribute to the regulation of food and water intake in a more complex fashion. Cholinergic stimulation—the local application of acetylcholine—of an area in the temporal lobe of the brain did not cause sated animals to drink but did significantly increase the water consumption of animals which had been deprived of water for some time. Injections of noradrenaline—adrenergic stimulation—into the same region of the brain similarly failed to elicit feeding behaviour but made hungry animals eat even more. The chemical coding of both regulatory systems was retained, but this portion of the brain appeared to influence basic motivational processes only indirectly by facilitating other parts of the system.

One should not conclude from these observations that all adrenergic or cholinergic systems in the brain contribute to the regulation of hunger or thirst—nothing could be further from the truth, as we shall see in a moment. It even appears premature to assume that all aspects of the regulation of food or water intake are necessarily part of an adrenergic or cholinergic circuit. What has been established quite firmly is the practically important fact that wherever the hunger and thirst circuits intermingle so extensively as to lose geographic identity, a specific chemical 'code' maintains functional specificity. So far, this code has been constant throughout all portions of the brain which we have investigated, making it possible for us to study the properties of each system individually and learn a great deal about their operation.

Emotional reactions

As we have seen, the components of the system concerned with two of the basic drives, hunger and thirst, are extensively interconnected. The complex neural circuit which they form includes most, if not all of the 'old' portion—in the evolutionary sense—of the brain. This is particularly interesting since essentially the same circuit *(see Fig. 3)* has been implicated in the regulation of a variety

EXPLORING THE BRAIN WITH CHEMICALS

of emotional reactions. Thus, electrical stimulation or damage to all areas in question influences an animal's reactions to painful or pleasant stimulation.

We know now that long lasting changes in emotional behaviour can be caused by small changes in the chemical composition of some part of this circuit. Observations from our own laboratory demonstrate, for instance, that a single injection of acetylcholine into a specific portion of the temporal lobe induces long lasting behavioural changes which suggest a profound alteration in the animal's emotional make-up. Previously friendly cats became vicious and attacked men as well as other cats, rats, and dogs. Many of them also showed electrophysiological and behavioural seizures similar to those seen in epilepsy. The response to a single injection lasted for months: spontaneous electrophysiological and behavioural seizure attacks were recorded as late as six months after the initial injection and the animals continued to react excessively to any environment stimulation (see Figs. 4 and 5).

One of our recent investigations of the rôle of the septal area provides an example of a more short-lived and reversible change in emotionality following chemical stimulation of a specific part of the brain. Normal rats rapidly learn to jump over a small hurdle in order to avoid a painful electric shock to the feet. Following the injection of acetylcholine into part of the septal area, our rats did not show any fear of the light which signalled the electric shock and could not be trained to avoid the painful stimulus in many hundreds of trials. The impairment appeared to be specifically related to emotional reactivity since the same injections increased general activity and caused the animals to work harder to obtain access to water. Moreover, the rats were perfectly capable of hurdling the barrier in response to the painful shock itself and performed the response efficiently and promptly.

Chemical factors in arousal

Chemical stimulation procedures are also being used to investigate the functions of the *reticular formation,* a diffuse network of nerve cells which forms the core of the brain. This complex structure is connected to all other portions of the central nervous system and has recently attracted much interest as a possible site for basic 'activation' or 'arousal' processes which may be an essential ingredient of all behavioural reactions.

Electrical stimulation of the reticular formation arouses a sleeping animal and

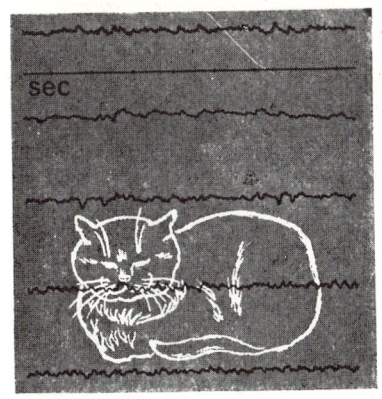

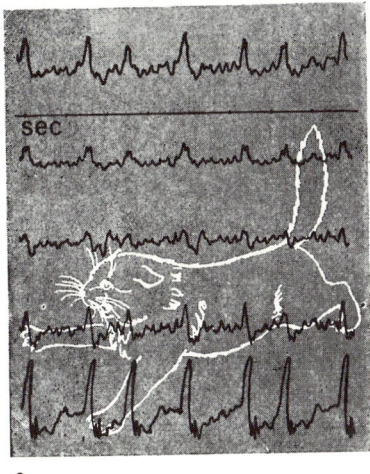

Fig 4 CHANGES in the emotional make-up of a cat after acetylcholine has been injected into the temporal lobe of its brain. (a) is a record of the brain-waves just before the injection, (b) immediately afterwards, when the cat became vicious, and (c) several hours after the stimulation during an epileptic-like seizure

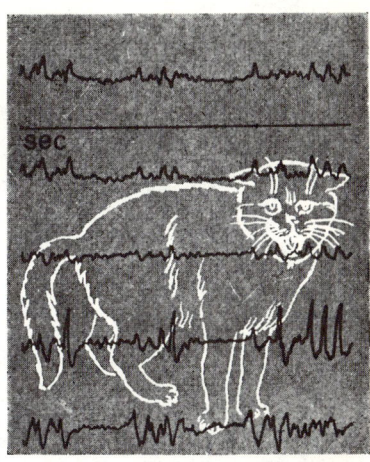

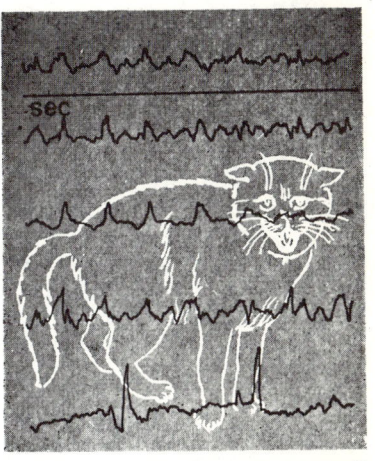

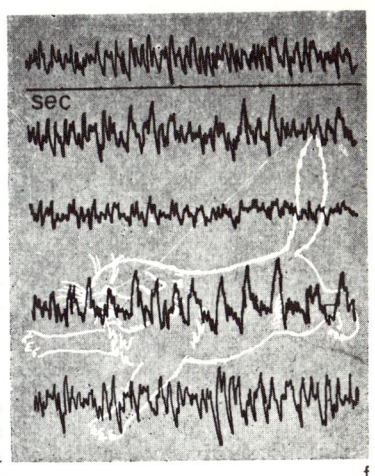

Fig 5 LONGER-TERM effects of a single injection of acetylcholine into the temporal lobe of a cat. 24 hours (d) and even 5 months (e) after the injection the brain-waves are still abnormal and the cat remains vicious. In addition, the cat is still subject to violent seizures, with brain-waves as in (f), 5 months after injection

extensive damage to almost any of its components produces lethargy and coma. The rôle of this mechanism in the control of more complex behaviours has been difficult to study in the past, since it is impossible to stimulate the brain electrically for the long periods of time required to assess the effects of a general increase in reactivity. We have just completed a series of studies which demonstrate that the properties of the reticular formation can be studied by means of chemostimulation.

The first group of experiments was concerned with the rôle of the uppermost portion of this system, the midline and reticular nuclei of the thalamus. We found that injections of acetylcholine into both regions inhibited all recently learned behaviours: hungry and thirsty animals consumed normal quantities of food and water but failed to perform simple instrumental responses (such as lever pressing or running through a T maze) to obtain bits of food or drops of water. Similarly, all animals escaped promptly and efficiently from painful electric shock but did not learn to perform a simple hurdle-jumping response to a warning signal which would have permitted complete avoidance of the painful experience.

Injections of *atropine,* a drug which blocks the action of acetylcholine, also reduced the animals' output on the food- or water-rewarded tasks, but apparently for quite different reasons. Whereas the acetylcholine-treated animals seemed particularly quiet and showed less exploratory activity than normal control subjects, the atropine-treated animals dashed about excitedly and found little time to stop and operate the food- or water-rewarded levers.

Injections of atropine in the midline region of the thalamus produced effects on avoidance behaviour which were opposite to those seen after stimulation with acetylcholine. Atropine-treated animals learned to avoid the painful shock faster than normal subjects and performed the response more promptly and reliably throughout many weeks of daily testing. Atropine injections into the area of the reticular nuclei, on the other hand, produced essentially the same effects as cholinergic stimulation—an apparently paradoxical finding which suggests that a general, nonspecific excitation of this portion of the brain may produce disruptive effects.

Another group of studies recently completed in our laboratories investigated the effect of the injection of acetylcholine on lower portions of the reticular system. Here, cholinergic stimulation raised the organism's overall level of reactivity and produced a general lowering of the threshold to any form of sensory stimulation. The animal's performance of a standard escape-avoidance task was improved, apparently because of the increased reaction to the painful shock. The increased reactivity to the environment interfered with the performance of simple behaviours rewarded by food and water such as lever pressing or running through a maze.

Many questions remain to be answered before the complexity of the human brain can be understood. Chemostimulation procedures have opened a new avenue of approach to this intricate problem and have contributed significantly to our understanding of a number of brain functions which could not be investigated with more conventional techniques. A closer understanding of the chemical events which are directly responsible for the processing of information in the brain will be an essential waystation, not only for neurophysiologists, but also for all those concerned with the behaviour of man.

LEARNING OF VISCERAL AND GLANDULAR RESPONSES

Recent experiments on animals show the fallacy of an ancient view of the autonomic nervous system.

NEAL E. MILLER

Rockefeller University

There is a strong traditional belief in the inferiority of the autonomic nervous system and the visceral responses that it controls. The recent experiments disproving this belief have deep implications for theories of learning, for individual differences in autonomic responses, for the cause and the cure of abnormal psychosomatic symptoms, and possibly also for the understanding of normal homeostasis. Their success encourages investigators to try other unconventional types of training. Before describing these experiments, let me briefly sketch some elements in the history of the deeply entrenched, false belief in the gross inferiority of one major part of the nervous system.

Historical Roots and Modern Ramifications

Since ancient times, reason and the voluntary responses of the skeletal muscles have been considered to be superior, while emotions and the presumably involuntary glandular and visceral responses have been considered to be inferior. This invidious dichotomy appears in the philosophy of Plato (*1*), with his superior rational soul in the head above and inferior souls in the body below. Much later, the great French neuroanatomist Bichat (*2*) distinguished between the cerebrospinal nervous system of the great brain and spinal cord, controlling skeletal responses, and the dual chain of ganglia (which he called "little brains") running down on either side of the spinal cord in the body below and controlling emotional and visceral responses. He indicated his low opinion of the ganglionic system by calling it "vegetative"; he also believed it to be largely independent of the cerebrospinal system, an opinion which is still reflected in our modern name for it, the autonomic nervous system. Considerably later, Cannon (*3*) studied the sympathetic part of the autonomic nervous system and concluded that the different nerves in it all fire simultaneously and are incapable of the finely differentiated individual responses possible for the cerebrospinal system, a conclusion which is enshrined in modern textbooks.

Many, though not all, psychiatrists have made an invidious distinction between the hysterical and other symptoms that are mediated by the cerebrospinal nervous system and the psychosomatic symptoms that are mediated by the autonomic nervous system. Whereas the former are supposed to be subject to a higher type of control that is symbolic, the latter are presumed to be only the direct physiological consequences of the type and intensity of the patient's emotions (see, for example, *4*).

Similarly, students of learning have made a distinction between a lower form, called classical conditioning and thought to be involuntary, and a superior form variously called trial-and-error learning, operant conditioning, type II conditioning, or instrumental learning and believed to be responsible for voluntary behavior. In classical conditioning, the reinforcement must be by an unconditioned stimulus that already elicits the specific response to be learned; therefore, the possibilities are quite limited. In instrumental learning, the reinforcement, called a reward, has the property of strengthening any immediately preceding response. Therefore, the possibilities for reinforcement are much greater; a given reward may reinforce any one of a number of different responses, and a given response may be reinforced by any one of a number of different rewards.

Finally, the foregoing invidious distinctions have coalesced into the strong

---

Reprinted from *Science*, Vol. 163, January 31, 1969. Copyright 1969 by the American Association for the Advancement of Science.

61

traditional belief that the superior type of instrumental learning involved in the superior voluntary behavior is possible only for skeletal responses mediated by the superior cerebrospinal nervous system, while, conversely, the inferior classical conditioning is the only kind possible for the inferior, presumably involuntary, visceral and emotional responses mediated by the inferior autonomic nervous system. Thus, in a recent summary generally considered authoritative, Kimble (5) states the almost universal belief that "for autonomically mediated behavior, the evidence points unequivocally to the conclusion that such responses can be modified by classical, but not instrumental, training methods." Upon examining the evidence, however, one finds that it consists only of failure to secure instrumental learning in two incompletely reported exploratory experiments and a vague allusion to the Russian literature (6). It is only against a cultural background of great prejudice that such weak evidence could lead to such a strong conviction.

The belief that instrumental learning is possible only for the cerebrospinal system and, conversely, that the autonomic nervous system can be modified only by classical conditioning has been used as one of the strongest arguments for the notion that instrumental learning and classical conditioning are two basically different phenomena rather than different manifestations of the same phenomenon under different conditions. But for many years I have been impressed with the similarity between the laws of classical conditioning and those of instrumental learning, and with the fact that, in each of these two situations, some of the specific details of learning vary with the specific conditions of learning. Failing to see any clear-cut dichotomy, I have assumed that there is only one kind of learning (7). This assumption has logically demanded that instrumental training procedures be able to produce the learning of any visceral responses that could be acquired through classical conditioning procedures. Yet it was only a little over a dozen years ago that I began some experimental work on this problem and a somewhat shorter time ago that I first, in published articles (8), made specific sharp challenges to the traditional view that the instrumental learning of visceral responses is impossible.

Some Difficulties

One of the difficulties of investigating the instrumental learning of visceral responses stems from the fact that the responses that are the easiest to measure —namely, heart rate, vasomotor responses, and the galvanic skin response —are known to be affected by skeletal responses, such as exercise, breathing, and even tensing of certain muscles, such as those in the diaphragm. Thus, it is hard to rule out the possibility that, instead of directly learning a visceral response, the subject has learned a skeletal response the performance of which causes the visceral change being recorded.

One of the controls I planned to use was the paralysis of all skeletal responses through administration of curare, a drug which selectively blocks the motor end plates of skeletal muscles without eliminating consciousness in human subjects or the neural control of visceral responses, such as the beating of the heart. The muscles involved in breathing are paralyzed, so the subject's breathing must be maintained through artificial respiration. Since it seemed unlikely that curarization and other rigorous control techniques would be easy to use with human subjects, I decided to concentrate first on experiments with animals.

Originally I thought that learning would be more difficult when the animal was paralyzed, under the influence of curare, and therefore I decided to postpone such experiments until ones on nonparalyzed animals had yielded some definitely promising results. This turned out to be a mistake because, as I found out much later, paralyzing the animal with curare not only greatly simplifies the problem of recording visceral responses without artifacts introduced by movement but also apparently makes it easier for the animal to learn, perhaps because paralysis of the skeletal muscles removes sources of variability and distraction. Also, in certain experiments I made the mistake of using rewards that induced strong unconditioned responses that interfered with instrumental learning.

One of the greatest difficulties, however, was the strength of the belief that instrumental learning of glandular and visceral responses is impossible. It was extremely difficult to get students to work on this problem, and when paid assistants were assigned to it, their attempts were so half-hearted that it soon became more economical to let them work on some other problem which they could attack with greater faith and enthusiasm. These difficulties and a few preliminary encouraging but inconclusive early results have been described elsewhere (9).

Success with Salivation

The first clear-cut results were secured by Alfredo Carmona and me in an experiment on the salivation of dogs. Initial attempts to use food as a reward for hungry dogs were unsuccessful, partly because of strong and persistent unconditioned salivation elicited by the food. Therefore, we decided to use water as a reward for thirsty dogs. Preliminary observations showed that the water had no appreciable effects one way or the other on the bursts of spontaneous salivation. As an additional precaution, however, we used the experimental design of rewarding dogs in one group whenever they showed a burst of spontaneous salivation, so that they would be trained to increase salivation, and rewarding dogs in another group whenever there was a long interval between spontaneous bursts, so that they would be trained to decrease salivation. If the reward had any unconditioned effect, this effect might be classically conditioned to the experimental situation and therefore produce a change in salivation that was not a true instance of instrumental learning. But in classical conditioning the reinforcement must elicit the response that is to be acquired. Therefore, conditioning of a response elicited by the reward could produce either an increase or a decrease in salivation, depending upon the direction of the unconditioned response elicited by the reward, but it could not produce a change in one direction for one group and in the opposite direction for the other group. The same type of logic applies for any unlearned cumulative aftereffects of the reward; they could not be in opposite directions for the two groups. With instrumental learning, however, the reward can reinforce any response that immediately precedes it; therefore, the same reward can be used to produce either increases or decreases.

The results are presented in Fig. 1, which summarizes the effects of 40 days of training with one 45-minute training session per day. It may be seen that in this experiment the learning proceeded slowly. However, statistical analysis showed that each of the trends in the predicted rewarded direction was highly reliable (10).

Since the changes in salivation for the two groups were in opposite directions, they cannot be attributed to classical conditioning. It was noted, however, that the group rewarded for increases seemed to be more aroused and active than the one rewarded for decreases. Conceivably, all we were doing was to change the level of activation of the dogs, and this change was, in turn, affecting the salivation. Although we did not observe any specific skeletal responses, such as chewing movements or panting, which might be expected to elicit salivation, it was difficult to be absolutely certain that such movements did not occur. Therefore, we decided to rule out such movements by paralyzing the dogs with curare, but we immediately found that curare had two effects which were diastrous for this experiment: it elicited such copious and continuous salivation that there were no changes in salivation to reward, and the salivation was so viscous that it almost immediately gummed up the recording apparatus.

Heart Rate

In the meantime, Jay Trowill, working with me on this problem, was displaying great ingenuity, courage, and persistence in trying to produce instrumental learning of heart rate in rats that had been paralyzed by curare to prevent them from "cheating" by muscular exertion to speed up the heart or by relaxation to slow it down. As a result of preliminary testing, he selected a dose of curare (3.6 milligrams of d-tubocurarine chloride per kilogram, injected intraperitoneally) which produced deep paralysis for at least 3 hours, and a rate of artificial respiration (inspiration-expiration ratio 1:1; 70 breaths per minute; peak pressure reading, 20 cm-H_2O) which maintained the heart at a constant and normal rate throughout this time.

In subsequent experiments, DiCara and I have obtained similar effects by starting with a smaller dose (1.2 milligrams per kilogram) and constantly infusing additional amounts of the drug, through intraperitoneal injection, at the rate of 1.2 milligrams per kilogram per hour, for the duration of the experiment. We have recorded, electromyographically, the response of the muscles, to determine that this dose does indeed produce a complete block of the action potentials, lasting for at least an hour after the end of infusion. We have found that if parameters of respiration and the face mask are adjusted carefully, the procedure not only maintains the heart rate of a 500-gram control animal constant but also maintains the vital signs of temperature, peripheral vasomotor responses, and the pCO_2 of the blood constant.

Since there are not very many ways to reward an animal completely paralyzed by curare, Trowill and I decided to use direct electrical stimulation of rewarding areas of the brain. There were other technical difficulties to overcome, such as devising the automatic system for rewarding small changes in heart rate as recorded by the electrocardiogram. Nevertheless, Trowill at last succeeded in training his rats (11). Those rewarded for an increase in heart rate showed a statistically reliable increase, and those rewarded for a decrease in heart rate showed a statistically reliable decrease. The changes, however, were disappointingly small, averaging only 5 percent in each direction.

The next question was whether larger changes could be achieved by improving the technique of training. DiCara and I used the technique of shaping—in other words, of immediately rewarding first very small, and hence frequently occurring, changes in the correct direction and, as soon as these had been learned, requiring progressively larger changes as the criterion for reward. In this way, we were able to produce in 90 minutes of training changes averaging 20 percent in either direction (12).

Key Properties of Learning: Discrimination and Retention

Does the learning of visceral responses have the same properties as the learning of skeletal responses? One of the important characteristics of the instrumental learning of skeletal responses is that a discrimination can be learned, so that the responses are more likely to be made in the stimulus situations in which they are rewarded than in those in which they are not. After the training of the first few rats had convinced us that we could produce large changes in heart rate, DiCara and I gave all the rest of the rats in the experiment described above 45 minutes of additional training with the most difficult criterion. We did this in order to see whether they could learn to give a greater response during a "time-in" stimulus (the presence of a flashing light and a tone) which indicated that a response in the proper direction would be rewarded than during a "time-out" stimulus (absence of light and tone) which indicated that a correct response would not be rewarded.

Figure 2 shows the record of one of the rats given such training. Before the beginning of the special discrimination training it had slowed its heart from an initial rate of 350 beats per minute to a rate of 230 beats per minute. From the top record of Fig. 2 one can see that, at the beginning of the special discrimination training, there was no appreciable reduction in heart rate that was specifically associated with the time-in stimulus. Thus it took the rat

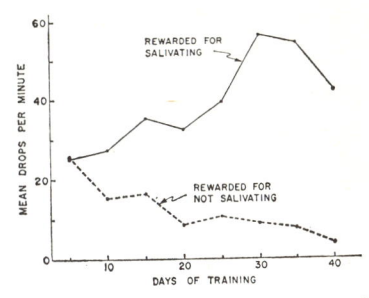

Fig. 1. Learning curves for groups of thirsty dogs rewarded with water for either increases or decreases in spontaneous salivation. [From Miller and Carmona (10)]

considerable time after the onset of this stimulus to meet the criterion and get the reward. At the end of the discrimination training the heart rate during time-out remained approximately the same, but when the time-in light and tone came on, the heart slowed down and the criterion was promptly met. Although the other rats showed less change than this, by the end of the relatively short period of discrimination training their heart rate did change reliably ($P < .001$) in the predicted direction when the time-in stimulus came on. Thus, it is clear that instrumental visceral learning has at least one of the important properties of instrumental skeletal learning—namely, the ability to be brought under the control of a discriminative stimulus.

Another of the important properties of the instrumental learning of skeletal responses is that it is remembered. DiCara and I performed a special experiment to test the retention of learned changes in heart rate (13). Rats that had been given a single training session were returned to their home cages for 3 months without further training. When curarized again and returned to the experimental situation for nonreinforced test trials, rats in both the "increase" and "decrease" groups showed good retention by exhibiting reliable changes in the direction rewarded in the earlier training.

Escape and Avoidance Learning

Is visceral learning by any chance peculiarly limited to reinforcement by the unusual reward of direct electrical stimulation of the brain, or can it be reinforced by other rewards in the same way that skeletal learning can be? In order to answer this question, DiCara and I (14) performed an experiment using the other of the two forms of thoroughly studied reward that can be

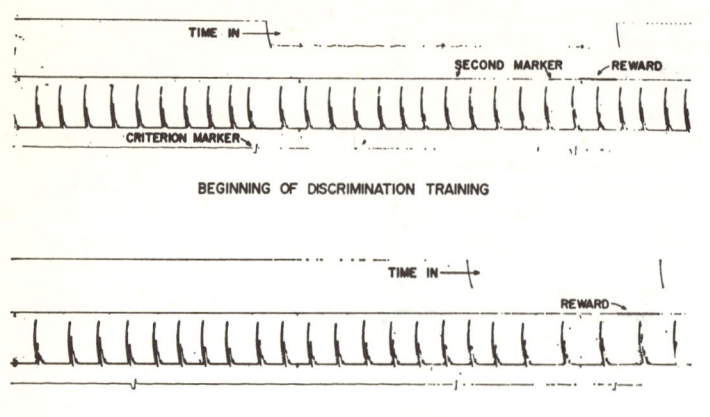

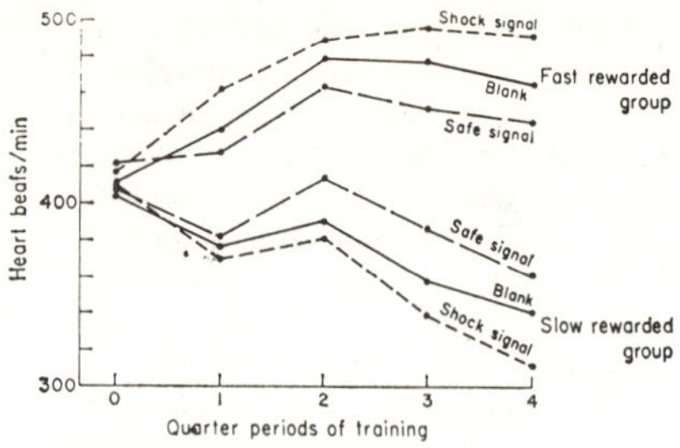

Fig. 2 (left). Electrocardiograms at the beginning and at the end of discrimination training of curarized rat rewarded for slow heart rate. Slowing of heart rate is rewarded only during a "time-in" stimulus (tone and light). [From Miller and DiCara (*12*)] Fig. 3 (above). Changes in heart rate during avoidance training. [From DiCara and Miller (*14*)]

conveniently used with rats which are paralyzed by curare—namely, the chance to avoid, or escape from, mild electric shock. A shock signal was turned on; after it had been on for 10 seconds it was accompanied by brief pulses of mild electric shock delivered to the rat's tail. During the first 10 seconds the rat could turn off the shock signal and avoid the shock by making the correct response of changing its heart rate in the required direction by the required amount. If it did not make the correct response in time, the shocks continued to be delivered until the rat escaped them by making the correct response, which immediately turned off both the shock and the shock signal.

For one group of curarized rats, the correct response was an increase in heart rate; for the other group it was a decrease. After the rats had learned to make small responses in the proper direction, they were required to make larger ones. During this training the shock signals were randomly interspersed with an equal number of "safe" signals that were not followed by shock; the heart rate was also recorded during so-called blank trials—trials without any signals or shocks. For half of the rats the shock signal was a tone and the "safe" signal was a flashing light; for the other half the roles of these cues were reversed.

The results are shown in Fig. 3. Each of the 12 rats in this experiment changed its heart rate in the rewarded direction. As training progressed, the shock signal began to elicit a progressively greater change in the rewarded direction than the change recorded during the blank trials; this was a statistically reliable trend. Conversely, as training progressed, the "safe" signal came to elicit a statistically reliable change in the opposite direction, toward the initial base line. These results show learning when escape and avoidance are the rewards; this means that visceral responses in curarized rats can be reinforced by rewards other than direct electrical stimulation of the brain. These rats also discriminate between the shock and the "safe" signals. You will remember that, with noncurarized thirsty dogs, we were able to use yet another kind of reward, water, to produce learned changes in salivation.

Transfer to Noncurarized State: More Evidence against Mediation

In the experiments discussed above, paralysis of the skeletal muscles by curare ruled out the possibility that the subjects were learning the overt performance of skeletal responses which were indirectly eliciting the changes in the heart rate. It is barely conceivable, however, that the rats were learning to send out from the motor cortex central impulses which would have activated the muscles had they not been paralyzed. And it is barely conceivable that these central impulses affected heart rate by means either of inborn connections or of classically conditioned ones that had been acquired when previous exercise had been accompanied by an increase in heart rate and relaxation had been accompanied by a decrease. But, if the changes in heart rate were produced in this indirect way, we would expect that, during a subsequent test without curare, any rat that showed learned changes in heart rate would show the movements in the muscles that were no longer paralyzed. Furthermore, the problem of whether or not visceral responses learned under curarization carry over to the noncurarized state is of interest in its own right.

In order to answer this question, DiCara and I (*15*) trained two groups of curarized rats to increase or decrease, respectively, their heart rate in order to avoid, or escape from, brief pulses of mild electric shock. When these rats were tested 2 weeks later in the non-curarized state, the habit was remembered. Statistically reliable increases in heart rate averaging 5 percent and decreases averaging 16 percent occurred. Immediately subsequent retraining without curare produced additional significant changes of heart rate in the rewarded direction, bringing the total overall increase to 11 percent and the decrease to 22 percent. While, at the beginning of the test in the noncurarized state, the two groups showed some differences in respiration and activity, these differences decreased until, by the end of the retraining, they were small and far from statistically reliable ($t = 0.3$ and 1.3, respectively). At the same time, the difference between the two groups with respect to heart rate was increasing, until it became large and thus extremely reliable ($t = 8.6$, d.f. $= 12$, $P < .001$).

In short, while greater changes in heart rate were being learned, the response was becoming more specific, involving smaller changes in respiration and muscular activity. This increase in specificity with additional training is another point of similarity with the instrumental learning of skeletal responses. Early in skeletal learning, the rewarded correct response is likely to be accompanied by many unnecessary movements. With additional training during which extraneous movements are not rewarded, they tend to drop out.

It is difficult to reconcile the foregoing results with the hypothesis that the differences in heart rate were mediated primarily by a difference in either respiration or amount of general activity. This is especially true in view of the research, summarized by Ehrlich and Malmo (*16*), which shows that muscular activity, to affect heart rate in the rat, must be rather vigorous.

While it is difficult to rule out completely the possibility that changes in heart rate are mediated by central impulses to skeletal muscles, the possibility of such mediation is much less attractive for other responses, such as intestinal contractions and the formation of urine by the kidney. Furthermore, if the learning of these different responses can be shown to be specific in enough visceral responses, one runs out of different skeletal movements each eliciting a specific different visceral response (*17*). Therefore, experiments were performed on the learning of a variety of different visceral responses and on the specificity of that learning. Each of these experiments was, of course, interesting in its own right, quite apart from any bearing on the problem of mediation.

Specificity: Intestinal versus Cardiac

The purpose of our next experiment was to determine the specificity of visceral learning. If such learning has the same properties as the instrumental learning of skeletal responses, it should be possible to learn a specific visceral response independently of other ones. Furthermore, as we have just seen, we might expect to find that, the better the rewarded response is learned, the more specific is the learning. Banuazizi and I worked on this problem (*18*). First we had to discover another visceral response that could be conveniently recorded and rewarded. We decided on intestinal contractions, and recorded them in the curarized rat with a little balloon filled with water thrust approximately 4 centimeters beyond the anal sphincter. Changes of pressure in the balloon were transduced into electric voltages which produced a record on a polygraph and also activated an automatic mechanism for delivering the reward, which was electrical stimulation of the brain.

The results for the first rat trained, which was a typical one, are shown in Fig. 4. From the top record it may be seen that, during habituation, there were some spontaneous contractions. When the rat was rewarded by brain stimulation for keeping contractions below a certain amplitude for a certain time, the number of contractions was reduced and the base line was lowered. After the record showed a highly reliable change indicating that relaxation had been learned (Fig. 4, second record from the top), the conditions of training were reversed and the reward was delivered whenever the amplitude of contractions rose above a certain level. From the next record (Fig. 4, middle) it may be seen that this type of training increased the number of contractions and raised the base line. Finally (Fig. 4, two bottom records) the reward was discontinued and, as would be expected, the response continued for a while but gradually became extinguished, so that the activity eventually returned to approximately its original base-line level.

After studying a number of other rats in this way and convincing ourselves that the instrumental learning of intestinal responses was a possibility, we designed an experiment to test specificity. For all the rats of the experiment, both intestinal contractions and heart rate were recorded, but half the rats were rewarded for one of these responses and half were rewarded for the other response. Each of these two groups of rats was divided into two subgroups, rewarded, respectively, for increased and decreased response. The rats were completely paralyzed by curare, maintained on artificial respiration, and rewarded by electrical stimulation of the brain.

The results are shown in Figs. 5 and 6. In Fig. 5 it may be seen that the group rewarded for increases in intestinal contractions learned an increase, the group rewarded for decreases learned a decrease, but neither of these groups showed an appreciable change in heart rate. Conversely (Fig. 6), the group rewarded for increases in heart rate showed an increase, the group rewarded for decreases showed a decrease, but neither of these groups showed a change in intestinal contractions.

The fact that each type of response changed when it was rewarded rules out the interpretation that the failure to secure a change when that change was not rewarded could have been due to either a strong and stable homeostatic regulation of that response or an inability of our techniques to measure changes reliably under the particular conditions of our experiment.

Each of the 12 rats in the experiment showed statistically reliable changes in the rewarded direction; for 11 the changes were reliable beyond the $P < .001$ level, while for the 12th the changes were reliable only beyond the .05 level. A statistically reliable negative correlation showed that the better the rewarded visceral response was learned, the less change occurred in the other, nonrewarded response. This greater specificity with better learning is what we had expected. The results showed that visceral learning can be specific to an organ system, and they clearly ruled out the possibility of mediation by any

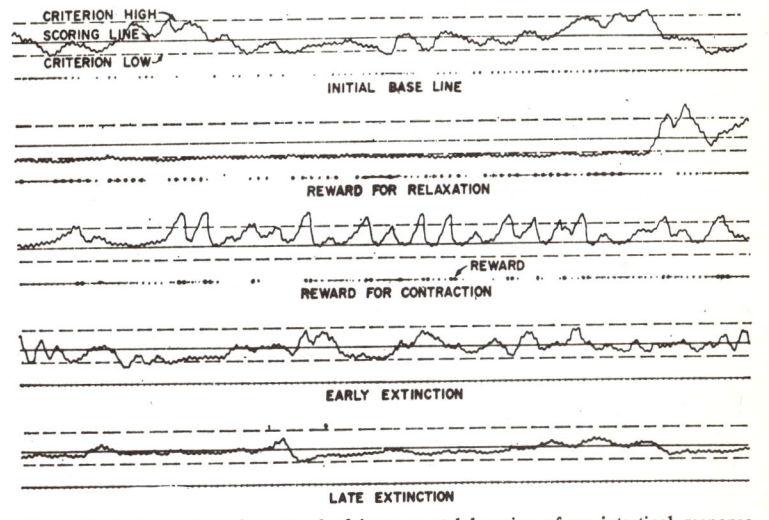

Fig. 4. Typical samples of a record of instrumental learning of an intestinal response by a curarized rat. (From top to bottom) Record of spontaneous contraction before training; record after training with reward for relaxation; record after training with reward for contractions; records during nonrewarded extinction trials. [From Miller and Banuazizi (*18*)]

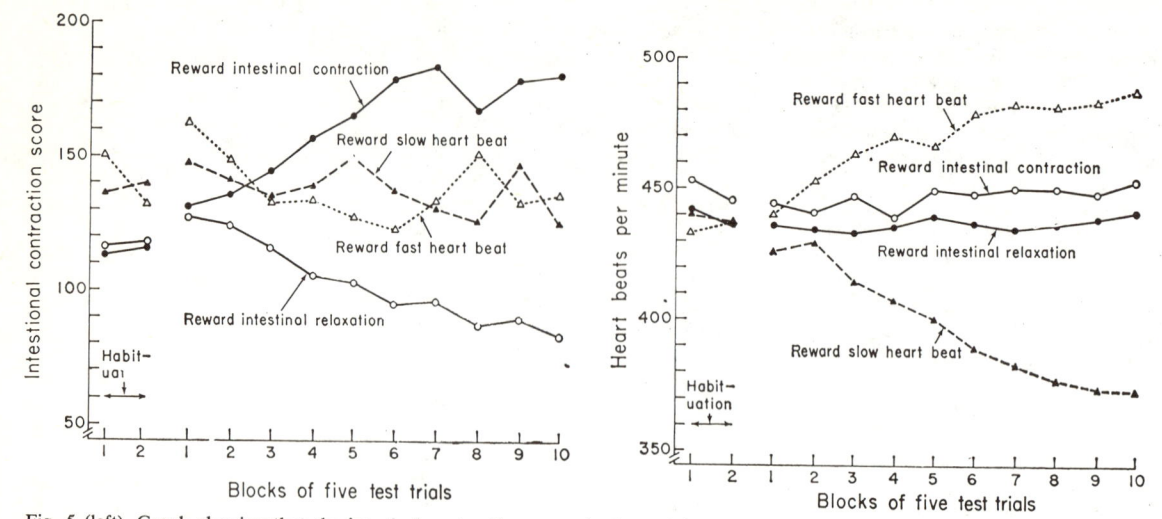

Fig. 5 (left). Graph showing that the intestinal contraction score is changed by rewarding either increases or decreases in intestinal contractions but is unaffected by rewarding changes in heart rate. [From Miller and Banuazizi (18)] Fig. 6 (right). Graph showing that the heart rate is changed by rewarding either increases or decreases in heart rate but is unaffected by rewarding changes in intestinal contractions. Comparison with Fig. 5 demonstrates the specificity of visceral learning. [From Miller and Banuazizi (18)]

single general factor, such as level of activation or central commands for either general activity or relaxation.

In an additional experiment, Banuazizi (19) showed that either increases or decreases in intestinal contractions can be rewarded by avoidance of, or escape from, mild electric shocks, and that the intestinal responses can be discriminatively elicited by a specific stimulus associated with reinforcement.

Kidney Function

Encouraged by these successes, DiCara and I decided to see whether or not the rate of urine formation by the kidney could be changed in the curarized rat rewarded by electrical stimulation of the brain (20). A catheter, permanently inserted, was used to prevent accumulation of urine by the bladder, and the rate of urine formation was measured by an electronic device for counting minute drops. In order to secure a rate of urine formation fast enough so that small changes could be promptly detected and rewarded, the rats were kept constantly loaded with water through infusion by way of a catheter permanently inserted in the jugular vein.

All of the seven rats rewarded when the intervals between times of urine-drop formation lengthened showed decreases in the rate of urine formation, and all of the seven rats rewarded when these intervals shortened showed increases in the rate of urine formation. For both groups the changes were highly reliable ($P < .001$).

In order to determine how the change in rate of urine formation was achieved, certain additional measures were taken. As the set of bars at left in Fig. 7 shows, the rate of filtration, measured by means of ^{14}C-labeled inulin, increased when increases in the rate of urine formation were rewarded and decreased when decreases in the rate were rewarded. Plots of the correlations showed that the changes in the rates of filtration and urine formation were not related to changes in either blood pressure or heart rate.

The middle set of bars in Fig. 7 shows that the rats rewarded for increases in the rate of urine formation had an increased rate of renal blood flow, as measured by ^3H-p-aminohippuric acid, and that those rewarded for decreases had a decreased rate of renal blood flow. Since these changes in blood flow were not accompanied by changes in general blood pressure or in heart rate, they must have been achieved by vasomotor changes of the renal arteries. That these vasomotor changes were at least somewhat specific is shown by the fact that vasomotor responses of the tail, as measured by a photoelectric plethysmograph, did not differ for the two groups of rats.

The set of bars at right in Fig. 7 shows that when decreases in rate of urine formation were rewarded, a more concentrated urine, having higher osmolarity, was formed. Since the slower passage of urine through the tubules would afford more opportunity for reabsorption of water, this higher concentration does not necessarily mean an increase in the secretion of antidiuretic hormone. When an increased rate of urine formation was rewarded, the urine did not become more diluted—that is, it showed no decrease in osmolarity; therefore, the increase in rate of urine formation observed in this experiment cannot be accounted for in terms of an inhibition of the secretion of antidiuretic hormone.

From the foregoing results it appears that the learned changes in urine formation in this experiment were produced primarily by changes in the rate of filtration, which, in turn, were produced primarily by changes in the rate of blood flow through the kidneys.

Gastric Changes

In the next experiment, Carmona, Demierre, and I used a photoelectric plethysmograph to measure changes, presumably in the amount of blood, in the stomach wall (21). In an operation performed under anesthesia, a small glass tube, painted black except for a small spot, was inserted into the rat's stomach. The same tube was used to hold the stomach wall against a small glass window inserted through the body wall. The tube was left in that position. After the animal had recovered, a bundle of optical fibers could be slipped snugly into the glass tube so that the light beamed through it would shine out through the unpainted spot in the tube inside the stomach, pass through the stomach wall, and be recorded by a photocell on the other side of the glass window. Preliminary tests indicated that, as would be expected, when the amount of blood in the stomach wall increased, less light would pass through. Other tests showed that stomach contractions elicited by injections of insulin did not affect the amount of light transmitted.

In the main experiment we rewarded curarized rats by enabling them to avoid or escape from mild electric shocks. Some were rewarded when the amount of light that passed through the stomach wall increased, while others were rewarded when the amount decreased. Fourteen of the 15 rats showed changes in the rewarded direction. Thus, we demonstrated that the stomach wall, under the control of the autonomic nervous system, can be modified by instrumental learning. There is strong reason to believe that the learned changes were achieved by vasomotor responses affecting the amount of blood in the stomach wall or mucosa, or in both.

In another experiment, Carmona (22) showed that stomach contractions can be either increased or decreased by instrumental learning.

It is obvious that learned changes in the blood supply of internal organs can affect their functioning—as, for example, the rate at which urine was formed by the kidneys was affected by changes in the amount of blood that flowed through them. Thus, such changes can produce psychosomatic symptoms. And if the learned changes in blood supply can be specific to a given organ, the symptom will occur in that organ rather than in another one.

Peripheral Vasomotor Responses

Having investigated the instrumental learning of internal vasomotor responses, we next studied the learning of peripheral ones. In the first experiment, the amount of blood in the tail of a curarized rat was measured by a photoelectric plethysmograph, and changes were rewarded by electrical stimulation of the brain (23). All of the four rats rewarded for vasoconstriction showed that response, and, at the same time, their average core temperature, measured rectally, decreased from 98.9° to 97.9°F. All of the four rats rewarded for vasodilatation showed that response and, at the same time, their average core temperature increased from 99.9° to 101°F. The vasomotor change for each individual rat was reliable beyond the $P < .01$ level, and the difference in change in temperature between the groups was reliable beyond the .01 level. The direction of the change in temperature was opposite to that which would

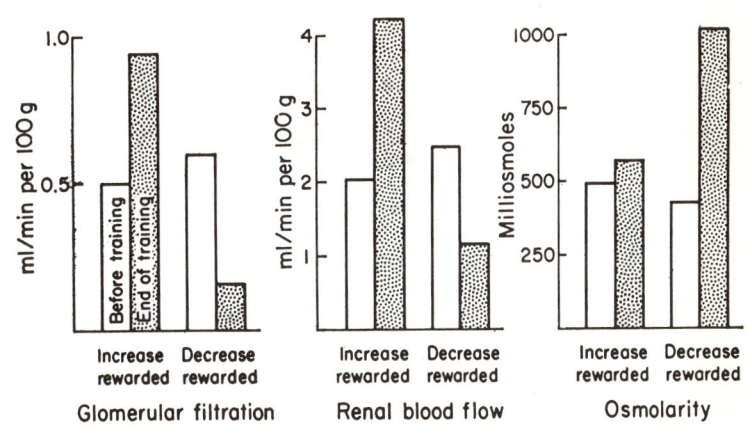

Fig. 7. Effects of rewarding increased rate of urine formation in one group and decreased rate in another on measures of glomerular filtration, renal blood flow, and osmolarity. [From data in Miller and DiCara (20)]

be expected from the heat conservation caused by peripheral vasoconstriction or the heat loss caused by peripheral vasodilatation. The changes are in the direction which would be expected if the training had altered the rate of heat production, causing a change in temperature which, in turn, elicited the vasomotor response.

The next experiment was designed to try to determine the limits of the specificity of vasomotor learning. The pinnae of the rat's ears were chosen because the blood vessels in them are believed to be innervated primarily, and perhaps exclusively, by the sympathetic branch of the autonomic nervous system, the branch that Cannon believed always fired nonspecifically as a unit (3). But Cannon's experiments involved exposing cats to extremely strong emotion-evoking stimuli, such as barking dogs, and such stimuli will also evoke generalized activity throughout the skeletal musculature. Perhaps his results reflected the way in which sympathetic activity was elicited, rather than demonstrating any inherent inferiority of the sympathetic nervous system.

In order to test this interpretation, DiCara and I (24) put photocells on both ears of the curarized rat and connected them to a bridge circuit so that only differences in the vasomotor responses of the two ears were rewarded by brain stimulation. We were somewhat surprised and greatly delighted to find that this experiment actually worked. The results are summarized in Fig. 8. Each of the six rats rewarded for relative vasodilatation of the left ear showed that response, while each of the six rats rewarded for relative vasodilatation of the right ear showed that response. Recordings from the right and left forepaws showed little if any change in vasomotor response.

It is clear that these results cannot be by-products of changes in either heart rate or blood pressure, as these would be expected to affect both ears equally. They show either that vasomotor responses mediated by the sympathetic nervous system are capable of much greater specificity than has previously been believed, or that the innervation of the blood vessels in the pinnae of the ears is not restricted almost exclusively to sympathetic-nervous-system components, as has been believed, and involves functionally significant parasympathetic components. In any event, the changes in the blood flow certainly were surprisingly specific. Such changes in blood flow could account for specific psychosomatic symptoms.

Blood Pressure Independent of Heart Rate

Although changes in blood pressure were not induced as by-products of rewarded changes in the rate of urine formation, another experiment on curarized rats showed that, when changes in systolic blood pressure are specifically reinforced, they can be learned (25). Blood pressure was recorded by means of a catheter permanently inserted into the aorta, and the reward was avoidance of, or escape from, mild electric shock. All seven rats rewarded for increases in blood pressure showed further increases, while all seven rewarded for decreases showed decreases, each of the changes, which were in opposite directions, being reliable beyond the $P < .01$ level. The increase was from 139 mm-Hg, which happens to be roughly comparable to

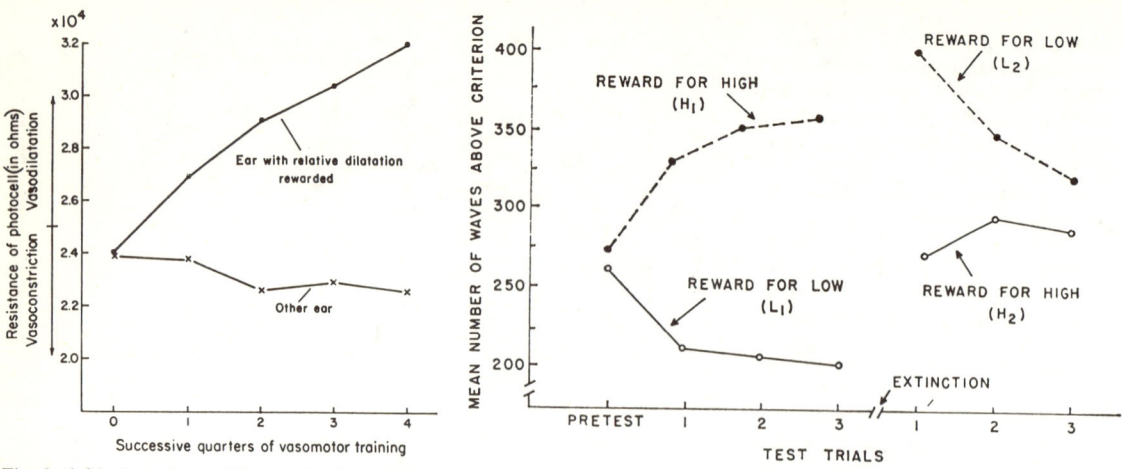

Fig. 8 (left). Learning a difference in the vasomotor responses of the two ears in the curarized rat. [From data in DiCara and Miller (24)]   Fig. 9 (right). Instrumental learning by curarized rats rewarded for high-voltage or for low-voltage electroencephalograms recorded from the cerebral cortex. After a period of nonrewarded extinction, which produced some drowsiness, as indicated by an increase in voltage, the rats in the two groups were then rewarded for voltage changes opposite in direction to the changes for which they were rewarded earlier. [From Carmona (29)]

the normal systolic blood pressure of an adult man, to 170 mm-Hg, which is on the borderline of abnormally high blood pressure in man.

Each experimental animal was "yoked" with a curarized partner, maintained on artificial respiration and having shock electrodes on its tail wired in series with electrodes on the tail of the experimental animal, so that it received exactly the same electric shocks and could do nothing to escape or avoid them. The yoked controls for both the increase-rewarded and the decrease-rewarded groups showed some elevation in blood pressure as an unconditioned effect of the shocks. By the end of training, in contrast to the large difference in the blood pressures of the two groups specifically rewarded for changes in opposite directions, there was no difference in blood pressure between the yoked control partners for these two groups. Furthermore, the increase in blood pressure in these control groups was reliably less ($P < .01$) than that in the group specifically rewarded for increases. Thus, it is clear that the reward for an increase in blood pressure produced an additional increase over and above the effects of the shocks per se, while the reward for a decrease was able to overcome the unconditioned increase elicited by the shocks.

For none of the four groups was there a significant change in heart rate or in temperature during training; there were no significant differences in these measures among the groups. Thus, the learned change was relatively specific to blood pressure.

Transfer from Heart Rate to Skeletal Avoidance

Although visceral learning can be quite specific, especially if only a specific response is rewarded, as was the case in the experiment on the two ears, under some circumstances it can involve a more generalized effect.

In handling the rats that had just recovered from curarization, DiCara noticed that those that had been trained, through the avoidance or escape reward, to increase their heart rate were more likely to squirm, squeal, defecate, and show other responses indicating emotionality than were those that had been trained to reduce their heart rate. Could instrumental learning of heart-rate changes have some generalized effects, perhaps on the level of emotionality, which might affect the behavior in a different avoidance-learning situation? In order to look for such an effect, DiCara and Weiss (26) used a modified shuttle avoidance apparatus. In this apparatus, when a danger signal is given, the rat must run from compartment A to compartment B. If he runs fast enough, he avoids the shock; if not, he must run to escape it. The next time the danger signal is given, the rat must run in the opposite direction, from B to A.

Other work had shown that learning in this apparatus is an inverted U-shaped function of the strength of the shocks, with shocks that are too strong eliciting emotional behavior instead of running. DiCara and Weiss trained their rats in this apparatus with a level of shock that is approximately optimum for naive rats of this strain. They found that the rats that had been rewarded for decreasing their heart rate learned well, but that those that had been rewarded for increasing their heart rate learned less well, as if their emotionality had been increased. The difference was statistically reliable ($P < .001$). This experiment clearly demonstrates that training a visceral response can affect the subsequent learning of a skeletal one, but additional work will be required to prove the hypothesis that training to increase heart rate increases emotionality.

Visceral Learning without Curare

Thus far, in all of the experiments except the one on teaching thirsty dogs to salivate, the initial training was given when the animal was under the influence of curare. All of the experiments, except the one on salivation, have produced surprisingly rapid learning—definitive results within 1 or 2 hours. Will learning in the normal, noncurarized state be easier, as we originally thought it should be, or will it be harder, as the experiment on the noncurarized dogs suggests? DiCara and I have started to get additional evidence on this problem. We have obtained clear-cut evidence that rewarding (with the avoidance or escape reward) one group of freely moving rats for reducing heart rate and rewarding another group for increasing heart rate produces a difference between the two groups

(27). That this difference was not due to the indirect effects of the overt performance of skeletal responses is shown by the fact that it persisted in subsequent tests during which the rats were paralyzed by curare. And, on subsequent retraining without curare, such differences in activity and respiration as were present earlier in training continued to decrease, while the differences in heart rate continued to increase. It seems extremely unlikely that, at the end of training, the highly reliable differences in heart rate ($t = 7.2$; $P < .0001$) can be explained by the highly unreliable differences in activity and respiration ($t = .07$ and 0.2, respectively).

Although the rats in this experiment showed some learning when they were trained initially in the noncurarized state, this learning was much poorer than that which we have seen in our other experiments on curarized rats. This is exactly the opposite of my original expectation, but seems plausible in the light of hindsight. My hunch is that paralysis by curare improved learning by eliminating sources of distraction and variability. The stimulus situation was kept more constant, and confusing visceral fluctuations induced indirectly by skeletal movements were eliminated.

Learned Changes in Brain Waves

Encouraged by success in the experiments on the instrumental learning of visceral responses, my colleagues and I have attempted to produce other unconventional types of learning. Electrodes placed on the skull or, better yet, touching the surface of the brain record summative effects of electrical activity over a considerable area of the brain. Such electrical effects are called brain waves, and the record of them is called an electroencephalogram. When the animal is aroused, the electroencephalogram consists of fast, low-voltage activity; when the animal is drowsy or sleeping normally, the electroencephalogram consists of considerably slower, higher-voltage activity. Carmona attempted to see whether this type of brain activity, and the state of arousal accompanying it, can be modified by direct reward of changes in the brain activity (28, 29).

The subjects of the first experiment were freely moving cats. In order to have a reward that was under complete control and that did not require the cat to move, Carmona used direct electrical stimulation of the medial forebrain bundle, which is a rewarding area of the brain. Such stimulation produced a slight lowering in the average voltage of the electroencephalogram and an increase in behavioral arousal. In order to provide a control for these and any other unlearned effects, he rewarded one group for changes in the direction of high-voltage activity and another group for changes in the direction of low-voltage activity.

Both groups learned. The cats rewarded for high-voltage activity showed more high-voltage slow waves and tended to sit like sphinxes, staring out into space. The cats rewarded for low-voltage activity showed much more low-voltage fast activity, and appeared to be aroused, pacing restlessly about, sniffing, and looking here and there. It was clear that this type of training had modified both the character of the electrical brain waves and the general level of the behavioral activity. It was not clear, however, whether the level of arousal of the brain was directly modified and hence modified the behavior; whether the animals learned specific items of behavior which, in turn, modified the arousal of the brain as reflected in the electroencephalogram; or whether both types of learning were occurring simultaneously.

In order to rule out the direct sensory consequences of changes in muscular tension, movement, and posture, Carmona performed the next experiment on rats that had been paralyzed by means of curare. The results, given in Fig. 9, show that both rewarded groups showed changes in the rewarded direction; that a subsequent nonrewarded rest increased the number of high-voltage responses in both groups; and that, when the conditions of reward were reversed, the direction of change in voltage was reversed.

At present we are trying to use similar techniques to modify the functions of a specific part of the vagal nucleus, by recording and specifically rewarding changes in the electrical activity there. Preliminary results suggest that this is possible. The next step is to investigate the visceral consequences of such modification. This kind of work may open up possibilities for modifying the activity of specific parts of the brain and the functions that they control. In some cases, directly rewarding brain activity may be a more convenient or more powerful technique than rewarding skeletal or visceral behavior. It also may be a new way to throw light on the functions of specific parts of the brain (30).

Human Visceral Learning

Another question is that of whether people are capable of instrumental learning of visceral responses. I believe that in this respect they are as smart as rats. But, as a recent critical review by Katkin and Murray (31) points out, this has not yet been completely proved. These authors have comprehensively summarized the recent studies reporting successful use of instrumental training to modify human heart rate, vasomotor responses, and the galvanic skin response. Because of the difficulties in subjecting human subjects to the same rigorous controls, including deep paralysis by means of curare, that can be used with animal subjects, one of the most serious questions about the results of the human studies is whether the changes recorded represent the true instrumental learning of visceral responses or the unconscious learning of those skeletal responses that can produce visceral reactions. However, the able investigators who have courageously challenged the strong traditional belief in the inferiority of the autonomic nervous system with experiments at the more difficult but especially significant human level are developing ingenious controls, including demonstrations of the specificity of the visceral change, so that their cumulative results are becoming increasingly impressive.

Possible Role in Homeostasis

The functional utility of instrumental learning by the cerebrospinal nervous system under the conditions that existed during mammalian evolution is obvious. The skeletal responses mediated by the cerebrospinal nervous system operate on the external environment, so that there is survival value in the ability to learn responses that bring rewards such as food, water, or escape from pain. The fact that the responses mediated by the autonomic nervous system do not have such direct action on the external environment was one of the reasons for believing that they are not subject to instrumental learning. Is the learning ability of the autonomic nervous system something that has no normal function other than that of providing my students with subject matter for publications? Is it a mere accidental by-product of the survival value of cerebrospinal learning, or does the instrumental learning of autonomically mediated responses have some adaptive function, such as helping to maintain that constancy of the internal environment called homeostasis?

In order for instrumental learning to function homeostatically, a deviation away from the optimum level will have to function as a drive to motivate learning, and a change toward the optimum level will have to function as a reward to reinforce the learning of the particular visceral response that produced the corrective change.

When a mammal has less than the optimum amount of water in his body, this deficiency serves as a drive of thirst to motivate learning; the overt consummatory response of drinking functions as a reward to reinforce the learning of the particular skeletal responses that were successful in securing the water that restored the optimum level. But is the consummatory response essential? Can restoration of an optimum level by a glandular response function as a reward?

In order to test for the possible rewarding effects of a glandular response, DiCara, Wolf, and I (32) injected albino rats with antidiuretic hormone (ADH) if they chose one arm of a T-maze and with the isotonic saline vehicle if they chose the other, distinctively different, arm. The ADH permitted water to be reabsorbed in the kidney, so that a smaller volume of more concentrated urine was formed. Thus, for normal rats loaded in advance with H_2O, the ADH interfered with the excess-water excretion required for the restoration of homeostasis, while the control injection of isotonic saline allowed the excess water to be excreted. And, indeed, such rats learned to select the side of the maze that assured them an injection of saline so that their glandular response could restore homeostasis.

Conversely, for rats with diabetes insipidus, loaded in advance with hypertonic NaCl, the homeostatic effects of the same two injections were reversed; the ADH, causing the urine to be more concentrated, helped the rats to get rid of the excess NaCl, while the isotonic saline vehicle did not. And, indeed, a group of rats of this kind learned the opposite choice of selecting the ADH side of the maze. As a further control on the effects of the ADH per se, normal rats which had not been given H_2O or NaCl exhibited no learning. This experiment showed that an excess of either H_2O or NaCl functions as a drive and that the return to the normal concentration produced by the appropriate response of a gland, the kidney, functions as a reward.

When we consider the results of this experiment together with those of our experiments showing that glandular and visceral responses can be instrumentally learned, we will expect the animal to learn those glandular and visceral responses mediated by the central nervous system that promptly restore homeostasis after any considerable deviation. Whether or not this theoretically possible learning has any practical significance will depend on whether or not the innate homeostatic mechanisms control the levels closely enough to prevent any deviations large enough to function as a drive from occurring. Even if the innate control should be accurate enough to preclude learning in most cases, there remains the intriguing possibility that, when pathology interferes with innate control, visceral learning is available as a supplementary mechanism.

Implications and Speculations

We have seen how the instrumental learning of visceral responses suggests a new possible homeostatic mechanism worthy of further investigation. Such learning also shows that the autonomic nervous system is not as inferior as has been so widely and firmly believed. It removes one of the strongest arguments for the hypothesis that there are two fundamentally different mechanisms of learning, involving different parts of the nervous system.

Cause of psychosomatic symptoms. Similarly, evidence of the instrumental learning of visceral responses removes the main basis for assuming that the psychosomatic symptoms that involve the autonomic nervous system are fundamentally different from those functional symptoms, such as hysterical ones, that involve the cerebrospinal nervous system. Such evidence allows us to extend to psychosomatic symptoms the type of learning-theory analysis that Dollard and I (7, 33) have applied to other symptoms.

For example, suppose a child is terror-stricken at the thought of going to school in the morning because he is completely unprepared for an important examination. The strong fear elicits a variety of fluctuating autonomic symptoms, such as a queasy stomach at one time and pallor and faintness at another; at this point his mother, who is particularly concerned about cardiovascular symptoms, says, "You are sick and must stay home." The child feels a great relief from fear, and this reward should reinforce the cardiovascular responses producing pallor and faintness. If such experiences are repeated frequently enough, the child, theoretically, should learn to respond with that kind of symptom. Similarly, another child whose mother ignored the vasomotor responses but was particularly concerned by signs of gastric distress would learn the latter type of symptom. I want to exphasize, however, that we need careful clinical research to determine how frequently, if at all, the social conditions sufficient for such theoretically possible learning of visceral symptoms actually occur. Since a given instrumental response can be reinforced by a considerable variety of rewards, and by one reward on one occasion and a different reward on another, the fact that glandular and visceral responses can be instrumentally learned opens up many new theoretical possibilities for the reinforcement of psychosomatic symptoms.

Furthermore, we do not yet know how severe a psychosomatic effect can be produced by learning. While none of the 40 rats rewarded for speeding up their heart rates have died in the course of training under curarization, 7 of the 40 rats rewarded for slowing down their heart rates have died. This statistically reliable difference (chi square = 5.6, $P < .02$) is highly suggestive, but it could mean that training to speed up the heart helped the rats resist the stress of curare rather than that the reward for slowing down the heart was strong enough to overcome innate regulatory mechanisms and induce sudden death. In either event the visceral learning had a vital effect. At present, DiCara and I are trying to see whether or not the learning of visceral responses can be carried far enough in the noncurarized animal to produce physical damage. We are also investigating the possibility that there may be a critical period in early infancy during which visceral learning has particularly intense and long-lasting effects.

Individual and cultural differences. It is possible that, in addition to producing psychosomatic symptoms in extreme cases, visceral learning can account for certain more benign individual and cultural differences. Lacey and Lacey (34) have shown that a given individual may have a tendency, which is stable over a number of years, to respond to a variety of different stresses with the same profile of autonomic responses, while other individuals may have statistically reliable tendencies to respond with different profiles. It now seems possible that differential conditions of learning may account for at least some of these individual differences in patterns of autonomic response.

Conversely, such learning may account also for certain instances in which the same individual responds to the same stress in different ways. For example, a small boy who receives a severe bump in rough-and-tumble play may learn to inhibit the secretion of tears in this situation since his peer group will punish crying by calling it "sissy." But the same small boy may burst into tears when he gets home to his mother, who will not punish weeping and may even reward tears with sympathy.

Similarly, it seems conceivable that different conditions of reward by a culture different from our own may be responsible for the fact that Homer's adult heroes so often "let the big tears fall." Indeed, a former colleague of mine, Herbert Barry III, has analyzed cross-cultural data and found that the amount of crying reported for children seems to be related to the way in which the society reacts to their tears (35).

I have emphasized the possible role of learning in producing the observed individual differences in visceral responses to stress, which in extreme cases may result in one type of psychosomatic symptom in one person and a different type in another. Such learning does not, of course, exclude innate individual differences in the susceptibility of different organs. In fact, given social conditions under which any form of illness will be rewarded, the symptoms of the most susceptible organ will be the most likely ones to be learned. Furthermore, some types of stress may be so strong that the innate reactions to them produce damage without any learning. My colleagues and I are currently investigating the psychological variables involved in such types of stress (36).

Therapeutic training. The experimental work on animals has developed a powerful technique for using instrumental learning to modify glandular and visceral responses. The improved training technique consists of moment-to-moment recording of the visceral function and immediate reward, at first, of very small changes in the desired direction and then of progressively larger ones. The success of this technique suggests that it should be able to produce therapeutic changes. If the patient who is highly motivated to get rid of a symptom understands that a signal, such as a tone, indicates a change in the desired direction, that tone could serve as a powerful reward. Instruction to try to turn the tone on as often as possible and praise for success should increase the reward. As patients find that they can secure some control of the symptom, their motivation should be strengthened. Such a procedure should be well worth trying on any symptom, functional or organic, that is under neural control, that can be continuously monitored by modern instrumentation, and for which a given direction of change is clearly indicated medically—for example, cardiac arrhythmias, spastic colitis, asthma, and those cases of high blood pressure that are not essential compensation for kidney damage (37). The obvious cases to begin with are those in which drugs are ineffective or contraindicated. In the light of the fact that our animals learned so much better when under the influence of curare and transferred their training so well to the normal, nondrugged state, it should be worth while to try to use hypnotic suggestion to achieve similar results by enhancing the reward effect of the signal indicating a change in the desired direction, by producing relaxation and regular breathing, and by removing interference from skeletal responses and distraction by irrelevant cues.

Engel and Melmon (38) have reported encouraging results in the use of instrumental training to treat cardiac arrhythmias of organic origin. Randt, Korein, Carmona, and I have had some success in using the method described above to train epileptic patients in the laboratory to suppress, in one way or another, the abnormal paroxysmal spikes in their electroencephalogram. My colleagues and I are hoping to try learning therapy for other symptoms—for example, the rewarding of high-voltage electroencephalograms as a treatment for insomnia. While it is far too early to promise any cures, it certainly will be worth while to investigate thoroughly the therapeutic possibilities of improved instrumental training techniques.

References and Notes

1. *The Dialogues of Plato*, B. Jowett, Transl. (Univ. of Oxford Press, London, ed. 2, 1875), vol. 3, "Timaeus."
2. X. Bichat, *Recherches Physiologiques sur la Vie et le Mort* (Brosson, Gabon, Paris, 1800).
3. W. B. Cannon, *The Wisdom of the Body* (Norton, New York, 1932).
4. F. Alexander, *Psychosomatic Medicine: Its Principles and Applications* (Norton, New York, 1950), pp. 40–41.
5. G. A. Kimble, *Hilgard and Marquis' Conditioning and Learning* (Appleton-Century-Crofts, New York, ed. 2, 1961), p. 100.
6. B. F. Skinner, *The Behavior of Organisms* (Appleton-Century, New York, 1938); O. H. Mowrer, *Harvard Educ. Rev.* **17**, 102 (1947).
7. N. E. Miller and J. Dollard, *Social Learning and Imitation* (Yale Univ. Press, New Haven, 1941); J. Dollard and N. E. Miller, *Personality and Psychotherapy* (McGraw-Hill, New York, 1950); N. E. Miller, *Psychol. Rev.* **58**, 375 (1951).
8. N. E. Miller, *Ann. N.Y. Acad. Sci.* **92**, 830 (1961); ———, in *Nebraska Symposium on Motivation*, M. R. Jones, Ed. (Univ. of Nebraska Press, Lincoln, 1963); ———, in *Proc. 3rd World Congr. Psychiat.*, Montreal, 1961 (1963), vol. 3, p. 213.
9. ———, in "Proceedings, 18th International Congress of Psychology, Moscow, 1966," in press.
10. ——— and A. Carmona, *J. Comp. Physiol. Psychol.* **63**, 1 (1967).
11. J. A. Trowill, *ibid.*, p. 7.
12. N. E. Miller and L. V. DiCara, *ibid.*, p. 12.
13. L. V. DiCara and N. E. Miller, *Commun. Behav. Biol.* **2**, 19 (1968).
14. ———, *J. Comp. Physiol. Psychol.* **65**, 8 (1968).
15. ———, *ibid.*, in press.
16. D. J. Ehrlich and R. B. Malmo, *Neuropsychologia* **5**, 219 (1967).
17. "It even becomes difficult to postulate enough different thoughts each arousing a different emotion, each of which in turn innately elicits a specific visceral response. And if one assumes a more direct specific connection between different thoughts and different visceral responses, the notion becomes indistinguishable from the ideo-motor hypothesis of the voluntary movement of skeletal muscles." [W. James, *Principles of Psychology* (Dover, New York, new ed., 1950), vol. 2, chap. 26].
18. N. E. Miller and A. Banuazizi, *J. Comp. Physiol. Psychol.* **65**, 1 (1968).
19. A. Banuazizi, thesis, Yale University (1968).
20. N. E. Miller and L. V. DiCara, *Amer. J. Physiol.* **215**, 677 (1968).
21. A. Carmona, N. E. Miller, T. Demierre, in preparation.
22. A. Carmona, in preparation.
23. L. V. DiCara and N. E. Miller, *Commun. Behav. Biol.* **1**, 209 (1968).
24. ———, *Science* **159**, 1485 (1968).
25. ———, *Psychosom. Med.* **30**, 489 (1968).
26. L. V. DiCara and J. M. Weiss, *J. Comp. Physiol. Psychol.*, in press.
27. L. V. DiCara and N. E. Miller, *Physiol. Behav.*, in press.
28. N. E. Miller, *Science* **152**, 676 (1966).
29. A. Carmona, thesis, Yale University (1967).
30. For somewhat similar work on the single-cell level, see J. Olds and M. E. Olds, in *Brain Mechanisms and Learning*, J. Delafresnaye, A. Fessard, J. Konorski, Eds. (Blackwell, London, 1961).
31. E. S. Katkin and N. E. Murray, *Psychol. Bull.* **70**, 52 (1968); for a reply to their criticisms, see A. Crider, G. Schwartz, S. Shnidman, *ibid.*, in press.
32. N. E. Miller, L. V. DiCara, G. Wolf, *Amer. J. Physiol.* **215**, 684 (1968).
33. N. E. Miller, in *Personality Change*, D. Byrne and P. Worchel, Eds. (Wiley, New York, 1964), p. 149.
34. J. I. Lacey and B. C. Lacey, *Amer. J. Psychol.* **71**, 50 (1958); *Ann. N.Y. Acad. Sci.* **98**, 1257 (1962).
35. H. Barry III, personal communication.
36. N. E. Miller, *Proc. N.Y. Acad. Sci.*, in press.
37. Objective recording of such symptoms might be useful also in monitoring the effects of quite different types of psychotherapy.
38. B. T. Engel and K. T. Melmon, personal communication.
39. The work described is supported by U.S. Public Health Service grant MH 13189.

Section Three

Motivation and Emotion

When one is deprived of food, a number of physiological changes take place in the body. Blood sugar level drops, gastric motility increases, body temperature changes, and so on. Professor Schachter, in the first paper of this section, asks whether activation of this biological machinery is the basis of feeling hungry and eating. The several experiments he reports suggest that this may be the case in normal people, but that in overweight individuals external or nonvisceral cues such as smell, taste, and the sight of others eating are of primary importance.

In the second paper, William Dement explores the purpose of dreams, and what happens when a person is prevented from dreaming. In this study an attempt is made to answer these questions using REMs (rapid eye movements) to identify dream periods. The results show that dreams are more than random activity of the mind. Psychological symptoms increase with dream deprivation, as does the tendency to dream.

The third paper in this section deals with cognitive development, and particularly with implications for the stimulation of early cognitive learning. Hunt focuses his attention on changes in intrinsic motivation that occur before the child learns to talk. By "intrinsic motivation" he is referring to motivation that originates *within* the organism, in contrast to motivation that stems from external stimuli.

The author identifies three stages of intrinsic motivation. In the first of these, there is an "orienting response," an innate tendency to attend to any change in visual or auditory stimulation. In the second stage, repeated encounters with similar perceptual stimulation lead to recognition, which is a source of pleasure and a basis for affectional attachment. The third stage involves a transition from an interest in the familiar to an interest in the novel. At this point repeatedly encountered objects, places, and events become "old stuff," and the infant becomes interested in novelty.

Cognitive learning, Hunt believes, is directly dependent upon the type of sensory stimulation provided the infant during these various stages of development. In this paper he outlines some of the procedures which, if followed, conceivably could lead to the enhancement of cognitive development.

In the next paper in this section, Schachter and Singer note that when we are emotionally aroused we are aware of certain profound changes in the internal physiology of the body. Fear causes the heart to pound and we may feel "butterflies" in the stomach. Love seems to be accompanied by other changes and anger by still others. But is this really true? For a long time psychologists have searched for physiological differentiators of emotion. With the exception of fear and anger, however, the search has not been successful. The authors suggest that, while there may be some differences in physiological patterns from emotion to emotion, a person labels and interprets a generalized "stirred-up" state in terms of the characteristics of the precipitating situation. In other words, it is one's *knowledge* of the situation that determines whether the state of internal arousal is labeled "anger," "fear," "joy," or something else.

In the final paper of this section, Dr. Paul Ekman discusses the results of an extensive cross-cultural project aimed at still another facet of emotion-facial expression. His project was designed to determine the extent to which various facial expressions are associated with particular emotions. The point of this may not be clear at first to the student but it should be noted that for a long time psychologists have believed that facial displays of emotion are learned, and therefore culturally variable. Using photographs of facial expressions associated with six different emotions in this country, the investigators set out to see if people living in Japan, Brazil, New Guinea, and Borneo could also identify the emotions involved. Their results indicated similar recognitions for happiness, anger, and fear in all cultures tested. The other three emotions, disgust, surprise, and sadness were less accurately judged but there was still enough agreement even with these to suggest that there is less cultural variability in emotional facial expressions than previously believed.

OBESITY AND EATING

Internal and external cues differentially affect the eating behavior of obese and normal subjects.

STANLEY SCHACHTER
Columbia University

Current conceptions of hunger control mechanisms indicate that food deprivation leads to various peripheral physiological changes such as modification of blood constituents, increase in gastric motility, changes in body temperature, and the like. By means of some still debated mechanism, these changes are detected by a hypothalamic feeding center. Presumably some or all facets of this activated machinery lead the organism to search out and consume food. There appears to be no doubt that peripheral physiological changes and activation of the hypothalamic feeding center are inevitable consequences of food deprivation. On the basis of current knowledge, however, one may ask, when this biological machinery is activated, do we necessarily describe ourselves as hungry, and eat? For most of us raised on the notion that hunger is the most primitive of motives, wired into the animal and unmistakable in its cues, the question may seem far-fetched, but there is increasing reason to suspect that there are major individual differences in the extent to which these physiological changes are associated with the desire to eat.

On the clinical level, the analyst Hilde Bruch (*1*) has observed that her obese patients literally do not know when they are physiologically hungry. To account for this observation she suggests that, during childhood, these patients were not taught to discriminate between hunger and such states as fear, anger, and anxiety. If this is so, these people may be labeling almost any state of arousal "hunger," or, alternatively, labeling no internal state "hunger."

If Bruch's speculations are correct, it should be anticipated that the set of physiological symptoms which are considered characteristic of food deprivation are not labeled "hunger" by the obese. In other words the obese literally may not know when they are physiologically hungry. For at least one of the presumed physiological correlates of food deprivation, this does appear to be the case. In an absorbing study, Stunkard (*2, 3*) has related gastric motility to self-reports of hunger in 37 obese subjects and 37 subjects of normal size. A subject, who had eaten no breakfast, came to the laboratory at 9 a.m.; he swallowed a gastric balloon, and for 4 hours Stunkard continuously recorded gastric motility. Every 15 minutes the subject was asked if he was hungry. He answered "yes" or "no," and that is all there was to the study. We have, then, a record of the extent to which a subject's self-report of hunger corresponds to his gastric motility. The results show (i) that obese and normal subjects do not differ significantly in degree of gastric motility, and (ii) that, when the stomach is not contracting, the reports of obese and normal subjects are quite similar, both groups reporting hunger roughly 38 percent of the time. When the stomach is contracting, however, the reports of the two groups differ markedly. For normal subjects, self-report of hunger coincides with gastric motility 71 percent of the time. For the obese, the percentage is only 47.6. Stunkard's work seems to indicate that obese and normal subjects do not refer to the same bodily state when they use the term *hunger*.

Effects of Food Deprivation and Fear

If this inference is correct, we should anticipate that, if we were to directly manipulate gastric motility and the other symptoms that we associate with hunger, we would, for normal subjects, be directly manipulating feelings of hunger and eating behavior. For the obese there would be no correspondence between manipulated internal state and eating behavior. To test these expectations, Goldman, Gordon, and I (*4*) performed an experiment in which bodily state was manipulated by two means—(i) by the obvious technique of manipulating food deprivation, so that some subjects had empty stomachs and others had full stomachs before eating; (ii) by manipulating fear, so that some subjects were badly frightened and others were quite calm immediately before eating. Carlson (5) has indicated that fear inhibits gastric motility; Cannon (6) also has demonstrated that fear inhibits motility, and has shown that it leads to the liberation, from the liver, of sugar into the blood. Hypoglycemia and gastric contractions are generally considered the chief peripheral physiological correlates of food deprivation.

Our experiment was conducted under the guise of a study of taste. A subject came to the laboratory in mid-afternoon or evening. He had been called the previous evening and asked not to eat the meal (lunch or dinner) preceding his appointment at the laboratory. The experiment was introduced as a study of "the interdependence of the basic human senses—of the way in which the stimulation of one sense affects another." Specifically, the subject was told that this study would be concerned with "the effects of tactile stimulation on the way things taste."

It was explained that all subjects had been asked not to eat a meal before coming to the laboratory because "in any scientific experiment it is necessary that the subjects be as similar as possible in all relevant ways. As you probably know from your own experience," the experimenter continued, "an important factor in determining how things taste is what you have recently eaten." The introduction over, the experimenter then proceeded as follows.

For the "full stomach" condition he said to the subject, "In order to guarantee that your recent taste experiences are similar to those of other subjects who have taken part in this experiment, we should now like you to eat exactly the same thing they did. Just help yourself to the roast beef sandwiches on the table. Eat as much as you want—till you're full."

For the "empty stomach" condition, the subjects, of course, were not fed.

Next, the subject was seated in front of five bowls of crackers and told, "We want you to taste five different kinds of crackers and tell us how they taste to you." The experimenter then gave the subject a long set of rating scales and said, "We want you to judge each cracker on the dimensions (salty, cheesy, garlicky, and so on) listed on this sheet. Taste as many or as few of the crackers of each type as you want in making your judgments; the important thing is that your ratings be as accurate as possible."

Before permitting the subject to eat, the experimenter continued with the next stage of the experiment—the manipulation of fear.

"As I mentioned," he said, "our primary interest in this experiment is the effect of tactile stimulation on taste. Electric stimulation is the means we use to excite your skin receptors. We use this method in order to carefully control the amount of stimulation you receive."

For the "low fear" condition the subject was told, "For the effects in which we are interested, we need to use only the lowest level of stimulation. At most you will feel a slight tingle. Probably you will feel nothing at all. We are only interested in the effect of very weak stimulation."

For the "high fear" condition the experimenter pointed to a large black console loaded with electrical junk and said, "That machine is the one we will be using. I am afraid that these shocks will be painful. For them to have any effect on your taste sensations, the voltage must be rather high. There will, of course, be no permanent damage. Do you have a heart condition?" A large electrode connected to the console was then attached to each of the subject's ankles, and the experimenter concluded, "The best way for us to test the effect of tactile stimulation is to have you rate the crackers now, before the electric shock, and then rate them again, after the shock, to see what changes in your ratings the shock has made."

The subject then proceeded to taste and rate crackers for 15 minutes, under the impression that this was a taste test; meanwhile we were simply counting the number of crackers he ate (7). We then had measures of the amounts eaten by subjects who initially had either empty or full stomachs and who were initially either frightened or calm. There were of course, two types of subjects: obese subjects (from 14 percent to 75 percent overweight) and normal subjects (from

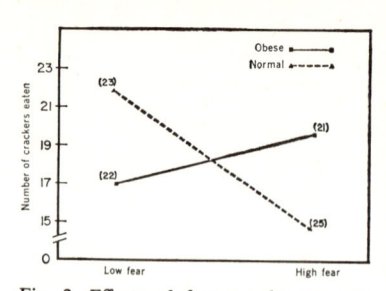

Fig. 2. Effects of fear on the amounts eaten by normal and obese subjects. Numbers in parentheses are numbers of subjects.

8 percent underweight to 9 percent overweight).

To review expectations: If we were correct in thinking that the obese do not label as hunger the bodily states associated with food deprivation, then our several experimental manipulations should have had no effects on the amount eaten by obese subjects; on the other hand, the eating behavior of normal subjects should have directly paralleled the effects of the manipulations on bodily state.

It will be a surprise to no one to learn, from Fig. 1, that the normal subjects ate considerably fewer crackers when their stomachs were full than when their stomachs were empty. The results for obese subjects stand in fascinating contrast. They ate as much —in fact, slightly more—when their stomachs were full as when they were empty (interaction $P < .05$). Obviously the actual state of the stomach has nothing to do with the eating behavior of the obese.

In Fig. 2, pertaining to the effect of fear, we note an analogous picture. Fear markedly decreased the number of crackers the normal subjects ate but had no effect on the number eaten by the obese (interaction $P < .01$). Again, there was a small, though nonsignificant, reversal: the fearful obese ate slightly more than the calm obese.

It seems clear that the set of bodily symptoms the subject labels "hunger" differs for obese and normal subjects. Whether one measures gastric motility, as Stunkard did, or manipulates it, as I assume my co-workers and I have done, one finds, for normal subjects, a high degree of correspondence between the state of the gut and eating behavior and, for obese subjects, virtually no correspondence. While all of our manipulations have had a major effect on the amounts eaten by normal subjects, nothing that we have done has had a substantial effect on the amounts eaten by obese subjects.

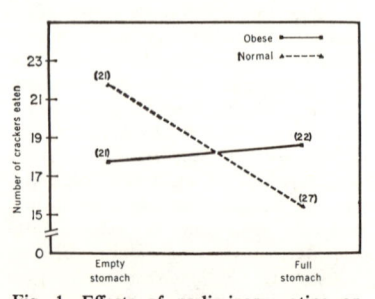

Fig. 1. Effects of preliminary eating on the amounts eaten during the experiment by normal and obese subjects. Numbers in parentheses are numbers of subjects.

OBESITY AND EATING

Effects of the Circumstances of Eating

With these facts in mind, let us turn to the work of Hashim and Van Itallie (8) of the Nutrition Clinic, St. Luke's Hospital, New York City. Their findings may be summarized as follows: virtually everything these workers do seems to have a major effect on the eating behavior of the obese and almost no effect on the eating behavior of the normal subject.

These researchers have prepared a bland liquid diet similar to commercial preparations such as vanilla-flavored Nutrament or Metrecal. The subjects are restricted to this monotonous diet for periods ranging from a week to several months. They can eat as much or as little of it as they want. Some of the subjects get a pitcher full and pour themselves a meal any time they wish. Other subjects are fed by a machine which delivers a mouthful every time the subject presses a button. With either feeding technique, the eating situation has the following characteristics. (i) The food itself is unappealing. (ii) Eating is entirely self-determined: whether or not the subject eats, how much he eats, and when he eats are matters decided by him and no one else. Absolutely no pressure is brought to bear to limit his consumption. (iii) The eating situation is devoid of any social or domestic trappings. It is basic eating; it will keep the subject alive, but it's not much fun.

To date, six grossly obese and five normal individuals have been subjects in these studies. In Fig. 3 the eating curves for a typical pair of subjects over a 21-day period are plotted. Both subjects were healthy people who lived in the hospital during the entire study. The obese subject was a 52-year-old woman, 5 feet 3 inches (1.6 meters) tall, who weighed 307 pounds (138 kilograms) on admission. The normal subject was a 30-year-old male, 5 feet 7 inches tall, who weighed 132 pounds.

The subject's estimated daily caloric intake before entering the hospital (as determined from a detailed interview) is plotted at the left in Fig. 3. Each subject, while in the hospital but before entering upon the experimental regime, was fed a general hospital diet. The obese subject was placed on a 2400-calorie diet for 7 days and a 1200-calorie diet for the next 8 days. As may be seen in Fig. 3, she ate everything on her tray throughout this 15-day period. The normal subject was placed on a 2400-calorie diet for 2 days, and he too ate everything.

With the beginning of the experiment proper, the difference in the eating behavior of the two subjects was dramatic and startling. The food consumption of the obese subject dropped precipitately the moment she entered upon the experimental regime, and it remained at an incredibly low level for the duration of the experiment. This effect is so dramatic that the weight of one obese subject who took part in the experiment for 8 months dropped from 410 to 190 pounds. On the other hand, the food consumption of the normal subject of Fig. 3 dropped slightly on the first 2 days, then returned to a fairly steady 2300 grams or so of food a day. The curves for these two subjects are typical. Each of the six obese subjects has manifested this marked and persistent decrease in food consumption during the experiment; each of the normal subjects has steadily consumed about his normal amount of food.

Before suggesting possible interpretations, I should note certain marked differences between these two groups of subjects. Most important, the obese subjects had come to the clinic for help in solving their weight problem and were, of course, motivated to lose weight. The normal subjects were simply volunteers. Doubtless this difference could account for the observed difference in eating behavior during the experiment, and until obese volunteers, unconcerned with their weight, are used as subjects in similar studies, we cannot be sure of the interpretation of this phenomenon. However, I think we should not, solely on grounds of methodological fastidiousness, dismiss these findings. It was concern with weight that brought these obese subjects to the clinic. Each of them, before entering the hospital and while in the hospital before being put on the experimental diet, was motivated to lose weight. Yet, despite this motivation, none of these subjects had been capable of restricting his diet at home, and each of them, when fed the general hospital diet, had eaten everything on his tray. Only when the food was dull and the act of eating was self-initiated and devoid of any ritual trappings did the obese subject, motivated or not, severely limit his consumption.

Internal and External Control

On the one hand, then, our experiments indicate virtually no relationship between internal physiological state and the eating behavior of the obese subject; on the other hand, these case studies seem to indicate a close tie between the eating behavior of the obese and what might be called the circumstances of eating. When the food is dull and the eating situation is uninteresting, the obese subject eats virtually nothing. For the normal subject, the situation is just the reverse: his eating behavior seems directly linked to his physiological state but is relatively unaffected by the external circumstances or the ritual associated with eating.

Given this set of facts it seems clear that eating is triggered by different sets of stimuli in obese and normal subjects. Indeed, there is growing reason to suspect that the eating behavior of the obese is relatively unrelated to any internal state but is, in large part, under external control, being initiated and terminated by stimuli external to the organism. Let me give a few examples. A person whose eating behavior is under external control will stroll by a pastry shop, find the food in the window irresistible, and, even if he has recently eaten, go in and buy something. He will pass by a hamburger stand, smell the broiling meat, and, even though he has just eaten, buy a hamburger. Obviously such external factors—smell, sight, taste, other people's actions—to some extent affect anyone's eating. However, in normal individuals such external factors interact with internal state. They may affect what, where, and how much the normal individual eats, but they do so chiefly when he is in a state of physiological hunger. For the obese, I suggest, internal state is irrelevant and eating is determined largely by external factors.

This hypothesis obviously fits the data presented here, as well it should, since it is an *ad hoc* construction designed specifically to fit these data. Let us see, then, what independent support there is for the hypothesis, and where the hypothesis leads.

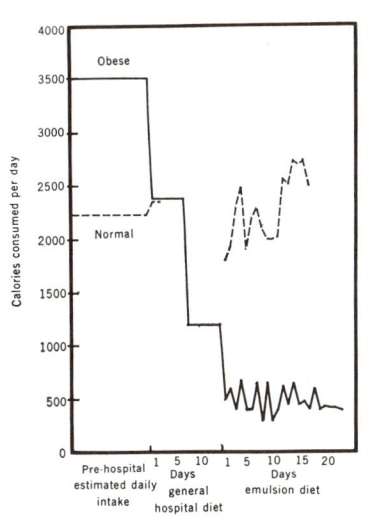

Fig. 3. The effects of an emulsion diet on the amounts eaten by an obese and a normal subject.

Effects of Manipulating Time

Among the multitude of external food-relevant cues, one of the most intriguing is the passage of time. Everyone "knows" that 4 to 6 hours after eating his last meal he should eat his next one. Everyone "knows" that, within narrow limits, there are set times for eating regular meals. We should, then, expect that if we manipulate time we should be able to manipulate the eating behavior of the obese subjects. In order to do this, Gross and I (9) simply gimmicked two clocks so that one ran at half normal speed and the other, at twice normal speed. A subject arrives at 5:00 p.m., ostensibly to take part in an experiment on the relationship of base levels of autonomic reactivity to personality factors. He is ushered into a windowless room containing nothing but electronic equipment and a clock. Electrodes are put on his wrists, his watch is removed "so that it will not get gummed up with electrode jelly," and he is connected to a polygraph. All this takes 5 minutes, and at 5:05 he is left alone, with nothing to do for a true 30 minutes, while ostensibly we are getting a record of galvanic skin response and cardiac rate in a subject at rest. There are two experimental conditions. In one, the experimenter returns after a true 30 minutes and the clock reads 5:20. In the other, the clock reads 6:05, which is normal dinner time for most subjects. In both cases the experimenter is carrying a box of crackers and nibbling a cracker as he comes into the room; he puts the box down, invites the subject to help himself, removes the electrodes from the subject's wrists, and proceeds with personality testing for exactly 5 minutes. This done, he gives the subject a personality inventory which he is to complete and leaves him alone with the box of crackers for another true 10 minutes. There are two groups of subjects—normal and obese—and the only datum we collect is the weight of the box of crackers before and after the subject has had a chance at it.

If these ideas on internal and external controls of eating behavior are correct, normal subjects, whose eating behavior is presumably linked to internal state, should be relatively unaffected by the manipulation and should eat roughly the same number of crackers regardless of whether the clock reads 5:20 or 6:05. The obese, on the other hand, whose eating behavior is presumably under external control, should eat very few crackers when the clock reads 5:20 and a great many crackers when it reads 6:05.

The data of Fig. 4 do indeed indicate that the obese subjects eat almost twice as many crackers when they think the time is 6:05 as they do when they believe it to be 5:20. For normal subjects, the trend is just the reverse (interaction $P = .002$)—an unanticipated finding but one which seems embarrassingly simple to explain, as witness the several normal subjects who thought the time was 6:05 and politely refused the crackers, saying, "No thanks, I don't want to spoil my dinner." Obviously cognitive factors affected the eating behavior of both the normal and the obese subjects, but there was a vast difference. While the manipulation of the clock served to trigger or stimulate eating among the obese, it had the opposite effect on normal subjects, most of whom at this hour were, we presume, physiologically hungry, aware that they would eat dinner very shortly, and unwilling to spoil their dinner by filling up on crackers.

Effects of Taste

In another study, Nisbett (10) examined the effects of taste on eating behavior. Nisbett reasoned that taste, like the sight or smell of food, is essentially an external stimulus to eating. Nisbett, in his experiment, also extended the range of weight deviation by including a group of underweight subjects as well as obese and normal subjects. His purpose in so doing was to examine the hypothesis that the relative potency of external versus internal controls is a dimension directly related to the degree of overweight. If the hypothesis was correct, he reasoned, the taste of food would have the greatest impact on the amounts eaten by obese subjects and the least impact on the amounts eaten by underweight subjects. To test this, Nisbett had his subjects eat as much as they wanted of one of two kinds of vanilla ice cream; one was a delicious and expensive product, the other an acrid concoction of cheap vanilla and quinine which he called "vanilla bitters." The effects of taste are presented in Fig. 5, in which the subjects ratings of how good or bad the ice cream is are plotted against the amount eaten. As may be seen in Fig. 5, when the ice cream was rated "fairly good" or better, the obese subjects ate considerably more than the normal subjects did; these, in turn, ate more than the underweight subjects did. When the ice cream was rated "not very good" or worse, the ordering tended to reverse: the underweight subjects ate more than either the normal or the obese subjects. This experiment, then, indicates that the external, or at least nonvisceral, cue *taste* does have differential effects on the eating behavior of underweight, normal, and obese subjects.

The indications, from Nisbett's experiment, that the degree of dependence on external cues relative to internal cues varies with deviation from normal weight are intriguing, for, if further work supports this hypothesis, we may have the beginnings of a plausible explanation of why the thin are thin and the fat are fat. We know from Carlson's work (5) that gastric contractions cease after a small amount of food has been introduced into the stomach. To the extent that such contractions are directly related to the hunger "experience"—to the extent that a person's eating is under internal control—he should "eat like a bird," eating only enough to stop the contractions. Eating beyond this point should be a function of external cues—the taste, sight, and smell of food. Individuals whose eating is externally controlled, then, should find it hard to stop eating. This hypothesis may account for the notorious "binge" eating of the obese (11) or the monumental meals described in loving detail by students (12) of the great, fat gastronomic magnificoes.

This rough attempt to explain why the obese are obese in itself raises intriguing questions. For example, does the external control of eating behavior inevitably lead to obesity? It is evident, I believe, that not only is such a linkage logically not inevitable but that the condition of external control of eating may in rare but specifiable circumstances lead to emaciation. A person whose eating is externally controlled should eat and grow fat when food-related cues are abundant and when he is fully aware of them. However, when such cues are lacking or when for some reason, such as withdrawal or depression, the individual is unaware of the cues, the person under external control would, one would expect, not eat, and, if the condition persisted, would grow "concentration-camp" thin. From study of the clinical literature one does get the impression that there is an odd but distinct relationship between obesity and extreme emaciation. For example, 11 of 21 subjects of case studies discussed by Bliss and Branch in *Anorexia Nervosa* (13) were, at some time in their lives, obese. In the case of eight of these 11 subjects, anorexia was preceded and accompanied by either marked withdrawal or intense depression. In contrast, intense attacks of anxiety or nervousness [states which our experiment (4) suggests would inhibit eating in normal individuals] seem to be associated with the development of anorexia among most of the ten subjects who were originally of normal size.

At this point, these speculations are

OBESITY AND EATING

simply idea-spinning—fun, but ephemeral. Let us return to the results of the studies described so far. These can be quickly summarized as follows.

1) Physiological correlates of food deprivation, such as gastric motility, are directly related to eating behavior and to the reported experience of hunger in normal subjects but unrelated in obese subjects (*3, 4*).

2) External or nonvisceral cues, such as smell, taste, the sight of other people eating, and the passage of time, affect eating behavior to a greater extent in obese subjects than in normal subjects (*8–10*).

Obesity and Fasting

Given these basic facts, their implications have ramifications in almost any area pertaining to food and eating, and some of our studies have been concerned with the implications of these experimental results for eating behavior in a variety of nonlaboratory settings. Thus, Goldman, Jaffa, and I (*14*) have studied fasting on Yom Kippur, the Jewish Day of Atonement, on which the orthodox Jew is supposed to go without food for 24 hours. Reasoning that, on this occasion, food-relevant external cues are particularly scarce, one would expect obese Jews to be more likely to fast than normal Jews. In a study of 296 religious Jewish college students (defined as Jewish college students who had been to a synagogue at least once during the preceding year on occasions other than a wedding or a bar mitzvah), this proves to be the case, for 83.3 percent of obese Jews fasted, as compared with 68.8 percent of normal Jews ($P < .05$).

Further, this external-internal control schema leads to the prediction that fat, fasting Jews who spend a great deal of time in the synagogue on Yom Kippur will suffer less from fasting than fat, fasting Jews who spend little time in the synagogue. There should be no such relationship for normal fasting Jews. Obviously, there will be far fewer food-related cues in the synagogue than on the street or at home. Therefore, for obese Jews, the likelihood that the impulse to eat will be triggered is greater outside of the synagogue than within it. For normal Jews, this distinction is of less importance. In or out of the synagogue, stomach pangs are stomach pangs. Again, the data support the expectation. When the number of hours in the synagogue is correlated with self-ratings of the unpleasantness of fasting, for obese subjects the correlation is $-.50$, whereas for normal subjects the correlation is only $-.18$. In a test of the difference between correlations, $P = .03$.

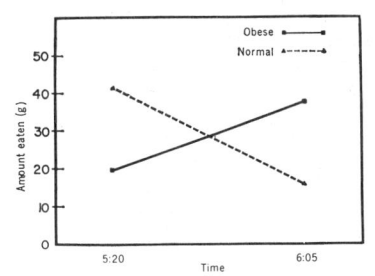

Fig. 4. The effects of manipulation of time on the amounts eaten by obese and normal subjects.

Obviously, for the obese, the more time the individual spends in the synagogue, the less of an ordeal fasting is. For normals, the number of hours in the synagogue has little to do with the difficulty of the fast.

Obesity and Choice of Eating Place

In another study (*14*) we examined the relationship of obesity to choice of eating places. From Nisbett's findings on taste, it seemed a plausible guess that the obese would be more drawn to good restaurants and more repelled by bad ones than normal subjects would be. At Columbia, students have the option of eating in the university dining halls or in any of the many restaurants that surround the campus. At Columbia, as probably at every similar institution in the United States, students have a low opinion of the institution's food. If a freshman elects to eat in a dormitory dining hall, he may, if he chooses, join a prepayment food plan at the beginning of the school year. Any time after 1 November he may, by paying a penalty of $15, cancel his food

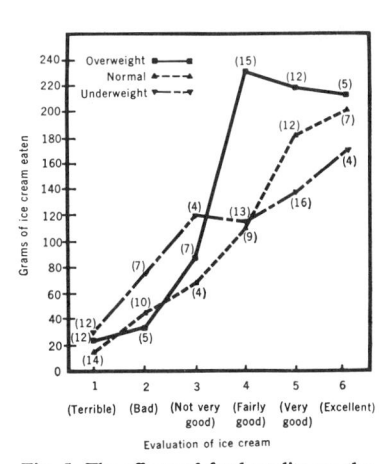

Fig. 5. The effects of food quality on the amounts eaten by obese, normal, and underweight subjects. Numbers in parentheses are numbers of subjects.

contract. If we accept prevailing campus opinion of the institution's food as being at all realistically based, we should anticipate that those for whom taste or food quality is most important will be the most likely to let their food contracts expire. Obese freshmen, then, should be more likely to drop out of the food plan than normal freshmen. Again, the data support the expectation: 86.5 percent of fat freshmen cancel their contracts as compared with 67.1 percent of normal freshmen ($P < .05$). Obesity does to some extent serve as a basis for predicting who will choose to eat institutional food.

Obesity and Adjustment to New Eating Schedules

In the final study in this series (*14*) we examined the relationship of obesity to the difficulty of adjusting to new eating schedules imposed by time-zone changes. This study involved an analysis of data collected by the medical department of Air France in a study of physiological effects of time-zone changes on 236 flight personnel assigned to the Paris–New York and Paris–Montreal flights. Most of these flights leave Paris around noon, French time; fly for approximately 8 hours; and land in North America sometime between 2:00 and 3:00 p.m. Eastern time. Flight-crew members eat lunch shortly after takeoff and, being occupied with landing preparations, are not served another meal during the flight. They land some 7 hours after their last meal, at a time that is later than the local lunch hour and earlier than the local dinner time.

Though this study was not directly concerned with eating behavior, the interviewers systematically noted all individuals who volunteered the information that they "suffered from the discordance between their physiological state and meal time in America" (*15*). One would anticipate that the fatter individuals, being sensitive to external cues (local meal hours) rather than internal ones, would adapt most readily to local eating schedules and be least likely to complain of the discrepancy between American meal times and physiological state.

Given the physical requirements involved in the selection of aircrews, there are, of course, relatively few really obese people in this sample. However, the results of Nisbett's experiment (*10*) indicate that the degree of reliance on external relative to internal cues may well be a dimension which varies with the degree of deviation from normal weight. It seems reasonable, then, to anticipate that, even within a restricted sample, there will be differences in response between the heavier and the lighter members of the sample. This is the case. In comparing the 101 flight personnel who are overweight (0.1 to 29 percent overweight) with the 135 who are not overweight (0 to 25 percent underweight), we find that 11.9 percent of the overweight complain as compared with 25.3 percent of the non-overweight ($P < .01$). It does appear that the fatter were less troubled by the effects of time changes on eating than the thinner flyers (16).

These persistent findings that the obese are relatively insensitive to variations in the physiological correlates of food deprivation but highly sensitive to environmental, food-related cues is, perhaps, one key to understanding the notorious long-run ineffectiveness of virtually all attempts to treat obesity (17). The use of anorexigenic drugs such as amphetamine or of bulk-producing, nonnutritive substances such as methyl cellulose is based on the premise that such agents dampen the intensity of the physiological symptoms of food deprivation. Probably they do, but these symptoms appear to have little to do with whether or not a fat person eats. Restricted, low-calorie diets should be effective just so long as the obese dieter is able to blind himself to food-relevant cues or so long as he exists in a world barren of such cues. In the Hashim and Van Itallie study (8), the subjects did, in fact, live in such a world. Restricted to a Metrecal-like diet and to a small hospital ward, all the obese subjects lost impressive amounts of weight. However, on their return to normal living, to a man they returned to their original weights.

References and Notes

1. H. Bruch, *Psychiat. Quart.* **35**, 458 (1961).
2. A. Stunkard, *Psychosomat. Med.* **21**, 281 (1959).
3. ———— and C. Koch, *Arch. Genet. Psychiat.* **11**, 74 (1964).
4. S. Schachter, R. Goldman, A. Gordon, *J. Personality Soc. Psychol.*, in press.
5. A. J. Carlson, *Control of Hunger in Health and Disease* (Univ. of Chicago Press, Chicago, 1916).
6. W. B. Cannon, *Bodily Changes in Pain, Hunger, Fear and Rage* (Appleton, New York, 1915).
7. It is a common belief among researchers in the field of obesity that the sensitivity of their fat subjects makes it impossible to study their eating behavior experimentally—hence this roundabout way of measuring eating; the subjects in this study are taking a "taste test," not "eating."
8. S. A. Hashim and T. B. Van Itallie, *Ann. N. Y. Acad. Sci.* **131**, 654 (1965).
9. S. Schachter and L. Gross, *J. Personality Soc. Psychol.*, in press.
10. R. E. Nisbett, *ibid.*, in press.
11. A. Stunkard, *Amer. J. Psychiat.* **118**, 212 (1961).
12. L. Beebe, *The Big Spenders* (Doubleday, New York, 1966).
13. E. L. Bliss and C. H. Branch, *Anorexia Nervosa* (Hoeber, New York, 1960).
14. R. Goldman, M. Jaffa, S. Schachter, *J. Personality Soc. Psychol.*, in press.
15. J. Lavernhe and E. Lafontaine (Air France), personal communication.
16. Obviously, I do not mean to imply that the *only* explanation of the results of these three nonlaboratory studies lies in this formulation of the external-internal control of eating behavior. These studies were deliberately designed to test implications of this general schema in field settings. As with any field research, alternative explanations of the findings are legion, and, within the context of any specific study, impossible to rule out. Alternative formulations of this entire series of studies are considered in the original papers [see Schachter *et al.* (*4* and *9*), Nisbett (*10*), and Goldman *et al.* (*14*)].
17. A. Stunkard and M. McLaren-Hume, *Arch. Internal Med.* **103**, 79 (1959); A. R. Feinstein, *J. Chronic Diseases* **11**, 349 (1960).
18. Much of the research described in this article was supported by grants G23758 and GS732 from the National Science Foundation.

THE EFFECT OF DREAM DEPRIVATION

The need for a certain amount of dreaming each night is suggested by recent experiments.

WILLIAM DEMENT

Mount Sinai Hospital, New York, N.Y.

About a year ago, a research program was initiated at the Mount Sinai Hospital which aimed at assessing the basic function and significance of dreaming. The experiments have been arduous and time-consuming and are still in progress. However, the results of the first series have been quite uniform, and because of the length of the program, it has been decided to issue this preliminary report.

In recent years, a body of evidence has accumulated which demonstrates that dreaming occurs in association with periods of rapid, binocularly synchronous eye movements (1–3). Furthermore, the amount and directional patterning of these eye movements and the associated dream *content* are related in such a way as to strongly suggest that the eye movements represent scanning movements made by the dreamer as he watches the events of the dream (3). In a study of undisturbed sleep (4), the eye-movement periods were observed to occur regularly throughout the night in association with the lightest phases of a cyclic variation in depth of sleep, as measured by the electroencephalograph. The length of individual cycles averaged about 90 minutes, and the mean duration of single periods of eye movement was about 20 minutes. Thus, a typical night's sleep includes four or five periods of dreaming, which account for about 20 percent of the total sleep time.

One of the most striking facts apparent in all the works cited above was that a very much greater amount of dreaming occurs normally than had heretofore been realized—greater both from the standpoint of frequency and duration in a single night of sleep and in the invariability of its occurrence from night to night. In other words, dreaming appears to be an intrinsic part of normal sleep and, as such, although the dreams are not usually recalled, occurs every night in every sleeping person.

A consideration of this aspect of dreaming leads more or less inevitably to the formulation of certain rather fundamental questions. Since there appear to be no exceptions to the nightly occurrence of a substantial amount of dreaming in every sleeping person, it might be asked whether or not this amount of dreaming is in some way a necessary and vital part of our existence. Would it be possible for human beings to continue functioning normally if their dream life were completely or partially suppressed? Should dreaming be considered necessary in a psychological sense or a physiological sense or both?

The obvious attack on these problems was to study subjects who had somehow been deprived of the opportunity to dream. After a few unsuccessful preliminary trials with depressant drugs, it was decided to use the somewhat drastic method of awakening sleeping subjects immediately after the onset of dreaming and to continue this procedure throughout the night, so that each dream period would be artificially terminated right at its beginning.

Subjects and Method

The data in this article are from the first eight subjects in the research program, all males, ranging in age from 23 to 32. Eye movements and accompanying low-voltage, nonspindling electroencephalographic patterns (4) were used as the objective criteria of dreaming. The technique by which these variables are recorded, and their precise

---

Reprinted from *Science*, Vol. 131, No. 3415, June 10, 1960. Copyright 1960 by the American Association for the Advancement of Science.

relationship to dreaming, have been extensively discussed elsewhere (2, 4). Briefly, the subjects came to the laboratory at about their usual bedtime. Small silver-disk electrodes were carefully attached near their eyes and on their scalps; then the subjects went to sleep in a quiet, dark room in the laboratory. Lead wires ran from the electrodes to apparatus in an adjacent room upon which the electrical potentials of eye movements and brain waves were recorded continuously throughout the night.

Eye movements and brain waves of each subject were recorded throughout a series of undisturbed nights of sleep, to evaluate his base-line total nightly dream time and over-all sleep pattern. After this, recordings were made throughout a number of nights in which the subject was awakened by the experimenter every time the eye-movement and electroencephalographic recordings indicated that he had begun to dream. These "dream-deprivation" nights were always consecutive. Furthermore, the subjects were requested not to sleep at any other time. Obviously, if subjects were allowed to nap, or to sleep at home on any night in the dream-deprivation period, an unknown amount of dreaming would take place, offsetting the effects of the deprivation. On the first night immediately after the period of dream deprivation, and for several consecutive nights thereafter, the subject was allowed to sleep without disturbance. These nights were designated "recovery nights." The subject then had a varying number of nights off, after which he returned for another series of interrupted nights which exactly duplicated the dream-deprivation series in number of nights and number of awakenings per night. The only difference was that the subject was awakened in the intervals between eye-movement (dream) periods. Whenever a dream period began, the subject was allowed to sleep on without interruption, and was awakened only after the dream had ended spontaneously. Next, the subject had a number of recovery nights of undisturbed sleep equal to the number of recovery nights in his original dream-deprivation series. Altogether, as many as 20 to 30 all-night recordings were made for each subject, most of them on consecutive nights. Since, for the most part, tests could be made on only one subject at a time, and since a minute-by-minute all-night vigil was required of the experimenter to catch each dream episode immediately at its onset, it can be understood why the experiments have been called arduous and time-consuming.

Table 1 summarizes most of the pertinent data. As can be seen, the total number of base-line nights for the eight subjects was 40. The mean sleep time for the 40 nights was 7 hours and 2 minutes, the mean total nightly dream time was 82 minutes, and the mean percentage of dream time (total dream time to total sleep time $\times$ 100) was 19.4. Since total sleep time was not held absolutely constant, percentage figures were routinely calculated as a check on the possibility that differences in total nightly dream time were due to differences in total sleep time. Actually, this is not a plausible explanation for any but quite small differences in dream time, because the range of values for total sleep time for each subject turned out to be very narrow throughout the entire study. When averaged in terms of individuals rather than nights, the means were: total sleep time, 6 hours 50 minutes; total dream time, 80 minutes; percentage of dream time, 19.5; this indicates that the figures were not skewed by the disparate number of base-line nights per subject. The remarkable uniformity of the findings for individual nights is demonstrated by the fact that the standard deviation of the total nightly dream time was only plus or minus 7 minutes.

Progressive Increase in Dream "Attempts"

The number of consecutive nights of dream deprivation arbitrarily selected as a condition of the study was five. However, one subject left the study in a flurry of obviously contrived excuses after only three nights, and two subjects insisted on stopping after four nights but consented to continue with the recovery nights and the remainder of the schedule. One subject was pushed to seven nights. During each awakening the subjects were required to sit up in bed and remain fully awake for several minutes. On the first nights of dream deprivation, the return to sleep generally initiated a new sleep cycle, and the next dream period was postponed for the expected amount of time. However, on subsequent nights the number of forced awakenings required to suppress dreaming steadily mounted. Or, to put it another way, there was a progressive increase in the number of attempts to dream. The number of awakenings required on the first and last nights of deprivation are listed in Table 1. *All* the subjects showed this progressive increase, although there was considerable variation in the starting number and the amount of the increase. An important point is that each awakening was preceded by a minute or two of dreaming. This represented the time required for the experimenter to judge the emerging record and make the decision to awaken the subject after he first noticed the beginning of eye movements. In some cases the time was a little longer, as when an eye-movement period started while the experimenter was looking away from the recording apparatus. It is apparent from this that the method employed did not constitute absolute dream deprivation but, rather, about a 65- to 75-percent deprivation, as it turned out.

Nightly Dream Time Elevated after Deprivation

The data on the first night of the dream deprivation recovery period are summarized for each subject in Table 1. As was mentioned, one subject had quit the study. The mean total dream time on the first recovery night was 112 minutes, or 26.6 percent of the total mean sleep time. If the results for two subjects who did not show marked increases on the first recovery night are excluded, the mean dream time is 127 minutes or 29 percent, which represents a 50-percent increase over the group base-line mean. For all seven subjects together, on the first recovery night the increase in percentage of dream time over the base-line mean (Table 1, col. 3, mean percentage figures; col. 10, first recovery night percentages) was significant at the $p < .05$ level in a one-tail Wilcoxin matched-pairs signed-ranks test (5).

It is important to mention, however, that one (S.M. in Table 1) of the two subjects alluded to above as exceptions was not really an exception because, although he had only 1 hour 1 minute of dreaming on his first recovery night, he showed a marked increase on *four* subsequent nights. His failure to show a rise on the first recovery night was in all likelihood due to the fact that he had imbibed several cocktails at a party before coming to the laboratory so that the expected increase in dream time was offset by the depressing effect of the alcohol. The other one of the two subjects (N.W. in Table 1) failed to show a significant increase in dream time on any of five consecutive recovery nights and therefore must be considered the single exception to the over-all results. Even so, it is hard to reconcile his lack of increase in dream time on recovery nights with the fact that during the actual period of dream deprivation he showed the largest build-up in number of awakenings required to suppress dreaming (11 to 30) of any subject in this group. One may only suggest that, although he was strongly affected by the dream loss, he could not increase his dream time on recovery nights because of an unusually stable basic sleep cycle that resisted modification.

Table 1. Summary of experimental results. *TST*, total sleep time; *TDT*, total dream time.

Mean and range, base-line nights			Dream-deprivation nights (No.)	Awakenings (No.)		Dream-deprivation recovery nights				First control recovery night		
TST	TDT	Percent		First night	Last night	No.	First night			TST	TDT	Percent
							TST	TDT	Percent			
Subject W. T. (4 base-line nights)												
6ʰ36ᵐ	1ʰ17ᵐ	19.5	5	8	14	1	6ʰ43ᵐ	2ʰ17ᵐ	34.0	6ʰ50ᵐ	1ʰ04ᵐ	15.6
6ʰ24ᵐ–6ʰ48ᵐ	1ʰ10ᵐ–1ʰ21ᵐ	17.0–21.3										
Subject H. S. (5 base-line nights)												
7ʰ27ᵐ	1ʰ24ᵐ	18.8	7	7	24	2	8ʰ02ᵐ	2ʰ45ᵐ	34.2	8ʰ00ᵐ	1ʰ49ᵐ	22.7
7ʰ07ᵐ–7ʰ58ᵐ	1ʰ07ᵐ–1ʰ38ᵐ	15.4–21.8										
Subject N. W. (7 base-line nights)												
6ʰ39ᵐ	1ʰ18ᵐ	19.5	5	11	30	5	6ʰ46ᵐ	1ʰ12ᵐ	17.8	7ʰ10ᵐ	1ʰ28ᵐ	20.2
5ʰ50ᵐ–7ʰ10ᵐ	1ʰ11ᵐ–1ʰ27ᵐ	17.4–22.4										
Subject B. M. (6 base-line nights)												
6ʰ59ᵐ	1ʰ18ᵐ	18.6	5	7	23	5	7ʰ25ᵐ	1ʰ58ᵐ	26.3	7ʰ48ᵐ	1ʰ28ᵐ	18.8
6ʰ28ᵐ–7ʰ38ᵐ	0ʰ58ᵐ–1ʰ35ᵐ	14.8–22.2										
Subject R. G. (10 base-line nights)												
7ʰ26ᵐ	1ʰ26ᵐ	19.3	5	10	20	5	7ʰ14ᵐ	2ʰ08ᵐ	29.5	7ʰ18ᵐ	1ʰ55ᵐ	26.3
7ʰ00ᵐ–7ʰ57ᵐ	1ʰ13ᵐ–1ʰ46ᵐ	16.9–22.7										
Subject W. D. (4 base-line nights)												
6ʰ29ᵐ	1ʰ21ᵐ	20.8	4	13	20	3	8ʰ53ᵐ	2ʰ35ᵐ	29.0			
5ʰ38ᵐ–7ʰ22ᵐ	1ʰ08ᵐ–1ʰ32ᵐ	17.8–23.4										
Subject S. M. (2 base-line nights)												
6ʰ41ᵐ	1ʰ12ᵐ	17.9	4	22	30	6	5ʰ08ᵐ	1ʰ01ᵐ	19.8	6ʰ40ᵐ	1ʰ07ᵐ	16.8
6ʰ18ᵐ–7ʰ04ᵐ	1ʰ01ᵐ–1ʰ23ᵐ	16.2–19.3					6ʰ32ᵐ*	1ʰ50ᵐ*	28.1*			
Subject W. G. (2 base-line nights)												
6ʰ16ᵐ	1ʰ22ᵐ	20.8	3	9	13							
6ʰ08ᵐ–6ʰ24ᵐ	1ʰ17ᵐ–1ʰ27ᵐ	20.7–20.9										

*Second recovery night (see text).

The number of consecutive recovery nights for each subject in this series of tests was too small in some cases, mainly because it was naively supposed at the beginning of the study that an increase in dream time, if it occurred, would last only one or two nights. One subject had only one recovery night, another two, and another three. The dream time was markedly elevated above the base-line on all these nights. For how many additional nights each of these three subjects would have maintained an elevation in dream time can only be surmised in the absence of objective data. All of the remaining four subjects had five consecutive recovery nights. One was the single subject who showed no increase, two were nearing the base-line dream time by the fifth night, and one still showed marked elevation in dream time. From this admittedly incomplete sample it appears that about five nights of increased dreaming usually follow four or five nights of dream suppression achieved by the method of this study.

Effect Not Due to Awakening

Six of the subjects underwent the series of control awakenings—that is, awakenings during non-dream periods. This series exactly duplicated the dream-deprivation series for each subject in number of nights, total number of awakenings, and total number of awakenings per successive night. The dream time on these nights was slightly below base-line levels as a rule. The purpose of this series was, of course, to see if the findings following dream deprivation were solely an effect of the multiple awakenings. Data for the first recovery nights after nights of control awakenings are included in Table 1. There was no significant increase for the group. The mean dream time was 88 minutes, and the mean percentage was 20.1. Subsequent recovery nights in this series also failed to show the marked rise in dream time that was observed after nights of dream deprivation. A moderate increase found on four out of a total of 24 recovery nights for the individuals in the control-awakening group was felt to be a response to the slight reduction in dream time on control-awakening nights.

Behavioral Changes

Psychological disturbances such as anxiety, irritability, and difficulty in concentrating developed during the period of dream deprivation, but these were not catastrophic. One subject, as was mentioned above, quit the study in an apparent panic, and two subjects insisted on stopping one night short of the goal of five nights of dream deprivation, presumably because the stress was too great. At least one subject exhibited serious anxiety and agitation. Five subjects developed a marked increase in appetite during the period of dream deprivation; this observation was supported by daily weight measurements which showed a gain in weight of 3 to 5 pounds in three of the subjects. The psychological changes disappeared as soon as the subjects were allowed to dream. The most important fact was that *none* of the observed changes were seen during the period of control awakenings.

The results have been tentatively interpreted as indicating that a certain amount of dreaming each night is a necessity. It is as though a pressure to dream builds up with the accruing dream deficit during successive dream-deprivation nights—a pressure which is first evident in the increasing frequency of attempts to dream and then, during the recovery period, in the marked increase in total dream time and percentage of dream time. The fact that this increase may be maintained over four or more successive recovery nights suggests that there is a more or less quantitative compensation for the deficit. It is possible that if the dream suppression were carried on long enough, a serious disruption of the personality would result [6].

References and Notes

1. E. Aserinsky and N. Kleitman, *J. Appl. Physiol.* **8**, 1 (1955); W. Dement and E. Wolpert, *J. Nervous Mental Disease* **126**, 568 (1958); D. Goodenough, A. Shapiro, M. Holden, L. Steinschriber, *J. Abnormal Social Psychol.* **59**, 295 (1959); E. Wolpert and H. Trosman, *A.M.A. Arch. Neurol. Psychiat.* **79**, 603 (1958).
2. W. Dement, *J. Nervous Mental Disease* **122**, 263 (1955).
3. ——— and N. Kleitman, *J. Exptl. Psychol.* **53**, 339 (1957); W. Dement and E. Wolpert, *ibid.* **55**, 543 (1958).
4. W. Dement and N. Kleitman, *Electroencephalog. and Clin. Neurophysiol.* **9**, 673 (1957).
5. S. Siegel, *Nonparametric Statistics for the Behavioral Sciences* (McGraw-Hill, New York, 1956).
6. The research reported in this paper was aided by a grant from the Foundations' Fund for Research in Psychiatry.

10

THE EPIGENESIS OF INTRINSIC MOTIVATION AND EARLY COGNITIVE LEARNING[1]

J. McV. Hunt
University of Illinois

Even as late as 15 years ago, a symposium on the stimulation of early cognitive learning would have been almost impossible. It would have been taken by most people as a sign that both participants and members of the audience were too soft-headed to be considered seriously. Even as late as 15 years ago, there was simply no point in talking about such a matter, for no possibility of altering cognitive capacity, or intelligence, was conceived to exist. To be sure, there was, before World War II, some evidence that suggested, even strongly, that cognitive capacities might be modified by early experience; but such evidence as existed was "too loose" to convince anyone who embraced the assumptions that intelligence is fixed and that development is predetermined (see Hunt, 1961). These two assumptions—and I believed and taught them just as did most of us—were considered to be among the marks of a "sound" and "hard-headed" psychologist. Had we psychologists absorbed the implications of Johannsen's (1903) distinction between the genotype and the phenotype and his notion that the phenotype is always a product of continuous, on-going, organism–environment interaction, we should never have held these two assumptions with such certainty; but of the two fathers of the science of genetics we knew only Mendel. Since World War II, however, the various investigations of the effects of infantile experience has piled up sufficient evidence to nearly destroy the credibility of these two dominant assumptions of our post-Darwinian tradition.

The change in conceptions started with the work of Sigmund Freud, but it has recently taken some abrupt new turns. Freud's (1905) theory of psychosexual development attributed great importance to the effects of early infantile experience and especially to the preverbal fates of instinctive modes of pleasure-getting. The earliest studies of the effects of infantile experience assumed these effects to be on the emotional rather than on the intellectual aspects of personality (Hunt, 1941).

[1] This paper was originally prepared for the symposium on the Stimulation of Early Cognitive Learning, chaired by J. R. Braun and presented at the Annual Meeting of the American Psychological Association, Philadelphia, Pennsylvania, 30 August 1963. It was written with the support of Public Health Service Grant MH K6–18,567.

Yet the studies of the effects of the richness of environmental variations encountered during infancy on adult maze-learning ability in rats (Hebb, 1947) and in dogs (Thompson & Heron, 1954) have proved to be most regularly reproducible. These studies stemmed from the neuropsychological theorizing of Donald Hebb (1949) and his distinction between "early learning," in which "cell-assemblies" are developed, and "later learning," in which these assemblies are connected in various kinds of "phase sequences." The studies showed that those rats encountering the larger number of environmental variations during infancy received higher scores on the Hebb-Williams (1946) maze-test of animal intelligence than did those encountering fewer variations (see Forgays & Forgays, 1952; Forgus, 1954; Hymovitch, 1952).

In Hebb's (1947) original study of this kind, the number of variations in environment ranged from the many supplied by pet-reared rats in a human home to the few supplied by cage-rearing in the laboratory. A similar approach was employed by Thompson & Heron (1954), and dogs pet-reared from weaning until eight months of age proved to be markedly superior in performance on the Hebb-Williams test at 18 months of age (after ten months with their cage-reared litter-mates in a dog pasture) to those litter-mates individually cage-reared from weaning to eight months. In fact, the pet-reared dogs appeared to differ more from their cage-reared litter-mates than did the pet-reared rats from their litter-mates. From this I am inclined to infer that the degree of the adult effect of such infantile experience increases as one goes up the vertebrate scale. I tend to attribute this apparent increase in the effect of infantile experience to the increasing proportion of the brain that is without direct connections with receptor input and/or motor output (see Pribram, 1960). I refer here, of course, to the notion of the A/S ratio first put forth by Hebb (1949).

This notion, that the degree of effect of the richness of variations in environment encountered during infancy on adult cognitive capacities increases with the size of the A/S ratio, suggests that the results of these animal studies should probably generalize to the human species. Incontrovertible evidence concerning this suggestion is hard to come by. Nevertheless, a combination of observations strongly supports the suggestion that such early experience has marked effects on the rate of human development and perhaps also has effects on the level of adult intellectual ability.

First, the evidence concerning effects of early experience upon the rate of human intellectual development is fairly compelling. It has long been noted that children being reared in orphanages show retardation in both their functional development and their motivational apathy. These observations were long discounted because of the notion that only those genotypically inferior remain in orphanages, but the well-known studies of René Spitz (1945, 1946) helped to rule out this attribution of the retardation to a selection of genotypes. Unfortunately, Spitz's observations could be discounted on other grounds (see Pinneau, 1955). More recently, however, Wayne Dennis (1960), whose prejudices would appear from his previous writings to favor the traditional assumptions of "fixed intelligence" and "predetermined development," has found two orphanages in Teheran where retardation is even more extreme than that reported by Spitz. Of those infants in their second year, 60 percent were still unable to sit up alone; of those in their fourth year, 85 percent were still unable to walk alone. Moreover, while children typically creep on all fours rather than scoot, as did the children in a third orphanage in Teheran (one for demonstration purposes), those in these two typically chose scooting. By way of explanation, Spitz emphasized the emotional factors associated with lack of mothering (a one-to-one interpersonal relationship) as the basis for the greater retardation observed at "foundling home" than at "nursery." Dennis, on the other hand, has attributed the extreme retardation in sitting and walking to lack of learning opportunities, or more specifically, to the "paucity of handling, including failure of attendants to place children in the sitting position and the prone position" (1960, p. 58). These may well be important factors, but I suspect that yet another factor is of sufficient importance to deserve specific investigative attention—namely, a paucity of variation in auditory and visual inputs, or, perhaps I should say a paucity of meaningful variation in these inputs. On the visual side, these Teheran infants (i.e., those in the orphanages in which 90 percent of the children are recorded as having been under one month of age at the time of admission) had plenty of light, but they continually faced homogeneous off-whiteness interrupted only by passing attendants who seldom stopped to be perceived. On the auditory side, while the noise level of the surrounding city was high and cries of other children were numerous, seldom did clear variations in sound come with such redundancy as to become recognizable and very seldom did such sound variations herald any specific changes in visual input. Thus, opportunities for the development of specific variations in either type of input and opportunities for auditory-visual coordinations were lacking. Moreover, since no toys were provided, the children had little opportunity to develop intentional behavior calculated to make interesting spectacles last. Dennis has reported the most extreme case of mass retardation of which I know. Although signs of malnutrition were present, Dennis was inclined not to consider it a major factor because of the vigor he observed in such automatisms as head shaking and rocking back and forth, and because he could see no way in which malnutrition could call forth scooting rather than creeping. Moreover, the role of heredity was minimized by the facts that the children in the demonstration orphanage, where retardation was much less marked, came from the one admitting neonates, and that they were probably chosen from those most retarded at the time of transfer.

Second, the evidence concerning the permanence of such effects is highly suggestive if less compelling than that concerning rate of development. Whether or not such retardation as that observed in Teheran inevitably leaves a permanent deficit cannot be stated with certainty. You will recall that Dennis observed that once these children in the orphanage learned to walk, they appeared to walk and run as well as other children do. But do not most intellectual and social functions demand a much more broadly integrated and more finely differentiated set of autonomous central processes than do such motor functions as walking and running? Certainly this is suggested by the fact that the dogs pet-reared by Thompson and Heron (1954) are much superior to those cage-reared in solving various problems in the Hebb-Williams mazes even after a period of ten months of running free in the dog pasture. Moreover, permanence of the effects of infantile experience is also strongly suggested by the results of Goldfarb's (see 1955) studies, in which adolescents, orphanage-reared for approximately their first three years, showed lower IQs, less rich fantasies, less tendency to take and hold onto a task, and more social problems than did adolescents (matched with those orphanage-reared for educational and socioeducational status of their mothers) who were reared in foster homes for those first three years. And again, permanence of intellectual deficit is also suggested by the finding in Israel that children of Jewish immigrants from the Orient persist in their scholastic inferiority to children of Jewish immigrants from Western countries, and by the observations that children from the slums in America persist in scholastic inferiority to children from middle-class parents even though the slum children may be advanced at least in motor development at ages from one to two years. In spite of these strong suggestions, it would be exceedingly interesting to have direct evidence from test performances at adolescence of these orphanage-reared Iranians for comparison with the test performances of family-reared Iranians or of adolescents reared in the demonstration orphanage. It is also important to determine whether the intellectual deficit from defective early experience is irreversible, or persists because of the way in which human children are usually treated once they achieve certain ages. If the latter alternative is the case, it should be possible to devise corrective experiences to overcome the deficit. This would be re-studying the issues that concerned Itard and Seguin. Getting the evidence necessary to decide such issues is exceedingly difficult.

Early Cognitive Learning and the Development of Intrinsic Motivation

Combining such bits of evidence as I have indicated with the geneticist's conception of genotype-environment interaction and with the biologist's notion of organism-environment interaction now makes it quite sensible to attempt to stimulate early cognitive learning. This evidence, however, hardly indicates how to go about it. Perhaps the most fruitful source of suggestions about how to proceed comes from an examination of the relationship between the development of intrinsic motivation and early cognitive learning.

CHANGES IN TRADITIONAL ASSUMPTIONS OF MOTIVATION

One of the leading traditional assumptions about motivation, namely, that painful stimulation during infancy leads inevitably (through something like Pavlovian conditioning) to increased proclivity to anxiousness and to reduced capacity for adaptation or learning, has been called into serious question by evidence from studies of the effects of painful infantile experience. Various investigators have found that rats submitted to painful electric shock, like those handled and petted, defecate and urinate less in an unfamiliar situation than do those left unmolested in the maternal nest (see Denenberg, 1959, 1962; Denenberg & Karas, 1960; Denenberg, Morton, Kline, & Grota, 1962; Levine, 1956, 1957, 1958, 1959). If proneness to defecate or urinate in an unfamiliar situation is an index to anxiousness, these findings appear to deny the notion that anxiousness is an inevitable consequence of painful stimulation and to suggest that painful stimulation may be a special case of the principle that variation in inputs helps to immunize an animal to fear of the strange. Moreover, investigators have found that encounters with electric shock before weaning may increase the adult ability of rats to learn, at least when this ability is indexed by means of the number of trials required to establish an avoidance response to painful stimulation (see Brookshire, 1958; Brookshire, Littman, & Stewart, 1961; Denenberg, 1959; Denenberg & Bell, 1960; Denenberg & Karas, 1960; Levine, 1956, 1958; Levine, Chevalier, & Korchin, 1956). Encounters with painful electric shock in infancy appear to share with petting and handling the same kind of effects upon avoidance conditioning just as they share similar effects upon later defecation and urination in an unfamiliar situation. At least, this appears to be true for rats, but it may not be true for mice (see Lindzey, Lykken, & Winston, 1960).

Perhaps this surprising similarity in the effects of painful stimulation and in the effects of petting and handling is an artifact of comparing the effects of each of these kinds of encounters with the effects of leaving the infant rat unmolested in the maternal nest. In such comparisons, painful shock, petting, and handling all constitute variations in receptor inputs or in environmental encounters. It has been argued that these various kinds of input are equivalent in their effects on still unweaned rat pups and that it is only stimulation per se that counts in early infancy (Levine, 1959). This, however, can hardly be so, for Salama & Hunt (1964) have found that rats shocked daily during their second ten days of life show substantially less "fixation" effect of shock at the choice-point in a T-maze than do their litter-mates that were petted or handled. The petted and handled rats in this experiment showed "fixation" effects that did not differ significantly from those of litter-mates left unmolested in the maternal nest. The findings of this experiment show that some of the effects of shock in early infancy differ markedly from those of petting and handling, but the fact that shock in infancy reduces rather than increases the "fixation" effects of shock at the choice-point in the maze is again highly dissonant with the assumption that painful stimulation must inevitably increase proclivity to anxiousness. Long ago, the Spartans based their child-rearing on the principle that infants should be exposed to pain and cold to toughen them against future encounters with such exigencies. The evidence may indicate that they were not entirely wrong. On the other hand, the status of this issue is hardly such as to warrant any abrupt change in our tradition of protective tenderness toward our young.

Another change in our conception of motivation derives from recognition that there is a motivating system inherent in an organism's informational interaction with the environment. Although it is quite clear that painful stimulation, homeostatic needs, and sex all constitute genuine motivating systems, a very large share of an organism's interaction with the environment is informational in character. It occurs through the distance receptors, the eyes and the ears, and, to a much lesser degree, through touch. Elsewhere I have documented the basis for the notion that a motivating system inheres within this informational interaction (Hunt, 1963a). For instance, the Russian investigators have found both an emotional aspect and an attentional aspect to even an infant mammal's response to change in visual or auditory input. This is what they call the "orienting response." The emotional aspect of this "orienting response" can be registered by such expressive indicators as vascular changes (plethysmograph), changes in blood pressure (sphygmomanometer), changes in heart rate (cardiotachometer), changes in palmar sweating (electrical conductance of the skin), changes in muscular tension (electromyograph), and changes in brain potentials (electroencephalogram). For these changes, see Razran (1961). The attentional aspect can be seen in the cessation of ongoing activities and the efforts to turn to the source of input. The fact that this "orienting response" is present at birth, or as soon as the ears are cleared and the eyes are open, indicates that it is a fundamental, ready-made mechanism. The fact that this response has both emotional and attentional aspects indicates, at least to me, that it is motivational, and the fact that the "orienting response" occurs to changes of ongoing inputs through the eyes and ears indicates that its motivational power is intrinsic within the organism's informational interaction with the environment.

STAGE ONE IN THE EPIGENESIS OF INTRINSIC MOTIVATION: THE "ORIENTING RESPONSE"

Indications of the motivational importance of this "orienting response" and of encounters with variations in inputs derive from the marked retardation observed in children whose auditory and visual inputs have been severely restricted. Here the extreme retardation observed by Dennis (1960) in the Teheran orphanages has the dramatic import, if I am correct, that the major factor in its causation lies in homogeneity of reception input. Furthermore, in light of our traditional behavioristic belief that the observable motor response is all-important in development, it is worth noting that the marked retardation that I am attributing to homogeneity of input does not occur with inhibition of motor function during the first year. Again, this latter observation is by Dennis, or by Dennis & Dennis (1940). You will recall that the distribution of ages for the onset of walking in Hopi children cradled for their first year did not differ from the distribution of ages for onset of walking in Hopi children reared in an unrestrained fashion. While the motions of the legs and arms of the cradled infants were restrained during most of their waking hours, the fact that these cradled infants were often carried about once they were 40 days old, means that they probably encountered an enriched variety of redundant changes in auditory and visual input. Such a comparison suggests that it may be changes in perceptual input rather than opportunity for motor response that is most important in the motivation of psychological development during the earliest months (see also Fiske & Maddi, 1961).

First Suggestion for Stimulating Early Cognitive Learning

This brings me to my first concrete suggestion for stimulating cognitive development during the earliest months, and the process can begin at the child's birth. I suggest that the circumstances be so arranged that the infant will encounter a high variety of redundant changes of auditory, visual, and tactual inputs.

But this suggestion needs elaboration. While changes in ongoing stimulation are probably of basic motivational importance, it may not be mere change in itself that is sufficient to foster cognitive development; redundance of the input changes and of intermodal sequences of input changes are probably necessary. Piaget's (1936) observations of his own infants suggest that, during approximately the first half-year, one of the major accomplishments of interaction with the environment consists in the coordination of what are at birth largely independent sensorimotor systems. According to Piaget, these systems include sucking, listening, looking, grasping, vocalizing, and wriggling. Without use, any one of these systems will wane. As is well known to any farm boy who has pail-fed a calf, the sucking wanes after ten days or two weeks of pail-feeding and the calf can be trusted completely among fresh cows with full udders. Moreover, the work of Alexander Wolf (1943) and of Gauron & Becker (1959) on the effects of depriving infant rats of audition and vision on the readiness of these systems to respond in adulthood, coupled with the work of Brattgård (1952) and of Riesen (1947, 1958, 1961) showing that the visual system fails to develop properly when rabbits and chimpanzees are reared in darkness, indicates that this principle holds for listening and looking as well as sucking. Parenthetically, I should add that the role of organism-environment interaction in early development appears also to be tied biochemically with later capacity to synthesize RNA, as the work of Brattgård (1952), Hydén (1959), and others (see Riesen, 1961) appears to indicate. Perhaps the earliest of such interactions serve chiefly to sustain and to strengthen and develop the individual ready-made sensorimotor organizations or, as Piaget terms them, the "reflexive schemata." Very shortly, under typical circumstances, however, the sounds that evoke listening come to evoke looking, and the things seen come to evoke grasping and reaching, and the things grasped come to evoke sucking, etc. Such changes indicate progress in the coordination of the originally separate systems. During this phase, which is the second stage in Piaget's (1936) system, the progressive organization of schemata consists chiefly in such coordination, and it appears to consist in sequential organization, of which Pavlov's *conditioning* and Guthrie's *contiguity learning* are special cases.

If one tries to imagine how one can introduce redundant changes in visual and auditory inputs in order to provide for the sequential coordination of listening with looking, of looking with reaching, etc., one finds it no easy matter without actually having on hand human beings whose approaches and withdrawals supply the auditory-input changes that are regularly followed by visual-input changes. I have found myself wondering if the emphasis on mothering may not have a somewhat justified explanation in that it is the human infant's informational interaction with this coming and going of the mother that provides the perceptual basis for this coordination of relatively independent schemata.

STAGE TWO IN THE EPIGENESIS OF INTRINSIC MOTIVATION

But the nature of this intrinsic motivational process changes with experience. Any attempt to stimulate early cognitive learning must, I believe, take this change in form, or epigenesis, into account if it is to be at all successful. Moreover, if this epigenesis is taken into account, the circumstances encountered by the infant should not only motivate a rapid rate of cognitive development but should contribute substantially to the satisfaction the infant gets from life. As observers of infant development have long noted, the human infant appears to learn spontaneously, that is, in the absence of the traditional extrinsic motivators, and to get superb enjoyment from the process (see Baldwin, 1895; Bühler, 1918, 1928; Hendrick, 1943; Mittlemann, 1954). This is a new notion to most of us, but it is also old. For instance, it was implicit in the "self-activity" of Froebel (1887) and in the "intrinsic interest" of Dewey (1900). Moreover, Maria Montessori (1909), to whose work I shall return shortly, built her system of education for young children on the notion that children have a spontaneous interest in learning.

In what appears to be the first major transition in the structure of intrinsic motivation, the infant, while continuing to respond to changes in ongoing stimulation, comes to react toward the cessation of inputs which have been encountered repeatedly in a fashion designed to continue them or to bring them back into perceptual ken. Piaget (1936) called this a "reversal transformation." He considered it to be the beginnings of intention. Each of you who has ever dandled an infant on your knee is familiar with at least one example: when you stop your motion, the infant starts a motion of his own that resembles yours, and when you start again, the infant stops. The prevalence of infants' actions that are instigated by an absence of repeatedly encountered changes in input suggests, at least to me, that the repeated encounters with a given pattern of change in receptor input lead to recognition that provides one basis, and I believe it an important one, for cathexis, emotional attachment, and positive reinforcement (see Hunt, 1963b). My colleague Morton Weir prefers to refer to what attracts the infant as "predictability." Perhaps this is the better term. I have, however, preferred "recognition" because I suspect that what is happening is that the repeated encounters with a pattern of change in ongoing input serve to build into the storage of the posterior intrinsic system of the cerebrum a coded schema that can be matched to an input from the repeatedly encountered pattern of change. As the pattern is becoming recognizable, or when it is newly recognized, I suspect it provides a joyful basis of cathexis and positive reinforcement. I believe, at least tentatively, that it is this recognition that is one of the most consistent evokers of the infant's smile. Such an interpretation gains some support from the fact that maternal separation and encounters with unfamiliar persons bring little emotional disturbance, anxiety, or grief until the second half of the first year of life (Freud & Burlingham, 1944). In fact, these observations of emotional disturbance are important indicators that the cathexis or maternal attachment has been formed. It is this emotional disturbance that supports the observation that an infant acts to retain or to obtain a pattern of familiar input that attests his cathexis of that pattern. Moreover, it should be noted that emotional distress accompanies maternal deprivation only after the age at which objects have begun to acquire permanence for the child. Presumably this permanence of objects is based on the development, in the course of repeated encounters with a pattern of change in input, of a set of semiautonomous central processes that can represent the pattern deriving from an encounter with an object.

Parenthetically, may I suggest also that the following-response within what is called "imprinting" may well be a special case of this more general principle that emotional attachment grows out of the recognition coming from repeatedly encountering an object, place, or person; the fact that the following-response occurs after a shorter period of perceptual contact with an object in a species such as the grey-leg goose, or in the sheep or deer, than is required in species such as the chimpanzee or man suggests that the number of encounters, or duration of perceptual contact, required may well be a matter of the portion of the brain without direct connections with receptors or motor units, or what Hebb (1949) has termed the A/S ratio.

Out of such observations comes the empirical principle, which I have imbibed from Piaget (1936), that "the more an infant has seen and heard, the more he wants to see and hear." The avidity of an infant's interest in the world may be seen to be in large part a function of the variety of situations he has encountered repeatedly. Moreover, it would appear to be precisely the absence of such avid interest that constitutes the regularly observed apathy of orphanage-reared children who have encountered only a very limited variety of situations. It may well be that this seeking of inputs that have been made familiar by repeated encounters is what motivates the behavior Dennis & Dennis (1941) have termed "autogenous." Outstanding examples of such behavior are the hand-watching and the repetitive vocalizations called "babbling." It is, apparently, seeking to see the hands that motivates the motions to keep them within view, thereby providing the beginnings of eye-hand coordination. It is, apparently, seeking to hear voice sounds that motivates spontaneous vocalizing and keeps it going, thereby providing the infant with a beginning of ear-vocal coordination.

Second Suggestion for the Stimulation of Early Cognitive Learning

This brings me to my second suggestion for fostering early cognitive learning. It comes in connection with the development of intrinsically motivated intentions or plans, as the terms *intention* and *plan* are utilized by Miller, Galanter, & Pribram (1960). In fact, it is in connection with this development of intrinsically motivated intentions or plans that one basis for this change in the conception of motivation may be seen. Psychologists and psychoanalysts have conceived of actions, habits, defenses, and even of every thought system, as an attempt to reduce or eliminate stimulation or excitation within the nervous system arising out of painful stimulation, homeostatic need, or sex. To anyone who has observed and pondered the struggle of a young infant to reach and grasp some object he sees, it is extremely difficult to find such an extrinsic motivational basis for his reaching and grasping. What is suggested by Piaget's observations is that in the course of repeated encounters with an object, there comes a point at which seeing that object becomes an occasion for grasping it. In this co-ordination between looking and grasping, it would appear that grasping the object becomes a goal even though it is quite unrelated to pain, to homeostatic need, or to sex. Once an infant has the grasping goal of an object he has seen repeatedly, his various other motor schemata of striking, pushing, and even locomotion become also means to achieve this goal. Anyone who ponders this phenomenon in the light of the traditional theory of extrinsic motives will ask, "but why grasp the object?" And, "why grasp one object rather than another?" My tentative answer to these questions is that the object has become attractive with the new-found recognition that comes with repeated visual or auditory encounters. While reading Piaget's (1936, 1937) observations, one gets the impression that a smile very frequently precedes the effort to grasp, as if the infant were saying, "I know what you are, I'll take hold of you." Of course, nothing is so explicit; he has no language; he is merely manifesting a kind of primordial plan or intention. It is my hypothesis that this primordial intention is instigated by recognitive perception. If this hypothesis is true, then once an infant is ready to grasp things and to manipulate them, it is important that he have perceptual access to things he can grasp. It is important that there be a variety of such things that he has encountered earlier. The more varied the objects that are available, the more interest the infant will have in his world and the more sources of attractive novelty he will have later on.

As already indicted, it is probably also important that the infant have an opportunity to interact with human beings as well as with inanimate objects. Perhaps one of the chief functions of early interaction with human beings is to make the vocalized phones of the parental language and the gestures of communication familiar, for one of the most common forms of action designed to hold onto newly recognized inputs is imitation.[2] Such imitation is important for socialization and for intellectual development because the roots of human culture reside in the sounds of language and the various gestures of communication. An infant imitates first those phones and gestures that are highly familiar to him. In fact, one of the most feasible ways to start an interactive relationship with a young infant is to make one of the sounds that he is making regularly or to perform one of his characteristic gestures. The very fact that the sounds or gestures are the infant's helps to insure his recognition of them. Seeing them in another person commonly brings delighted interest and, not infrequently, imitative effort to recover them when the adult has stopped. The infant's jouncing in the dandling relationship is a special case of such imitative effort. Again we have a kind of encounter hard to arrange without involving human beings. This paucity of encounters that can be arranged without human beings supports the idea that the stories of feral men, including Romulus and Remus, are probably myths.

---

[2] This conception of imitation differs radically from that given by Miller & Dollard (1941), but it does not deny that their conception may be true under certain circumstances.

STAGE THREE IN THE EPIGENESIS OF INTRINSIC MOTIVATION

The second major transformation in intrinsic motivation appears to occur when repeatedly encountered objects, places, and events become "old stuff." The infant then becomes interested in *novelty*. The breakdown of the meaning of a given input with repeated perceptual encounters and the monotony that comes with repeated participation in given events are phenomena that psychologists have long observed (see Titchener, 1926, p. 425). Hebb (1949, p. 224), moreover, has observed that a major source of pleasure resides in encountering something new within the framework of the familiar. The sequence—of "orienting response" to stimulus change, recognition with repeated encounters, and interest in the variations within the familiar—may well be one in the interaction of an organism with each completely new class of environmental phenomena. What look like stages in the development of the first year may possibly be derived from the fact that an infant tends to be repeatedly encountering a fairly extended variety of situations at a fairly consistent rate. In any event, in his observations of his own children, Piaget (1936) noted that this interest in novelty appears toward the end of the first year.

There are those who dislike the very notion of such an epigenesis in the structure of motivation. There are those who seek single explanatory principles. Some have tried to explain this series of transformations in terms either of a process in which the new is continually becoming familiar or of a process whereby the earlier interest in the familiar exists because recognizability itself is novel at this phase. We may someday get a biochemical understanding of this phenomenon, but such attempts to find a unitary psychological principle of explanation are probably doomed to failure. Numerous studies indicate very clearly that organisms first respond to change in ongoing inputs. It is less certain that they next prefer the familiar, but the evidence is abundant that they later prefer objects and situations that are relatively less familiar than others available (see Dember, Earl, & Paradise, 1957; Hebb & Mahut, 1955; Montgomery, 1952, 1953a.) There is one instance in which a study shows that the lowly rat will endure even the pain of electric shock to get from his familiar nest-cage to an unfamiliar situation where there are novel objects to manipulate (Nissen, 1930). Studies also exist, moreover, in which organisms withdrew in fear from "familiar objects in an unfamiliar guise." These were objects that could never have been associated with painful stimulation in their previous experience because the animals had been reared under known conditions at the Yerkes Primate Laboratory. Festinger (1957) has, also, found people withdrawing from information dissonant with their strong held beliefs, plans, or commitments.

It is no easy matter to characterize properly what is essential in that glibly called "novelty." I believe, however, that we can say that novelty resides within the organism's informational interaction with its environment. I have termed this essence "incongruity" (Hunt, 1963a); Berlyne (1960) has written of the "collative variables" underlying "arousal potential"; Festinger (1957) has talked of "dissonance"; Hebb (1949) has written of the stage of development in cortical organization; and Munsinger & Kessen (1964), are using the term "uncertainty." Whatever this essence is called, too much of it gives rise to withdrawal and gestures commonly connoting fear. Too little appears to be associated with boredom. That novelty that is attractive appears to be an optimum of discrepancy in this relationship between the informational input of the moment and the information already stored in the cerebrum from previous encounters with similar situations.

Once interest in novelty appears, it is an important source of motivation. Perhaps it is the chief source of motivation for cognitive learning. Interest in novelty appears to motivate the improvement of locomotor skills, for the novel objects "needing" examination or manipulation are typically out of reach. It appears to motivate imitation of unfamiliar verbal phones and unfamiliar gestures and even of fairly complex actions. Imitated vocalizing of unfamiliar phones and vocal patterns appears to be exceedingly important in the acquisition of language. The notion that all infants vocalize all the phones of all languages (Allport, 1924) has long been hard to believe. The social side of language acquisition appears to be more than the mere reinforcing with approval or notice of those vocal patterns characteristic of the parents' language. If the interest in novelty provides an intrinsic motivational basis for (imitatively) vocalizing phones that have never been a part of the infant's vocal repertoire, then we have a believable explanation for the fact that most of the first pseudo-words are approximations of adult vocalizations that have occurred repeatedly in connection with novel and exciting events. Repetition of encounters with a given class of events may be presumed gradually to establish central processes representative of that class of event, that is, *images*, if you will. Imitation of the novel phones verbalized by adults in association with the class of events may provide the infant with a vocalization that can serve him as a sign of his image. Later, reinforcement, partially based on approval-disapproval and partially based on growing cognitive differentiation, may lead gradually to images and phonemic combinations that are sufficiently like those of the people taking care of an infant to permit communication.

Once language is acquired, the human child comes into basically the same existential situation in which all of us find ourselves. He then has two major sources of informational input: first, the original one of perceiving objects and events and, second, the new one of learning about them through the language of others. One of his major intellectual tasks is to make what he learns about the "real world" through the communications of others jibe with what he learns about it directly through his own receptors. This is a creative task of no mean proportion, and it is not unlike the task with which mature men of science are continuously concerned. This is one of George Kelly's (1955) major points.

The considerations already outlined in connection with my suggestions concerning repeated encounters with a given class of stimulus change and "recognition" show again the basis for the principle that "the more a child has seen and heard, the more he wants to see and hear" and do. If an infant has encountered a wide variety of changes in circumstances during his earliest days, and if he has encountered them repeatedly enough to become attached to them through recognition, and if he has had ample opportunity to act upon them and to manipulate them, he will become, I believe, ready to be intrigued by novel variations in an ample range of objects, situations, and personal models.

The fact that too much novelty or incongruity can be frightening and too little can be boring, however, creates a problem for those who would stimulate cognitive development. They must provide for encounters with materials, objects, and models that have the proper degree of that incongruity (Hunt, 1963a). This is one aspect of what I have termed the "problem of the match" (Hunt, 1961b, pp. 267ff.).

Third Suggestion for the Stimulation of Early Cognitive Learning

Consideration of the problem of the match brings me to my third concrete suggestion for stimulating cognitive learning in the very young. I must confess that I have borrowed this suggestion from Montessori (1909; see also Fisher, 1912). The first portion of this suggestion is that careful observation be made of what it is in the way of objects, situations, and models for imitation that interests the infant. Once it is clear what objects and models are of interest, then I suggest providing each infant with an ample variety of them and with an opportunity to choose spontaneously the ones that intrigue him at a given time. This latter suggestion assumes, of course, that the infant is already comfortable, that he feels safe, and that he is satisfied so far as homeostatic needs are concerned. I really feel that we do not have to worry too much about gratifying the sex appetite of a child under three years of age.

When I wrote *Intelligence and Experience* (1961b), this problem of providing a proper match between the materials with which a child is confronted by teachers and what he already has in his storage loomed large because of our tremendous ignorance of the intricacies involved. This ignorance is a major challenge for investigation; in the meantime, however, as Jan Smedslund pointed out to me in a conversation in Boulder last summer, Montessori long ago provided a practical solution. She based her system of education on intrinsic motivation, but she called it "spontaneous learning." She provided young children with a wide variety of materials, graded in difficulty and roughly calculated to be the range of materials that would provide a proper match for children of ages three to six if they were given opportunity for choice. She also gave each of the children in her school an opportunity to occupy himself or herself with those materials of his or her own individual choice. To do this, she broke the lock-step in the educational process. A Montessori school was socially so structured that the children were obviously expected to occupy themselves with the materials provided. Moreover, by having together within a single room children ranging in age from three to six years, she provided a graded series of models for the younger children and an opportunity for some of the older children to learn by teaching the younger ones how to do various things. You will be interested to know that a substantial proportion of the slum children in Montessori's school began reading and writing before they were five years old. In the Casa di Bambini, which Montessori founded in 1907 in the basement of a slum apartment-house in Rome, the teacher was the apartment-house superintendent's 16-year-old daughter who had been trained by Montessori. You will also be interested to know that the old nursery school bugaboo that children have very brief spans of attention did not hold. Dorothy Canfield Fisher (1912)—the novelist who spent the winter of 1910–1911 at the original Casa di Bambini—has written that it was common to see a three-year-old continuously occupied with such a mundane task as buttoning and unbuttoning for two or more hours at a stretch.

Montessori's contributions to the education of the very young were discussed with excitement in America until the time of World War I. Thereafter the discussion ended almost completely. I suspect that this occurred because Montessori's theoretical views were so dissonant with what became about then the dominant views of American psychologists and American educators. Her theory that cognitive capacity could be modified by proper education was dissonant with the dominant and widely-prevailing notions of "fixed intelligence" and "predetermined development." These notions were implicit in the doctrine of a constant IQ. Her notion of spontaneous learning was sharply dissonant with the doctrine that all behavior is extrinsically motivated by painful stimulation, or homeostatic need, or sex. Moreover, the importance she attributed to sensory training was dissonant with what became the prevailing presumption that it is the observable motor response that counts. We need to reexamine her contributions in the light of the theoretical picture that has been emerging since World War II. I am grateful to Jan Smedslund for calling her contributions to my attention.

My discourse has skipped roughly half of the second year and all of the third year of life, because interest in novelty typically makes its earliest appearance toward the end of the first year or early in the second. (Montessori's schools took children only at three years of age or older.) I suspect that the basic principle involved in stimulating cognitive learning is fairly constant once the interest in novelty appears. On the other hand, I would not be surprised if it were precisely during this period between 18 months and three years of age that lower-class families typically most hamper the kind of cognitive learning that is later required for successful performance in school and in our increasingly technological culture. Let me explain briefly.

During the first year, the life of an infant in a family crowded together in one room—as Oscar Lewis (1961) has described such living in his *Children of Sanchez* and as I have observed it in the slums of New York—probably provides a fairly rich variety of input. On the other hand, once an infant begins to use his new-found locomotor and linguistic skills, his circumstances in a lower-class setting probably become anything but conducive to appropriate cognitive learning. Using his new locomotor skills gets him in the way of problem-beset adults and, all too likely, may bring punishment which can be avoided only by staying out of their way. This in turn deprives the infant of the opportunity to hear and imitate the verbal phones that provides the basis for spoken language. If a slum child should be lucky enough to acquire the "learning set" that things have names and to begin his repetitive questioning about "what's that?", he is not only unlikely to get answers but also likely to get his ears cuffed for asking such silly questions. Moreover, in the slum setting of lower-class family life, the models that an infant has to imitate are all too often likely to result in the acquisition of sensorimotor organizations and attitudes that interfere with rather than facilitate the kinds of cognitive learning that enable a child to succeed in school and in a technological culture such as ours. How long such interference with development can last without resulting in a permanent reduction in cognitive potential remains an unsolved problem. It is likely, however, that day-care centers and nursery schools prepared to face such children with situations, materials, and models that are not too incongruous with the schemata and attitudes that they have already acquired, can counteract much of the detrimental effect of lower-class life. Such pre-school experience during the second and third, and possibly even during the fourth, years of life can perhaps serve well as an antidote to this kind of cultural deprivation (see Hunt, 1964).

Summary: I have limited my discussion to the implications, for the stimulation of early cognitive learning, of the epigenesis of intrinsic motivation that I believe I can see taking place during preverbal development. I have identified three stages of intrinsic motivation that are separated by two major "reversal transformations." In the first of these, repeated encounters with patterns of change in perceptual input lead to recognition that I now believe to be a source of pleasure and a basis for cathexis or for affectional attachment. The second consists in a transition from an interest in the familiar to an interest in the novel. During the first few months, when the child is responsive chiefly to changes in the character and intensity of ongoing stimulation, I suspect it is most important to provide for repeated encounters with as wide a variety as possible of changes in receptor input. It may also be important to provide for sequential arrangements of these inputs that will provide a basis for a coordination of all combinations of the ready-made reflexive sensorimotor systems. As the infant becomes attached to objects, people, and situations by way of the hypothetical joys of new-found recognition, it is probably most important to provide opportunities for him to utilize his own repertoire of intentional activities to retain or elicit or manipulate the objects, people, and situations, again in as wide a variety as is feasible. Once interest in novelty appears, I suspect it is most important to give the child access to a variety of graded materials for manipulation and coping and to a variety of graded models for imitation. With what little we now know of what I call the "problem of the match," I suspect it is important to follow Montessori's principle of trusting to a considerable degree in the spontaneous interest of the individual infant instead of attempting to regiment his learning process in any lock-step method of preschool education.

COGNITIVE, SOCIAL, AND PHYSIOLOGICAL DETERMINANTS OF EMOTIONAL STATE[1]

STANLEY SCHACHTER

Columbia University

JEROME E. SINGER

State University of New York at Stony Brook

The problem of which cues, internal or external, permit a person to label and identify his own emotional state has been with us since the days that James (1890) first tendered his doctrine that "the bodily changes follow directly the perception of the exciting fact, and that our feeling of the same changes as they occur *is* the emotion" (p. 449). Since we are aware of a variety of feeling and emotion states, it should follow from James' proposition that the various emotions will be accompanied by a variety of differentiable bodily states. Following James' pronouncement, a formidable number of studies were undertaken in search of the physiological differentiators of the emotions. The results, in these early days, were almost uniformly negative. All of the emotional states experimentally manipulated were characterized by a general pattern of excitation of the sympathetic nervous system but there appeared to be no clear-cut physiological discriminators of the various emotions. This pattern of results was so consistent from experiment to experiment that Cannon (1929) offered, as one of the crucial criticisms of the James-Lange theory, the fact that "the same visceral changes occur in very different emotional states and in non-emotional states" (p. 351).

More recent work, however, has given some indication that there may be differentiators. Ax (1953) and Schachter (1957) studied fear and anger. On a large number of indices both of these states were characterized

[1] This experiment is part of a program of research on cognitive and physiological determinants of emotional state which is being conducted at the Department of Social Psychology at Columbia University under PHS Research Grant M-2584 from the National Institute of Mental Health, United States Public Health Service. This experiment was conducted at the Laboratory for Research in Social Relations at the University of Minnesota.

The authors wish to thank Jean Carlin and Ruth Hase, the physicians in the study, and Bibb Latané and Leonard Weller who were the paid participants.

Reprinted from *Psychological Review*, Vol. 69, No. 5, September, 1962. Copyright 1962, American Psychological Association, Inc.

by a similarly high level of autonomic activation but on several indices they did differ in the degree of activation. Wolf and Wolff (1947) studied a subject with a gastric fistula and were able to distinguish two patterns in the physiological responses of the stomach wall. It should be noted, though, that for many months they studied their subject during and following a great variety of moods and emotions and were able to distinguish only two patterns.

Whether or not there are physiological distinctions among the various emotional states must be considered an open question. Recent work might be taken to indicate that such differences are at best rather subtle and that the variety of emotion, mood, and feeling states are by no means matched by an equal variety of visceral patterns.

This rather ambiguous situation has led Ruckmick (1936), Hunt, Cole, and Reis (1958), Schachter (1959) and others to suggest that cognitive factors may be major determinants of emotional states. Granted a general pattern of sympathetic excitation as characteristic of emotional states, granted that there may be some differences in pattern from state to state, it is suggested that one labels, interprets, and identifies this stirred-up state in terms of the characteristics of the precipitating situation and one's apperceptive mass. This suggests, then, that an emotional state may be considered a function of a state of physiological arousal[2] and of a cognition appropriate to this state of arousal. The cognition, in a sense, exerts a steering function. Cognitions arising from the immediate situation as interpreted by past experience provide the framework within which one understands and labels his feelings. It is the cognition which determines whether the state of physiological arousal will be labeled as "anger," "joy," "fear," or whatever.

In order to examine the implications of this formulation let us consider the fashion in which these two elements, a state of physiological arousal and cognitive factors, would interact in a variety of situations. In most emotion inducing situations, of course, the two factors are completely interrelated. Imagine a man walking alone down a dark alley, a figure with a gun suddenly appears. The perception-cognition "figure with a gun" in some fashion initiates a state of physiological arousal; this state of arousal is interpreted in terms of knowledge about dark alleys and guns and the state of arousal is labeled "fear." Similarly a student who unexpectedly learns that he has made Phi Beta Kappa may experience a state of arousal which he will label "joy."

Let us now consider circumstances in which these two elements, the physiological and the cognitive, are, to some extent, independent. First, is the state of physiological arousal alone sufficient to induce an emotion? Best evidence indicates that it is not. Marañon[3] (1924), in a fascinating study, (which was replicated by Cantril & Hunt, 1932, and Landis & Hunt, 1932) injected 210 of his patients with the sympathomimetic agent adrenalin and then simply asked them to introspect. Seventy-one percent of his subjects simply reported their physical symptoms with no emotional overtones; 29% of the subjects responded in an apparently emotional fashion. Of these the great majority described their feelings in a fashion that Marañon labeled "cold" or "as if" emotions, that is, they made statements such as "I feel *as if* I were afraid" or "*as if* I were awaiting a great happiness." This is a sort of emotional "déjà vu" experience; these subjects are neither happy nor afraid, they feel "as if" they were. Finally a very few cases apparently reported a

---

[2] Though our experiments are concerned exclusively with the physiological changes produced by the injection of adrenalin, which appear to be primarily the result of sympathetic excitation, the term physiological arousal is used in preference to the more specific "excitation of the sympathetic nervous system" because there are indications, to be discussed later, that this formulation is applicable to a variety of bodily states.

[3] Translated copies of Marañon's (1924) paper may be obtained by writing to the senior author.

genuine emotional experience. However, in order to produce this reaction in most of these few cases, Marañon (1924) points out:

> One must suggest a memory with strong affective force but not so strong as to produce an emotion in the normal state. For example, in several cases we spoke to our patients before the injection of their sick children or dead parents and they responded calmly to this topic. The same topic presented later, during the adrenal commotion, was sufficient to trigger emotion. This adrenal commotion places the subject in a situation of 'affective imminence' (pp. 307–308).

Apparently, then, to produce a genuinely emotional reaction to adrenalin, Marañon was forced to provide such subjects with an appropriate cognition.

Though Marañon (1924) is not explicit on his procedure, it is clear that his subjects knew that they were receiving an injection and in all likelihood knew that they were receiving adrenalin and probably had some order of familiarity with its effects. In short, though they underwent the pattern of sympathetic discharge common to strong emotional states, at the same time they had a completely appropriate cognition or explanation as to why they felt this way. This, we would suggest, is the reason so few of Marañon's subjects reported any emotional experience.

Consider now a person in a state of physiological arousal for which no immediately explanatory or appropriate cognitions are available. Such a state could result were one covertly to inject a subject with adrenalin or, unknown to him, feed the subject a sympathomimetic drug such as ephedrine. Under such conditions a subject would be aware of palpitations, tremor, face flushing, and most of the battery of symptoms associated with a discharge of the sympathetic nervous system. In contrast to Marañon's (1924) subjects he would, at the same time, be utterly unaware of why he felt this way. What would be the consequence of such a state?

Schachter (1959) has suggested that precisely such a state would lead to the arousal of "evaluative needs" (Festinger, 1954), that is, pressures would act on an individual in such a state to understand and label his bodily feelings. His bodily state grossly resembles the condition in which it has been at times of emotional excitement. How would he label his present feelings? It is suggested, of course, that he will label his feelings in terms of his knowledge of the immediate situation.[4] Should he at the time be with a beautiful woman he might decide that he was wildly in love or sexually excited. Should he be at a gay party, he might, by comparing himself to others, decide that he was extremely happy and euphoric. Should he be arguing with his wife, he might explode in fury and hatred. Or, should the situation be completely inappropriate he could decide that he was excited about something that had recently happened to him or, simply, that he was sick. In any case, it is our basic assumption that emotional states are a function of the interaction of such cognitive factors with a state of physiological arousal.

This line of thought, then, leads to the following propositions:

1. Given a state of physiological arousal for which an individual has no immediate explanation, he will "label" this state and describe his feelings in terms of the cognitions available to him. To the extent that cognitive factors are potent determiners of emotional states, it could be anticipated that precisely the same state of physiological arousal could be labeled "joy" or "fury" or "jealousy" or any of a great diversity of emotional labels depending on the cognitive aspects of the situation.

2. Given a state of physiological arousal for which an individual has a completely appropriate explanation (e.g., "I feel this way because I have just received an injection of adrenalin") no evaluative needs will arise

---

[4] This suggestion is not new for several psychologists have suggested that situational factors should be considered the chief differentiators of the emotions. Hunt, Cole, and Reis (1958) probably make this point most explicitly in their study distinguishing among fear, anger, and sorrow in terms of situational characteristics.

and the individual is unlikely to label his feelings in terms of the alternative cognitions available.

Finally, consider a condition in which emotion inducing cognitions are present but there is no state of physiological arousal. For example, an individual might be completely aware that he is in great danger but for some reason (drug or surgical) remain in a state of physiological quiescence. Does he experience the emotion "fear"? Our formulation of emotion as a joint function of a state of physiological arousal and an appropriate cognition, would, of course, suggest that he does not, which leads to our final proposition.

3. Given the same cognitive circumstances, the individual will react emotionally or describe his feelings as emotions only to the extent that he experiences a state of physiological arousal.[5]

PROCEDURE

The experimental test of these propositions requires (*a*) the experimental manipulation of a state of physiological arousal, (*b*) the manipulation of the extent to which the subject has an appropriate or proper explanation of his bodily state, and (*c*) the creation of situations from which explanatory cognitions may be derived.

In order to satisfy the first two experimental requirements, the experiment was cast in the framework of a study of the effects of vitamin supplements on vision. As soon as a subject arrived, he was taken to a private room and told by the experimenter:

In this experiment we would like to make various tests of your vision. We are particularly interested in how certain vitamin compounds and vitamin supplements affect the visual skills. In particular, we want to find out how the vitamin compound called 'Suproxin' affects your vision.

What we would like to do, then, if we can get your permission, is to give you a small injection of Suproxin. The injection itself is mild and harmless; however, since some people do object to being injected we don't want to talk you into anything. Would you mind receiving a Suproxin injection?

If the subject agrees to the injection (and all but 1 of 185 subjects did) the experimenter continues with instructions we shall describe shortly, then leaves the room. In a few minutes a physician enters the room, briefly repeats the experimenter's instructions, takes the subject's pulse and then injects him with Suproxin.

Depending upon condition, the subject receives one of two forms of Suproxin—epinephrine or a placebo.

Epinephrine or adrenalin is a sympathomimetic drug whose effects, with minor exceptions, are almost a perfect mimicry of a discharge of the sympathetic nervous system. Shortly after injection systolic blood pressure increases markedly, heart rate increases somewhat, cutaneous blood flow decreases, while muscle and cerebral blood flow increase, blood sugar and lactic acid concentration increase, and respiration rate increases slightly. As far as the subject is concerned the major subjective symptoms are palpitation, tremor, and sometimes a feeling of flushing and accelerated breathing. With a subcutaneous injection (in the dosage administered to our subjects), such effects usually begin within 3–5 minutes of injection and last anywhere from 10 minutes to an hour. For most subjects these effects are dissipated within 15–20 minutes after injection.

Subjects receiving epinephrine received a subcutaneous injection of ½ cubic centimeter of a 1 : 1000 solution of Winthrop Laboratory's Suprarenin, a saline solution of epinephrine bitartrate.

Subjects in the placebo condition received a subcutaneous injection of ½ cubic centimeter of saline solution. This is, of course, completely neutral material with no side effects at all.

Manipulating an Appropriate Explanation

By "appropriate" we refer to the extent to which the subject has an authoritative, unequivocal explanation of his bodily condition. Thus, a subject who had been informed by the physician that as a direct consequence of the injection he would feel palpitations, tremor, etc. would be considered to have a completely appropriate explanation. A subject who had been informed only that the injection would have no side effects would have no appropriate explanation of his state. This dimension of appropriateness was manipulated in three experimental conditions which shall be called: Epinephrine Informed (Epi Inf), Epinephrine Ignorant (Epi Ign), and Epinephrine Misinformed (Epi Mis).

Immediately after the subject had agreed to the injection and before the physician entered the room, the experimenter's spiel in each of these conditions went as follows:

---

[5] In his critique of the James-Lange theory of emotion, Cannon (1929) also makes the point that sympathectomized animals and patients do seem to manifest emotional behavior. This criticism is, of course, as applicable to the above proposition as it was to the James-Lange formulation. We shall discuss the issues involved in later papers.

Epinephrine Informed. I should also tell you that some of our subjects have experienced side effects from the Suproxin. These side effects are transitory, that is, they will only last for about 15 or 20 minutes. What will probably happen is that your hand will start to shake, your heart will start to pound, and your face may get warm and flushed. Again these are side effects lasting about 15 or 20 minutes.

While the physician was giving the injection, she told the subject that the injection was mild and harmless and repeated this description of the symptoms that the subject could expect as a consequence of the shot. In this condition, then, subjects have a completely appropriate explanation of their bodily state. They know precisely what they will feel and why.

Epinephrine Ignorant. In this condition, when the subject agreed to the injection, the experimenter said nothing more relevant to side effects and simply left the room. While the physician was giving the injection, she told the subject that the injection was mild and harmless and would have no side effects. In this condition, then, the subject has no experimentally provided explanation for his bodily state.

Epinephrine Misinformed. I should also tell you that some of our subjects have experienced side effects from the Suproxin.

These side effects are transitory, that is, they will only last for about 15 or 20 minutes. What will probably happen is that your feet will feel numb, you will have an itching sensation over parts of your body, and you may get a slight headache. Again these are side effects lasting 15 or 20 minutes.

And again, the physician repeated these symptoms while injecting the subject.

None of these symptoms, of course, are consequences of an injection of epinephrine and, in effect, these instructions provide the subject with a completely inappropriate explanation of his bodily feelings. This condition was introduced as a control condition of sorts. It seemed possible that the description of side effects in the Epi Inf condition might turn the subject introspective, self-examining, possibly slightly troubled. Differences on the dependent variable between the Epi Inf and Epi Ign conditions might, then, be due to such factors rather than to differences in appropriateness. The false symptoms in the Epi Mis condition should similarly turn the subject introspective, etc., but the instructions in this condition do not provide an appropriate explanation of the subject's state.

Subjects in all of the above conditions were injected with epinephrine. Finally, there was a placebo condition in which subjects, who were injected with saline solution, were given precisely the same treatment as subjects in the Epi Ign condition.

Producing an Emotion Inducing Cognition

Our initial hypothesis has suggested that given a state of physiological arousal for which the individual has no adequate explanation, cognitive factors can lead the individual to describe his feelings with any of a diversity of emotional labels. In order to test this hypothesis, it was decided to manipulate emotional states which can be considered quite different—euphoria and anger.

There are, of course, many ways to induce such states. In our own program of research, we have concentrated on social determinants of emotional states and have been able to demonstrate in other studies that people do evaluate their own feelings by comparing themselves with others around them (Schachter 1959; Wrightsman 1960). In this experiment we have attempted again to manipulate emotional state by social means. In one set of conditions, the subject is placed together with a stooge who has been trained to act euphorically. In a second set of conditions the subject is with a stooge trained to act in an angry fashion.

Euphoria

Immediately [6] after the subject had been injected, the physician left the room and the experimenter returned with a stooge whom he introduced as another subject, then said:

> Both of you have had the Suproxin shot and you'll both be taking the same tests of vision. What I ask you to do now is just wait for 20 minutes. The reason for this is simply that we have to allow 20 minutes for the Suproxin to get from the injection site into the bloodstream. At the end of 20 minutes when we are certain that most of the Suproxin has been absorbed into the bloodstream, we'll begin the tests of vision.

The room in which this was said had been deliberately put into a state of mild disarray. As he was leaving, the experimenter apologetically added:

> The only other thing I should do is to apologize for the condition of the room. I just didn't have time to clean it up. So, if you need any scratch paper or rubber bands or pencils, help yourself. I'll be back in 20 minutes to begin the vision tests.

---

[6] It was, of course, imperative that the sequence with the stooge begin before the subject felt his first symptoms for otherwise the subject would be virtually forced to interpret his feelings in terms of events preceding the stooge's entrance. Pretests had indicated that, for most subjects, epinphrine-caused symptoms began within 3–5 minutes after injection. A deliberate attempt was made then to bring in the stooge within 1 minute after the subject's injection.

As soon as the experimenter had left, the stooge introduced himself again, made a series of standard icebreaker comments, and then launched his routine. For observation purposes, the stooge's act was broken into a series of standard units, demarcated by a change in activity or a standard comment. In sequence, the units of the stooge's routine were the following:

1. Stooge reaches for a piece of paper and starts doodling saying, "They said we could use this for scratch, didn't they?" He doodles a fish for some 30 seconds, then says:
2. "This scrap paper isn't even much good for doodling" and crumples paper and attempts to throw it into wastebasket in far corner of the room. He misses but this leads him into a "basketball game." He crumples up other sheets of paper, shoots a few baskets, says "Two points" occasionally. He gets up and does a jump shot saying, "The old jump shot is really on today."
3. If the subject has not joined in, the stooge throws a paper basketball to the subject saying, "Here, you try it."
4. Stooge continues his game saying, "The trouble with paper basketballs is that you don't really have any control."
5. Stooge continues basketball, then gives it up saying, "This is one of my good days. I feel like a kid again. I think I'll make a plane." He makes a paper airplane saying, "I guess I'll make one of the longer ones."
6. Stooge flies plane. Gets up and retrieves plane. Flies again, etc.
7. Stooge throws plane at subject.
8. Stooge, flying plane, says, "Even when I was a kid, I was never much good at this."
9. Stooge tears off part of plane saying, "Maybe this plane can't fly but at least it's good for something." He wads up paper and making a slingshot of a rubber band begins to shoot the paper.
10. Shooting, the stooge says, "They [paper ammunition] really go better if you make them long. They don't work right if you wad them up."
11. While shooting, stooge notices a sloppy pile of manila folders on a table. He builds a tower of these folders, then goes to the opposite end of the room to shoot at the tower.
12. He misses several times, then hits and cheers as the tower falls. He goes over to pick up the folders.
13. While picking up, he notices, behind a portable blackboard, a pair of hula hoops which have been covered with black tape with a few wires sticking out of the tape. He reaches for these, taking one for himself and putting the other aside but within reaching distance of the subject. The stooge tries the hula hoop, saying, "This isn't as easy as it looks."
14. Stooge twirls hoop wildly on arm, saying, "Hey, look at this—this is great."
15. Stooge replaces the hula hoop and sits down with his feet on the table. Shortly thereafter the experimenter returns to the room.

This routine was completely standard, though its pace, of course, varied depending upon the subject's reaction, the extent to which he entered into this bedlam and the extent to which he initiated activities of his own. The only variations from this standard routine were those forced by the subject. Should the subject originate some nonsense of his own and request the stooge to join in, he would do so. And, he would, of course, respond to any comments initiated by the subject.

Subjects in each of the three "appropriateness" conditions and in the placebo condition were submitted to this setup. The stooge, of course, never knew in which condition any particular subject fell.

Anger

Immediately after the injection, the experimenter brought a stooge into the subject's room, introduced the two and after explaining the necessity for a 20 minute delay for "the Suproxin to get from the injection site into the bloodstream" he continued, "We would like you to use these 20 minutes to answer these questionnaires." Then handing out the questionnaires, he concludes with, "I'll be back in 20 minutes to pick up the questionnaires and begin the tests of vision."

Before looking at the questionnaire, the stooge says to the subject,

I really wanted to come for an experiment today, but I think it's unfair for them to give you shots. At least, they should have told us about the shots when they called us; you hate to refuse, once you're here already.

The questionnaires, five pages long, start off innocently requesting face sheet information and then grow increasingly personal and insulting. The stooge, sitting directly opposite the subject, paces his own answers so that at all times subject and stooge are working on the same question. At regular points in the questionnaire, the stooge makes a series of standardized comments about the questions. His comments start off innocently enough, grow increasingly querulous, and finally he ends up in a rage. In sequence, he makes the following comments.

1. Before answering any items, he leafs quickly through the questionnaire saying, "Boy, this is a long one."
2. Question 7 on the questionnaire requests, "List the foods that you would eat in a typical day." The stooge comments, "Oh for Pete's sake, what did I have for breakfast this morning?"
3. Question 9 asks, "Do you ever hear

bells? ———. How often? ———."
The stooge remarks, "Look at Question 9. How ridiculous can you get? I hear bells every time I change classes."

4. Question 13 requests, "List the childhood diseases you have had and the age at which you had them" to which the stooge remarks, "I get annoyed at this childhood disease question. I can't remember what childhood diseases I had, and especially at what age. Can you?"

5. Question 17 asks "What is your father's average annual income?" and the stooge says, "This really irritates me. It's none of their business what my father makes. I'm leaving that blank."

6. Question 25 presents a long series of items such as "Does not bathe or wash regularly," "Seems to need psychiatric care," etc. and requests the respondent to write down for which member of his immediate family each item seems most applicable. The question specifically prohibits the answer "None" and each item must be answered. The stooge says, "I'll be damned if I'll fill out Number 25. 'Does not bathe or wash regularly'—that's a real insult." He then angrily crosses out the entire item.

7. Question 28 reads:
"How many times each week do you have sexual intercourse?" 0–1 ——— 2–3 ——— 4–6 ——— 7 and over ———. The stooge bites out, "The hell with it! I don't have to tell them all this."

8. The stooge sits sullenly for a few moments then he rips up his questionnaire, crumples the pieces and hurls them to the floor, saying, "I'm not wasting any more time. I'm getting my books and leaving" and he stamps out of the room.

9. The questionnaire continues for eight more questions ending with: "With how many men (other than your father) has your mother had extramarital relationships?"
4 and under ———: 5–9 ———: 10 and over ———.

Subjects in the Epi Ign, Epi Inf and Placebo conditions were run through this "anger" inducing sequence. The stooge, again, did not know to which condition the subject had been assigned.

In summary, this is a seven condition experiment which, for two different emotional states, allows us (a) to evaluate the effects of "appropriateness" on emotional inducibility and (b) to begin to evaluate the effects of sympathetic activation on emotional inducibility. In schematic form the conditions are the following:

EUPHORIA	ANGER
Epi Inf	Epi Inf
Epi Ign	Epi Ign
Epi Mis	Placebo
Placebo	

The Epi Mis condition was not run in the Anger sequence. This was originally conceived as a control condition and it was felt that its inclusion in the Euphoria conditions alone would suffice as a means of evaluating the possible artifactual effect of the Epi Inf instructions.

Measurement

Two types of measures of emotional state were obtained. Standardized observation through a one-way mirror was the technique used to assess the subject's behavior. To what extent did he act euphoric or angry? Such behavior can be considered in a way as a "semiprivate" index of mood for as far as the subject was concerned, his emotional behavior could be known only to the other person in the room—presumably another student. The second type of measure was self-report in which, on a variety of scales, the subject indicated his mood of the moment. Such measures can be considered "public" indices of mood for they would, of course, be available to the experimenter and his associates.

Observation

Euphoria. For each of the first 14 units of the stooge's standardized routine an observer kept a running chronicle of what the subject did and said. For each unit the observer coded the subject's behavior in one or more of the following categories:

Category 1: Joins in activity. If the subject entered into the stooge's activities, e.g., if he made or flew airplanes, threw paper basketballs, hula hooped, etc., his behavior was coded in this category.

Category 2: Initiates new activity. A subject was so coded if he gave indications of creative euphoria, that is, if, on his own, he initiated behavior outside of the stooge's routine. Instances of such behavior would be the subject who threw open the window and, laughing, hurled paper basketballs at passersby; or, the subject who jumped on a table and spun one hula hoop on his leg and the other on his neck.

Categories 3 and 4: Ignores or watches stooge. Subjects who paid flatly no attention to the stooge or who, with or without comment, simply watched the stooge without joining in his activity were coded in these categories.

For any particular unit of behavior, the subject's behavior was coded in one or more of these categories. To test reliability of coding two observers independently coded two experimental sessions. The observers agreed completely on the coding of 88% of the units.

Anger. For each of the units of stooge behavior, an observer recorded the subject's responses and coded them according to the following category scheme:

Category 1: Agrees. In response to the stooge the subject makes a comment indicating that he agrees with the stooge's standardized comment or that he, too, is irked by a particular item on the questionnaire. For example, a subject who responded to the stooge's comment on the "father's income" question by saying, "I don't like that kind of personal question either" would be so coded (scored +2).

Category 2: Disagrees. In response to the stooge's comment, the subject makes a comment which indicates that he disagrees with the stooge's meaning or mood; e.g., in response to the stooge's comment on the "father's income" question, such a subject might say, "Take it easy, they probably have a good reason for wanting the information" (scored −2).

Category 3: Neutral. A noncommittal or irrelevant response to the stooge's remark (scored 0).

Category 4: Initiates agreement or disagreement. With no instigation by the stooge, a subject, so coded, would have volunteered a remark indicating that he felt the same way or, alternatively, quite differently than the stooge. Examples would be "Boy I hate this kind of thing" or "I'm enjoying this" (scored +2 or −2).

Category 5: Watches. The subject makes no verbal response to the stooge's comment but simply looks directly at him (scored 0).

Category 6: Ignores. The subject makes no verbal response to the stooge's comment nor does he look at him; the subject, paying no attention at all to the stooge, simply works at his own questionnaire (scored −1).

A subject was scored in one or more of these categories for each unit of stooge behavior. To test reliability, two observers independently coded three experimental sessions. In order to get a behavioral index of anger, observation protocol was scored according to the values presented in parentheses after each of the above definitions of categories. In a unit-by-unit comparison, the two observers agreed completely on the scoring of 71% of the units jointly observed. The scores of the two observers differed by a value of 1 or less for 88% of the units coded and in not a single case did the two observers differ in the direction of their scoring of a unit.

Self Report of Mood and Physical Condition

When the subject's session with the stooge was completed, the experimenter returned to the room, took pulses and said:

Before we proceed with the vision tests, there is one other kind of information which we must have. We have found, as you can probably imagine, that there are many things beside Suproxin that affect how well you see in our tests. How hungry you are, how tired you are, and even the mood you're in at the time—whether you feel happy or irritated at the time of testing will affect how well you see. To understand the data we collect on you, then, we must be able to figure out which effects are due to causes such as these and which are caused by Suproxin.

The only way we can get such information about your physical and emotional state is to have you tell us. I'll hand out these questionnaires and ask you to answer them as accurately as possible. Obviously, our data on the vision tests will only be as accurate as your description of your mental and physical state.

In keeping with this spiel, the questionnaire that the experimenter passed out contained a number of mock questions about hunger, fatigue, etc., as well as questions of more immediate relevance to the experiment. To measure mood or emotional state the following two were the crucial questions:

1. How irritated, angry or annoyed would you say you feel at present?

I don't feel at all irritated or angry (0)	I feel a little irritated and angry (1)	I feel quite irritated and angry (2)	I feel very irritated and angry (3)	I feel extremely irritated and angry (4)

2. How good or happy would you say you feel at present?

I don't feel at all happy or good (0)	I feel a little happy and good (1)	I feel quite happy and good (2)	I feel very happy and good (3)	I feel extremely happy and good (4)

To measure the physical effects of epinephrine and determine whether or not the injection had been successful in producing the necessary bodily state, the following questions were asked:

1. Have you experienced any palpitation (consciousness of your own heart beat)?

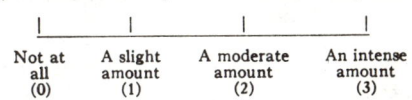

Not at all (0)	A slight amount (1)	A moderate amount (2)	An intense amount (3)

2. Did you feel any tremor (involuntary shaking of the hands, arms or legs)?

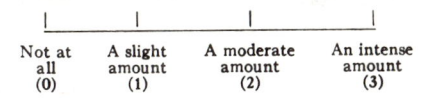

Not at all (0)	A slight amount (1)	A moderate amount (2)	An intense amount (3)

To measure possible effects of the instructions in the Epi Mis condition, the following questions were asked:

1. Did you feel any numbness in your feet?
2. Did you feel any itching sensation?
3. Did you experience any feeling of headache?

To all three of these questions was attached a four-point scale running from "Not at all" to "An intense amount."

In addition to these scales, the subjects were asked to answer two open-end questions on other physical or emotional sensations they may have experienced during the experimental session. A final measure of bodily state was pulse rate which was taken by the physician or the experimenter at two times—immediately before the injection and immediately after the session with the stooge.

When the subjects had completed these questionnaires, the experimenter announced that the experiment was over, explained the deception and its necessity in detail, answered any questions, and swore the subjects to secrecy. Finally, the subjects answered a brief questionnaire about their experiences, if any, with adrenalin and their previous knowledge or suspicion of the experimental setup. There was no indication that any of the subjects had known about the experiment beforehand but 11 subjects were so extremely suspicious of some crucial feature of the experiment that their data were automatically discarded.

Subjects

The subjects were all male, college students taking classes in introductory psychology at the University of Minnesota. Some 90% of the students in these classes volunteer for a subject pool for which they receive two extra points on their final exam for every hour that they serve as experimental subjects. For this study the records of all potential subjects were cleared with the Student Health Service in order to insure that no harmful effects would result from the injections.

Evaluation of the Experimental Design

The ideal test of our propositions would require circumstances which our experiment is far from realizing. First, the proposition that: "A state of physiological arousal for which an individual has no immediate explanation will lead him to label this state in terms of the cognitions available to him" obviously requires conditions under which the subject does not and cannot have a proper explanation of his bodily state. Though we toyed with such fantasies as ventilating the experimental room with vaporized adrenalin, reality forced us to rely on the disguised injection of Suproxin—a technique which was far from ideal for no matter what the experimenter told them, some subjects would inevitably attribute their feelings to the injection. To the extent that subjects did so, differences between the several appropriateness conditions should be attenuated.

Second, the proposition that: "Given the same cognitive circumstances the individual will react emotionally only to the extent that he experiences a state of physiological arousal" requires for its ideal test the manipulation of states of physiological arousal and of physiological quiescence. Though there is no question that epinephrine effectively produces a state of arousal, there is also no question that a placebo does not prevent physiological arousal. To the extent that the experimental situation effectively produces sympathetic stimulation in placebo subjects, the proposition is difficult to test, for such a factor would attenuate differences between epinephrine and placebo subjects.

Both of these factors, then, can be expected to interfere with the test of our several propositions. In presenting the results of this study, we shall first present condition by condition results and then evaluate the effect of these two factors on experimental differences.

RESULTS

Effects of the Injections on Bodily State

Let us examine first the success of the injections at producing the bodily state required to examine the propositions at test. Does the injection of epinephrine produce symptoms of sympathetic discharge as compared with the placebo injection? Relevant data are presented in Table 1 where it can be immediately seen that on all items subjects who were in epinephrine conditions show considerably more evi-

TABLE 1
THE EFFECTS OF THE INJECTIONS ON BODILY STATE

Condition	N	Pulse Pre	Pulse Post	Self-rating of Palpitation	Tremor	Numbness	Itching	Headache
Euphoria								
Epi Inf	27	85.7	88.6	1.20	1.43	0	0.16	0.32
Epi Ign	26	84.6	85.6	1.83	1.76	0.15	0	0.55
Epi Mis	26	82.9	86.0	1.27	2.00	0.06	0.08	0.23
Placebo	26	80.4	77.1	0.29	0.21	0.09	0	0.27
Anger								
Epi Inf	23	85.9	92.4	1.26	1.41	0.17	0	0.11
Epi Ign	23	85.0	96.8	1.44	1.78	0	0.06	0.21
Placebo	23	84.5	79.6	0.59	0.24	0.14	0.06	0.06

dence of sympathetic activation than do subjects in placebo conditions. In all epinephrine conditions pulse rate increases significantly when compared with the decrease characteristic of the placebo conditions. On the scales it is clear that epinephrine subjects experience considerably more palpitation and tremor than do placebo subjects. In all possible comparisons on these symptoms, the mean scores of subjects in any of the epinephrine conditions are greater than the corresponding scores in the placebo conditions at better than the .001 level of significance. Examination of the absolute values of these scores makes it quite clear that subjects in epinephrine conditions were, indeed, in a state of physiological arousal, while most subjects in placebo conditions were in a relative state of physiological quiescence.

The epinephrine injection, of course, did not work with equal effectiveness for all subjects; indeed for a few subjects it did not work at all. Such subjects reported almost no palpitation or tremor, showed no increase in pulse and described no other relevant physical symptoms. Since for such subjects the necessary experimental conditions were not established, they were automatically excluded from the data and all further tabular presentations will not include such subjects. Table 1, however, does include the data of these subjects. There were four such subjects in euphoria conditions and one of them in anger conditions.

In order to evaluate further data on Epi Mis subjects it is necessary to note the results of the "numbness," "itching," and "headache" scales also presented in Table 1. Clearly the subjects in the Epi Mis condition do not differ on these scales from subjects in any of the other experimental conditions.

Effects of the Manipulations on Emotional State

Euphoria: Self-report. The effects of the several manipulations on emotional state in the euphoria conditions are presented in Table 2. The scores recorded in this table are derived, for each subject, by subtracting the value of the point he checks on the irritation scale from the value of the point he checks on the happiness scale. Thus, if a subject were to check the point "I feel a little irritated and angry" on the irritation scale and the point "I feel very happy and good" on the happiness scale, his score would be +2. The higher the positive value, the happier and better the subject reports himself as feeling. Though we employ an index for expositional simplicity, it should be noted that the two components of the index each yield results completely consistent with those obtained by use of this index.

Let us examine first the effects of the appropriateness instructions. Comparison of the scores for the Epi Mis and Epi Inf conditions makes it immediately clear that the experimental differences are not due to artifacts resulting from the informed instructions. In both conditions the subject was warned to expect a variety of symptoms as a consequence of the injection. In the Epi Mis condition, where the symptoms were inappropriate to the subject's bodily state the self-report score is almost twice that in the Epi Inf condition where the symptoms were completely appropriate to the subject's bodily state. It is reasonable, then, to attribute differences between informed subjects and those in other conditions to differences in manipulated appropriateness rather than to artifacts such as introspectiveness or self-examination.

It is clear that, consistent with expectations, subjects were more susceptible to the stooge's mood and consequently more euphoric when they had no explanation of their own bodily states than when they did. The means of both the Epi Ign and Epi Mis conditions are considerably greater than the mean of the Epi Inf condition.

It is of interest to note that Epi Mis subjects are somewhat more euphoric than are Epi Ign subjects. This pattern repeats itself in other data shortly to be presented. We would attribute this difference to differences in the appropriateness dimension. Though, as in the Epi Ign condition, a subject is not provided with an explanation of his

TABLE 2

SELF-REPORT OF EMOTIONAL STATE IN THE EUPHORIA CONDITIONS

Condition	N	Self-Report scales	Comparison	p[a]
Epi Inf	25	0.98	Epi Inf vs. Epi Mis	<.01
Epi Ign	25	1.78	Epi Inf vs. Epi Ign	.02
Epi Mis	25	1.90	Placebo vs. Epi Mis, Ign, or Inf	ns
Placebo	26	1.61		

[a] All p values reported throughout paper are two-tailed.

bodily state, it is, of course, possible that he will provide one for himself which is not derived from his interaction with the stooge. Most reasonably he could decide for himself that he feels this way because of the injection. To the extent that he does so he should be less susceptible to the stooge. It seems probable that he would be less likely to hit on such an explanation in the Epi Mis condition than in the Epi Ign condition for in the Epi Mis condition both the experimenter and the doctor have told him that the effects of the injection would be quite different from what he actually feels. The effect of such instructions is probably to make it more difficult for the subject himself to hit on the alternative explanation described above. There is some evidence to support this analysis. In open-end questions in which subjects described their own mood and state, 28% of the subjects in the Epi Ign condition made some connection between the injection and their bodily state compared with the 16% of subjects in the Epi Mis condition who did so. It could be considered, then, that these three conditions fall along a dimension of appropriateness, with the Epi Inf condition at one extreme and the Epi Mis condition at the other.

Comparing the placebo to the epinephrine conditions, we note a pattern which will repeat itself throughout the data. Placebo subjects are less euphoric than either Epi Mis or Epi Ign subjects but somewhat more euphoric than Epi Inf subjects. These differences are not, however, statistically significant. We shall consider the epinephrine-placebo comparisons in detail in a later section of this paper following the presentation of additional relevant data. For the moment, it is clear that, by self-report manipulating appropriateness has had a very strong effect on euphoria.

Behavior. Let us next examine the extent to which the subject's behavior was affected by the experimental manipulations. To the extent that his mood has been affected, one should expect that the subject will join in the stooge's whirl of manic activity and initiate similar activities of his own. The relevant data are presented in Table 3. The column labeled "Activity index" presents summary figures on the extent to which the subject joined in the stooge's activity. This is a weighted index which reflects both the nature of the activities in which the subject engaged and the amount of time he was active. The index was devised by assigning the following weights to the subject's activities: 5—hula hooping; 4—shooting with slingshot; 3—paper airplanes; 2—paper basketballs; 1—doodling; 0—does nothing. Pretest scaling on 15 college students ordered these activities with respect to the degree of euphoria they represented. Arbitrary weights were assigned so that the wilder the activity, the heavier the weight. These weights are multiplied by an estimate of the amount of time the subject spent in

TABLE 3

BEHAVIORAL INDICATIONS OF EMOTIONAL STATE IN THE EUPHORIA CONDITIONS

Condition	N	Activity index	Mean number of acts initiated
Epi Inf	25	12.72	.20
Epi Ign	25	18.28	.56
Epi Mis	25	22.56	.84
Placebo	26	16.00	.54

p value

Comparison	Activity index	Initiates[a]
Epi Inf vs. Epi Mis	.05	.03
Epi Inf vs. Epi Ign	ns	.08
Plac vs. Epi Mis, Ign, or Inf	ns	ns

[a] Tested by X^2 comparison of the proportion of subjects in each condition initiating new acts.

each activity and the summed products make up the activity index for each subject. This index may be considered a measure of behavioral euphoria. It should be noted that the same between-condition relationships hold for the two components of this index as for the index itself.

The column labeled "Mean number of acts initiated" presents the data on the extent to which the subject deviates from the stooge's routine and initiates euphoric activities of his own.

On both behavioral indices, we find precisely the same pattern of relationships as those obtained with self-reports. Epi Mis subjects behave somewhat more euphorically than do Epi Ign subjects who in turn behave more euphorically than do Epi Inf subjects. On all measures, then, there is consistent evidence that a subject will take over the stooge's euphoric mood to the extent that he has no other explanation of his bodily state.

Again it should be noted that on these behavioral indices, Epi Ign and Epi Mis subjects are somewhat more euphoric than placebo subjects but not significantly so.

Anger: Self-report. Before presenting data for the anger conditions, one point must be made about the anger manipulation. In the situation devised, anger, if manifested, is most likely to be directed at the experimenter and his annoyingly personal questionnaire. As we subsequently discovered, this was rather unfortunate, for the subjects, who had volunteered for the experiment for extra points on their final exam, simply refused to endanger these points by publicly blowing up, admitting their irritation to the experimenter's face or spoiling the questionnaire. Though as the reader will see, the subjects were quite willing to manifest anger when they were alone with the stooge, they hesitated to do so on material (self-ratings of mood and questionnaire) that the experimenter might see and only after the purposes of the experiment had been revealed were many of these subjects willing to admit to the experimenter that they had been irked or irritated.

This experimentally unfortunate situation pretty much forces us to rely on the behavioral indices derived from observation of the subject's presumably private interaction with the stooge. We do, however, present data on the self-report scales in Table 4. These figures are derived in the same way as the figures presented in Table 2 for the euphoria conditions, that is, the value checked on the irritation scale is subtracted from the value checked on the happiness scale. Though, for the reasons stated above, the absolute magnitude of these figures (all positive) is relatively meaningless, we can, of course, compare condition means within the set of anger conditions. With the happiness-irritation index employed, we should, of course, anticipate precisely the reverse results from those obtained in the euphoria conditions; that is, the Epi Inf subjects in the anger conditions should again be less susceptible to the stooge's mood and should, therefore, describe themselves as in a somewhat happier frame of mind than subjects in the Epi Ign condition. This is the case; the Epi Inf subjects average 1.91 on the self-report scales while the Epi Ign subjects average 1.39.

Evaluating the effects of the injections, we note again that, as anticipated, Epi Ign subjects are somewhat less happy than Placebo subjects but, once more, this is not a significant difference.

Behavior. The subject's responses to the stooge, during the period when both were filling out their questionnaires, were systematically coded to provide a behavioral index of anger. The coding scheme and the numerical

TABLE 4

SELF-REPORT OF EMOTIONAL STATE IN THE ANGER CONDITIONS

Condition	N	Self-Report scales	Comparison	p
Epi Inf	22	1.91	Epi Inf vs. Epi Ign	.08
Epi Ign	23	1.39	Placebo vs. Epi Ign or Inf	ns
Placebo	23	1.63		

values attached to each of the categories have been described in the methodology section. To arrive at an "Anger index" the numerical value assigned to a subject's responses to the stooge is summed together for the several units of stooge behavior. In the coding scheme used, a positive value to this index indicates that the subject agrees with the stooge's comment and is growing angry. A negative value indicates that the subject either disagrees with the stooge or ignores him.

The relevant data are presented in Table 5. For this analysis, the stooge's routine has been divided into two phases—the first two units of his behavior (the "long" questionnaire and "What did I have for breakfast?") are considered essentially neutral revealing nothing of the stooge's mood; all of the following units are considered "angry" units for they begin with an irritated remark about the "bells" question and end with the stooge's fury as he rips up his questionnaire and stomps out of the room. For the neutral units, agreement or disagreement with the stooge's remarks is, of course, meaningless as an index of mood and we should anticipate no difference between conditions. As can be seen in Table 5, this is the case.

For the angry units, we must, of course, anticipate that subjects in the Epi Ign condition will be angrier than subjects in the Epi Inf condition. This is indeed the case. The Anger index for the Epi Ign condition is positive and large, indicating that these subjects have become angry, while in the Epi Inf condition the Anger index is slightly negative in value indicating that these subjects have failed to catch the stooge's mood at all. It seems clear that providing the subject with an appropriate explanation of his bodily state greatly reduces his tendency to interpret his state in terms of the cognitions provided by the stooge's angry behavior.

Finally, on this behavioral index, it can be seen that subjects in the Epi Ign condition are significantly angrier than subjects in the Placebo condition. Behaviorally, at least, the injection of epinephrine appears to have led subjects to an angrier state than comparable subjects who received placebo shots.

Conformation of Data to Theoretical Expectations

Now that the basic data of this study have been presented, let us examine closely the extent to which they conform to theoretical expectations. If our hypotheses are correct and if this experimental design provided a perfect test for these hypotheses, it should be anticipated that in the euphoria conditions the degree of experimentally produced euphoria should vary in the following fashion:

Epi Mis $\geq$ Epi Ign $>$ Epi Inf $=$ Placebo

And in the anger conditions, anger should conform to the following pattern:

Epi Ign $>$ Epi Inf $=$ Placebo

In both sets of conditions, it is the case that emotional level in the Epi Mis and Epi Ign conditions is considerably greater than that achieved in the corresponding Epi Inf conditions. The results for the Placebo condition, however, are ambiguous for consistently the Placebo subjects fall between the Epi Ign and the Epi Inf subjects. This is a particularly troubling pattern for it makes it impossible to evaluate unequivocally the effects of the state of physiological arousal and indeed raises serious questions about our entire theoretical structure. Though the emo-

TABLE 5

BEHAVIORAL INDICATIONS OF EMOTIONAL STATE IN THE ANGER CONDITIONS

Condition	N	Neutral units	Anger units
Epi Inf	22	+0.07	−0.18
Epi Ign	23	+0.30	+2.28
Placebo	22[a]	−0.09	+0.79

Comparison for anger units	p
Epi Inf vs. Epi Ign	<.01
Epi Ign vs. Placebo	<.05
Placebo vs. Epi Inf	ns

[a] For one subject in this condition the sound system went dead and the observer could not, of course, code his reactions.

tional level is consistently greater in the Epi Mis and Epi Ign conditions than in the Placebo condition, this difference is significant at acceptable probability levels only in the anger conditions.

In order to explore the problem further, let us examine the experimental factors identified earlier, which might have acted to restrain the emotional level in the Epi Ign and Epi Mis conditions. As was pointed out earlier, the ideal test of our first two hypotheses requires an experimental setup in which the subject has flatly no way of evaluating his state of physiological arousal other than by means of the experimentally provided cognitions. Had it been possible to physiologically produce a state of sympathetic activation by means other than injection, one could have approached this experimental ideal more closely than in the present setup. As it stands, however, there is always a reasonable alternative cognition available to the aroused subject—he feels the way he does because of the injection. To the extent that the subject seizes on such an explanation of his bodily state, we should expect that he will be uninfluenced by the stooge. Evidence presented in Table 6 for the anger condition and in Table 7 for the euphoria conditions indicates that this is, indeed, the case.

As mentioned earlier, some of the Epi Ign and Epi Mis subjects in their answers to the open-end questions clearly attributed their physical state to the injection, e.g., "the shot gave me the shivers." In Tables 6 and 7 such subjects are labeled "Self-informed." In Table 6 it can be seen

TABLE 6

The Effects of Attributing Bodily State to the Injection on Anger in the Anger Epi Ign Condition

	N	Anger index
Self-informed subjects	3	−1.67
Others	20	+2.88
Self-informed versus Others		$p = .05$

TABLE 7

The Effects of Attributing Bodily State to the Injection on Euphoria in the Euphoria Epi Ign and Epi Mis Conditions

Epi Ign

	N	Activity index
Self-informed subjects	8	11.63
Others	17	21.14
Self-informed versus Others		$p = .05$

Epi Mis

	N	Activity index
Self-informed subjects	5	12.40
Others	20	25.10
Self-informed versus Others		$p = .10$

that the self-informed subjects are considerably less angry than are the remaining subjects; indeed, they are not angry at all. With these self-informed subjects eliminated the difference between the Epi Ign and the Placebo conditions is significant at the .01 level of significance.

Precisely the same pattern is evident in Table 7 for the euphoria conditions. In both the Epi Mis and the Epi Ign conditions, the self-informed subjects have considerably lower activity indices than do the remaining subjects. Eliminating self-informed subjects, comparison of both of these conditions with the Placebo condition yields a difference significant at the .03 level of significance. It should be noted, too, that the self-informed subjects have much the same score on the activity index as do the experimental Epi Inf subjects (Table 3).

It would appear, then, that the experimental procedure of injecting the subjects, by providing an alternative cognition, has, to some extent, obscured the effects of epinephrine. When account is taken of this artifact, the evidence is good that the state of physiological arousal is a necessary component of an emotional experience for when self-informed subjects are removed, epinephrine subjects give consistent indications of greater emotionality than do placebo subjects.

Let us examine next the fact that consistently the emotional level, both reported and behavioral, in Placebo conditions is greater than that in the Epi Inf conditions. Theoretically, of course, it should be expected that the two conditions will be equally low, for by assuming that emotional state is a joint function of a state of physiological arousal and of the appropriateness of a cognition we are, in effect, assuming a multiplicative function, so that if either component is at zero, emotional level is at zero. As noted earlier this expectation should hold if we can be sure that there is no sympathetic activation in the Placebo conditions. This assumption, of course, is completely unrealistic for the injection of placebo does not prevent sympathetic activation. The experimental situations were fairly dramatic and certainly some of the placebo subjects gave indications of physiological arousal. If our general line of reasoning is correct, it should be anticipated that the emotional level of subjects who give indications of sympathetic activity will be greater than that of subjects who do not. The relevant evidence is presented in Tables 8 and 9.

As an index of sympathetic activation we shall use the most direct and unequivocal measure available—change in pulse rate. It can be seen in Table 1 that the predominant pattern in the Placebo condition is a decrease in pulse rate. We shall assume, therefore, that

TABLE 8

SYMPATHETIC ACTIVATION AND EUPHORIA IN THE EUPHORIA PLACEBO CONDITION

Subject whose:	N	Activity index
Pulse decreased	14	10.67
Pulse increased or remained same	12	23.17
Pulse decreasers versus pulse increasers or same		$p = .02$

TABLE 9

SYMPATHETIC ACTIVATION AND ANGER IN ANGER PLACEBO CONDITION

Subjects whose:	N[a]	Anger index
Pulse decreased	13	+0.15
Pulse increased or remained same	8	+1.69
Pulse decreasers versus pulse increasers or same		$p = .01$

[a] N reduced by two cases owing to failure of sound system in one case and experimenter's failure to take pulse in another.

those subjects whose pulse increases or remains the same give indications of sympathetic activity while those subjects whose pulse decreases do not. In Table 8, for the euphoria condition, it is immediately clear that subjects who give indications of sympathetic activity are considerably more euphoric than are subjects who show no sympathetic activity. This relationship is, of course, confounded by the fact that euphoric subjects are considerably more active than noneuphoric subjects—a factor which independent of mood could elevate pulse rate. However, no such factor operates in the anger condition where angry subjects are neither more active nor talkative than calm subjects. It can be seen in Table 9 that Placebo subjects who show signs of sympathetic activation give indications of considerably more anger than do subjects who show no such signs. Conforming to expectations, sympathetic activation accompanies an increase in emotional level.

It should be noted, too, that the emotional levels of subjects showing no signs of sympathetic activity are quite comparable to the emotional level of subjects in the parallel Epi Inf conditions (see Tables 3 and 5). The similarity of these sets of scores and their uniformly low level of indicated emotionality would certainly make it appear that both factors are essential to an emotional state. When either the level of sympathetic arousal is low or a completely appropriate cognition is available, the level of emotionality is low.

Discussion

Let us summarize the major findings of this experiment and examine the extent to which they support the propositions offered in the introduction of this paper. It has been suggested, first, that given a state of physiological arousal for which an individual has no explanation, he will label this state in terms of the cognitions available to him. This implies, of course, that by manipulating the cognitions of an individual in such a state we can manipulate his feelings in diverse directions. Experimental results support this proposition for following the injection of epinephrine, those subjects who had no explanation for the bodily state thus produced, gave behavioral and self-report indications that they had been readily manipulable into the disparate feeling states of euphoria and anger.

From this first proposition, it must follow that given a state of physiological arousal for which the individual has a completely satisfactory explanation, he will not label this state in terms of the alternative cognitions available. Experimental evidence strongly supports this expectation. In those conditions in which subjects were injected with epinephrine and told precisely what they would feel and why, they proved relatively immune to any effects of the manipulated cognitions. In the anger condition, such subjects did not report or show anger; in the euphoria condition, such subjects reported themselves as far less happy than subjects with an identical bodily state but no adequate knowledge of why they felt the way they did.

Finally, it has been suggested that given constant cognitive circumstances, an individual will react emotionally only to the extent that he experiences a state of physiological arousal. Without taking account of experimental artifacts, the evidence in support of this proposition is consistent but tentative. When the effects of "self-informing" tendencies in epinephrine subjects and of "self-arousing" tendencies in placebo subjects are partialed out, the evidence strongly supports the proposition.

The pattern of data, then, falls neatly in line with theoretical expectations. However, the fact that we were forced, to some extent, to rely on internal analyses in order to partial out the effects of experimental artifacts inevitably makes our conclusions somewhat tentative. In order to further test these propositions on the interaction of cognitive and physiological determinants of emotional state, a series of additional experiments, published elsewhere, was designed to rule out or overcome the operation of these artifacts. In the first of these, Schachter and Wheeler (1962) extended the range of manipulated sympathetic activation by employing three experimental groups— epinephrine, placebo, and a group injected with the sympatholytic agent, chlorpromazine. Laughter at a slapstick movie was the dependent variable and the evidence is good that amusement is a direct function of manipulated sympathetic activation.

In order to make the epinephrine-placebo comparison under conditions which would rule out the operation of any self-informing tendency, two experiments were conducted on rats. In one of these Singer (1961) demonstrated that under fear inducing conditions, manipulated by the simultaneous presentation of a loud bell, a buzzer, and a bright flashing light, rats injected with epinephrine were considerably more frightened than rats injected with a placebo. Epinephrine-injected rats defecated, urinated, and trembled more than did placebo-injected rats. In nonfear control conditions, there were no differences between epinephrine and placebo groups, neither group giving any indication of fear. In another study, Latané and Schachter (1962) demonstrated that rats injected with epinephrine were notably more capable of avoidance learning than were rats injected with a placebo. Using a modified Miller-Mowrer shuttlebox, these investigators found that during an experimental period involving 200 massed trials, 15 rats injected with epinephrine avoided shock an average of 101.2 trials while 15 placebo-injected rats averaged only 37.3 avoidances.

Taken together, this body of studies

does give strong support to the propositions which generated these experimental tests. Given a state of sympathetic activation, for which no immediately appropriate explanation is available, human subjects can be readily manipulated into states of euphoria, anger, and amusement. Varying the intensity of sympathetic activation serves to vary the intensity of a variety of emotional states in both rats and human subjects.

Let us examine the implications of these findings and of this line of thought for problems in the general area of the physiology of the emotions. We have noted in the introduction that the numerous studies on physiological differentiators of emotional states have, viewed en masse, yielded quite inconclusive results. Most, though not all, of these studies have indicated no differences among the various emotional states. Since as human beings, rather than as scientists, we have no difficulty identifying, labeling, and distinguishing among our feelings, the results of these studies have long seemed rather puzzling and paradoxical. Perhaps because of this, there has been a persistent tendency to discount such results as due to ignorance or methodological inadequacy and to pay far more attention to the very few studies which demonstrate *some* sort of physiological differences among emotional states than to the very many studies which indicate no differences at all. It is conceivable, however, that these results should be taken at face value and that emotional states may, indeed, be generally characterized by a high level of sympathetic activation with few if any physiological distinguishers among the many emotional states. If this is correct, the findings of the present study may help to resolve the problem. Obviously this study does *not* rule out the possibility of physiological differences among the emotional states. It is the case, however, that given precisely the same state of epinephrine-induced sympathetic activation, we have, by means of cognitive manipulations, been able to produce in our subjects the very disparate states of euphoria and anger.

It may indeed be the case that cognitive factors are major determiners of the emotional labels we apply to a common state of sympathetic arousal.

Let us ask next whether our results are specific to the state of sympathetic activation or if they are generalizable to other states of physiological arousal. It is clear that from our experiments proper, it is impossible to answer the question for our studies have been concerned largely with the effects of an epinephrine created state of sympathetic arousal. We would suggest, however, that our conclusions are generalizable to almost any pronounced internal state for which no appropriate explanation is available. This suggestion receives some support from the experiences of Nowlis and Nowlis (1956) in their program of research on the effects of drugs on mood. In their work the Nowlises typically administer a drug to groups of four subjects who are physically in one another's presence and free to interact. The Nowlises describe some of their results with these groups as follows:

At first we used the same drug for all 4 men. In those sessions seconal, when compared with placebo, increased the checking of such words as expansive, forceful, courageous, daring, elated, and impulsive. In our first statistical analysis we were confronted with the stubborn fact that when the same drug is given to all 4 men in a group, the N that has to be entered into the analysis is 1, not 4. This increases the cost of an already expensive experiment by a considerable factor, but it cannot be denied that the effects of these drugs may be and often are quite contagious. Our first attempted solution was to run tests on groups in which each man had a different drug during the same session, such as 1 on seconal, 1 on benzedrine, 1 on dramamine, and 1 on placebo. What does seconal do? Cooped up with, say, the egotistical benzedrine partner, the withdrawn, indifferent dramimine partner, and the slightly bored lactose man, the seconal subject reports that he is distractible, dizzy, drifting, glum, defiant, languid, sluggish, discouraged, dull, gloomy, lazy, and slow! This is not the report of mood that we got when all 4 men were on seconal. It thus appears that the moods of the partners do definitely influence the effect of seconal (p. 350).

It is not completely clear from this description whether this "contagion" of mood is more marked in drug than in placebo groups, but should this be the case, these results would certainly support the suggestion that our findings are generalizable to internal states other than that produced by an injection of epinephrine.

Finally, let us consider the implications of our formulation and data for alternative conceptualizations of emotion. Perhaps the most popular current conception of emotion is in terms of "activation theory" in the sense employed by Lindsley (1951) and Woodworth and Schlosberg (1958). As we understand this theory, it suggests that emotional states should be considered as at one end of a continuum of activation which is defined in terms of degree of autonomic arousal and of electroencephalographic measures of activation. The results of the experiment described in this paper do, of course, suggest that such a formulation is not completely adequate. It is possible to have very high degrees of activation without a subject either appearing to be or describing himself as "emotional." Cognitive factors appear to be indispensable elements in any formulation of emotion.

Summary

It is suggested that emotional states may be considered a function of a state of physiological arousal and of a cognition appropriate to this state of arousal. From this follows these propositions:

1. Given a state of physiological arousal for which an individual has no immediate explanation, he will label this state and describe his feelings in terms of the cognitions available to him. To the extent that cognitive factors are potent determiners of emotional states, it should be anticipated that precisely the same state of physiological arousal could be labeled "joy" or "fury" or "jealousy" or any of a great diversity of emotional labels depending on the cognitive aspects of the situation.

2. Given a state of physiological arousal for which an individual has a completely appropriate explanation, no evaluative needs will arise and the individual is unlikely to label his feelings in terms of the alternative cognitions available.

3. Given the same cognitive circumstances, the individual will react emotionally or describe his feelings as emotions only to the extent that he experiences a state of physiological arousal.

An experiment is described which, together with the results of other studies, supports these propositions.

References

Ax, A. F. Physiological differentiation of emotional states. *Psychosom. Med.*, 1953, **15**, 433–442.

Cannon, W. B. *Bodily changes in pain, hunger, fear and rage.* (2nd ed.) New York: Appleton, 1929.

Cantril, H., & Hunt, W. A. Emotional effects produced by the injection of adrenalin. *Amer. J. Psychol.*, 1932, **44**, 300–307.

Festinger, L. A theory of social comparison processes. *Hum. Relat.*, 1954, **7**, 114–140.

Hunt, J. McV., Cole, M. W., & Reis, E. E. Situational cues distinguishing anger, fear, and sorrow. *Amer. J. Psychol.*, 1958, **71**, 136–151.

James, W. *The principles of psychology.* New York: Holt, 1890.

Landis, C., & Hunt, W. A. Adrenalin and emotion. *Psychol. Rev.*, 1932, **39**, 467–485.

Latané, B., & Schachter, S. Adrenalin and avoidance learning. *J. comp. physiol. Psychol.*, 1962, **65**, 369–372.

Lindsley, D. B. Emotion. In S. S. Stevens (Ed.), *Handbook of experimental psychology.* New York: Wiley, 1951. Pp. 473–516.

Marañon, G. Contribution à l'étude de l'action émotive de l'adrénaline. *Rev. Francaise Endocrinol.*, 1924, **2**, 301–325.

Nowlis, V., & Nowlis, H. H. The description and analysis of mood. *Ann. N. Y. Acad. Sci.*, 1956, **65**, 345–355.

Ruckmick, C. A. *The psychology of feeling and emotion.* New York: McGraw-Hill, 1936.

Schachter, J. Pain, fear, and anger in hypertensives and normotensives: A psychophysiologic study. *Psychosom. Med.*, 1957, **19**, 17–29.

Schachter, S. *The psychology of affiliation.* Stanford, Calif.: Stanford Univer. Press, 1959.

Schachter, S., & Wheeler, L. Epinephrine, chlorpromazine, and amusement. *J. abnorm. soc. Psychol.*, 1962, **65**, 121–128.

Singer, J. E. The effects of epinephrine, chlorpromazine and dibenzyline upon the fright responses of rats under stress and non-stress conditions. Unpublished doctoral dissertation, University of Minnesota, 1961.

Wolf, S., & Wolff, H. G. *Human gastric function.* New York: Oxford Univer. Press, 1947.

Woodworth, R. S., & Schlosberg, H. *Experimental psychology.* New York: Holt, 1958.

Wrightsman, L. S. Effects of waiting with others on changes in level of felt anxiety. *J. abnorm. soc. Psychol.*, 1960, **61**, 216–222.

12

PAN-CULTURAL ELEMENTS IN FACIAL DISPLAYS OF EMOTION

Paul Ekman
Langley Porter Neuropsychiatric Institute, San Francisco, California

E. Richard Sorenson
National Institute of Neurological Diseases and Blindness, Bethesda, Maryland

Wallace V. Friesen
Langley Porter Neuropsychiatric Institute

Abstract. Observers in both literate and preliterate cultures chose the predicted emotion for photographs of the face, although agreement was higher in the literate samples. These findings suggest that the pan-cultural element in facial displays of emotion is the association between facial muscular movements and discrete primary emotions, although cultures may still differ in what evokes an emotion, in rules for controlling the display of emotion, and in behavioral consequences.

In studies in New Guinea, Borneo, the United States, Brazil, and Japan we found evidence of pan-cultural elements in facial displays of affect. Observers in these cultures recognize some of the same emotions when they are shown a standard set of facial photographs. This finding contradicts (i) the theory (1) that facial displays of emotion are socially learned and therefore culturally variable; and (ii) the findings from studies within a single culture that observers of the face alone do not achieve either accuracy or high agreement in recognizing different emotional states (2).

Bruner and Taguiri (3) said: "The best evidence available [from 30 years of research] seems to indicate that there is no invariable pattern (or at least no innate invariable pattern of expression) accompanying specific emotions." In contrast, our findings support Darwin's (4) suggestion that facial expressions of emotion are similar among humans, regardless of culture, because of their evolutionary origin.

Our study was based in part on Tomkins' (5) theory of personality, which emphasized the importance of affect and which postulated innate subcortical programs linking certain evokers to distinguishable, universal facial displays for each of the primary affects—interest, joy, surprise, fear, anger, distress, disgust-contempt, and shame. Ekman and Friesen (6) reasoned that past impressions of cultural differences in facial displays of affect may represent a failure to distinguish what is pan-cultural (the association of facial muscular movements with each primary affect) from what is culturally variable (learned affect evokers, behavioral consequences of an affect display, and the operation of display rules).

Display rules were defined as procedures learned early in life for the management of affect displays and include deintensifying, intensifying, neutralizing, or masking an affect display. These rules prescribe what to do about the display of each affect in different social settings; they vary with the social role and demographic characteristics, and should vary across cultures.

To uncover the pan-cultural elements

Reprinted from *Science*, Vol. 164, April 4, 1969. Copyright 1969 by the American Association for the Advancement of Science.

in facial displays of affect, the investigator must obtain samples (photographs) of facial expression that are free of cultural differences because of learned evokers, display rules, and consequences. We attempted to select such photographs and to prove that observers from different cultures recognize the same affect from the same photograph. Because similarities in the recognition of emotion among literate cultures might be attributed to learning their own or each other's facial affect cues from a shared visual source (television, movies, or magazines), it was necessary to obtain data also from visually isolated cultures, preferably preliterate cultures.

Photographs were selected from over 3000 pictures to obtain those which showed only the pure display of a single affect. The selection was guided by a study in which Ekman, Friesen, and Tomkins (7) developed a procedure for scoring facial affects that was based on a compilation of lists of cues particular to each primary affect. The scoring procedure had not been completed when the photographs were selected for this cross-cultural study, but the partial lists provided the basis for choosing pictures which contained cues distinctive for happiness, surprise, fear, anger, disgust-contempt, and sadness. This list of affects includes all of Tomkins' primary affect categories except for interest and shame; it also includes almost all of the affect states, discriminable within any one culture.

The most common reasons for rejecting photographs were that they showed the influence of display rules or blends of the cues of one affect with those of one or more other affects rather than single-affect pictures. Thirty photographs met our criteria; they showed male and female Caucasians, adults and children, professional and amateur actors, and mental patients. The stimuli were reproduced as 35-mm slides and photographs (13 by 18 cm) cropped to include only the face and neck.

The observers' task was to select a word from a list of six affects for each picture. In the United States, Brazil, and Japan, slides were projected one at a time for 20 seconds each to groups of freshmen college students from whom the foreign-born had been eliminated. The photographic prints (13 by 18 cm) were shown one at a time to each observer in New Guinea and Borneo. The affect words were translated into the locally understood languages (Japanese, Portuguese, Neo-Melanesian Pidgin, Fore, and Bidayuh). There were no Neo-Melanesian Pidgin equivalents for disgust-contempt or surprise, and in these cases a phrase was submitted (looking at something which stinks, looking at something new).

For our isolated, non-Western preliterate samples we attempted to find those least affected by the modern technological, commercial, and ideological currents. The New Guinea sample was the Fore linguistic-cultural group (8) who until 12 years ago were an isolated Neolithic material culture. We studied the Fore most influenced by contacts with Westerners (government, missionaries, and others) as well as those least influenced by these recent contacts who have preferred to remain in their isolated hamlets in the mountains.

We report in detail only on the most Westernized Fore; we summarize the results on the less Westernized Fore, whose unfamiliarity with certain tasks required development of specialized judgment procedures and conducting a number of additional experiments. There were two subsamples in the most Westernized Fore; one subsample performed the judgment task by using Pidgin translations of the affect terms, and the other subsample used the affect terms of their own Fore language.

The Borneo sample was the Sadong, a Bidayuh-speaking group of Hill Dyaks in southwest Sarawak. These people still lived in their traditional long houses and maintained their traditional agrarian way of life. Only one man spoke English, most men spoke some Malay, and many had seen a few movies in a commercial center located about a day's walk from their village.

The distribution of six responses to each category (affect) of photographs was tallied, and the most frequent judgment response for each affect category was converted into a percentage of the total responses to the stimuli which represented that category (Table 1). The data from the three literate samples support our contention of a pan-cultural element in facial affect display. Agreement and accuracy were far higher in each group than had been reported for recognition of emotions within cultures, and the same affect term was the most frequent response in the United States and Brazil for all of the stimuli and for 29 out of the 30 stimuli when Japan is compared. Three literate cultures are not a sufficient sample to proclaim universality; however, Izard (9), who worked independently at the same time as we, but with his own set of facial photographs obtained results for eight other literate cultures that are substantially the same as ours.

When exposure to common visual input is controlled (to answer the argument that such similarities among literate cultures only reflect learned recognitions from mass media) the agreement and accuracy were lower in the preliterate cultures than in the literate ones. We believe that this is because of the enormous obstacles imposed by language barriers and task unfamiliarity in preliterate cultures (even with the more Westernized observers). Despite such handicaps, there were similar

Table 1. Rates of recognition of six affects among samples from the United States, Brazil, Japan, New Guinea, and Borneo.

Affect category	United States	Brazil	Japan	New Guinea* Pidgin responses	New Guinea* Fore responses	Borneo*
Happy (H)	97 H	97 H	87 H	99 H	82 H	92 H
Fear (F)	88 F	77 F	71 F	46 F	54 F	40 F
			26 Su	31 A	25 A	33 Su
Disgust-contempt (D)	82 D	86 D	82 D	29 D	44 D	26 Sa
				23 A	30 A	23 H
Anger (A)	69 A	82 A	63 A	56 A	50 A	64 A
	29 D		14 D	22 F	25 F	
Surprise (SU)	91 Su	82 Su	87 Su	38 Su	45 F	36 Su
				30 F	19 A	23 F
Sadness (SA)	73 Sa	82 Sa	74 Sa	55 Sa	56 A	52 Sa
				23 A		
Number of observers	99	40	29	18	14	15
Number of stimuli for which most frequent response was predicted response	30/30	30/30	29/30	11/24	12/24	18/23
Number of stimuli for which 70 percent of the observers agreed	25/30	26/30	23/30	7/24	6/24	6/23
Chi-square†	10,393	3818	2347	532	261	427
Chi-square excluding happy stimuli†	5718	2119	1241	188	92	211

* A few photographs, mostly happy pictures, were eliminated in work with preliterate observers in order to make the task shorter.   † All chi-squares were significant beyond $P=.01$.

recognitions of happiness, anger, and fear in all samples, and for disgust, surprise, and sadness in two out of three samples (Table 1). An affect category was never misidentified by the majority of observers in more than one of the preliterate samples. Our studies of other much less Westernized Fore observers yielded similar results, with the exception of the sadness category, and we also obtained additional support in studies in progress on how these affects are expressed in the Fore. The possibility that the data on the preliterate samples might have been biased by the use of Caucasoid faces as stimuli was negated by additional studies in which Melanesian (South Fore) faces were shown to the South Fore observers and results similar to those reported here were obtained. The proposition that there are pan-cultural elements in human affect displays appears to be largely supported, both in the literate cultures that we and Izard have studied, and for the most part in the preliterate cultures that we have investigated. Those who deem it important to have maximum control for shared visual input to limit the opportunity to learn common affect recognitions might still want the further evidence on the less Westernized samples of Fore to be reported later.

References and Notes

1. For example, O. Klineberg, *Social Psychology* (Holt, New York, 1940); W. La Barre, *J. Personality* **16**, 49 (1947).
2. Although the semantic dimensions which may underlie the judgment of emotions are similar across cultures, it has not been demonstrated that the face displays the same emotion in the same way across cultures. H. Schlosberg, *Psychol. Rev.* **61**, 81 (1954); C. E. Osgood, *Scand. J. Psychol.* **7**, 1 (1966); H. C. Triandis and W. W. Lamber, *J. Abnorm. Soc. Psychol.* **56**, 321 (1958).
3. J. S. Bruner and R. Taguiri, "The perception of people," in *Handbook of Social Psychology*, G. Lindzey, Ed. (Addison-Wesley, Cambridge, Mass., 1954), vol. 2, pp. 634–654.
4. C. Darwin, *The Expression of the Emotions in Man and Animals* (Murray, London, 1872).
5. S. S. Tomkins, "The positive affects," *Affect, Imagery, Consciousness* (Springer, New York, 1962), vol. 1; "The negative affects," *Affect, Imagery, Consciousness* (Springer, New York, 1963), vol. 2; —— and R. McCarter, *Percept. Motor Skills* **18** (Monogr. Suppl. No. 1-V18), 119 (1964).
6. P. Ekman and W. V. Friesen, "Origins, usage and coding of nonverbal behavior, in *Communication Theory and Linguistic Models in the Social Sciences*, E. Vernon, Ed. (Di Tella, Buenos Aires, 1968); "The repertoire of nonverbal behavior," *Semiotica*, in press.
7. P. Ekman, W. V. Friesen, S. S. Tomkins, "A facial affect scoring technique; and initial validity study," in preparation.
8. D. C. Gajdusek, *Trans. Roy. Soc. Trop. Med. Hyg.* **57** (No. 3), 151 (1963); E. R. Sorenson and D. C. Gajdusek, *Pediatrics* **37** (No. 1), 149 (1966).
9. C. E. Izard, "The emotions and emotion constructs in personality and culture research," in *Handbook of Modern Personality Theory*, R. D. Cattell, Ed. (Aldine, Chicago, in press).

17 October 1968; revised 16 January 1969

Section Four

Sensation and Perception

In the first paper of this section, Dr. White and his associates report the results of experiments designed to restore sight to the blind through replacement of the visual function in blind subjects. They have developed a tactile television system in which a television camera image is converted into a pattern of electrical stimulation through an array of electrodes in contact with the skin. With this newly developed tactile image converter, blind and blindfolded subjects have tracked the direction and rate of moving targets and have determined the position, relative size, shape, number and orientation of visible objects.

In the second paper, Lettvin and his associates report the results of research in which they were trying to learn more about the types of sensory information relayed from the eye to the brain. Frogs were used in this study, for several reasons explained in the paper. Basically, the visual system in the frog is much simpler than in the human being and, consequently, easier to study.

The most important finding of this research was that the eye transmits information to the brain which is already highly organized and interpreted. It does not simply transmit a more or less accurate copy of the distribution of light on the receptors. The system, as they describe it, is admirably suited to the type of life led by the frog.

In the next paper in this section Professor E. R. Hilgard summarizes much of what we know about the sense of pain, and in addition, he describes several experiments conducted at Stanford in which the search was for objective indicators of pain. These experiments were also designed to tell us more about the effects of hypnotic analgesia (suggestions, during hypnosis, that no pain is felt). Using blood pressure as a tentative objective indicator of pain, Hilgard found that under hypnosis pain can, in fact, be completely removed. Blood pressure, it should be noted, was found to rise sharply as the non-hypnotized subject felt pain. In hypnotic analgesia, however, no blood pressure rise was observed under some circumstances.

In the next paper, Singh, Johnston, and Klosterman discuss the effects of differences in early visual experiences on perception in later life. A number of psychologists have shown that when rats are raised in an "enriched environment" both behavioral and biochemical changes can be produced. In most cases, however, it has been difficult to specify the variables that bring about such changes. Handling, living together with other rats, and visual stimulation have often been confounded in these experiments.

Singh and his associates report the results of an experiment in which the sole independent variable was variation in the visual stimuli to which the rats were exposed. Some saw a pattern of black and white stripes, while others could look only at a flat white surface. Surprisingly, those exposed to the stripes gained weight faster than the others, and there were significant differences in brain chemistry as well. The experimenters concluded that the nature of visual impact in infancy may cause enduring alterations in some basic physiological mechanisms.

The next paper deals with interpersonal perception. Wilkins and de Charms studied authoritarian and non-authoritarian individuals in terms of the cues they used in evaluating others. The authoritarian person—the individual who respects strength, authority, and power—tends to react to others more in terms of external than internal cues. That is, his perception of other persons is guided more by such things as the type of house in which the person lives, his income, and so on than by the person's traits, mannerisms, and values. The non-authoritarian, on the other hand, tends to perceive others more in terms of internal cues such as values and personal characteristics.

The final paper in the section deals with an entirely different aspect of perception. Here the investigator was trying to account for the apparent narrowness of perception in the person holding extreme political views. Such persons are notoriously intolerant of the views of others and tend, typically, to perceive stands on political issues in black or white, all-or-none terms. Several different experiments reported in this paper show that one's position on an issue tends to be an anchoring point in perceiving and judging other stands. The more extreme that position, the more intolerant the individual becomes of views other than his own. Not only do the findings reported in this paper help us to understand perception in the political extremist, but they have important implications for attitude or opinion change as well. To change the attitudes of those holding extreme views, it is suspected, may only be accomplished in small steps. Presenting markedly different positions may actually further entrench the listener's beliefs.

SEEING WITH THE SKIN

BENJAMIN W. WHITE
FRANK A. SAUNDERS
LAWRENCE SCADDEN
PAUL BACH-Y-RITA
CARTER C. COLLINS
Pacific Medical Center

Twelve years have passed since the publication of Geldard's (1957) provocative paper in which the potentialities of the skin as a communication channel were demonstrated. Since that time, Geldard and his colleagues have refined their technique of presenting highly discriminable vibrotactile stimuli to various parts of the body. In a recent report, Geldard (1968) describes the application of nine vibrators at widely separated body sites, each one triggered by one photocell in a linear array scanning typed and printed characters. It is hoped that this system will enable trained Ss to read at speeds comparable to those that Geldard reported earlier, using a set of five vibrators mounted on the chest and capable of delivering signals at three intensities and three durations. After a few hours of training with this sytem, Ss were able to receive material at a rate approximately twice that of proficient Morse code operators.

Geldard's efforts have been oriented exclusively toward the use of the skin to receive a set of known and clearly discriminable characters, whose optimal coding has been determined by psychophysical techniques. The possibility of using the skin as a channel for *pictorial* material has not been systematically explored, though devices capable of presenting dynamic two-dimensional tactile images exist (Linville & Bliss, 1968; Strakiewicz & Kulizewski, 1965). The potential utility of such devices as visual substitution systems for the blind is immediately apparent. It is surprising that in this day of advanced technology, the blind are still moving about in the world using a cane, a guide dog, a sighted companion, or an outstretched hand.

In addition to its value as an aid for the blind, such a tactile image system provides an opportunity to explore a number of such perceptual phenomena as size constancy or space perception that heretofore have been considered uniquely visual. Also, the problems people encounter in gaining facility with this novel system should throw light on aspects of perceptual learning that have thus far been difficult to investigate.

For the past year, we have been working with a sensory substitution system that converts a visual image into a tactile one. It is the purpose of this report to present some of the initial findings from this work and to discuss their implications for perceptual theory.

METHODS

The theoretical neurophysiological basis (Bach-y-Rita, 1967) and the physical

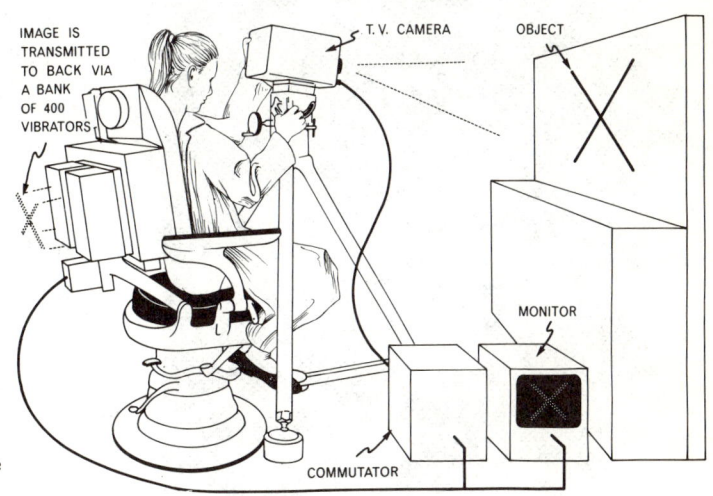

Fig. 1. Schematic representation of the tactile television system.

Reprinted from *Perception and Psychophysics*, Vol. 7 (1), 1970. Copyright 1970, Psychonomic Journals, Inc., Austin, Texas.

concept of the instrumentation (Collins, 1967) for the vision substitution system have been discussed previously. Preliminary results in training blind Ss to use the apparatus have been briefly reported (Bach-y-Rita et al, 1969a; Bach-y-Rita et al, 1969b; Scadden, 1969; Saunders, 1969).

As shown in Fig. 1, the "eye" of the system consists of a television camera. This camera, which is mounted on a tripod, is manipulated by the S, who can aim the zoom lens at any part of the room, in order to localize and identify objects or persons. Stimuli can also be presented on a back-lit screen by slide or motion picture projection. The video image is electronically transformed and sent to a 20 by 20 matrix of solenoid vibrators mounted in the back of a stationary dental chair. The 400 stimulators, spaced 12 mm apart with 1-mm-diam tips, cover an area approximately 10 in. square. Each solenoid is designed to vibrate at 60 Hz when its locus is within an illuminated region of the camera field. The on-off activity of the vibrators can be monitored visually on an oscilloscope as a two-dimensional pictorial display.

The Ss for this series of experiments were young adults, many of whom were from a nearby college. Twenty-five congenitally blind men and women have been tested in the apparatus, in addition to five adults who were blinded later in childhood. Over 50 sighted Ss have also been examined. Not all of these Ss have been put through all the procedures described below. Eight blind Ss have had over 40 h of training in the chair, while others have come in to serve as Ss for a single experiment.

RESULTS

Subjects are able to perceive certain simple displays with this tactile system, almost as soon as they have been introduced to it. If a white circular target, capable of activating approximately three-quarters of the tactors, is placed before the camera, Ss have no difficulty in centering the image on the tactor array by manipulating the camera. If a vertical white stripe is moved from side to side, the S is able to describe the motion accurately or to imitate it with an appropriate hand gesture. Similarly, a propeller motion of the stripe can be accurately followed or described. Ss can also discriminate between a stationary vertical or horizontal stripe. When given control of the wheels controlling camera position on the tripod, the horizontal-vertical discrimination becomes even easier since only motion orthogonal to stripe orientation produces a detectable change in the tactile display. If a diagonal stripe is presented, Ss are able to report whether the upper end is on the left or the right. They are also able to adjust the camera so that one end of the line is centered. Ss are able to report the orientation of a curved line (a 60-deg arc with a 4-deg radius of curvature) with reasonable accuracy.

On none of these tasks was the performance of the blind Ss significantly different from that of the sighted Ss who were, of course, blindfolded while being tested.

Form Discrimination

Initial experiments with form discrimination showed that performance rapidly improved when Ss were allowed to scan the figures by moving the camera and were given immediate correction after a wrong response. When asked to identify a circle, square, or triangle, Ss' performance remained near chance levels after 60 trials when no correction was given and no camera movement was allowed. With correction, accuracy reached 60% after 54 trials, with a mean response latency of 6 sec. Significant improvement was found between each 18-trial block. When the Ss were allowed to pan the camera over the forms and given correction, they achieved 100% accuracy in the third block of 18 trials with a latency of 1 sec or less (Bach-y-Rita et al, 1969). The discrimination was even more rapidly established when the figures were initially presented in pairs for the S to inspect after telling him, "The square is on the right and the circle on the left." After as little as 10 min of such training, some Ss could achieve 100% accuracy in identifying these three simple forms. Particularly in early stages of training, Ss panned the camera so that the figure came into and passed out of the field, suggesting that the discrimination is largely based upon contour changes in the leading edge of the figure.

Acuity Judgments

Six blind Ss were asked to judge the vertical-horizontal orientation of slide-projected displays consisting of from 4 to 12 pairs of parallel black and white lines. The five displays were presented in random order for a total of 40 presentations, and the Ss were allowed to scan them with the camera before making a judgment. Five of

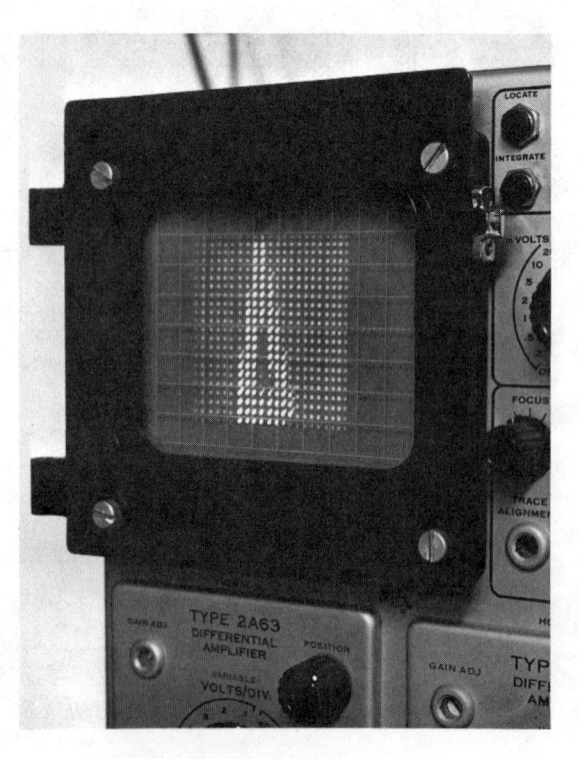

Fig. 2. Representation of the visual display which continuously monitors the state of the 400 tactors.

these Ss were congenitally blind, and the sixth lost sight before the age of 4. They had had from 15 to 40 h of experience in the vision substitution system. The performance of the blind Ss using the tactile input was compared with the performance of six sighted Ss who made the same judgments, not from the tactile input, but from the visual display seen on the oscilloscope monitor. Figure 2 shows the kind of visual display the sighted Ss were given.

The two groups showed remarkably similar performance. There was only one incorrect judgment out of a total of 480. The blind Ss had a mean latency to correct response of 1.2 sec as compared to 1.1 sec for the sighted group Though both groups were instructed in the control of the camera and encouraged to move it before making a judgment, neither group did so to any great extent.

Slant Judgments

The same groups of blind and sighted Ss were asked to make slant judgments based again upon slide-projected displays of a checkerboard that had been photographed at a 70-deg slant from frontal parallel. This slide was projected in one of four orientations by simply rotating the slide in the projector. On 40 such randomized presentations, the S was asked to judge whether the checkerboard tilted away to the top, bottom, left, or right. The results for this task are shown in Table 1. The blind Ss using the tactile display made significantly more errors and took significantly longer to make their judgments than the sighted Ss using the visual display. Unlike the vertical-horizontal bar orientation task, the blind Ss all used scanning of the camera to make the slant judgment. Since this scanning had to be done by turning two wheels on the tripod, this probably accounts for much of the latency difference. The accuracy of the experienced blind Ss is high on this task and the accuracy of the sighted Ss is not perfect. This would indicate that the limitations on the tactile system thus far probably are more a function of the resolution of the display than of the sensitivity of the back.

Observations of Experienced Blind Ss

Seven congenitally blind Ss have each had over 40 h of experience in the vision substitution system. These men and women have been studied intensively because they proved adept with the apparatus and were able to provide valuable insights about its capacities and limitations.

These Ss were given extended practice in the identification of a collection of some 25

Table 1
Comparison of Tactile
and Visual Slant Judgments

	Accuracy	Latency
Blind Os Tactile Display	83% (n = 240)	8.4 sec
Sighted Os Visual Display	97% (n = 240)	2.8 sec

"things"—a coffee cup, a telephone, a stuffed animal. They were encouraged to scan these objects by manipulating the camera and to try to describe them. Initial scanning was prolonged, a new object often requiring up to 15 min of exploration before correct identification. This latency dropped steadily with repeated presentations until the Ss were often able to identify an object within 10 sec on its fifth presentation. A "learning to learn" phenomenon was evident, since new objects took less and less time to identify as the vocabulary of objects increased.

The experienced Ss, after they had gained facility in identifying a number of objects, were asked to describe arbitrary arrangements of objects placed upon a table top. The table was placed so that the camera looked down at it from an angle of approximately 20 deg off horizontal. The Ss were able both to identify the objects on the table top and to describe their arrangement even though their placement on occasion was such that objects at the rear were partially occluded by those in front.

Obviously judgments of this sort must make use of the sort of information that in classical texts is called "cues for distance." Particularly useful in making judgments about the position of the object in depth was its vertical position on the display. The higher up it was, the farther back on the table top. This is precisely the information that Roberts (1963) found so useful in his program enabling a computer to construct a three-dimensional representation of an object using only the two-dimensional representation of it as input.

The congenitally blind person has never directly experienced the relationship between the visual angle subtended by an object and its distance from the observer. One of the experienced blind Ss was a psychologist who had explained this relationship to introductory psychology classes for several years. One day, while in the chair, he experienced the change in size of a tactile image as an object was brought closer and closer to the camera, and the sudden perceptual realization of this size-distance relationship came as a genuine "aha" experience. This evidence of size constancy has been found in other Ss as well. Perhaps of greater interest have been the occasions when Ss have given startled ducks of the head when the tactile image was suddenly magnified by a sudden turn of the zoom lever on the camera.

One discrimination that some of the Ss found most difficult to achieve was that of internal detail. For such Ss, the detection of facial features in photographs or folds in fabric followed by many hours the ability to recognize objects on the basis of outside contour alone. There appear, however, to be profound individual differences in this respect, and one S, on his first session in the chair, was able not only to detect an internal hole in an object, but to describe its shape accurately.

Further evidence of the existence of powerful three-dimensional organization of tactile information presented in this unusual manner is seen in the response some Ss have made spontaneously to a kinetic depth display. A modified version of the Metzger apparatus was used, consisting of a turntable on which two vertical white rods were mounted. This was rotated slowly before the camera and the Ss were asked to describe what they "saw." Some sighted Ss, upon first tactile presentation of this moving display, have spontaneously described it as moving in depth. Several blind Ss were given experience with a yoked pair of turntables. On one of these, an object was placed within view of the camera, while the S turned the other freely, experiencing the transformations that the object underwent with the rotation. After an hour's experience with this equipment, they could report accurately the eccentric placement of two and three objects on the turntable, and could also experience rotation in depth with the Metzger display.

DISCUSSION

This sytem was constructed in order to find out whether or not people could make sufficient use of it to warrant its serious consideration as a visual substitution system for the blind. The most striking feature of the initial results with the system is that Ss, blind and sighted, are able, after only relatively short training periods, to identify familiar objects and to describe their arrangement in depth. Such results are the basis for cautious optimism about the ultimate utility of a visual substitution system. Evidently even a crude 400-tactor system is capable of providing sufficient information to permit construction of what is usually called the visual world. The limits thus far encountered are attributable to the poverty of the display rather than to limitations in the capacity of the tactile perceptual system.

It will be important in subsequent models of the system to employ a lighter sensor than the present cumbersome television camera, a sensor that can be head-mounted so the S can scan his environment in a more congenial fashion. It will also be important to explore new factor configurations. Questions of optimal spacing of tactors and the resolution required in order to perform various tasks will require extensive investigation. Recent experiments in detection of small inner detail indicate that turning off half the tactors in the array makes surprisingly little difference. A second version of the system, presently under construction, will embody both a light head-mounted camera and a tactor array built in a wheel chair, thus giving the user a modest degree of mobility and making it possible to evaluate the system under a much wider range of conditions than has been possible thus far.

It is clear from these first tests with the visual substitution system that three-dimensional organization of the information in the dynamic tactile array is easily achieved. The demonstrations of the kinetic depth effect on the skin, and the instances of startle response to tactile looming are clear examples of such organization in this modality.

In addition to the three-dimensional interpretation of motion in tactile displays, the results thus far point to the great importance of self-generated motions on the part of the observer. When asked to identify static forms with camera fixed, Ss have a very difficult time; but when they are free to turn the camera to explore the figures, the discrimination is quickly established. With fixed camera, Ss report experiences in terms of feelings on their backs, but when they move the camera over the displays, they give reports in terms of externally localized objects in front of them. The camera motion here is analogous to eye movements in vision and this finding raises the interesting possibility that external localization of percepts may depend critically upon such movements.

It is at least a plausible hypothesis that a translation of the input that is precisely correlated with self-generated movement of the sensor is the necessary and sufficient condition for the experienced phenomena to be attributed to a stable outside world. The converse of this hypothesis should also hold—that a lack of correspondence between a translation of the input array and self-generated sensor movements should result in experiences that are attributed either to nonrigid conditions in the external world, or to phenomena that have their perceived origin within the observer. It would be of some interest to examine protocols from stabilized retinal-image experiments. Such a stabilization eliminates all correlation between eye movement and translations of the optic array. The finding that stabilized images fade has usually been interpreted to mean that fine eye movements are necessary in order to generate stable visual forms. It is possible that the stabilized retinal-image results may be due to the fact that the percepts arising under such conditions of stimulation are localized within the observer rather than in the outside world. As von Békésy (1967) points out, we are adept at tuning out such internal information as the taste of our own saliva or the sound of the blood in our ears. Perhaps we are equally adept at tuning out visual phenomena that are uncorrelated with eye movements. Certainly afterimages are apt to disappear abruptly and then reappear several times before they fade for good, and the motes in our eyes are seen only under special circumstances.

Whether or not this hypothesis about the basis for external localization of percepts is valid, the fact remains that Ss with this visual substitution system were seriously handicapped when they could not move the camera. At first we erroneously assumed that little or no significant form discrimination was possible with fixed camera, but later experiments disproved this when experienced blind Ss were able to make quick and accurate judgments of grill orientation without moving the camera. Static judgments of orientation of the checkerboard patterns were rare, however. The experienced blind Ss found it relatively easy to determine the plane of the tilt, a judgment similar to the bar-orientation task, but had considerable difficulty telling which edge of the display was near or far. For this, they all employed many scanning movements of the camera. This suggests that there may be some aspects of tactile information pickup that depend heavily upon changes in the tactile array, and in this respect operate differently from vision.

The tactor matrix in this system was arranged in four quadrants, as shown in Fig. 3. With such an arrangement, the space between the center columns of tactors was at least twice as wide as the spacing of the other columns. Interestingly enough, this wide silent area was not evident to any of the Ss. If a narrow vertical stripe was moved horizontally from one side of the field to the other, its path was perceived perfectly smooth with no jump in the middle, even though the tactile image had travelled twice as far in the same time when it crossed the center of the tactor matrix. The fissure in the tactor array is not comparable to the blind spot in the eyes since in the latter case this is a gap in the sensor so that information is not received in this region, while in the tactor-array case there is no gap in the camera field, just an irregularity in the spacing of the tactors. Both, however, seem to be invisible. It would be of some interest to see how far apart the two halves of the tactor matrix could be placed on the body before a S would report a gap.

Thus far there have been no salient differences between the blind and the sighted Ss in their acquisition of skill on this visual substitution system. As was mentioned previously, the relationship between visual angle subtended by an object and distance from the S is one that the blind have not experienced directly and thus have to be introduced to as a "cue" for distance. Some blind Ss have never been taught the shapes of the letters of the alphabet, so in order to teach the discrimination of such forms they have to be given an opportunity to handle cutout letters. But on the whole, the similarities between the performance of the two groups are far more striking than the differences.

The visual substitution system offers a unique vehicle for the study of perceptual learning. If one accepts a Hebbian position on the manner in which visual form discrimination is established, one would be inclined to expect that proficiency with this tactile system would be tediously acquired, especially for congenitally blind Ss who have had no previous opportunity to create the

Fig. 3. The 20 x 20 tactor array.

cell assemblies and phase sequences that Hebb postulates as the basis for visual form discrimination. Another more recent line of evidence on the neurophysiological basis of certain visual discriminations in lower animals suggests that they may be dependent upon highly specialized and surprisingly peripheral feature detectors in the visual system (Hubel & Wiesel, 1962; Lettvin et al, 1959). If such detectors are also to be found in the human eye, it might be predicted that detection of such features from tactile inputs would be difficult, if not impossible, since such detectors in all probability would not be found in the skin.

The Gibsonian (1966) view of perceptual learning would probably predict that, to the extent a tactile array contained the same temporal and spatial adjacencies to be found in the optic array, learning to respond to "the higher order invariances" in tactile stimulation should present no overwhelming difficulty. Also, Gibson would expect performance with the system to improve markedly when the observer was free to probe the environment to pick up information. Gibson has repeatedly stressed the importance of such exploratory activity in perception.

The results to date with the visual substitution system support the conclusion that facility is quite rapidly attained and that some Ss are able to make highly sophisticated discriminations with it almost as soon as they are put in the chair. One completely naive S, for example, was able to report accurately the shape of a hollow tetrahedron, complete with shape of the space that formed an internal detail. The learning seen thus far is certainly not of the prolonged sort postulated by Hebb in initial visual form discrimination. Nor have there been marked differences between the congenitally blind and sighted Ss, which might also be expected by empiricists like Hebb or Taylor (1962). Also, the results do not lend support to a theory of visual form perception that postulates highly specialized feature detectors at the retinal level, though the drastically impoverished display in the present tactual system makes any conclusions in this regard only tentative.

In the past, many efforts at providing information to the blind have been based upon hopelessly old-fashioned ideas about the way the perceptual system works. In psychological prehistory there used to be a distinction between sensation and perception. The former had to do with stimulation of end organs that sent their messages to the brain where they were synthesized and correlated through long experience until a percept emerged. Many efforts at creating sensory aids are still hung up on this antique notion and set out to provide a set of maximally discriminable sensations. With this approach, one almost immediately encounters the problem of overload—a sharp limitation in the rate at which the person can cope with the incoming information. It is the difference between landing an aircraft on the basis of a number of dials and pointers that provide readings on such things as airspeed, pitch, yaw, and roll, and landing a plane with a contact analog display. It is the difference between Skinner and John Holt. It is the difference between Titchener and Koffka. Visual perception thrives when it is flooded with information, when there is a whole page of prose before the eye, or a whole image of the environment; it falters when the input is diminished, when it is forced to read one word at a time, or when it must look at the world through a mailing tube. It would be rash to predict that the skin will be able to see all the things the eye can behold, but we would never have been able to say that it was possible to determine the identity and layout in three dimensions of a group of familiar objects if this system had been designed to deliver 400 maximally discriminable sensations to the skin. The perceptual systems of living organisms are the most remarkable information-reduction machines known. They are not seriously embarrassed in situations where an enormous proportion of the input must be filtered out or ignored, but they are invariably handicapped when the input is drastically curtailed or artificially encoded. Some of the controversy about the necessity of preprocessing sensory information stems from disappointment in the rates at which human beings can cope with discrete sensory events. It is possible that such evidence of overload reflects more an inappropriate display than a limitation of the perceiver. Certainly the limitations of this system are as yet more attributable to the poverty of the display than to taxing the information-handling capacities of the epidermis.

REFERENCES

BACH-y-RITA, P. Sensory plasticity: Applications to a vision substitution system. Acta Neurologica Scandinavica, 1967, 43, 417-426.
BACH-y-RITA, P., & COLLINS, C. C. Sensory plasticity and tactile image projection (abstract). Investigations in Ophthalmology, 1967, 6, 669.
BACH-y-RITA, P., COLLINS, C. C., WHITE, B. W., SAUNDERS, F., SCADDEN, L., & BLOMBERG, R. A tactile vision substitution system. American Journal of Optometry, 1969, 46, 109-111.
BACH-y-RITA, P., COLLINS, C. C., SAUNDERS, F., WHITE, B. W., & SCADDEN, L. Vision substitution by tactile image projection. Nature, 1969, 221, 963-964.
BÉKÉSY, G. von. Sensory inhibition. Princeton, N.J.: Princeton University Press, 1967.
COLLINS, C. C. Tactile image projection (abstract). National Symposium on Information Display, 1967, 8, 290.
GELDARD, F. A. Adventures in tactile literacy. American Psychologist, 1957, 12, 115-124.
GELDARD, F. A. Body English. Psychology Today, 1968, 2, 42-47.
GIBSON, J. J. *The senses considered as perceptual systems.* Boston: Houghton Mifflin Co., 1966.
HEBB, D. O. *Organization of behavior.* New York: Wiley, 1949.
HUBEL, D. H., & WIESEL, T. N. Receptive fields, binocular interaction, and functional architecture in the cat's visual cortex. Journal of Physiology, 1962, 160, 106-154.
LETTVIN, J. Y., MATURANA, H. R., McCULLOCH, W. S., & PITTS, W. H. What the frog's eye tells the frog's brain. Proceedings of the Institute of Radio Engineers, 1959, 47, 1940-1951.
LINVILLE, J. G., & BLISS, J. C. A direct translation reading aid for the blind. Proceedings of the Institute of Electrical & Electronics Engineers, 1966, 54, 40-51.
ROBERTS, L. G. Machine perception of three-dimensional solids. Technical Report No. 315, 1963, Lincoln Laboratory, M.I.T., Cambridge, Massachusetts.
SAUNDERS, F. Tactile television: Characteristics of visuo-spatial information. Proceedings of the A.F.B. Tactile Display Conference, Palo Alto, Calif., April 1969.
SCADDEN, L. The reception of visual images through the skin. New Scientist, 1969, 41, 677-678.
STARKIEWICZ, W., & KULIZEWSKI, T. Progress report on the electroftalm mobility aid. *Proceedings of the Rotterdam Mobility Research Conference.* New York: American Foundation for the Blind, 1965.
TAYLOR, J. G. *The behavioral basis of perception.* New Haven, Conn.: Yale University Press, 1962.

NOTES

1. Supported by DHEW, Social and Rehabilitation Service Grant No. RD-2444-S; USPHS Research Career Award No. 5 K3 NB-14,094 to P. Bach-y-Rita; Rosenberg Foundation grant; USPHS General Research Support Grant No. 5 S01 FR 05566; T. B. Walker Foundation; and Trust in Memory of Beatrice and James J. Ingels. We wish to thank Mrs. Betty Hart for valuable editorial assistance.

2. Address: Smith-Kettlewell Institute of Visual Sciences, Pacific Medical Center, San Francisco, California.

WHAT THE FROG'S EYE* TELLS THE FROG'S BRAIN

J. W. LETTVIN†
H. R. MATURANA‡
W. S. McCULLOCH‖
W. H. PITTS‖

Massachusetts Institute of Technology

Summary—In this paper, we analyze the activity of single fibers in the optic nerve of a frog. Our method is to find what sort of stimulus causes the largest activity in one nerve fiber and then what is the exciting aspect of that stimulus such that variations in everything else cause little change in the response. It has been known for the past 20 years that each fiber is connected not to a few rods and cones in the retina but to very many over a fair area. Our results show that for the most part within that area, it is not the light intensity itself but rather the pattern of local variation of intensity that is the exciting factor. There are four types of fibers, each type concerned with a different sort of pattern. Each type is uniformly distributed over the whole retina of the frog. Thus, there are four distinct parallel distributed channels whereby the frog's eye informs his brain about the visual image in terms of local pattern independent of average illumination. We describe the patterns and show the functional and anatomical separation of the channels. This work has been done on the frog, and our interpretation applies only to the frog.

INTRODUCTION

Behavior of a Frog

A FROG hunts on land by vision. He escapes enemies mainly by seeing them. His eyes do not move, as do ours, to follow prey, attend suspicious events, or search for things of interest. If his body changes its position with respect to gravity or the whole visual world is rotated about him, then he shows compensatory eye movements. These movements enter his hunting and evading habits only, *e.g.*, as he sits on a rocking lily pad. Thus his eyes are actively stabilized. He has no fovea, or region of greatest acuity in vision, upon which he must center a part of the image. He also has only a single visual system, retina to colliculus, not a double one such as ours where the retina sends fibers not only to colliculus but to the lateral geniculate body which relays to cerebral cortex. Thus, we chose to work on the frog because of the uniformity of his retina, the normal lack of eye and head movements except for those which stabilize the retinal image, and the relative simplicity of the connection of his eye to his brain.

The frog does not seem to see or, at any rate, is not concerned with the detail of stationary parts of the world around him. He will starve to death surrounded by food if it is not moving. His choice of food is determined only by size and movement. He will leap to capture any object the size of an insect or worm, providing it moves like one. He can be fooled easily not only by a bit of dangled meat but by any moving small object. His sex life is conducted by sound and touch. His choice of paths in escaping enemies does not seem to be governed by anything more devious than leaping to where it is darker. Since he is equally at home in water and on land, why should it matter where he lights after jumping or what particular direction he takes? He does remember a moving thing providing it stays within his field of vision and he is not distracted.

---

* Original manuscript received by the IRE, September 3, 1959. This work was supported in part by the U. S. Army (Signal Corps), the U. S. Air Force (Office of Sci. Res., Air Res. and Dev. Command), and the U. S. Navy (Office of Naval Res.); and in part by Bell Telephone Labs., Inc.
† Res. Lab. of Electronics and Dept. of Biology, Mass. Inst. Tech., Cambridge, Mass.
‡ Res. Lab. of Electronics, Mass. Inst. Tech., Cambridge, Mass., on leave from the University of Chile, Santiago, Chile.
‖ Res. Lab. of Electronics, Mass. Inst. Tech., Cambridge, Mass.

Reprinted from the *Proceedings of the Institute of Radio Engineers*, Vol. 47, No. 11, November, 1959.

WHAT THE FROG'S EYE TELLS THE FROG'S BRAIN

Anatomy of Frog Visual Apparatus

The retina of a frog is shown in Fig. 1(a). Between the rods and cones of the retina and the ganglion cells, whose axons form the optic nerve, lies a layer of connecting neurons (bipolars, horizontals, and amacrines). In the frog there are about 1 million receptors, $2\frac{1}{2}$ to $3\frac{1}{2}$ million connecting neurons, and half a million ganglion cells [1]. The connections are such that there is a synaptic path from a rod or cone to a great many ganglion cells, and a ganglion cell receives paths from a great many thousand receptors. Clearly, such an arrangement would not allow for good resolution were the retina meant to map an image in terms of light intensity point by point into a distribution of excitement in the optic nerve.

There is only one layer of ganglion cells in the frog. These cells are half a million in number (as against one million rods and cones). The neurons are packed together tightly in a sheet at the level of the cell bodies. Their dendrites, which may extend laterally from $50\,\mu$ to $500\,\mu$, interlace widely into what is called the inner plexiform layer, which is a close-packed neuropil containing the terminal arbors of those neurons that lie between receptors and ganglion cells. Thus, the amount of overlap of adjacent ganglion cells is enormous in respect to what they see. Morphologically, there are several types of these cells that are as distinct in their dendritic patterns as different species of trees, from which we infer that they work in different ways. The anatomy shown in the figures is that found in standard references. Further discussion of anatomical questions and additional original work on them will appear in a later publication.

Physiology as Known up to This Study

Hartline [2] first used the term *receptive field* for the region of retina within which a local change of brightness would cause the ganglion cell he was observing to discharge. Such a region is sometimes surrounded by an annulus, within which changes of brightness affect the cell's response to what is occurring in the receptive field, although the cell does not discharge to any event occurring in the annulus alone. Like Kuffler [4], we consider the receptive field and its interacting annulus as a single entity, with apologies to Dr. Hartline for the slight change in meaning. Hartline found three sorts of receptive field in the frog: ON, ON-OFF, and OFF. If a small spot of light suddenly appears in the receptive field of an ON-cell, the discharge soon begins, increases in rate to some limit determined by the intensity and area of the spot, and thereafter slowly declines. Turning off the spot abolishes the discharge.

If the small spot of light suddenly appears or disappears within the field of an ON-OFF cell, the discharge is short and occurs in both cases.

If the spot of light disappears from the field of an OFF cell, the discharge begins immediately, decreases slowly in frequency, and lasts a long time. It can be abolished promptly by turning the spot of light on again.

For all three sorts of field, sensitivity is greatest at the center of each field and least at the periphery.

Barlow [3] extended Hartline's observations. He observed that the OFF cells have an adding receptive field, *i.e.*, the response occurs always to OFF at both center and periphery of that field, and that the effect of removing light from the periphery adds to the effect of a reduction of light at the center, with a weight decreasing with distance.

The ON-OFF cells, however, have differencing receptive fields. A discharge of several spikes to the appearance of light in the center is much diminished if a light is turned on in the extreme periphery. The same interaction occurs when these lights are removed. Thus, an ON-OFF cell seems to be measuring inequality of illumination within its receptive field. (Kuffler [4] at the same time showed a similar mutual antagonism between center and periphery in each receptive field of ganglion cells in the eye of a cat, and later Barlow, Kuffler and Fitzhugh [5] showed that the size of the cat's receptive fields varied with general illumination.) Barlow saw that ON-OFF cells were profoundly sensitive to movement within the receptive field. The ON cells have not been characterized by similar methods.

These findings of Hartline and Barlow establish that optic nerve fibers (the axons of the ganglion cells) do not transmit information only about light intensity at single points in the retina. Rather, each fiber measures a certain feature of the whole distribution of light in an area of the receptive field. There are three sorts of function, or areal operation, according to these authors, so that the optic nerve looks at the image on the retina through three distributed channels. In any one channel, the overlap of individual receptive fields is very great. Thus one is led to the notion that what comes to the brain of a frog is this: for any visual event, the OFF channel tells how much dimming of light has occurred and where; the ON-OFF channel tells where the boundaries of lighted areas are moving, or where local inequalities of illumination are forming; the ON channel shows (with a delay) where brightening has occurred. To an unchanging visual pattern, the nerve ought to become fairly silent after a while.

Consider the retinal image as it appears in each of the three distributed channels. For both the OFF and ON channels, we can treat the operation on the image by supposing that every point on the retina gives rise to a blur about the size of a receptive field. Then the OFF channel tells, with a long decay time, where the blurred image is darkened, and the ON channel tells with a delay and long decay where it is brightened. The third channel, ON-OFF, principally registers moving edges. Having the mental picture of an image as it appears through the three kinds of channel, we are still faced with the question of how the animal abstracts what is useful to him from his surroundings. At this point, a safe position would be that a fair amount of data reduction has in fact been accomplished by the retina and that the interpretation is the work of the brain, a yet-to-be unravelled mystery. Yet the nagging worries remain: why are there two complementary projections of equally poor resolution? Why is the mosaic of receptors so uselessly fine?

Initial Argument

The assumption has always been that the eye mainly senses light, whose local distribution is transmitted to

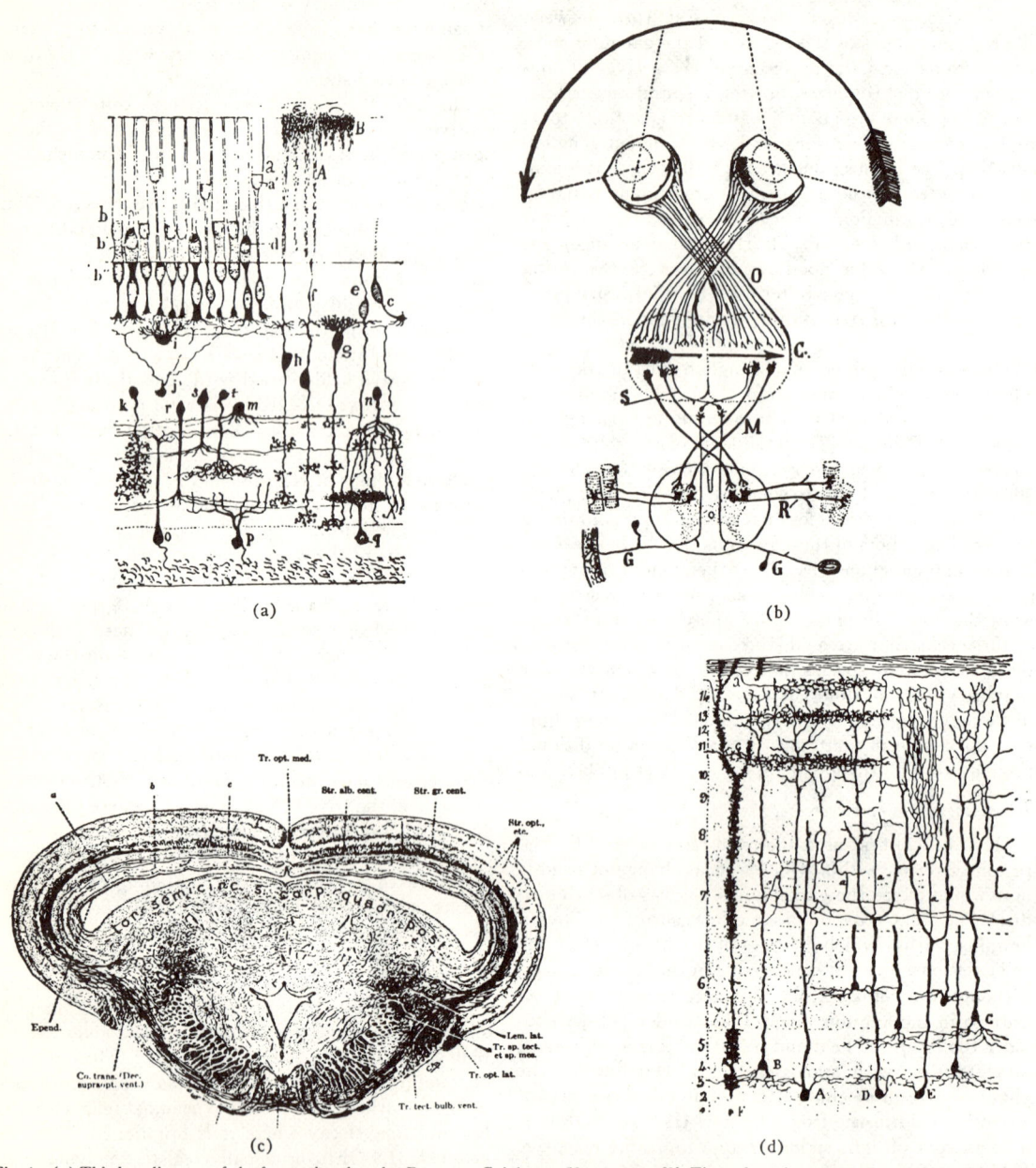

Fig. 1—(a) This is a diagram of the frog retina done by Ramon y Cajal over 50 years ago [9]. The rods and cones are the group of elements in the upper left quarter of the picture. To their bushy bottom ends are connected the bipolar cells of the intermediate layer, for example, *f*, *g*, and *h*. Lateral connecting neurons, called *horizontal* and *amacrine* cells, also occur in this layer, for example, *i*, *j* and *m*. The bipolars send their axons down to arborize in the inner plexiform layer, roughly the region bounded by cell *m* above and the bodies of the ganglion cells, *o*, *p* and *q*, below. In this sketch, Ramon has the axons of the bipolar cells emitting bushes at all levels in the plexiform layer; in fact, many of them branch at only one or two levels.
  Compare the dendrites of the different ganglion cells. Not only do they spread out at different levels in the plexiform layer, but the patterns of branching are different. Other ganglion cells, not shown here, have multiple arbors spreading out like a plane tree at two or three levels. If the terminals of the bipolar cells are systematically arranged in depth, making a laminar operational map of the rods and cones in terms of very local contrast, color, ON, OFF, etc., then the different shapes of the ganglion cells would correspond to different combinations of the local operations done by the bipolars. Thus would arise the more complex operations of the ganglion cells as described in the text. (b) This is Ramon y Cajal's diagram of the total decussation or crossing of the optic nerve fibers in the frog [9]. He made this picture to explain the value of the crossing as preserving continuity in the map of the visual world. *O* is the optic nerve and *C* is the *superior colliculus* or *optic tectum* (the names are synonymous). (c) This is Ariens-Kapper's picture of the cross section of the brain of a frog through the colliculus, which is the upper or dorsal part above the enclosed space. (d) This is Pedro Ramon Cajal's diagram of the nervous organization of the tectum of a frog. The terminal bushes of the optic nerve fibers are labelled *a*, *b*, and *c*. *A*, *B*, *C*, *D* and *E* are tectal cells receiving from the optic nerve fibers. Note that the axons of these cells come off the dendrites in stratum 7, which we call the *palisade* layer. The endings discussed in this paper lie between the surface and that stratum.

the brain in a kind of copy by a mosaic of impulses. Suppose we held otherwise, that the nervous apparatus in the eye is itself devoted to detecting certain patterns of light and their changes, corresponding to particular relations in the visible world. If this should be the case, the laws found by using small spots of light on the retina may be true and yet, in a sense, be misleading. Consider, for example, a bright spot appearing in a receptive field. Its actual and sensible properties include not only intensity, but the shape of its edge, its size, curvature, contrast, etc.

We decided then how we ought to work. First, we should find a way of recording from single myelinated and unmyelinated fibers in the intact optic nerve. Second, we should present the frog with as wide a range of visible stimuli as we could, not only spots of light but things he would be disposed to eat, other things from which he would flee, sundry geometrical figures, stationary and moving about, etc. From the variety of stimuli we should then try to discover what common features were abstracted by whatever groups of fibers we could find in the optic nerve. Third, we should seek the anatomical basis for the grouping.[1]

(Actual) Methods

Using a variant of Dowben and Rose's platinum black-tipped electrode described in another paper of this issue, we then began a systematic study of fibers in the optic nerve. One of the authors (H. R. M.) had completed the electron microscopy of optic nerve in frogs [8], and with his findings we were able to understand quickly why certain kinds of record occurred. He had found that the optic nerve of a frog contains about half a million fibers (ten times the earlier estimates by light microscopy). There are 30 times as many unmyelinated axons as myelinated, and both kinds are uniformly distributed throughout the nerve. The axons lie in small densely packed bundles of five to 100 fibers with about 100 A between axons, each bundle surrounded by one or more glial cells [8]. But along the nerve no bundle maintains its identity long, for the component fibers so braid between bundles that no two fibers stay adjacent. Thus the place a fiber crosses one section of the nerve bears little relation to its origin in the retina and little relation to where it crosses another section some distance away.

Fibers are so densely packed that one might suppose such braiding necessary to prevent serious interactions. On the other hand, the density makes the recording easier. A glial wall surrounds groups rather than single fibers, and penetration of the wall brings the tip among really bare axons each surrounded by neighbors whose effect is to increase the external impedance to its action currents, augmenting the external potential in propor-

tion. Thus, while we prefer to use platinum black tips to improve the ratio of signal to noise, we recorded much the same population with ordinary sharp microelectrodes of bright Pt or Ag. The method records equally well from unmyelinated and myelinated fibers.

We used *Rana pipiens* in these experiments. We opened a small flap of bone either just behind the eye to expose the optic nerve, or over the brain to expose the superior colliculus. No further surgery was done except to open the membranes of connective tissue overlying the nervous structure. The frog was held in extension to a cork platform and covered with moist cloth. An animal in such a position, having most of his body surface in physical contact with something, goes into a still reaction—*i.e.*, he will not even attempt to move save to pain, and except for the quick small incision of the skin at the start of the operation our procedure seems to be painless to him. With the animal mounted, we confront his eye with an aluminum hemisphere, 20 mils thick and 14 inches in diameter, silvered to a matte grey finish on the inner surface and held concentric to the eye. On the inner surface of this hemisphere, various objects attached to small magnets can be moved about by a large magnet moved by hand on the outer surface. On our hemisphere, 1° is slightly less than an eighth of an inch long. In the tests illustrated, we use as stimulating objects a dull black disk almost 1° in diameter and a rectangle 30° long and 12° wide. However, in the textual report, we use a variety of other objects. As an indicator for the stimulus, we first used a phototube looking at an image of the hemisphere taken through a camera lens and focussed on the plane of a diaphragm. (Later we used a photomultiplier, so connected as to give us a logarithmic response over about 4 decades.) Thus we could vary how much of the hemisphere was seen by the stimulus detector and match that area in position and size against the receptive field of the fiber we were studying. The output of this arrangement is the stimulus line in the figures.

Findings

There are four separate operations on the image in the frog's eye. Each has its result transmitted by a particular group of fibers, uniformly distributed across the retina, and they are all nearly independent of the general illumination. The operations are: *1) sustained contrast detection; 2) net convexity detection; 3) moving edge detection; and 4) net dimming detection*. The first two are reported by unmyelinated fibers, the last two by myelinated fibers. Since we are now dealing with events rather than point excitations as stimuli, receptive fields can only be defined approximately, and one cannot necessarily distinguish concentric subdivisions. The fibers reporting the different operations differ systematically not only in fiber diameter (or conduction velocity) but also in rough size of receptive field, which ranges from about 2° diameter for the first operation, to about 15° for the last. The following description of these groups is definite.

1) Sustained Contrast Detectors

An unmyelinated axon of this group does not respond when the general illumination is turned on or off. If the

---

[1] This program had started once before in our laboratory with A. Andrew [6], [7] of Glasgow who unfortunately had to return to Scotland before the work got well under way. However, he had reported in 1957 that he found elements in the colliculus of the frog that were sensitive to movement of a spot of light (a dot on an oscilloscope screen) even when the intensity of the spot was so low that turning it on and off produced no response. In particular, the elements he observed showed firing upon movement away from the centers of their receptive fields, but not to centripetal movements. As will appear later, this sort of response is a natural property of OFF fibers.

sharp edge of an object either lighter or darker than the background moves into its field and stops, it discharges promptly and continues discharging, no matter what the shape of the edge or whether the object is smaller or larger than the receptive field. The sustained discharge can be interrupted (or greatly reduced) in these axons by switching all light off. When the light is then restored, the sustained discharge begins again after a pause.

Indeed the response to turning on a distribution of light furnished with sharp contrast within the field is exactly that reported by Hartline for his ON fibers. In some fibers of this group, a contrast previously within the field is "remembered" after the light is turned off, for they will keep up a low mutter of activity that is not present if no contrast was there before. That this is not an extraordinary sensitivity of such an element in al-

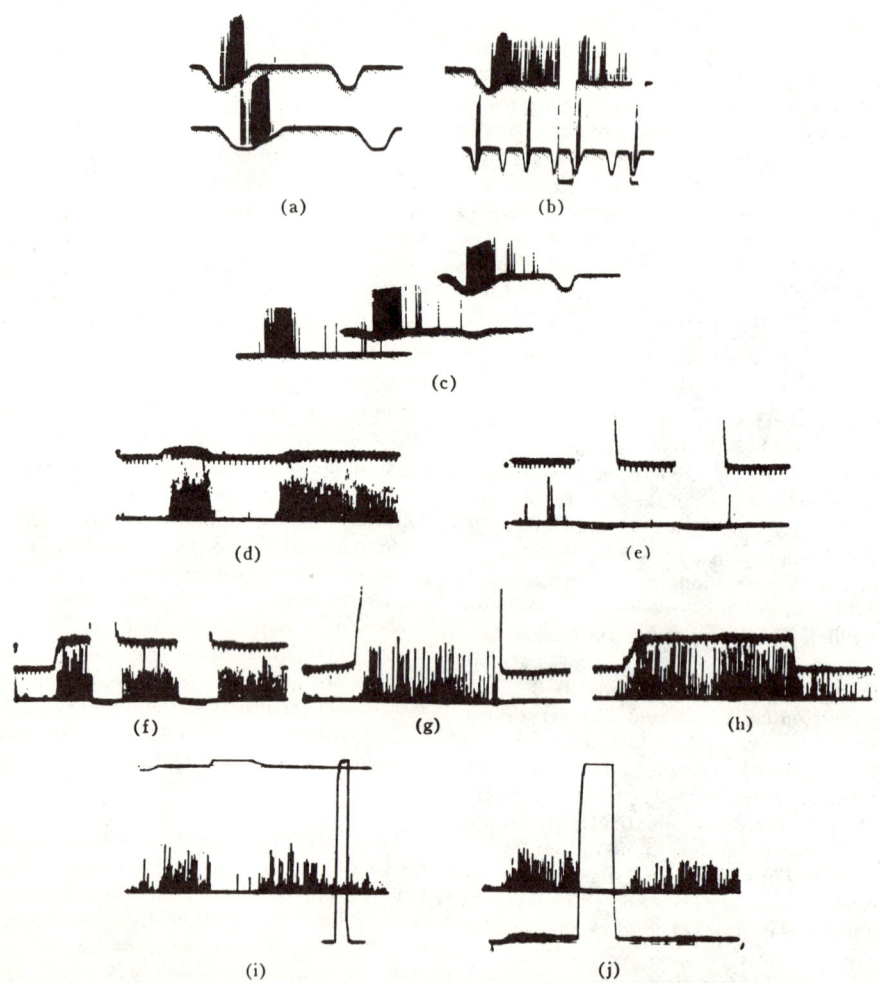

Fig. 2—Operation 1)—contrast detectors. The records were all taken directly with a Polaroid camera. The spikes are clipped at the lower end just above the noise and brightened on the screen. Occasional spikes have been intensified by hand for purposes of reproduction. The resolution is not good but we think that the responses are not ambiguous. Our alternate recording method is by means of a device which displays the logarithm of pulse interval of signals through a pulse height pick-off. However, such records would take too much explanation and would not add much to the substance of the present paper. (a) This record is from a single fiber in the optic nerve. The base line is the output of a photocell watching a somewhat larger area than the receptive field of the fiber. Darkening is given by downward deflection. The response is seen with the noise clipped off. The fiber discharge to movement of the edge of a 3° black disk passed in one direction but not to the reverse movement. (Time marks, 20 per second.) (b) The same fiber shown here giving a continued response when the edge stops in the field. The response disappears if the illumination is turned off and reappears when it is turned on. Below is shown again the asymmetry of the response to a faster movement. (Time marks, 20 per second.) (c) The same fiber is stimulated here to show asymmetrical response to the 3° black object moved in one direction, then the reverse and the stimuli are repeated under a little less than a 3-decade change of illumination in two steps. The bottom record is in extremely dim light, the top in very bright light. (Time marks, 20 per second.) (d) In the bottom line, a group of endings from such fibers is shown recorded from the first layer in the tectum. A black disk 1° in diameter is moved first through the field and then into the field and stopped. In the top line, the receptive field is watched by a photomultiplier (see text) and darkening is given by upward deflection. (Time marks, 5 per second for all tectal records.) (e) OFF and ON of general illumination has no effect on these fibers. (f) A 3° black disk is moved into the field and stopped. The response continues until the lights are turned OFF but reappears when the lights are turned ON. These fibers are nonerasable. (g) A very large black square is moved into the field and stopped. The response to the edge continues so long as the edge is in the field. (h) The 3° disk is again moved into the field and stopped. When it leaves, there is a slight after-discharge. (i) A 1° object is moved into the field, stopped, the light is then turned off, then on, and the response comes back. The light is, however, a little less than 300✕ dimmer than in the next frame. Full ON and OFF are given in the rectangular calibration on the right. (j) The same procedure as in Fig. 2(i) is done under very bright light. The return of response after reintroducing the light seems more prolonged—but this is due only to the fact that, in Fig. 2(i), the edge was not stopped in optimal position.

most complete darkness can be shown by importing a contrast into its receptive field after darkening in the absence of contrast. No mutter occurs then. This memory lasts for at least a minute of darkness in some units.

In Fig. 2 we see the response of such a fiber in the optic nerve. We compare these responses with full illumination (a 60-watt bulb and reflector mounted a foot away from the plane of the opening of the hemisphere) to those with less than 1/300 as much light (we put a variable resistance in series with the bulb so that the color changed also). We are struck by the smallness of the resulting change. In very dim light where we can barely see the stimulating object ourselves, we still get very much the same response.

2) Net Convexity Detectors

These fibers form the other subdivision of the unmyelinated population, and require a number of conditions to specify when they will respond. To our minds, this group contains the most remarkable elements in the optic nerve.

Such a fiber does not respond to change in general illumination. It does respond to a small object (3° or less) passed through the field; the response does not outlast the passage. It continues responding for a long time if the object is imported and left in the field, but the discharge is permanently turned off (erased) by a transient general darkness lasting 1/10 second or longer. We have not tried shorter obscurations.

The fiber will not respond to the straight edge of a dark object moving through its receptive field or brought there and stopped. If the field is about 7° in diameter, then, if we move a dark square 8° on the side through it with the edge in advance there is no response, but if the corner is in advance then there is a good one. Usually a fiber will respond indefinitely only to objects which have moved into the field and then lie wholly or almost wholly interior to the receptive field. The discharge is greater the greater the convexity, or positive curvature, of the boundary of the dark object until the object becomes as small as about ½ the width of the receptive field. At this point, we get the largest response on moving across that field, and a good, sustained response on entering it and stopping. As one uses smaller and smaller objects, the response to moving across the field begins to diminish at a size of about 1°, although the sustained response to coming in and stopping remains. In this way we find the smallest object to which these fibers respond is less than 3 minutes of arc. A smooth motion across the receptive field has less effect than a jerky one, if the jerks recur at intervals longer than ½ second. A displacement barely visible to the experimenter produces a marked increase in response which dies down slowly.

Any checked or dotted pattern (in the latter case, with dots no further apart than half the width of the receptive field) moved as a whole across the receptive field produces little if any response. However, if any dot within the receptive field moves differentially with respect to the background pattern, the response is to that dot as if it were moving alone. A group of two or three distinct spots enclosed within the receptive field and moved as a whole produce less direct response to movement and much less sustained response on stopping than if the spots are coalesced to a single larger spot.

A delightful exhibit uses a large color photograph of the natural habitat of a frog from a frog's eye view, flowers and grass. We can move this photograph through the receptive field of such a fiber, waving it around at a 7-inch distance: there is no response. If we perch with a magnet a fly-sized object 1° large on the part of the picture seen by the receptive field and move only the object we get an excellent response. If the object is fixed to the picture in about the same place and the whole moved about, then there is none.

Finally, the response does not depend on how much darker the object is than its background, so long as it is distinguishably so and has a clear-cut edge. If a disk has a very dark center and merges gradually into the grey of the background at the boundary, the response to it is very much less than to a uniform grey disk only slightly darker than the background. Objects lighter than the background produce almost no response unless they have enough relief to cast a slight shadow at the edge.

All the responses we have mentioned are relatively independent of illumination, and Fig. 3 taken as described in the caption shows the reactions to a 3° object and the large rectangle under some of the conditions described.

General Comments on Groups 1) and 2)

The two sorts of detectors mentioned seem to include all the unmyelinated fibers, with conduction velocities of 20 to 50 cm. The two groups are not entirely distinct. There are transition cases. On one hand, some convexity detectors respond well to very slightly curved edges, even so far as to show an occasional sustained response if that edge is left in the field. They may also not be completely erasable (though very markedly affected by an interruption of light) for small objects. On the other hand, others of the same group will be difficult to set into an indefinitely sustained response with any object, but only show a fairly long discharge, acting thereby more as detectors of edges although never reacting to straight edges. Nevertheless the distribution of the unmyelinated axons into two groups is very marked. Any fiber of either group may show a directional response— *i.e.*, there will be a direction of movement that may fail to excite the cell. For the contrast fibers, this will also appear as a nonexciting angle of the boundary with respect to the axis of the frog. Such null directions and angles cancel out in the aggregate.

3) Moving-Edge Detectors

These fibers are myelinated and conduct at a velocity in the neighborhood of 2 meters per second. They are the same as Hartline's and Barlow's ON-OFF units. The receptive field is about 12° wide. Such a fiber responds to any distinguishable edge moving through its receptive field, whether black against white or the other way around. Changing the extent of the edge makes little difference over a wide range, changing its speed a great one. It responds to an edge only if that edge moves, not otherwise. If an object wider than about 5°

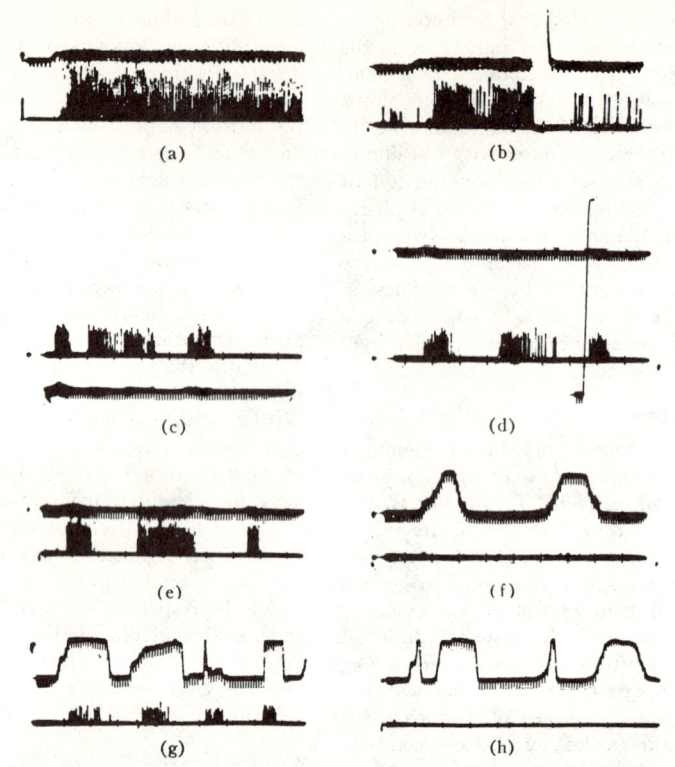

Fig. 3—Operation 2)—convexity detectors. The photomultiplier is used, and darkening is an upward deflection. (a) These records are all from the second layer of endings in the tectum. In the first picture, a 1° black disk is imported into the receptive field and left there. (b) The same event occurs as in Fig. 3(a), but now the light is turned off then on again. The response is much diminished and in the longer record vanishes. These fibers are erasable. (c) The 1° disk, is passed through the field first somewhat rapidly, then slowly, then rapidly. The light is very bright. (d) The same procedure occurs as in Fig. 3(c), but now the light has been dimmed about 300✕. The vertical line shows the range of the photomultiplier which has been adjusted for about 3½ decades of logarithmic response. (e) A 1° black disk is passed through the field at three speeds. (f) A 15° black strip is passed through at two speeds edge leading. (g) A 15° black strip is passed through in various ways with corner leading. (h) The same strip as in Fig. 3(g) is passed through, edge leading.

moves smoothly across the field, there are separate responses to the leading and trailing edges, as would be expected from Barlow's formulation. These fibers generally show two or three regularly spaced spikes, always synchronous among different fibers to turning the light on or off or both. The response to moving objects is much greater than to changes in total illumination and varies only slightly with general illumination over a range of 1/300. The frequency of the discharge increases with the velocity of the object within certain limits (see Fig. 4).

4) Net Dimming Detectors

These are Hartline's and Barlow's OFF fibers. But they have some properties not observed before. They are myelinated and the fastest conducting afferents, clocked at 10 meters per second.[2] One such fiber responds to sudden reduction of illumination by a prolonged and regular discharge. Indeed, the rhythm is so much the same from fiber to fiber that in recording from several at once after sudden darkening, the impulses assemble in groups, which break up only after many seconds. Even then the activity from widely separated retinal areas seems to be related. We observe that the surface potential of the colliculus shows a violent and prolonged oscillation when the light is turned off. This oscillation, beginning at about 18 per second and breaking into 3 to 5 per second after several seconds, seems to arise from these fibers from the retina; the same record is seen when the optic nerve is severed and the recording electrode placed on the retinal stump. See Fig. 5.

The receptive field is rather large—about 15°—and works as Barlow describes. Darkening of a spot produces less response when it is in the periphery of the field than when it is at the center. The effect of a moving object is directly related to its size and relative darkness. The response is prolonged if a large dark object stops within the field. It is almost independent of illumination, actually increasing as the light gets dimmer. There is a kind of erasure that is complementary to that of group 2). If the general lighting is sharply dimmed, but not turned off entirely, the consequent prolonged response is diminished or abolished after a dark object passes through the receptive field. In this case, the reasons for erasure are apparent. Suppose one turns off the light and sets up a prolonged response. Then the amount of light which must be restored to interrupt the response gets less and less the longer one

---

[2] The even faster fibers, with velocities up to 20 meters per second, we presently believe to be the efferents to the retina, but although there is some evidence for this, we are not yet quite certain.

WHAT THE FROG'S EYE TELLS THE FROG'S BRAIN

waits. That is, the sensitivity of the OFF discharge to the ON of light increases with time. If we darken the general lighting only by a factor of 100, we also get a prolonged discharge. However, if we turn off the light completely a few seconds after the 100/1 dimming and then turn it back on to the same dim level, the discharge is increased by the second dimming and is completely or almost completely abolished by the relighting. The effect of moving a dark object through the field after dimming is to impose a second dimming pulse followed by brightening as the object passes.

Others

Lastly, there is a small group of afferent fibers which does not seem to have distinct receptive fields. They each measure the absolute degree of darkness over a wide area with a long time constant. That is, the frequency of discharge is greater the darker it is. They have a complement in that some of the moving edge detectors have a resting discharge of very low frequency if the illumination is extremely bright

Discussion

Let us compress all of these findings in the following description. Consider that we have four fibers, one from each group, which are concentric in their receptive fields. Suppose that an object is moved about in this concentric array:

1) The contrast detector tells, in the smallest area of all, of the presence of a sharp boundary, moving or still, with much or little contrast.

2) The convexity detector informs us in a somewhat

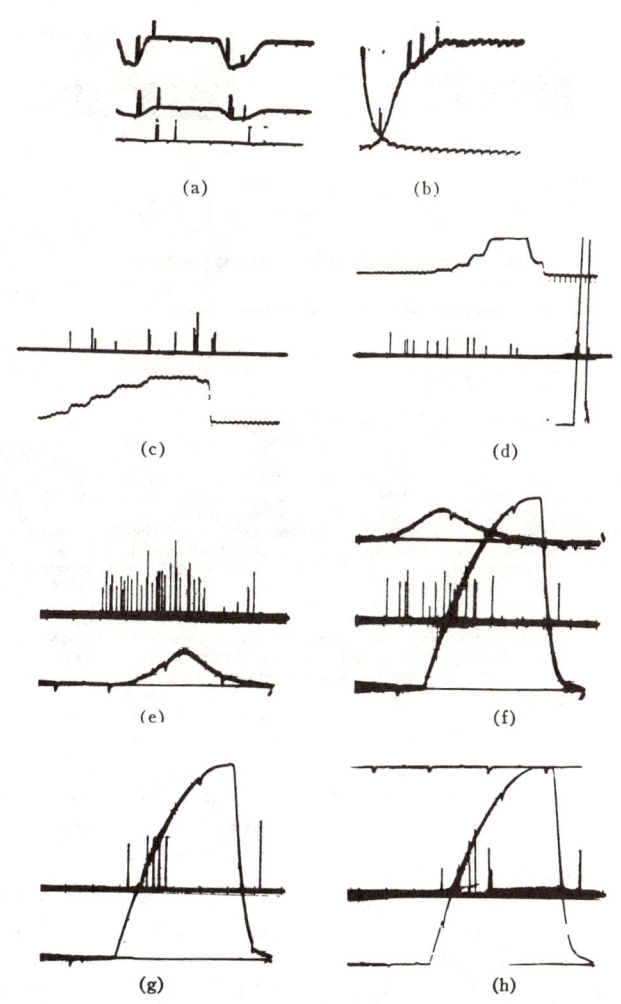

Fig. 4—Operation 3)—moving-edge detectors. The first two pictures are taken from a single fiber in the optic nerve. (a) Shows a 7° black disk moving through the receptive field (the photocell was not in registration with the field). There is a response to the front and back of the disk independent of illumination. There is about a 300/1 shift of illumination between top and bottom of the record. Darkening is a downward deflection with the photocell record. (Time marks, 5 per second.) (b) OFF and ON of general lighting. (Time marks, 50 per second.) Note double responses and spacing. (c) This and succeeding records are in the third layer of endings in the tectum. Several endings are recorded but not resolved. Darkening is an upward deflection of the photomultiplier record. The response is shown to the edge of a 15° square moved into and out of the field by jerks in bright light. (d) The same procedure occurs as in Fig. 4(c), but in dim light. Calibration figure is at the right. (e) The response is shown to a 7° black disk passed through the receptive fields under bright light. The sweep is faster, but the time marks are the same. (f) The same procedure as for Fig. 4(e), but under dim light. The OFF and ON of the photomultiplier record was superimposed for calibration. (g) OFF and ON response with about half a second between ON and OFF. (h) Same as Fig. 4(g), but with 2 seconds between OFF and ON.

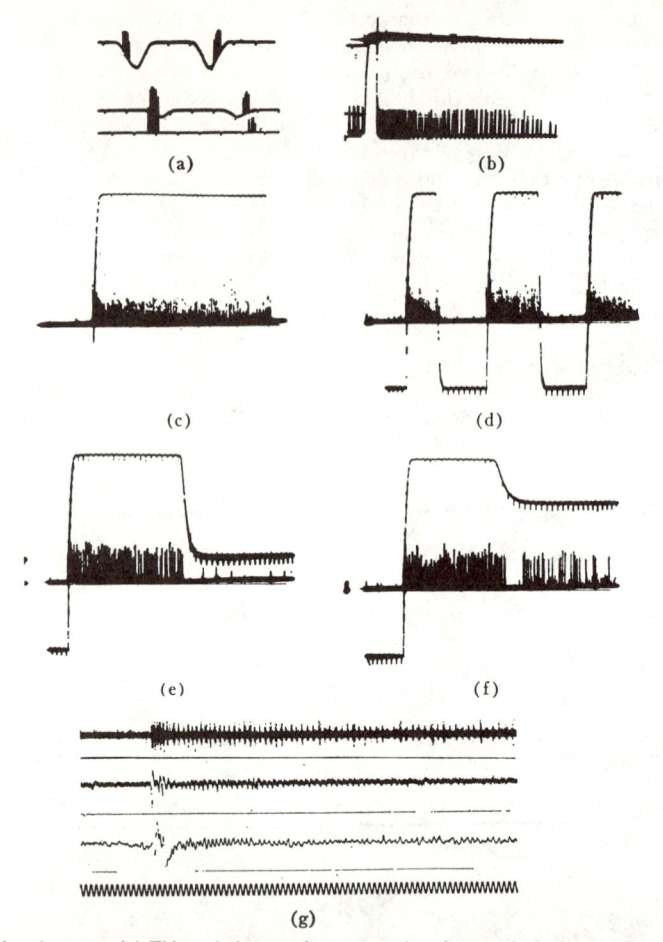

Fig. 5—Operation 4)—dimming detectors. (a) This and the next frame are taken from a single fiber in the optic nerve. Here we see the response to a 7° black disk passing through the receptive field. The three records are taken at three illumination levels over a 300:1 range. In the phototube record, darkening is a downward deflection. (Time marks, 5 per second.) (b) OFF and ON of light. The OFF was done shortly after one sweep began, the ON occurred a little earlier on the next sweep. The fiber is silenced completely by the ON. (Time marks, 5 per second.) (c) In this and the next three frames, we are recording from the fourth layer of endings in the tectum. This frame shows the response to turning OFF the general illumination. (d) OFF and ON of light at regular intervals. (e) OFF then ON of the light to a lesser brightness. (f) OFF then ON of the light to a still lesser brightness. The level to which the ON must come to abolish activity decreases steadily with time. (g) The synchrony of the dimming detectors as described in the text. At the top are three or four fibers recorded together in the optic nerve when the light is suddenly turned off. The fibers come from diverse areas on the retina. In the second line are the oscillations recorded from the freshly cut retinal stump of the optic nerve when the light is suddenly turned off. In the third line are the oscillations recorded on the surface of the tectum, the visual brain, before the nerve was cut. Again the light is suddenly turned off. The last line is 20 cps. These records of synchrony were obviously not all made at the same time, so that comparing them in detail is not profitable.

larger area whether or not the object has a curved boundary, if it is darker than the background and moving on it; it remembers the object when it has stopped, providing the boundary lies totally within that area and is sharp; it shows most activity if the enclosed object moves intermittently with respect to a background. The memory of the object is abolished if a shadow obscures the object for a moment.

3) The moving-edge detector tells whether or not there is a moving boundary in a yet larger area within the field.

4) The dimming detector tells us how much dimming occurs in the largest area, weighted by distance from the center and by how fast it happens.

All of the operations are independent of general illumination. There are 30 times as many of the first two detectors as of the last two, and the sensitivity to sharpness of edge or increments of movement in the first two is also higher than in the last two.

Results in the Tectum

As remarked earlier, the optic nerve fibers are all disordered in position through the nerve. That is, the probability that any two adjacent fibers look at the same region in the retina is very small. However, when the fibers terminate in the superior colliculus they do so in an orderly way such that the termini exhibit a continuous map of the retina. Each optic nerve crosses the base of the skull and enters the opposite tectum [Fig. 1(b)] via two bundles—one rostromedial, the other caudalateral. The fibers sweep out over the tectum in the superficial neuropil in what grossly appears to be a laminated

WHAT THE FROG'S EYE TELLS THE FROG'S BRAIN

way [Fig. 1(c)]. The detail of ending is not known, and there is some reason to think Pedro Ramon's drawing [9] is too diagrammatic [Fig. 1(d)], however well it fits with our data.

In any case, the outer husk of neuropil, roughly about half the thickness of the optic tectum, is formed of the endings of the optic fibers mixed with dendrites of the deeper lying cells, and in this felting lie few cell bodies.

We have found it singularly easy to record from these terminal bushes of the optic fibers. That is, if an electrode is introduced in the middle of one bush, the external potential produced by action currents in any branch increases in proportion to the number of branches near the electrode. Since the bushes are densely interdigitated everywhere, it is not difficult to record from terminal arbors anywhere unless one kills or blocks them locally, as is easily done by pressure, etc.

One may inquire how we can be sure of recording from terminal arbors, and not from cells and their dendrites. The argument is this. First, there are about four layers of cells in the depths of the tectum [Fig. 1(d)], and only their dendrites issue into the superficial neuropil wherein lie very few cells indeed. There are about 250,000 of these cells in all, compared to 500,000 optic fibers. In the outer thickness of the tectum, among the terminating fibers, almost every element we record performs one of the four operations characterizing the fibers in the nerve, and has a corresponding receptive field. Now as the electrode moves down from the surface in one track, we record 5 to 10 cells in the deepest half of the tectum. Not a single cell so recorded shows activity even remotely resembling what we find in the superficial neuropil. Among the cells, none show optic nerve operations, and the smallest receptive fields we find are over 30° in diameter. If the active elements in the upper layers are cells (one will see about 20 to 30 active elements in one electrode track before reaching the cell layer), which cells can they be? Or if they are dendrites, to what neurons do they belong? We regard these considerations as conclusive enough.

Figs. 2–5 show that the four operational groups of fibers terminate in four separate layers of terminals, each layer exhibiting a continuous map of the retina (we confirm Gaze's diagram of the projection [10]) and all four maps are in registration. Most superficial lie the endings for the contrast detectors, the slowest fibers. Beneath them, but not so distinctly separate, are the convexity detectors. Deeper, and rather well separated, are the moving-edge detectors admixed with the rare and ill-defined axons that measure the actual level of darkness. Deepest (and occasionally contaminated with tectal cells or their axons) lie the dimming detectors. Thus the depth at which these fibers end is directly related to their speed of conduction.

Such an arrangement makes experiment easy, for all the fibers of one operation performed on the same field in the retina end in one place in the tectum and can be recorded as a group. It is very useful to see them this way, for then the individual variations among similar units cancel one another and only the common properties remain. We made the tectal records shown in the accompanying figures with a single electrode in two penetrations (to get decent separation of contrast and convexity detectors which lie just below the pia), to show how clear-cut the arrangement is.

CONFIRMATION OF SPERRY'S PROPOSAL

The existence of a fourfold map of the retina in the tectal neuropil led us, naturally, to repeat Sperry's initial experiment on the regeneration of cut optic nerve [11]. Since the nerve is as scrambled as it can be originally, we saw no point in turning the eye around 180° but simply cut one nerve in a few frogs, separated the stumps to be sure of complete severance, and waited for about 3 months. At the end of this time, after it was clear that the cut nerves were functioning again, we compared the tectal maps of the cut and uncut nerves in some of them. We confirmed (as did Gaze [12]) Sperry's proposal that the fibers grew back to the regions where they originally terminated in mapping the retina [13]. But we also found a restoration of the four layers with no error or mixing. In one frog, after 90 days, the fibers had grown back best at the entrance of the two brachia to the colliculus, and least at the center, yet there were no serious errors. The total area of retina communicating with one point of the collicular neuropil (*i.e.*, the sum of the receptive fields of the fibers recorded from that point) had increased three or four times, from a diameter of about 15° to a diameter of about 30°. But there was no admixture of fibers with receptive fields in widely separated regions. In another frog, after 120 days, the area seen from one point was barely twice normal.

GENERAL DISCUSSION

What are the consequences of this work? Fundamentally, it shows that the eye speaks to the brain in a language already highly organized and interpreted, instead of transmitting some more or less accurate copy of the distribution of light on the receptors. As a crude analogy, suppose that we have a man watching the clouds and reporting them to a weather station. If he is using a code, and one can see his portion of the sky too, then it is not difficult to find out what he is saying. It is certainly true that he is watching a distribution of light; nevertheless, local variations of light are not the terms in which he speaks nor the terms in which he is best understood. Indeed, if his vocabulary is restricted to types of things that he sees in the sky, trying to find his language by using flashes of light as stimuli will certainly fail. Now, since the purpose of a frog's vision is to get him food and allow him to evade predators no matter how bright or dim it is about him, it is not enough to know the reaction of his visual system to points of light. To get useful records from individual receptors (the rods and cones), assuming that they operate independently and under no reflex control, this stimulus may be adequate. But when one inspects responses that are a few nervous transformations removed from the receptors, as in the optic nerve, that same choice of stimulus is difficult to defend. It is equivalent to assuming that all of the interpretation is done further on in the nervous system. But, as we have seen, this is false.

One might attempt to measure numerically how the response of each kind of fiber varies with various properties of the successions of patterns of light which evoke them. But to characterize a succession of patterns in space requires knowledge of so many independent variables that this is hardly possible by experimental enumeration of cases. To examine the effect of curvature alone we should have to explore at least the response to all configurations of three spots moving in a large variety of ways. We would prefer to state the operations of ganglion cells as simply as possible in terms of whatever *quality* they seem to detect and, instead, examine the bipolar cells in the retina, expecting to find there a dissection of the operations into combinations of simpler ones performed at intermediate stages. For example, suppose that there are at least two sorts of rods and cones, one increasing its voltage with the log of light at one color, the other decreasing its voltage with the log of light at some other color. If bipolars connect to several contiguous rods or cones of opposing reactions and simply add voltages, some bipolars will register a large signal only if an appropriate contrast occurs. We have in fact found something of the sort occurring, for it seems that the inner plexiform layer of the retina is stratified to display several different local properties, one layer indicating local differences in intensity of light. Some of Svaetichin's [14] data can be adduced here. The different dendritic distribution of the ganglion cells, as in Fig. 1(a), may signify that they extract differently weighted samples of simple local operations done by the bipolars, and it is on this that we are now working.

But there is another reason for a reluctance to make accurate measurements on the activity of ganglion cells in the intact animal. A significant efferent outflow goes to the retina from the brain. We now know to a certain extent how the cells in the tectum handle the four inputs to them which are described in this paper. There are at least two distinct classes of these cells, and at least one of them issues axons back into the optic nerve. We have recorded this activity there. Such axons enter the retina and we think some effects of their activity on the sensitivity of ganglion cells are noticeable.

The way that the retina projects to the tectum suggests a nineteenth century view of visual space. The image on the retina, taken at the grain of the rods and cones, is an array of regularly spaced points at each of which there is a certain amount of light of a certain composition. If we know the position of every point and the values of light at every point, we can physically reconstruct the image, and looking at it understand the picture. If, however, we are required to establish continuities within the picture only from the numerical data on position and light at independent points, it becomes a very difficult task. The retina projects onto the tectum in four parallel sheets of endings, each sheet mapping continuously the retina in terms of a particular areal operation, and all four maps are in registration. Consider the dendrite of a tectal cell extending up through the four sheets. It is looking at a point in the image on the retina, but that point is now seen in terms of the properties of its neighborhood as defined by the operations. Since the overlap of receptive fields within any operation is very great, it now seems reasonable to erect simple criteria for finding continuities. For example, if an area over which there is little change in the fourfold signature of a moving object is bounded by regions of different signature, it seems likely that that area describes the image of a single object.

By transforming the image from a space of simple discrete points to a congruent space where each equivalent point is described by the intersection of particular qualities in its neighborhood, we can then give the image in terms of distributions of combinations of those qualities. In short, every point is seen in definite contexts. The character of these contexts, genetically built in, is the physiological synthetic *a priori*. The operations found in the frog make unlikely later processes in his system of the sort described by two of us earlier [15], for example, dilatations; but those were adduced for the sort of form recognition which the frog does not have. This work is an outgrowth of that earlier study which set the question.

CONCLUSION

The output from the retina of the frog is a set of four distributed operations on the visual image. These operations are independent of the level of general illumination and express the image in terms of: 1) local sharp edges and contrast; 2) the curvature of edge of a dark object; 3) the movement of edges; and 4) the local dimmings produced by movement or rapid general darkening. Each group of fibers serving one operation maps the retina continuously in a single sheet of endings in the frog's brain. There are four such sheets in the brain, corresponding to the four operations, and their maps are in registration. When all axonal connections between eye and brain are broken and the fibers grow back, they reconstitute the original retinal maps and also arrange themselves in depth in the original order with no mistakes. If there is any randomness in the connections of this system it must be at a very fine level indeed. In this, we consider that Sperry [11] is completely right.

We have described each of the operations on the retinal image in terms of what common factors in a large variety of stimuli cause response and what common factors have no effect. What, then, does a particular fiber in the optic nerve measure? We have considered it to be how much there is in a stimulus of that quality which excites the fiber maximally, naming that quality.

The operations thus have much more the flavor of perception than of sensation if that distinction has any meaning now. That is to say that the language in which they are best described is the language of complex abstractions from the visual image. We have been tempted, for example, to call the convexity detectors "bug perceivers." Such a fiber [operation 2] responds best when a dark object, smaller than a receptive field, enters that field, stops, and moves about intermittently thereafter. The response is not affected if the lighting changes or if the background (say a picture of grass and flowers) is moving, and is not there if only the background, moving or still, is in the field. Could one better describe a system for detecting an accessible bug?

Acknowledgment

We are particularly grateful to O. G. Selfridge whose experiments with mechanical recognizers of pattern helped drive us to this work and whose criticism in part shaped its course.

Bibliography

[1] H. R. Maturana, "Number of fibers in the optic nerve and the number of ganglion cells in the retina of Anurans," *Nature*, vol. 183, pp. 1406–1407; May 16, 1959.

[2] H. K. Hartline, "The response of single optic nerve fibres of the vertebrate eye to illumination of the retina," *Amer. J. Physiol.*, vol. 121, pp. 400–415; February, 1938.
Also, "The receptive fields of the optic nerve fibers," *Amer. J. Physiol.*, vol. 130, pp. 690–699; October, 1940.

[3] H. B. Barlow, "Summation and inhibition in the frog's retina," *J. Physiol.*, vol. 119, pp. 69–88; January, 1953.

[4] S. W. Kuffler, "Discharge patterns and functional organization of mammalian retina," *J. Neurophysiol.*, vol. 16, pp. 37–68; January, 1953.

[5] H. B. Barlow, R. Fitzhugh, and S. W. Kuffler, "Change of organization in the receptive fields of the cat's retina during dark adaptation," *J. Physiol.*, vol. 137, pp. 338–354; August, 1957.

[6] A. M. Andrew, "Report on Frog Colliculus," Res. Lab. of Electronics, Mass. Inst. Tech., Cambridge, Quarterly Progress Rept., pp. 77–78; July 15, 1955.

[7] A. M. Andrew, "Action potentials from the frog colliculus," *J. Physiol.*, vol. 130, p. 25P; September 23–24, 1955.

[8] H. R. Maturana, "The Fine Structure of the Optic Nerve and Tectum of Anurans. An Electron Microscope Study," Ph.D. dissertation, Harvard University, Cambridge, Mass.; 1958.

[9] Pedro Ramon Cajal, "Histologie du Systeme Nerveux," Ramon y Cajal, Maloine, Paris, France; 1909–1911.

[10] R. M. Gaze, "The representation of the retina on the optic lobe of the frog," *Quart. J. Exper. Physiol.*, vol. 43, pp. 209–214; March, 1958.

[11] R. Sperry, "Mechanisms of neural maturation," in "Handbook of Experimental Psychology," S. S. Stevens, Ed., John Wiley and Sons, Inc., New York, N. Y.; 1951.

[12] R. M. Gaze, "Regeneration of the optic nerve in *Xenopus laevi*," *J. Physiol.*, vol. 146, p. 40P; February 20–21, 1959.

[13] H. R. Maturana, J. Y. Lettvin, W. S. McCulloch, and W. H. Pitts, "Physiological evidence that cut optic nerve fibers in the frog regenerate to their proper places in the tectum," *Science*; 1959 (in press).

[14] G. Svaetichin and E. F. NcNichol Jr., "Retinal mechanisms for chromatic and achromatic vision," *Ann. N. Y. Acad. Sci.*, vol. 74, pp. 385–404; November, 1958.

[15] W. S. McCulloch and W. H. Pitts, "How we know universals. The perception of auditory and visual forms," *Bull. Math. Biophysics*, vol. 9, pp. 127–147; June, 1947.

PAIN AS A PUZZLE FOR PSYCHOLOGY AND PHYSIOLOGY[1]

ERNEST R. HILGARD

Stanford University

PAIN is so familiar that we take it for granted, but this does not lessen its importance. Pain reduction is a primary task of the physician, second only to the preservation of life. The ubiquity of pain is clear enough from the many advertisements which pit one pain killer against another. Because pain is so important, and interest in pain is so great, it is surprising how little firm knowledge there is about pain.

What Is Puzzling about Pain?

The very familiarity of pain may cause us to acknowledge it without questioning it. Pain appears to warn us of tissue damage, and it is easy to assign a superficial interpretation that it is merely "the cry of an injured nerve." When one does begin to question pain, however, there are many mysteries that remain to be unraveled. I wish to mention some of these before reporting some of our own experiments on pain and its reduction.

[1] The preparation of this article and the investigations here reported have been supported by the National Institute of Mental Health, Public Health Service, Grant MH-3859, and by a contract with the United States Air Force Office of Research (Contract AF 49 [638]-1436). Requests for reprints should be sent to Hilgard, Department of Psychology, Stanford University, Stanford, California 94305.

1. *Is pain a sensory modality?* The first question is this: Shall we consider pain to be a sensory modality like vision or audition? If you cut your finger or stub your toe, pain behaves very much as if it were an ordinary sensory modality. That is, there is a stimulus, there are receptors in the fingers and toes, there is an afferent transmission of impulses, a central processing of data, a perceptual response appropriate to the stimulus, and perhaps some verbal accompaniment, such as "Ouch." The perceptual response of felt pain localized in a finger or a toe is analogous to seeing a light off to the left or of hearing a sound off to your right. Perceptual responses give knowledge of environmental events, and you guide your actions accordingly. Furthermore, the stimulus to pain can be graduated, as by an electric shock of varying intensity, or by water at different degrees of hot or cold, with subsequent changes in felt pain. All that I have said thus far qualifies pain as a sensory modality.

But there are other considerations which make it less easy to assign pain the status of a sensory modality. Most defined sensory modalities have definite stimuli, definite receptors, specific sensory tracts, and localized receptive areas within the cortex. Not so for pain. Any stimulus can qualify to produce pain if it is intense enough; loud sounds and very bright lights are painful. The receptors are unspecified, despite the role traditionally assigned to free nerve endings. While there are pathways for cutaneous pain, there are at least two afferent systems, and they operate quite differently (Melzack & Wall, 1965). And there is no one pain center that has been localized in the brain.

A further problem arises in that there are so many differences in the quality of felt pain that it may be as dubious to consider pain a single sense as to consider all cutaneous experiences as belonging to a single sense of touch. Even the attempt to define pain has met numerous obstacles (e.g., Beecher, 1959; Melzack, 1968). One of the puzzles is how to deal with the distinction between mild sensory pain and the intense pains that are described as suffering or anguish; under frontal lobe operations, for example, the anguish may be reduced even though the pain remains.

We must therefore give a qualified answer to the question whether or not pain can be counted as a sensory modality.

2. *Are there any satisfactory physiological indicators of pain?* We know about pain through a subject's verbal reports, but if we expect to objectify the amount of pain he feels we would be happy to have some physiological indicators by which to compare his pain with that of others who suffer. Our second question is, then: Do satisfactory indicators exist?

A satisfactory physiological indicator of pain is one which is present (or increased) when pain is felt, and absent (or reduced) when pain is not felt. The correlation between the physiological indicator and the verbal report has to be established both positively and negatively if the indicator is to be used in confidence in the absence of supplementary verbal report. Without attempting at this time a literature review, may I simply summarize the state of our knowledge of the physiological correlates of pain by saying that there is at present *no single accepted indicator of pain* that can be counted to vary in an orderly way with degrees of pain and absence of pain.[2] While in many experiments some kind of average difference in a physiological response can be detected with increase in pain, individual differences in the patterning of responses, and some individual response stereotypy to different kinds of stress, complicate the problem.

3. *Where is the pain that is felt?* My third question about the puzzle of pain is this: Where is the pain that the subject reports? A subject locates the pain of an injury at the site of the injury or noxious stimulation by the same sorts of local signs and environmental references that he uses in localizing other sources of stimulation. I say: "I feel pain in my finger." My listener sees that the finger is bleeding, and replies: "No wonder you feel pain in your finger; you cut it." The pain is in my finger just as the word I read is on the printed page. The psychoneural *conditions* of feeling pain and of seeing words are within me, but it would be as uninformative to say that the pain is in my head as to say that the word I read is in my head. We have to distinguish between the *conditions* of the perception and the *informative aspect* of the perception itself. The *information* is of a pain in my finger and of a word on the printed page.

The trouble about pain as informative is that there are at least three kinds of pain which make us wonder whether or not to accept information conferred by the localized pain. The first of these is *referred* pain, in which the source of irritation is one place and the pain is felt at another place, as in heartburn as the result of indigestion. The second is *psychosomatic* pain, in which the stimulus conditions may be vague, as in a headache following a political argument. The third kind is *phantom-limb* pain, where the pain is felt in a part of the body which has been amputated from it. Of these, phantom-limb pain is particularly interesting. Our tendency to revert to a strict sensory analogy is very strong; hence we would expect phantom-limb pain to be the result of referring the stimulation of a cut nerve in the stump to the limb from which it originally received its impulses. However, phantom-limb pain probably has more to do with body image than with local signs (Melzack, 1968; Sternbach, 1968; Szasz, 1957). The reply to our question must then be that, *as information* (even if it be false), the best we can do is to accept that the pains are where they are felt, including the phantom-limb pains; as *conditions* for pain, there are many complex events within the nervous system.

4. *How account for the great individual differences in felt pain?* My fourth and final question about the puzzle of pain has to do with the *lack* of relationship between the conditions of

---

[2] There have been a great many reviews of the literature on pain, of which Melzack (1968) and Sternbach (1968) can serve as recent representatives and as sources of citations of earlier reviews.

noxious stimulation and the amount of pain that is felt. This is primarily a matter of individual differences, but they are very impressive. I am not talking about the extreme cases of people who are born with practically complete lack of sensitivity to cutaneous or other pains. These people correspond in their own way to the totally blind or the totally deaf. Within the normal population, however, there are widespread differences, and it is these which concern us now.

In the relief of postsurgical pain through morphine, Beecher (1959) and his associates have found results that may be summarized roughly as follows: about a third of the patients gain relief of pain through morphine that is greater than the relief following a placebo; about a third get as much relief from a placebo as they do from morphine; the final third are relieved neither by placebo nor by morphine in doses considered safe to use.

Differences in pain responses are found to be related to cognitive styles by Petrie (1967). She reports that subjects selected on the basis of a test of kinesthetic aftereffects can be classified as *augmenters* or *reducers:* the augmenters exaggerate their pain responses and the reducers tend to inhibit theirs.

Differences in pain responsiveness, particularly complaints about pain, have been found to be associated with social class, ethnic groups, and family constellation. For example, Gonda (1962a, 1962b) found that those from the working class complain more to the nurses in hospitals than do those from white-collar classes, an observation confirmed in England as well as in the United States.

Finally, pain responses in the laboratory appear to follow some of the theories of cognitive consistency, in that the pain corresponds to the amount of reward offered for participating in pain experiments—the greater the reward the greater the pain—as though some suffering is consistent with the higher pay for participation (Lewin, 1965; Zimbardo, Cohen, Weisenberg, Dworkin, & Firestone, 1966; Zimbardo, 1969).

By raising these four questions, about pain as a sensory modality, about the physiological indicators of pain, about where pain is felt, and about individual differences in pain responsiveness, I hope that you will now agree that there are sufficient unsolved problems to make a concerned attack on pain a fruitful scientific enterprise.

Pain as a Sensory Modality: Cold Pressor Response and Ischemic Pain in the Normal Waking State [3]

We have used two sources of noxious stimulation in the experiments I am about to report. In the first of these pain is produced by placing the subject's hand and forearm in circulating cold water at several temperatures. This arrangement is commonly referred to as the *cold pressor test* (Greene, Boltax, Lustig, & Rogow, 1965; Hines & Brown, 1932; Wolf & Hardy, 1941). In the second method pain is produced by first placing a tourniquet just above the elbow, and then asking the subject to squeeze a dynamometer a standard number of times. After he quits working and is quiet, the pain begins to mount. This we call *ischemic pain,* following the practice of Beecher and his associates (Beecher, 1966; Smith, Lawrence, Markowitz, Mosteller, & Beecher, 1966). Their method is a modification of the method initiated by Lewis, Pickering, and Rothschild (1931).

First, the cold pressor test. I shall not report here the details of experimental arrangements, which will appear in due course in the form of journal articles. Suffice it to say that there are base-line conditions: first, a *vigilance* condition, in which the subject keeps alert by pressing the appropriate one of a pair of buttons, to turn off that one of two discriminable sounds which happens to be sounding; this is followed by a condition of *relaxation* for several minutes prior to the immersion of the hand and forearm in the cold water; the *immersion period,* usually of 40 seconds; then, after the hand and arm are removed from the water and dried, a repetition of the vigilance and relaxation conditions. Except as part of the situational background, the base-line conditions are not important for the present psychophysical account, but they are important for the physiological measures which were taken concomitantly with the

---

[3] Among the professional workers in the Laboratory of Hypnosis Research who have contributed most directly to the pain studies reported here the author wishes to mention Leslie M. Cooper, Arthur F. Lange, John R. Lenox, Arlene H. Morgan, Lewis B. Sachs, Toshimasa Saito, and John Voevodsky. A number of others have assisted in the record reading and data analysis. The author wishes to express his appreciation to these co-workers for permitting him to make use of the results of joint efforts as they have appeared in reports already published, and as they will appear in other reports in which the participants will be coauthors.

verbal reports. While the hand and forearm are immersed in the cold water, the subject reports his felt pain on a scale of 0 to 10, 0 being no pain, and 10 being a pain so severe that he would wish to remove his hand. We refer to this as a *critical level*, for it is the tolerance level for the pain, without special encouragement to continue to suffer. If a subject has reached the pain level of 10 before the immersion period is over, he is persuaded to keep his hand in the water a little longer and to keep on counting. This he is able to do, and the result is of course a pain report beyond 10.

That such verbal pain reports yield an orderly relationship to the conditions of stimulation, both to the temperature of the water, and to the time in the water, is shown by the mean results for 0, 5, 10, and 15 degrees Centigrade as plotted in Figure 1. The means of the pain-state reports in each of the temperatures differ significantly from each of the other temperatures by t tests, with significances of at least $p = .05$.

These data appear orderly enough to provide a test of standard psychophysical models. The model chosen is Stevens' (1966) power function

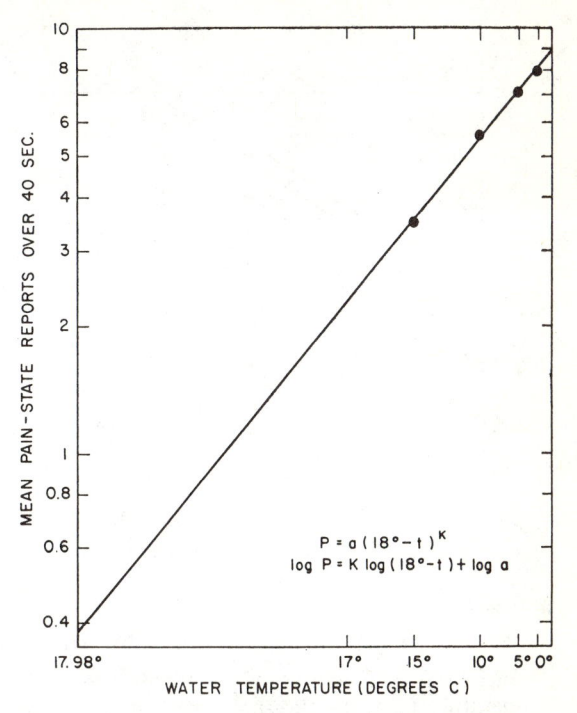

FIG. 2. Pain as a power function of the differences in water temperature from the threshold value of 18 degrees Centigrade.

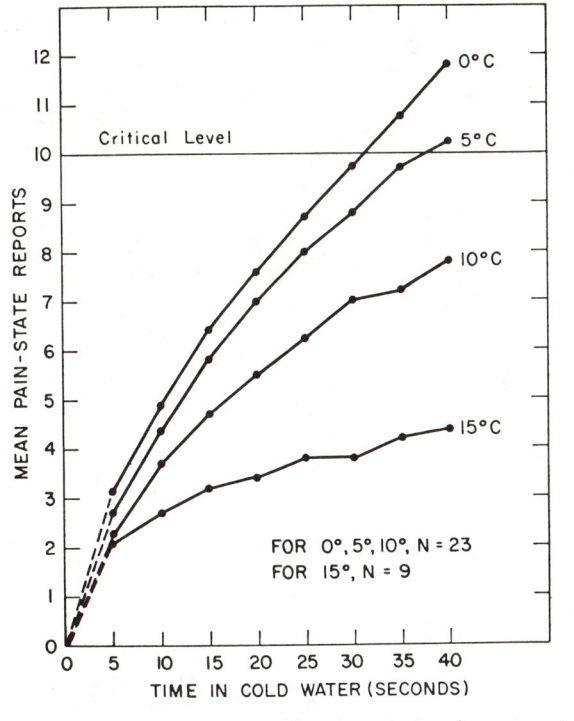

FIG. 1. Reported pain as a function of time in water at temperatures of 0, 5, 10, and 15 degrees Centigrade.

because it proves to fit better than the standard Fechner logarithmic function. The test is quite simple. If both the numerical pain report and some measure of the intensity of stimulation are plotted logarithmically, the power function fits if a straight-line function results.

There is the single scale for verbal pain reports, but there are two possibilities for describing the intensity of stimulation: one, the *temperature* of the water, on the simple assumption that the colder the water the greater the pain; two, the *time* in the water, on the assumption that the pain mounts the longer the hand and forearm are exposed to the cold. The two measures have a common intermediary, which is the relationship between cold and pain, but there is no a priori reason for both of them to fit the same mathematical function.

Let us first see how pain varies as a function of water temperature. Other workers have found that the threshold for cold pressor pain is near 18 degrees Centigrade. This is well below skin temperature, but water can feel cold without feeling painful. If we then plot the average pain-state reports at 15, 10, 5, and 0 degrees on a scale which as-

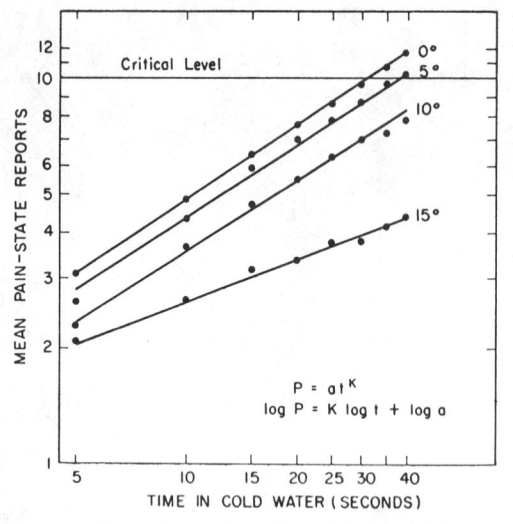

FIG. 3. Pain as a power function of time in cold water.

sumes that as the water gets colder the pain will be a power function of the difference in water temperature from the threshold value of 18 degrees we get the plot shown in Figure 2. The four plotted points fall quite well along a straight line, and the line projects to a threshold value of pain near 18 degrees.

Now we may ask whether a similar result will be obtained if we plot pain as a power function of the time in water of a given temperature. Because we have four temperatures, we have a family of four lines, as shown in Figure 3. Again the straight lines fit well enough to indicate the appropriateness of the power function.[4]

Turning now to ischemia, as our second form of laboratory pain, and using the same scale of pain reports, we again find a power function with time, although now the time units are in minutes rather than in seconds (Figure 4).

Thus far I have shown that pain reported verbally on a simple numerical scale yields not only orderly results, but valid results, in the sense that the pain reported bears a systematic relationship to the temperature of the water and to the time of exposure to the noxious stimulus. The lawfulness is supported by the fit of the power function which holds within so many other perceptual modalities.

I emphasize these findings as a reply to those who would degrade the subject's statements as being "merely" verbal reports, as though some sort of physiological response would be sounder. I wish to assert flatly that there is no physiological measure of pain which is either as discriminating of fine differences in stimulus conditions, as reliable upon repetition, or as lawfully related to changed conditions, as the subject's verbal report.

Physiological Accompaniments of Pain

If I seem to disparage physiological indicators of pain, it is not because we have not studied them, nor indeed because results are negative, for I shall have some positive results to report. We have studied a number of measures, but I shall confine my discussion to one indicator, systolic blood pressure as measured from a finger on the hand opposite to that which is suffering the pain. We place a small inflatable cuff around one finger, with a plethysmographic transducer on the finger tip to indicate when the pulse is occluded. Another plethysmograph on an adjacent finger helps us to

[4] There are limitations in the fit of the power functions for both the cold pressor response and the ischemic response, when the stimulating conditions endure too long. In the cold pressor response numbing begins to set in at about 60 seconds for 0 degrees Centigrade water; in the case of ischemia there may be a sudden upturn of pain as the critical tolerance level is passed. We have elsewhere proposed a more complex function which can be used when there are inflections in the rate of change of pain or when the pain change is not monotonic (Voevodsky, Cooper, Morgan, & Hilgard, 1967).

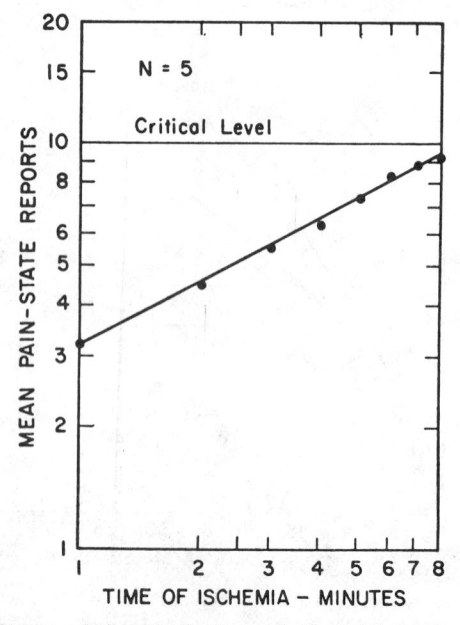

FIG. 4. Pain as a function of time of ischemia.

monitor heart responses. An automatically operated air pump inflates the finger cuff until the circulation is cut off, as indicated by the record from the plethysmograph on that finger, and then a device automatically releases the air from the cuff until the pulse again appears and is restored to normal, when the cycle automatically repeats itself. Thus a record is obtained on the polygraph of the systolic blood pressure every 10 seconds or so. By connecting these measurements as they appear on the polygraph we have an essentially continuous record of the blood pressure.

The rise in pain in the cold water is accompanied by a rise in blood pressure, and the rise in ischemic pain is also accompanied by a rise in blood pressure. Thus, under appropriate conditions, blood pressure appears to be the kind of indicator of pain for which we have been searching. A record of the blood pressure rise within cold water at four temperatures is given in Figure 5, which corresponds closely to the verbal pain reports earlier shown in Figure 1. The average results hold also for individual subjects. That is, those who suffer less at a given temperature also show less rise in blood pressure. Thus, for water at 0 degrees Centigrade, a correlation between mean pain reports and blood pressure rise for 22 subjects reaches $r = .53$, a satisfactorily significant correlation ($p = .02$). Others have reported similar findings (e.g., Tétreault, Panisset, & Gouger, 1964).

Blood pressure also rises as pain rises in ischemia. Rise in pain reports and rise in blood pressure yield the curves shown in Figure 6. These are means for 11 subjects. The abscissa has been converted to ratios of time in ischemia in order to plot the several subjects in comparable units. The

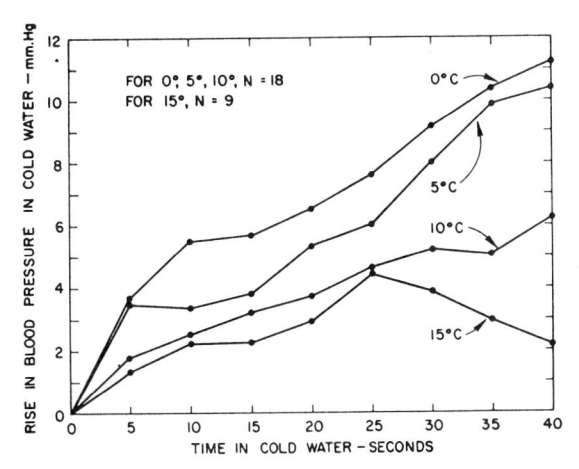

FIG. 5. Blood pressure as a function of time in water at temperatures of 0, 5, 10, and 15 degrees Centigrade.

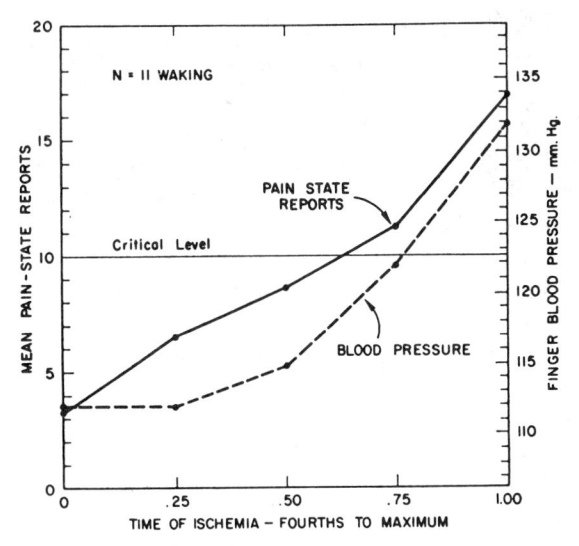

FIG. 6. Pain reports and blood pressure as a function of time in ischemia. (The tourniquet was removed when pain became intolerable, which varied from 12 to 32 minutes for these 11 subjects. Hence the time to intolerable pain was divided into fourths for purposes of obtaining the means that are plotted.)

time to maximum tolerable pain (at which the tourniquet had to be removed) fell between 12 and 32 minutes, by contrast with the water pain which was measured over a fraction of a minute only.

Thus we have established blood pressure as a candidate to serve as an indicator of pain. At least, in two stressful situations, it mounts as the pain mounts. As we shall see later, this does not satisfy all the requisites for a physiological pain indicator.

Pain Reduction under Hypnosis: Cold Pressor Response

Now I wish to turn to the reduction of pain, under the identical physical conditions of stressful stimulation, when that reduction is by way of hypnosis.[5] First we shall consider reduction of cold pressor pain.

[5] The experimental literature on pain reduction (and pain production) in hypnosis is very confused, despite the well-established clinical successes in childbirth, dentistry, major surgery, and the successful relief of pain through hypnosis in severe burns and terminal cancer. A few of the major reports from other laboratories of experimental studies are listed here for the benefit of those who may care to explore this literature: Barber and Hahn (1962, 1964), Brown and Vogel (1938), Doupe, Miller, and Keller (1939), Dudley, Holmes, Martin, and Ripley (1964, 1966), Dynes (1932), Levine (1930), Sears (1932), Shor (1962), Sutcliffe (1961), West, Neill, and Hardy (1952), Wolff and Goodell (1943).

College students or high school students who come to the laboratory for their first experience of hypnosis differ widely in their responses to a standard induction procedure followed by a standard list of suggestions. By making use of some scales earlier standardized in our laboratory (Weitzenhoffer & Hilgard, 1959, 1962, 1967) we are able to sort our subjects according to their degree of hypnotic susceptibility before they take part in the experiments concerned with pain. Then, at some later time, they experience the cold pressor pain in the waking condition, and learn to use the verbal pain report to indicate how much pain they feel. On a subsequent occasion we may hypnotize them, without suggesting any pain reduction, and then expose them to immersion in the cold water, or we may hypnotize them and tell them that they will feel no pain in the cold water. This is the condition which we call attempted hypnotic analgesia. The subjects who entered the ice water experiments had had very little experience of hypnosis, and they were not trained in pain reduction. Our purpose was not to see how completely we could wipe out pain, but rather to see what individual differences in pain reduction would appear under standard conditions.

Because we did not have blood pressure measures on the subjects of our first reported experiment,[6] I shall turn to our second experiment which was partially a replication of the first one, but also introduced some modifications. We used high school students as subjects in this second investigation, instead of college students, largely because they were conveniently available in large numbers during the summer when the experiment was conducted. The subjects had already served in the experiment with water at different temperatures, in the normal waking state, so that they came to the hypnotic portion of the experiment well familiar with reports of pain on the verbal pain-state scale. They served three days, one in the normal waking condition, one in hypnosis without analgesia, and one in hypnosis with suggested analgesia; the orders of the latter two days were randomized, to correct for any demand characteristics associated with having the hand in ice water in the midst of hypnosis. The advantages of comparing a day of hypnosis *without* suggested analgesia and hypnosis *with* analgesia are twofold. In the first place, this arrangement separates out any physiological effects that are attributable to the hypnosis as distinct from those associated with the stressful stimulus, and, in the second place, it rules out the effect upon pain of whatever relaxation is associated with hypnotic induction. It is well known that relaxation may itself reduce pain. The results for the three days are shown in Figure 7, plotted separately for the subjects low in hypnotic susceptibility and for those high in susceptibility. What we see from the figure is that hypnosis alone did not reduce pain appreciably for either group, but the suggested analgesia did indeed produce a reduction in verbally reported pain, slightly for the low hypnotizables, more for the high hypnotizables. In Figure 7 the high and low susceptibles are the extremes of

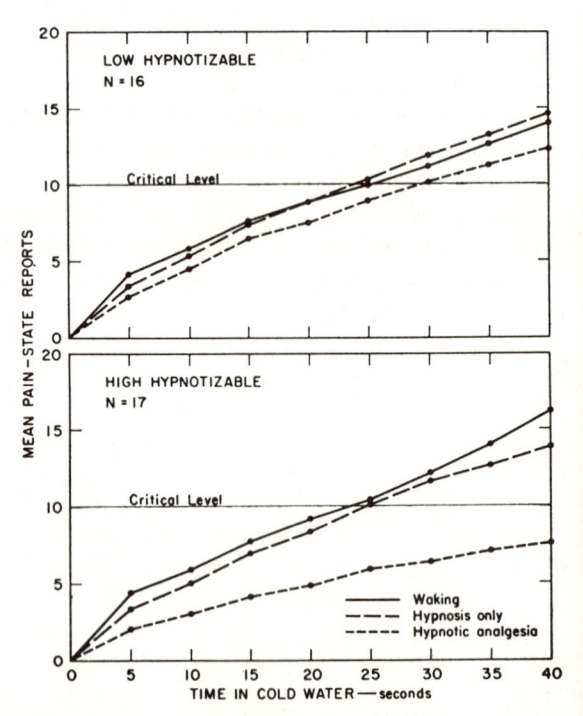

FIG. 7. Pain as a function of time in water of 0 degrees Centigrade in waking state, and following attempted hypnotic induction without analgesia instructions and with analgesia instructions. (Low subjects, scores of 0–9 on combined Forms A and C—Mean = 7.1; High subjects, scores of 18–24 on combined Forms A and C—Mean = 21.6.)

---

[6] Hilgard (1967). In this first experiment of the series with the cold pressor response, reactions from 55 college students were reported. The correlation between the amount of pain reduction under hypnotic analgesia and susceptibility to hypnosis was reported as $r = .37$ ($p = .01$). If one very discordant subject is eliminated, this rises to $r = .46$. See also Hilgard, Cooper, Lenox, Morgan, and Voevodsky (1967).

a larger distribution, so that a correlational analysis is not appropriate. For a smaller group of 19 subjects, unselected for hypnosis, and including moderates as well as highs and lows, the correlation between hypnotic susceptibility as tested prior to the pain experiment and the pain reduction under hypnosis turned out to be $r = .60$ ($p = .01$).

The verbal pain reports thus yield an orderly picture of pain reduction under hypnotic analgesia, with the greatest reduction found for those who are the most hypnotizable. Now what of the blood pressure measures? Will they continue to correlate with pain reports under these conditions? To our surprise, the blood pressure *rises* under hypnosis and is highest under the analgesic condition, for both high and low hypnotizable subjects (Figure 8). It may be noted that, particularly for the high hypnotizable subjects, the blood pressure rises before the hands are placed in the ice water, so that the initial readings are above those of the less hypnotizable.[7]

We are thus led to two propositions about the relationship between blood pressure and pain:

1. When pain is felt there is a tendency for blood pressure to rise in an amount correlated with the amount of experienced pain.

2. Blood pressure may rise in a stressful situation independent of the amount of felt pain.

The second of these statements is my reason for asserting that blood pressure is not a completely satisfactory physiological indicator of pain. It works in some situations, but not in others. There is nothing very surprising about this, because we know that there are many controls over blood pressure of which pain is but one. The two propositions, taken together, show that we have to be careful not to identify a *correlate* of pain, found in some special arrangement, with the pain itself. We may note also that we have to avoid a superficial interpretation of pain reduction under hypnosis by claiming that the effects of hypnotic analgesia rest entirely on the reduction of anxiety; it appears that excitation, possibly with some anxiety over the impending stress, may keep the blood pressure high, even while the pain is reduced.

---

[7] The initial differences in blood pressure between waking and hypnosis days were not found in ischemia (Figure 9), and this discrepancy sets problems for further investigation. The conclusion holds, however, that blood pressure rises in the cold pressor test even when no pain is felt.

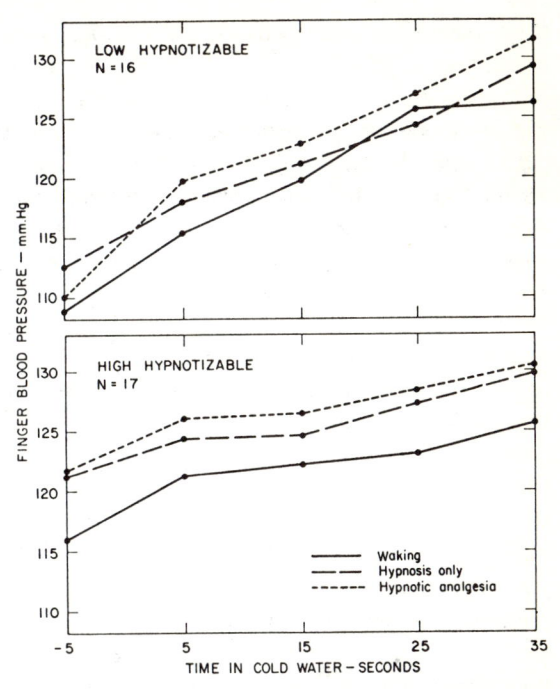

FIG. 8. Blood pressure as a function of time in water of 0 degrees Centigrade in waking state, and following attempted hypnotic induction without analgesia instructions and with analgesia instructions. (Same subjects as in Figure 7.)

Pain Reduction under Hypnosis: Ischemic Pain

The relationship between blood pressure and pain reduction under hypnosis turned out quite differently in ischemia. It is fortunate that we performed both experiments, for had we performed only one of them we might have produced misleading generalizations. There are several differences in the experiments to be noted. First, the cold water has the stress of cold, in addition to pain, while the cold is lacking in the ischemia experiment. Second, ischemic pain tends to mount very slowly at first, so that there is time for the hypnotic subject to achieve a confident analgesic state, while the shock of the ice water is immediate. Third, in the experiments to be reported the subjects were much more highly selected for their ability to reduce pain in hypnosis than they were in the cold pressor experiment, in which they were not selected at all. Still, the subjects in the ischemia experiments were selected from those in the cold pressor experiment, so we are not dealing with idiosyncrasies that can be accounted for on the basis of subject differences. These subjects behaved differently in ischemia from the way that they themselves had behaved in the ice water experiment.

It turns out that in the ischemia experiment these highly responsive subjects were able not only to rid themselves completely of pain for a matter of 18–45 minutes, but their blood pressure, which rose sharply in the waking state, *did not rise in ischemia or rose very little* even though the stressful condition was continued for many minutes beyond the time, in the waking condition, when the pain was too severe to be further endured. Results for six subjects, all of whom suffered greatly in the waking state but were able to maintain their analgesia throughout in the hypnotic state, are shown in Figure 9. The time to unbearable pain in the waking state is taken as unity; under hypnotic analgesia the tourniquet was kept on well beyond the time at which the intolerable pain would have been found in the waking state. Two subjects were unable to remain analgesic throughout; their blood pressures showed changes beyond the subjects reported in Figure 9. While they were eliminated from Figure 9, statistical treatment with them left in shows a significant difference ($t = 3.12$, $df = 7$, $p = .01$) between the rise in blood pressure in the waking state over hypnotic analgesia for the whole group of subjects tested.

The three additional subjects, whose responses to ischemia in the waking state were reported earlier (in Figure 6), were subjects refractory to hypnosis, who were intended to be used as simulators in the hypnotic analgesia experiment, according to the experimental design recommended by Orne (1959, 1962). It turned out that the stress was too great, however, and none of them could tolerate the pain for the time required to parallel the behavior of the "true" hypnotic analgesia subjects. While this in some respects spoiled the experimental design, the conclusions are the same regarding the reality of the hypnotic analgesia for the "true" subjects, substantiated by the lack of any appreciable rise in blood pressure.

We are now prepared to add a third proposition regarding the relationship between blood pressure and pain:

3. When stressful conditions which normally lead both to reported pain and to an increase in blood pressure do not lead to an increase in blood pressure, it may be assumed that pain is absent.

This now brings us to a conclusion regarding the reality of hypnotic analgesia and to a summary assertion about the role of blood pressure. The absence of pain, reported by the hypnotically analgesia subject, is confirmed by the absence of a rise in blood pressure. Thus we have a physiological validation for the reality of hypnotic analgesia, but the validator works in one direction only. That is, *absence* of the blood pressure rise may be taken as an indication of absent pain under specified conditions, but pain may be absent *even if blood pressure rises*. This is a logical problem which has caused a good deal of confusion in earlier efforts to deal with the question of pain reduction under hypnotic analgesia (see especially Barber, 1963; Barber & Hahn, 1962; Sutcliffe, 1961).

Clinical Relevance of the Laboratory Study of Pain and Hypnotic Analgesia

I wish to close my remarks with a few comments on the practical implications of the kind of experiments I have reported. There are continuing arguments over the relative amounts of money and energy to be expended on basic research and on research aimed at the applications of science. There are those who take the position that basic research is an end in itself, designed to satisfy curiosity, to seek the truth, to discover and order knowledge for its own sake. There are others who take the position that basic science will ultimately pay off in its contributions to society, although immediate payoff is not to be expected; this is the essence of the position that "there is nothing so practical as a good theory." On the more general

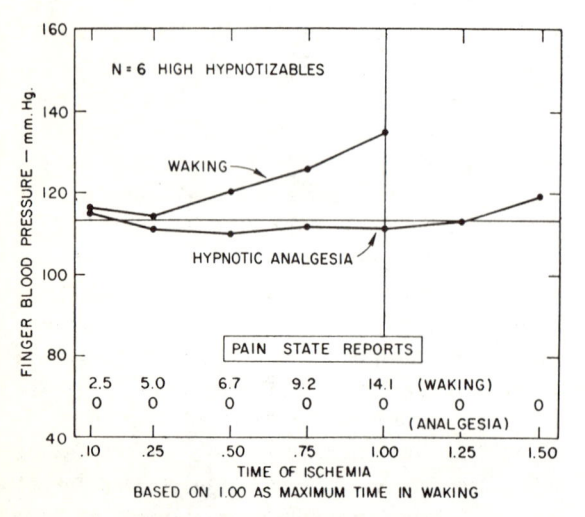

FIG. 9. Blood pressure in ischemia, in waking state and in hypnotic analgesia (Mean, 6 subjects).

issues, I take a moderate position: I believe that science has multiple aims, that there is a division of labor along the spectrum from pure science to the arts of practice, that there should be mutual respect and encouragement for those who work at any point along this spectrum, so long as their work is imaginative and sound.

When, however, there is an evident application for laboratory results I believe there is an obligation on the scientific enterprise as a whole to provide the bridging investigations that move from the laboratory to the real world. Thus the psychology of learning is incomplete if it is not reflected in educational practices, and the study of pain is incomplete if it does not contribute to the relief of pain outside the laboratory.

One may well ask how the experiments which I have reported bear upon the relief of pain through hypnosis by dentists, obstetricians, surgeons, and others who are confronted with the practical problems of suffering people. The answer is that the studies alone will not make much of a contribution unless they are extended to deal with the practical problems, either by those within laboratories such as ours, or by others who build upon our findings.

The potential contributions fall along the following lines:

1. First, our hypnotic susceptibility scales make it possible to determine what kinds of responsiveness to hypnosis are essential if a patient is to profit from the use of hypnosis in pain reduction. Not all people can be helped, and one obligation upon science is to be diagnostic regarding those who can be served by particular applications. It must be pointed out, however, that until normative data are obtained in the practical setting, the scales cannot be used effectively.

2. Second, the further study of the physiological consequences of pain, and the alterations of these consequences by hypnotic analgesia, can yield better understanding of what is happening in otherwise stressful conditions, such as the preparation for surgery or surgery itself. If hypnosis can reduce surgical pain or postoperative shock, it is important to know what is happening inside the body. Again, unless these studies are carried out eventually in the hospital, the information gained in the laboratory will tend to be idle and useless.

We have accepted this as part of the responsibility of our own laboratory, and have undertaken studies of some patients suffering the pains of terminal cancer, others with migraine headaches. Clinicians are at present far ahead of our laboratories in the hypnotic reduction of pain, but the laboratory worker has a contribution to make. The contribution will be made, however, only if he takes his obligation seriously, and goes to the necessary trouble to tailor his findings to the needs of the world outside the laboratory.

REFERENCES

BARBER, T. X. The effects of "hypnosis" on pain: A critical review of experimental and clinical finding. *Psychosomatic Medicine,* 1963, 24, 303–333.

BARBER, T. X., & HAHN, K. W., JR. Physiological and subjective responses to pain-producing stimulation under hypnotically suggested and waking-imagined "analgesia." *Journal of Abnormal and Social Psychology,* 1962, 65, 411–418.

BARBER, T. X., & HAHN, K. W., JR. Experimental studies in "hypnotic" behavior: Physiologic and subjective effects of imagined pain. *Journal of Nervous and Mental Disease,* 1964, 139, 416–425.

BEECHER, H. K. *Measurement of subjective responses.* New York: Oxford University Press, 1959.

BEECHER, H. K. Pain: One mystery solved. *Science,* 1966, 151, 840–841.

BROWN, R. R., & VOGEL, V. H. Psychophysiological reactions following painful stimuli under hypnotic analgesia contrasted with gas anesthesia and Novocain block. *Journal of Applied Psychology,* 1938, 22, 408–420.

DOUPE, J., MILLER, W. R., & KELLER, W. K. Vasomotor reactions in the hypnotic state. *Journal of Neurology and Psychiatry,* 1939, 2, 97–106.

DUDLEY, D. L., HOLMES, T. H., MARTIN, C. J., & RIPLEY, H. S. Changes in respiration associated with hypnotically induced emotion, pain, and exercise. *Psychosomatic Medicine,* 1964, 24, 46–57.

DUDLEY, D. L., HOLMES, T. H., MARTIN, C. J., & RIPLEY, H. S. Hypnotically induced facsimile of pain. *Archives of General Psychiatry,* 1966, 15, 198–204.

DYNES, J. B. Hypnotic analgesia. *Journal of Abnormal and Social Psychology,* 1932, 27, 79–88.

GONDA, T. A. The relation between complaints of persistent pain and family size. *Journal of Neurology, Neurosurgery, and Psychiatry,* 1962, 25, 277–281. (a)

GONDA, T. A. Some remarks on pain. *Bulletin, British Psychological Society,* 1962, 47, 29–35. (b)

GREENE, M. A., BOLTAX, A. J., LUSTIG, G. A., & ROGOW, E. Circulatory dynamics during the cold pressor test. *American Journal of Cardiology,* 1965, 16, 54–60.

HILGARD, E. R. A quantitative study of pain and its reduction through hypnotic suggestion. *Proceedings of the National Academy of Sciences,* 1967, 57, 1581–1586.

HILGARD, E. R., COOPER, L. M., LENOX, J., MORGAN, A. H., & VOEVODSKY, J. The use of pain-state reports in the study of hypnotic analgesia to the pain of ice water. *Journal of Nervous and Mental Disease,* 1967, 144, 506–513.

HINES, E. A., & BROWN, G. E. A standard stimulus for measuring vasomotor reactions: Its application in the study of hypertension. *Proceedings of Staff Meetings, Mayo Clinic*, 1932, **7**, 332.

LEVINE, M. Psychogalvanic reaction to painful stimuli in hypnotic and hysterical anesthesia. *Bulletin Johns Hopkins Hospital*, 1930, **46**, 331–339.

LEWIN, I. The effect of reward on the experience of pain. In, *Dissertations in cognitive processes*. Detroit, Mich.: Center for Cognitive Processes, Wayne State University, 1965.

LEWIS, T., PICKERING, G. W., & ROTHSCHILD, P. Observations upon muscular pain in intermittent claudication. *Heart*, 1931, **15**, 359–383.

MELZACK, R. Pain. *International Encyclopedia of the Social Sciences*. Vol. 11. New York: Macmillan and Free Press, 1968. Pp. 357–363.

MELZACK, R., & WALL, P. D. Pain mechanisms: A new theory. *Science*, 1965, **150**, 971–979.

ORNE, M. T. The nature of hypnosis: Artifact and essence. *Journal of Abnormal and Social Psychology*, 1959, **58**, 277–299.

ORNE, M. T. On the social psychology of the psychological experiment: With particular reference to demand characteristics and their implications. *American Psychologist*, 1962, **17**, 776–783.

PETRIE, A. *Individuality in pain and suffering*. Chicago: University of Chicago Press, 1967.

SEARS, R. R. Experimental study of hypnotic anesthesia. *Journal of Experimental Psychology*, 1932, **15**, 1–22.

SHOR, R. E. Physiological effects of painful stimulation during hypnotic analgesia under conditions designed to minimize anxiety. *International Journal of Clinical and Experimental Hypnosis*, 1962, **8**, 151–163.

SMITH, G. M., LAWRENCE, D. E., MARKOWITZ, R. A., MOSTELLER, F., & BEECHER, H. K. An experimental pain method sensitive to morphine in man: The submaximum effort tourniquet technique. *Journal of Pharmacology and Experimental Therapeutics*, 1966, **154**, 324–332.

STERNBACH, R. A. *Pain: A psychophysiological analysis*. New York: Academic Press, 1968.

STEVENS, S. S. Matching functions between loudness and ten other continua. *Perception and Psychophysics*, 1966, **1**, 5–8.

SUTCLIFFE, J. P. "Credulous" and "skeptical" views of hypnotic phenomena: Experiments on esthesia, hallucination, and delusion. *Journal of Abnormal and Social Psychology*, 1961, **62**, 189–200.

SZASZ, T. S. *Pain and pleasure*. New York: Basic Books, 1967.

TÉTREAULT, L., PANISSET, A., & GOUGER, P. Étude des facteurs, émotion et douleur dans la réponse tensionnelle au "cold pressor test." *L'Union Médicale du Canada*, 1964, **93**, 177–180.

VOEVODSKY, J., COOPER, L. M., MORGAN, A. H., & HILGARD, E. R. The measurement of suprathreshold pain. *American Journal of Psychology*, 1967, **80**, 124–128.

WEITZENHOFFER, A. M., & HILGARD, E. R. *Stanford Hypnotic Susceptibility Scales, Forms A and B*. Palo Alto, Calif.: Consulting Psychologists Press, 1959

WEITZENHOFFER, A. M., & HILGARD, E. R. *Stanford Hypnotic Susceptibility Scales, Form C*. Palo Alto, Calif.: Consulting Psychologists Press, 1962.

WEITZENHOFFER, A. M., & HILGARD, E. R. *Revised Stanford Profile Scales of Hypnotic Susceptibility, Forms I and II*. Palo Alto, Calif.: Consulting Psychologists Press, 1967.

WEST, L. J., NEILL, K. C., & HARDY, J. D. Effects of hypnotic suggestions on pain perception and galvanic skin response. *Archives of Neurology and Psychiatry*, 1952, **68**, 549–560.

WOLF, S., & HARDY, J. D. Studies on pain: Observations on pain due to local cooling and on factors involved in the "cold pressor" effect. *Journal of Clinical Investigation*, 1941, **20**, 521–533.

WOLFF, H. G., & GOODELL, H. The relation of attitude and suggestion to the perception of and reaction to pain. *Proceedings of the Association for Research in Nervous and Mental Disease*, 1943, **23**, 434–448.

ZIMBARDO, P. G. *Cognitive control of motivation*. Chicago: Scott, Foresman, 1969.

ZIMBARDO, P. G., COHEN, A. R., WEISENBERG, M., DWORKIN, L., & FIRESTONE, I. Control of pain motivation by cognitive dissonance. *Science*, 1966, **151**, 217–219.

EFFECT ON BRAIN ENZYME AND BEHAVIOUR IN THE RAT OF VISUAL PATTERN RESTRICTION IN EARLY LIFE

DEVENDRA SINGH
RICHARD J. JOHNSTON
HAROLD J. KLOSTERMAN

University of Texas and North Dakota State University

Several studies have shown that certain behavioural and biochemical changes can be produced in rats if they are raised in an "enriched environment" or subjected to stress or handling during infancy.[1] Typically, an enriched environment is created by placing some small objects or mates in the cage of the animal or by handling the animal every day for a specified period of time. All these manipulations require an extended period of physical contact either with other animals, with the experimenter or with both. When animals are handled or permitted to live together, the resulting temperature differential alone can produce physiological changes,[2] so it is not clear whether some behavioural or physiological changes can be produced in an adult animal by manipulating just the visual or auditory environment in infancy. By eliminating group living and handling, and manipulating only the visual complexity of the environment in which rats were raised, we found significant differences in body weight, brain cholinesterase (ChE) activity and sensory conditioning.

Nineteen litter-mate female Holtzman albino rats, weaned at 30 days of age and matched for body weight, were randomly assigned to either a visual pattern (VP) or a restricted visual pattern (RVP) group. The visual environment of both groups was restricted by a wooden enclosure extending 30·48 cm. beyond the front of the cage. The enclosure of the VP group had alternate black and white stripes painted on it, while the enclosure of the RVP group was painted flat white. Each animal was placed in an individual wire mesh cage and remained in its experimental environment, and was supplied with unlimited food and water until it was 90 days of age. The overhead fluorescent illumination diffused light evenly over all cages and a 12 h light-dark cycle was maintained. The animals were never touched nor were their cages removed throughout the experimental period except when the animals were weighed and rated for emotionality[3] at 60 days of age. The original experiment which contained only seven rats (four in the VP and three in the RVP group) was replicated with

---

Reprinted from *Nature*, Vol. 216, No. 5122, pp. 1337–1338, December 30, 1967. This study was supported in part by a research grant from the U. S. National Institute of Mental Health.

TABLE 1

Rearing Condition	Body Weight (g)	Age (days) 30	60	90	101
VP	Mean	92·3	206·8	251·3	273·2
	σM	2·76	3·43	5·85	9·82
RVP	Mean	92·2	199·9	237·8	248·5
	σM	2·82	3·26	2·49	4·35
Difference		0·1	6·9*	13·5*	23·7*

*Significant at 0·05 level.

Mean body weights for restricted visual pattern group (RVP) and visual pattern group (VP) for the four weighing periods.

twelve rats (six in each group). Because the trend of behavioural tests and weight gain was identical for original and replicated experiments, all the data have been pooled.

At 90 days of age all animals were weighed and rated for emotionality a second time. The animals did not differ in emotionality rating either when 60 or 90 days old. The VP group, however, gained significantly more body weight than did the RVP group at both 60 and 90 days of age. As evident from Table 1, the VP group also maintained its higher weight gains than the RVP group at 101 days of age when final body weights were obtained.

We also tested all animals for spontaneous activity in a photoelectric activity cage for 12 h each day for three consecutive days, but within-group variability was excessive and the differences in activity were not significant. Finally, we tested all animals for sensory reinforcement for 7 days, at the conclusion of which the animals were killed and their brains were removed for measurement of ChE activity.

The sensory reinforcement test consists of conditioning an animal to perform a specific task, usually touching a lever, when the only reward is a flash of light in a light-proof chamber in which the animal is working.[4] We used a sound- and light-proof chamber (28·57 cm × 19·68 cm × 23·49 cm) which contained a stationary lever on one side, 8·89 cm above the floor. The lever was connected to a contact relay which, when touched, could activate a flash of light (6 W) for 0·75 sec in the box and a counter. Each animal was placed for 25 min daily for 7 consecutive days and the number of times the lever was touched was recorded. For the first 3 (adaptation) and last 3 (extinction) days, touching the lever did not activate the light in the box, but the number of touches was recorded. On the 2 days of conditioning, however, the flash of light accompanied each touch of the lever. There were no significant differences between the groups on adaptation and extinction days, but the VP group made significantly more responses than the RVP group ($P = 0.05$) on the days of conditioning (Fig. 1).

Measures of brain ChE activity were obtained for only the twelve animals which were used in the replication. Animals were decapitated and their brains were removed. The brains were weighed and cut into equal anterior and posterior halves. For each half, the cortical (lateral, ventral and dorsal) and subcortical tissues were divided. The four samples thus obtained for each rat (anterior cortex, posterior cortex, anterior subcortex and posterior subcortex) were individually weighed and frozen in dry ice. All samples were then coded so that the analyst could determine whether the tissue was cortical or subcortical, but he was unaware from which

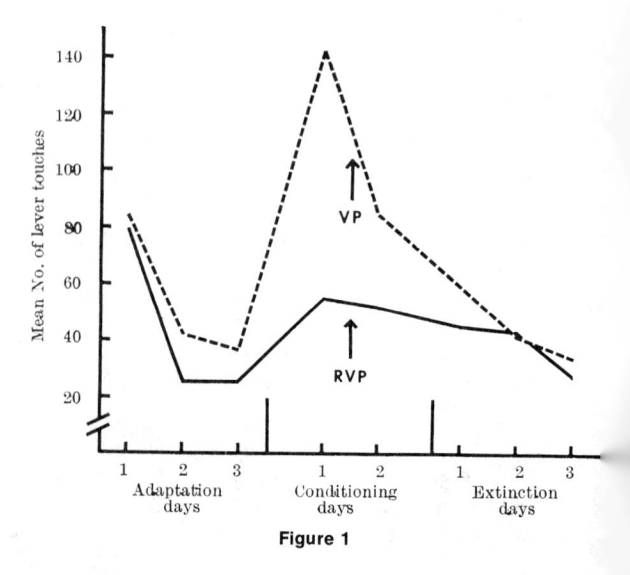

Figure 1

TABLE 2

Rearing Condition	ChE Activity*	Anterior Cortex	Posterior Cortex	Total Cortex
VP	Mean	55·00	55·80	53·09
	σM	7·90	4·55	4·45
RVP	Mean	38·67	27·33	33·00
	σM	5·11	6·06	4·02
Difference		16·33†	28·47	20·00‡

*All ChE values are in moles ACh $\times 10^{10}$ hydrolysed/min/mg of tissue.
†Significant at 0·05 level.
‡Significant at 0·01 level.
The ChE activity for restricted visual pattern group (RVP) and visual pattern group (VP).

group the tissue was taken. The ChE activity was determined by the rate of hydrolysis of acetylcholine perchlorate (ACh). The procedure employed was identical to that of Rosenzweig, Krech and Bennett.[5]

Because the subcortical ChE activity between VP and RVP groups was not significantly different, Table 2 presents the ChE activity for the cortical tissue samples only. The posterior cortex sample, which contained the visual cortex, showed significantly greater ChE activity for the VP group than for the RVP group. The ChE activity between anterior and posterior cortical samples within a group, either VP or RVP, did not show significant differences. When the total cortex between the groups was compared, however, the ChE activity for the VP group was much higher than that for the RVP group. Our findings are not in agreement with those of Rosenzweig et al.[1]; they found decreased ChE activity in the cortex and increased activity in the subcortex of those rats which were raised in an enriched environment. Our brain samples are not strictly comparable with those in their study, however, because our cortical samples contained lateral, dorsal and ventral portions of cortex, while in their study only the lateral portion of the cortex was used.[1]

The results of our study strongly suggest that visual pattern restriction or enrichment in early life may be a critical factor in those studies which have shown behavioural, physiological and biochemical changes in the adult animals raised in groups or handled during infancy. The fact that greater body weight and increased ChE activity of brain can be induced by manipulating visual patterns indicates that the nature of visual input in infancy may cause enduring alteration in some basic physiological mechanisms.

References

1. Rosenzweig, M. R., Krech, D., Bennett, E. L., and Diamond, M. C., *J. Comp. Physiol. Psychol.*, **55**, 429 (1962); Levine, S., and Lewis, G. W., *Science*, **129**, 42 (1959); Denenberg, V. M., and Karas, G. G., *Science*, **130**, 629, (1959).
2. Schaffer, T., Weingarten, F. S., and Towne, J. C., *Science*, **135**, 41 (1962).
3. King, F. A., *J. Nerv. Ment. Dis.*, **126**, 57 (1958).
4. Kish, G. B., in *Operant Behavior: Areas of Research and Application* (edit. by Honig, W. K.), 109 (Appleton-Century-Crofts, New York, 1966).
5. Rosenzweig, M. R., Krech, D., and Bennett, E. L., in *Ciba Foundation Symposium on the Neurological Basis of Behavior*, 337 (J. and A. Churchill, London, 1958).

AUTHORITARIANISM AND RESPONSE TO POWER CUES[1]

EDWARD J. WILKINS
Brandeis University

RICHARD deCHARMS
Washington University, St. Louis, Missouri

The present study is an attempt to investigate two dimensions of stimuli presented by a standard stimulus person (SP) and the relation of these dimensions to personality characteristics of *S*s. The hypotheses are derived from Heider's (1958) "naïve analysis of action" and especially from his discussion of the concept of "can" in the attribution of causality in social interaction. Heider stresses the distinction between the attribution of social causality to internal personality characteristics or to external factors in the environment. Thus a person "can" engage in a specific behavior only when internal factors are strong enough to overcome external environmental factors. A person may be seen as being able to do something because his internal characteristics are strong or because the external characteristics are weak or favorable for him. "Therefore, though 'can' is a resultant of two contributing sources, it is sometimes ascribed more to the person and sometimes more to the environment" (Heider, 1958, p. 89).

Power is seen by Heider primarily as the personal or internal component of "can" or ability. However, he points out that power

[1] This study was carried out under Contract Nonr—816 (11) between the Office of Naval Research and the Small Groups Laboratory, Social Science Institute at Washington University. The report is based on a Master's thesis submitted to Washington University by the first author. The authors wish to thank Drs. W. W. Charters, Jr., R. L. Hamblin, and G. P. Stone for their helpful criticism.

Reprinted from *Journal of Personality*, Vol. 30, No. 3, September, 1962.

may be derived from at least two sources—personal characteristics or social status.

Power is ... highly affected by attitudes of self-confidence, attitudes that assert, "I can do something worthwhile here."

Certainly a person's apparent self-confidence often influences our judgment of his abilities.

Moreover, social and legal status often affects what a person can and cannot do by determining the strength of the environmental forces....

Nevertheless, social and legal status is often felt to be a personal characteristic. It "follows the person around" in a wide variety of situations and in this sense becomes attached to him.... Attribution of status, therefore, is less univocal than is attribution of ability, personality or attitudes. The latter generally "belong to" the person. But a person's status may sometimes be felt to be part of his essence and in other cases to be detached from him as a person.

The question of attribution of such action possibilities is not as clear-cut as it may seem. Though possessions are definitely "outside the person's skin" and typically are felt to be a part of the environment, not infrequently the actions they permit are ascribed to the person (pp. 94-96).

In light of this analysis of power it seems feasible to predict that power cues deriving from internal and from external sources may be of differential importance to different types of people. Specifically, the power dimensions may be systematically related to authoritarianism. The Authoritarian Personality (Adorno, Frenkel-Brunswik, Levinson, & Sanford, 1950) is characterized by a general "fear of weakness." This general characteristic appears to underlie such subsyndromes as anti-intraception, concealment of softness, striving for power or status, rejection of weak out-groups, exaggerated assertions of strength and toughness, preoccupation with dominance-submission and the "strong" and "weak." It will be assumed here that a central feature involved in all of these characteristics of the high authoritarian is concern for power, i.e., the ability to control the behavior of others, and fear that others will be able to control one's behavior.

The distinction between internal and external power will be conceptualized as follows. Internal power will be considered power accruing to the individual qua individual. This type of power is perceived by others through an individual's personal mannerisms, traits, and expressed values. External power will be considered power, accruing to the individual in accordance with the positions the individual holds and his possession of societally-valued material objects or experiences. An example of an internal power cue would be a confident tone of voice; an example of an external power cue would be the type of house a person lives in.

Past research has indicated that power cues affect the reactions of Ss. Thibaut and Riecken (1955a) manipulated the status of an SP and found greater liking for the high-status SP who complied to a request made by the S. In another study instigation to aggression resulted in the most expressed aggression when high authoritarians were instigated by a low-status person (Thibaut and Riecken,

1955b). Scodel and Mussen (1953) have found that high authoritarians do not perceive low authoritarians as having F scores which are significantly different from their own, while low authoritarians estimate the high authoritarians' F scores to be significantly higher than their own. The high authoritarians appear to be less accurate in estimating others' F scores. The authors conclude that high authoritarians show a general lack of insight into others and a relatively high need to consider themselves members of the ingroup, leading to the perception of similar attitudes and personality characteristics in others. In other words, Scodel and Mussen propose a functional basis for the selective perceptions and types of inferences made by the high authoritarians.

Results from a study by Roberts and Jessor (1958) indicate that there are some conditions, at least, in which there may not be differential perception of power cues by high and low authoritarians. When Ss were asked to judge the occupation, income, and education of each SP, no differences were found between the responses of high and low authoritarians. Thus, what will be called here external power cues were recognized equally well by both high and low authoritarians.

Internal or psychological power cues were the focus of an experiment by Jones (1954) concerning the relationship between authoritarianism and impression formation. Contrary to the author's original hypotheses, the high authoritarians in this study were not more sensitive than the low authoritarians to psychological dimensions such as personal power or forcefulness of the SP. In fact, they were significantly less sensitive. Jones did find, however, that authoritarians showed a greater tendency than nonauthoritarians to differentiate their social environment in terms of power-related concepts, and authoritarians were significantly more positive in their evaluations of a leader regardless of his personal (internal) characteristics. Both of these findings are in accord with the Adorno *et al.* (1950) presentation of the general authoritarian syndrome.

The results of these and other studies led us to differentiate between internal and external power cues. In addition, it was noted that there are at least three different levels at which a stimulus may be analytically considered in the experimental setting. First, the stimulus must be "objectively" present. By this is meant a cue that is manipulated by the experimenter and directly perceivable by an observer. Second, there is the level of perception; that is, the stimulus as perceived by an individual. Finally, there is the usage level; the stimulus as used by the individual in describing a person, situation, or event. Before a person can use an incoming cue he must have perceived it; before he can perceive a given cue it must be there objectively.

The experiment was designed to manipulate independently internal and external power cues and to measure usage of power cues in descriptions, and evaluation of the SPs by high and low authoritarians. In addition, an attempt was made to measure grossly the accuracy of perception of external power cues. The major hypotheses are as follows:

Hypothesis 1. There is no significant difference between high and low authoritarians with respect to the perception of external power-relevant cues. This hypothesis stems primarily from Roberts and Jessor's (1958) findings as discussed earlier. It merely assumes that both high and low authoritarians are equally aware of the factual class content presented by any given SP.

Hypothesis 2. High authoritarians use more external factors in descriptive statements about a SP than do low authoritarians.

Hypothesis 3. High authoritarians use fewer internal factors in descriptive statements about the SP than do low authoritarians.

Hypothesis 4. In making positive evaluations of others, high authoritarians rely more on external power cues than do low authoritarians. Statistically, this hypothesis predicts an interaction between level of authoritarianism in the S and external power cues presented by the SP as determinants of evaluation scores. It was expected that high authoritarians would give more positive evaluations of the high external power SP than of the low external power SP. This would be less true in the case of low authoritarians. Evaluation is used broadly here to refer to ratings on a scale covering several dimensions of personality characteristics.

Hypothesis 5. In making positive evaluation of others, low authoritarians rely more on internal power cues than do high authoritarians. Statistically, this predicts an interaction between level of authoritarianism and internal power cues. It was expected that low authoritarians would give more positive evaluations of the high internal power SP than of the low internal power SP. This would be less true in the case of high authoritarians.

Method

Subjects and Design

The 80 Ss used in the experiment were undergraduate college males recruited from Army and Air Force Reserve Officer Training Corps classes. These Ss ranged between the ages of 17 and 21.

The design of the experiment was a $2 \times 2 \times 2$ analysis of variance incorporating two levels (by a median split) of Ss' authoritarianism, and the four combinations of manipulated internal and external power cues presented by the SP.

Independent Variables and General Procedure

In order to measure authoritarianism, a variant of the California F scale (cf. Adorno *et al.* 1950, forms 40 and 45) was administered to the Ss. Following this, each group of Ss heard one of four tape recordings. These four tape recordings represent the four experimental variations of the present study. They may be described as follows.

High internal–high external. This is what might be referred to, for brevity's sake, as the "tycoon." A man who has inherited the top rung in the ladder of success, he is a member of the upper class, but one who has retained a high degree of vigor and force. He is decisive, confident, and not afraid of responsibility. His answers are straightforward and direct. There is no uneasiness or faltering about his manner.

High internal–low external. This can be called "the young man on his way up," or more simply "the go-getter." Here is a person of definitely lower economic, occupational, and educational background, with few initial advantages in life except his own "will to power." He has not arrived but he is trying hard. He is an individual characterized by decisiveness, vigor, forcefulness, and self-confidence.

Low internal–high external. This person may be called the "decadent-aristocrat." This is an individual who, although he is at the top of the class hierarchy, has "gone to seed" personally. Indecisiveness, lack of conviction, lack of definite goals, lack of aggressiveness and self-confidence, are applicable characteristics.

Low internal–low external. This final category of SP may be called "shiftless trash." A person of the lower class, but one who lacks the fire and determination of the "go-getter." There is a certain uneasiness and faltering in his speech. He is not sure of himself and he has little if any interest in improving his lot.

These four tape recordings were made by two individuals whose voice qualities differed drastically, being at either end of the high internal–low internal continuum, i.e., one had a deep, full voice, the other a higher and weak-sounding voice. The voice of the interviewer was the same on all tapes. The person with the deep voice played the role of the high internal power cue SP making two tapes on both of which he responded confidently. The weaker-voiced SP made the other two tapes, responding hesitantly and without confidence.

The tapes were made up of two sections, corresponding to the two dimensions of power. The four possible combinations of the two types of each section resulted in four tapes representing the four combinations of high and low internal and external power cues. In the first section of each tape, the "general information interview," the external power cues were manipulated. Both SPs made one tape on which they responded to questions concerning socio-economic status as a high external person (high SES). The questions asked about the SP's parents' occupation, income, education, etc., and his occupation, income, and education. Each SP made a second tape on which he responded as a low external person (low SES).

The second section of each tape variation was presented as a "general attitude discussion." It was here that the difference in confidence or self-esteem of the high internal vs. low internal power cue SPs was reinforced. In the "general attitude discussion" the high internal SP showed no hesitancy in answering, took a strong stand, and gave definite conventional reasons for his answers. The low internal SP gave very hesitant answers, often qualifying or saying he wasn't sure. His reasons were usually weak and often hinged on whether people would tend to like or dislike the person in the situation presented in the question. Three of the questions dealt with self-esteem, e.g., "Many of the people I meet don't think too much of me." To this type of question the high internal SP responded as a person with high self-esteem, whereas the low internal SP responded as a person with low self-esteem. The low internal SP presented himself as persuasible, which he felt was a bad personal characteristic, whereas the high internal SP presented himself as nonpersuasible especially when right.

Some of the questions asked on this part of the tapes were taken from the California *F* scale.[2] None of these questions, however, were ones which were used in assessing the level of authoritarianism in the *S*s. Three questions dealt with conventional morality ("An insult to the honor should always be punished"), two dealt with anti-intraception ("Nowadays more and more people are prying into matters that should remain personal and

---

[2] This constitutes a methodological flaw the consequences of which will be assessed in the discussion.

private."), two dealt with strictness of leadership ("Any good leader should be strict with people under him in order to gain their respect."), and one dealt with attitudes toward science ("Science has its place, but there are many important things that can never possibly be understood by the human mind"). The high internal SP responded to these questions as a person with high authoritarianism would. He gave a definite answer and a reasonable explanation. The low internal SP answered as would a person with low authoritarianism, gave unsure answers and weak explanations.

These manipulations on the tape were intended to present the high internal SP as a person with high self-esteem, not swayed by other people's opinions, and with definite, well-substantiated, and rather conventional ideas. The low internal SP was intended to be the opposite of the above.[3]

Each S heard only one of the four tapes. It was introduced by E as "something we have left over from a study we did a couple of years ago. It is part of some interviews we made with people from all walks of life. Some are students just like you. Some are businessmen, some are professional people, some are retired, some are unemployed—all kinds. Since we still have these recordings, we decided not to let them go to waste, but to use them instead to find out how people size other people up. What we want you to do is very simple: just listen to this recording and afterwards answer some questions about the person on the tape."

After E answered any questions the Ss might have had they listened to one of the four recordings described above. Groups of from 2 to 7 Ss were randomly assigned to the four experimental variations by the following procedure. Before the arrival of each group in the laboratory two coins were tossed producing four possible outcomes: heads-heads, tails-tails, heads-tail, and tails-heads. Each of these four possible outcomes represented one of the four experimental variations. Thus, it was possible to assign most Ss randomly to each of the experimental variations.

Measurement of the Dependent Variables

When the recording had finished playing the Ss were given four forms to fill out with regard to "John," the SP. The order in which they were completed is the order presented here.

(*a*) *The free comment form* asked the S to "list the five most important things you would mention in describing John to a friend." The results from this form were categorized as to whether they referred to internal or external power cues. A percentage score for each was derived for each S. Interscorer reliability was 91.2 per cent.

(*b*) *The acceptance scale* presented 32 adjectives or descriptive phrases on which "John" was to be rated using a seven-point scale.[4] The items were intended to measure general acceptance of the SP and were primarily items dealing with positive character traits, likeability, or approachability. A *post hoc* analysis was performed on the scale by means of a factor analysis of the data collected from all Ss.

(*c*) *The perceptual accuracy form* asked the Ss six questions about the factual information presented on the tape. All questions dealt with external power cues. Thus the perceptual accuracy score (the percentage of ques-

---

[3] Actual typescripts of the tapes can be obtained by writing R. deCharms, Social Science Institute, Washington University.

[4] The items were: (1) ambitious, (2) assertive, (3) conceited, (4) confident, (5) courageous, (6) decided, (7) dependable, (8) does a good job, (9) enjoyable to work under, (10) firm, (11) forceful, (12) friendly, (13) gets things done, (14) has definite goals, (15) has social interests, (16) has to be respected, (17) intelligent, (18) knows where he's going, (19) likeable, (20) mature, (21) natural leader, (22) obnoxious, (23) open-minded, (24) popular, (25) sense of humor, (26) sincere, (27) strong character, (28) thinks ahead, (29) thinks for himself, (30) uses his head, (31) warm, (32) would make a good friend.

tions answered correctly) refers only to the manipulation of external power cues.

(d) *The class and status questionnaire* asked for information on Ss' parents' income, education, and occupation.

Results

Hypothesis 1 predicts no significant difference between high and low authoritarians with respect to the perception of external power cues.

Table 1 presents the relevant data. High authoritarians attain a mean perceptual accuracy score of 87.3 per cent correct which does not differ significantly from low authoritarians with 83.8 per cent correct. The analysis of variance shows, however, that perceptual accuracy is related to both external and internal cues. The means show that a high level of either external or internal cues leads to greater perceptual accuracy.

Hypothesis 2 predicts that high authoritarians use more external factors in descriptive statements about the SP than do low authoritarians. Table 2 presents the relevant means and analysis of variance. Here the percentage of external comments used by high authoritarians is almost twice that used by low authoritarians (high mean = 37.4, low mean = 17.1, $p < .0005$).[5] This result is highly

[5] Tables 1 and 2 reveal heterogeneity of variance. Under these conditions .01 was used as a conservative level of significance in testing the major hypotheses.

TABLE 1
Perceptual Accuracy Scores
(percentage correct)

a. *Means by treatment conditions*

| Stimulus persons' power cues || Subjects' F scale scores ||||||||
External	Internal	N	$\bar{X}$	s^2	N	$\bar{X}$	s^2	N	$\bar{X}$
		\multicolumn{3}{c	}{High}	\multicolumn{3}{c	}{Low}	\multicolumn{2}{c}{Total}
High	High	12	94.4	1353	8	93.7	504	20	94.2
High	Low	13	88.4	1290	7	85.7	1347	20	87.5
Low	High	10	86.7	4267	10	85.0	5237	20	85.8
Low	Low	11	78.8	3318	9	72.2	5090	20	75.8
Total		46	87.3		34	83.8		80	85.8
High External		25	91.3		15	90.0		40	90.81
Low External		21	82.6		19	78.9		40	80.84
High Internal		22	90.9		18	88.9		40	90.00
Low Internal		24	84.0		16	78.1		40	81.64

b. *Analysis of variance*

Source of variance[a]	df	Mean Square	F	p
Authoritarianism	1	17.1	0.51	—
External Cues	1	195.0	5.77	<.025
Internal Cues	1	150.5	4.45	<.05
Residual	72	33.8		

[a] All interactions nonsignificant.

TABLE 2
Percentage of External Comments Used in Description of Stimulus Person

a. *Means by treatment conditions*

Stimulus persons' power cues		Subjects' F scale scores							
		High			Low			Total	
External	Internal	N	$\bar{X}$	s^2	N	$\bar{X}$	s^2	N	$\bar{X}$
High	High	12	20.0	4000	8	7.5	750	20	15.0
High	Low	13	38.5	13969	7	17.1	3543	20	31.0
Low	High	10	44.0	4640	10	26.0	5640	20	35.0
Low	Low	11	49.1	5891	9	15.6	3022	20	34.0
Total		46	37.4		34	17.1		80	28.8
High External		25	29.6		15	12.0		40	23.0
Low External		21	46.7		19	21.1		40	34.5
High Internal		22	30.9		18	17.8		40	25.0
Low Internal		24	43.4		16	16.3		40	32.6

b. *Analysis of variance*

Source of variation[a]	df	Mean Square	F	p
Authoritarianism	1	911.7	15.23	<.0005
External Cues	1	332.8	5.56	<.025
Internal Cues	1	65.0	1.09	—
Residual	72	59.9		

[a] All interactions nonsignificant.

significant, confirming the hypothesis. In addition, the analysis of variance demonstrates that people in general, whether high or low in authoritariansim, use more external cues to describe the low external power SP than the high external power SP. It should be remembered that the means in this table present the number of external factors listed and not their validity; i.e., whether they refer to high or low external power cues.

Hypothesis 3 predicts that high authoritarians use fewer internal factors in descriptive statements about the SP than do low authoritarians. Table 3 presents the relevant means and analysis of variance. The result is again highly significant in the predicted direction (high mean = 52.9, low mean = 78.2, $p < .0005$). The analysis of variance demonstrates a significant interaction between external and internal power cues. This interaction does not invalidate the confirmation of Hypothesis 3 since, even if the interaction mean square is used as an estimate of residual variance, the mean square for authoritarianism remains significant. The means reveal that the interaction is a result of a big difference in internal comments about the high internal power SP as a function of high vs. low external power cues: internal attributes are much more frequent when the SP has high external power.

TABLE 3
PERCENTAGE OF INTERNAL COMMENTS USED IN DESCRIPTION OF STIMULUS PERSON

a. *Means by treatment conditions*

| Stimulus persons' power cues | | Subjects' F scale scores ||||||||
| External | Internal | \multicolumn{3}{c}{High} | \multicolumn{3}{c}{Low} | \multicolumn{2}{c}{Total} |
		N	$\bar{X}$	s^2	N	$\bar{X}$	s^2	N	$\bar{X}$
High	High	12	71.2	5967	8	85.0	2200	20	76.7
High	Low	13	50.8	15692	7	80.0	4000	20	61.0
Low	High	10	36.0	6240	10	68.0	4960	20	52.0
Low	Low	11	50.9	5891	9	82.2	2756	20	65.0
Total		46	52.9		34	78.2		80	63.7
High External		25	60.6		15	82.7		40	68.9
Low External		21	43.8		19	74.7		40	58.5
High Internal		22	55.2		18	75.6		40	64.4
Low Internal		24	50.8		16	81.2		40	63.0

b. *Analysis of variance*

Source of variation[a]	df	Mean Square	F	p
Authoritarianism	1	1466	21.28	<.0005
External Cues	1	286	4.15	<.05
Internal Cues	1	0	0.00	—
External × Internal Cues	1	345	5.01	<.05
Residual	72	68.9		

[a] All other interactions non-significant.

Hypothesis 4 deals with evaluations of the SP on the acceptance scale. This hypothesis predicts an interaction between the level of authoritarianism of the S and the external power cues presented by the SP. Such an interaction is obvious in the lower portion of Table 4 which shows means for high and low external power cues broken down as to high and low authoritarianism of the S. The means reveal that the high external SP receives much higher acceptance scores from the high authoritarians than the low external SP. This difference is in the same direction but not as marked for the Ss with low authoritarianism. Analysis of variance demonstrates that this interaction is significant at the .025 level of significance. The analysis also reveals no over-all difference between Ss with high and low authoritarian scores, but shows that Ss in general are much more accepting of both types of high power SP than either type of low power SP.

Hypothesis 5 predicts a statistical interaction between the level of authoritarianism and internal power cues with regard to the acceptance scale. The means in Table 4 show only a slight trend in favor of the hypothesis and the analysis of variance shows that the interaction is nonsignificant.

A factor analysis of the acceptance scale data revealed two major

TABLE 4
Acceptance of Stimulus Persons

a. *Means by treatment conditions*

| Stimulus persons' power cues ||| Subjects' F scale scores ||||||||
External	Internal	\multicolumn{3}{c}{High}	\multicolumn{3}{c}{Low}	\multicolumn{2}{c}{Total}
		N	$\bar{X}$	s^2	N	$\bar{X}$	s^2	N	$\bar{X}$
High	High	12	150.9[a]	6341	8	141.8	9432	20	147.3
High	Low	13	127.2	5336	7	115.7	4755	20	123.2
Low	High	10	107.8	4570	10	130.6	5334	20	119.2
Low	Low	11	74.4	3531	9	83.7	6438	20	78.6
Total		46	116.5		34	117.8		80	117.1
High External		25	138.6		15	129.6		40	135.2
Low External		21	90.3		19	108.4		40	98.9
High Internal		22	131.3		18	135.6		40	133.2
Low Internal		24	103.0		16	97.7		40	100.9

b. *Analysis of variance*

Source of variation[b]	df	Mean Square	F	p
Authoritarianism	1	17	0.26	—
External Cues	1	2419	36.60	<.0005
Internal Cues	1	2116	32.01	<.0005
Authoritarianism × External Cues	1	347	5.25	<.025
Authoritarianism × Internal Cues	1	32	0.48	—
Residual	72	66.1		

[a] The higher the score, the greater the degree of acceptance.
[b] All other interactions nonsignificant.

factors and three minor ones. Factor I included 19 items from the scale (all with loading above .50).[6]

Analysis of variance of scores based on the total of these items reveals significant effects attributable to the variation of external power cues (high external SP mean = 77.22, low mean = 60.85, $p < .0005$), internal power cues (high internal SP mean = 89.98, low mean = 48.10, $p < .0005$), and F scale score of S (high F mean = 73.37, low mean = 64.70, $p < .05$).

Factor II included 7 items from the acceptance scale (all with loadings above .65).[7] The analysis of variance of total scores derived from these items reveals a significant interaction between the external and internal power SPs (high external–high internal mean = 23.65, high–low mean = 32.80, low–high mean = 31.40, low–low mean = 22.65, $p < .0005$).

Factor III included 2 items ("Has social interests" and "Sincere"). The analysis of variance reveals a significant interaction between the external and internal power SPs (high external–high

---

[6] These items are numbers 1, 2, 3, 4, 5, 6, 10, 11, 13, 14, 16, 17, 18, 20, 21, 27, 28, 29, and 30 in footnote 4.
[7] These items are numbers 9, 12, 19, 24, 25, 31, and 32 in footnote 4.

internal SP mean = 9.60, high–low mean = 10.10, low–high mean = 9.10, low–low = 6.55, $p < .005$).

Factor IV included 2 items ("Obnoxious" which was reverse-scored, and "Open-minded"). Analysis of variance revealed a significant interaction between the external and internal power SPs (high external–high internal mean = 7.00, high–low mean = 11.00, low–high mean = 9.30, low–low mean = 8.00, $p < .0005$).

Factor V included 2 items ("Dependable" and "Does a good job"). Analysis of variance reveals a significant interaction between the external and internal power SPs and a significant effect attributable to internal SPs over and above the interaction (high external–high internal mean = 11.55, high–low mean = 8.40, low–high mean = 10.90, low–low mean = 4.55, $p < .005$).

The Ss were asked to report their parents' income in thousands of dollars. This measure of socio-economic status was intended as a control to check that Ss came from approximately the same socio-economic class. However, there turned out to be a significant difference in reported parents' income between Ss who heard the high external power SP and Ss who heard the low external power SP. A further check on socio-economic status of the Ss asked them to report the number of years of schooling of their parents and also parents' occupation. The significant difference between Ss exposed to the high external power SP versus the low also obtained for the data on number of years of schooling reported by the Ss. The result was still significant; however, the difference was not as great. If index scores of father's occupation are used (Hollingshead, 1949) the difference between high and low external power SPs becomes significant.

One further finding relates authoritarianism of Ss to major field in college. Of the 80 Ss in the experiment, 70 were enrolled either in the school of liberal arts or the school of engineering. A Chi square relating high and low F scale split at the median to liberal arts or engineering enrollment demonstrated a significant relationship (Chi square = 9.66, $p < .005$). The significant Chi square is a result of the fact that approximately three times as many of the students enrolled in engineering fell above the median as those who fell below the median on the F scale, while more liberal arts students fell below the median on the F scale.

Discussion

The results as presented strongly confirm the hypotheses in all but one instance, that being the predicted interaction between authoritarianism and internal power on the acceptance scale. The level of authoritarianism of a S does not affect the accuracy of his perception and/or recall of relevant external power cues of a SP (Hypothesis 1). It should be emphasized that the perceptual accuracy measure is clearly not sensitive enough to pick up slight differences. It appears, however, that the sections of the stimulus tapes had differential effects on accuracy scores. Thus the two tapes containing high external power cues led to significantly greater accuracy scores than did the two containing low external power cues. The same relationship holds for the tapes containing high and low internal power cues. These results may indicate that (*a*) the sections of the tapes were actually different as to clarity, (*b*) items on the perceptual accuracy form favored the high tapes, or (*c*) for some reason *S*s tended to distort or misperceive the data presented about the low internal and low external SP. It is impossible to determine exactly what led to these results, but it is clear that the effect was not related to the level of authoritarianism of the *S*.

As predicted, high authoritarian *S*s used more external power cues in descriptions of the SPs than did low authoritarians (Hypothesis 2). Thus, they apparently differed as to how they used the perceived external power cues. In general, however, *S*s used fewer external power cues to characterize the high external power SP than the low external power SP. This is a surprising result, but again is not related to the authoritarianism of the *S*. It is suggested that the reason for this discrepancy lies in the fact that the degree of poverty evidenced by the low external power SPs was more at variance with the experience of the *S*s than was the material well-being presented by the high external power SP. This being the case the low external power SP elicited more comment from the *S*s.

As to the use of internal power cues in describing the SP, low authoritarians used more than high authoritarians (Hypothesis 3). Here we have no check on differential perception of the cues, since we have no measure of perceptual accuracy of internal cues.

The results indicate that external power cues of the SP and the interaction between the internal and external power cues of the SP provide sources of variation which are statistically significant. It may be seen from Table 3 that the two extreme experimental variations, high internal–high external and low internal–low external, elicited the highest percentages of internal comments on the description sheets. The two "mixed" experimental variations, low internal–high external and high internal–low external, elicited significantly lower percentages of internal comments in the *S*s' descriptions. It may be that the "pure" types, i.e., high–high and low–low, represent expected and psychologically congruent combinations of the manipulated variables. The "mixed" types, i.e., low–high and high–low, represent unexpected and psychologically incongruent combinations. The *S*s presented with the mixed variations note the discrepancy and are less willing to make comments on the SP's psychological and less objectifiable characteristics. At the same time, however, they are required to make descriptive statements concerning the SP and, therefore, rely more heavily on his more obvious external characteristics.

With regard to the acceptance scale, it was found as predicted that high authoritarians tended to show high acceptance scores for high external power SPs and low acceptance scores for low external power SPs. The difference was in the same direction for the low authoritarian Ss but small. This interaction was predicted by Hypothesis 4.

One caution may be in order in evaluating the above findings. The manipulation of internal power cues was primarily accomplished by differences in decisiveness, tone of voice, etc. However, on the tapes the high internal power SP was made to agree with F scale items asked during the tape, while the low internal SP disagreed with them. Thus, the high authoritarian Ss probably agreed with the answers given by the high internal power SP and may have seen him as more similar to themselves than did the low authoritarian Ss. The intent of this manipulation was to strengthen the perception of the high internal SP as a self-confident person with strong conventional attitudes. However, one might argue that the main effect influencing the results with regard to the manipulation of internal power cues was attributable to the fact that the high authoritarian Ss were presented with a SP with similar attitudes to their own, while the low authoritarians were presented with a SP with differing attitudes. On the assumption that high authoritarians would tend to give higher evaluations to an SP with similar attitudes, it might be expected that the highs would evaluate the high internal SP more highly and the low internal SP less than the low authoritarians. However, the similarity of attitude factor seems not to have been a very potent determinant of evaluation, since it was the low authoritarians who gave the highest acceptance scores to the high internal power SP and the lowest to the low internal power SP.

In general, these results show that high and low authoritarians do not differ in acceptance of others but in what they base their acceptance upon. For high authoritarians the class cues of the SP provide the keystone for acceptance or rejection, while low authoritarians were most influenced by internal or psychological cues. In a sense, high authoritarians do not find it necessary to go "into" the persons they are evaluating while low authoritarians do.

The results of the factor analysis make it clear that the Ss evaluations of the SP on the acceptance scale are in fact a composite of ratings primarily of strength of character and friendliness. When the factors are analyzed separately authoritarianism no longer interacts significantly with external power cues. This could be the results of the fact that none of the subscales are as sensitive as the total score, or possibly the over-all evaluation including several factors gives a better picture of the general attitude toward the SP.

Analyses of the five subscales gives us data on inferences drawn by Ss in general from the stimulus dimensions and hence tells us something about how different types of power are perceived. Strong main effects were found for each subscale showing that the different SPs elicited precise and meaningful distinctions from the Ss. These differential effects are remarkable since it will be remembered that each S was presented with only one SP and hence the distinctions do not come from comparisons made by the Ss but from reactions of different groups of Ss to each SP.

The subscale from factor I is similar to the "potency" factor reported Osgood, Suci, and Tannenbaum (1957). Since it is not identical, we shall call it "strength of character." It has an obvious relationship to the perception of power. As might be expected, high authoritarian Ss give higher ratings on this scale, in general, than do low authoritarians. This is the only effect involving authoritarianism found in the analyses of the subscales. Both internal and external power cues affected the ratings on the "strength of character" subscale. It was most highly related to variation in internal power cues.

The remaining subscales resulted in interesting interactions between external and internal power cues. Thus, the Ss apparently perceived four distinct SPs, not two orthogonal dimensions. For this reason we shall discuss these results using the colloquial names introduced earlier.

Factor II refers to the "friendliness" of the SP and may be related to Osgood, Suci, and Tannenbaum's (1957) evaluation scale. On this factor the "tycoon" (high external–high internal SP) and the "shiftless trash" (low–low) are seen as less friendly than the "go-getter" or the "decadent aristocrat." As to social interests and sincerity (factor III), "shiftless trash" is seen as far below the other SPs.

Factor IV is a combination of open-mindedness and nonobnoxiousness. Here the "decadent aristocrat" is seen as least obnoxious and most open-minded while the "tycoon" is the most obnoxious and closed-minded. As might be expected the "tycoon" and the "go-getter" are high on dependability (factor V) and the "shiftless trash" is very low, i.e., indeed "shiftless."

These results demonstrate that Ss were quite sensitive to the characteristics of the SPs and responded with typical cultural values. The "tycoon" was strong and dependable but obnoxious, closed-minded, and unfriendly. The "go-getter" was strong, dependable, and friendly. The "decadent aristocrat" was evidently not seen as decadent. He was open-minded, nonobnoxious and friendly. "Shiftless trash" was lowest on every scale except that he surpassed the "tycoon" slightly in open-mindedness and nonobnoxiousness.

The data here reported clearly support Heider's contention that perceived power of a SP may be derived from personal characteristics and/or social status of the SP. In addition, these two types of power cues have strong effects on the reactions of Ss to the SP both in general and in interaction with the authoritarianism of the S.

The two types of power cues are not necessarily perceived independently of each other. Thus the four combinations of external and internal cues evidently lead to four distinct types in the perception of the Ss with regard to such aspects as friendliness, sincerity, open-mindedness, and dependability.

The income, education, and occupation data reported by the Ss for their parents at the conclusion of the experiment were originally intended to check whether or not the Ss fell between the class positions defined by the high and low external power SPs. A significant difference was found, however, between Ss who heard the high and those who heard the low external stimulus tape. This finding is discrepant with the careful randomization of Ss in various cells of the experiment. It is possible that hearing the tape had an effect on the Ss' subsequent reports of their parents' incomes. Thus one might argue that this direct variation of reported parental income with income of the SP is a variety of distortion based on what Veblen (1899) has called an invidious comparison.

An independent check on the Ss' reports of their parents' occupations was made possible by access to records maintained elsewhere in the university. Unfortunately, only the occupational data were available. However, these data, which could not have been affected by the experimental manipulation, show no significant differences between experimental groups. It seems probable that Ss were influenced to change the reported income of their parents to be more in accord with the income reported by the SP that they heard.

Ss enrolled in the liberal arts school tended to have lower F scale scores than did Ss enrolled in the engineering school. One could say that liberal arts is in reality attracting "liberal" people. As a *post hoc* explanation the high authoritarians' preference for engineering may be a result of their anti-intraception, rejection of emotion, and desire for predictability and control over the environment. This result seems to be a matter of selection rather than a particular academic field molding authoritarian attitudes since the majority of the Ss in this experiment were first-semester freshmen.

Summary

Eighty Ss participated in an experimental investigation of the relationship between authoritarianism of the S and his reactions to standard SPs presented to him. The SPs differed as to the types of power or status they appeared to possess. Internal power cues were manipulated through forcefulness and decisiveness of speech. External power cues were manipulated by the SP's reported socio-economic status. These power dimensions were derived from Heider's (1958) discussion of power. The Ss' accuracy of perception, acceptance, and free description of the SP constituted the dependent variables. The following relationships were found.

There was no significant difference between high and low authoritarians with respect to the perception of external power-relevant cues. High authoritarians relied more on external factors in their descriptions of others than did low authoritarians who relied on internal factors. The SP with high external power cues was evaluated highest by all Ss, but high authoritarians make the sharpest distinction (in evaluating a person) between high and low external power cues. It was hypothesized that internal power cues would be a more important factor in the acceptance scores of the low than the high authoritarians. This hypothesis was not confirmed. The high (internal) power SP was quite uniformly preferred.

The results generally support the theoretical position that high authoritarians are not necessarily more sensitive to external power cues, but are more influenced by them in making inferences about other persons. Low authoritarians are less influenced by external power cues in evaluating others, and use more internal factors in describing others.

REFERENCES

Adorno, T. W., Frenkel-Brunswik, Else, Levinson, D. J., & Sanford, R. N. *The authoritarian personality*. New York: Harper, 1950.

Heider, F. *The psychology of interpersonal relations*. New York: Wiley, 1958.

Hollingshead, A. B. *Elmtown's youth*. New York: Wiley, 1949.

Jones, E. E. Authoritarianism as a determinant of first-impression formation. *J. Pers.*, 1954, **23**, 107-127.

Osgood, C. E., Suci, G. J., and Tannenbaum, P. H. *The measurement of meaning*. Urbana, Ill., Univ. Illinois Press, 1957.

Roberts, A. H., & Jessor, R. Authoritarianism, punitiveness, and perceived social status. *J. abnorm soc. Psychol.*, 1958, **56**, 311-314.

Scodel, A., & Mussen, P. H. Social perceptions of authoritarians and nonauthoritarians. *J. abnorm. soc. Psychol.*, 1953, **48**, 181-184.

Thibaut, J. W., & Riecken, H. W. Authoritarianism, status, and the communication of aggression. *Hum. Relat.*, 1955, **8**, 95-120. (a).

Thibaut, J. W., & Riecken, H. W. Some determinants and consequences of the perception of social causality. *J. Pers.* 1955, **24**, 113-133. (b).

Veblen, T. *Theory of the leisure class*. (1899) New York: Modern Library, 1934.

18

PERCEPTION AND JUDGMENT IN THE POLITICAL EXTREMIST[1]

JAMES O. WHITTAKER
Pennsylvania State University

The tendency for individuals holding extreme positions on controversial issues to characterize these issues in all-or-none, dichotomous terms, has long been apparent to those involved in studies of communication and persuasion. The strong Republican, for example, seems unable to differentiate Socialism and Communism as economic systems, and in fact, if his position is on the ultra-right, he is likely to place Democrats and moderate Republicans in the same category with Socialists and Communists. It would appear that his own attitudes in some way affect his perception of the stands of others. He seems unable to discriminate between positions at the other end of the continuum, and therefore lumps all these positions together in the same category.

Until the recent work of Muzafer Sherif, Carl Hovland [2], and others [5], this latter statement was simply conjecture. In these experiments, however, it has been demonstrated that one's perception of positions on any issue, is determined to a great extent by one's own position on the issue.

Sherif and Hovland [2] conceive of an individual's stand on an issue in terms of a *range* or a *latitude of acceptance*. This includes not only the specific position which comes closest to his

---

[1] The research by the present author which is reported in this paper was supported by a grant (AF-AFOSR 62-188) from the United States Air Force Office of Scientific Research. The author wishes to thank Professor Muzafer Sherif of the Pennsylvania State University for his helpful comments and criticisms offered during the conduct of this study, and the Yale University Press for permission to print Tables 1, 2, and 3 from Sherif, M. and C. Hovland, SOCIAL JUDGMENT. Copyright © 1961 by Yale University. All rights reserved.

TABLE 1
Hypothetical latitudes of acceptance and rejection of subjects holding each position[2]

Positions rated	Subject's own position								
	A	B	C	D	E	F	G	H	I
A	√√	√	0	X	X	XX	XX	XX	XX
B	√	√√	√	0	X	X	X	X	X
C	0	√	√√	√	0	X	X	X	X
D	X	0	√	√√	√	0	X	X	X
E	X	X	0	√	√√	√	0	X	X
F	X	X	X	0	√	√√	√	0	X
G	X	X	X	X	0	√	√√	√	0
H	X	X	X	X	X	0	√	√√	√
I	XX	XX	XX	XX	X	X	0	√	√√

own but other positions which he is willing to tolerate as well. Implicit in this conception of course, is a *latitude of rejection* as well. This latitude includes not only the *most* unacceptable position, but other positions which the individual also rejects.

These investigators hypothesized that as one's position moves from neutral to extreme, his tolerance for stands other than his own is reduced. With neutrals or moderates then, tolerance for other positions is considerably greater than with those at either extreme. In line with this hypothesis they have presented the empirical model of latitudes of acceptance and rejection shown in Table 1.

Nine different positions on a hypothetical issue are shown in "A" through "I". The subject's own position (the position he finds most acceptable) is represented by "√√". Other stands which he evaluates as acceptable are represented by a single "√". Completely unacceptable stands are represented by "XX", while other unacceptable stands are indicated with a single "X". Stands neither accepted nor rejected are indicated by the zero ("0").

This model predicts that subjects holding position "A" or "I" would find acceptable far fewer positions than they reject. Note however, that with subjects holding moderate or intermediate positions, the latitude of acceptance is of about the same magnitude as the latitude of rejection. Such subjects in other words, are far more tolerant of positions other than their own, than are subjects at the extremes.

To test this model, nine statements pertaining to the 1956 Presidential campaign were selected on the basis of trials with twenty-five individuals whose stands were known to the experimenters. The nine statements ranged from strong pro-Republican (designated as "A") through middle of the road (designated as "E") to strong pro-Democratic (designated as "I").

---

[2] From Sherif, M. and C. Hovland. SOCIAL JUDGMENT. New Haven, Conn.: Yale University Press, 1961, p. 143.

TABLE 2
*Percent of Positions on the Election Issue
included in the Latitudes of Acceptance and Rejection*[3]

Position checked most acceptable	Latitude of acceptance (√√ + √)	Latitude of rejection (XX + X)	Not checked (0)
A	37.02	51.38	11.60
B	33.37	52.29	14.34
C	35.19	48.56	16.25
D	33.33	40.33	26.33
E	32.24	38.43	29.32
F	40.66	39.56	19.78
G	36.46	43.65	19.89
H	35.21	53.72	11.07
I	30.56	55.56	13.88

These statements were presented to 406 college students in three southwest universities. Each subject was asked to check the *most acceptable* statement from his point of view, and others that he also found acceptable. Then he was asked to check the *most objectionable* statement and others to which he also objected. The experimenters indicated that it was not necessary to respond to every statement.

The results of this experiment are shown in Table 2. Note that when a subject checked either statement A (strong pro-Republican) or statement I (strong pro-Democrat) as the most acceptable, he tended to reject considerably more positions than he accepted. With those checking intermediate stands, however, the tendency in this regard is considerably less.

In other experiments it has been demonstrated that these findings are valid not only in the case of political issues but with other issues as well [1]. For example, prior to a referendum in Oklahoma to determine the fate of its prohibition laws, a large number of statements relating to the use of alcohol were selected from newspapers and other sources. From these statements, nine were selected by twenty-five judges as representing positions from wet to dry. The statements were as follows:

A Since alcohol is the curse of mankind, the sale and use of alcohol, including light beer, should be completely abolished.

B Since alcohol is the main cause of corruption in public life, lawlessness, and immoral acts, its sale and use should be prohibited.

C Since it is hard to stop at a reasonable moderation point in the use of alcohol, it is safer to discourage its use.

D Alcohol should not be sold or used except as a remedy for snake bites, cramps, colds, fainting, and other aches and pains. *

E The arguments in favor and against the sale and use of alcohol are nearly equal.

F The sale of alcohol should be so regulated that it is available in limited quantities for special occasions.

---

[3] From Sherif, M. and C. Hovland. SOCIAL JUDGMENT. New Haven, Conn.: Yale University Press, 1961, p. 139.

G The sale and use of alcohol should be permitted with proper state controls, so that the revenue from taxation may be used for the betterment of schools, highways, and other state institutions.

H Since prohibition is a major cause of corruption in public life, lawlessness, immoral acts, and juvenile delinquency, the sale and use of alcohol should be legalized.

I It has become evident that man cannot get along without alcohol; therefore, there should be no restriction whatsoever on its sale and use.

As in the experiment cited above, subjects were asked to check the one statement closest to their own stand; others not objectionable to them, the most objectionable statement, and others that they also found objectionable. "Dry" subjects in this experiment were from the Women's Christian Temperance Union, Salvation Army, and strict denominational colleges in Oklahoma. A group of 25 individuals personally known to the experimenters were selected as the "wet" subjects.

The results of this experiment are shown in Table 3. Again it will be noted that tolerance for positions other than one's own is considerably less among the extreme subjects than among those holding intermediate stands.

In another experiment demonstrating similar results, the issue involved attitudes toward government controls in American agriculture [5]. This experiment was conducted when the Kennedy Administration Farm Bill advocating greater production and marketing controls was being debated in Congress and in all news media. The two major farm groups in the country had come out with opposing stands—the Farm Bureau opposing the bill and the Farmer's Union favoring it.

As in the previous studies, nine statements were selected which represented a continuum of positions from pro through neutral to con. These statements were mimeographed on a single sheet and given to subjects attending Farm Bureau meetings, Farmer's union meetings, or college classes. The instructions were the same as in the experiments previously discussed.

The results of this experiment, shown in Table 4, corroborate the findings of the previous studies. Again, those holding extreme positions tend to be less tolerant of positions other than

TABLE 3
Acceptability of Statements in Relation to Subjects' Positions on Alcohol Issue[4]

Subjects' positions	N	Mean number of items acceptable	Mean number of items not checked	Mean number of items rejected
Extreme (A, B, G, H, I)	193	2.81	1.48	4.71
Intermediate (C, D, E, F) p = < .03	37	3.05	2.24	3.70

[4] From Sherif, M. and C. Hovland. SOCIAL JUDGMENT. New Haven, Conn.: Yale University Press, 1961, p. 135.

TABLE 4
Acceptability of Statements in Relation to Subjects' Positions on Farm Issue[5]

Positions	N	Mean number of items acceptable	Mean number of items not checked	Mean number of items rejected
Extreme (A, B, H, I)	37	1.97	3.05	3.97
Intermediate (C, D, E, F, G)	141	2.86	2.74	3.40
$p = < .01$				

their own, while moderates show a greater tendency to accept alternative positions.

These experiments have a number of important implications. First, they help us to better understand the behavior of the radical—the person with extreme views. For example, when we hear someone call President Eisenhower a "conscious agent of the Communist conspiracy," it may be difficult for us to believe that the person making the statement actually believes the statement himself. We may simply dismiss such a person as some kind of "political nut." These experiments, however, suggest that it is entirely possible for a person making such a statement to strongly believe it. When one holds extreme views, as we have seen, he does not in fact discriminate the shades of gray discriminated by the less extreme individual. Thus, in his mind he tends to dichotomize issues, i.e., "you are either for us or against us."

Another implication relates to methods of changing attitudes. Since tolerance for other positions is reduced among those holding extreme attitudes, it stands to reason that presenting markedly different positions will bring about little or no change. In fact it has recently been demonstrated that such attempts may actually *reinforce* the listener's beliefs [3]. To change the attitudes of those holding extreme views, we suspect that it may only be accomplished in small steps. By presenting a series of arguments, each one only slightly different from the position of the listener, it may be possible to move the extremist to a more moderate position.

The final implication of these studies relates to understanding our own behavior. When we understand that our perception and judgment of others' positions is colored by our own attitudes, we may perceive the positions of others a little more objectively. For those concerned with public opinion, this is an absolute necessity.

REFERENCES

1. Hovland, C., O. Harvey, and M. Sherif. Assimilation and contrast effects in reaction to communication and attitude change. JOURNAL OF ABNORMAL AND SOCIAL PSYCHOLOGY 55 (1957) pp. 244–252.

---

[5] From Whittaker, J. Cognitive Dissonance and the Effectiveness of Persuasive Communications. PUBLIC OPINION QUARTERLY 28 (1964) pp. 547–555.

2. Sherif, M. and C. Hovland. SOCIAL JUDGMENT. New Haven, Conn.: Yale University Press, 1961.
3. Whittaker, J. Opinion change as a function of communication—attitude discrepancy. PSYCHOLOGICAL REPORTS 13 (1963) pp. 763–772.
4. Whittaker, J. Parameters of social influence in the autokinetic situation. SOCIOMETRY 27 (1964) pp. 88–95.
5. Whittaker, J. Cognitive Dissonance and the Effectiveness of Persuasive Communications. PUBLIC OPINION QUARTERLY 28 (1964) pp. 547–555.

Section Five

Learning and Retention

How should different learning situations be classified or categorized? One customary distinction has been between classical and instrumental conditioning. Bitterman, however, in the first article in this section, uses three categories: "Thorndikian Situations, Pavlovian Situations, and Avoidance Situations." Each is sufficiently different from the others, he believes, to warrant considering the use of three rather than two categories, as mentioned above.

Dodwell and Bessant, in the second article of the section, present new evidence relating to another issue of long standing in psychology—the issue as to whether or not perceptual learning occurs. Can animals, in other words, learn associations between stimuli or does learning always involve associations between stimuli and responses? This experiment seems to show that learning is not always of the S-R type.

The third article deals with the effects of punishment on behavior. Skinner, in an experiment conducted a number of years ago, concluded that punishment does not serve to extinguish responses but rather only temporarily inhibits the response rate. Boe and Church, on the other hand, in a recent series of experiments have demonstrated that the extent to which punishment reduces the number of responses in extinction is dependent upon the intensity of the punishment and the number of training trials. The recovery of responses when punishment ceased, observed by Skinner, did not occur in the present experiments.

In the next article of the section, Thelen discusses the educational issue of conditioning versus insight, particularly with reference to programmed instruction. Should *any* instruction in the school utilize simple repetition and reinforcement, characteristic of conditioning? Thelen argues that simply increasing the verbal repertoire of the student is not or should not be the goal of education. Conditional learning of a very large number of fragments of information does not contribute to the development of character, ability to think critically, ability to apply principles, or development of interests. Rather than pursue such learning, it is suggested, the primary emphasis should be on "insight" learning—seeking principles and then moving systematically to demonstrate the principles.

The fifth article of this section deals with problems relating to the most effective type of pre-school program for the disadvantaged. Karnes and her associates compared five programs over a period of several years. These included the Traditional Nursery School, a Community-Integrated Program, a Montessori Program, an Ameliorative Program, and a Direct Verbal Program. At the end of the pre-school year, students enrolled in the latter two programs —both heavily emphasizing verbal skills—showed a mean gain in IQ of 13 points. Those in the other three groups showed more modest gains. By the end of the following year (Kindergarten year) children in the Direct Verbal Program were significantly superior to those in the other four groups in terms of language gains. Even more important, at the end of the first grade, serious learning deficits had all but been eliminated among children who had been enrolled in the Ameliorative and Direct Verbal Pre-School Program. The study shows clearly that pre-school educational programs for the disadvantaged must be aimed primarily at improving language or verbal skills.

At first glance, the results of this study may seem to contradict those of Thelen, reported in the second article in the section. It should be noted however, that a certain *minimum* level of verbal or language ability is absolutely necessary for pursuit of conventional classroom work. Here Karnes is talking about a means for bringing disadvantaged students up to this level, and Thelen is talking about education for those already at or above the minimal level in verbal or language skills.

New research in the area of retention is examined by A. L. Jacobson in the final paper. He points out that about 1950 the attention of psychologists began to focus on RNA (ribonucleic acid), a large molecule found in all living cells and similar in structure to DNA. Early experiments with planaria, a type of flat worm, had suggested that RNA is actually the substance of memory. When taken from trained animals and injected into the untrained, learning also appeared to be transferred. Further injection of a chemical which destroys RNA *prevented* the transfer of learning. The next step was to see if learning could be transferred through RNA injections in higher animals. Using rats, Jacobson attempted the same thing, and was successful. RNA, then, seems to be the stuff of which memories are made. But many questions still remain. What is the nature of the behavioral effects transferred? What produces the effects? How does training affect RNA or protein so as to make the transfer effect possible?

TECHNIQUES FOR THE STUDY OF LEARNING IN ANIMALS: ANALYSIS AND CLASSIFICATION

M. E. BITTERMAN

Bryn Mawr College

Although many different techniques for the study of learning in animals have been developed in the 60 years or so since the problem of animal intelligence first was brought into the laboratory, their interrelations never have been carefully defined. Crude dichotomies have been proposed—"respondent conditioning" versus "operant conditioning" by Skinner (1935, 1937), "classical conditioning" versus "instrumental conditioning" by Hilgard and Marquis (1940)—and, more recently, a trichotomy—"classical conditioning" versus "instrumental conditioning" versus "selective learning" by Spence (1956)—but the diversity of method is too great to be encompassed in any such one-way analysis. While certain differences among the techniques to be classified *must* be ignored if the number of categories is to be smaller than the number of techniques, the quest for parsimony seems to have been carried too far.

Classification is not merely a matter of taste. When one can find no objective basis for evaluating the conviction that a given difference in technique should be stressed or that another safely may be disregarded, it is only because the proper experiments have not been performed. Consider, for example, the question of whether the difference between flexion conditioning with avoidable as compared with unavoidable shock should be reflected in a classification of techniques. The answer is "Yes" for Hilgard and Marquis, who emphasize the contingency of reinforcement on response. They classify flexion conditioning as "classical" when shock is unavoidable and as "instrumental" when shock is avoidable. The answer is "No" for Spence, who emphasizes the degree of control afforded the experimenter over the

[1] This paper grows out of a program of research on the comparative psychology of learning supported by Contract Nonr 2829 (01) with the Office of Naval Research and by Grant M-2857 from the United States Public Health Service. Its reproduction in whole or in part is permitted for any purpose of the United States Government.

appearance of the response to be learned. Ignoring the contingency of shock upon failure of response to the CS, Spence treats avoidance conditioning as a special case of classical conditioning in which the pattern of reinforcement gradually shifts from consistent to intermittent. Such a disagreement surely need not remain long in the realm of opinion. One has only to compare the behavior of an animal trained with avoidable shock and that of a control animal trained with shock that is unavoidable but simply withheld on whichever trials the first animal avoids; if response contingency is unimportant, the course of learning in the two animals should be the same.

In general, a classification of techniques may be treated as the expression of a set of hypotheses about the functional significance of differences in technique—a distinction between two techniques as an assertion that they yield results which differ in some fundamental respect, and a failure to distinguish between two techniques as an assertion that they may be used interchangeably in the analysis of learning. This is not to say that a classification may not be preferred on historical, or on pedagogical, or even on esthetic grounds, but only that a functional interpretation is available which provides a basis for empirical evaluation. Methodological and functional considerations have, in fact, been linked rather closely in the past. Methodological distinctions have been taken as points of departure for dual-process analyses of learning, while strivings for a unitary conception have been reflected in the blurring of methodological distinctions. One may even point to experiments designed explicitly to provide a functional comparison of different methods (Youtz, 1938a, 1938b, 1939), although the empirical study of methodological interrelations certainly has not been carried very far.

Functional considerations play a central role in the classification to be offered here, which grows out of a program of comparative research (Bitterman, 1960). The first step in the program is to assess the phyletic generality of certain theoretically significant phenomena of learning which have been established in work with the rat (hitherto the principal subject of research on learning), and to that end a variety of simple animals must be studied under conditions analogous to those which have been used for the study of the rat; but what are "analogous" conditions? Clearly, the answer to this question requires some hypotheses about the essential properties of the various techniques which have been used for the rat. As will later be indicated, the comparative enterprise not only motivates further methodological analysis but constitutes a new source of data in terms of which the outcome may be evaluated.

Thorndikian Situations

It seems reasonable to begin the analysis with a set of closely interrelated techniques which date back to the turn of the century and which have yielded most of the information on which contemporary conceptions of animal learning are based. The adjective *Thorndikian* is appropriate both because of Thorndike's pioneering role in their development and because their operation is predicated on an empirical law of effect. Familiar examples are the problem box and the maze. In each of these situations, traditionally, the experimenter sets out to change behavior by manipulating its consequences, that is, by arranging a contingency between some motivationally significant state of affairs ("reinforcement") and the behavior in question. Thus, pulling a loop in a problem box or turning to the left in a T maze may be encouraged with food or discouraged with shock. Indeed, the motivational significance of any event may be assessed in terms of its effect on the response which produces it in such a situation. An event that facilitates the occurrence of a response upon which it is contingent is called a *reward;* an event that has the opposite effect is called a *punishment;* while an event that produces no measurable change in behavior is motivationally insignificant or neutral. An aversive stimulus is one whose onset is punishing, and in what is called *escape training* the offset of such a stimulus serves as a reward.

Unitary and Choice Situations

An important distinction between two main types of Thorndikian situation may be illustrated by a comparison of the problem box and the maze. In both these apparatuses, the animal is afforded numerous possibilities for action, one of which the experimenter chooses to reward. The main difference between them has to do with the treatment of irrelevant responses. In work with the problem box, the experimenter may take some qualitative notice of the variety of fruitless activities which appear, but his interest is centered on the rewarded response and the readiness with which it comes to expression. The basic datum is time. In the maze, by contrast, the unrewarded behavior of the animal is structured more clearly; certain major alternatives to correct response are delineated, and the interest of the experimenter is centered on their decline and disappearance. The basic datum is error. Time may be recorded, but it does not as clearly reflect progress in the choice among alternative courses of action, the aspect of selective learning which the maze is so well suited to display.

The designation *unitary* Thorndikian situation (or T-1 situation) will be used here for the problem box and for any other Thorndikian situation in which but a single course of action is defined and the readiness with which it comes to expression is measured. The designation Thorndikian *choice* situation (or T-2 situation) will be used for the maze and for any other Thorndikian situation in which two or more incompatible courses of action are defined and choice among them is studied. The nature of the responses delineated and the general properties of the environments in which they appear are ignored in this classification. Thus, a problem box which offers a choice of manipulanda is classed with the maze as a T-2 situation, while the runway is classed as a T-1 situation despite its structural resemblance to the maze. The runway may, of course, provide a measure of error, as in the early works of Hicks (1911), who plotted the learning of a culless maze in terms of retracing, while the potentialities of the maze for the study of choice may be ignored, as in the early work of Thorndike (1898), who, measuring only time, used the maze as though it were just another problem box. In such cases, the classification is based on the use to which the apparatus actually is put in a given experiment. For the most part, however, contradictions between potentiality and use are rare. An investigator interested in choice among alternative courses of action is not likely to use a runway, nor, unless he is interested specifically in choice among alternative courses of action, is he likely (today) to use a maze.

Both T-1 and T-2 situations may be "chained." The most common example of a chained T-2 situation is the maze of many choice-points, once very much the mode, but rarely encountered today, perhaps because of the conviction, expressed by Lashley (1918), that the single-unit maze is quite as sensitive as the multiple-unit maze to the effects of significant variables and much less costly in time and effort. (The two kinds of apparatus are not, of course, fully equivalent; certain problems—such as that of correction versus noncorrection, first studied by Lashley—arise only when the number of choice points is reduced to one, while other problems—such as that of serial order—disappear.) Chained T-1 situations never have been widely used. An example may be found in a string of problem boxes, each presenting one manipulandum, with the first giving access to the second, the second to the third, and so on, until the reward finally is attained (Herbert & Arnold, 1947). For certain purposes, conceivably, mixed chains (composed both of T-1 and of T-2 units) might be used.

Generalized and Discriminative Situations

Each of the two types of Thorndikian situation already distinguished —*unitary* and *choice*—may occur in *discriminative* as well as in *generalized* form. This new distinction, which is orthogonal to the first, will be conveyed by adding the letters g (for generalized) and d (for discriminative) to the symbols for unitary and choice: T-1g, T-1d, T-2g, T-2d. In a discriminative problem, the experimental environment is varied systematically from trial to trial, and with it the consequences of response, the capacity of the animal to discriminate the change being inferred from a corresponding variation in behavior. In a generalized problem, there may be some variation in the experimental environment from trial to trial (intentional or unintentional), and there may be some variation in the consequences of response (as in work on partial reinforcement), but there is (by definition) no correlation between the two kinds of change, and hence there is no objective basis for systematic variation in behavior.

In the simplest T-1d case, a single defined response is rewarded under one set of conditions but not rewarded (or punished) under another set of conditions, and the readiness with which the response comes to expression under the two conditions is compared. For example, response in a single-window jumping apparatus is rewarded when a white card is displayed but punished when the card displayed is black (Solomon, 1943). Performance in a T-1d problem may be expressed in terms of "error," but a temporal criterion is implied. For example, in an early experiment by Thorndike (1898), cats were fed for climbing to the top of their cage in response to the words "I must feed those cats," but not for making the same response to the words "Tomorrow is Tuesday," an error being recorded whenever they climbed up (promptly) to the second phrase or failed (in a reasonable period of time) to climb up in response to the first. Similarly, Grice (1949), working with another T-1d situation, computed the median response time for a series of trials and counted as an error any response to the negative stimulus faster than the median or any response to the positive stimulus slower than the median. A clear distinction should be made between error thus defined and erroneous choice in a T-2d situation.

In a T-2d problem, two or more alternative responses are defined—two in the simplest case. One of the responses is rewarded and the second unrewarded (or punished) under a given set of conditions, while the consequences of the two courses of action are reversed under another set of conditions, and erroneous choices are counted. For example, in a conventional jumping apparatus, a jump to the right window is rewarded when the card in the right window is white and the card in the left window is black, but a jump to the left window is rewarded when the positions of the two cards are interchanged; or, in the same apparatus, response to the right window is rewarded when two white cards are displayed, but response to the left window is rewarded when two black cards are displayed. (Problems of the first kind have been termed "simultaneous" while problems of the second kind have been termed "successive," an adjective applied as well to T-1d problems; considerable confusion has resulted from the failure to distinguish between T-1d and successive T-2d problems.) The so-called "higher order" discriminations—oddity, matching-from-sample, and multiple choice—also may be classified as T-2d problems, although they seem to make demands which go far beyond those of the simpler problems first exemplified. The T-1d and T-2d categories actually are rather coarse ones which themselves invite careful analysis and subdivision.

Like T-2g situations, T-2d situations may be "chained"—as when an animal is required to make a series of choices based on brightness before the reward is attained (Stone, 1928). Meaningful T-1d chains also are possible, although no instance of such a chain is to be found in the literature. For example, response to a manipulandum in one unit gives immediate access to the next unit when the positive stimulus is present; when the negative stimulus is present, access to the next unit is given after a predetermined period of time whether or not the animal responds.

Discrete and Continuous Situations

There has been little clarity on the relation of Skinner's technique to other techniques for the study of learning in animals. It has been asserted by Woodworth (1938), for example, that the Skinner box "bridges the gap" between the problem box and the classical conditioning situation, and a similar view is met again in Spence (1956), who places the Skinner box on a continuum at a point intermediate between the methods of Thorndike and Pavlov; but the notion of continuity is difficult to justify. Skinner (1935, 1937) certainly has succeeded very well in drawing a sharp line between his method and that of Pavlov on the basis of criteria which fail to distinguish his method from that of Thorndike.

Skinnerian situations are Thorndikian situations as the term is defined here. The original Skinner box differs from the older problem box only in that it delivers food to the response compartment (instead of admitting the animal to a separate feeding compartment) when the defined response is made, a feature which eliminates handling of the animal between trials. Equipped with a retractable lever, which is introduced to begin each trial and withdrawn after response, the Skinner box may be used in exactly the same manner as the older problem box; in fact, a retractable manipulandum which delivered food to the responding animal was developed for the monkey by Thorndike himself (1901). Skinner (1932), of course, has preferred to use his apparatus as a "repeating" problem box—his own adjective—inverting the traditional measure of performance, and substituting for time per response on discrete trials number of responses per unit time (rate of response) to a continuously available lever. Either way, a Skinner box containing one lever may be classified as a T-1 situation. A single response is delineated, its consequences are manipulated, and the readiness with which it comes to expression is measured. With two levers and the study of choice, the Skinner box becomes a T-2 situation.

It seems reasonable, nevertheless, to make a formal distinction between Thorndikian situations in which latencies or choices are measured in discrete trials and their Skinnerian counterparts in which rates of response are measured under conditions of continuous opportunity to respond. Situations of the first kind will be designated as *discrete*, while those of the second kind will be designated as *continuous*, and for symbolic purposes the subscripts d (for discrete) or c (for continuous) will be added to the T for Thorndikian, as, for example, in T_d-2g (discrete, choice, generalized) or in T_c-1d (continuous, unitary, discriminative). The discrete-continuous distinction reflects the hypothesis that rate of response, despite its close mathematical relation to latency, has a functional significance which is to a certain extent unique, and some interesting evidence for this view comes from comparative studies of the effect of inconsistent reinforcement on resistance to extinction. In the rat, discrete and continuous techniques both give the so-called paradoxical effect (greater resistance to extinction after inconsistent than after consistent reinforcement). In the fish, initial resistance to extinction is greater after consistent reinforcement in the discrete case (Longo & Bitterman, 1960; Wodinsky & Bitterman, 1959, 1960); but some as yet unpublished data show greater resistance to extinction after inconsistent reinforcement in the continuous case. Whether the difference in outcome may be traced to a difference in the functional properties of the two techniques, or whether it is a product of certain parametric differences between the two sets of experiments, remains to be determined. The matter is introduced here only to suggest the possibility that techniques which are functionally equivalent for one species may not be so for others. In this connection it is worth noting, perhaps, that the potentialities of the rate measure seem to be realized fully only when inconsistency of reinforcement is introduced.

A General Definition of Thorndikian Situations

In each of the Thorndikian situations considered thus far, a change in behavior is measured which springs from a contingency between some defined response and some motivationally significant state of affairs. Experiments on latent learning suggest, however, that a Thorndikian situation may be characterized without reference either to the actual occurrence of change in behavior or to the motivational significance of the consequences of response. In the T-1 case, an investigator may set out deliberately to minimize the motivational significance of the consequences of response in an effort to minimize the extent of change in behavior. For example, a hungry rat is trained in a runway which leads to an empty end box or to one which contains only water. To arrange a set of end-box conditions which are entirely without motivational significance is not, of course, always very easy, but it can be done (Gonzalez & Diamond, 1960). In the T-2 case, the consequences of alternative responses, whether motivationally significant or not, may be balanced in an effort to forestall the development of a preference for one or the other response. For example, a hungry rat is run in a simple T maze with both end boxes empty, or one empty and the other containing only water, or one containing food and the other both food and water; or a rat that is both hungry and thirsty is run in a T maze with one end box containing food and the other containing water. Such situations are intended merely to provide occasions for learning whose effects are estimated in later tests. The tests always involve a change in the motivational significance of the consequences of response: for example, food is added to a previously empty end box; or the end box is associated with food in direct feedings; or the prevailing condition of deprivation is altered, and with it the relevance of previously encountered incentives. Nevertheless, despite the careful attention which must be paid to motivational significance in evaluating the outcome of exposure to a Thorndikian situation, the situation itself may be defined without reference to motivational significance. What is essential only is *a contingency of some specified event or circumstance on some measurable bit of behavior*—a contingency arranged by an investigator who is interested in studying its effects on the animal.[2]

PAVLOVIAN SITUATIONS

Well before Pavlov's experiments on conditioning became widely known, other investigators were led

---

[2] No treatment of Thorndikian techniques would be complete without some mention of a set of situations closely related to the problem box (calling for string-pulling, rake-wielding, box-stacking, and the like) which figured prominently in the work of certain of Thorndike's critics, beginning with Hobhouse (1901), who did not think that Thorndike's apparatus provided a representative picture of animal intelligence. Designed to be fully "surveyable" (to conceal nothing from the animal) and, although simple in principle, to render "chance" solutions unlikely, these (Hobhousian) situations present Thorndikian contingencies of a rather loose sort and *may* be used, like Thorndike's problem boxes, to study the way in which the experience of such contingencies affect subsequent behavior. Their principal use, however, has been in inquiries into the ability of animals to discover appropriate modes of behavior in advance of reinforcement—that is, in quests for evidence of "productive" or "inferential" as contrasted with "reproductive" or learned solutions.

quite independently, by an interest in associative learning, to experiments of essentially the same kind. As far back as the turn of the century, a distinction was made between what was called "trial-and-error" or "selective learning"—the modification of behavior as a function of its consequences—and what was called "association of stimuli" or "substitution" —the acquisition by one stimulus of some of the behavioral properties of a second stimulus as a function of the pairing of the two stimuli. Primarily concerned though he was with selective learning, Thorndike (1898) himself made use of paired stimulation; when a verbal statement such as "I must feed those cats" was followed regularly by the presentation of food, he reported, the words alone would bring the animals to the feeding place. It seems fitting nonetheless—in view of the scope of Pavlov's (1927) contribution—that the method should bear his name.

In the traditional Pavlovian experiment, as in the traditional Thorndikian experiment, the behavior of the animal is altered by the introduction of some motivationally significant stimulus such as food or shock ("reinforcement"), but there are important differences. In a Thorndikian experiment, reinforcement is contingent on response; doing one thing leads to food or to shock, doing another does not. In a Pavlovian experiment, reinforcement is scheduled without regard to response; the experimenter does not set out to mold behavior in some predetermined fashion, but only to study the way in which the functional properties of one stimulus are altered by virtue of its contiguity with another. Because their introduction is not contingent on the animal's behavior, Pavlovian reinforcements cannot be treated as rewards or punishments in any meaningful manner, nor can rewards and punishments be distinguished in a Pavlovian experiment. Another difference between the two techniques is worth noting. In a Thorndikian experiment, the choice of the behavior which is to serve as the index of learning is independent of the choice of reinforcement; any of a large variety of responses which the animal is likely to make may be encouraged with food or discouraged with shock. In a Pavlovian experiment, the choice of reinforcement restricts the choice of a behavioral indicator; while the conditioned and unconditioned responses are not always (as Pavlov thought) identical, the investigator must be guided in his search for evidence of learning by the functional properties of the reinforcing stimulus. Sharp as the distinction may be between the traditional Thorndikian and Pavlovian procedures, it has been ignored very often by theorists preoccupied with the task of deriving all of the data of learning from the operation of a single process. Pavlov himself claimed, of course, that all instances of learning could be analyzed as instances of conditioning, although Thorndike, committed as he was to the generality of the law of effect, never was satisfied that Pavlov's procedure could be cast in the same mold as his own.

Coordinate with the unitary Thorndikian (or T-1) situation is the unitary Pavlovian (or P-1) situation, in which the tendency for a CS to produce some defined effect is measured in terms of latency or magnitude. The defined effect may be a response which is reflexly elicited by the US, as in the salivary conditioning experiment, or something quite different, as when the rate of fixed-interval responding in a Skinnerian situation is depressed by shock and by a stimulus paired with shock (Estes & Skinner, 1941). A P-1 situation may be generalized (P-1g) or discriminative (P-1d); in the discriminative case, the CS is varied systematically from trial to trial and with it the likelihood that the US will be presented (as, for example, when a bright light always is followed by food but a dim light never is). With two unconditioned stimuli, each eliciting a different response, it is possible to set up a P-2 situation, the Pavlovian analogue of the Thorndikian choice situation.

(A T-2 situation may be constituted with but a single reinforcer, which is another interesting difference between Pavlovian and Thorndikian techniques.) The discriminative (P-2d) case is perhaps the easier to conceive than the generalized (P-2g). For example, one CS is paired with acid introduced into the mouth of a dog, while another CS is paired with meat-powder (Pavlov, 1927). The P-2g case must involve some inconsistency of reinforcement (which is, or course, not true of T-2g). For example, a CS is paired with shock to the right forelimb on a random 75% of trials and with shock to the left forelimb on the remaining 25% of trials. This is the Pavlovian analogue of a kind of T-2 situation in which there has been much interest of late. For example, a right turn at the choice point of a maze leads to food on a random 75% of trials while a left turn leads to food on the remaining 25% of trials (Brunswik, 1939).

The discrete-continuous dichotomy, which was developed in the analysis of Thorndikian procedures, seems to have no Pavlovian parallel; Pavlovian training is an affair of discrete trials. Nor does the notion of "chaining" have any application to Pavlovian procedures.

A Pavlovian situation, like a Thorndikian situation, may serve merely as an occasion for learning whose effects are measured in subsequent tests. One such case, well known to Pavlov, is that in which the presentation of CS and US is strictly simultaneous; only when the training procedure is altered can the effects of pairing be assessed. A second is that of "sensory preconditioning"—conceived originally by Thorndike (1898) himself as a check on the existence of "representations"—which is analogous to the Thorndikian experiment with consequences of response which are lacking in motivational significance; neutral stimuli are paired, then one is given some behavioral property, and the effects of the pairing are estimated from response to the other. A third case is that in which attention is centered on the acquisition, not of response-eliciting properties, but of rewarding properties (Williams, 1929); for example, an animal is fed repeatedly in a distinctive box (that is, box and food are paired), after which access to the empty box is made contingent upon response in a Thorndikian situation. In one variety of experiment which has considerable theoretical importance, the order of these experiences is reversed; the contingency of access to the empty box upon some response is displayed, after which the animal is fed in the box, and the effect on response is measured (Gonzalez & Diamond, 1960). In general, then, a Pavlovian situation may be defined without reference either to the occurrence in that situation of any particular kind of behavioral change, or to the functional properties of the stimuli which are paired. What is essential only is *a sequence or conjunction of stimuli whose contiguity is independent of the animal's response.*

Avoidance Situations

The only learning situations which cannot be classified unequivocally as Pavlovian or Thorndikian are those which involve the avoidance of aversive stimulation. In them, Pavlovian and Thorndikian features are closely intertwined. On the one hand, a neutral stimulus is paired with an aversive stimulus, thereby acquiring certain arousing properties. The pairing is not, on the other hand, entirely independent of the animal's behavior—the aversive stimulus is introduced only if the CS fails to elicit some defined response, whose likelihood of occurrence (low at the outset) the pairing serves to increase. This contingency of reinforcement on response is not displayed on the very first trial, as it is in a pure Thorndikian situation. In avoidance training, the contingency is a negative one, which (since the mere possibility of avoidance cannot influence the animal) does not become manifest until the Pavlovian procedure has taken effect.

There is another Thorndikian contingency which operates in some (though not in all) avoidance situations, this one making itself felt from the very first trial: termination of the aversive stimulus may be contingent on some defined response, often—but not always—the same response as that which avoids the aversive stimulus. In flexion conditioning, when shock to the limb is administered through a grid on which the limb of the animal rests, and when the scheduled duration of shock is substantial, flexion both escapes and avoids shock. In the shuttle box, too, the conditions of training may be such that changing compartments both escapes and avoids shock, although, as Warner (1932) noted early, the response which escapes shock may be different from that which avoids it (for example, leaping over a hurdle as compared with crawling under). It is possible, of course, to set up an avoidance situation in which there is no escape at all. In flexion conditioning, shock may be administered through a bracelet attached to the limb, and a control circuit so arranged that the CR will forestall the shock but the UR will not alter its scheduled duration. In the shuttle box, the shock may be very brief, terminating quite independently of any response the animal may make to it (Hunter, 1935). Even without escape, however, there remains the contingency of aversive stimulation on failure of response to the CS, an essential feature of avoidance training which distinguishes it from Pavlovian training, while the paired stimulation which is responsible for the emergence of response to the CS distinguishes it from Thorndikian training. Avoidance training seems to require a major category of its own.

In its most common use, the shuttle box may be classified as an A_d-1g situation (A for avoidance); a single course of action is defined, and its latency is measured in discrete trials without systematic variation in sensory conditions. The corresponding discriminative (A_d-1d) situation also may be generated in the shuttle box; for example, a bright light is followed by shock unless the defined response is made, but a dim light never is followed by shock. In such a situation, it may be noted, discrimination can progress only as the animal fails to respond to the dim light, since the consequences of response to the two lights are identical. (In a T-1d situation, by contrast, the consequences of response to the stimuli to be discriminated are different, and discrimination therefore is facilitated by response to the negative stimulus; in a P-1d situation, discrimination may progress quite independently of response.)

Choice among alternative courses of action also may be studied in avoidance situations. Suppose, for example, that shock from a grid in the floor of a T maze is scheduled x seconds after an animal is placed in the starting box. In the generalized (A_d-2g) case, shock is avoided by prompt entrance into the end box on the right, but not by entrance into the end box on the left. In the discriminative (A_d-2d) case, a turn to the right avoids shock when the stem of the maze is black, while a turn to the left avoids shock when the stem is white. Two unconditioned stimuli are not required to generate an A-2 situation as they are to generate a P-2 situation, but two unconditioned stimuli may be used. For example, one signal is followed by avoidable shock to the right limb, while a second is followed by avoidable shock to the left limb (James, 1947).

The discrete-continuous dichotomy developed in the analysis of Thorndikian situations is applicable also to avoidance training. An A_c-1g situation may be constituted in a modified Skinner box or a shuttle box. In a design developed by Sidman (1953), no exteroceptive warning signal is used, but shock is scheduled every x seconds by a clock which the defined response resets. (The lack of an exteroceptive signal does not, of course, subvert the definition of avoidance training as originating in a quasi-Pavlovian contiguity of stimuli; as Pavlov himself showed, internal processes correlated with the passage of time since the occurrence of a specified event may be cast in the role of CS). In the corresponding discriminative (A_e-1d) case, the clock which schedules shock runs only under one of two sensory conditions. Avoidance situations of the continuous type which do involve exteroceptive signaling also are feasible. In the A_e-1g case, for example, shock from a grid in the floor of a Skinner box is scheduled x seconds after the onset of a light and avoided by response on a variable-ratio schedule. A_e-2 situations, both generalized and discriminative, may be generated when alternative courses of action are defined.

Like Thorndikian situations, avoidance situations may be chained. Just as an animal may learn to run a simple T maze under threat of shock, so it may learn to run a multiple T maze. An example of chaining in an avoidance situation of the continuous type is the following: with the onset of the CS, response to one manipulandum is followed, on a variable-ratio schedule, by access to a second manipulandum, response to which, again on a variable-ratio schedule, terminates the CS and avoids shock.

Although the term implies threat of an aversive condition which the animal learns to forestall, avoidance training, like Thorndikian and Pavlovian training, may be characterized without reference to the nature of the stimuli employed or to the occurrence of behavioral change. It would be possible, for example, to train an animal with some neutral stimulus rather than shock in a shuttle box designed to produce a substantial frequency of spontaneous crossing, and then to test for learning after the neutral stimulus has been paired with shock. Irrespective of outcome, the conception of such an experiment is sufficient to delineate what is here regarded as the essential feature of avoidance training: *a sequence of stimuli is scheduled with the occurrence of the second contingent upon the failure of the animal to make some specified response to the first.*

Terminology

While there need be no detailed comparison of the classification here proposed with earlier ones, it may be worth while, in the interest of preserving whatever compatible usages may exist, to consider how well some of the broader methodological designations which now are current will serve the needs of the new classification. Since current terminology derives from earlier classifications, the major differences in emphasis must become quite apparent in the process.

The term "conditioning" usually is used for the kind of training here called Pavlovian, but that term also is used rather widely to designate techniques which are not here classified as Pavlovian, and often as a synonym for "learning" itself. The term "classical conditioning" is closer to what is here intended by Pavlovian, although in some contexts it has a narrower meaning (suggesting a harnessed animal) and in other contexts a broader one (encompassing avoidance). Avoidance remains a useful term, but "instrumental conditioning" is too ambiguous, since it has been applied indiscriminately both to avoidance training and to pure Thorndikian training. The term "operant conditioning" is even more ambiguous; it has a narrow (Skinnerian) sense in which it is tied to a questionable distinction between "elicited" and "emitted" behavior, as well as a more general sense in which it is equivalent to instrumental conditioning. The term "selective learning" has a pure Thorndikian connotation, but it seems to designate a process of learning rather than a method of studying it.

In general, there is little to salvage in the current terminology. Specific situational designations, such as maze, problem box, and runway, continue to be useful, but the broader classificatory terms are unsuitable because they are geared to methodological dichotomy rather than to trichotomy. Even if dichotomy should in time give way to trichotomy, of course, it is likely that many of the older terms will continue to be used with altered meanings and with considerable consequent confusion. The terms for the subcategories here defined—unitary and choice situations, generalized and discriminative situations, discrete and continuous situations—fortunately do not compete with established usages and therefore create less opportunity for confusion, although it is possible that a clearer notation might be found. Reflection will show, however, that complexity of notation is to a certain extent an inevitable consequence of the amount of information to be conveyed.

It is natural that a new classification should require a new terminology, although a change in classification does not, of course, necessarily imply an advance in conception. Whether the classification here proposed represents an advance in thinking about the interrelations among learning situations cannot now be told. Classification is more, ultimately, than a matter of taste, but there is little else on which to depend at the present time. It is to be hoped that a renewed concern with problems of classification will stimulate further research on methodological interrelations.

REFERENCES

BITTERMAN, M. E. Toward a comparative psychology of learning. *Amer. Psychologist*, 1960, **15**, 704–712.

BRUNSWIK, E. Probability as a determiner of rat behavior. *J. exp. Psychol.*, 1939, **25**, 175–197.

ESTES, W. K., & SKINNER, B. F. Some quantitative properties of anxiety. *J. exp. Psychol.*, 1941, **29**, 390–400.

GONZALEZ, R. C., & DIAMOND, L. A test of Spence's theory of incentive motivation. *Amer. J. Psychol.*, 1960, **73**, 396–403.

GRICE, G. R. Visual discrimination learning with simultaneous and successive presentation of stimuli. *J. comp. physiol. Psychol.*, 1949, **42**, 365–373.

HERBERT, M. J., & ARNOLD, W. J. A reaction chaining apparatus. *J. comp. physiol. Psychol.*, 1947, **40**, 227–229.

HICKS, V. C. The relative values of different curves of learning. *J. anim. Behav.*, 1911, **1**, 138–156.

HILGARD, E. R., & MARQUIS, D. G. *Conditioning and learning.* New York: Appleton-Century, 1940.

HOBHOUSE, L. T. *Mind in evolution.* London: Macmillan, 1901.

HUNTER, W. S. Conditioning and extinction in the rat. *Brit. J. Psychol.*, 1935, **26**, 135–148.

JAMES, W. T. The use of work in developing a differential conditioned reaction of antagonistic reflex systems. *J. comp. physiol. Psychol.*, 1947, **40**, 177–182.

LASHLEY, K. S. A simple maze: With data on the relation of the distribution of practice to the rate of learning. *Psychobiology*, 1918, **1**, 353–367.

LONGO, N., & BITTERMAN, M. E. The effect of partial reinforcement with spaced practice on resistance to extinction in the fish. *J. comp. physiol. Psychol.*, 1960, **53**, 169–172.

PAVLOV, I. P. *Conditioned reflexes: An investigation of the physiological activity of the cerebral cortex.* London: Oxford Univer. Press, 1927.

SIDMAN, M. Avoidance conditioning with brief shock and no exteroceptive warning signal. *Science*, 1953, **118**, 157–158.

SKINNER, B. F. On the rate of formation of a conditioned reflex. *J. gen. Psychol.*, 1932, **7**, 274–285.

SKINNER, B. F. Two types of conditioned reflex and a pseudo type. *J. gen. Psychol.*, 1935, **12**, 66–76.

SKINNER, B. F. Two types of conditioned reflex: A reply to Konorski and Miller. *J. gen. Psychol.*, 1937, **16**, 272–282.

SOLOMON, R. L. Latency of response as a measure of learning in a "single-door" discrimination. *Amer. J. Psychol.*, 1943, **56**, 422–432.

SPENCE, K. W. *Behavior theory and conditioning.* New Haven: Yale Univer. Press, 1956.

STONE, C. P. A multiple discrimination box and its use in studying the learning ability of rats: I. Reliability of scores. *J. genet. Psychol.*, 1928, **35**, 557–573.

THORNDIKE, E. L. Animal intelligence: An experimental study of the associative processes in animals. *Psychol. Rev. monogr. Suppl.*, 1898, **2**(4, Whole No. 8).

THORNDIKE, E. L. The mental life of monkeys. *Psychol. Rev. monogr. Suppl.*, 1901, **3**(5, Whole No. 15).

WARNER, L. H. The asociation span of the white rat. *J. gen. Psychol.*, 1932, **41**, 57–89.

WILLIAMS, K. A. The reward value of a conditioned stimulus. *U. Calif. Publ. Psychol.*, 1929, **4**, 31–55.

WODINSKY, J., & BITTERMAN, M. E. Partial reinforcement in the fish. *Amer. J. Psychol.*, 1959, **72**, 184–199.

WODINSKY, J., & BITTERMAN, M. E. Resistance to extinction in the fish after extensive training with partial reinforcement. *Amer. J. Psychol.*, 1960, **73**, 429–434.

WOODWORTH, R. S. *Experimental psychology.* New York: Henry Holt, 1938.

YOUTZ, R. E. P. The change with time of a Thorndikian response in the rat. *J. exp. Psychol.*, 1938, **23**, 128–140. (a)

YOUTZ, R. E. P. Reinforcement, extinction, and spontaneous recovery in a non-Pavlovian reaction. *J. exp. Psychol.*, 1938, **22**, 305–318. (b)

YOUTZ, R. E. P. The weakening of one Thorndikian response following the extinction of another. *J. exp. Psychol.*, 1939, **24**, 294–304.

LEARNING WITHOUT SWIMMING IN A WATER MAZE

P. C. Dodwell
D. E. Bessant

Queen's University, Kingston, Ontario, Canada

Thorndike has outlined a program of experiments designed to establish or refute the validity of expectancy-type theories of learning (Thorndike, 1946). The experiments suggested by Thorndike are such that the subjects (animals) should, according to any expectancy theory, learn without actually performing any instrumental responses; he implies that, in his view, such experiments would yield negative results. One of his suggestions is:

> Put the rat, in a little wire car, in the entrance chamber of a maze, run it through the correct path of a simple maze and into the food compartment. Release it there and let it eat the morsel provided. Repeat ten to a hundred times according to the difficulty of the maze under ordinary conditions. The rat has had an opportunity to form expectancies that presence in the food compartment is followed by food, that the last correct turn is followed by the food chamber, and so on. Then put it in the entrance chamber free to go wherever it is inclined and observe what it does. Compare the behavior of such rats with that of rats run in the customary manner (p. 278).

Several experiments (Bugelski, 1958; Gleitman, 1955; McNamara, Long, & Wike, 1956) have aimed at establishing whether learning can occur under conditions similar to those suggested in the above quotation. Gleitman investigated preferences of groups of rats for places at which previously (1) shock was started, (2) no shock was received, and (3) shock was terminated. He demonstrated a significant preference for (3) over (1) but not for (3) over (2) or for (2) over (1). Bugelski's results (not published in detail) were inconclusive, and those of McNamara, Long, and Wike demonstrated learning of an elevated T maze without performance, but only when extra-maze cues are present.

The two studies which yielded positive results are restricted to relatively simple situations. No demonstration has yet been given of the formation of "expectancies" in more complex mazes, where one might expect that "curiosity" drive could enter as an important variable (MacCorquodale & Meehl, 1954). In the absence of precise definition of the situations in which expectancies are supposed to be formed by rats, one could argue two possibilities: first, that expectancies are only formed in relatively simple choice situations, or secondly, that simple situations yield such rapid learning anyway that a very sensitive measure would be needed to show differences between "expectation" and "no expectation" goups. Taking the first position, one would predict no learning without performance in a complex maze, and taking the second, that any effect of expectancies (provided they can be formed in complex choice situations) should be more easily measurable in a complex situation than in a simple one. It seemed worth investigating whether in fact learning without performance of instrumental responses could be demonstrated in a complex maze.

Reprinted from *The Journal of Comparative and Physiological Psychology*, Vol. 53, No. 5, 1960.

LEARNING WITHOUT SWIMMING IN A WATER MAZE

Method

Apparatus

A water maze with eight choice points was used (see Fig. 1). It appears that there is, generally, a rather sharp increase in maze difficulty for rats when eight choice points or more are present (Munn, 1950). The walls of the alleys (12 in. high) and the depth of water (5½ in.) were such that the rats could neither stand in an alley, nor jump out of it, with ease. A wooden trolley was constructed, 4½ in. long, 2¾ in. wide, and 5¾ in. high, with casters fixed to its underside, so that its upper surface was ¼ in. above the water when placed in the maze. It could be propelled through the maze with a long wooden handle.

Subjects

The Ss were 16 male hooded rats of two different strains, which had previously been used in discrimination experiments with a Lashley-type jumping stand. The strains were Long-Evans, and an unknown strain from a local breeder; both types of rat were present in both experimental conditions, and there were no differences in the performances of the two strains.

Procedure

The Ss were randomly assigned to two groups, experimental (E) and control (C). The control animals swam through the maze to a criterion of 3 errorless trials. Five trials were given in the first day of training, and the remaining trials on the second day. Intertrial intervals within days were short; the animal was left for about a minute in the goal box after swimming the maze, and then replaced at the start. The experimental animals were propelled through the maze on the trolley, at approximately the swimming speed of a rat, for the mean number of trials required by the control group to learn the maze, i.e., 10. They then learned the maze by swimming through it in the ordinary way. Five trials riding the trolley were given on the first day, the second 5 riding trials and all swimming trials on the second day. Intertrial intervals and time in goal box were the same for riding as for swimming trials. The number of swimming trials required to reach the criterion, and the number of errors made, were recorded. Before learning the maze, Group C rats were run back and forth on the trolley in Section A of the maze (see Fig. 1) 50 times, to ensure that both groups had approximately equal familiarity with the close proximity of water on the first swimming trials. In a preliminary test (with different rats) it had been established that rats prefer to sit on a raft rather than swim in 5½ in. of water. This does not mean that Group E was as well motivated to learn the maze as Group C, but it indicates that they were motivated to avoid being in the maze, which is further demonstrated by the fact that they invariably left the trolley on arrival at the goal box.

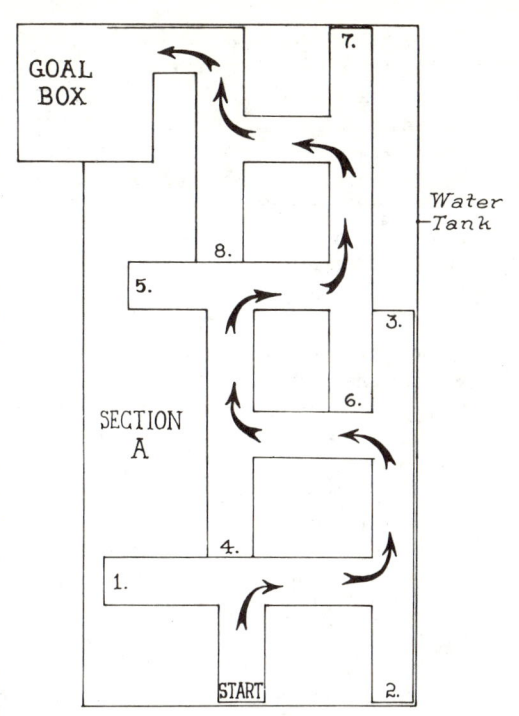

FIG. 1. Diagram of the apparatus.

Results

The learning of Group E was superior to that of Group C, both in terms of number of trials and of errors. The mean numbers of trials for the C and E groups were 9.6 (range, 8 to 11) and 5.6 (range, 4 to 7), respectively, and the mean number of errors 96.4 (range, 55 to 130) and 18.9 (range, 10 to 45), respectively. Since the distributions are mutually exclusive in both cases no statistical test of the significance of this result was deemed necessary.

The behavior of the two groups differed considerably, especially in the first two or three swims through the maze. Whereas Group C rats swam through the maze vigorously from the start, Group E showed characteristic "startle" behavior, remaining still for long periods and then moving jerkily through the maze. They also tended to jump out of the maze much more frequently than control rats; no correlation was found between learning scores and number of jumps out of the maze in Group E, so it appears unlikely that this was an important factor in the over-all superiority of the experimental group. Jumps out of the maze are included as errors in the numbers cited above. If they were not included, the error score would differentiate the two groups even more sharply, since jumps out of the maze were very infrequent in Group C (less than 1 per rat, compared with a mean of 8.3 per rat in Group E).

The behavior of Group E rats on the trolley was interesting. After the first three or four trials they showed definite anticipation of the next correct turn in the maze. Not only did they very frequently turn their heads in the correct direction at, or just before, each choice point, but also this behavior became more marked as the goal box was approached: the rats moved up to the front of the trolley, and in some cases jumped off the trolley into the water just before the goal box was reached. No quantitative measure of the number of correct anticipations was made, but the phenomenon is very striking, and was found in all rats in Group E.

Discussion

Clearly the Group E rats were making responses while on the trolley, so it is arguable that learning without performance has not been demonstrated. However, these responses were not instrumental, and since the experimental design satisfies Thorndike's paradigm, we may assert that performance (of instrumental responses) is not a necessary condition of learning the maze, and that "expectancies" can be formed in their absence. The head-turning and subsequent rapid learning of the maze both support this assertion. The rats used in this experiment were experimentally sophisticated, and had been trained in visual discrimination. This may have induced more searching for visual cues than would be found in naive animals. However, theories of expectancy learning make no specific requirements vis-a-vis sophistication, and a Hullian-type theory would require performance for learning to occur, no matter how sophisticated the Ss. It should be noted that, in a sense, the head-turning was a performance which was (fortuitously) reinforced, hence a Hullian might argue that the findings here reported could in fact be predicted from Hull's theory. The logical fallacies involved in this sort of argument have been exposed by Deutsch (1956).

No attempt was made to eliminate extramaze cues; this may be an important factor, and undoubtedly the nature of the anticipations formed would be better understood if some control over such cues had been exercised. By far the most frequently entered blind alley for Group E was Number 5, which indicates that, apart from being able to make specific anticipations at a choice point, they also had a "general notion" of the position of the goal box. It also indicates that the findings cannot be explained in terms of a "curiosity" drive; if faster learning were due simply to lack of curiosity about blind alleys already inspected from the trolley, there should be no differential tendency to enter some blind alleys rather than others. It is concluded, therefore, that rats previously trained in visual discriminations can subsequently form "expectancies" in a moderately complex maze when no instrumental responses are elicited, and that these "expectancies" significantly affect the speed with which the correct maze path can be learned. The writers have not, as yet, attempted to demonstrate the phenomenon with naive rats.

Summary

An experiment was performed with two groups of rats, one of which was allowed to learn a moderately complex maze by swimming through it in the ordinary way, the other being run through the maze on a trolley before learning to swim through. The number of runs through on the trolley for each rat in the second group was equal to the mean number of trials required to learn the maze by the first group. On subsequently learning to swim through the maze, the second group showed significantly better performance than the first, both in terms of the number of trials needed and the number of errors made. This finding is held to support the contention that learning can occur, by the formation of "expectancies," without the elicitation of instrumental responses.

REFERENCES

Bugelski, B. R. *Psychology of learning*. New York: Holt, 1958.

Deutsch, J. A. The inadequacy of the Hullian derivations of reasoning and latent learning. *Psychol. Rev.*, 1956, **63**, 389–399.

Gleitman, H. Place learning without prior performance. *J. comp. physiol. Psychol.*, 1955, **48**, 77–79.

Hilgard, E. R. *Theories of learning*. New York: Appleton-Century-Crofts, 1956.

McNamara, H. J., Long, J. B., & Wike, E. L. Place learning without performance. *J. comp. physiol. Psychol.*, 1956, **49**, 477–480.

MacCorquodale, K., & Meehl, P. E. Edward C. Tolman. In W. K. Estes, K. MacCorquodale, P. E. Meehl, C. G. Mueller, Jr., W. N. Schoenfeld, & W. S. Verplanck (Eds.), *Modern learning theory*. New York: Appleton-Century-Crofts, 1954.

Munn, N. L. *Handbook of psychological research on the rat*. New York: Houghton Mifflin, 1950.

Thorndike, E. K. Expectation. *Psychol. Rev.*, 1946, **53**, 277–281.

PERMANENT EFFECTS OF PUNISHMENT DURING EXTINCTION[1]

Erling E. Boe[2]
Russell M. Church

Brown University

The results of two experiments (Estes, 1944, Experiment A; Skinner, 1938, p. 154) indicate that a brief period of punishment at the beginning of extinction will not reduce the total number of responses emitted during the course of extinction, even though the immediate effect of punishment is to depress response rate. For these results to occur, punished Ss must emit more responses than control Ss during postpunishment extinction sessions to compensate for their reduced output during punishment. For convenience, this phenomenon will henceforth be referred to as compensatory recovery.

On the basis of other experiments (B, C, D, F, G, & J) in which compensatory recovery did not occur, Estes (1944) drew the general conclusion that "The extent to which the total number of unreinforced elicitations of a response necessary for extinction at a given level of drive can be reduced by punishment is a joint function of the conditions of punishment and the conditions of previous positive reinforcement [p. 34]." Compensatory recovery was not found in other experiments (Akhtar, 1963; Boe, 1964) as well. Thus, the conditions under which it is observed appear to be much narrower than the conditions under which it is not. The present experiments were designed first to reproduce compensatory recovery, if possible, and then to identify various conditions necessary for its demonstration.

Experiment 1

Boe (1964) found that the extent to which punishment reduced the total number of responses during extinction was inversely related to punishment intensity and directly related to the number of training trials. In this experiment rats were trained to enter the right goal box of a modified Y maze and then, during the first 10 of 30 extinction trials, they were punished with a brief shock. Compensatory recovery was not found in any of the nine relevant groups in Boe's experiment, although it might be found in a free-responding situation, at least under optimal conditions. Consequently, Experiment 1 was designed

[1] This investigation was supported by a United States Public Health Service Fellowship (PHS 1-F2-MH-28233) and Research Grant MH-08123 from the National Institute of Mental Health.
[2] Now at the University of Pennsylvania.

to replicate as exactly as possible the procedures used by Estes (1944) in Experiment A where compensatory recovery has been previously reported. In addition to his "mild" shock group, several groups with higher voltage levels were added so that the range of shock intensities over which the phenomenon occurs could be observed.

Method

Subjects. The Ss were 60 naive, male, albino, Norway rats of hysterectomy-derived, barrier-sustained stock that arrived from the Charles River Breeding Laboratories at 49 days of age. They were about 125 days old at the beginning of the experiment and weighed 215–295 gm.

Apparatus. A force of about 15 gm. was required to operate the lever in six standard lever boxes. Electrical stimulation was applied through a grid floor with a matched-impedance ac source (150 K ohm in series with Ss).

Design. The 60 Ss were randomly assigned to six groups differing only in the intensity (0, 35, 50, 75, 120, or 220 v.) of the .1-sec. electric shocks. One S in the 50-v. group was eliminated because of failure to acquire the lever-pressing response. The Ss in a particular group were punished with the same voltage throughout the punishment phase. The least severe shock (35 v.) was barely strong enough to elicit a reliable UR in pilot animals that were stimulated noncontingently, while the 220-v. shock elicited a strong UR. According to Campbell and Teghtsoonian (1958), the threshold for aversion in rats is 30 v. for the matched-impedance source used here.

Procedure. The Ss were housed in individual cages with water always accessible, and were handled daily. For the first 7 days, food was available ad lib; thereafter, Ss were given daily feedings of about 12 gm. of dry Purina chow mixed with about 25 cc of water.

On the first experimental day all Ss were trained to approach the food cup following the activation of the pellet dispenser by automatically dispensing one 45-mg. Noyes food pellet each minute until 60 pellets had been delivered. On Day 2, each S was continuously reinforced for the first 30 lever responses and then returned to its home cage. Thereafter, all sessions were 60 min. long and each S was run at approximately the same time each day.

For the next three sessions, lever pressing was reinforced on a 4-min. FI schedule. Extinction commenced on the following (sixth) session and was continued for nine 1-hr. sessions in all. Shock was contingent upon lever pressing during Minutes 5–20 of the first extinction session only. During the 15-min. punishment phase, the stimulator was reset every 30 sec. and the next response was punished. Thus, a maximum of 30 shocks could be delivered to a particular S if sufficient responding were maintained.

Upon completion of the nine extinction sessions, three 1-hr. retraining sessions were scheduled. The first five responses during the first retraining session were reinforced with a food pellet; thereafter, reinforcement was delivered on the original 4-min. FI schedule.

The procedures employed from magazine training through the first three extinction sessions were identical to those reported by Estes (1944) for his Experiment A. In the present experiment, however, there were six additional extinction sessions, and then three retraining sessions that replicated the procedure used by Estes in his Experiment C.

Dependent variable. The number of responses during the last session of reinforced training was highly correlated with the number of responses emitted during the nine sessions of extinction (rank-order correlations for 10-S groups = .53–.94, with a median of .76; for ρ of .55, $p < .05$, one-tailed). Since the purpose of the experiment was to examine performance differences during extinction as a function of punishment intensity, it was desirable to reduce the effect of performance level prior to treatment on performance level during extinction. Therefore, the number of responses during various segments of extinction for a particular S was divided by the number of responses that S made during the last session of reinforced training ($M = 722$), and the ratio was then multiplied by 100, hereafter called the response percentage, and it is the dependent variable used for reporting most of the results. The response percentage measure is virtually independent of variation in reinforced response rate (the median ρ for 10-S groups = $-.17$; for 2 of 12, $\rho < .55$).

Results

Median response percentages for the six groups of Ss are presented in cumulative form for the nine sessions of extinction in Figure 1. It is obvious that there was both an immediate (i.e., during the punishment period) and a permanent (i.e., during nine sessions of extinction) decrease in responding, with the amount of decrease depending upon punishment intensity. Although response rate increased somewhat upon discontinuation of punishment in the three most intensely punished groups, there was no evidence of compensatory recovery.

The relationship between response per-

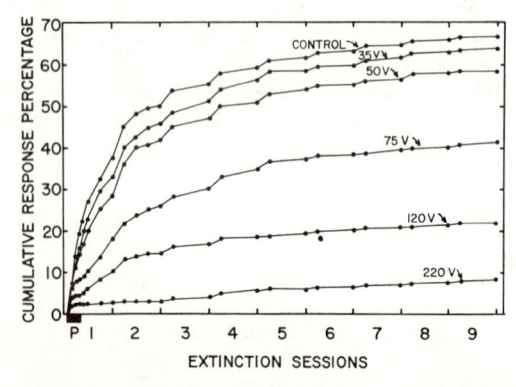

FIG. 1. Cumulative median response percentage during extinction. (Punishment, P, was contingent upon lever pressing during Minutes 5–20 of the first extinction session.)

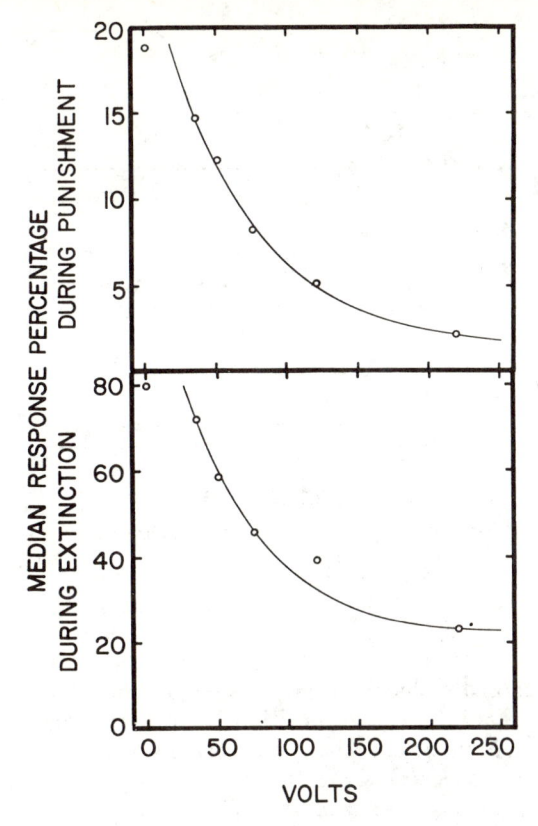

FIG. 2. Median response percentage during the 15-min. punishment period (upper panel) and during nine extinction sessions (lower panel) as a function of punishment intensity (voltage). (The formulas for the exponential function fit to the observed values are $R = 23.01e^{-.015V} + 1.25$, and $R = 96.40e^{-.018V} + 21.30$, respectively, where R represents response percentage and V represents voltage.)

centage during the 15-min. punishment period and voltage of the punishing shocks is shown in the upper section of Figure 2. An exponential curve was fitted to the observed values. The observed value for the unpunished control group was not included in the curve-fitting procedure because the threshold for the punishing effect of an electric shock obviously lies somewhere above zero voltage. Extrapolation of the curve upward to the control group's level of response percentage suggests that the punishment threshold is approximately 17 v. under the conditions of this experiment. A Kruskal-Wallis analysis of variance test of the six observed medians indicated that their differences were highly significant ($H = 44.9$, $df = 5$, $p < .001$). In addition, individual tests showed that both the 35-v. and 50-v. groups were significantly below the control group (Mann-Whitney one-tailed U test, $p < .05$ in both cases).

The effect of variation in punishment intensity on total responses during extinction is shown in the lower section of Figure 2. An exponential curve similar to that shown in the upper section again fits the observed values well, and the overall effect of variation in punishment intensity was highly significant (Kruskal-Wallis analysis of variance, $H = 25.2$, $df = 5$, $p < .001$). For the reasons presented above, the value for the control group was not used in fitting the curve. Compensatory recovery obviously did not occur in the more intense punishment groups, and there are two substantial reasons for concluding that it did not occur in the 35-v. and 50-v. groups as well. The first reason is that the observed values for both groups are below the control group and fall near the exponential function. The second reason is that the differences between the control and the two mild punishment groups increased following the discontinuation of punishment instead of decreasing as required for compensatory recovery to occur. Whereas the 35-v. and 50-v. groups were 4.2 and 6.6 percentage points, respectively, lower than the control group after 15 min. of punishment, they dropped an additional 4.3 and 12.3 percentage points, respectively, lower during the subsequent 8 hr. and 40 min. of extinction.

Since punishment was programmed on a 30-sec. interval schedule, the number of punishments received was not necessarily correlated with the amount of responding, i.e., a slow but steady rate of responding would be sufficient to produce the maximum of 30 punishments in the 15-min. punishment period. Slow but steady response rates were not maintained during punishment, however, and the number of punishments delivered was also an exponential function of shock intensity. Median number of punishments delivered, beginning with the 35-v. group and in order of intensity thereafter, were 26.5, 25.0, 16.0, 9.8, and 4.2. Control Ss responded at a rate that would have produced a median of 28.8 of a possible 30.0 punishments. The effect of variation in shock intensity was again highly significant (Kruskal-Wallis analysis of variance, $H = 42.5$, $df = 5$, $p < .001$).

In an important sense, the relationship

between shock intensity and response percentage reported in Figure 2 does not represent the full effect of increasing intensity, because punishment frequency simultaneously diminishes. A more meaningful measure might be the amount of response suppression produced per punishment. This measure was computed by first subtracting the response percentage of each of the punished groups from the response percentage of the control group as reported in the upper section of Figure 2, and then dividing this difference by the actual number of punishments delivered. The subtraction yields the amount of suppression as a function of punishment intensity, and the division yields the measure of suppression per punishment. This variable is plotted as a function of shock intensity in Figure 3, both in terms of raw units and of their logarithms. The power function fit to the observed values closely resembles those found in psychophysical experiments of the relationship between current and the subjective estimation of shock intensity by human Ss (Kalikow, 1966; Sternbach & Tursky, 1964; Stevens, Carton, & Shickman, 1958).

Although compensatory recovery did not occur in most of Estes' (1944) experiments, he reported that punishment did not reduce the amount of time needed for extinction in some of these. While the present data also indicate that a time measure of extinction was much less sensitive to experimental manipulations than the response percentage measure, an effect on the time measure was detected. Most Ss (90%) reached the criterion of less than 2% within nine extinction sessions (overall median equaled about five sessions). The median sessions to this criterion for each group from control to most severely punished (220 v.) were 6.0, 7.5, 5.3, 4.5, 3.2, and 3.5 (Kruskal-Wallis analysis of variance, $H = 11.7$, $df = 5$, $p < .05$).

Except for Ss in the most intense (220-v.) punishment group, the results reported above in terms of medians are representative of the response patterns of individual Ss. The large individual differences that appeared in the 220-v. group are shown in Figure 4. Each extinction curve is based upon the performance of a single S following the discontinuation of punishment (i.e., responses during the first 20 min. of the first extinction session are not included in the figure). Differences between these curves were not related to performance levels during the immediately preceding punishment period.

Two Ss in the 220-v. punishment group (D20 and D36) resumed responding almost immediately after punishment was discontinued, and they gradually diminished their response rate over the subsequent extinction sessions (Figure 4). This pattern was characteristic of the perform-

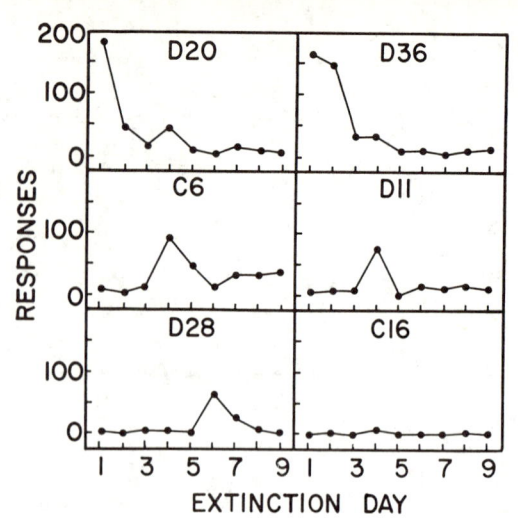

Fig. 4. Number of lever-pressing responses as a function of extinction session for six individual Ss in the 220-v. punishment group.

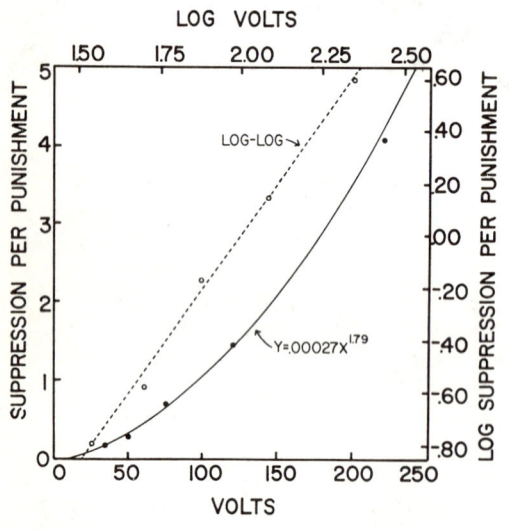

Fig. 3. Amount of suppression per punishment in response percentage units as a function of punishment intensity (voltage) presented in two ways. (The solid, curved line is plotted against the scales at the left and lower margins, while the dashed, straight line is plotted against the logarithmic transformation of those scales located at the top and right margins.)

ance of the 49 Ss in all the other groups. Three Ss (C6, D11, and D28) had a delayed onset of extinction. After three or more sessions of almost complete suppression, these Ss increased their response rate and then reduced it. Obviously, punishment had not eliminated response strength entirely, but it apparently had reduced it. The third pattern of responding is illustrated by C16, and it was characteristic of the remaining 4 Ss in the 220-v. group. The brief period of intense punishment appears to have eliminated lever pressing (i.e., reduced it to operant level or below). At the very least, an enduring suppression was produced by intense punishment in half of the Ss exposed to it.

Differences in rate of responding during retraining as a function of punishment intensity (and total responses during extinction, too, since they are related) were also examined. Medians for each of the six groups were computed for response percentage during the first 15 min. of the first hourly session, during the first 30 min. of the first session, during the entire first session, and during all three sessions combined. None of the probability levels produced by the Kruskal-Wallis analysis of variance tests even approached conventional levels of significance. Furthermore, the 5 Ss that were almost completely suppressed by punishment in the 220-v. group were comparable to the other 5 Ss that were not. All Ss simply reconditioned rapidly. The failure of a compensatory increase in response rate during retraining to be proportional to the amount of suppression during extinction is further evidence that punishment permanently reduced response strength in direct relation to its intensity.

Experiment 2

A question of considerable theoretical importance is whether or not the permanent reduction in number of responses produced by punishment during extinction is a function of the correlation between the lever-pressing response and shock. Although Estes (1944) concluded that "The result of a period during which a disturbing stimulus is associated with the stimuli which normally act as an occasion for the occurrence of the response is a depression in strength of the response during subsequent periods of extinction very similar to that produced by a period of actual punishment of the response [p. 35]" on the basis of his Experiments I and J, he also recognized that the response contingency characteristic of punishment was relevant to its suppressing effect under some conditions. With respect to recovery from punishment, the importance of shock being contingent upon responses in comparison to its being contingent upon discriminative stimuli has been demonstrated by Hunt and Brady (1955) and by Azrin (1956). However, more rapid recovery occurred after punishment than noncontingent shock in the Hunt and Brady experiment, while punishment prolonged the period of suppression in the Azrin experiment. Since experimental procedures of Estes, Hunt and Brady, and Azrin differed in many respects, it is impossible to determine the source of these widely differing results. Although the weight of more recent research clearly indicates that punishment is more suppressive than noncontingent shock during the period of its application, no new data on their relative rates of recovery have been forthcoming. Experiment 2 was designed to provide further information on the unsettled question of contingency effects on recovery from punishment.

Method

The kind and number of Ss, apparatus, and the training procedures were like those reported for Experiment 1. The experimental design (but not all procedural details) of Estes' (1944) Experiment J (Part 2) was used.

The 60 Ss were first randomly assigned in equal numbers to the six conditions of a 2 × 3 factorial experiment. The independent variable at two levels was the administration (or not) of a session with the lever removed; the variable at three levels was shock condition (punishment, noncontingent shock, unpunished control). On the day following the third hourly session of reinforced training, a 20-min. extinction session was conducted in which (a) the lever-pressing response was punished for 20 Ss in the punishment condition, (b) shocks were periodically delivered independent of responding for 20 Ss in the noncontingent shock condition, and (c) simple extinction was given to 20 Ss in the control condition. As in Experiment 1, all shocks (120 v. at .1 sec.) were delivered during Minutes 5–20 of the first extinction session. Under the punishment condition, lever-pressing responses were shocked on the 30-sec. intermittent schedule used in Experiment 1. Under the noncontingent shock condition, the electrical stimulus was automatically delivered every 30 sec. without regard to responding.

An hourly session in the box with the lever removed was conducted the next day for 10 Ss in each of the punishment, noncontingent shock, and control conditions. The other 10 Ss in each condition were simply removed from their living cages, handled briefly, and then returned to their cages. Hourly extinction sessions with the lever present were conducted for the remaining 9 days of the experiment.

Results

Since the session in the leverless box produced little or no effect on resistance to extinction, the two groups of 10 Ss each given punishment, the two groups given noncontingent shock, and the two groups given simple extinction were combined. The main results are therefore reported for three groups of 20 Ss each in Figure 5. Both punishment and noncontingent shock reduced response rate during the 15-min. punishment session. During several of the subsequent extinction sessions, however, the response rate of punished Ss continued to be suppressed in comparison with the control group, while the noncontingently shocked Ss were not suppressed following the discontinuation of shock. Instead, they resumed responding almost immediately at a rate comparable to that of the control group.

Median response percentages and tests of significance at selected times during extinction are presented in Table 1. These data confirm the impressions given in Figure 5, viz., that the punishment and noncontingent shock groups were similar during the 20-min. punishment period and were both suppressed in relation to the control group, while the control and noncontingent shock groups were similar as soon as shock was discontinued and both had higher response rates than the punishment group. The suppressing effect of punishment seemed to be relatively enduring, while the suppression produced by noncontingent shock rapidly disappeared.

Although the punishment and noncontingent shock groups did not differ in overall response percentage during the 15-min. punishment period (see Table 1), examination of this period in Figure 5 shows that the response rate of the punishment group was considerably more suppressed during the last segments. Consequently, the significance of this observed difference between median response percentages was computed for each of the three 5-min. blocks during the 15-min. punishment period. The two groups were not significantly different during the first 5-min. block, but on each of the second two blocks, punishment Ss were significantly (U test, $p < .001$) more suppressed although they received only about one-third as many shocks as the noncontingent Ss (median of 8.8 shocks vs. a uniform 30 for noncontingent Ss).

TABLE 1
MEDIAN RESPONSE PERCENTAGE DURING EXTINCTION

Session	Punishment	NC shock	Control
Punishment period	4.2[a]	7.0[b]	16.4[a, b]
First postpunishment extinction session	8.8[a, b]	19.4[a]	21.0[b]
All extinction sessions	36.8[a, b]	51.8[a]	58.8[b]

Note.—The medians tabulated in each row differ significantly from each other at the .001 level (Kruskal-Wallis analysis of variance).

[a, b] Medians differ significantly ($p < .001$) from each other (Mann-Whitney U tests).

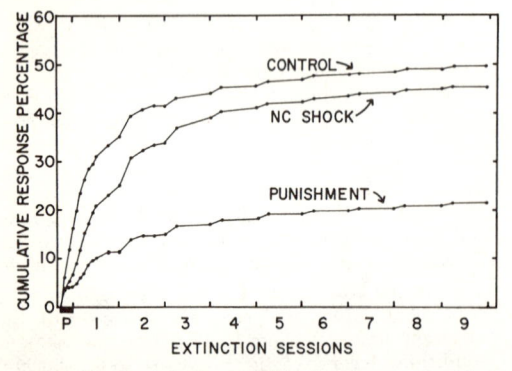

FIG. 5. Cumulative median response percentage during extinction. (Punishment, P, was contingent upon lever pressing during Minutes 5–20 of the 20-min. initial extinction session.)

DISCUSSION

Observations that a brief period of punishment at the beginning of extinction merely depresses performance temporarily but does not reduce the total number of responses emitted during the course of extinction have provided the strongest empirical basis for rejection of Thorndike's (1913) early view (hereafter referred to as the suppression hypothesis) that punishment subtracts strength from a learned connection. The results of Experiment 1, an attempt to replicate the conditions of an experiment in which compensatory recovery was reported (Estes, 1944, Experiment A), are consistent with the results of a number of other experiments (Akhtar, 1963; Boe, 1964; Estes, 1944) in suggesting that the range of conditions under which compensatory recovery can be reproduced, if at all, is very narrow. Thus a major reason for rejection of the suppression hypothesis is removed. This is not to suggest, however, that the suppression hypothesis provides a complete account of the results, e.g., the acceleration in rate shortly after the punishment was discontinued that was particularly prominent in the 75-v. and 120-v. groups. An adequate explanation of punishment effects must entail several different principles, one of which might be the suppression hypothesis.

Perhaps the discrepancy between the present results and those of Skinner (1938) and Estes (1944, Experiment A) can be reconciled on the basis of differences in intensity of the punishing stimulus. It is possible that the punishing stimulus used by Estes (a condenser discharge) was milder than the lowest intensity used in the present experiment, since he did not report that his mild shock produced statistically significant suppression; the stimuli used by Skinner (a kickback of the lever combined with a "fairly loud click") may also have been milder than the lowest intensity used in the present experiment since a moderate response rate was maintained despite the fact that each response was followed by the stimulus. Compensatory recovery may occur only when responses are followed by stimuli that serve to change the stimulus context (i.e., external inhibitors) but that are not aversive (punishing) stimuli.

Current theories of punishment may be classified into those for which a correlation between instrumental responding and punishment is necessary and those for which such a correlation is irrelevant (Church, 1963). Results of Experiment 2 indicate that the correlation between response and shock was of major importance both during punishment and following its discontinuation. Noncontingent shock suppressed responding considerably (though not as much as punishment) during the treatment period, but had no detectable effect on the course of subsequent extinction. These results, as well as others, suggest that an adequate theoretical account of punishment must entail at least two factors, one of which requires response contingency and one that does not.

REFERENCES

Akhtar, M. The role of counterconditioning in intermittent reinforcement. *Dissert. Abstr.*, 1963, **23,** 4428–4429.

Azrin, N. H. Some effects of two intermittent schedules of immediate and non-immediate punishment. *J. Psychol.*, 1956, **42,** 3–21.

Boe, E. E. Extinction as a function of intensity of punishment, amount of training, and reinforcement of a competing response. *Canad. J. Psychol.*, 1964, **18,** 328–342.

Campbell, B. A., & Teghtsoonian, R. Electrical and behavioral effects of different types of shock stimuli on the rat. *J. comp. physiol. Psychol.*, 1958, **51,** 185–192.

Church, R. M. The varied effects of punishment. *Psychol. Rev.*, 1963, **70,** 369–402.

Estes, W. K. An experimental study of punishment. *Psychol. Monogr.*, 1944, **57**(3, Whole No. 263).

Hunt, H. F., & Brady, J. V. Some effects of punishment and intercurrent "anxiety" on a simple operant. *J. comp. physiol. Psychol.*, 1955, **48,** 305–310.

Kalikow, D. N. The effects of innervation density on the psychophysical function for electrocutaneous stimulation. Unpublished master's thesis, Brown University, 1966.

Skinner, B. F. *The behavior of organisms.* New York: Appleton-Century, 1938.

Sternbach, R. A., & Tursky, B. On the psychophysical power function in electric shock. *Psychon. Sci.*, 1964, **1,** 217–218.

Stevens, S. S., Carton, A. S., & Shickman, G. M. A scale of apparent intensity of electric shock. *J. exp. Psychol.*, 1958, **56,** 328–344.

Thorndike, E. L. *Educational psychology.* Vol. 2. *The psychology of learning.* New York: Teachers College, Columbia University, 1913.

PROGRAMED INSTRUCTION: INSIGHT vs. CONDITIONING

H. A. THELEN

University of Chicago

Suppose I want you to learn that the chemical symbol for Sodium is Na, for Potassium, K, for Calcium, Ca, and so on down through a list of 25 elements. By "learn" I mean becoming able, without hesitation, to respond with "Na" when I say "Sodium," with "K" when I say "Potassium."

Probably the simplest way to teach you is through drill. You would read the list of elements and symbols and would try to memorize the connections. Then I would give you a list of elements and you would try to write the correct symbols. I would correct your mistakes and you would try again. We could also drill orally, with me naming the elements, you responding, me correcting. Or we could conduct the drill on a machine which would give you immediate "feedback" of "right" or "wrong."

CONDITIONING

This sort of learning occurs through repetition and "reinforcement"—some sort of feedback or response which tends to "fix" the connection between element and symbol in your mind. The objective is to develop the specific habit of associating names and symbols. This process is called "conditioning."

Conditioning is the only process through which nonsense (or near-nonsense) can be learned. It can also be used to teach pigeons to tread on the right lever in order to get grain. It is an efficient way to learn *isolated* bits of information, such as the year in which Columbus discovered America, the months of the year, and the density of lead.

It is hoped that being told your response is correct will make you want to make further effort; but, if you don't really care about it, then we will fall back on the notion that generally speaking, if a person makes a response (never mind for what reason) he is more likely to make the same response the next time the stimulus is presented. Programers say that such learning tactics "increase the verbal repertoire."

AN EXPERIMENT

Let us consider another type of task. Suppose I want you to learn the quantitative law "governing" the period of back-and-forth oscillation of a pendulum. I can give you a ball of twine, an assortment of weights (different sizes, shapes, weights, and colors), and a support from which you can hang the weights by means of the twine. I would probably also give you a yardstick and a stopwatch, although I might prefer to wait until you asked for them.

My instructions would be to play with the things I had just given you and see if you could discover what it is that determines how

PROGRAMED INSTRUCTION: INSIGHT VS. CONDITIONING

rapidly the pendulum will swing back and forth; and also just what the relationship is between this factor and the rate of swing.

You would probably begin by using a piece of string to hang one of the weights from the support, and you would set it in motion and notice its regular rate of swing. Your next move would probably be either to lengthen or to shorten the string and see what happened. You would soon get the notion that changing the weights (color, weight, shape) made no difference, but lengthening or shortening the string resulted in the pendulum swinging slower or faster.

You would then use the yardstick to measure the length of the string, and the watch to time the swings. You would make several measurements and you would find that the shorter the string the faster the pendulum, but not in direct proportion.

I might have to give you a hint about trying the square root of the length. But we would keep at it until you found the relationship that worked—which would also mean you would have to realize that you had to measure from the "middle" (center of gravity) of the weight rather than from the hook on its top.

We would discuss what you had done, and I would be interested both in your findings and in your strategy. I would probably want to see next if you could make use of the law you have discovered to work some problems, and if you could use the strategy of controlled experimentation more efficiently in another discovery situation.

"INSIGHT" LEARNING

The kind of learning process I have been describing is "insight" learning. You explore various hunches and at some point you are aware of the principle. Then you move systematically to demonstate the principle. You cannot make "mistakes" because each "mistake" furthers your inquiry by eliminating an unfruitful possibility.

This sort of insight learning is most effective for the learning of principles (the law of the pendulum) as distinguished from discrete bits of information (how many seconds a 12-inch pendulum requires to swing back and forth once). Principles learned through this sort of discovery tend to be "internalized"; they can be used in many unfamiliar or different situations later.

If I had merely told you the principle, you would memorize my words, but all you would have learned is the answer to the specific question: What is the law of the pendulum?

If I had told you the principle and then given you some problems to work you would learn to use the formula for making calculations, but it would not necessarily be useful to you for any other purpose.

If I had tried to develop the principle through question and answer discussion with you, you might develop the insight required to use it as part of verbal expositions, but you would not be very likely to "see" its operation in a wide range of situations in nature later (when I was not there).

Eightly per cent of present programs (those using Skinner-linear and Crowder-branching rules) teach by the first method, conditioning. The remaining twenty per cent teach by a miscellaneous variety of rules, but tend more toward their authors' conceptions of insight learning. There is considerable controversy about the worth and usefulness of the eighty per cent. (The twenty per cent have mostly not been available to the public. Their turn will come later.)

THE MAJOR ISSUE

It seems clear to me that the major issue concerning programed learning is primarily the large educational issue of conditioning versus insight. This issue, unresolved for two thousand years, is still unresolved. Teaching programs, educational television, the place and nature of achievement tests, the differences between education for the masses and for the elite—answers to these questions hinge on one's position about conditioning versus insight learning as the means of education.

To say this does not mean that there isn't plenty to criticize about present learning programs even for conditioning, but I do not think that is the main issue. The issue is whether "increasing the verbal repertoire" is a legitimate educational objective; whether conditioned learning of a very large number of fragments of information can in any way contribute to the development of character, ability to think critically, ability to apply principles, development of interests, and so on.

This is yet to be demonstrated; and it will be hard to demonstrate because we do not have the sort of evaluation devices and techniques we need to assess most of these major educational objectives.

THREE COURSES OF ACTION

Not having the necessary assessment instruments to measure the significant objectives, what shall we do? Three courses of action are possible.

One is to develop the instruments, but the pattern of "achievement tests" is so well entrenched at present that I don't have much immediate hope.

The second course of action is to give up our educational mission and settle for a lesser one. For the most part this is what the programers are trying to persuade us to do: a good program, they would have us believe, is one that does as good a job as an average teacher in teaching the things that are typically measured on achievement tests. This seems to me to be a cynical view, the counsel of despair.

The third alternative is the oldest and best; it is actually the basis of most teaching. This is to study the experiences of the children *during* the learning activity. Thus one may assume that if students work absorbedly, come up with ideas that are new to them, try to build on each other's ideas, think up alternative ways to do things, offer and evaluate conclusions drawn from experiences they can describe—in such a case we would probably say they were having "worth-while educative experiences" even though we have *not* yet given them a "test."

What we are working from is a model in our minds of what productive study looks and feels like. As long as a classroom full of students fits the teacher's model (even though he doesn't know he has one) the teacher simply tries to maintain interaction as it is; but the moment the experiences begin to lose their thrust or go sour, the teacher acts to change the situation and get back on the track.

The best model for classrooms is that of educated people utilizing knowledge effectively to conduct inquiries into problems, questions and issues that they feel are important. This model assumes that one becomes educated by acting more and more like an educated person.

The teacher is satisfied if he believes the children are doing this as well as they can, given their immature status, lack of experience, and present skills. If the teacher has no sound internalized image of such an operation, then he will act in accordance with some noneducative substitute, such as simply being comfortable and polite, becoming an audience for his play-acting of the expert or executive, becoming a congregation for his moralizing, becoming glibly informed with a lot of talk about (rather than understanding of) phenomena, becoming "independent" (which usually boils down to getting over being immobilized in an anarchic situation).

As I say, the big question is what we really *mean* by education—as shown by our actions as teachers. What is the nature of an educative situation?

THE BEST POLICY

There is little doubt that most competent opinion by people who have no vested interest in particular materials or in the sacred traditions of public schools is that we should maximize insight learning and minimize conditioned learning as much as possible.

There are both theoretical and practical objections to conditioned learning as the way to useful and utilizable knowledge (even though most attitudes and many skills are learned through conditioning in the family). There are only practical objections (too much work) to insight learning.

SOME HELPFUL DEDUCTIONS

As applied to programing of materials, the following deductions may serve as a starting set:

1. The student would be able to define his purpose in using the materials, terms of a question to be answered, a relationship to be sought, a skill to be learned, and he would have solid reasons which, for him, justify his learning of these things.

2. The materials would present reasonably large or molar "situations" containing many elements, and the student would devise his own path through these elements, taking them in any order he chooses, going back and forth among them, having free choice.

3. Each of these molar situations would involve at least two phases: discovery of the pattern followed by immediate application, summarizing, prediction, or raising of further questions that occurred to the student as he was working.

4. During the "search" phase, the student would get immediate feedback when he had classified each element appropriately.

5. During the application or assimilation phase, feedback could not be built into the program because any of a large number of speculations or answers might be right—at least from the point of view of the student. The feedback for this phase would have to be reserved for a non-material third phase: class discussion which begins with the testimony of several students.

6. The programed materials thus would lead into class discussion; the reported speculations and difficulties of the students during the second phase would be testimony from which the agenda for discussion is generated.

7. The discussion would be concerned both with the students' speculations and conclusions and with the way in which the students arrived at these answers.

8. Diagnosis of the discussion would lead into the formation of what the students need to study next, and a variety of activities as appropriate, including further work with programed materials, would then be initiated.

THE EFFECTS OF FIVE PRESCHOOL INTERVENTIONS*

MERLE B. KARNES
University of Illinois

In the broad social concern with the poor and disadvantaged of our population which has characterized the 1960s, no program has appeared more hopeful than preschool education. Here, if anywhere, it seemed, was the point at which the cycle of deprivation might be broken, the predictable sequence of academic failure and early drop-out interrupted. The assumption that preschool experience would allow disadvantaged children to compete more favorably in the formal school setting was embodied in federal social policy through the support of Head Start without any real agreement, however, about the educational approaches most appropriate for this purpose.

It has long been supposed that traditional nursery schools prepare children in important ways for the educational experience they are soon to undertake in the public schools. Little research has, in fact, been done on the question of whether nursery school experience does have a lasting effect upon school adjustment and academic success, but we may assume that for children of middle-class backgrounds the preschool is at least moderately relevant to their later and more formal education. Such nursery schools can obviously assume the conventional advantages of middle-class life in the children who come to them, and they can count as well upon the support and interest of the parents, who are sure to have conventional academic aspirations for their children.

When we turn to the question of preschool education for children who are socially and economically disadvantaged, however, these facts are changed. By definition these children do not have the kind of background which middle-class children bring to the preschool. The cumulative deficiency in language development of the disadvantaged child (Deutsch, 1963), particularly as it relates to the acquisition of more formal language structures in the academic setting (Bernstein, 1961; Jensen, 1963; John and Goldstein, 1964) and to the development of the more abstract cognitive abilities (Ausubel, 1964), is generally accepted as the major challenge to preschool programming. Further limitations on the school progress of the disadvantaged child may be imposed by inadequate perceptual development (Deutsch, 1965), by reduced ability to concentrate and persevere (Deutsch, 1960), by inadequate motivation toward school success (Gordon and Wilkerson, 1966, p. 17), and by a depressed self-concept (Goff, 1954; Silverman, 1963). Whether the traditional nursery school experience can overcome these debilitating effects on learning ability of a disadvantaged environment or whether special educational programs must be designed has not been clearly resolved.

Our studies generally focused on four major questions concerning the educational development of the disadvantaged preschool child:

1. What kind of classroom intervention is most effective?

2. How long must special classroom inter-

---

*U.S. Office of Education, Bureau of Research, 1969.

vention be maintained to stabilize effective functioning?

3. At what age must educational intervention be initiated to prevent learning disabilities associated with cultural deprivation?

4. Can effective educational development be achieved by paraprofessional classroom teachers and mothers at home?

A major area of investigation was the comparative evaluation of five preschool interventions initiated with four-year-old disadvantaged children selected to represent a wide range of ability levels. These classroom interventions were chosen to represent levels of structure along a continuum from the traditional nursery school to the highly structured preschool. The effects of the five interventions were evaluated at the end of the preschool year and again at the end of the kindergarten year. For three of these interventions it was possible to obtain follow-up data at the end of first grade. The two studies presented here then, are an evaluation of the immediate effectiveness of these interventions as well as the stability of improved performance as reflected in subsequent academic achievement in the public schools. Since preliminary results were differential as well as highly encouraging for the more structured programs, one of these (the Ameliorative preschool) provided a framework for the subsequent investigation of related variables: (a) the effects of initiating the Ameliorative program with three-year-old children and with low IQ children and (b) the feasibility of using paraprofessional staff as teachers in the Ameliorative preschool. Finally, in an effort to bring the advantages of preschool training to children at a still earlier age, a series of studies was undertaken to provide instructional programs for children under three years of age and to develop techniques that could be used in training mothers to intervene at home in the educational development of their children.

SUMMARY I. The Effects of Five Preschool Interventions: Evaluations over Two Years

This study was designed to evaluate the differential effects of five preschool interventions through batteries of standardized tests administered prior to the intervention, following the preschool year, and one year later at the end of kindergarten. The classroom interventions were chosen on theoretical as well as practical bases to represent levels of structure along a continuum from the traditional nursery to the highly structured preschool. The nature of teacher-child interaction was considered to be the critical dimension of structure: as the specificity and intensity of this interaction increases so does the degree of structure. Two programs (Traditional and Community-Integrated) represented the less structured end of the continuum; a third (Montessori) embodied an established theory which includes much that can be identified with a child-centered or traditional approach and a methodology which incorporates considerable structure; the fourth (Ameliorative) and the fifth (Direct Verbal) programs fell at the highly structured end of the continuum.

METHOD

The Five Programs of Preschool Intervention

During the first year of the study, 75 disadvantaged children, five class units of 15 children each, participated. Two class units were assigned to the Traditional program, two the Ameliorative program, and one class unit to the Direct Verbal program. In the second year, an additional class unit was enrolled in the Direct Verbal program and a class unit was enrolled in each of the remaining intervention programs (Community-Integrated and Montessori). Children attended daily sessions of approximately two hours and fifteen minutes for a period of no less than seven or more than eight months.

The five programs of classroom intervention may be distinguished as follows:

1. Major goals of the *Traditional* nursery school program were to promote the personal, social, motor, and general language development of the children. Teachers were instructed to capitalize on opportunities for incidental and informal learning, to encourage the children to talk and to ask questions, and to stimulate their interest in the world around them. Music, story, and art activities were scheduled regularly. Outdoor play was a part of the daily routine; indoor play focused on a doll and housekeeping center, a vehicle and block center, and a small toy center.

2. The *Community-Integrated* program, operated at four neighborhood centers, provided a traditional nursery school experience similar to the one above. These centers were licensed by the state and were sponsored by community groups, and classes were composed predominantly of middle- and upper-class Caucasian children. Two to four disadvantaged children from the research class unit attended sessions at one of these four centers. Socio-economic integration was the pertinent variable rather than racial integration which was achieved in all programs. Central to the altered classroom dynamics in the Community-Integrated program was the presence of an advantaged-peer language model in addition to the teacher model provided in all programs. To the extent that children in a traditional nursery school acquire language from each other, the Community-Integrated program provided the optimum setting for verbal development.

3. The *Montessori* program was administered by the local society, and staff and classroom materials met Montessori standards. The daily schedule began with a routine health check and toileting. The group then met "on the line" for conversation, songs, finger plays, and exercises. The next half hour was devoted to "spontaneous choice" of approved materials and was followed by a second period on the line devoted to musical activities, stories, and games. A "practical life" demonstration, juice time, toileting, the silence exercise, and tidying the classroom occupied the next half hour. The final ten or twenty minutes of the session were given over the playground activities or supervised short walks. The specific nature of the "prepared environment" raised the level of structure within the Montessori classroom beyond that of the two traditional programs. The Montessori teacher did not, however, maintain the high level of specific control over the actions of the children required by the teachers in the two highly structured programs. Structure in the Montessori program derived not from direct teacher-child interaction but from the prescribed manner in which the child learned from the materials.

4. In the *Ameliorative* program, verbalizations in conjunction with the manipulation of concrete materials were considered to be the most effective means of establishing new language responses. A game format (card packs, lotto games, models and miniatures, sorting, matching, and classifying games) created situations where *verbal responses could be made repeatedly in a productive, meaningful context* without resorting to rote repetition; often the child could visually and motorically assess the correctness of his thinking before he made an appropriate verbalization. If the child was unable to make a verbal response, the teacher supplied an appropriate model; when he began to initiate such responses, the teacher had the opportunity to correct, modify, and expand his verbalizations.

Each class unit (N = 15) was divided into three groups on the basis of Binet IQ with one teacher for each group. The daily schedule was divided into three 20-minute structured learning periods: math concepts, language arts and reading readiness, and science-social studies. A large room where the 15 children could gather for group activities was available; however, instruction took place in cubicles which contained materials appropriate to the three content areas, and each teacher moved from one cubicle to another with her group of five children. Concepts taught during the structured periods were reinforced during directed play and especially during the music period.

The low pupil-teacher ratio allowed for differentiation of instruction to provide a high success ratio for each child. Immediate correction of incorrect responses (often through the repetition of model sentences or through duplicate layouts of small manipulative materials) and reinforcement of appropriate responses (usually through praise) assured the children of their competencies in handling curricular requirements and enhanced their intrinsic motivation to learn. Frequent review extended content previously presented and provided opportunities to use further the vocabulary and sentence structures which had been taught.

5. In the *Direct Verbal* program intensive oral drill in verbal and logical patterns was chosen as the mode for instruction since disadvantaged children were considered adequate in perceptual and motoric skills but inadequate in verbal and abstract skills. The class unit was divided into three groups of five children, initially on the basis of Stanfort-Binet IQ scores and teacher evaluation. Each of the three teachers conducted a 20-minute learning period (language, arithmetic, or reading) for the three groups. The general instructional strategy was that of rule followed by application. A verbal formula was learned by rote and then applied to a series of analogous examples of increasing difficulty.

The language program focused on the minimum essentials of language competence. The objective was a kind of basic English that teacher and child may use in the conduct of elementary education—a basic English which does not embody all the concepts a child should master but which provides a medium through which those concepts may be learned. The process began by teaching a basic identity statement applied to familiar objects: "This is a_____. This is not a _____." When this statement was mastered, new language patterns were introduced: plurals, polar sets, prepositional phrases, sub-class nouns, active verbs, common tenses, and personal pronouns. The program culminated in the use of language for deductive reasoning.

The arithmetic program emphasized a "science of counting" without reference to phenomena that can be interpreted arithmetically. The disadvantaged child was assumed to lack the verbal and logical sophistication necessary to abstract arithmetic principles from everyday experiences. After the initial teaching of counting, arithmetic was taught through equations emphasizing the idea that any equation could be read as a statement of fact and also as an instruction that told how the fact could be established through a counting operation. The kind of pattern drill used in the language program to teach basic grammatical rules was also used in arithmetic.

The children were taught to read with a modified Initial Teaching Alphabet. Innovations had to do with the formation of long-vowel sounds and the convention for blending words. As early as possible, the children were introduced to controlled-vocabulary stories written by the reading staff.

Songs were especially written for the music period and provided practice in language operations which had been taught. Storytelling also provided additional practice in language operations and involved more question-and-answer activity than is common in reading stories to children.

Selection of Subjects

The subjects for this study were selected from the preschool population of the economically depressed neighborhoods of Champaign-Urbana, a community of 100,000 in central Illinois. Families judged by public aid and school authorities to be economically and educationally deprived were canvassed for children who had no previous preschool experience and who would be four years old before the first of December, an age appropriate for enrollment in public kindergarten the following year. A home interviewer determined final eligibility after she had completed a detailed family history. In addition, interviewers canvassed certain acutely disadvantaged sections of the city to locate children new to the community or otherwise unknown to the referring agencies.

The 1960 Stanford-Binet Intelligence Scale was administered to eligible children who were then stratified on the basis of their intelligence quotients into three groups: IQ scores 100 and above, 90 through 99, and 70 through 89. The children were assigned to class units (N = 15) in which one-third of each class consisted of children who had scored in the "high" IQ range; one-third, the "middle" range; one-third, the "low" range. Mean intelligence quotients were then computed for the three strata and for each class unit. These means were evaluated for comparability between class units as a whole and for strata between classes. Class units were examined to assure comparability of sex and race. When necessary, substitutions were made between classes to maintain an approximate ratio of 67% Negro children and 33% Caucasian children and a ratio of approximately 50% male and 50% female children. Finally, each class unit was randomly assigned to a particular intervention program.

Evaluation Procedures

Since the intent of this study was to evaluate over a two-year period the effectiveness of five classroom interventions upon the overall school readiness of disadvantaged children, evaluations were made prior to the intervention, at the end of the preschool year, and at the end of the kindergarten year in the following areas:

1. Intellectual functioning as measured by the 1960 Stanford-Binet Individual Intelligence Scale, Form L-M.

2. Language development as measured by the Illinois Test of Psycholinguistic Abilities, experimental edition, 1961.

3. Vocabulary comprehension as measured by the Peabody Picture Vocabulary Test.

In addition, the Frostig Developmental Test of Visual Perception and the Metropolitan Readiness Tests were administered at the time of the second and third batteries.

RESULTS AT THE END OF THE PRESCHOOL YEAR

The two highly structured programs (Ameliorative and Direct Verbal) demonstrated a substantial mean gain (13 points) in *intellectual functioning* (Binet IQ). No child in either program failed to make an IQ gain. On test two 92% of the children in the Ameliorative group and 74% of the children in the Direct Verbal group fell in the high intelligence strata. The other three groups made more modest mean gains (5 to 8 points) and from 15 to 24% of these children regressed. Clearly, the test-two performance of the Ameliorative and Direct Verbal groups on the Stanford-Binet was superior to the performances of the other three groups. Although the Traditional group was not significantly lower than the Ameliorative or Direct Verbal group, neither was it significantly higher than the Community-Integrated or Montessori group.

On the initial assessment of *language development* (ITPA) the children in this study were most deficient on the three subtests related to verbal expressive abilities: Vocal Encoding, Auditory-Vocal Automatic, and Auditory-Vocal Association. The Ameliorative group eliminated a major initial deficiency on each of these three subtests, and the Direct Verbal group eliminated a major deficiency on two of these three subtests. The Traditional group did relatively well in this area. The performances of the Community-Integrated and Montessori groups on these three subtests were static at best, and their substantial deficits remained at the time of test two. On the ITPA total the Ameliorative group was significantly higher than the Community-Integrated and Montessori groups but did not differ significantly from the Direct Verbal and Traditional groups. The Direct Verbal and Traditional groups were significantly higher than the Montessori group only.

The magnitude of the gains of the Ameliorative group on the nine subtests of the ITPA and the consistency with which it made these gains resulted in an essentially nondeficit test-two performance. The Traditional group made consistent but more modest gains and had no major deficits (deficits in excess of 6 months) at the time of test two. The Direct Verbal group made somewhat larger gains than the Traditional group but made these gains somewhat less consistently and had major deficits on two subtests at test two. The Community-Integrated and Montessori groups generally made smaller and less consistent gains than the other three groups. The movement of the Montessori group was somewhat regressive while that of the Community-Integrated group was more nearly static.

There were no significant differences among the five groups in *vocabulary comprehension* as measured by the Peabody Picture Vocabulary Test. The performance of the Ameliorative group in *visual perception* (Frostig) was significantly higher than those of the other four groups. On test two, over 75% of the children in the Traditional, Montessori, and Community-Integrated groups earned scores indicating a need for remediation; in the Direct Verbal group 43% of the children earned such scores. Only 21% of the children in the Ameliorative group scored at this low level. An assessment of *school readiness* (Metropolitan) indicated the statistical superiority of the Ameliorative and Direct Verbal groups in number readiness only.

CONCLUSIONS AT THE END OF THE PRESCHOOL YEAR

Since the five intervention programs were chosen to represent points along a continuum of structure, one might assume that the results would order themselves along this continuum to the extent that structure is a valid dimension in effecting change. Such was not the case. The children in the Ameliorative and Direct Verbal programs (high on the structure continuum) generally showed the greatest gains. Those who participated in the Traditional program (low on the structure continuum) showed more modest gains. Children in the Community-Integrated program (also low on the structure continuum) and those who participated in the Montessori program (midway on the structure continuum) showed the least progress.

The failure of the Montessori children to demonstrate appreciable progress seems to invalidate the notion that the level of structure relates to the progress made by the disadvantaged child. The Montessori program provided a high degree of structure in terms of careful planning for the kinds of motor-sensory activity appropriate to the development of an adequate base from which language and cognitive skills arise, and these provisions may be considered comparable to the activities used to elicit verbal responses (the game format) in the Ameliorative program or to the pattern drill employed in the Direct Verbal program. The Montessori teacher provided a "prepared environment" but did not systematically engage the child in verbalizations or require such verbalizations as part of the definition of productive involvement. This failure of the Montessori program resulted, at least during the intervention interval, in somewhat regressive language behavior. Structured emphasis on motor-sensory development without similar concern for verbal development programmatically moves in the wrong direction for the disadvantaged child.

The expectation that children in the Community-Integrated group would show progress equal to or greater than that of the children in the Traditional group was not substantiated. The disadvantaged children in the Community-Integrated program failed to incorporate the language model of their advantaged peers because they did not reciprocate in verbal interactions at any significant level. The homogeneity of the Traditional group, on the other hand, required these children to respond verbally during certain activities. Their teachers necessarily accommodated these activities to the verbal level of the children and gradually developed more acceptable and extended responses. The progress in verbal expressive ability made by the children in the Traditional program reflects this accommodation.

The very real progress made by the children in the Traditional program must be viewed against the generally superior performance of the children in the two highly structured programs. The effectiveness of directly teaching specific content was illustrated by the superior performance of the Ameliorative and Direct Verbal groups on the number readiness test of the Metropolitan. The magnitude and consistency of their gains in intellectual functioning (Binet IQ) clearly endorse the importance of providing a setting in which the child is required to make appropriate and increasingly complex verbalizations. There is some evidence that obtaining these verbalizations in conjunction with productive, manipulative experiences (Ameliorative program) more effectively developed visual perceptual skills (Frostig) as well as the visual-motor skills involved in certain ITPA subtests (Visual Decoding, Visual-Motor Sequencing, and Motor Encoding). In addition, children who made verbal responses concurrent with meaningful, manipulative experiences more effectively incorporated syntactical constructs into their verbal repertoire (Auditory-Vocal Automatic subtest). On the other hand, verbal pattern drills (Direct Verbal program) provided unique opportunities to develop the auditory reception of structured aspects of language (Auditory-Vocal Association and Auditory Decoding subtests).

THE SECOND YEAR OF THE STUDY

Interventions During the Kindergarten Year

During their second year in the study the children in the Traditional, Community-

Integrated, Montessori, and Ameliorative programs attended public kindergarten for a half day where no research intervention was made. The children in the Ameliorative program attended public kindergarten in the morning and, in addition, participated in a one-hour supportive program at the research center in the afternoon. According to the research design, children in the Direct Verbal program were not to attend public kindergarten and were to return to the research center for a half-day program.

The children in the *Ameliorative supportive program* were divided into two classes of twelve children each. The one-hour session consisted of two periods—language development/reading readiness and mathematics concepts. An effort was made to avoid repeating activities which had already been provided in the morning public kindergarten and to emphasize activities directly related to first-grade academic success. Because the test-two performance of the Ameliorative group on all ITPA subtests had been essentially nondeficit, the major orientation of the supportive program was toward school readiness rather than language development. Since these children had demonstrated competence in visual perceptual skills (Frostig) and a mean Binet IQ substantially above 100 (only two children scored below 100) and because they were approaching an age appropriate to more specific academic endeavors, this shift in program emphasis seemed reasonable.

The *Direct Verbal* program in the second year of the study offered an extension of the first year's curriculum, and the children were again grouped by ability for 25-minute instructional periods in reading, arithmetic, and language. The language program included concepts of measure, the formal use of function words, and the vocabulary engendered by a study of part-whole relationships of over 100 objects. The Direct Verbal staff developed a highly systematized reading method which emphasized sub-skills such as blending, rhyming, visual discrimination, left-to-right orientation and sequencing. The children were taught to recognize symbols as sounds and to combine these sounds, using the sub-skills, into words. In arithmetic the children received further work in the curriculum initiated the first year, and no significant alterations were made.

RESULTS AT THE END OF THE KINDERGARTEN YEAR

At the end of the second year of intervention, statistical comparisons were made between data from batteries one and three, but only inferences can be drawn between data from batteries two and three. Clearly the performance of the Direct Verbal group in *intellectual functioning* (Binet IQ) was superior to that of the other four groups. Only the children in the Direct Verbal group made a substantial gain during the second year (6 points). The four groups that attended public kindergarten the second year basically maintained the gains in intellectual functioning made during the first year, and losses or additional gains did not exceed 3 points. Although the supportive program for the Ameliorative group was unsuccessful in fostering further IQ gains, it may have been responsible for maintaining the relatively large gain of this group.

On the initial *language development* assessment (ITPA) these children were most deficient on three subtests requiring verbal expressive abilities: Vocal Encoding, Auditory-Vocal Automatic, and Auditory-Vocal Association. Of the three groups who attended only public kindergarten the second year, the Community-Integrated group demonstrated the least change on these three subtests. The Traditional group, although they had shown relatively good progress on these three subtests during the preschool year, tended to regress during the kindergarten year. The Montessori group, on the other hand, which had demonstrated a regressive pattern the first year, made substantial gains during the kindergarten year. The regressive performance during the second year of the fourth group who attended public kindergarten (Ameliorative) is particularly distressing since these children also attended the one-hour supportive program. The Direct Verbal group was the only group that showed continued and appreciable progress over the two-year period and was at or above its chronological age on the three subtests related to verbal expressive abilities. These results, together with the results on intellectual functioning, may be an indictment of public school programming for disadvantaged children but are clearly an endorsement of continued special programming.

On the ITPA total the performance of the

Direct Verbal group was significantly higher than those of the other four groups. Differences between test-one and test-three performances for these four groups were negligible, and only the Direct Verbal group showed a substantial gain (7 months). Over the two-year period the Direct Verbal group consistently made gains which resulted in a nondeficit test-three performance on all ITPA subtests. The Ameliorative group made no appreciable regressions but its gains were more modest. On five subtests the Ameliorative group was above its chronological age at test three, but four major deficits (6 to 12 months) remained. The gains of the Traditional group were not of sufficient magnitude to result in any test-three performance above chronological age, and three of its deficits were of major proportions. The performance of the Montessori group was somewhat more erratic than that of the Traditional group; major deficits remained on three subtests, but on three subtests the Montessori group scored above its chronological age. At test three the Community-Integrated group had major deficits on eight subtests, two of which exceeded twelve months.

At the time of test three the Traditional group was significantly lower than the other four groups on the test of *visual perception* (Frostig). The Traditional group made no progress during the second year while the Montessori and Community-Integrated groups made substantial growth in this area during their year in public kindergarten. The Ameliorative group, which had been significantly superior at test two, showed modest but continued growth. The mean of the Direct Verbal group which had ranked second at test two now closely approximated that of the Ameliorative group. Children in the public kindergarten did indeed make gains in this area; however, the groups which participated in the structured academically-oriented programs had a considerably smaller percentage of children prone to reading failure, to the extent that reading failures are related to visual perceptual inadequacies.

On the assessment of school readiness (Metropolitan) the reading readiness performance of the Ameliorative group was significantly higher than those of the other four groups. This result is rather surprising in view of the Direct Verbal group's superiority in intellectual functioning (Binet) and language development (ITPA). The failure of the Direct Verbal group to achieve a performance superior to those of the other groups, especially the three groups who attended public kindergarten only, is puzzling since its curriculum included an intensive two-year reading program. A major intent of the Ameliorative supportive program had been to prepare children for formal reading instruction, and this focus appropriately developed reading readiness skills as measured by the Metropolitan. Thirty-eight percent of the children in the Ameliorative program achieved a superior reading readiness status, and 67% of the children in this group were rated high normal and above. No child in the other four programs earned a superior rating, and from 15 to 31% of the children in these groups were in the high normal range. Nearly equal percentages of the children in these four groups fell in the high, average, and low ranges. The favorable reading prediction for the large number of children in the Ameliorative program is complemented by the few children who received low-normal ratings, less than one-fourth the percentage of any other group.

On the Metropolitan Number Readiness Test the Ameliorative and Direct Verbal groups were significantly higher at test three than the other groups. A substantially higher percentage of the children in the Ameliorative group (83%) achieved a superior number readiness status; however, the percentages of children in the Ameliorative and Direct Verbal groups who were rated high normal and above (91%) were identical and higher than those of the other three groups (48 to 64%). Apparently, disadvantaged children of preschool and kindergarten age profit from academically-oriented instruction in mathematics, and both programs seemed appropriate and effective with these children.

The children who participated in the Traditional, Community-Integrated, and Montessori programs the first year and who attended only the public kindergarten the second year generally demonstrated the least progress on the *total battery*. The performance of the Traditional group at the end of the first year more nearly approximated those of the two structured groups than those of the Community-Integrated and Montessori groups which changed little during the preschool intervention. The regression of the Traditional group and the modest progress of the Montessori group during the second year (the kindergarten year) resulted in similar test-three performances. The Community-Integrated group regressed substantially in important areas during the second year. The children in the Ameliorative group made progress equal or superior to that of the Direct Verbal group during the first year but regressed substantially in critical areas the second year. The one-hour supportive program was successful in fostering further development of school readiness (Metropolitan) and visual perception (Frostig). Only the Direct Verbal group made consistent and continued progress in all areas over the two-year period.

CONCLUSIONS AT THE END OF THE KINDERGARTEN YEAR

Only at the end of the first year of the study can differential results be directly attributed to the specifics of preschool intervention, since only then were the five programs comparable in terms of class unit composition, teacher-pupil ratio, and time. The second year of this study introduces new variables and cannot be viewed merely as a follow-up of the five preschool programs. For those interested in preschool programming for disadvantaged children, the data obtained at the end of the preschool year *must* remain of primary relevance.

It seems clear that one year of preschool programming, no matter how immediately effective, did not equip disadvantaged children to maintain performance in the kindergarten setting. Regardless of the progress made in preschool by the four groups of children which attended public kindergarten, their relative performances deteriorated during the second year, and the efficacy of kindergarten programming for disadvantaged children seems open to question. Since one of the principal findings of the first year was that intensive teacher-child interaction is critical to maximum language development and since this kind of interaction cannot occur with the teaching ratio of the public kindergarten, the deterioration in language development is not surprising. Only children in the Direct Verbal program, which maintained a low pupil-teacher ratio and intensive pupil-teacher interaction the second year, made continuing progress in language development.

During the first year of the study, Ameliorative programming was appropriate and highly effective, and children made remarkable progress in all areas, particularly those of initial inadequacy. This encouraging educational prognosis contributed to a shift in emphasis from language development to school readiness in the one-hour supportive program. The marked regression in verbal expressive abilities experienced by these children during the kindergarten year suggests that this shift in emphasis was ill advised or at least premature. The additional one-hour supportive program did indeed promote superior academic readiness but failed to maintain the level of language functioning achieved in the Ameliorative preschool.

Only children who attended the Direct Verbal preschool were provided low pupil-teacher ratios and intensive language programming over the two-year period, and only these children made continued growth in all aspects of the test battery. The second year IQ gain is particularly encouraging as are the remarkable two-year gains in verbal expressive abilities made by children in this group. Only in the area of reading readiness did these children fail to achieve the superior performance, and this study offers no direct evidence to support the early introduction of reading instruction to disadvantaged children.

SUMMARY II. A Follow-Up of Three of the Five Preschool Interventions: Evaluations over Three Years

Because all interventions were not initiated during the first year of the study, data at the end of first grade are not available for the Montessori and Community-Integrated groups or for the second Direct Verbal class unit. Follow-up data are, however, available for the Traditional group (N = 25), the Ameliorative group (N = 24), and the first class unit of the Direct Verbal group (N = 10). *The available N for the Direct Verbal group, therefore, is reduced from 23 to 10, and conclusions based on data obtained during the third year for this group must be tentative.* Since the implications of the first two years were discussed in the preceding report, the major intent of this study will be to evaluate the status of the three groups at the completion of first grade.

Evaluations were made in the following areas prior to the intervention, at the end of the preschool year, at the end of the kindergarten year, and at the end of first grade:

1. Intellectual functioning as measured by the 1960 Stanford-Binet Individual Intelligence Scale, Form L-M.

2. Language development as measured by the Illinois Test of Psycholinguistic Abilities, experimental edition, 1961.

3. Visual perception as measured by the Frostig Developmental Test of Visual Perception.

In addition, the Peabody Picture Vocabulary Test was included in the first three batteries, the Metropolitan Readiness Tests were administered at the end of the preschool and kindergarten years, and the California Achievement Tests, Lower Primary Form W, were given at the end of the first grade.

The first intervention embodied the traditionalist point of view: a nursery school experience which worked in conventional ways to improve the personal, social, motor, and general language development of the children was followed by a traditional kindergarten under the auspices of the public school. The Direct Verbal program radically departed from the established view: The traditional preschool and kindergarten were seen as inadequate and inappropriate to the task of insuring the academic competencies of the disadvantaged child, and the experimental Direct Verbal preschool was provided for the two years prior to first grade. The Ameliorative program represented a middle ground: Amelioration of deficits related to school inadequacies began during the preschool year so that the disadvantaged child might benefit fully from the traditional kindergarten. The public kindergarten with a one-hour supportive program, it was assumed, would then be an appropriate prelude to first grade. Children from the three intervention programs attended first-grade classes under the sole supervision of the public schools, and all children were given the fourth battery of tests in the late spring of the third year of the study.

RESULTS AT THE END OF FIRST GRADE

School Achievement

Although important interim evaluations were made at the end of the preschool and kindergarten years, school achievement at the end of first grade was understood to be a critical criterion in assessing program effectiveness. The *reading achievement* of the Ameliorative and Direct Verbal groups as measured by the California Achievement Tests was significantly higher than that of the Traditional group. Two years of reading instruction in the Direct Verbal program prior to first grade seem to have been only as effective as the extensive readiness preparation in the Ameliorative program in producing accelerated reading development. This study provides little evidence to support the introduction of early reading programs for disadvantaged children.

The California *language* test assessed capitalization, punctuation, word usage, and spelling skills and bears little relation to language development as it is discussed elsewhere in this report. The performance of the Ameliorative group was significantly higher on this language test than that of the Traditional group. The performance of the Direct Verbal group approximated that of the Ameliorative group but failed to achieve significance. Since the skills required for successful performance on this test were not taught at the preschool or kindergarten levels (with the exception of limited spelling instruction for Direct Verbal children), the differential nature of this performance may reflect the superiority of the Ameliorative and Direct Verbal groups in general school readiness as evidenced on the Metropolitan Readiness Tests at the end of the kindergarten year.

The results of the Metropolitan Number Readiness Test at the end of the kindergarten year indicated that the two structured groups were better prepared for the more formal work of first-grade mathematics. The Ameliorative and Direct Verbal groups were significantly higher than the Traditional group on the California *arithmetic* test at the end of the first grade, confirming this prediction.

Intellectual Functioning

The Binet performances of the three groups were clearly differentiated over the three-year period. The performance of the Ameliorative and Direct Verbal groups was significantly superior to that of the Traditional group at the end of the pre-school year. At the end of the kindergarten year, the Binet performance of the Direct Verbal group was significantly superior to that of the other two groups. (The Ameliorative group was very nearly significantly higher than the Traditional group.) At the end of the third year of the study, when all children were completing the first grade, there were no significant differences among the three groups. The modest preschool gain (8 points) of the Traditional group remained relatively stable during the following two years (5 points at the end of the first grade). Although the one-hour supportive program was unsuccessful in fostering a further gain for the Ameliorative group, it may have been responsible for maintaining the relatively large preschool gain (14 points). The Ameliorative group did, however, lose 6 points of this gain during the kindergarten and first-grade years. Only the Direct Verbal group received sustained special programming during the preschool and kindergarten years, and only the Direct Verbal group made large and continuing gains (13 and 10 points) during the first two years of the study. When special programming terminated and these children entered the first grade of the public schools, they experienced a sizeable loss (11 points).

Language Development

Initial ITPA total language age deficits for the three groups were four to five months. At the end of the preschool year, the groups were performing very nearly at their respective chronological ages. The Traditional group maintained a small deficit, and the Direct Verbal group achieved a modest acceleration. The Ameliorative group made the largest gain and was functioning nearly three months above its mean chronological age. During the second year of the study, only the Direct Verbal group made continued gains, and its ITPA total performance was significantly higher than those of the Ameliorative and the Traditional groups. The losses of the Ameliorative group during the kindergarten year resulted in a test-three performance two months below its chronological age while the losses of the Traditional group resulted in a test-three deficit which very nearly equaled its initial deficit. There were no statistical differences among the ITPA total performances of the three groups at the end of the third year of the study. All groups regressed during the first-grade year. The extent of the losses of the Traditional and Ameliorative groups during the kindergarten and first-grade years exceeded the gains they had made in the preschool year. Although the Direct Verbal group was performing at its chronological age, the loss experienced by this group during the first grade exceeded its gain of the kindergarten year and does not support an encouraging language prognosis.

Visual Perception

At the end of the preschool year, the performance of the Ameliorative group on the Frostig Developmental Test of Visual Perception was significantly higher than that of the Traditional group only. During the kindergarten year, the Ameliorative and Direct Verbal groups made continuing progress and were significantly higher than the Traditional group which regressed slightly. All groups made progress during the first-grade year; however, the Traditional group made a substantial gain and there were no longer significant differences among the groups. Initially, nearly all of the children fell in the lowest quartile on this instrument. At the end of the first grade, only 8% of the children in the Ameliorative group scored in the lowest quartile while 20% of the Direct Verbal children and 48% of the Traditional children earned such scores.

CONCLUSIONS AT THE END OF FIRST GRADE

No intervention program was entirely successful in providing the impetus necessary to sustain at the end of first grade the gains in intellectual functioning and language development made during the preschool years. In spite of the disappointments of some of the longitudinal data, however, a major accomplishment of this study remains: Serious learning deficits of the disadvantaged children in the Ameliorative and Direct Verbal groups were eliminated during the preschool year. In the Direct Verbal program, where an extensive intervention was sustained over a two-year period, continued growth occurred. The deterioration in language and intellectual functioning which occurred at the termination of intensive programming demonstrates the need for continued intervention characterized by low pupil-teacher ratios which make possible the interaction necessary for language development and which provide the opportunity to design and implement learning experiences to achieve specific goals.

Although these three short-term interventions (even a two-year classroom intervention is essentially a short-term effort) did not differentially alter intellectual functioning in any permanent fashion, two aspects of the Binet data have important implications. The sizeable gain of the low strata children in the Ameliorative group remained stable, most pertinently, during first grade when no research intervention was provided. It seems justifiable to conclude that the Ameliorative program offered particular opportunities to develop the intellectual functioning of low-normal and slow-learning children. The small number in each stratum of the Direct Verbal group preclude discussion of gains by strata. The IQ losses experienced by the high strata children in both the Traditional and Ameliorative groups during the first grade are of real concern and resulted in an IQ change in a negative direction over the three-year period. The modest gain of the Traditional high stratum and the substantial gain of the Ameliorative high stratum during the preschool year remained constant through the kindergarten year but were lost during the first grade. It seems reasonable to assume that in important ways the public schools during first grade failed disadvantaged children with demonstrated potential. This assumption is further supported by the substantial regression during first grade of 24 of the 26 children from the three intervention groups who had scored 110 and above at the end of kindergarten.

Since the intent of preschool intervention for disadvantaged children is to alter in positive ways later school performance, both structured programs must be judged successful. Virtually all of the children in the two structured programs were making at least adequate academic progress. In spite of two years of traditional preschool programming, nearly half of the children in the Traditional group obtained California scores which indicated sharply limited school achievement. This differential achievement level demonstrates the potential for school success among disadvantaged children which can be developed through structured preschool experiences. Functioning effectively in the public school setting is a critical first step in altering the life circumstances of the disadvantaged child to the end that he may participate more fully in the educational and economic opportunities of a democratic culture.

CHEMICAL TRANSFER OF LEARNING

New experiments involve injecting brain material, principally RNA, from trained animals into untrained animals. The resulting changes in the behavior of the untrained animals support a chemical explanation of memory.

A. L. JACOBSON
University of California, Los Angeles

Scientists may be on the verge of a major break-through in the problem of memory. For at least a hundred years, physiologists and psychologists have pondered over and investigated the manner in which an organism's experience is stored and later used. Certain general features of the process have been worked out, but the nature of the hypothetical 'memory trace' or 'engram' has remained frustratingly elusive. In the 1930s and 1940s, Karl Lashley, an eminent neuropsychologist, conducted an extensive series of investigations aimed at discovering just where memory is stored in the brain. One of Lashley's basic techniques involved ablating or removing cortical tissues from various parts of rats' brains and finding out whether these lesions interfered with the animals' memory for previously-learned tasks. But Lashley's search for the engram failed: although he found deficits in performance, they appeared to be more related to the *amount* of cortical tissue removed than to the particular location of the tissue. This work suggested that the engram, whatever its nature, must be rather widely represented in the brain. Later investigations have shown that the amount of memory impairment produced by such lesions depends on several variables, including the nature of the task employed.

This question of localization of memories has also been investigated by electrophysiological techniques. Dr Wilder Penfield of McGill University in Montreal, in the course of his neurosurgical operations on conscious humans, has discovered that direct electrical stimulation of certain portions of the brain can evoke particular experiences or memories in great detail. Penfield reports, "The sights and sounds, and the thoughts, of a former day pass through the man's mind again." In contrast to Lashley's results, this finding suggests particular locations in the brain for at least certain memories.

Two brains in one

Quite recently, the above ablation technique has been employed in a somewhat different way. Cutting the corpus callosum, the major bundle of nerve fibres connecting the two cerebral hemispheres, produces a *split-brain* preparation. An animal treated in this way behaves essentially normally in most situations, since the input to the two hemispheres is the same. However, if a particular input is given to only *one* hemisphere, the habit taught is apparently restricted to that particular half of the brain; if the stimulus is given to the other hemisphere, the animal reveals no indication of prior training. In fact, the two hemispheres can be taught diametrically opposed solutions to the same problem; the animal's response is then determined by which side of the brain receives the triggering stimulus.

Much of the split-brain research has been conducted by Dr Roger Sperry of the California Institute of Technology. The usual subjects have been cats and monkeys, but Dr Sperry has also studied the behaviour of two humans, who had had a split-brain operation to reduce the intensity of epileptic seizures. These patients, though normal in their everyday behaviour, show 'dissociation' effects in the laboratory similar to those of split-brain animals—so much so that Dr Sperry claims these subjects appear to have two separate 'spheres of consciousness.' One example will suffice. In humans, the speech function is typically confined to one hemisphere. When Sperry blindfolded one of his subjects and placed an object in the hand connected to the 'mute' hemisphere, the subject could use the object appropriately, but was totally unable to identify it verbally. The information reaching the mute hemisphere was quite unavailable to the hemisphere controlling speech.

The ablation technique, then, has revealed many aspects of brain functioning and has suggested how different parts of the brain interact in the process of memory storage. But it tells us little about the actual nature of this process or about the nature of the engram itself. One approach, the *consolidation hypothesis* has thrown some light on the former problem. Proposed in 1900, this hypothesis asserts that, following a learning experience, a period of time is required for the effects of the experience to become established in the brain via continuing neural activity. Such an explanation has been used to account for the limited amnesias of human accident victims—a traumatic experience during the consolidation period might disrupt the laying down of the memory trace. The consolidation hypothesis has been tested by administering electroconvulsive shocks (ECS) to the brains of rats shortly after a learning experience. In one recent experiment, for example, this treatment interfered with learning if the ECS was given as much as 30 seconds after a training trial, but not if the delay was 60 seconds or more.

Another intriguing implication of the consolidation hypothesis is that appropriate action after the learning experience may help, rather than hinder, the process of learning. And, in fact, post-trial injection of the neural stimulant strychnine sulphate does produce more rapid learning in some cases, presumably by virtue of its effect on the neural activity involved in consolidation.

Does RNA 'encode' memory?

Such experiments provide us with valuable information about the laying down of the memory trace. But what, exactly, is being laid down or consolidated? Here we must resort primarily to theory, for experimental facts are scarce. The most dominant view for many years has been that the behavioural changes we call learning are correlated with some physiological change within our brains, most probably at the synapse—the

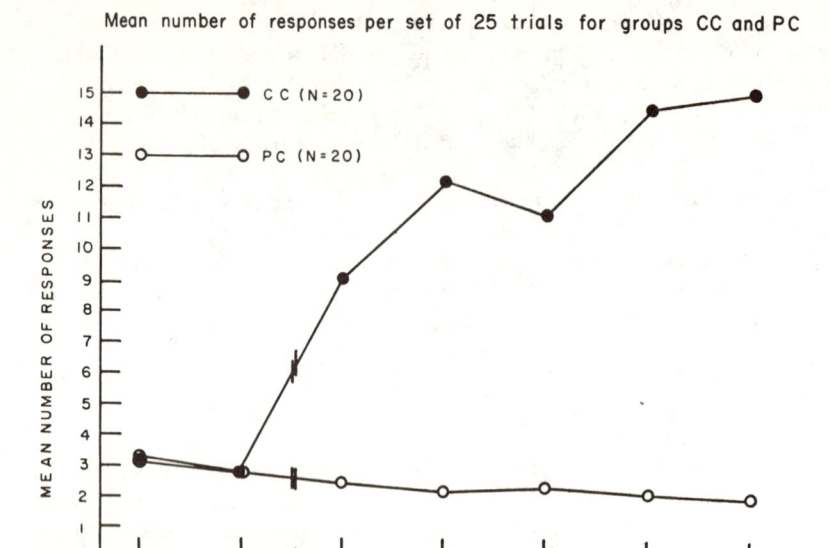

Fig 1 CLASSICAL CONDITIONING in planarians. Group CC (classically-conditioned) worms were trained to respond to light by pairing the light with an electric shock, while group PC (pseudo-conditioned) received randomly interspersed light and shock. Only the classically-conditioned worms learned the response, 'anticipating' the electric shock. L_1 and L_2 are trial sets during which no shock was given

junction between two neurons. Since behaviour is dictated by neural activity, changes in behaviour must involve changes in neural activity. And the synapse, as the key decision point in a neural network, is a logical site for such neural changes. These changes would make the passage of impulses across particular synapses more efficient, and thus selectively aid the activation of hypothetical neural chains mediating certain behaviours.

The very vagueness of the above explanation reflects our ignorance in this critical area. Observation of synaptic changes accompanying learning is extremely difficult—where, for instance, should one look? The mammalian brain is discouragingly complex. One way to get around this problem is to study simpler organisms which are still capable of learning. Thus, Dr J. V. Luco has studied the manner in which a cockroach, deprived of its forelegs, learns to use its middle legs efficiently in cleaning the antennae. Dr Luco has observed that accompanying this behavioural change is a change in the electrical reaction of the cockroach's nervous system, which he interprets as an effect occurring at a single synapse. Such correlations of behavioural change and synaptic change are rarely found, however, and suggestive at best. Lowered synaptic resistance is generally conceded to be a likely basis for memory, but we must not lose sight of the fact that data in support of this contention are practically non-existent.

Around 1950, a new way of thinking arose which may one day be considered the turning point in man's understanding of his own brain. Molecular biologists had identified DNA as the carrier of genetic instructions, and certain of them had noted a basic conceptual similarity between heredity and memory: namely, that both involve information storage. The information in one case is passed on from generation to generation, while in the other it concerns the experience of the individual organism. This similarity suggested that the information storage or coding process in the two cases might be at least analogous.

Of all the possible chemical substances which might encode memory, ribonucleic acid, or RNA, appears in

CHEMICAL TRANSFER OF LEARNING

many respects the most attractive candidate. RNA is a large molecule present in all living cells and similar in structure to DNA. Furthermore, in theory RNA has a large enough storage capacity for information to account for the facts of memory, and it does not directly serve as a repository of genetic information in the same manner as DNA. For these reasons, the hypothesis that RNA encodes memory was proposed. Of course this hypothesis does not contradict the notion of synaptic change as a basis of learning; even if experience is encoded in RNA, one must still explain the manner in which such stored information exerts an influence on subsequent behaviour—an explanation which might well include changes in neural action. The RNA hypothesis, as typically stated, asserts that learning produces changes in RNA which then mediate or monitor (via protein synthesis) the synaptic alterations which presumably underlie modifications of behaviour.

In the last ten years a number of experiments have been performed which seem to implicate RNA in learning and memory functions. Noteworthy among these is the work of Dr Holger Hydén of Sweden, who has found changes in the RNA in the brains of rats occurring at the same time as behavioural changes. Another line of research has shown that chemical agents which interfere with RNA activity also have adverse effects on learning. The approach which will be the concern of the remainder of this article, however, is quite different. Recent experiments have demonstrated that material transferred from trained animals can produce specific behavioural changes in untrained animals, such that the recipient animals appear to have acquired some of the training of the donors. The evidence gathered so far suggests that in many of these cases RNA is involved in the transfer process.

Pavlovian worms

The planarian is a common, water-dwelling flatworm, about half an inch long, which has a rudimentary nervous system (including a brain) and also has remarkable powers of regeneration—if a planarian is cut into several pieces, each piece will regenerate into a complete planarian. Some ten years ago, Dr James McConnell and Dr Robert Thompson at the University of Texas reported that they had successfully established a Pavlovian-type conditioned response in planarians. Initially, if they presented a light flash, the animals made little obvious response. An electric current passed through the water, however, would evoke a contraction of the planarian's body. If the light flash was now repeatedly presented immediately before the shock, the planarians came to make more and more observable responses to the light, *before* the shock was given. It appeared, in other words, as though they were 'anticipating' the shock, much as Pavlov's dogs 'anticipated' food when a tone was sounded.

Several years later McConnell, Daniel Kimble and I conditioned planarians in the fashion described above, and then cut each conditioned planarian in half across the body. After each half had

Fig 2 INJECTING RNA into a planarian, which is anaesthetized by dry ice under the watch glass. The RNA is obtained from other planarians which have been classically-conditioned; the injected worm is then tested to discover if the response learned by the donor worms has been transferred
Courtesy of Worm Runners' Digest

regenerated, we trained the 'new' planarians in the same manner as the original worms. These regenerated worms, whether derived from the head half or tail half of the original worms, acquired the conditioned response much faster than had the originals. Thus, to some extent, the tendency to react to the light had apparently been passed on to both 'offspring'.

McConnell proposed that the conditioning process had produced some *chemical* change in the animal, and he posed a further question: could the response to light produced by training be transferred to an entirely different planarian, rather than to an asexual offspring? McConnell, R. Jacobson and B. Humphries tested this notion by taking advantage of the fact that hungry planarians will eat other planarians—particularly if the latter are damaged. They conditioned one group of worms, then cut them up and fed them to untrained cannibal worms (identified as group 1). A second group of victim worms which received no training was fed to a second group of untrained cannibal worms (group 2). When the cannibal worms were subsequently tested, the group 1 animals were significantly more responsive to the light than were group 2 worms. Clearly, the cannibals' ingestion of the trained worms had affected their response to light. Incidentally, I should add that this study was conducted in 'blind' fashion—that is, the experimenter did not know during testing whether a given cannibal had ingested trained or untrained victims. Such a procedure lessens the chance of the results' being inadvertently biased.

This cannibalism study raised a question of interpretation: was the observed behavioural effect actually an instance of true learning being transferred from one animal to another, or might the same effect have been observed if control victims, instead of being untreated, had been stimulated with shock and light but not specifically trained? In other words, did the transfer effect depend on training or only on sheer stimulation of the victim worms? In addition, could the transfer effect be ascribed to a particular chemical substance, possibly RNA in the victim worms' bodies?

Inducing a response by injection

Drs E. R. John and W. Corning, at the University of Rochester, reasoned that if the RNA hypothesis is correct, then it might be possible to 'erase' memories by applying a chemical substance which breaks down RNA. Their experiment showed, in fact, that such a substance, the enzyme ribonuclease, apparently does 'wipe out' a classically-conditioned response in regenerating planarians.

These findings led C. Fried, S. Horowitz and me to perform an experiment designed to analyze the role of RNA in the planarian transfer effect more thoroughly. We trained one group of planarians (classically-conditioned, or CC) to respond to light by pairing the light with electric shock. A second group (pseudo-conditioned, or PC), we gave randomly interspersed lights and shocks, and a third group (non-conditioned, or NC) received no training at all. Thus, at the end of this stage of the experiment only the first group was responding to the light (*see Fig. 1*). We then extracted RNA from each of the three groups, and injected it into three groups of 25 untrained planarians (*see Fig. 2*). Each of these 75 injected planarians was then given 25 exposures to the light and was scored on whether or not it responded to each exposure. Naturally, we ran this part of the experiment 'blind'. The result (*see Fig. 3*) was that planarians which received RNA from the CC group consistently made more responses to the light than did recipients of RNA from the two control groups, PC and NC. We have repeated this experiment successfully and have done other tests which suggest more strongly that RNA is the effective agent. We have, it seems, induced a response to a stimulus by injection!

Acquisition of a conditioned response, however, is only one aspect of behavioural change. Horowitz, Fried, and I wondered how the loss (or extinction) of the conditioned response might de-

CHEMICAL TRANSFER OF LEARNING

Distribution of scores (responses per 25 trials) for injected planarians

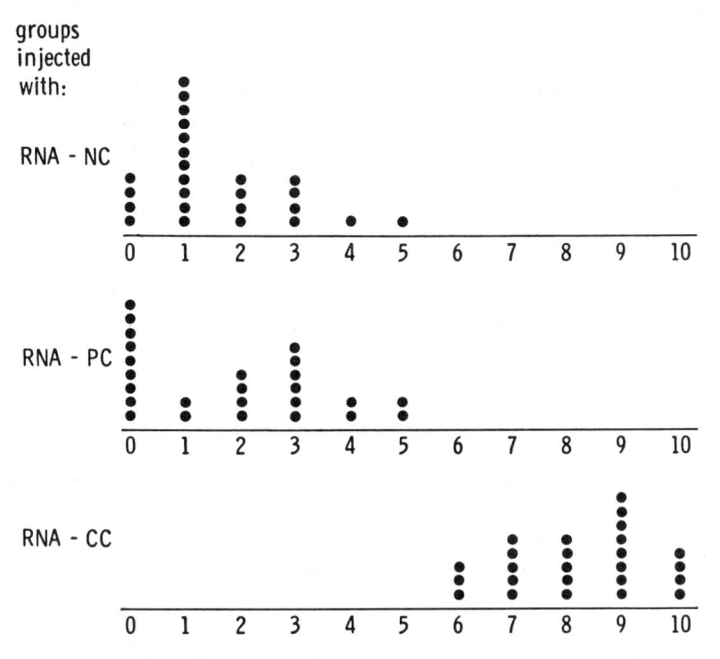

Fig 3 RESPONSES to light of untrained planarians which have been injected with RNA from donor worms. Three groups of donor worms were used; classically-conditioned (CC), pseudo-conditioned (PC) and non-conditioned (NC). The injected worms receiving RNA from the classically-conditioned group were markedly more responsive to the light than were the others

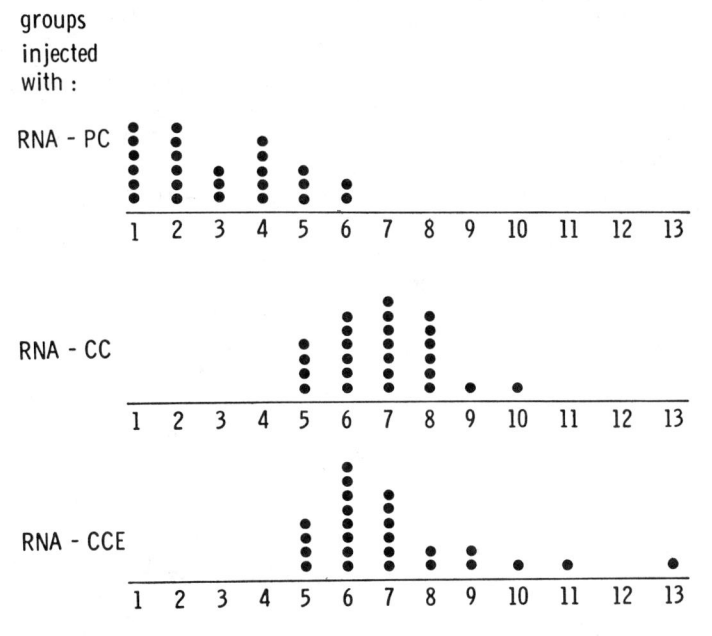

Fig 4 EXTINGUISHING the conditioned response of the donor worms (by giving repeated presentations of light without shock) before RNA extraction, appears not to reduce the RNA transfer effect in recipient worms (CCE). Recipients of RNA from both CC and CCE groups of donor worms made a greater number of responses than recipients of RNA from control worms

pend on RNA changes. We trained two groups of planarians as before, one with paired (CC) and the other with randomly interspersed light and shock (PC). Immediately before RNA extraction, we gave one half of the CC group an extended series of light bursts which were *not* followed by an electric shock. This process extinguished the conditioned response; that is, the planarians ceased to respond to the light. We then extracted RNA, injected, and tested as before. Once again, the recipients from CC worms were more responsive to the light than were recipients from PC worms. But the recipients from CCE worms (conditioned, then extinguished) were just as responsive as the CC recipients (*see Fig. 4*)! The extinction process, although it had wiped out the donors' response to light, had not reduced the RNA transfer effect. The interpretation of this finding will require considerable further analysis, but it certainly appears that in this case extinction is not simply an 'undoing' of the presumed chemical changes produced during acquisition.

Rats in place of worms

The planarian makes an ideal simple system for the study of learning. Recently, however, experiments on mammals analogous to those on planarians have been reported from several laboratories. Dr D. Albert performed one of the first of these studies. His basic experiment is quite ingenious. A treatment known as 'spreading depression' can put one hemisphere of a rat's brain temporarily out of action. If one hemisphere (say hemisphere A) is made nonfunctional in this way, and the rat then learns an avoidance task, only hemisphere B receives the training. Thus, when the rat is later tested with hemisphere B out of action it behaves like an untrained animal, taking just as long to learn the task the second time as it did the first. Albert removed tissue from the trained hemisphere B and injected it back into the donor rat, with the result that the second learning, with hemisphere A, was markedly faster. He also found that only tissue from a certain region of the trained hemisphere would produce this facilitation effect—an interesting contrast to Lashley's work. Albert then investigated the effects of different treatments on the brain tissue before it was injected. He found that ribonuclease eliminated the transfer effect, whereas the enzyme trypsin, which breaks down proteins, did not—a strong indication that RNA rather than a protein was producing the transfer effect.

In our laboratories at the University of California, we have conducted several experiments on the transfer of behaviour in rats. My wife Ann and I collaborated on this work with F. Babich and S. Bubash, who started the project and discovered the basic phenomenon. In our first experiment, we trained rats to run to the food cup of an experimental chamber (Skinner box) when a distinct click was sounded. With each click, a small pellet of food dropped into the food cup, rewarding the rat for its approach (*see Fig. 5*). When training was completed, these animals were killed, and RNA extracted from their brains was injected into the body cavities of other, untrained rats. A control group of rats received RNA from the brains of rats which had not been trained in the Skinner box. We then tested the experimental and control recipients in blind fashion in the Skinner box to see whether the click had any effect. Each animal was given 25 clicks (but no pellets) and was scored each time on whether or not it approached the cup area. Overall, the experimental rats approached the cup far more often than did control rats (*see Fig. 6*). We concluded tentatively that the original training had changed the brain RNA, which in turn had exerted effects on the behaviour of the injected animals. We did not rule out the possibility, however, that traces of other material in the extract had produced the effects.

Transfer of specific effects

But what sort of effects? Were these effects specific or general? Was it in fact *learning* that we were transferring? We attempted in two further experiments to answer these questions—at least in part. In the first we trained two groups

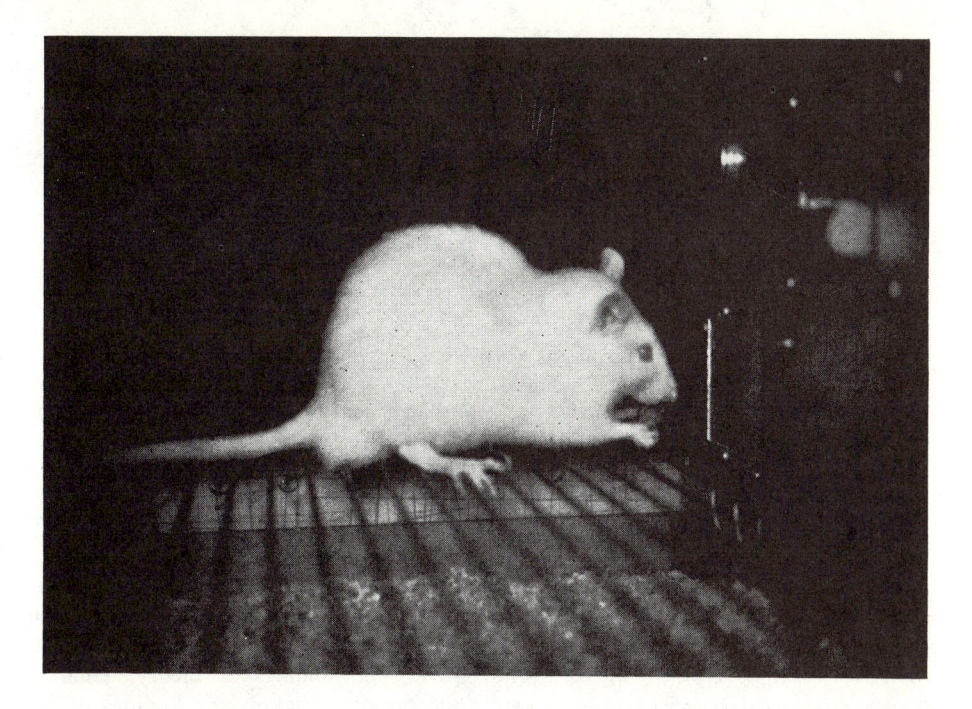

Fig 5 REWARDING a rat with food when it approaches the food cup in a Skinner's box. Rats were trained to run to the food cup when a distinct click was sounded. When training was completed, these animals were killed, and RNA extracted from their brains was injected into the body cavity of other, untrained rats. A control group of rats received RNA from the brains of rats which had not been trained. Both experimental and control recipients were then tested in the Skinner box in a similar way to see whether the click had any effect

of rats to approach the food cup, one in response to the click and the other in response to a blinking light. As before, RNA from these rats was injected into untrained rats. We then tested each untrained rat with both the click and the blinking light, and on the average the animals responded predominantly to the stimulus with which their particular donor rats had been trained (*see Fig. 7*). That is, when the donors had been trained with the click, the recipients responded more to the click than to the light, and conversely for training with the light. Thus, to some extent the transfer effect was specific—a conclusion which strengthens the hypothesis that the effect being transferred is related to learning.

In a second experiment a discrimination apparatus rather than a Skinner box was used. Together with C. Goren, we trained one group of rats with food reward to select alternative A, and another group to select alternative B, in a type of simple maze. Alternatives A and B were differentiated by several cues, including floor colour, position, and so on. When the task was well learned, we extracted RNA from the brains of the trained rats and injected it into untrained rats. Each untrained rat was then placed in the maze 25 times and allowed to select one alternative each time. We gave no food reward during testing—as in both the planarian studies and the rat Skinner box studies, we did not allow new learning to occur. Each injected rat was said to have a 'preference' for the alternative it chose 13 or more times (out of the 25 choices) during testing. On the whole, recipient rats tended to 'prefer' the alternative which their respective donors had been trained to select. Thus we have additional evidence that the RNA transfer effect is specific in nature, and also that it can occur in different behavioural situations.

Since RNA injections affect behaviour in animals as disparate as rats and planarians, it would seem theoretically possible to use recipients and donors of

Distribution of scores (responses per 25 trials) for injected rats

Rat donor   ● = experimental Ss
                ○ = control Ss

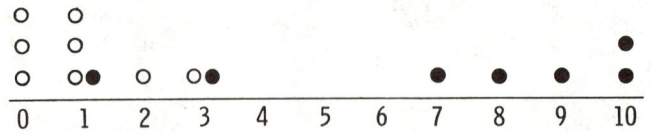

```
○  ○
○  ○                                               ●
○  ○●  ○  ○●           ●   ●   ●   ●
─────────────────────────────────────────
0  1   2  3   4   5   6   7   8   9   10
```

Fig 6 DISTRIBUTION OF SCORES for recipient rats approaching the food cup in a Skinner box, as shown in Figure 5. Each animal was given 25 clicks and was scored each time on whether or not it approached the cup. The experimental rats, injected with RNA from the brains of trained rats, scored much higher than the control animals which received RNA from untrained rats

different species. We attempted to do this. The experiment was similar to our first rat experiment in the Skinner box, except that in this case the donor animals were hamsters. And, as was predicted, rats receiving RNA from trained hamsters approached the food cup much more than rats receiving RNA from untrained hamsters (*see Fig. 8*). We had succeeded in transferring 'learning' from one species to another!

Crucial questions for the future

Not uncommonly in science a discovery is made simultaneously in independent laboratories. This is not entirely accidental—the activities of the various investigators have in such cases often been inspired by the same previous experimental findings or theory. Thus in the present situation, the findings of Dr G. Ungar and C. Oceguera-Navarro of Baylor University and of Drs H. H. Roigaard-Petersen, E. J. Fjerdingstad, and Th. Nissen of the University of Copenhagen should be mentioned. Drs Ungar and Oceguera-Navarro adapted rats to a repeated mechanical stimulus, then injected tissue from their brains into mice. These mice were found to adapt more quickly to the stimulus than were control mice. The Danish group

Total number of responses per animal on the 25 test trials with click (C) and on the 25 test trials with light (L)

group receiving RNA - C		group receiving RNA - L	
R's to C	R's to L	R's to C	R's to L
2	3	0	7
3	4	0	7
5	2	0	3
5	2	1	3
6	1	0	2
7	1	0	2
7	0	0	1
11	2	7	5
46	15	8	30

Fig 7 TRANSFER of specific learning is shown by training the donor rats to respond specifically to either a light or a click. Rats injected with RNA taken from donors trained with a click (left side of chart) show a greater response to a click than a light. The opposite occurs when the donor rats are trained with a light (right)

Hamster donor

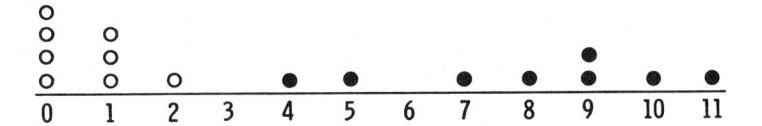

```
o
o   o
o   o
o   o   o       •   •       •   •   •   •   •
0   1   2   3   4   5   6   7   8   9  10  11
```

Fig 8 SCORES for recipient rats approaching the food cup as in Figure 6 above. This time however the donor animals were hamsters. Rats receiving RNA from trained hamsters approached the food cup much more than rats receiving injections of RNA taken from untrained hamsters. Thus it would appear that 'learning' has been transferred from one species to another

trained rats to select either the lighted or dark path in a discrimination apparatus. RNA from the brains of these rats helped recipient rats to learn this same discrimination. These different research groups were all apparently unaware of each other's activities; the major catalysts of this particular coincidence were the RNA hypothesis and the cannibalistic transfer results in planarians.

A further aspect of the 'chemical transfer of learning' must be considered. Since the experiments mentioned above, other laboratories have undertaken similar investigations. Not all of them have been successful, and some with negative results regard their results as casting doubt upon the successful efforts. However, the growing number of positive results is encouraging, and we believe that the inconsistency of findings simply reflects our incomplete knowledge of the critical variables rather than a fundamental misconception. When we know enough to reconcile the successes with the failures, we will be well on our way to understanding the transfer effects.

Certain crucial questions still remain. What is the precise nature of the behavioural effects transferred and can we attribute them to learning? What produces the effects—are we sure it is RNA and only RNA? Although I have spoken glibly of 'RNA' being extracted and injected, typically such RNA preparations contain traces of other substances as well. At the moment we do not have definite evidence that these substances can be safely disregarded. For example, Ungar and Oceguera-Navarro believe that in their experiment the effective transfer agent was some small protein. Finally, even if we were quite convinced that the effect transferred is a specific learned response, and even if we could identify the effective agent in each experiment beyond doubt, we are still faced with bewildering theoretical questions. How does the injected material act upon the recipient animal? How does training affect RNA or protein so as to make the transfer effect possible? How might alterations in RNA or protein affect synaptic resistance? How can we account for the specificity of neural circuits that would seem necessary in learning?

In 1950, considering his 30 years of brilliant work, Karl Lashley mused, "I sometimes feel, in reviewing the evidence on the localization of the memory trace, that the necessary conclusion is that learning just is not possible." The problem of learning and memory is no less complex today than it ever was; indeed, it may appear that the new biochemical approaches raise more questions than they answer. But a more important consideration is that the new questions show promise of being the right ones to ask.

Section Six

The Development of Behavior

For a long time psychologists believed that development of motor skills such as walking and talking occurred largely as a result of the physical growth or maturation of the child. In the first paper of this section, however, Professor Dennis presents research evidence obtained from institutions in Iran showing that extreme restriction of opportunities for practice precludes "normal" development. His research shows clearly that both experience *and* growth processes interact in determining normal development.

In the second paper of this section, Jerome Kagan discusses the determinants of attention in the infant. Since obtaining knowledge of the environment is so closely related to how the infant distributes his attention, and for how long, it is important for the psychologist to know what determines or influences these processes. Kagan reviews several experiments aimed at finding answers to this question and, in addition, discusses briefly the implications of such research.

Luther S. Distler, in the third paper, discusses the "generation gap"—not in terms of the "inevitable conflict" between parents and adolescents stemming from adolescent striving for independence—but rather in terms of cultural evolution. He argues that Western culture is evolving away from a "patristic" value orientation with an emphasis on success and achievement, and toward a "matristic" emphasis on feelings, intimacy, sensory experiences, and self-exploration.

EFFECTS OF LIMITED PRACTICE ON THE MATURATION OF MOTOR SKILLS

WAYNE DENNIS

Brooklyn College, Brooklyn, New York

A. INTRODUCTION

Considerable interest has recently been shown in the fact that in some institutions for children there occurs a decided retardation in behavioral development. The observations of Spitz (8, 9, 10) in particular have received much notice, chiefly because of the interpretations which Spitz has placed upon his data. In our opinion, the primary importance of these observations lies in their challenge to the theory that infant development consists largely of the maturation of a motor sequence which is little affected by learning.

Aside from the investigations of Spitz, studies of behavioral retardation among institutional children have been few in number. The scarcity of such studies is due in large part to the fact that institutions in which conditions comparable to those described by Spitz can be found are not numerous. In many countries institutional care has been replaced by other methods of caring for dependent children. However, institutions in which behavioral development is retarded can still be found in countries which are "underdeveloped" not only in regard to modern technology but also in respect to newer methods for the care of foundlings and other homeless infants.

The present paper reports studies of development in three institutions in Tehran, the capital of Iran. In two of these institutions, children are exceedingly retarded in their motor development. In the third little retardation is present. It is believed that comparisons of child care in these institutions, and of behavioral development in them, will throw considerable light upon the nature of the environmental factors which influence motor development. This paper supplements a recent report on behavioral retardation in a Leb-

---

Reprinted by permission from *The Journal of Genetic Psychology*, Vol. 96, pp. 47–59, 1960.

anese institution by Dennis and Najarian (4). In the earlier report attention was directed primarily to motor development in the first year of life, whereas in the present instance the period from one year to four years of age is the one with which we are mainly concerned. Preliminary observations indicated that development during the first year in the two Iranian institutions in which retardation occurs is essentially the same as in the Lebanese institution described in the previous paper. For this reason in the present study attention is given chiefly to the age period to which little attention was directed in the earlier report.

B. Description of the Institutions

The two institutions in which marked retardation occurs, which will be called Institutions I and II, are supported chiefly by public funds; the third institution, to be labeled III, is supported by private funds. Several other children's institutions both public and private, exist in Tehran. The present report should not be taken to imply that retardation prevails in the majority of Iranian institutions.

It is worthy of note that the number of children to be found in institutions in Tehran is quite large. This number is explained by several factors. For one thing, Tehran is a large city, having approximately two million inhabitants. The recent growth of Tehran has taken place in the main through migration from villages. This has led to a considerable amount of social disorganization which has increased the number of illegitimate children, foundlings, abandoned children, orphans and half-orphans. Furthermore in Tehran at the present time, provisions for the care of dependent children, other than by institutionalization, are quite inadequate. Consequently, almost all children not living with parents or relatives are to be found in institutions.

1. *Institution I*

Institution I feels obligated to accept all foundlings and all abandoned children under three years of age who are brought to it. The population of the institution varies from day to day because of departures and admissions. During the time of the present study (September, 1958) the average daily population was about 600; of these about 275 were between birth and one year of age, 135 were between one and two years of age, and about 110 were between two and three years of age. While children above three years are generally transferred to other institutions, a few remain in Institution I beyond this age.

The excess of younger children over older children in Institution I may be due to several causes, including an increased intake rate in recent years, a higher death rate during the first year than in later years, return of older children to relatives, and transfer of older children to other institutions. The data at our disposal do not permit an assignment of relative weights to these factors.

More than nine-tenths of the children in Institution I are recorded as having been under one month of age at the time of their admission. When the actual date of birth is not known, an estimate of age at admission, based on weight, size, and appearance is made and placed in the child's record.

The mother never accompanies the child to Institution I nor sees him after admission.

In general children are placed in individual cribs, although at times, because of over-crowding, two infants temporarily occupy the same crib. In such instances, the heads of the two babies are placed at opposite ends of the bed.

A child is bathed on alternate days. Except when being bathed, the younger children spend practically their entire time in their cribs. They are given milk and other liquids while lying in bed, the bottle being supported by a small pillow. When semi-solid foods are introduced, infants are sometimes held by an attendant and sometimes fed in bed. The children are placed in bed in the supine position. They are never placed prone and seldom get themselves into this position.

The paucity of handling is due primarily to the attendant-child ratio. On the average there were eight children per attendant. In addition to feeding the children, bathing them, and changing clothing and diapers, the attendants are also responsible for changing the bed-linen and cleaning the rooms, and have some responsibilities for preparing food. Each attendant is on duty 12 hours per day. In general there are 32 children and four attendants to a room, although this varies somewhat according to the size of the room. There is no assignment of attendants to particular children. The attendants have no special training for their work and are poorly paid. The emphasis on the part of the supervisors seems to be on neatness in the appearance of the rooms, with little attention to behavioral development.

In his crib the child is not propped up, and is given no toys. The child who can pull himself to sitting, and hence is in some danger of falling from his shallow crib, is placed, when awake, on a piece of linoleum on the composition stone floor of the room. Until he himself achieves the sitting position he remains in bed. In two rooms some of the children who can sit are seated in a row on a bench which has a bar across the front to prevent falling. Aside from these two benches and the frames for the cribs, the rooms have no children's furniture and no play equipment of any kind.

2. *Institution II*

This institution accepts children over three years of age. The children in this institution come mainly from Institution I. Child care practices in II are a continuation of the practices existing in I, but sanitation and cleanliness are poorer and the appearance of the children suggests that nutrition and health are poorer. However, in neither I nor II are there any records of growth in height or weight, and it was not possible for us to obtain any objective assessment of nutritional status.

3. *Institution III*

Institution III was established only one year prior to the present study. It was started primarily to demonstrate improved methods of institutional care. The children in III come from Institution I but are selected for transfer in the early months of life. It seems likely that those sent to Institution III are chosen from among the more retarded children. They remain in III until three years of age unless adopted before that date. The number of children per attendant is 3–4. Children are held in arms while being fed, are regularly placed prone during part of the time they are in their cribs, are propped up in a sitting position in their cribs at times and are placed in play pens on the floor daily when above four months of age. Numerous toys are provided. Attendants are coached in methods of child care, and supervisors emphasize behavioral development as well as nutrition and health.

Individual growth charts are available for each child in Institution III and show without exception that these children are much below prevailing weight norms on arrival but attain normal weight within a few months.

C. Types of Behavioral Data

Quantitative observations on the behavioral status of the groups described above were made only with regard to motor coördinations. Some general observations on social and emotional behavior will be presented after motor behavior has been discussed.

In respect to motor development, each child who was a subject of this study was classified with regard to his ability to meet each of the following behavioral criteria:

1. *Sit alone.* The child was placed in a sitting position on the floor. He was scored as sitting alone if he maintained this position for one minute. However, if a child could maintain this position at all he ordinarily could maintain it indefinitely.

2. *Creep or Scoot.* The child was placed sitting on the floor and was encouraged to locomote by having the attendant hold a cookie, or extend her arms, toward the child at a distance of about six feet. He was scored as passing the test if he covered the distance in any manner. If he locomoted, his mode of progression was recorded. The modes of locomotion will be discussed at a later point.

3. *Stand by holding.* The child was held under the arms and placed adjacent to the horizontal bars of a child's bed. It was observed whether or not he grasped the bars and maintained a standing position.

4. *Walk by holding.* The child who could stand by holding was observed for some minutes to determine whether he took steps while holding. He was urged to walk by the attendant.

5. *Walk alone.* The child who could walk by holding objects was placed standing without support and was encouraged to walk to the outstretched arms of the attendant. The child was scored as walking alone if he took at least two steps without support.

In the above tests one of the attendants with whom the child was familiar was coached to make the tests while the experimenter remained at a distance of six feet or more from the child and somewhat behind him. This procedure was followed because it was found that the child's unfamiliarity with the experimenter often inhibited the child's behavior if he was tested by the examiner himself. Communication between the attendant and the examiner was conducted via an Iranian interpreter. Tests were conducted among the children of a given room only after the experimenter and the interpreter had made several visits to the room and somewhat decreased the children's shyness. If a child failed a test, the attendant was asked whether or not he could usually perform the required response. If the answer was positive, renewed efforts were made to elicit a successful performance. The experimenter is convinced that subjects who were scored as failing a test were actually unable to perform the required task.

The numbers of children tested at each age level in each institution are shown in Table 1. In Institutions I and II the total number of children tested was 123. In selecting children to provide this sample, the children of appropriate ages were selected at random from each of several rooms, the rooms so far as we could determine not being unusual in any respect. However,

EFFECTS OF LIMITED PRACTICE ON MATURATION OF MOTOR SKILLS

TABLE 1
Per Cent of Each Group Passing Each Test

Institutions	I	I	II	III	III
N	50	40	33	20	31
Ages	1.0-1.9	2.0-2.9	3.0-3.9	1.0-1.9	2.0-2.9
Sit alone	42	95	97	90	100
Creep or Scoot	14	75	97	75	100
Stand holding	4	45	90	70	100
Walk holding	2	40	63	60	100
Walk alone	0	8	15	15	94

we excluded from testing any child who had sensory or motor defects, who was ill or who had recently been ill. In Institution III all children between age one and three were tested. They totaled 51.

D. Results of Tests

Table 1 shows the per cent of each group which passed each test. The reader is asked to direct his attention first to the retardation which is evident in Institutions I and II. Among those children in Institution I who were between 1.0–1.9 years of age, fewer than half could sit alone and none could walk alone. In normative studies, of home-reared children, such as those conducted by Jones (6), Gesell (5), Dennis and Dennis (2) and others, it has been found that by nine months of age all normal non-institutional American children can sit alone. By two years of age nearly all can walk alone. A majority of the children of Institution I cannot perform these responses at ages at which almost all home-reared children can perform them. It will be noted that even between 2.0–2.9 years of age only 8 per cent of the children in Institution I are able to walk alone and only 15 per cent of those children in Institution II who are 3.0–3.9 years of age are able to walk alone. We are not aware that any groups so retarded as Groups I and II have previously been reported.

In Institution III the picture is different. Of those children between 2.0–2.9 years of age nearly every child is able to walk unaided. While these children do not equal the performance of home-reared children, their motor behavior is much superior to that of children in Institutions I and II. In other words it is not institutionalization per se which handicaps Groups I and II since Group III children who are also institutionalized are but slightly retarded in motor development. The records of Group III also show that motor retardation is not a general characteristic of Tehran children.

Of special note is the difference in types of pre-walking locomotion between Institutions I and II on the one hand and Institution III on the other.

Of the 67 children in Institutions I and II who engaged in creeping or scooting, only 10 did so by creeping, i.e., going on hands and knees or on hands and feet. All others progressed by "scooting," i.e., their locomotion took place in the sitting position, the body being propelled forward by pushing with the arms aided by propulsion from the legs. Many children who could not walk were quite adept at scooting.

Since tests for creeping or scooting were made when the child was in a sitting position, it might seem that the frequency of scooting was due to the nature of the starting position. To test the effect of starting position, many subjects who were "scooters" were placed prone and offered a cookie at some distance, a powerful incentive for locomotion in these children. In each case the child first pushed himself to a sitting position and then scooted. Scooting was definitely the preferred mode of locomotion even when the child was placed prone. So far as we could determine, the majority of the scooters were completely unfamiliar with creeping.

In Institution III, the reverse situation prevailed. Of 15 children who were observed to creep or scoot, all progressed by creeping. No scooting whatsoever was seen in this institution, yet tests were made from the sitting position as with Groups I and II. When placed sitting and encouraged to locomote, the children leaned forward, got themselves on hands and knees, and crept.

E. Interpretative Comments on Motor Development

Let us examine now the probable reasons why the children in Institutions I and II were so severely retarded relative to home-reared children and why they were so much more retarded than children in Institution III. Several different possibilities need to be considered.

Attention should first be directed to malnutrition as a possible cause of retarded motor development. As noted earlier there can be no doubt that many of the children in Group I were much smaller and lighter than non-institutional children and children of the same age in Group III. There can be no doubt, too that malnutrition can be so severe as to interfere with motor performance and motor progress. But the question at stake is not whether malnutrition can affect motor functions but whether malnutrition was in fact a major cause of the retardation of Groups I and II.

We are inclined to think that undernourishment was not the major factor. The following considerations have led us to this interpretation: In the first place, Groups I and II were not entirely listless and inactive. In this connection we need to bring out a fact that we have not noted in earlier sections, namely that these children engaged to a considerable extent in automatisms such as head shaking and rocking back and forth. In many cases, these actions were quite vigorous. These activities tend to indicate that these children were not slow in motor development simply because of motor weakness.

The second consideration is somewhat similar to the first, namely, that the locomotor activities in which the children in Groups I and II engaged seem to require as much as or more energy than the locomotor activities which are usual at their respective ages, but in which they did not engage. For example, while few two-year-olds in Group I walked, three-fourths of them locomoted, chiefly by scooting. No physiological data are available, but it seems likely that the metabolic cost of covering a certain distance by scooting is as great as, or even greater than, the effort required to go the same distance by walking. Certainly this would be true for an adult, but of course one cannot argue from the adult to the child. At any rate the possibility exists that the reason that these children scooted was because this was the only form of locomotor skill which they had learned, not that they were too weak to walk.

This interpretation seems to be borne out by the fact that the pre-walking methods of locomotion were different in different groups. The retarded groups scooted. It is difficult to believe that malnutrition can lead to scooting rather than creeping. It is far from obvious that scooting is "easier" than creeping. If it is, why should not all children choose the easier method? In other words, the differences between groups seem to us to be due to the outcome of different learning situations rather than to differences in nutritional status.

What were the differences in the situations faced by Groups I and II and Group III which may account for the development of two different types of locomotion and different degrees of retardation? We suggest the following:

In Group III and in many homes infants are propped up in a sitting position, or held in a sitting position. In this position the child can raise his head and can partially raise his shoulders for short periods and can relax these efforts without falling. He can thus practice some elements of sitting. On the other hand, the child who remains on his back has no such opportunities to learn to sit. In some respects it is surprising that children who are never propped up or held on the lap are able to learn to sit at all. But it will be remembered that in Groups I and II some children could not sit until they were more than two years of age. Until they could sit alone, all forms of locomotion were impossible for them, because they were not placed in a position in which creeping was possible.

This is not true in Group III. In this group and in many homes, the child is frequently placed prone in bed or on the floor. In this position he can raise his head from the surface, push with his arms, raise his chest, pull his arms and legs beneath his body—in other words, he can practice acts which are employed in creeping. The child who lies on his back nearly every moment of the day is denied such practice. Thus one specific item of child care, i.e., occasionally placing the child face downward, may well contribute to the development of creeping in most children and its absence may account for the lack of creeping in Groups I and II.

The question may be raised as to why children in Institutions I and II did not get themselves into the prone position in their cribs. Repeated observations of these infants in their cribs showed that few ever attained the prone position. The probable reasons are the small size of the cribs and the softness of the beds, both of which made turning over very difficult.

It is likely that this item, i.e., absence of placement in the prone position, may lead to delayed development not only in regard to creeping but also in respect to walking. The child who can creep can go to a piece of furniture, grasp it and pull to his knees. This may lead to walking on his knees while holding furniture. Many children go from knee walking to walking by holding to furniture and thence to walking alone. In contrast to the child who creeps, the child who scoots to a piece of furniture is sitting when he arrives at his goal and can attain a higher position only by lifting his entire weight by his arms. In our opinion, the lack of creeping accounts in large measure for the retardation in walking of Groups I and II.

We are well-aware that some persons have interpreted the behavioral retardation of institutional infants to emotional factors rather than to a paucity of learning opportunities. Some have even suggested that under certain conditions institutional infants simply "waste away" from psychological, not from medical causes, a process called marasmus.

If marasmus actually exists, it has somehow been escaped by several hundred children in Iranian institutions living under conditions which are supposed to foster it. Although the prevailing emotional tone of children in Institutions I and II is dysphoric, it is difficult to conceive of mechanisms whereby their unhappiness retards their motor development and causes them to scoot rather than to creep.

There remains the necessity of relating the results of the present study to certain findings reported earlier by the present author. We refer to a study which found no apparent effect of cradling upon the motor development of Hopi children (3) and a study which indicated that infant development can proceed normally under conditions described as "minimal social stimulation" (1). On the surface these results seem contradictory to those here reported, because the former studies found that environmental deprivations had but little effect whereas the present study reports that major consequences can ensue from them. In fact, however, the studies are not contradictory but complementary. To bring the results of these studies into harmony, one needs only to examine the kinds of deprivation which were involved and their severity. Certain differences among these studies seem to us to be crucial. The Hopi children were limited in regard to learning opportunities only *while on the cradleboard*. As we pointed out in our original report, they were on the cradleboard chiefly during these sleeping hours, when in any case little learning is expected to occur. When awake they were handled, held upright against the mother, placed sitting on her lap, and placed prone. Their deprivation of learning opportunities was much less than that encountered by the children in Institution I who 24 hours per day for many months remained in a supine position.

A similar contrast exists between Rey and Del, the subjects of an experiment in environmental deprivation, and children in Institutions I and II. Rey and Del were not deprived to the same degree nor in the same manner as the institutional children described above. As the original report shows (1), Del and Rey, beginning at nine months, were regularly placed in a prone position on a pad on the floor. After it was found that they could not sit alone they were given special practice in sitting. Del and Rey were also given special training in supporting their weight when held upright. Such training was not given in Institutions I and II.

These experiences with special training given to Del and Rey suggest that the retardation of the institutional children could be fairly rapidly remedied if intensive specialized practice were given them. Unfortunately it was not possible for us to undertake such experiments while we were in Tehran. The speed with which delayed skills can be developed remains an important problem for future researches with institutional children.

So far as the permanency of motor deficiencies is concerned it should be noted that Institution II had many children between ages 6 and 15 years who presumably were as retarded at ages two and three as were the children whose behavior was described above. Yet these children were attending school, playing games, doing chores, and being trained in difficult skills, such as the weaving of Persian rugs. There was nothing in their general behavior to suggest that any permanent consequences issued from the extreme retardation in motor development during the early years. To be sure, we have no direct evidence that these children were retarded at two and three years of age, but so far as we could ascertain there has been no change in the child care offered by Institutions I and II and no reason to suppose that their early development was different from that of their counterparts in the present study.

Finally let us note that the results of the present study challenge the widely-held view that motor development consists in the emergence of a behavioral sequence based primarily upon maturation. Shirley's chart of the motor sequence is a textbook favorite. It shows sitting alone at seven months, creeping at 10 months, and walking alone at 15 months. The present study shows that these norms are met only under favorable environmental conditions. Among the children of Institution I not only was sitting alone greatly retarded but in many cases creeping did not occur. Instead, an alternate form of locomotion was employed. These facts seem to indicate clearly that experience affects not only the ages at which motor items appear but also their very form. No doubt the maturation of certain structures, which as yet cannot be identified, is necessary before certain responses can be learned, but learning also is necessary. Maturation alone is insufficient to bring about most post-natal developments in behavior. This is also the conclusion which we reached in the Del-Rey experiment, but the present study supports this position more dramatically because the limitations of learning in Institutions I and II are more drastic and more long-continued than were those in the Del-Rey study.

F. Social and Emotional Behavior

Only incidental observations were made relative to social and emotional behavior. Several of these had to do with the infants' reactions to visitors.

In the weeks preceding our tests, it appears that Institution I seldom had visitors. The children of Institution II formerly had few visitors but several weeks before our arrival a volunteer social service group, aware of the isolation of these children, began to make periodic visits to them, taking them from their beds, holding them, and carrying them about. Institution III also had several visitors, partly because of the demonstration nature of this orphanage.

Children in Institution I, probably because of their unfamiliarity with visitors, were somewhat afraid of us during our first visit. They did not smile with us and, in most cases, would cry if we picked them up. On repeated visits, however, they became more friendly, smiled at us, and before our work was completed some of them would hold out their arms to be carried.

Most of the children in Institution II were positive to visitors at the beginning of our work. Several employed attention-seeking devices before visitors and cried if other children were selected for attention. In contrast in Group III, probably because of the greater time spent with attendants and because of their familiarity with visitors, there was little fear of strangers and only limited attention seeking.

Eagerness for food appeared to be greatest in Institution II. In this institution there was much crying before meal time. Children of this group handled cups and spoons quite well. In general there was very little wasting of food on the part of these children. Cups of milk were reached for eagerly, handled carefully, and drunk rapidly. There were attempts, sometimes successful, on the part of those who had finished eating to obtain the food of others, and hitting, pinching, and biting were sometimes the outcomes of such clashes. Children who could not walk could nevertheless manage to attack others and to defend themselves with considerable skill. After feeding they became much more jovial and nearly every child could be made to smile or laugh by an adult who shook him lightly or tickled him.

G. Summary

This paper has presented data concerning behavioral development among 174 children, aged one year to four years, in three Iranian institutions. In Institutions I and II infant development was greatly retarded. The behavioral progress of children in the third institution was much less retarded. The interpretations offered for these differences in behavior among the children of different institutions are as follows: the extreme retardation in Institutions I and II was probably due to the paucity of handling, including the failure of attendants to place the children in the sitting position and the prone position. The absence of experience in these positions is believed to have retarded the children in regard to sitting alone and also in regard to the onset of locomotion. The lack of experience in the prone positions seems in most cases to have prevented children from learning to creep; instead of creeping, the majority of the children in Institutions I and II, prior to walking, locomoted by scooting. In Institution III, in which children were frequently handled, propped in the sitting position, and placed prone, motor development resembled that of most home-reared children. The retardation of subjects in Institutions I and II is believed to be due to the restriction of specific kinds of learning opportunities. This interpretation was found to be congruent with the results of other studies in environmental deprivation. In the light of these findings, the explanation of retardation as being due primarily to emotional factors is believed to be untenable. The data here reported also show that behavioral development cannot be fully accounted for in terms of the maturation hypothesis. The important contributions of experience to the development of infant behavior must be acknowledged.

References

1. DENNIS, W. Infant development under conditions of restricted practice and of minimum social stimulation. *Genet. Psychol. Monog.*, 1941, **23**, 143-189.
2. DENNIS, W., & DENNIS, M. G. Behavioral development in the first year as shown by forty biographies. *Psychol. Rec.*, 1937, **1**, 349-361.
3. ———. The effect of cradling practices upon the onset of walking in Hopi children. *J. Genet. Psychol.*, 1940, **56**, 77-86.
4. DENNIS, W., & NAJARIAN, P. Infant development under environmental handicap. *Psychol. Monog.*, 1957, **71**, 1-13.
5. GESELL, A. Infancy and Human Growth. New York: Macmillan, 1928.
6. JONES, M. C. The development of early behavior patterns in young children. *Ped. Sem.*, 1926, **33**, 537-585.
7. SHIRLEY, M. M. The First Two Years: Vol. I. Postural and Locomotor Development. *Inst. Child Welfare Monog. Series*, No. 6. Minneapolis: Univ. Minn. Press, 1933.
8. SPITZ, R. A. Hospitalism, an inquiry into the genesis of psychiatric conditions in early childhood. *Psychoanal. Stud. Child*, 1945, **1**, 53-74.
9. SPITZ, R. A. Hospitalism: A follow-up report. *Psychoanal. Stud. Child*, 1946, **2**, 113-117.
10. SPITZ, R. A. Anaclitic depression. *Psychoanal. Stud. Child*, 1946, **2**, 313-342.

THE DETERMINANTS OF ATTENTION IN THE INFANT

The factors determining attention change during the first two years of life and throw light on later differences in cognitive functioning.

JEROME KAGAN

Harvard University

The evolution of a science is recorded in what are usually gradual but are sometimes abrupt changes in the central question asked, the concepts preferred, and the subject judged convenient for study. Nineteenth-century physiologists asked how sensory events were transferred from receptor surface to brain, conceived of a process requiring energy transmission, and studied animal forms with accessible afferent nerves. Physiologists now believe they know how a flash of light travels from the retina inward but remain puzzled over what happens when afferent nerves release their information at the end of the journey. This question has generated the concepts of inhibition and arousal and has attracted investigators to organisms whose brains are accessible to surgery and electrical recording.

Psychology too has experienced a dramatic shift in preferred question, process, and organism. Until recently behavioral scientists wanted to understand how an animal learned a new habit, be it running a maze or pressing a bar with its paw. The solution seemed to require theoretical and empirical inquiry into the phenomena surrounding motivation, reinforcement, and the hypothetical connections between external stimulus and response. This conception of the problem led naturally to the selection of small mammals which allowed close control of experimental conditions. Psychologists have recently redirected their interest from the puzzle of response acquisition to the mystery of mental processes. This shift is due to several factors. Neurophysiologists have found that the brain's electrical activity covaries more closely with states of attention than with patterns of behavior. The psycholinguists have reminded psychology of the profound chasm between knowing and acting: the young child understands sentences long before he utters them, and all of us possess the competence to generate many more rules than we will ever use. Piaget's lifetime effort to outline a developmental history of the stages of human reasoning has catalyzed inquiry into the structure of thought in the child.

These lines of investigation have been supplemented by events in other sectors. Existentialism, drug experience, and popularizations of psychopathology have aroused interest in the quality of inner feelings at the expense of concern with the pragmatic outcome of action. Public recognition that the majority of school failures are poor children has led public and private institutions to increase their support of scientific exploration of children's thought. And the concept of critical period, an idea born in experimental embryology and nurtured in comparative psychology, has prompted scientists to examine more carefully the early months of human development. These diverse forces have found a common aim in study of the mental processes of the young child.

A six-month-old infant displays a remarkable ability to focus his attention

Reprinted from *American Scientist*, Vol. 58, No. 3, May-June, 1970.

on interesting events, and he will maintain prolonged orientations to the face of a stranger, the movement of a leaf, or a lively conversation. He seems to be quietly absorbing information and storing it for future use. Since acquiring knowledge about the environment depends so intimately upon how the infant distributes his attention, and for how long, it is important to ask what governs these processes. This question has stimulated fruitful research from which an outline of preliminary principles is emerging.

Early determinants of fixation time: contrast and movement

The most obvious index of attentiveness to visual events is the length of orientation to an object—called fixation time. Like any response it has multiple determinants; the relative power of each seems to change as the infant grows. Ontogenetically, the earliest determinant of length of orientation to a visual event derives from the basic nature of the central nervous system. The infant is predisposed to attend to events that possess a high rate of change in their physical characteristics. Stimuli that move or possess light-dark contrast are most likely to attract and hold a newborn's attention. A two-day-old infant is more attentive to a moving or intermittent light than to a continuous light source; to a design with a high degree of black-white contrast than to one of homogeneous hue (Haith 1966; Salapatek and Kessen 1966; Fantz 1966; Fantz and Nevis 1967). These facts come from experiments in which stimuli varying, for example, in degree of black-white contrast (e.g. a black triangle on a white background versus a totally gray stimulus) are presented to infants singly or in pairs while observers or cameras record the length of orientation to each of the stimuli. In general, the newborn's visual search behavior seems to be guided by the following rules: (1) If he is alert and the light is not too bright, his eyes open. (2) Seeing no light, he searches. (3) Seeing light but no edges, he keeps searching. (4) Finding contour edges, his eyes focus on and cross them (Haith 1968).

The attraction to loci of maximal contrast and movement is in accord with knowledge about ganglion potentials in the retinas of vertebrates. Some ganglion cells respond to a light going on; others to its going off; still others to both. Since an object moving across a visual field stimulates a set of cells for a short period, it creates onset and offset patterns similar to those of an intermittent light. Figures that contain dark lines on light backgrounds serve better as onset stimuli than do solid patterns because the change in stimulation created by the border of dark on light elicits more frequent firing of nerve cells, and this phenomenon may facilitate sustained attention (Kuffler 1952, 1953).

The preference for attending to objects with high contrast is dependent, however, on the size of the figure; there seems to be an optimal area that maintains fixation at a maximum. Four-month-old infants shown designs of varying areas (Fig. 1) were most attentive to the moderately large designs (Fig. 2) (McCall and Kagan 1967). Similarly there is a non-linear relation between the total amount of black-white edge in a figure and attention. Consider a series of black-and-white checkerboards of constant area but varying numbers of squares. The total number of inches at which black borders white increases as the number of squares increases. Karmel (1966) has suggested, on the basis of studies with young infants, that the longest fixations are devoted to figures with a moderate amount of edge.

Fig. 1. One of a set of random designs shown to four-month infants

Although indices of attention to auditory events are more ambiguous than those to visual ones, intermittent tones, which have a high rate of change, elicit more sustained interest, as evidenced by motor quieting, than continuous tones (Eisenberg 1964; Brackbill 1966). Nature has apparently awarded the newborn an initial bias in his processing of experience. He does not have to learn what he should examine, as the nineteenth-century empiricists argued. The preferential orientation to change is clearly adaptive, for the source of change is likely to contain the most information about the presence of his mother or danger.

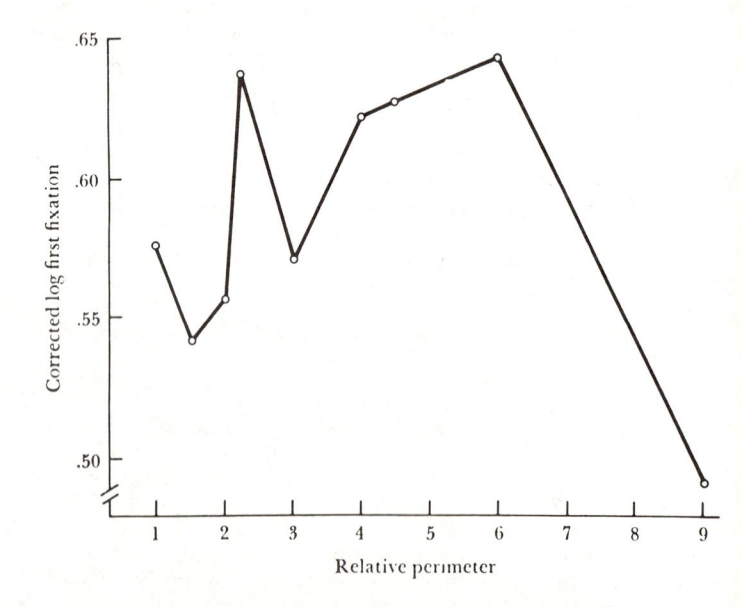

Fig. 2. Relation between fixation time and approximate area of random design in four-month infants

The role of discrepancy from schema

The initial disposition to attend to events with a high rate of change soon competes with a new determinant based on experience. The child's encounters with events result, inevitably, in some mental representation of the experience, called a schema. A schema is defined as an abstraction of a sensory event that preserves the spatial or temporal pattern of the distinctive elements of the event. A schema is to be regarded as a functional property of mind that permits an organism to recognize and retrieve information. The schema does not necessarily involve a motor response. It is neither a detailed copy of the event nor synonymous with the language label for the event. An example from a recent experiment may be useful here.

A four-year-old looked through a set of 50 magazine pictures illustrating objects, people, or scenes, many of which he had never seen before and could not name when asked. He spent only a few seconds on each picture and flipped through the 50 in less than three minutes. He was then shown 50 pairs of pictures; one of each pair was the picture he saw earlier, the other was new. He was asked to point to the picture he saw before. Although he could recall spontaneously only three or four, the average four-year-old recognized over 45 of the 50 pictures. Some children recognized them all. Since some of the pictures showed objects the child had never seen (say, a lathe or a slide rule), it is unlikely that his performance can be totally explained by assuming that each picture elicited a language label or a fragmentary motor response. What hypothetical entity shall we invoke to explain the child's ability to recognize over 90 percent of the scenes? If we use the concept schema to refer to the processes that permitted recognition, we can say that each picture contained a unique configuration of salient elements, and the schema preserved that configuration, without necessarily preserving an exact spatial analogue of the event. Some psychologists might use the older term memory engram to convey the meaning we attribute to schema. The schema for a visual event is not a photographic copy, for minor changes in the scenes viewed initially do not produce changes in the child's performance. Nor is the schema synonymous with a visual image, for the child is also able to recognize a series of different melodies or sound patterns after brief exposure to each. Early twentieth-century biologists used the concept of the gene to explain demonstrated properties of cells and nuclear material, though no one knew the gene's structure. We use the concept of schema to account for properties of mind, even though we cannot specify its structure.

The notion of schema helps to explain the older infant's distribution of attention. Toward the end of the second month, fixation time is influenced by the degree to which the child's memory for a particular class of events resembles the specific external event encountered originally. Thus the length of orientation to a picture of a strange face is dependent on the child's schema for the faces he has seen in the past. Events which are moderately discrepant from his schema elicit longer fixations than very familiar events or ones that are completely novel and bear no relation to the schema. The relation of fixation time to magnitude of discrepancy between schema and event is assumed to be curvilinear; this assumption is called the discrepancy hypothesis.

The neurophysiologist describes this attentional phenomenon in slightly different language.

> The prepotent role of novelty in evoking the orienting reflex suggests that this response is not initiated directly by a stimulus, in the customary sense of the term, but rather by a change in its intensity, pattern or other parameters. A comparison of present with previous stimulation seems of prime significance, with an orienting reflex being evoked by each point of disagreement. The concept of a cortical neuronal model ... accounts for this induction of the orienting reflex by stimuli whose characteristic feature is their novelty. This model preserves information about earlier stimuli, with

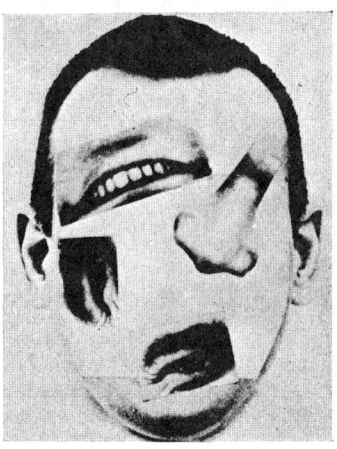

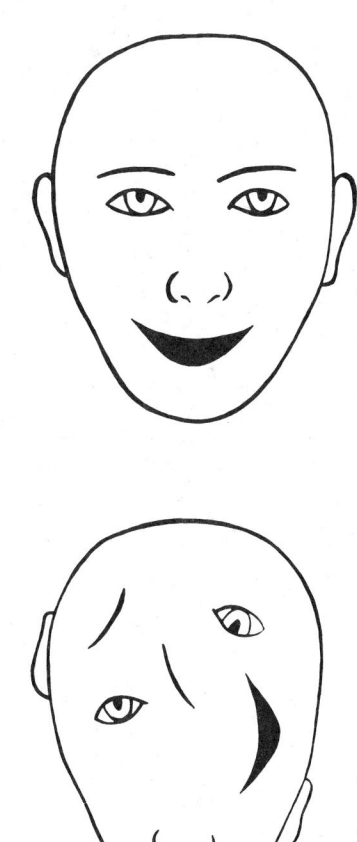

Fig. 3. Achromatic faces shown to infants

which aspects of novel stimulation may be compared. The orienting reflex is evoked whenever the parameters of the novel stimulus do not coincide with those of the model [Magoun 1969, p. 180].

Although an orienting reflex can often be produced by any change in quality or intensity of stimulation, duration of sustained attention seems to be influenced by the degree of discrepancy between event and related schema. Consider some empirical support for the discrepancy hypothesis. One- or two-week-old infants look equally long at a black-and-white outline of a regular face (upper right Fig. 3) and a meaningless design, for contrast is still the major determinant of attention at this early age. Even the eight-week-old attends equally long to a three-dimensional model of a head and an abstract three-dimensional form (Carpenter 1969). But four-month-old infants show markedly longer fixations to the two regular faces in Figure 3 than to the design in Figure 1 (McCall and Kagan 1967). The four-month-old has acquired a schema for a human face, and the achromatic illustrations are moderately discrepant from that schema. However, if the face is highly discrepant from the schema, as occurs when the components are rearranged (the lower faces in Fig. 3), fixation time is reduced (Wilcox 1969; Haaf and Bell 1967). The moderately discrepant face elicits more sustained attention than the extremely discrepant form at 16 weeks, but not during the first eight weeks of life (Fantz and Nevis 1967; Wilcox 1969; Lewis 1969). The differences in length of fixation to a normal face and to an equally complex but distorted face is greatest between three and six months of age, when infants normally display long fixations to faces. After six months fixation times to photographs of faces drop by over 50 percent and are equally long for both regular and irregular faces (Lewis 1969).

This developmental pattern confirms the discrepancy hypothesis. Prior to two months, before the infant has a schema for a human face, photographs of either regular or irregular faces are treated as nonsense designs and elicit equal periods of attention. Between two and four months the schema for a human face is established, and a photograph of a strange face is optimally discrepant from that schema. During the latter half of the first year, the schema for a face becomes so firmly established that photographs of regular or irregular faces, though discriminable, elicit short and equal fixations.

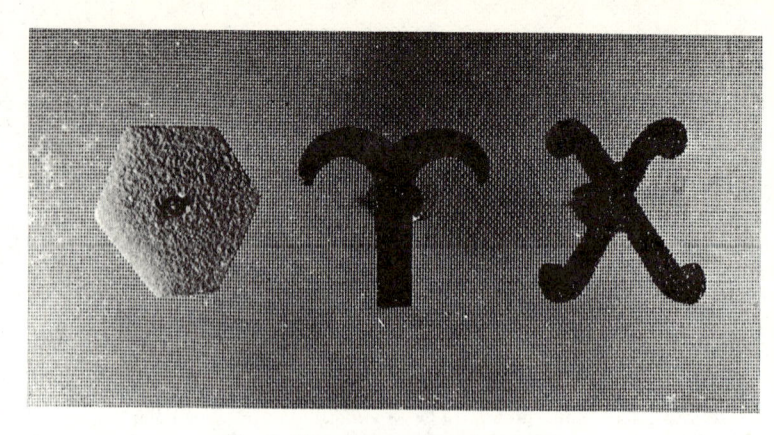

Fig. 4. One of the two standard mobiles shown to infants in the laboratory

A second source of support for the discrepancy hypothesis comes from experiments in which an originally meaningless stimulus is presented repeatedly (usually 5 to 10 times), and afterward a variation of the original stimulus is shown to the infant. Fixation time typically decreases with repetitions of the first stimulus; but when the variation is presented, fixation times increase markedly (McCall and Melson 1969). In one experiment four-month-old infants were shown a stimulus containing three objects (a doll, a bow, and a flower) for five 30-second presentations. On the sixth trial the infants saw a stimulus in which one, two, or all three objects were replaced with new ones. Most infants showed significantly longer fixations to the changed stimulus than to the last presentation of the original (McCall and Kagan 1970).

The most persuasive support for the curvilinear hypothesis comes from an experiment in which a new schema was established experimentally (Super, Kagan, Morrison, Haith, and Weiffenbach, unpublished). Each of 84 firstborn Caucasian infants, four months old, was shown the same three-dimensional stimulus composed of three geometric forms of different shape and hue for 12 half-minute periods (Fig. 4). Each infant was then randomly assigned to one of seven groups. Six of these groups were exposed at home to a stimulus that was of varying discrepancy from the standard viewed in the laboratory. The mother showed the stimulus, in the form of a mobile, to the child 30 minutes a day for 21 days. The seven experimental groups were as follows (Fig. 5):

Group 1: Control standard. These infants were exposed to the same stimulus they saw in the laboratory at four months.

Group 2: Subtraction. These infants were shown a four-element stimulus constructed by adding a fourth element to the three-element standard seen in the laboratory. ("Subtraction" referred to the later laboratory session [see below], which used only three elements.)

Group 3: Serial rearrangement. Infants exposed to a stimulus in which the three elements of the original standard were rearranged in the horizontal plane.

Group 4: Asymmetric rearrangement. Infants shown the three-element stimulus rearranged in an asymmetric form.

Group 5: Ninety-degree rotation. Infants shown a stimulus in which the three horizontal elements in the standard were rearranged in a vertical plane.

Group 6: Extreme discrepancy. Infants shown a mobile consisting of many more elements of different shapes and colors than those of the standard.

Group 7: No-mobile control. Infants exposed to no stimulus during the 21-day experimental period.

Three weeks later each subject was brought back to the laboratory and shown the same stimulus viewed initially at four months. The major dependent variable was the change in fixation time between the first and second test sessions. Figure 6 illustrates

THE DETERMINANTS OF ATTENTION IN THE INFANT

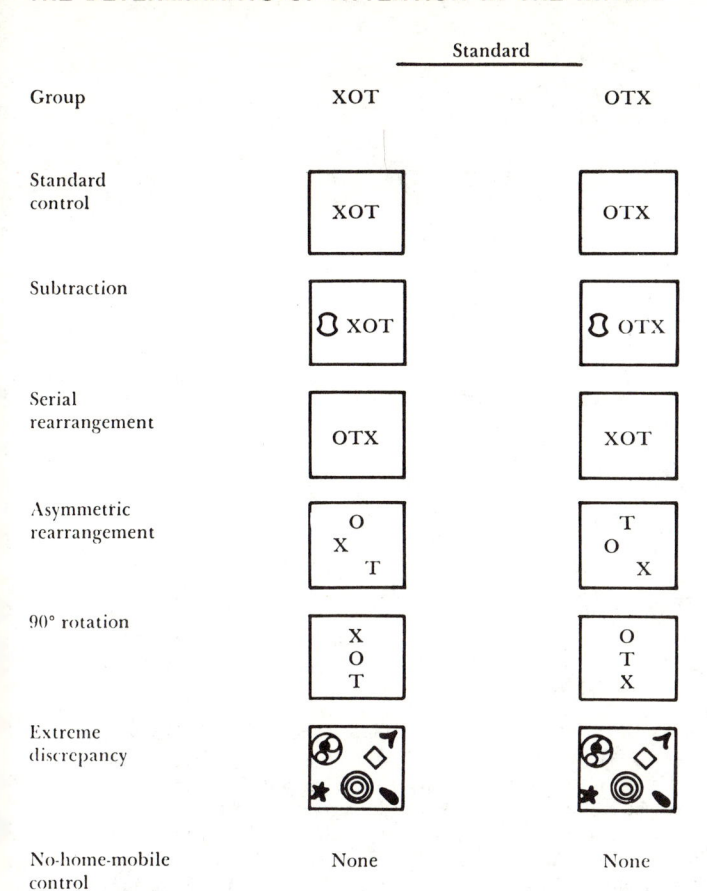

	Standard	
Group	XOT	OTX
Standard control	[XOT]	[OTX]
Subtraction	[Ω XOT]	[Ω OTX]
Serial rearrangement	[OTX]	[XOT]
Asymmetric rearrangement	[O / X / T staggered]	[T / O / X staggered]
90° rotation	[X/O/T vertical]	[O/T/X vertical]
Extreme discrepancy	[shapes]	[shapes]
No-home-mobile control	None	None

Fig. 5. Schematic illustration of the mobiles infants saw at home for 21 days

these change scores for total fixation time across the first six trials of each session.

The infants who saw no stimulus at home are the referent group to which all the other groups are to be compared. These infants showed no change in fixation time across the three weeks, indicating that the laboratory stimulus was as attractive on the second visit as on the first. The infants who developed a schema for the asymmetric and vertical rotation mobiles (moderate discrepancy) showed the smallest drop in interest across the three weeks. By contrast, the infants who experienced a minimal (groups 2 and 3) or major discrepancy (group 6) showed the greatest drop in interest. (Analysis of variance for total fixation time across the first six trials yielded an F ratio of 5.29 and a probability value of less than .05.) There was a curvilinear relation between attention and stimulus-schema discrepancy. Although the existing data are still not conclusive, they clearly support the discrepancy hypothesis.

The onset of a special reaction to discrepancy between two and three months is paralleled by other physiological and behavioral changes in the infant. Temporal characteristics of the cortical evoked potential to a visual stimulus approach adult form, growth of occipital neurons levels off, and the alpha rhythm of the electroencephalogram becomes recognizable (Ellingson 1967). The Moro reflex—the spreading and coming together of the arms when the head is suddenly dropped a few inches—begins to disappear, crying decreases, babbling increases, decreased attention to repeated presentations of a visual event becomes a reliable phenomenon (Dreyfus-Brisac 1958; Ellingson 1967), and three-dimensional representations of objects elicit longer fixations than two-dimensional ones (Fantz 1966). Perhaps the infant's capacity to react to discrepancy at this age reflects the fact that the brain has matured enough to permit the establishment of long-term memories and their activation by external events.

The effect of the infant's hypotheses

As the child approaches the end of the first year he acquires a new kind of cognitive structure which we call hypotheses. A hypothesis is an interpretation of some experience accomplished by mentally transforming an unusual event to the form the child is familiar with. The "form he is familiar with" is the schema. The cognitive structure used in the transformation is the hypothesis. Suppose a five-year-old notes a small bandage on his mother's face; he will attempt to find the reason for the bandage and may activate the hypothesis, "She cut her face." A five-month-old will recognize his mother in spite of the bandage but will not try to explain its presence.

To recognize that a particular sequence of sounds is human speech, rather than a telephone, requires a schema for the quality of a human voice. Interpretation of the meaning of the speech, on the other hand, requires the activation of hypotheses, in

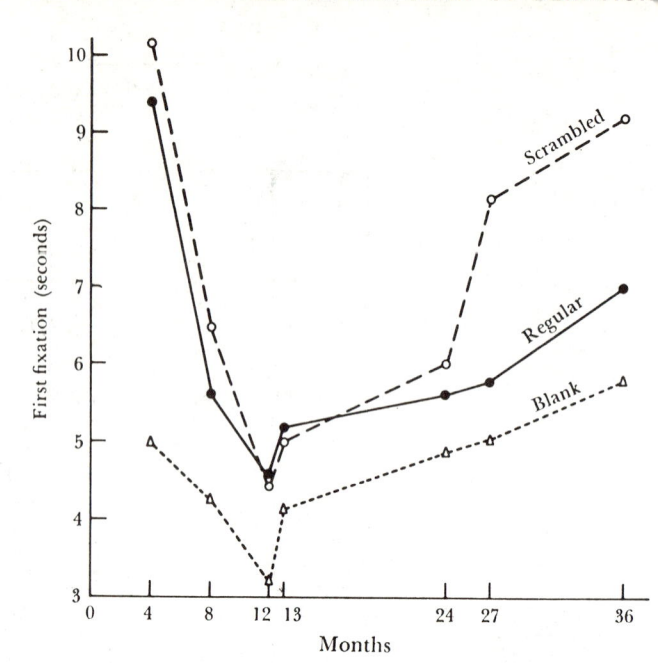

Fig. 6. Change in fixation time for each of the experimental groups

this case linguistic rules. The critical difference between a schema and a hypothesis resembles the difference between recognition and interpretation. Recognition is the assimilation of an event as belonging to one class rather than another. The performance of the four-year-old in the experiment with 50 pictures illustrates the recognition process. The child requires only a schema for the original event in order to answer correctly. Interpretation involves the additional process of activating hypotheses that change the perception of an event so that it can be understood. It is assumed that the activation of hypotheses to explain discrepant events is accompanied by sustained attention. The more extensive the repertoire of hypotheses— the more knowledge the child has— the longer he can work at interpretation and the more prolonged his attention. The child's distribution of attention at an art museum provides a final analogy. He may be expected to study somewhat unusual pictures longer than extremely realistic ones or surrealistic ones because he is likely to have a richer set of hypotheses for the moderately discrepant scenes. The richer the repertoire of hypotheses, holding discrepancy of event constant, the longer the child will persist at interpretation. There is as yet no body of empirical proof for these ideas, but data that we shall consider agree with these views.

In sum, three factors influence length of fixation time in the infant. High rate of change in physical aspects of the stimulus is primary during the opening weeks, discrepancy becomes a major factor at two months, and activation of hypotheses becomes influential at around 12 months. These three factors supplement each other; and a high-contrast, discrepant event that activates many hypotheses should elicit longer fixation times from an 18-month-old than a stimulus with only one or two of these attributes.

Two parallel investigations attest to the potential usefulness of the complementary principles of discrepancy and activation of hypotheses. In the first, one-, two-, and three-year-old children of middle class families in Cambridge, Massachusetts, and of peasant Indian families from a village in the Yucatan peninsula were shown color prints of male faces— Caucasian for the American children and Indian for the Mexican children (Finley 1967). Fixation time to the faces increased with age. The largest increase between two and three years of age occurred to the discrepant, scrambled face rather than to the nondiscrepant, regular face; the former required the activation of more hypotheses in order to be assimilated.

In the second study 180 white, firstborn boys and girls from the Cambridge area viewed the clay faces in Figure 7 repeatedly at 4, 8, 13, and 27 months of age. There was a U-shaped relation between age and fixation time. Fixation decreased from 4 to 13 months but increased between 13 and 27 months. The longer fixations at 4 months reflect the fact that these stimuli were discrepant from the infant's acquired schema for his parents' faces. Fixations decreased at 8 and 13 months because these masks were less discrepant but did not yet activate a long train of hypotheses in the service of assimilation. Between one and two years fixations rose because the child was activating hypotheses to resolve the discrepancy.

As with the first study, the largest increase in fixation time, between 13 and 27 months, occurred to the scrambled face. The children's spontaneous comments indicated that they were trying to understand how a face could be so transformed. "What happened to his nose? Who hit him in the nose?" asked a two-year-old. And, "Who that, Mommy? A monster, Mommy?" said another.

The function resulting from combining the data of the two studies is illustrated in Figure 8. The U-shaped relation between fixation time and age is concordant with the theoretical argument given earlier.

Social class and fixation time

The number of hypotheses surrounding a class of events should covary, in part, with language competence. Hence any experiences that promote

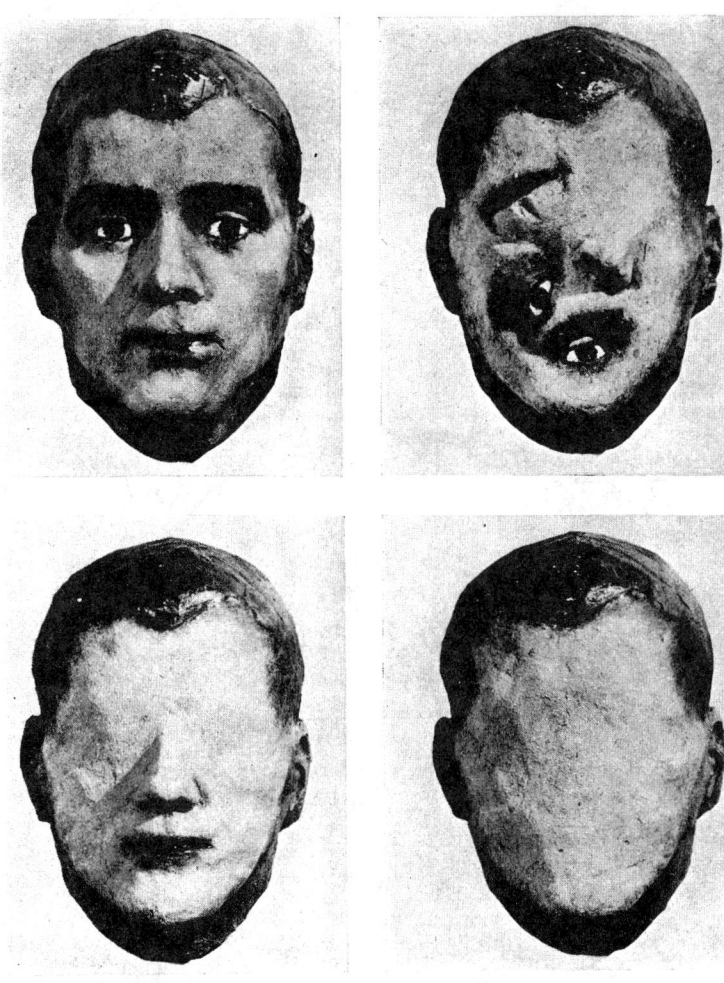

Fig. 7. Clay masks shown to children at 4, 8, 13, and 27 months

and the three-month-old infant's fixation time to photographs of faces in the laboratory. The association was positive for girls ($r = .61$, $p < .01$) and close to zero for boys. Hess, Shipman, Brophy, and Bear (1968, 1969) and Werner (1969) have reported more substantial correlations for girls than boys between maternal education or verbal ability, on the one hand, and the child's IQ or level of reading achievement on the other. There seems to be a general tendency for indexes of maternal intellectual ability and, by inference, maternal concern with the child's mental development, to be better predictors of cognitive development in daughters than sons.

One interpretation of this puzzling phenomenon rests on the fact that girls are biologically less variable than boys (Acheson 1966). This implies that fewer infant girls would display extreme degrees of irritability, activity, or attentiveness. Let us assume the following principle: the more often the mother attempts to interest her child in an event the stronger the child's tendency to develop a general sensitivity to change and a capacity for sustained attention to discrepancy. This principle is likely to be less valid for infants who temperamentally have a tendency toward apathy or hypervigilance. There are many functional relations in nature that lose their validity when one of the variables assumes an extreme value, and this may be another instance of that phenomenon.

An alternative explanation of the stronger covariation for girls than boys between maternal intelligence and the child's mental development assumes greater differences between well and poorly educated mothers in their treatment of daughters than of sons, especially in maternal actions that promote attention and language acquisition. A mother seems more likely to project her motives, expectations, and self-image on her daughter than on her son, and is more likely to assume that her daughter will come to resemble her. Many poorly educated mothers feel less competent than the college graduate and have greater doubts about their daughters' potential for intellectual accomplishment. Such a mother may set or supply lower standards and less enthusiastic as well as less consistent encouragement to her infant girl to learn new skills. The well educated mother sets higher aspirations and acts as though

acquisition of language should be associated with longer fixation times toward the end of the first year. The positive correlation between parental educational level and the child's linguistic competence is well known and well documented (see, for example, Cazden 1966). Thus a positive relation between parental education and fixation time should appear toward the end of the first year and grow with time. The data on 180 firstborns indicated that parental education was not highly related to fixation time to faces at 4 and 8 months but was moderately related (correlation coefficient [r] = about 0.4) at 13 and 27 months, and this relation was slightly stronger for girls than for boys. Since the majority of infants either increased in fixation time or showed no essential change between 13 and 27 months, we computed the change in first fixation between 13 and 27 months for each child and correlated that change with parental educational level as well as independent indexes of verbal ability at 27 months. There was a positive relation between increase in fixation time and parents' educational level for the girls ($r = .31$) but not for boys ($r = -.04$); 27-month-old girls with the highest vocabulary scores showed the largest increases in fixation time.

It is not clear why the relation between parental education and sustained attention should be stronger for girls than for boys. Other investigators have also reported closer covariation in girls than boys between social class and various indexes of cognitive development including IQ scores and school grades. Moss and Robson (1968) studied the relation between amount of face-to-face interaction mother and infant had in the home

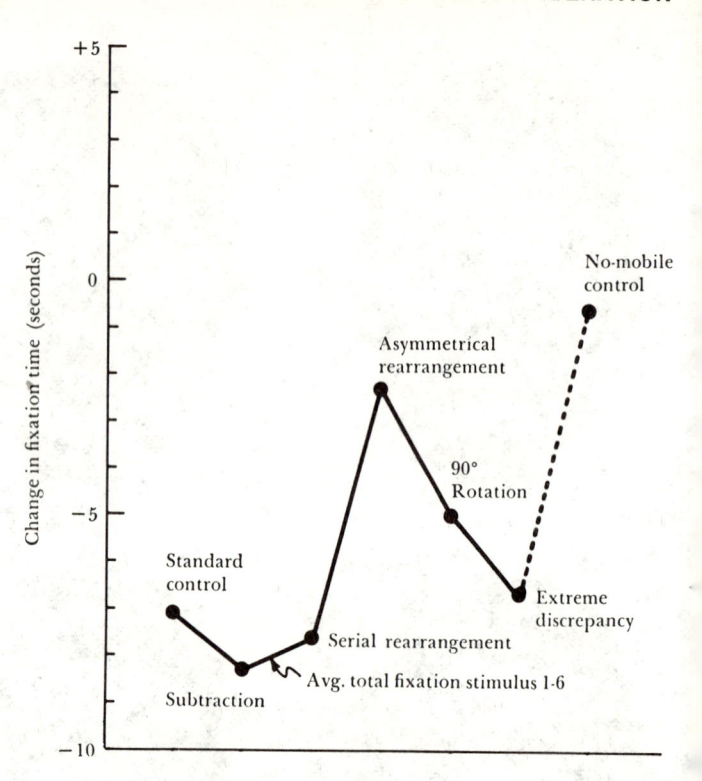

Fig. 8. Relation between fixation time to faces and age of child

she held the power to catalyze her child's development.

The situation with sons is somewhat different. Most mothers, regardless of class background, believe their sons will have to learn how to support a family and achieve some degree of independence. Hence mothers of all classes may be more alike in energizing the cognitive development of sons. The restricted range of acceleration of sons, compared with daughters, would result in closer covariation for girls between social class and indexes of cognitive development.

This argument finds support in observations of the mother-child interaction in the home. Well educated mothers are more likely to talk to their four-month-old daughters than mothers with less than a high school education. But this class difference in maternal "talkativeness" does not occur for sons. Observations of an independent sample of 60 mother-daughter pairs at 10 months of age (Tulkin, unpublished) also indicates that middle, in contrast to lower, class mothers spend significantly more time in face-to-face contact with their daughters, vocalize more often to them, and more frequently reward their attempts to crawl and stand. A final source of data is the home observations on some of the 180 children at 27 months. The observer noted each instance in which the mother reproved the child for disobeying a rule. Mothers of all social classes were more likely to reprove sons than daughters. However, reproval for incompetence at a task was most frequently meted out by the well educated mothers of daughters; there was no comparable class difference for mothers of sons.

Thus, independent and complementary evidence supports the idea that differential pressures toward intellectual competence are more likely to covary with social class for mother-daughter than for mother-son pairs. It has usually been assumed that the girl is more concerned with acceptance by parents and teachers than the boy, and that this particular motive for intellectual accomplishment covaries with social class; but intellectual achievement among boys is spurred by more varied motives, including hostility, power, and identification with competent male figures—motives less closely linked to social class. However valid these propositions, they are not operative during the first year of life.

Implications

The influence of contrast, discrepancy, and activation of hypotheses on distribution of attention is probably not limited to the first two years of life. Schools implicitly acknowledge the validity of these principles for older children by using books with contrasting colors and unusual formats and by emphasizing procedures whose aim is to ensure that the child has a relevant hypothesis available when he encounters a new problem. A child who possesses no hypothesis for solution of a problem is likely to withdraw from the task. Many children regard mathematics as more painful than English or social studies because they have fewer strategies to use with a difficult problem in arithmetic than for one in history or composition. The school might well give children more help in learning to generate hypotheses with which to solve problems, and put less pressure on them to accumulate facts.

The principles discussed in this paper are also related to the issue of incentives for acquiring new knowledge. The behaviorist, trying to preserve the theoretical necessity of the concept of reinforcement, has been vexed by the fact that the child acquires new knowledge in the absence of any demonstrable external reward. However, the process of assimilating a discrepant event to a schema has many of the characteristics of a pleasant experience and therefore is in accord with the common understanding of a reward. The central problem in educating children is to attract and maintain focused attention. The central theoretical problem in understanding mental growth is to discern the factors that are continually producing change in schema and hypothesis. Solution of these two problems is not to be found through analyses of the environment alone. We must decipher the relation between the perceiver and the space in which he moves, for that theme, like Ariadne's thread, gives direction to cognitive growth.

Acknowledgments

Preparation of this paper was supported in part by research grant HD04299 from NICHD, United States Public Health Service, and a grant from the Carnegie Corporation of New York.

References

Acheson, R. N. 1966. Maturation of the skeleton. In F. Falkner, ed. *Human development.* Philadelphia: W. B. Saunders, pp. 465–502.

Brackbill, Y., G. Adams, D. H. Crowell, and M. C. Gray. 1966. Arousal level in newborns and preschool children under continuous auditory stimulation. *J. Exp. Child Psychol.* 3:176–88.

Carpenter, G. C. Feb. 1969. Differential visual behavior to human and humanoid faces in early infancy. Presented at Merrill-Palmer Infancy Conference, Detroit, Mich.

Cazden, C. B. 1966. Subcultural differences in child language. *Merrill-Palmer Quart.* 12:185–219.

Dreyfus-Brisac, C., D. Samson, C. Blanc, and N. Monod. 1958. L'électroencéphlograme de l'enfant normal de moins de trois ans. *Etudes néo-natales* 7:143–75.

Eisenberg, R. B., E. J. Griffin, D. B. Coursin, and M. A. Hunter. 1964. Auditory behavior in the neonate. *J. Speech and Hearing Res.* 7:245–69.

Ellingson, R. J. 1967. Study of brain electrical activity in infants. In L. P. Lipsitt and C. C. Spiker, eds. *Advances in child development and behavior.* New York: Academic Press, pp. 53–98.

Fantz, R. L. 1966. Pattern discrimination and selective attention as determinants of perceptual development from birth. In A. H. Kidd and J. J. Rivoire, eds. *Perceptual development in children.* New York: International Universities Press.

Fantz, R. L., and S. Nevis. 1967. Pattern preferences in perceptual cognitive development in early infancy. *Merrill-Palmer Quart.* 13:77–108.

Finley, G. E. 1967. Visual attention, play, and satiation in young children: a cross cultural study. Unpublished doctoral dissertation, Harvard Univ.

Haaf, R. A., and R. Q. Bell. 1967. A facial dimension in visual discrimination by human infants. *Child Devel.* 38:893–99.

Haith, M. M. 1966. Response of the human newborn to visual movement. *J. Exp. Child Psychol.* 3:235–43.

Haith, M. M. March 1968. Visual scanning in infants. Paper presented at regional meeting of Society for Research in Child Development. Clark Univ., Worcester, Mass.

Hess, R. D., V. C. Shipman, J. E. Brophy, and R. M. Bear. 1968 and (follow-up phase) 1969. The cognitive environments of urban preschool children. Report to the Graduate School of Education, Univ. of Chicago.

Karmel, B. Z. 1966. The effect of complexity, amount of contour, element size and element arrangement on visual preference behavior in the hooded rat, domestic chick, and human infant. Unpublished doctoral dissertation, George Washington Univ., Washington, D. C.

Kuffler, S. W. 1952. Neurons in the retina: Organization, inhibition, and excitation problems. *Cold Spring Harbor Symposium in Quantitative Biology* 17:281–92.

Kuffler, S. W. 1953. Discharge patterns and functional organization of mammalian retina. *J. Physiol.* 16:37–68.

Lewis, M. 1969. Infants' responses to facial stimuli during the first year of life. *Devel. Psychol.* no. 2, pp. 75–86.

McCall, R. B., and J. Kagan. 1967. Attention in the infant: effects of complexity, contour, perimeter, and familiarity. *Child Devel.* 38:939–52.

McCall, R. B. and J. Kagan. 1970. Individual differences in the infant's distribution of attention to stimulus discrepancy. *Developmental Psychology* 2:90–98.

McCall, R. B., and W. H. Melson. March 1969. Attention in infants as a function of the magnitude of discrepancy and habituation rate. Paper presented at meeting of the Society for Research in Child Development. Santa Monica, Calif.

Magoun, H. W. 1969. Advances in brain research with implications for learning. In K. H. Pribram, ed., *On the biology of learning.* New York: Harcourt, Brace & World, pp. 171–90.

Moss, H. A. 1967. Sex, age and state as determinants of mother-infant interaction. *Merrill-Palmer Quart.* 13:19–36.

Moss, H. A., and K. S. Robson. 1968. Maternal influences on early social-visual behavior. *Child Devel.* 39:401–8.

Salapatek, P., and W. Kessen. 1966. Visual scanning of triangles by the human newborn. *J. Exp. Child Psychol.* 3:113–22.

Super, C., J. Kagan, F. Morrison, and M. Haith. An experimental test of the discrepancy hypothesis. Unpublished.

Tulkin, S. Social class differences in mother-child interaction. Unpublished.

Werner, E. E. 1969. Sex differences in correlations between children's IQs and measure of parental ability and environment ratings. *Devel. Psychol.* 1:280–85.

Wilcox, B. M. 1969. Visual preferences of human infants for representations of the human face. *J. Exp. Child Psychol.* 7:10–20.

THE ADOLESCENT "HIPPIE" AND THE EMERGENCE OF A MATRISTIC CULTURE

LUTHER S. DISTLER

University of California, Berkeley

There is a revolution going on, and it's happening first and most dramatically among our youth. Despite our fascination with youth culture in its more exotic and flamboyant aspects, most adults, including parents of today's adolescents, don't rationally understand and can't emotionally comprehend the new youth culture. There exists a generation gap of a new sort—a cultural generation gap. This culture shift is occurring along a continuum from a Patristic-instrumental culture to a more Matristic-expressive culture.

For the last two years we have been seeing many junior and senior high school age young people who have used drugs and are in some sense involved with, for want of a better characterization, the "hippie" identity. These young people have for the most part come on their own initiative to therapy-like groups held at the University Psychology Clinic. My clinical impressions have grown from these group experiences, conjoint family therapy with adolescent "hippies" and their parents, and a therapy-like group for parents of some of the young people being seen in the Clinic. I have also spent some time in that currently popular rationalization for marginal participation in youth culture—observation in the Haight-Ashbury district and Telegraph Avenue.

I will begin with an apology to the young people with whom I have worked and learned. In the title of my paper and throughout my presentation I will be referring to the "hippie" adolescent, with quotes around "hippie." "Hippie" is a term the mass media have coined and it is well entrenched. It is a stereotype. Neither I nor they thought of themselves as "hippie," and for that matter often enough I thought of them as young adults rather than adolescents. But the term "hippie" should help communicate in a general sense the admittedly heterogeneous cultural subgroup within which these young people functioned, and much of what I want to talk about has to do with the sociocultural aspect of generational conflict as I observed it in their dealings with and feelings about their parents and the dominant adult culture.

The concept of generation conflict has gained considerable attention in recent days. Since Dr. Baumrind suggested this symposium, a cover story on *Life* magazine featured an article which was the abstract of a popular book on the generation gap, and the Mid-Peninsula Free University at Palo Alto

---

This paper is based on a paper read at the American Psychological Association's 76th Convention, as part of a symposium on Adolescents and their Parents: Sources of Generational Conflict, August 31, 1968, San Francisco, California.

offered a Generation Gap Mediating Service. As might well be expected both of these phenomena are related to what might be considered, in Dr. Adelson's terms, an exceptional subgroup, the "hippie."

The central thesis which I would like to advance today is that there is a radical shift occurring in our dominant culture and that the impact of this change is most marked among our young people. The more usual developmental-generational conflicts (struggle for autonomy and disengagement from the family) are exacerbated by marked differences in the cultural evaluative system to which the parents of today's adolescents were socialized and the emerging culture which is shaping today's youth. This *cultural generation gap* is a central and dramatic aspect of intergenerational conflict between "hippie" adolescents and their parents. Individually and in the collective "hippie" subculture, generational conflict is explicitly emphasized, in such statements as "You can't trust anyone over 30 or maybe even 23," and that adults just don't know where they or it's "at." Many of these young people feel that they are in a fundamentally different place or world of meaning and experience than their parents and their parents' generation, and they often withdraw from confrontations or hassles with their parents because they feel that their parents just wouldn't understand anyway.

I began puzzling about what was happening when I found myself strangely out of touch with these young adolescent members of the "hippie" world. It came as rather a surprise to myself and my female co-therapist. I have had quite a bit of experience working with adolescents and thought I knew and understood them pretty well. We seemed to be able to communicate at the content level but they and we seemed to be operating in a different mode. At first we attributed these difficulties to their drug experiences—the sort of axiom that goes, "If you haven't dropped acid you can't possibly know how we experience things." But it seemed much more pervasive and built into the group culture.

Early in these efforts to understand the sources of generational distance between myself and these young people in our therapy-like groups I was struck by the relevance of Parson's analysis of *instrumental* and *expressive* modes. The group patiently helped me and my female co-therapist to sense that our implicitly instrumental orientation set us apart from them. We defined ourselves and them in terms of functional roles or part identities; we were the therapists, they were clients or patients; we were task-oriented and goal-directed, they were focused on experiencing themselves and each other. But our most annoying trait was our marked reliance on rationality—they would express things in images and sensory modes and we would analyze, relate, and try to synthesize their expressions into coherent meaningful packages. During the first sessions of this group one of its members shared an image that captured much of the dynamics. He saw the two therapists as Buddhist monks and the group was seen as chanting our names over and over to the tune of Greensleeves. He saw the group as sharing a pleasant experience, but we were seen in his fantasy as mildly displeased and impatiently waiting for something more meaningful to be talked about. The group resonated to his imagery and of course we analyzed it.

While much socialization, particularly during adolescence, occurs within the peer group, most of what they are dealing with is reactions to their early socialization within the nuclear family. The family provides a male, or paternal model, and a female, or maternal model. The use of both a male and female therapist in our groups in some ways created a family-like setting for the examination of parental projections. For example, in the group referred to above, they early expressed near unanimity in the assertion that "all fathers are fascists," but it wasn't until well along in the group that this hostility was experienced toward the male therapist. This hostility expressed a general rejection of the instrumental-rational role ascribed to males in the dominant adult culture. Socialization, particularly when seen in historical perspective, is intricately enmeshed in sex-linked terms. The experience of identity crises so characteristic of adolescence have long been most painfully experienced in terms of anxieties about one's sex-role identity. In western culture instrumental roles have been linked to males and expressive mode to females.

The "hippie" phenomenon is, I feel, but one reflection of a more general cultural shift from a *Patristic* to a *Matristic* culture. Before proceeding to an explication of Patristic and

Matristic, I would like to acknowledge my indebtedness to Nathan Adler, who first acquainted me with this conceptualization of cultural change. Dr. Adler has put forth a stimulating suggestion that in the history of western society there have been shifts back and forth along a Patristic-Matristic continuum, with the Matristic mode associated with periods of stress and instability. Our focus here, however, will be limited to a consideration of the relevance of this conceptualization to the understanding of current cultural changes. The terms Patristic and Matristic should not be confused with the description of cultures as Patriarchal and Matriarchal which is intended to reflect the relative power and dominance of males and females in the family structure. The Patristic-Matristic concept is a more dynamic concept, somewhat closer to the Jungian formation of Anima and Animus. These terms are intended to reflect that socialization is intricately enmeshed in sex-linked evaluative terms, and that the nuclear family with its paternal and maternal models provides a ready means for communicating these sex-linked evaluations of what is important and valued.

In Patristic cultures the male role is ascribed greater value—it is a man's world. The Patristic cultural ideal for *both* males and females is socialization to *instrumental* roles, but the male's role definition is sharper and more bound to the instrumental. The Patristic culture values achievement, goal-directedness, delay of gratification, rationality, autonomy and individual responsibility. One's sense of personal worth is closely related to what one does or becomes. Vocational choice, school performance, and attainment are important sources of one's self worth. Industry and competence are highly valued. Morality is based on authority—either social or religious, and control over impulse expression and intimacy is rewarded. Artistic expression in music, literature, fine arts is valued in terms of the quality of *products* rather than process. Involvement in social and religious groups is valued more in terms of fulfilling one's social responsibilities or status requirements than in terms of one's gregarious or affiliative needs. Most of human relations take on a task focus even within the family. The Patristic culture is well suited to attaining instrumental ends, such as in a frontier society engaged in a struggle for existence, or during the rapid growth of the industrial revolution. But with the beginning of the automation and electronic revolution increasingly large numbers of our society are not needed in instrumental roles. Technological disenfranchisement from the Patristic ideal of becoming someone with an important instrumental role is felt most sharply among the youth. The educational revolution which has kept larger and larger numbers of our young people in extended adolescent roles for longer and longer periods of time has contributed to the youths' disillusionment with Patristic culture.

The emerging Matristic culture values *expressive* roles. It values feelings, intimacy, sensory experiences, and self-exploration. It attempts to break loose from the prevalent emphasis on rationality and a consensually validated view of reality. In Jungian terms, cognitive processes are more feeling- than thinking-based. Personal meaning is felt more in terms of *being* than in doing or becoming, and the here and now is more important than the future. Spontaneity and the potential for playing is valued. Group activities are person- or experience-focused rather than task- or goal-focused. Artistic activity is seen more as a process of sharing the expression and participation. Participation in art and culture becomes more valued than the excellence of the created product. Morality is personal, interpersonal and relativistic. While values may be held strongly and concretely, their authority is based more on personal conviction than on institutional authorities. There is an affinity for the mystical, transcendental, and existential. Such traditionally maternal attributes as nurturance, succorance, affiliation, and the desire for close personal relationships are valued over such attributes as endurance, order, autonomy, independence.

The impact of this shift from Patristic to Matristic values on the generational conflicts of the "hippie" adolescent and his parents is compounded by the ambivalences of adolescent and parents alike to these value changes. The parents frequently give a mixed message approving greater expressiveness, but out of a sense of responsibility for socializing their child to adapt to the world as they know it they push for an acceptance of Patristic values.

The shift toward a Matristic culture is only in the early stages and is generally not articulated by the adolescent or even by his older peer models or intellectual "gurus" in terms of positive statements of Matristic values, but rather in the intermediate stage of a sort of negative identity—i.e., they are more articulately *anti-patristic*. They are surer of what they don't want than of what they do want. Their analyses of the faults and foibles of the Patristic culture are often incisive and telling.

The parents of our "hippie" adolescents are caught up in their ambivalence. Often the adolescents' rejection of Patristic values coincides with the parents' disillusionment and dissatisfaction with their roles in society. The most striking inconsistency is seen in the parents' criticisms of the schools and the lack of fulfillment they experience in their work, but they demand that their adolescent go along with the system. The parent worries about what will become of their child if he doesn't proceed toward attaining the roles in society that will assure him access to the materialistic comforts of our society. Often this covers a concern that their adolescents' rejection of the Patristic culture's emphasis on doing and becoming will result in a continued dependence on them that is exploitative if not parasitic. This is particularly difficult for the father who feels attacked and threatened by the explicit anti-patristic criticisms of his commitment to the Protestant work ethic, while at the same time he feels the responsibility to support his son's or daughter's dropping out.

Many parents expect their adolescents to be rebellious, but within the context of cultural values as they experienced them. Their expectations are based on their own recollections of their adolescent rebellion which didn't question the Patristic value system, but rather demanded entrance into adult instrumental roles or the material rewards of adult status in an instrumental society—e.g., independence from adult authority, etc. They can't understand their adolescent's rejection of the Patristic culture. As one father put it, "I could understand it if my son was stealing cars, or cheating on tests, or challenging my authority. But he just doesn't seem interested in anything." This father tried to bribe his son to put up with school by promising him the sports car he (the father) had wanted, and just couldn't comprehend his son's lack of interest.

Another common fear amongst parents who don't understand the nature of the emerging Matristic culture is that their son is going to be an effeminate, passive homosexual, and not just because of the significance of long hair and clothes styles, but because of the rejection of masculine instrumental roles.

Mothers in the families I have worked with often seem somewhat more sympathetic or empathetic with their adolescents' search for a more Matristic identity—I suspect, because often they are somewhat closer to the expressive orientation to life themselves. But they feel confused and torn between their loyalties to their husbands and their own commitment to Patristic-instrumental roles. Often this increases the stress within the family and particularly in the marital relationship. There are pressures to take sides in the family struggle which make therapeutic interventions more difficult, particularly for the male therapist who because of his humanistic-expressive orientation often further challenges the father's role in the family. On the other hand, while the mothers are often covertly encouraging the adolescents' anti-patristic expressions she is the one more likely to get panicky, overemotional, and overprotective about much of the behavior which accompanies the adolescent's venture into a "hippie" identity, particularly with regard to explorations with drugs and sex, and to a lesser extent leaving school and home.

Since this formulation grew out of the context of therapy or therapy-like groups, it seems appropriate to touch briefly on what implications or consequences it has for our work with these young people. This sociocultural perspective helped us understand the nature of some of the distance and differences in modes of relating which we felt most uncomfortably in the early stages of our work. We cut back on our intellectual, integrative, analytic comments and expressed more directly, both in verbal and non-verbal ways, our feelings and reactions to them. In some senses an accommodation occurred. The therapists shifted in a more Matristic direction, at least stylistically, whereas the group became less vocally anti-Patristic. If one takes seriously the position that a cultural generation gap exists, then the thorny issue of whether the therapists' value commitments along the Patristic-Matristic dimension intrude on the goals one brings to work with these young people. Therapy goals could be stated in such ways as to implicitly constitute an effort to get them to adjust to the

Patristic culture, e.g., decrease use of drugs, get them back to school, etc. On the other hand, therapists with humanistic expressive orientations could and have described an array of therapy goals which are essentially affirmations of a Matristic orientation — e.g., self-actualization, interpersonal honesty, sensory awareness, etc. While we probably have tended to lean more in the latter direction, we have tried to maintain a studied and intentional ambivalence, hopefully leaving the adolescent freedom within the relationship to work out his own resolution of these generational and cultural conflicts.

The real value of this formulation has been in working with adolescent-parental relationships. In parent groups and conjoint family therapy I sometimes didactically presented aspects of this formulation as a conceptual tool for bridging the generation gap. This often served to clear the air; it often let them look at their conflicts and inabilities, and to communicate in a more comfortable and constructive way. It helped to put things in a broader context, to face more honestly aspects where they held different values, and to experience these differences with less feeling that they were rejecting each other.

The relevance of a hypothesized cultural shift from Patristic to Matristic values may be unique in some degree to "hippie" adolescents. However, given mass media influences on youth culture, I suspect that these observations may have general relevance to an understanding of some of the current sources of generational conflict between adolescents and their parents. Further, I suspect that part of the mass media popularity of "hippies" is their reflection of a broader disaffection with the current cultural stereotype of adult roles.

The hippie scene, and more broadly the slow shift away from a dominantly Patristic (instrumental) culture toward a more Matristic (expressive) culture, is not limited to adolescents, although the cultural contrast is perhaps seen most sharply in intergenerational differences. One could recast the generation gap concept into cultural evolutionary terms rather than in terms of the inherent and always-to-be-with-us conflict between parents and youth. As the culture changes the young are not as immersed in their socialization to the implicit and pervasive influences of earlier cultural values. Youth and "hippies" may represent in exaggerated form the future direction of our culture, hence the mass media's focus on them may serve the role of bearer of a new more Matristic-expressive culture. At least within the relatively affluent, broadly middle-class sector of our society, many of the crises of adaptation — for example, the breakdown of intimacy, the uses of leisure, and the loss of meaning in many jobs — reflect needs for which a more Matristic culture may provide potential solutions. The current popularity of encounter groups, sensory awareness, and self-actualization are other facets of the Patristic-Matristic cultural shift that are clearly not limited to youth culture or "hippies."

Bibliography

Adelson, Joseph. The myths of adolescence: A polemic. Paper read at Symposium: Adolescents and their parents: Sources of generational conflict, American Psychological Association, August 31, 1968, San Francisco, California.

Adler, Nathan. The antinomian personality: A typological construct. Unpublished paper, November, 1967.

Parsons, Talcott. Family structure and the socialization of the child. In T. Parsons and R. G. Bales (Eds.), *Family, socialization, and interaction process.* Glencoe, Illinois: Free Press, 1955.

Soskin, William F. Hippie: Bastard son of the beat generation. Memorandum for the Joint Commission on Mental Health of Children. December, 1967, Berkeley, California.

Section Seven

Thinking and Creativity

Thinking has been referred to as "man's most complex behavior." In this section of three papers, five psychologists probe this intricate area from the behavioral scientists' point of view. As we begin to understand the physiological correlates of what takes place in the brain during thinking, psychologists are concomitantly attempting to unravel the complex tangle of questions such as: If thinking is a skill, is it amenable to training? Can creativity be fostered? What is the impact of culture on how creative endeavors are valued? Is there a causal relation between creativity and conformity? Are there different kinds of intellectual ability? How is cognitive style shaped by social environment? These are but a very few of the problems which are being subjected to rigorous study.

In the first paper in this section, E. Paul Torrance addresses himself to the relationship between the values various cultures place on creative talent and endeavors, and their development and sustenance in those cultures. This extensive study, involving eleven cultures, yielded data from more than 8000 school children and their teachers. His results indeed indicate that "what is honored in a country will be cultivated there."

The next paper, by Vernon Allen and John Levine, investigates problems relating to the detrimental effects on creativity of social pressures to conform. They ask whether experimentally increased creativity might result in psychological changes of decreased conformity since the two seem to be inversely related. Seventy-six subjects who received a four week program of creativity training and 88 method control subjects who did not were compared for conformity to group pressure. The training achieved reduced conformity for low IQ subjects but not for average and high IQ subjects. Their results lead them to postulate a causal relationship between creativity and conformity.

Jacob Getzels and Philip Jackson have long been concerned about giftedness, its meaning, and environmental sources. In their research they sought to differentiate adolescent intellectual functioning into qualitative categories. Individuals described as "high IQ without concomitantly high creativity" differed along several social behavioral dimensions from those found to be highly creative but not high IQ. The family environments of these youngsters were subjected to careful scrutiny in an attempt to discover how differing environments work to shape cognitive style.

"WHAT IS HONORED IN A COUNTRY WILL BE CULTIVATED THERE"

E. PAUL TORRANCE

Department of Educational Psychology, The University of Georgia

In discussing my studies of creative talent, I have occasionally quoted Plato's famous statement that "what is honored in a country will be cultivated there" (Torrance, 1963, 1965). This has evoked two kinds of responses among critics of these studies. One group has contended that Plato's statement may have relevance for the cultivation of certain kinds of talent but not for creative talent. Their contention is that creative talent emerges only in response to efforts to suppress and discourage it. The other group has been willing to accept Plato's statement as relevant to the development of creative talent, but they have wanted empirical "proof" that specific ways of honoring creative talent are related to creative functioning and development in measurable ways.

In this paper, I shall present data concerning the relationship between level of creative functioning as measured by the *Torrance Tests of Creative Thinking* (Torrance, 1966) of children from grades one through six in eleven different cultures and two measures of the extent to which these cultures honor creative talent. One way a culture shows what it honors is through the kinds of behavior teachers and parents encourage or discourage. An attempt was made to assess the extent to which the cultures under study honor creative talent through the Ideal Pupil Checklist (Torrance, 1962, 1965). Another way a culture honors creative talent is by making available to its members a wide variety of employment opportunities in the creative arts and sciences. An attempt was made to assess this indicator of cultural differences through an analysis of the occupational choices of children in grades three through six in each of the subject cultures.

METHODS

Subjects

The basic plan of the study called for the administration of a battery of the *Torrance Tests of Creative Thinking Ability* to samples of children from grades one through six in each of eleven selected cultures or subcultures. From 500 to 1500 children were tested in each of these comparison groups. The teachers of these children were administered the Ideal Pupil Checklist and children in grades three through six were asked to indicate what kind of work they would like to do when they left school.

The cultures were chosen on the basis of clues concerning differences in the ways

---

Reprinted from *Gifted Children Quarterly*, Vol. 10, pp. 16-21, 1968.

they deal with creative behavior among children. The following eleven groups were studied:

1. A school representing the advantaged, dominant white culture of the United States. This school was located in a suburban community in Minneapolis, Minnesota, and drew its pupils from a rather heterogeneous but advantaged white population.
2. A school representing the disadvantaged Negro culture of the Deep South (U.S.A.). This was a segregated school in a relatively rural county in middle Georgia.
3. A school system representing a racially mixed, advantaged and disadvantaged culture in the United States. This school system was located near Los Angeles, California; samples were drawn from several different elementary schools in such a way as to represent the system.
4. Six schools in the near-primitive culture of Western Samoa. Three of these schools were Christian mission schools in the relatively populated areas of the island and three were isolated government schools.
5. Seven diverse schools in New Delhi, India, representing an underdeveloped but emerging culture. These schools represented Muslim, Hindu, Sikh, Christian mission, and Nationalistic subcultures.
6. Two schools in West Berlin to represent an advanced European culture with a long tradition of creative achievement. One school was located in a workingman's district of West Berlin and the other in a suburban community of West Berlin.
7. Two schools in Norway to represent a second European culture with a lesser reputation for creative achievement. One school was located in a suburb near Oslo and the other in an isolated mountain village in the northern part of the country, one speaking the Bokmäl dialect and the other the Landsmäl dialect.
8. Two schools in Western Australia representing an English-speaking culture other than the United States. One school was located in a predominantly agricultural area and the other in a suburban area near Perth.
9. Chinese schools in Singapore representing an old and relatively creative culture in a heterogeneous urban area.
10. Malayan schools in Singapore representing the native culture in this same heterogeneous urban area.
11. Tamil schools in Singapore representing a third culture located in this same heterogeneous urban area.

The details of the data collection have been described elsewhere (Torrance, 1967). In all instances, children were asked to respond in the language most familiar to them.

Tests of Creative Thinking Ability

The *Torrance Tests of Creative Thinking* (Torrance, 1966, 1967) were translated into the native languages of the subject and administered by native-speaking examiners. The battery consisted of three figural (Picture Construction, Picture Completion, and Repeated Figures) and six verbal (Ask Questions, Guess Causes, Guess Consequences, Product Improvement, Unusual Uses, and Just Suppose) test tasks. Only the figural tests were administered in the first and second grades and only the figural and the first three verbal tests were administered in the third grade. The rationale of the test tasks, scoring procedures, their reliability and validity, and comparison group norms have been presented elsewhere (Torrance, 1966).

Ideal Pupil Checklist

In developing the Ideal Pupil Checklist, I drew from over 50 empirical studies of the personalities of creative people compared with similar less creative people. The list consists of 62 characteristics and teachers were asked to respond to it according to the following instructions:

"Check each of the characteristics listed on this page which would describe the kind of person you would like to see the children you teach become. Doublecheck the five characteristics which you consider most important and believe should be especially encouraged. Draw a line through the characteristics which you consider undesirable and which should be discouraged or punished."

This procedure is easy to administer cross-culturally and requires only a few minutes. It was possible to obtain responses from the teachers of the subjects in all of the cultures or subcultures except Norway.

For any given sample rankings can be obtained for each of the characteristics by weighting the responses of each subject as follows:

Two points, each doublecheck (strongly encourage)
One point, each single check (encourage)
Zero, each unmarked response (neither encourage nor discourage)
Minus one, each "cross out" (discourage).

In separate studies it has been found that samples of teachers within a given culture, such as the dominant cultures of the United States and India (Torrance, 1965, 1967), produce sets of rankings that correlate quite closely with one another but moderately or low with rankings produced by teachers from other cultures.

A panel of ten advanced scholars of the creative personality were asked to rank the characteristics according to their importance to the productive, creative personality. The composite rankings obtained from this panel were then correlated with each of the sets of rankings obtained from the ten groups participating in this aspect of the study.

Occupational Choices and Aspirations

All subjects in grades three through six were asked to express their occupational choices or aspirations. An index was then developed by adding the percentage of the subjects who chose occupations outside of the 25 most popular occupations of a sample of 4,192 children in the United States (Torrance, 1965, 1967) to the percentages choosing occupations in visual art, writing, drama, dancing, music, and the sciences. The rationale for this index was that the extent to which a culture honors creative talent will be reflected in the diversity of the occupations perceived by the children of a culture as open to them and by the availability of creative outlets in the creative arts and sciences.

RESULTS

The level of measured creative functioning was determined by converting all mean raw scores at each grade level to standard or T-score equivalents based on the fifth grade data of the U.S.A. advantaged, dominant culture sample. The overall creativity index for each culture was computed by adding the figural and verbal means. Table 1 presents the overall creativity indexes and the rank-order coefficients of correlation and rankings between the rankings obtained from the experts and the teachers of each of the ten cultures for which these data were obtained.

When the two sets of rankings are correlated, a coefficient of .94 is obtained. It will be noted that all discrepancies are rather minor. From the correlations between the rankings given by the teachers and those of the experts, we would have expected the Australian children to have been less creative and the Malayans more creative. Only 1.1 standard-score points separated them, however. It is interesting to note that the three subcultures in Singapore attained almost identical indexes when their rankings were correlated with those of the expert panel. The Minnesota, California, and West German samples are definitely out ahead on both indexes and are ranked in the same order on both of them.

The creativity indexes based on occupational choices and aspirations, the rankings

TABLE 1. OVERALL CREATIVITY INDEXES AND RANKINGS AND IDEAL PUPIL INDEXES ON CREATIVITY CRITERIA AND RANKINGS FOR TEN DIFFERENT CULTURES

Culture or Subculture	Creativity Level Index	Creativity Level Ranking	Ideal Pupil Index	Ideal Pupil Ranking
Minnesota, U.S.A.	97.2	1	.43	1
California, U.S.A.	96.2	2	.40	2
West Germany	92.5	3	.37	3
Chinese, Singapore	84.5	4	.28	5
Tamils, Singapore	82.4	5	.28	5
Western Australia	82.1	6	.19	8
Malays, Singapore	81.0	7	.28	5
U.S.A. Negro	80.0	8.5	.21	7
India	80.0	8.5	.11	10
Western Samoa	79.3	10	.17	9

TABLE 2. OVERALL CREATIVITY INDEXES AND RANKINGS AND OCCUPATIONAL INDEXES ON CREATIVITY CRITERIA AND RANKINGS FOR NINE DIFFERENT CULTURES

Culture or Subculture	Creativity Level Index	Ranking	Occup. Aspirations Index	Ranking
Minnesota, U.S.A.	97.2	1	47	1
California, U.S.A.	96.2	2	31	2
West Germany	92.5	3	30	3
Norway	88.3	4	14	5
Singapore	82.6	5	11	6
Western Australia	82.1	6	21	4
U.S.A. Negro	80.0	7.5	10	7.5
India	80.0	7.5	10	7.5
Western Samoa	79.3	9	7	9

derived therefrom, and the overall creativity indexes and rankings are presented in Table 2. Because of the similarity of the creativity indexes of the three Singapore samples, the size of the samples, and the similarity of their occupational choices and aspirations, these three samples have been combined.

The two sets of rankings yield a rank-order coefficient of correlation of .95. Again there are only minor discrepancies. From the index based on occupational choices and aspirations, we would have expected the Australian children to have achieved a somewhat higher level of creative functioning than those in Norway and Singapore. Again, the Minnesota, California, and West German samples are clearly in front on both indexes and are ranked accurately.

SUMMARY AND DISCUSSION

One of the ways by which a culture honors creative talent is reflected in the ideals of the teachers of that culture and the kinds of behavior that they encourage and discourage among children. Using data supplied by the teachers in ten different cultures or subcultures concerning their concept of the ideal pupil, rankings were obtained concerning the extent to which 62 characteristics are encouraged or discouraged. These characteristics had been found in empirical studies to be associated with the productive, creative personality and had been rated on creativity criteria by a panel of ten advanced scholars of creative personality. Indexes of the extent to which the culture or subculture encourages or discourages creative behavior were obtained by correlating the composite rankings of the experts with the composite rankings of the teachers of each of the cultures or subcultures studied. The rank-order coefficient of correlation of .94 of this index with overall creativity indexes based on the *Torrance Tests of Creative Thinking* indicates a close correspondence between these two indexes and supports the idea that "what is honored in a country is cultivated there."

Another way that reflects the honor given creative talent in a culture or subculture is the availability of creative occupational outlets for its members. This was assessed by the variety of occupations chosen by children within the cultures in grades three through six (percentage of occupational choices outside the 25 most popular choices of a large U.S.A. group at the same grade levels) and the choice of occupations in the creative arts (visual art, writing, drama, music, dancing) and sciences. Rankings obtained from this index were correlated with the rankings obtained from the overall creativity index and a coefficient of .95 was obtained. Thus, there is a close correspondence between these two sets of rankings and this supports the idea that "what is honored in a country is cultivated there."

The data summarized in this paper identify two ways of looking at the ways cultures honor creative behavior. The findings suggest that the culture that desires to produce high levels of creative talent should seek to encourage those behaviors in children that facilitate creative functioning and discourage those characteristics that inhibit such functioning and should make available to its members a variety of occupational outlets and careers in the creative arts and sciences.

The indexes used in this study are relatively gross ones but are based on a great quantity of data from over 8,000 children and their teachers. Within each culture, however, there are great variations among both pupils and teachers. The commonalities within cultures, however, are striking and yield information that serves as general though not precise guides to understanding, predicting, and improving creative behavior.

References

Torrance, E. P.: *Guiding Creative Talent.* Englewood Cliffs, N. J.: Prentice-Hall, Inc., 1962.

Torrance, E. P.: *Education and the Creative Potential.* Minneapolis: University of Minnesota Press, 1963.

Torrance, E. P.: *Rewarding Creative Behavior.* Englewood Cliffs, N.J.: Prentice-Hall, Inc., 1965.

Torrance, E. P.: *Torrance Tests of Creative Thinking: Norms-Technical Manual (Research Edition).* Princeton, N.J.: Personnel Press, 1966.

Torrance, E. P.: *Understanding the Fourth-Grade Slump in Creative Thinking.* (Final Report on Cooperative Research Project 994) Athens, Ga.: Georgia Studies of Creative Behavior, University of Georgia, 1967.

CREATIVITY AND CONFORMITY

Vernon L. Allen
John M. Levine
University of Wisconsin

Creativity and conformity seem to be antithetical psychological processes. The generalization receives support from both casual observation and empirical research. Investigators in the Berkeley Creativity Project found that among many groups of persons differing in objectively assessed creativity, conformity was greatest in groups designated as least creative (Crutchfield, 1958). Other studies of more homogeneous groups have also found that persons who scored high on creativity indices conformed less than persons who scored low (Barron, 1952, 1953, 1955; Crutchfield, 1951, 1955). Thus, substantial evidence from empirical research confirms the assertion that creativity and conformity are inversely related.

Concluding that an inverse relation exists between creativity and conformity is not completely satisfying; a theoretical explanation is needed of the psychological basis for the deleterious effect of social pressure on creativity. A convincing theoretical analysis has been provided by Crutchfield (1962), who discusses two factors that might account for the association between conformity and creativity.

First, conformity pressure tends to create extrinsic, ego-involved motivation. Under extrinsic motivation, creativity is a means to some goal external to the solution of the immediate problem. Under intrinsic or task-involved motivation, by contrast, the creative process is a rewarding end in itself. Arousal of ego-involved or extrinsic motivation causes the individual to be concerned primarily with acceptance or rejection by the group, rather than with problem-solving. Research has shown that extremely high motivation—in this case anxiety about one's relationship to the group—leads to rigid cognitive processes detrimental to insightful problem solution. In sum, conformity pressure produces motivations that are incompatible with the cognitive flexibility essential to creative thinking.

Second, Crutchfield mentions personality traits of the conformist as linking conformity pressures and creativity. Conformers have been found to possess such traits as anxiety, rigidity, low ego strength, lack of spontaneity, intolerance of ambiguity, conventional attitudes, feelings of personal inferiority, dependence toward others, and orthodox values. These personality characteristics, typical of conformers, correlate negatively with creative thinking.

The theoretical analysis contributed by Crutchfield appears quite plausible; it seems reasonable that conformity pressure produces ego-involved motivation detrimental to creativity and that personality characteristics of conformers are inimical to creative thinking. Nevertheless, the relation between creativity and conformity is undoubtedly very complex, and the direction of causality certainly equivocal. For instance, would enhanced creativity result from induced resistance to group pressure? Conversely, would an increase in creative skills produce a concomitant increase in independence under group pressure? On the basis of the observed inverse relation between creativity and conformity, one might respond affirmatively to both questions. But the prediction is not as straightforward as it appears. The correlation between creativity and conformity does not, of course, designate a causal relation; some third variable might be responsible for both creativity and conformity. The present study was designed to shed light on the question of causality in the observed relation between creativity and conformity. Specifically, the study tests empirically whether experimentally enhanced creativity produces greater independence in the face of group pressure. Stating the problem in another way, we are concerned with whether experimentally increased creativity produces a psychological change which transfers to the social pressure situation, resulting in decreased conformity.

The design of the present study involved administering a creativity-training program to a group of Experimental subjects. Later, the subjects in the Experimental group and a matched Control group were subjected to social pressure from peers.

Programmed instructional material[2] developed by Crutchfield

---

2. Further information about the training material (Series One: General Problem Solving of *The Productive Thinking Program*) can be obtained from its distributor, Educational Innovation, P. O. Box 9248, Berkeley, California 94719.

and associates (Covington & Crutchfield, 1965; Crutchfield, 1966) was used to develop and facilitate creative thinking. The training material consists of an integrated series of one-hour lessons in the form of simple detective stories designed to hold the interest of fifth- and sixth-grade children. The stories are presented in cartoon format. Each child, working alone at his own speed, discovers solutions to problems by using a series of increasingly informative cues. The problems require use of various cognitive skills essential to problem-solving, without necessitating specialized or curriculum-bound knowledge.

The training material was designed to improve problem-solving skills, increase self-confidence, and strengthen positive attitudes toward problem-solving and creativity. One assumption underlying the training program was that creative thinking is a complex problem-solving process, incorporating the use and management of numerous cognitive skills. It was further assumed that such skills, possessed in varying degree by everyone, could be enhanced by proper training. Results of several previous studies with similar programmed creativity-training material have shown substantial and significant improvement on a variety of criterion tests of problem-solving and originality (Covington & Crutchfield, 1965; Crutchfield, 1966).

Method

Subjects

The subjects were 164 fifth-grade students, 78 males and 86 females, of the Racine, Wisconsin, Unified school district. The subjects ranged in age from nine to 13; 91 per cent were 10 or 11 years old. Subjects were tested together by class; six classes, each containing 27 to 32 pupils, were used. Three classes (76 subjects) received the creativity training (Experimental condition). Three other classes (88 subjects) followed the normal fifth-grade curriculum rather than the creativity program and were matched with the creativity group on Kuhlman-Anderson IQ scores, Stanford achievement scores, and socioeconomic status (Control condition).

Procedure

Creativity training program. The six classes in the present experiment were drawn from 47 classes used in a creativity training study conducted in the Racine school district.[3] The Racine study was designed to test the effectiveness of creativity-training material under adverse procedural conditions: massed lessons were administered by classroom teachers who gave no assistance to students. The training

---

3. The creativity project was jointly conducted by the Wisconsin Research and Development Center for Cognitive Learning at the University of Wisconsin, Madison, and the Creative Thinking Project at the University of California, Berkeley.

program consisted of 16 self-administering lessons completed at the rate of four per week for four weeks. The lessons were revised from earlier materials (Covington & Crutchfield, 1965).

Conformity testing. The conformity procedure was conducted approximately three weeks after the subjects completed the final creativity-training lesson. The subjects were unaware of any connection between the conformity procedure and the prior creativity-training study. After an introduction by the classroom teacher, one of the two male experimenters[4] gave the following instructions:

> We are making a survey of fifth-graders' judgments and opinions about a variety of things. We are comparing fifth-grade classes from several schools. We will give you answer sheets to record your answers to a number of questions. Each question will be shown on the screen in the front of the room, and I will also read the question aloud. Your job is to give the best answer on each question, by circling one of the answers provided for each question on your answer sheet. Please answer as quickly as possible, so as not to delay the entire class. No one in this school will see your individual answers, so be sure to do your own work. Please do not talk. Be sure to answer every question.

Twenty-four slides were presented; each remained on the screen for 10 seconds. The experimenter read aloud the question for each slide. At the completion of the series, the experimenters thanked the class and departed with the slide projector and screen. The subjects believed the experiment to be finished.

In approximately one hour, the experimenters returned to the classroom and gave the following instructions to the subjects:

> Now we'd like to give you the same questions a second time. People sometimes want to change their minds after they've had more time to think about a question. So you may change your mind on this second try, or you may not. In any case, we would like to know your judgment right now. Again, circle the one best answer for each question. Oh yes, we've looked at the answers given by the entire class and thought you might be interested to know what the class thought about each question. So, we'll tell you as we go along what answer the majority of the class gave. We will let you know later which class in all the schools we've tested did best on this exercise.

The series of 24 slides was again presented. In addition, a fictitious class norm purporting to represent majority opinion was given orally immediately after presentation of each slide. This norm was couched in the following terms: "Almost everyone in the class gave answer ———."

---

4. We are grateful to Barry W. Bragg for help in collecting the data.

A careful debriefing explaining both the methodology and purpose of the experiment followed the slide series.

Stimuli

The stimuli were 24 slides consisting of three general types of items: visual, attitude, and achievement. The visual perception items required judgment of relationships among visual stimuli. For instance, the subject had to determine which of nine rectangles was square. The attitude items, which were answered using a nine-point scale ranging from "strongly disagree" to "strongly agree," consisted of such statements as, "I like to read about science" and "I have a good sense of humor." The achievement items tapped factual knowledge, verbal skills, and numerical proficiency.

Sixteen of the 24 items used were critical (group pressure) items—six visual, four attitude, and six achievement. On the critical items, the purported class norm given by the experimenter was placed at the 95th percentile of responses given by a standardization group. That is, the stated norm was placed at or beyond the point at which only 5 per cent of the standardization group responded. The standardization group was composed of persons answering alone without seeing the responses of others. For achievement and attitude items, the standardization group was 30 fifth-grade students of the Evansville (Wisconsin) public school system. For the visual items, the standardization group was that used by Tuddenham, MacBride, and Zahn (1956).

The remaining eight stimuli were neutral items—three visual, two attitude, and three achievement. On these filler items, the reported class norm was actually the popular or correct answer.

Order of stimulus presentation was balanced in three ways. The 24 slides were divided into blocks of 12 stimuli; each block contained approximately one-half of both critical and neutral items of each of the three types (visual, attitude, and achievement). Second, the three types of items were counterbalanced within each block of 12. Finally, the critical and neutral items were counterbalanced within each block.

Items of each of the three types, can be divided into continuous-response and discrete-response categories. This distinction will prove important in data analysis. Continuous-response items provide several potential answers ordered along a size or intensity dimension. For instance, a continuous-response achievement item asking "How many meals do Americans eat per day?" offers answers ranging, in order, from one to six. Alternative answers for discrete-response stimuli, on the other hand, are not ordered along a continuum. For example, responses for an achievement item requiring identification of a spelling mistake are (1) trust, (2) mesure, (3) marble, and (4) simple. Of the 16 critical items, the continuous-response category contained three attitude, five visual, and one achievement; one attitude, one visual, and five achievement items were of the discrete-response type.

Method of Analysis

Conformity scores were computed and analyzed differently for the continuous- and discrete-response items. Using only continuous-response items, mean conformity scores for each subject were calculated separately for the three attitude and five visual items. Mean scores were computed because items were very similar in content and previous research has found significant positive correlations among conformity scores on items of each type. Mean scores were calculated by summing algebraic differences between initial responses and responses given under group pressure and dividing by the number of items used. (The single continuous-response achievement item was analyzed separately.)

Generally, three attitude and five visual items were employed in computing the two mean conformity scores for each subject. However, this was not always the case, because a subject's initial response occasionally fell at or beyond the simulated group norm on a particular item. In these instances, the subject was not subjected to group pressure by the experimenter's report, since the subject's private response was as extreme as that of the group. Hence, those few items on which the subject's initial response was located at or beyond the simulated group norm were eliminated from the calculations.

Using mean conformity scores for attitude and visual items, an analysis of variance was conducted; factors analyzed were sex, IQ, condition, and type of item. Duncan's New Multiple Range Test (Edwards, 1963) was then used to compare between selected means. In addition, intercorrelations were computed among mean conformity scores of both attitude and visual items in the Experimental and Control conditions.

Discrete-response items were analyzed individually because of their great variability in content and difficulty. For each item, a score was given indicating either that (a) the subject did not give the simulated group response in the first series, but did give this answer in the second series, or (b) the subject did not give the group's alleged response in either series. Subjects who gave the group response in the first series on a particular item were eliminated from calculations on that item, because they were not subject to group pressure on the later test. For each item, a mean conformity score was computed by summing across the subjects' scores and dividing by the number of subjects used. Finally, t tests were employed to compare conformity on a particular item in the Control and Experimental conditions.

Results

Creativity Training

Results of the Racine study are too extensive to permit complete presentation here; further detailed information is available elsewhere.[5] Although there were virtually no significant differences on pretraining creativity measures between subjects who subsequently received creativity training and those who did not,

---

5. "The Development of Productive Thinking Skills in Fifth-Grade Children," Tech. Report 34, Wisconsin Research and Development Center for Cognitive Learning, University of Wisconsin, Madison. This report contains details of design, programmed materials, and results.

trained subjects performed significantly better than controls on approximately 33 per cent of the posttraining creativity indices. Data indicated that the training program was more effective in enhancing convergent thinking (problem-solving ability) than divergent-thinking (originality). While the Racine program successfully increased creativity, results were not as dramatic as outcomes of earlier studies (Covington & Crutchfield, 1965; Crutchfield, 1966). We may conclude, however, that the training program did produce the desired effect of increasing problem-solving skill, even under adverse conditions.

Conformity

Attitude and visual items. The analysis of variance performed on the attitude and visual items yielded two significant interaction effects, indicating that results were quite complex. The Items × Condition interaction was significant at less than the .01 level ($F = 7.49$). Table 1 presents mean conformity scores on attitude and visual items in the Control and Experimental conditions for males and females. The Item × Condition means show that subjects in the Control condition conformed much more than Experimental subjects on the visual items; conversely, Experimental subjects conformed slightly more than Controls on attitude items.

The Items × Condition × Sex interaction was significant at less than the .05 level ($F = 4.63$). Results of the Duncan New Multiple Range Tests on data in Table 1 indicated that males conformed significantly more in the Control condition than in the Experimental condition on visual items (.74 vs. .19), while this difference for females did not reach statistical significance (.77 vs. .64).

Although the analysis of variance did not yield a significant overall IQ effect nor a Condition × IQ interaction, interesting and suggestive relations among the means make further analysis worthwhile. Let us now inspect closely the relation between conformity and IQ. Table 2 presents mean conformity scores across

Table 1. Mean conformity scores on attitude and visual items for males and females.

	Control	Experimental
Attitude		
Males	.53	.73
Females	.77	.74
Mean	.65	.73
Visual		
Males	.74	.19
Females	.77	.64
Mean	.75	.41

continuous-response items (attitude and visual) in the Control and Experimental conditions as a function of IQ level. Inspection of the overall mean conformity scores of subjects in the three IQ levels reveals an inverse relation between conformity and IQ; conformity decreases as IQ increases. To explore the relation between IQ and conformity, Duncan's New Multiple Range Tests were conducted. Results showed that for overall mean conformity scores, the Low IQ subjects conformed significantly more than the High IQ subjects ($<.05$). The Medium IQ subjects, who scored midway between the Highs and Lows on conformity, did not differ significantly from either of the two groups.

Data in Table 2 show that the inverse relation between conformity and IQ holds only for the Control condition (1.07, .60, and .44 for the Low, Medium, and High IQ levels, respectively). For Experimental subjects, conformity was not negatively related to IQ (.59, .62, and .51 for Low, Medium, and High IQ levels, respectively). Further, while conformity was considerably higher in the Control condition (1.07) than in the Experimental condition (.59) for Low IQ subjects, conformity was actually slightly higher in the Experimental condition for Medium and High IQ subjects. Results of the Duncan New Multiple Range Tests showed that the Low IQ Control subjects, who conformed significantly more than both the Medium ($<.10$) and High ($<.05$) IQ Control subjects, also conformed to a significantly greater degree than the Low IQ Experimental subjects ($<.10$). On the other hand, neither Medium nor High IQ Control subjects differed significantly in conformity from the corresponding subjects in the Experimental condition. It appears, then, that the Creativity training program successfully reduced conformity only among Low IQ subjects who yielded readily in the Control condition. In fact, conformity scores of Medium and High IQ Experimental subjects were slightly higher than in the Control condition.

Correlations among continuous-response items. The final results of the continuous-response items to be discussed are the intercorrelations among mean conformity scores. Table 3 presents the average intercorrelations of conformity scores on attitude

Table 2. Mean conformity scores on attitude and visual items as a function of IQ level.

	IQ level		
Condition	Low 1/3	Medium 1/3	High 1/3
Control	1.07	.60	.44
Experimental	.59	.62	.51
Mean	.83	.61	.47

and visual items in the Control and Experimental conditions. In the Control condition, average correlations among items of .39 and .43 were obtained for attitude and visual stimuli, respectively. In the Experimental condition, conformity scores among the attitude items revealed an average correlation of .20, while the average correlation among visual items was .13. Thus, the intercorrelation for both types of items was much higher in the Control condition than in the Experimental condition. Comparing the average correlations of attitude items in the Control and Experimental groups yielded a difference significant at less than the .02 level ($z = 2.10$). A similar comparison for visual items in the two conditions showed an even larger statistically significant difference ($z = 6.23$, $p < .001$). These results indicate that intercorrelations among conformity scores on both attitude and visual items were significantly greater in the Control condition than in the Experimental condition. That is, subjects in the Control condition reacted more uniformly across items to group pressure than did subjects who received Creativity training.

Conformity on other items. Let us now turn to the discrete-response items which were analyzed individually because of great variability in content and difficulty. (The single continuous-response achievement item will be included in this discussion.) Table 4 presents mean conformity scores of the eight individually analyzed items in the Control and Experimental conditions. Inspection of the data indicates that Control subjects conformed more than Experimental subjects on five of the eight items; conformity differences on three items (2, 4, 6) attained statistical significance. Of the three items on which Experimental subjects conformed more than Controls, only one item (7) yielded a statistically significant difference. These results support continuous-response data by showing generally more conformity in the Control condition than in the Experimental condition.

By dividing the eight items into those which have veridical answers and those which do not, additional meaning can be derived from the data. The first five items in Table 4 have only one veridical answer; for the last three items, no single clearly correct answer exists. Of the five items having correct answers, four showed greater conformity in the Control condition than in

Table 3. Average intercorrelations of conformity scores on attitude and visual items in control and experimental conditions.

Condition	Attitude	Visual
Control	.39	.43
Experimental	.20	.13

Table 4. Mean conformity scores of individually analyzed items in control and experimental conditions.

Item type	Control	Experimental	t
1. Information	.33	.20	1.24
2. Numerical	.28	.11	2.79***
3. Number series	.38	.32	.87
4. Spelling	.11	.04	1.85*
5. Synonyms	.20	.25	.66
6. Visual preference	.22	.09	2.09**
7. Visual insoluble	.32	.68	3.91***
8. Number series insoluble	.63	.72	1.12

*$p<.10$.
**$p<.05$.
***$p<.01$.
—All t tests are two-tailed.

the Experimental condition. Conversely, on two of the three items having indeterminate answers, Experimental subjects conformed more than Controls. These data indicate, then, that while Experimental subjects conformed more than Controls on ambiguous items, they conformed less on items which had a single objectively correct answer. Results closely parallel continuous-response findings reported earlier: conformity was greater on subjective items (attitudes) in the Experimental condition than in the Control, but on objective items (visual judgments) Controls conformed more than Experimental subjects.

Discussion

One interesting finding of the present study concerned the magnitude of the average intercorrelation among continuous-response items (visual and opinion) in the Experimental and Control conditions. Results indicated that Control subjects reacted more uniformly to group pressure across items of the same type than did subjects who received creativity training; that is, the Control subjects exhibited a stronger tendency either to generally accept or reject group pressure across similar types of items than did Experimental subjects. It is interesting to note that creativity training did not produce anticonformers who dissented from the group for the sake of dissent. Rather, subjects who received the training tended to utilize the groups' answers selectively, relying on the group on some items but not on others. Our findings for Control subjects corroborate previous research showing that subjects under social pressure respond quite consistently to group pressure (Crutchfield, 1955; Tuddenham, 1958). The inconsistency to group pressure exhibited by the Experimental subjects helps explain the limited overall conformity reduction produced by creativity training. Lack of consistent reaction to group pressure across items may actually have attenuated overall conformity reduction in the Experimental condition.

Turning now to other conformity data, the present study found that the relation between IQ level and conformity differed for the Control and the Experimental conditions. In the Control condition an inverse relation existed between IQ and conformity: amount of conformity increased as the level of IQ decreased. Previous investigations (Nakamura, 1958; Tuddenham, 1959) have also found a negative relation between IQ and conformity. Contrary to typical findings, Experimental subjects did not show an increase in conformity as IQ level decreased; the amount of conformity was quite uniform across IQ levels. The creativity training produced an overall decrease in susceptibility to group pressure for subjects having low IQ but not for subjects having average and high IQ. One explanation for the finding is that the training program increased positive attitudes toward creativity and improvement in problem-solving skills, both of which may have transferred to the conformity situation. The improvement in skills would transfer by increasing task-oriented, as opposed to social-oriented, motivation; low IQ subjects, who probably have the least task-oriented motivation, would benefit most. An improvement in both skills and attitude could indirectly affect response to group pressure by changing self-confidence. An increase in self-confidence would be expected to produce less conformity (Fagen, 1963; Hochbaum, 1954). Since it is probable that low IQ subjects are initially lowest in self-confidence (which might also help account for their high conformity in the Control condition), increasing confidence by creativity training would benefit low IQ subjects most.

Three additional factors may have been partially responsible for limiting the overall effect of creativity training primarily to low IQ subjects. First, the creativity training program produced less dramatic differences between trained and Control subjects than found in prior studies (Covington & Crutchfield, 1965; Crutchfield, 1966). It will be recalled that the Racine training materials were administered under less than optimal conditions for obtaining maximal enhancement of creativity. Had the effects of creativity training been stronger, a greater difference in overall conformity between Control and Experimental conditions might have been manifested with all IQ groups, instead of only the low IQ groups. Second, the conformity experiment was conducted three weeks after the conclusion of creativity training. Perhaps the effects of training dissipated somewhat during this interval, attenuating subsequent differences between Control and Experimental subjects in the conformity situation. Third, the group pressure technique used in the present study typically induces less conformity than other methods. In our study, subjects responded privately to an announced group norm. Previous research has found that greater conformity pressure is induced by public responding and face-to-face interaction with the group (Deutsch & Gerard, 1955). Techniques producing more intense social pressure would have caused greater conformity among the Control subjects at all IQ levels, thereby making possible a greater conformity difference between the Control and Experimental conditions.

The differential effect of creativity training by type of item sheds light on an interesting question: Precisely what aspects of the creativity training transferred to the conformity situation? Results showed that Control subjects conformed more than Experimentals on visual items, while Experimental subjects conformed slightly more than Controls on attitude items. The creativity training does not seem to produce a *general* effect on conformity to the group. Another instance of the selective efficacy of creativity training on conformity was found on the individually analyzed items. Control subjects conformed slightly more than Experimentals on items having objectively correct answers, but Experimental subjects conformed more than Controls on two of the three items having indeterminate answers.

It appears, then, that the transfer from creativity training to behavior in the social pressure situation was rather specific; subjects became more independent primarily on items having objectively correct answers. Thus, the problem-solving skills enhanced by creativity training transferred only to behavior requiring similar skills. Recall that results of the Racine program indicated that the training was more successful in increasing problem-solving skills (convergent thinking) than originality (divergent thinking). Thus, behavior of subjects under group pressure is congruent with findings for the creativity training.

Evidence from the present study suggests that the relation between conformity and creativity is complex and perhaps mediated by unconsidered variables. We can conclude, however, that creativity does seem causally related to conformity. Further research will be required to explicate fully the psychological mechanisms linking creativity and conformity.

Summary

Conformity to group pressure was compared for 76 subjects receiving a four-week program of creativity training and for 88 matched controls. Effect of creativity training on conformity was quite specific: conformity was reduced on items having correct answers, but not on subjective items. Results also showed that subjects receiving creativity training responded more selectively than controls to items similar in content, agreeing with the group on some items but not on others. In addition, the creativity training reduced overall conformity for low IQ subjects but not for subjects of average and high IQ levels. It was concluded that there is a causal relation between creativity and conformity, due to the transfer of common skills across the situations.

References

Barron, F. Some personality correlates of independence of judgment. *J. Pers.*, 1952, **21**, 287-297.

Barron, F. Complexity-simplicity as a personality dimension. *J. abnorm. soc. Psychol.*, 1953, **48**, 163-172.

Barron, F. The disposition toward originality. *J. abnorm. soc. Psychol.*, 1955, **51**, 478-485.

Covington, M. V., & Crutchfield, R. S. Experiments in the use of programmed instruction for the facilitation of creative problem solving. *Programmed Instruction*, 1965, **4**, 3-10.

Crutchfield, R. S. Assessment of persons through a quasi group-interaction technique. *J. abnorm. soc. Psychol.*, 1951, **46**, 577-588.

Crutchfield, R. S. Conformity and character. *Amer. Psychol.*, 1955, **51**, 629-636.

Crutchfield, R. S. Conformity and creative thinking. Paper read at "Symposium on Creative Thinking," Univer. of Colorado, Boulder, 1958.

Crutchfield, R. S. Detrimental effects of conformity pressures on creative thinking. *Psychologische Beitrage*, 1962, **6**, 464-471.

Crutchfield, R. S. Creative thinking in children: Its teaching and testing. In O. G. Brim, R. S. Crutchfield, & W. H. Holtzman, *Intelligence: Perspectives 1965*. New York: Harcourt, Brace, and World, 1966. Pp. 33-64.

Deutsch, M., & Gerard, H. B. A study of normative and informational social influences upon individual judgment. *J. abnorm. soc. Psychol.*, 1955, **51**, 629-636.

Edwards, A. L. *Experimental Design in Psychological Research*. New York: Holt, Rinehart and Winston, 1963.

Fagan, S. A. The effects of real and experimentally reported ability on confidence and conformity. *Amer. Psychologist*, 1963, **18**, 357-358. (Abstract)

Hochbaum, G. The relation between group members' self-confidence and their reactions to group pressures to uniformity. *Amer. sociol. Rev.*, 1954, **19**, 678-687.

Nakamura, C. V. Conformity and problem solving. *J. abnorm. soc. Psychol.*, 1958, **56**, 315-320.

Tuddenham, R. D. The influence of distorted group norm upon individual judgment. *J. Psychol.*, 1958, **46**, 227-241.

Tuddenham, R. D. Correlates of yielding to a distorted group norm. *J. Pers.*, 1959, **27**, 272-284.

Tuddenham, R. D., MacBride, P., & Zahn, V. Studies in conformity and yielding: I. Development of Standard Experimental Series-1. Tech. Rep. No. 1, ONR Contr. NR 170-159. Berkeley: Univer. of California, 1956.

FAMILY ENVIRONMENT AND COGNITIVE STYLE: A Study of the Sources of Highly Intelligent and of Highly Creative Adolescents*

Jacob W. Getzels
Philip W. Jackson
University of Chicago

From the time Binet first constructed his intelligence test with the resulting ubiquitous IQ metric to the present, the problem of intellectual ability and giftedness has remained largely a psychological issue. The important question has been a psychometric one: how can we obtain a precise measure of the general ability called intelligence or of a group of factors comprising so-called mental capacity? When sociologists have attempted to deal with differential cognitive functioning and giftedness, their efforts have most frequently been restricted to relating social class or ethnic variables to *amount* of mental ability as represented by the aforementioned IQ.

As we have had occasion to remark elsewhere,[1] involved in the IQ conception of intellectual functioning are several types of confusion, if not outright error. First, there is the limitation of the single metric itself, which not only restricts our perspective of the more general phenomenon, but places on the one concept a greater theoretical and predictive burden than it was intended to carry. Second, within the universe of intellectual functioning we have behaved as if the intelligence test represented an adequate sampling of *all* functions—the "gifted child," for example, has become synonymous with the "child with a high IQ." Third, we have so emphasized the measuring of different *amounts* of intellectual ability that we have neglected the understanding of different *kinds* of intellectual ability.

Despite its longevity there is nothing inevitable about the use of the IQ in defining

---

* This research was supported by a grant from the U.S. Office of Education. The present paper is a revision of a briefer report given at the American Sociological Association meetings, New York, August 31, 1960. The revision was prepared while the first-named author was at the Center for Advanced Study in the Behavioral Sciences, Stanford, California.

[1] J. W. Getzels and P. W. Jackson, "The Meaning of Giftedness: An Examination of an Expanding Concept," *Phi Delta Kappan,* 40 (November, 1959), pp. 75–78.

Reprinted from *American Sociological Review,* Vol. 26, No. 3, June, 1961, by permission of Phi Delta Kappan.

intellectual ability and potential giftedness. Indeed, it may be argued that in many ways this metric is only an historical accident—a consequence of the fact that early inquiries in the field of intellectual functioning had as their social context the classroom and as their criterion academic progress. If the initial context of inquiry into mental ability had not been the classroom, other qualities defining intellectual functioning might have been identified just as the qualities measured by the IQ apparently were in the classroom. Indeed, even without shifting the context of inquiry from the classroom, if only the original criterion of learning had been changed, the qualities defining intellectual functioning and giftedness might also have been changed. For example, if we recognized that learning involves the production of novelty as well as the remembrance of course-content, then measures of creativity as well as the IQ might become appropriate defining characteristics of mental ability and giftedness. It is, of course, a commonplace to recognize people who seem to be highly "intelligent" (as measured by the IQ) but apparently not "creative" (whatever that seems to mean in any particular case), and people who are "creative" but not necessarily "intelligent" (at least as measured by the conventional IQ).

The research project from which we are drawing our present report was directed toward the following three related tasks:

1. To identify two groups of subjects differing significantly in *kind* of intellectual functioning—in this case, "intelligence" and "creativity."

2. To examine the personal-social behavioral concomitants of the two kinds of intellectual functioning—for example, would the groups also differ in levels of achievement, patterns of interpersonal relations, types of career aspirations, etc.?

3. To study in some depth the family environment of the two groups.

DIFFERENTIATING COGNITIVE STYLE: SUBJECTS, METHODS, FINDINGS

The methods and findings with respect to the first two tasks have already been reported in detail elsewhere [2] and will be presented here only insofar as is necessary to clarify the issues and findings with respect to the third task—determining the relationship between type of intellectual functioning and family environment—which is the focus of this report.

The experimental groups were drawn from 449 adolescents comprising the total population of a Midwestern private secondary school [3] on the basis of performance on the following instruments:

1. Standard IQ tests, most usually the Binet itself.
2. Five Creativity measures, taken or adapted from Guilford and Cattell, or constructed especially for the study, as follows:
   a. Word Association. The subject was asked to give as many definitions as possible to fairly common stimulus-words, e.g., "bolt," "bark," "sack." His score depended on the absolute number of definitions and the number of different categories into which his definitions could be put.
   b. Uses for Things. The subject was required to give as many uses as he could for objects customarily having a single stereotyped function, e.g., "brick," "paperclip." His score depended on the number and originality of the uses he mentioned.
   c. Hidden Shapes. The subject was required to find a given geometric form hidden

---

[2] J. W. Getzels and P. W. Jackson, "The Highly Intelligent and the Highly Creative Adolescent: A Summary of Some Research Findings," in Calvin W. Taylor, editor, *Research Conference on the Identification of Creative Scientific Talent*, Salt Lake City: University of Utah Press, 1959, pp. 46–57; "Occupational Choice and Cognitive Functioning: Career Aspirations of Highly Intelligent and of Highly Creative Adolescents," *Journal of Abnormal and Social Psychology,* 61 (July, 1960), pp. 119–123; "The Study of Giftedness: A Multidimensional Approach," in Co-operative Research Monograph No. 2 of the U.S. Office of Education, *The Gifted Student*, Washington, D.C.: U.S. Office of Education, 1960, pp. 1–18.

[3] The children in this school come in large measure from families who are in the employ of an urban university, or from families who, although not employed by the university, prefer to reside in or near the university community, and to send their children to its school because of its presumed excellence. The children are much above average in ability, the mean IQ of the total school being 132, with a standard deviation of 15.1.

in more complex geometric forms or patterns.
d. Fables. The subject was required to provide a "moralistic," a "humorous," and a "sad" ending to each of four fables in which the last line was missing. His score depended on the number, appropriateness, and originality of the endings.
e. Make-Up Problems. The subject was presented with four complex paragraphs, each containing a number of numerical statements, e.g., "the costs in building a house." He was required to make up as many mathematical problems as he could that might be solved with the information given. His score depended upon the number, appropriateness, and originality of the problems.

What most of these verbal and numerical tests had in common was that the score depended not on a single pre-determined correct response as is frequently the case of the common intelligence test, but on the number, novelty, and variety of responses.

On the basis of the IQ measure and a summated score on the creativity measures, the two experimental groups were formed as follows:

1. The High Creativity Group. These were subjects at the top 20 per cent on the creativity measures when compared with same-sex age peers, but *below* the top 20 per cent in IQ. Their mean IQ was 127, with a range from 108 to 138. N = 26 (15 boys, 11 girls).

2. The High Intelligence Group. These were subjects in the top 20 per cent in IQ when compared with same-sex age peers, but *below* the top 20 per cent on the creativity measures. Their mean IQ was 150, with a range from 139 to 179. N = 28 (17 boys, 11 girls).[4]

---

[4] The initial samples of highly creative and highly intelligent subjects were larger than the final experimental groups. Because of the goals of the overall project, students who were also especially outstanding in qualities such as psychological health or morality were the subjects of independent study. In a sense, the present experimental groups may be said to represent relatively "pure" types since they do not include adolescents gifted as well in a number of these other characteristics. There were also students who were at once both "highly intelligent" and "highly creative." These too are not included in the present study.

Having thus identified two groups differing (at least by test score) in style of intellectual functioning—in effect, the objective of the first research task—we were ready to turn to our second task, which may now be put in the form of a direct question: What is the nature of the performance of the groups on the following personal-social variables: school achievement, perception by teachers, production of fantasies, and choice of adult career? The findings were quite straightforward:

1. *School achievement.* Although there is a 23 point difference in average IQ between the high IQ's and the high Creatives, the school achievement of the two groups as measured by standardized achievement tests was *equally superior* to the population from which they were drawn.

2. *Perception by teachers.* The teachers were asked to rate all students in the school on the degree they enjoyed having them in class. The high IQ student was rated as more desirable than the average student, the high Creative was not.

3. *Fantasy production.* Six Thematic Apperception Test-type pictures were shown, and the subjects were required to write four-minute stories to each of the pictures. The stories of the two groups were found to be strikingly different, the Creative making significantly greater use of *stimulus-free themes, unexpected endings, humor,* and *playfulness.*

4. *Career aspiration.* The two groups were asked to indicate their career aspirations and occupational choices. When these were analyzed into "conventional" (e.g., doctor, lawyer, engineer) and "unconventional" (e.g., adventurer, inventor, writer) categories, it was found that 16 per cent of the high IQ's and 62 per cent of the high Creatives had made "unconventional" career choices.

In short, two conclusions seemed clear from studying the children themselves: First, they could be differentiated by kind of preferred intellectual functioning, i.e., into high IQ and high Creativity groups. Second, when they were so differentiated, the two groups were equally superior in achievement to the population from which they were drawn, and they themselves differed significantly in a number of personal-social variables, including perception by teachers, fantasy production, and choice of career.

FAMILY ENVIRONMENT AND COGNITIVE STYLE: METHODS, SUBJECTS, FINDINGS

The central issue of the present report is: Do the two groups also vary systematically in the nature of their family environment? Accordingly, family inventories and 2–3 hour interviews were obtained from approximately 80 per cent of the mothers of the two groups. The analysis of these data may be discussed with respect to each of the following family variables:

1. Education and occupation of the parents.
2. Age of the parents.
3. Mother's recollection of her own family situation when she was her child's age.
4. Reading interests in the family, at least as represented by the number and type of magazines taken.
5. Parental satisfaction and dissatisfaction with the child and his school.
6. Parental satisfaction and dissatisfaction with their own child-rearing practices.
7. Mother's description of the kinds of friends preferred for her child.

1. *Education and occupation of parents.* Educational data were available for the parents of 24 of the 28 high IQ's and for 24 of the 26 high Creatives. When these data were analyzed by simply dichotomizing college graduates versus others, the result obtained could be summarized as in Table 1.

The data were also dichotomized by parents having at least some graduate training as against those having no graduate training. The results of this analysis are given in Table 2.

[1] Because of the exploratory nature of this phase of the research many of the comparisons presented here were derived from the obtained data. Therefore, the probability values attached to the chi-squares in this and the following Tables must be viewed with caution.

TABLE 1. NUMBER OF COLLEGE GRADUATES AMONG FATHERS AND MOTHERS OF THE TWO EXPERIMENTAL GROUPS

	Number of College Graduates			
	IQ (n=24)	Creative (n=24)	χ^2	p[1]
Father	21	15	4.0	.05
Mother	16	12	1.37	N.S.

TABLE 2. NUMBER OF PARENTS HAVING SOME GRADUATE TRAINING

	Having Graduate Training			
	IQ (n=24)	Creative (n=24)	χ^2	p
Father	19	13	3.38	.10
Mother	13	5	5.69	.02

Whichever analysis is undertaken, it seems that the parents of the high IQ child tend to have higher educational status than the parents of the high Creativity child. But what is perhaps more noteworthy is the *greater specialized training* of both the mother and the father of the high IQ's. The essential difference is probably not so much in the general level of cultivation, which is very high for both groups when compared to the general population, but in the significantly greater specialization of training or, if one will, "professionalization of education" of the high IQ group.

In this connection, the occupational data are relevant. The data for fathers are presented in Table 3, and for mothers in Table 4.

It appears that we are dealing not only with two different types of children but with two different types of parents. As might be anticipated from the data on educational status, a greater proportion of the high IQ fathers than of the high Creativity fathers are found in the academic or educational occupations. But it is noteworthy that despite their greater professional training, a greater proportion of the mothers of the high IQ children than of the high Creativity children are exclusively housewives, and do not hold other full- or part-time jobs. It would seem that the mothers of the high IQ subjects have more time to devote to their children than do the mothers of the high Creative subjects. In this connection, it will be

TABLE 3. OCCUPATIONAL STATUS OF THE FATHERS OF THE TWO EXPERIMENTAL GROUPS

Occupational Status	IQ (n=24)	Creative (n=24)	χ^2	p
University teaching, research, editing	15	7	6.15	.02
Business	4	11		
Medicine, law	5	6	....	...

TABLE 4. OCCUPATIONAL STATUS OF THE MOTHERS OF THE TWO EXPERIMENTAL GROUPS

Occupational Status	IQ (n=24)	Creative (n=24)	χ^2	p
Housewife only	18	11	4.27	.05
Full or part-time employment	6	13		

shown from other sources of data that the high IQ mothers are in fact likely to be more vigilant about the "correct" upbringing of their children than the high Creativity mothers.

2. *Age of parents.* The mean age is almost exactly the same for the two groups of mothers, and although the age of the fathers tended to be slightly greater for the high IQ group than for the high Creativity group, it was not significantly so. The significant and striking difference between the two groups was in the discrepancy or congruence between the age of the father and mother. If the data are dichotomized as one year or less age difference and two years or more age difference, the results may be summarized as in Table 5.

We may only conjecture at this time about the reasons for the age discrepancies or similarities between the parents of the present sample, and about the effects of these age factors on the family environment. But two reasons for a number of the discrepancies seem relevant: waiting to finish advanced academic training before risking marital responsibilities, and waiting to be satisfactorily "settled" to maintain a family in the "right" style. Both reasons suggest an apparently greater insecurity among the high IQ parents than among the high Creativity parents, a suggestion that is also supported by subsequent interview data.

3. *Mother's memories of own home.* The relevant interview question was: How would you describe the home you lived in as a child? The responses were long and detailed —the mothers seemed to enjoy relating their own real or imagined childhood experiences to their children's present situation. Here, for example, is a fairly typical response by one of the IQ mothers:[5]

> It was as typically Midwestern middle class American as one could find. Neither rich nor poor . . . The family belonged to important people in town. Father was the principal of the school, active in church and in the literary group. His was a large family, and there were many homes we could go to. Father died when I was thirteen. Mother began teaching school. We thought more about money. Then I worked while in college. I have some doubt about that—traumatic insecurity, especially financially. So abnormally thrifty ever since—keeping magazines . . . I hope children won't miss these highlights of our life even if disasters . . . .

The problem of quantifying this kind of material is of course formidable, and many differences that one "feels" as one reads the complete sets of interviews "wash out" as one attempts to categorize. Nonetheless, certain categorical differences may be noted. For example, seven of the 22 IQ mothers for whom interview material is available say specifically of their home that it was "middle class," and only one of the 18 Creative mothers for whom interview material is available says this. Eight of the 22 IQ mothers describe their family in rather global-emotional terms; 12 of the 18 Crea-

TABLE 5. AGE DIFFERENCE BETWEEN PARENTS FOR THE TWO EXPERIMENTAL GROUPS

Age Difference between Parents	IQ (n=24)	Creative (n=24)	χ^2	p
0–1 years	4	13	7.38	.01
2 or more years	20	11		

TABLE 6. MENTION OF FINANCIAL STATUS AND OF POVERTY IN DESCRIPTIONS OF OWN HOME LIFE BY MOTHERS OF THE TWO EXPERIMENTAL GROUPS

	IQ (n=22)	Creative (n=18)	χ^2	p
Mention of finances	16	7	4.64	.05
Emphasis on poverty, financial hardship	9	1	4.84*	.05

* Yates correction applied.

---

[5] Here and throughout the paper the mothers' statements are taken from notes recorded during the interview. At the time these interviews were made the parents of five other experimental groups were also being studied. The interviewers did not know into which of the seven groups any mother belonged. The present quotations have been altered in irrelevant details to maintain anonymity.

tive mothers seem to do this. That is, the IQ mothers tend to be more "stereotypic" in their descriptions (they tend to put themselves in "classes"); the Creative mothers attempt rather more rounded descriptions.

But the chief categorical difference—and a very relevant one—lies in their reference to the financial status of their home and childhood. As the data in Table 6 show, the high IQ parents tend not only to mention finances significantly more often than the high Creativity parents, but to emphasize financial hardship more often. Whatever else these responses imply about the different remembrance of things past and areas of latent concern, they do tend to support the suggestion of greater insecurity among the parents of the high IQ children than among the parents of the high Creativity children.

4. *Reading interests in the home.* It is almost impossible to obtain an exact measure of the reading habits of a family. Nonetheless, an attempt toward a partial assessment was made by asking the following interview questions: What magazines and newspapers do you subscribe to or buy regularly? What magazines do you read just once in a while?

Professional or scholarly journals, which would have increased the count for the high IQ parents, were omitted in the analysis. Despite this, there was a difference in the number of magazines coming into the homes of the high IQ and high Creativity subjects, a difference that is quite illuminating.

The 22 high IQ families reported reading "regularly" a total of 125 magazines, and "sometimes" 54 magazines. The 18 high Creative families reported reading "regularly" a total of 107 magazines, and "sometimes" 30 magazines. The respective means were 8.14 for the high IQ's and 5.94 for the high Creatives. If the families are divided into those mentioning six or fewer and those mentioning seven or more magazines, the relationship portrayed in Table 7 is observed.

TABLE 7. NUMBER OF MAGAZINES "TAKEN" OR READ IN HOMES OF THE TWO EXPERIMENTAL GROUPS

Number of Magazines	IQ (n=22)	Creative (n=18)	χ^2	p
6 or fewer	7	12	4.34	.05
7 or more	15	6		

There seem to be significant quantitative differences between the two groups. There are also some noteworthy qualitative trends in the data. For example, 21 of the 22 high IQ mothers report taking or reading 50 "Mass Media Magazines" (*Time, Life, Newsweek, Reader's Digest*). This is about 28 per cent of their total. Sixteen of the 18 high Creative mothers report taking or reading 27 "Mass Media Magazines," which is about 19 per cent of their total. Conversely, five of the 22 high IQ mothers mention seven "Magazines of Liberal Political Comment" (*Reporter, Nation, New Republic*)— about 3 per cent of the total—but seven of the 18 high Creative mothers mention ten magazines in this category, i.e., about 7 per cent of their total. Perhaps the most noteworthy difference is in the number of children's magazines (*Boys Life, Junior Natural History Magazine*, etc.) mentioned by the two groups. Ten of the 22 high IQ mothers mention 17 such magazines, three of the 18 high Creativity mothers mention five such magazines.

5. *Parental satisfaction and dissatisfaction with the child and with his school.* A crucial issue in the present study of family environment and giftedness is the reaction of the parent to any unusual qualities in the child and the type of education the child is getting. Two interview questions are relevant here:

a. During your child's earliest years in school, did the teachers call to your attention or did you yourself notice anything unusual about him and school?
b. As far as the present school is concerned, what are the things you like best about the education your child is getting? Is there anything about your child's education at this school that you are not satisfied with?

The replies to both questions are quite consistent and informative. They will be discussed in turn.

a. Although the high IQ and the high Creativity parents report the same number of total observations and the same number of favorable and unfavorable qualities in their children as seen by *teachers*, the high IQ parents report both a greater number of total observations (59 against 31) and a greater number of unfavorable qualities as seen by *themselves*. When the latter data are dichotomized into "not more than one

FAMILY ENVIRONMENT AND COGNITIVE STYLE

TABLE 8. NUMBER OF UNFAVORABLE QUALITIES OBSERVED IN THEIR CHILDREN BY MOTHERS OF THE TWO GROUPS

Number of Unfavorable Qualities Observed	IQ (n=23)	Creative (n=19)	χ^2	p
Not more than one	13	17	5.53	.02
More than one	10	2		

TABLE 10. MOTHERS' SATISFACTION AND DISSATISFACTION WITH THEIR OWN CHILD TRAINING PRACTICES

Opinion of Own Child Training Practice	IQ (n=23)	Creative (n=19)	χ^2	p
Satisfied	17	8	4.37	.05
Dissatisfied	6	11		

unfavorable quality" and "more than one unfavorable quality," the result is the relationship presented in Table 8.

What is noteworthy in these data is the greater "vigilance" and "critical" or at least "less accepting" attitude of the high IQ mothers—they both observe *more* about their children and they observe a greater number of *objectionable* qualities. It is as if they were on the look-out for things to improve about their children. (In this connection, the greater number of children's magazines the high IQ parents take is perhaps relevant.)

b. The same "vigilance" and critical attitude is seen in their attitudes toward the school their children are attending. Here again the high IQ parents report a greater number of total observations (138 against 95), and a significantly greater number of dissatisfactions, as shown in Table 9.

6. *Parental satisfaction with their child-rearing practices.* Despite the apparent greater misgiving and uncertainty of the high IQ mother toward her child and toward the school, she expresses fewer misgivings and uncertainties than does the high Creative mother regarding her own child training practices. It is almost as if she were critical of others but "smug" about herself. The relevant interview question was: As you look back on the ways you have tried to make your child responsible to you as far as bed-time, playing outside, leaving the house, homework and so forth were concerned, would you say you were too lenient, not lenient enough, or what? The results are presented in Table 10.

7. *Kinds of friends preferred for their children.* There is one final set of data that rounds out the differences between the family environment of the high IQ and the high Creativity families, at least as represented by the mothers' attitudes. The interview question was: What qualities do you like to see in your child's friends?

Again, the high IQ mothers had somewhat more to say. But the striking finding was the difference in what they said. When the qualities mentioned are divided into two categories, the one relating to "external" characteristics (e.g., "good family," "good manners," "studious"), the other to "internal" characteristics (e.g., "sense of values," "interest in something," "openness—not secretive"), the result is the relationship summarized in Table 11.

Several sample responses may give some greater substance to these tabular differences. Here, for example, are two high IQ mothers describing the qualities they would like to see in their child's friends: (a) "Sunday school children, religious, go to church every Sunday, of parents whose standards are ours. Honest, sincere, clean-minded and clean-mouthed. Studious." (b) "Right between the eyes—aware of my own inadequacies. Intelligence is certainly foremost—admit to my snobbism. Kind of cultural background, not money. A level of family. What I don't like—wild kid who doesn't know how to behave in a house—dirty talk —I've put up with it—a certain amount is acceptable—outside can use up energies. Neither extroverted nor introverted." Here are two high Creativity mothers describing the qualities they would like to see in their child's friends: (a) "Like what I want to see in E . . . [her child]—it's the same

TABLE 9. NUMBER OF UNFAVORABLE SCHOOL QUALITIES OBSERVED BY MOTHERS OF THE TWO EXPERIMENTAL GROUPS

Number of Unfavorable School Qualities Observed	IQ (n=23)	Creative (n=19)	χ^2	p
Not more than one	7	12	4.5	.05
More than one	16	7		

TABLE 11. CHARACTERISTICS PREFERRED FOR CHILDREN'S FRIENDS BY MOTHERS OF THE TWO GROUPS

Characteristics	IQ (n=23) $\bar{X}$[1]	S	Creative (n=19) $\bar{X}$	S	t	p
External—Specific, e.g., good family, manners, studious	2.48	1.20	1.58	1.07	2.56	.02
Internal—General, e.g., sense of values, interests, openness	.91	1.12	1.79	1.47	2.13	.05

[1] These means refer to the average number of characteristics mentioned.

thing. Valid sense of values—what a person is rather than what he appears to be. Satisfaction in creative constructive activity. Balance and maturity in interpersonal relations. Interest and enthusiasm for learning and reaching out beyond it to greater understanding." (b) "Openness—not secretive that old folks won't understand. Interest in something to do—not bored expression. Temperate in manners and habits. Frankness and honesty. Interest in living." It is here in the projections of desirable traits for their children's friends that we may perhaps see the most honest aspirations for their own children. As the high Creative mother says, "It's the same thing." And it is here, as we have seen, that we again find some very striking differences indeed.

DISCUSSION AND SUMMARY

It is clear that the intellectual functioning of adolescents can be differentiated not only into quantitative categories of high and low IQ but also into qualitative categories among which are "high IQ without concomitantly high Creativity" and "high Creativity without concomitantly high IQ." The intellectual functioning represented by these two categories bears resemblance to Guilford's factors of "convergent" and "divergent" thinking.[6] When adolescents representing these qualitative categories are identified it is found that they also differ on a number of significant personal-social variables. For example, although both are equally superior to the average student in school achievement, they are perceived differently by teachers, they differ in the nature of their fantasy productions, and they aspire to different career goals.

With respect to these initial findings, and before a study of the family environments was undertaken, we suggested that,

... the essence of the performance of our Creative adolescents lay in their ability to produce new forms, to risk conjoining elements that are customarily thought of as independent and dissimilar, to go off in new directions. The creative adolescent possesses the ability to free himself from the usual to "diverge" from the customary. He seemed to enjoy the risk and uncertainty of the unknown. In contrast, the high IQ adolescent seemed to possess to a high degree the ability and the need to focus on the usual, to be channelled and controlled in the direction of the right answer—the customary. He appeared to shy away from the risk and the uncertainty of the unknown and to seek out the safety and security of the known.[7]

In an attempt to relate the differences in intellectual behavior to a broader psycho-social context we found fruitful Maslow's formulations of Defense and Growth.[8] He writes:

Every human being has both sets of forces within him. One set clings to safety and defensiveness out of fear, tending to regress, hanging on to the past . . . afraid to take chances, afraid to jeopardize what he already has, afraid of independence, freedom, separation. The other set of forces impels him forward toward wholeness of self and uniqueness of self, toward full functioning of all his capacities, toward confidence in the

---

[6] J. P. Guilford, *A Revised Structure of Intellect*, Reports from the Psychological Laboratory, No. 19, Los Angeles: University of Southern California, April, 1957.

[7] See "The Highly Intelligent and the Highly Creative Adolescent: A Summary of Some Research Findings," *op. cit.*, p. 56.

[8] See "Occupational Choice and Cognitive Functioning: Career Aspirations of Highly Intelligent and of Highly Creative Adolescents," *op. cit.*, p. 122.

face of the external world at the same time that he can accept his deepest, real, unconscious Self ... This basic dilemma or conflict between the defensive forces and the growth trends I conceive to be existential, imbedded in the deepest nature of the human being, now and forever into the future. ... Therefore we can consider the process of healthy growth to be a never-ending series of free choice situations, confronting each individual at every point throughout his life, in which he must choose between the delights of safety and growth, dependence and independence ... Safety has both anxieties and delights; growth has both anxieties and delights.[9]

In these terms, the high IQ adolescent may be seen as preferring the anxieties and delights of "safety," the high Creativity adolescent the anxieties and delights of "growth."

We would maintain that the intellectual differences between these groups and the underlying psycho-social orientations have their source not only in the immediate school experience but in the family environment in which the adolescents grew up. The family environment of these students, at least as portrayed by the mothers' interviews, is consonant with the psycho-social formulations applied to the groups. The parents of the high IQ student tend to recall greater financial difficulties during their own childhood and hence, at least by inference, may be said to have experienced in the past, and perhaps the present, greater real or imagined personal insecurity than is true for the parents of the highly creative students. The high IQ parents seem to be more "vigilant" with respect to their children's behavior and their manifest academic performance. As compared with the parents of the highly creative adolescents, the parents of the high IQ students tend at once to be more critical of both their children and the school; it is as if their standards were always just one step ahead of attainment. Nor is their vigilance limited to concern for their child's educational progress. They appear equally concerned with the desirable qualities possessed by their children's friends. The qualities they would like to see in their children's friends, which may in a sense be conceived as projections of the qualities they would like to see in their own children, focus upon such immediately visible virtues as cleanliness, good manners, studiousness. In contrast, the parents of the creative adolescents focus upon less visible qualities such as the child's openness to experience, his values, and his interests and enthusiasms.

When these differences in the parents' attitudes and aspirations are combined with differences in educational specialization, the age discrepancy between father and mother, and the kind of reading material available in the home, the over-all impression of the high IQ family is one in which individual divergence is limited and risks minimized, the over-all impression of the high Creative family is one in which individual divergence is permitted and risks are accepted. In this sense, the concepts of Defense and Growth which were used to distinguish the high IQ adolescent and the high Creative adolescent, seem also useful in distinguishing between their family environment.

CONCLUSION

Several concluding comments seem in order, particularly since the type of data presented here lends itself rather easily to misinterpretation and overgeneralization. First, in describing the high IQ and the high Creativity adolescents, we do not intend to give the impression of the one as representing "good guys" and the other "bad guys." The distinction we are making is analytic not evaluative. Both convergent and divergent thinking are valuable in their separate ways. Second, in discussing the greater "vigilance" of the parents of the high IQ group, we do not intend to give support to the current unfortunate dichotomy between "bad" authoritarianism and "good" permissiveness. The issue is not all-or-none, either-or, but appropriate emphasis. Third, in adducing evidence for the greater "specialized education" and "bookishness" of the parents of the high IQ children as against the parents of the high Creativity children, we do not intend to suggest that the presence of books or specialized knowledge in the family leads inevitably to high

---

[9] A. H. Maslow, "Defense and Growth," *Merrill-Palmer Quarterly*, 3 (Fall, 1956), pp. 37–38.

IQ, the absence to high Creativity. It is not the presence of books or specialized knowledge but their use and meaning that make the difference. Finally, we should like to point out that at least as much by the issues raised as by the nature of the preliminary findings we have presented, the question of how types of cognition are shaped by types of family environment is a fruitful area for sociological examination.

Section Eight

Measurement and Individual Differences

In the first article of this section, Darrell Huff discusses statistics in a way never seen in college textbooks. Why are statistics important? How can they be used to mislead and misinform? What does the student need to know in order to become an intelligent *consumer* of statistics? This interesting and often amusing discussion of the subject should add to the student's initial understanding based on his reading of an introductory text in psychology and the lectures in his course.

The measurement of individual differences is considered in the second paper in this section. Professors Angoff and Anderson in this paper describe how tests are developed and standardized. In addition, they discuss some of the concepts associated with standardized tests such as norms and scaling. Following this paper, Henry Dyer discusses nine misconceptions about tests that often stand in the way of their proper use.

Among other things, Dyer points out that tests do not measure "native ability." In fact he says that such an inherent entity may not even exist, although studies such as those cited by Hirsch, below, support the idea. Misconceptions such as this often lead to the misuse of tests, and the result has been an increasing cry from critics that testing is a menace to education and should be dropped. Dyer, however, claims that this argument is specious. Rather than abandon the use of tests, he says, educators and others should learn to use them intelligently.

In the final paper, Jerry Hirsch notes that the organisms which psychologists study are intrinsically variable before they undergo differentiating experiences. But even though this is readily apparent to the geneticist, the author believes that the "opinion leaders" of two generations of psychologists literally excommunicated heredity from the behavioral sciences. Recently, however, new research and new methods of study have again focused the attention of behavioral scientists on the extent to which behavior may be genetically influenced.

PARLEZ-VOUS STATISTICS?

DARRELL HUFF

Carmel, California

"THERE ARE THREE KINDS OF LIES: lies, damned lies, and statistics."

These well-known words, attributed to Disraeli, represent a cynical view of statistical science. It is possible, of course, to lie with statistics. But abuses — and misuses — may easily stem from ignorance, misunderstanding or carelessness.

The position most of us have most of the time in relation to statistics is that of consumer. The analogy is almost literal truth. Consumption of faulty statistics, or over-hasty consumption of perfectly good statistics, can lead to a kind of mental indigestion. Its symptoms are hazy ideas and plain misconceptions leading to faulty judgments and, ultimately, to costly mistakes.

To reach a better understanding of how statistics functions, and of its limitations, weaknesses and dangers as well, let's look at statistics as a language. Like any language, it is both a means of communication and a way of thinking about things.

"Statistical thinking will one day be as necessary for efficient citizenship as the ability to read and write," wrote H. G. Wells, long ago. Like so many of Wells's bold predictions, this one has pretty much come true in our time.

Without the use of statistics the best of us must find it impossible — the human mind being limited in some respects and the human life span being all too short — to comprehend or talk about or reach decisions concerning things that come in large numbers. There lies the critical importance of statistics: It gives us power to deal with things that come in large numbers — like people, or dollars or atoms.

The tool of statistical understanding we use the most is the measure of central tendency. Its importance is shown by the place held in everyone's vocabulary by words like average, normal, usual, typical and common — all of which often, though by no means always, refer to a central tendency.

Most of the time when we speak of an average, what we have in mind is an arithmetic mean. It is familiar to all of us, and so is the method of deriving it by merely adding up all the terms and dividing by the number of them.

Since everyone understands the mean, it naturally gets used too much. It is a perfectly good measure for many things; in fact, it is indispensable. But unfortunately it is a highly deceptive measure of many other things, including some for which it is often used.

Good Arithmetic, Bad Statistics

Suppose, for example, you want to express the wage level in a small business. There are 10 production workers and a couple of clerical people, all earning between $75 and $120 a week. The proprietor pays himself a manager's salary — business being good at the moment — of $500 a week. The average salary, figured as an arithmetic mean, turns out to be about $122. Yet everyone in the place, with a single exception, is earning less than that. It is impeccable arithmetic but bad statistics, because it gives a misleading picture.

To get around this frequent problem a different kind of average was invented. It is called the median, and it, too, you meet almost every day. In any distribution of figures it is what you might refer to as the balance point. It is the middle figure in size if there is an odd number of terms; with an even number of terms there is no middle figure, so the midpoint between the two middle figures is the median. It is easiest to think of the median as the point below which half the distribution ranks.

When you meet a figure that is described as the average income of any group, you can be almost sure that it is a median, since this is what any reputable statistician would use for such a purpose most of the time.

Reprinted by permission from *THINK Magazine*, January, 1963, published by IBM. Copyright 1963 by International Business Machines Corporation.

283

Thus the Bureau of the Census, which prefers the term mean or median rather than average, came up in May of this year with the information that the median income of white families in California in 1959 was $6,857. This does not tell the whole story, but it tells quite a bit: Specifically, that half these families receive incomes below that figure and half above.

If the Bureau had been interested in impressing us with our prosperity rather than in imparting useful information, it could have done so by calculating the mean and calling it the average. Since that kind of average would be heavily weighted by the presence of a comparatively few very large incomes, it would be much bigger than the median.

Most income distributions are highly skewed. Draw a picture of a mass of figures that are equally distributed around their average and it will be symmetrical. It will be in the familiar shape of a bell. But a picture of a typical distribution of incomes will have a long tail on the right, representing a few very large incomes. Its shape will resemble that of half a teardrop split lengthwise with its nose to the left and its half-tail swooping to the right.

There are other situations in which neither mean nor median will serve.

Consider again a manufacturing plant, this time one in which the accident rate is a matter of concern. How could you describe the "average accident" in it if asked to do so?

You could, if you liked, find some quantitative factor about which to derive a mean or a median. It might be the number of man hours lost from each accident. Both mean and median would have some value for this purpose, but neither would tell management anything about the causes of the accidents.

The useful measure of central tendency here might be the mode. In a general way, this means just what it does in plain English: the most usual. Using this you could report the modal accident as, say, a crushed toe. That would be useful information, perhaps leading to introduction of metal-capped work shoes or some other specific accident preventive.

The mean, the median and the mode, then, are the three central measures you will most often meet as a businessman or citizen consumer of statistics. To avoid being misled, the first question to ask when confronted by an average is simply: What kind of average is this? The second is: How well does this type represent — or misrepresent — the data?

Even a properly chosen average cannot tell the whole story. Along with it you often need some indication of the range of figures on which the average is based. Otherwise you are still in a pretty good position to draw false conclusions.

Suppose you are planning the purchase of a bit of land on which to build a vacation house. You have narrowed your choice to a sea coast spot and one in the mountains, both of which you learn from weather bureau records have an average July maximum daily temperature of 78 degrees.

In which will you be more comfortable? The answer depends to a considerable extent upon a second important statistical measure: variation.

The measure of variation in common use today is the standard deviation. Mathematically it is a little complicate but in use it is easy to understand. The range from o standard deviation below the average to one standard dev tion above it will include approximately two-thirds of cases.

Applied to your alternative cabin sites, this measure w give valuable information. You might find that the standa deviation from 78 degrees is, for the sea coast location, degrees. For the mountain site it is 20 degrees. From t you can say that at the seashore on two days out of th in July the temperature will reach a maximum within comfortable range of 68 to 88 degrees. But at your mo tain spot two thirds of the days will vary within the wi range of 58 to 98. And, of course, it follows that one J day in three will be either colder than 58 or hotter than

The standard deviation has equal utility in connecti with all kinds of figures for which an average has been tained. It is useful to a shirt manufacturer in determin neck sizes to manufacture, to a buyer in comparing the c sistency of hardness of samples of steel from different sour of supply.

Other Clues in Standard Deviation

There are other helpful clues to be found in the stand deviation. Given a normal distribution, it tells you s more things about the total variation. Just as a sprea one standard deviation each way includes about two th (68 percent is slightly more exact) of the cases, a sprea two standard deviations each way will include approxima 95 percent. And three will include almost 100 percent

Another way of stating this last fact is this: The t range equals approximately six standard deviations.

Sampling studies lie behind a great part of the avera and other statistical figures that you encounter. They a necessity for reasons both of common sense and of c

Consider, for instance, the cost if Dr. Gallup's organ tion were to ask its questions of every American instea a sample of a few thousand.

A manufacturer of light bulbs naturally wishes to k the burning life of his product. But if he tested every b instead of a relatively tiny sample he would have noth left to sell.

The drawback to the sampling technique is that it o all too many opportunities to introduce errors resulting f badly chosen samples. People who do market and scien research and opinion polling carry on a constant ba against this source of bias. They do a remarkable job though, in the nature of things, they can never quite

Landon Over Roosevelt?

A famous instance of accidental bias, that of the las the old *Literary Digest* polls, has been a warning to polls ever since. Using a truly enormous sample — about ten lion people — the magazine predicted that in Novem 1936, it would be Landon over Roosevelt by more than to one. The sample, taken from lists of *Digest* subscri

PARLEZ-VOUS STATISTICS?

nd from telephone directories, was similar to one by which he magazine had successfully predicted outcomes of previous elections.

How, then, could it suddenly have gone so wrong?

Analysts later discovered that to an unprecedented degree voting in 1936 was along economic lines. By using a sample ot carefully selected from the whole voting population but merely from those relatively prosperous groups who subscribed to the *Digest* or had telephones, the editors had introduced a fatal bias.

For a more recent instance, analyze the leading paragraphs f a news story carried by a New York newspaper under the eading, "Doctors Reported for Security Plan."

"A recent poll in New Jersey indicates that most of the ountry's doctors would like to come under the Social Security Old Age and Survivors insurance program, according [a New Jersey source].

" . . . the poll, conducted by the Essex County Medical ociety, showed that New Jersey physicians favored inclusion y a 6-to-1 margin."

For a first source of bias, note that Essex County is assumed to represent the nation. It may, of course, but then gain it may not.

Reading the rest of the news story you find that the 6-to-1 fers to the doctors who returned a questionnaire post card. bout 78 percent did not answer. Is it safe to assume that ose who fired it into a wastebasket felt the same about e subject as those who took the trouble to send it in?

And there is a final relevant fact, omitted from the newsper account: The questionnaire was mailed along with a edical publication in which an article argued in favor of tending Social Security to doctors.

So the 6-to-1 opinion was hardly that of "most of the ountry's doctors." It might more realistically be described that of the 22 percent of Essex County, New Jersey, docrs who replied to a questionnaire accompanying an article voring one side of the subject.

There is a clear warning in these instances and in the numerable ones like them that appear regularly in print. hen presented with a statistic derived from a sampling dy, look closely at how the sample was chosen. Ask urself what factors may have operated to exclude certain oups.

Size of the sample is as significant as quality, and somenes it is even harder to judge. Useful research is often ssible with samples of a few dozen patients; and the whole pulation of the United States is adequately represented some opinion studies with a sample of a few hundred or ousand.

So when an early test of polio vaccine was set up with a mple of more than one thousand children, it seemed to be an impressively large scale. Vaccine was given to 450 ildren while 680 others in the community were left unated as controls. An epidemic came. And not one of the ccinated children contracted paralytic polio.

Not one of the control group did either.

What the experimenters had failed to take into account s the low incidence of paralytic polio even in an epidemic. ce the normal rate would have been only perhaps two cases in such a group, the experiment was doomed to mean inglessness from the start. That's why more recent work wit polio vaccine has been based on cases counted in the te thousands.

It is clear that we cannot judge the adequacy of sampl size on numbers alone. Nor is there any particular percen tage of the whole group that the sample must equal. Mathe matical methods are required.

The results of these you will find expressed as a leve of confidence or a statement of statistical significance.

Census Reports and Income

You might, for example, be reading a census report o the median income level of a certain group of families. I this is a sampling study you will naturally — and most prop erly — wonder how accurate the figure is. Your answer wi lie in a statement taking a form like this: "The chances ar 19 out of 20 that the average is correct within a range o $100 either way."

Why plus or minus $100? Why 19 out of 20?

Since the income figure we are given — say, $5,000 a yea — is only an estimate based on a sample, the true figure i almost surely something else. This true figure is the on that would have been obtained if every person in the popu lation in question had been interviewed to find the average

It seems that the size and nature of our particular sampl is such that statisticians have calculated its standard erro to be $50. Two standard errors then come to $100. It i a statistical fact that two standard errors in either directio must include approximately 95 percent of the possible range

Why 19 out of 20? You will recognize that as just an other way of saying 95 percent.

If this sounds familiar it is because standard error i analagous to standard deviation, which we were talking abou a few paragraphs back. The difference is that what we ar now dealing with is not variability within data but error du to sampling. Standard deviation and standard error are simi lar mathematically but they apply to different situations.

Correlation is another statistical measure in whose nam strange and wonderful things are often reported by unwar observers. All a correlation can be is a mathematical state ment of the degree to which specified phenomena tend to g together. It is in assuming that therefore one must hav caused the other that we most often go astray. You wi recognize this as just another form of the ancient fallacy i logic — that when one thing follows another it must hav been produced by it, or *post hoc, ergo propter hoc.*

Correlation: Cars and Accidents

What statistical correlation has added to this is a quan titative aspect. When there is no discoverable relationshi between two occurrences the correlation is said to be zerc If an increase in one is accompanied by a decrease in th other, the correlation is negative; it will be expressed a a decimal lying between zero and −1. The more usuall positive correlation is expressed as a decimal between zer and 1.

A correlation that is close to 1 indicates that one occurrence is almost invariably accompanied by the other — the kind of thing we often speak of as a "one-to-one relationship." A typical example would be the correlation between the number of cars on the road on a given weekend and the number of accidents. We know that as traffic density is doubled the number of accidents will approximately double also if other conditions remain unchanged.

The deceptive kind of correlation is the one that is mathematically true but essentially spurious. A classic instance is a demonstrably close numerical relationship between the salaries of Presbyterian ministers in Massachusetts and the price of rum in Havana.

But which has caused which? Are the ministers supporting the rum trade — or benefiting from it? The truth, of course, is that those salaries and those prices have both risen right along with all other prices and salaries as a part of the historic and world-wide increase in the price of practically everything over the last century.

The thing we must all keep in mind here is that things may consistently occur together without one having caused the other at all.

So far we've been talking about the use and meaning in some of the major statistical tools — the measures of central tendency, of variation, of confidence, of correlation — and some of the pitfalls of sampling.

A Working Girl's Salary

The *presentation* of statistical material has its traps, too. One of these is the attempt to make more of a conclusion than the data warrant.

One form this takes is impossible precision. When you swallow an overprecise figure you are led to believe that you have learned more than you have, more, in fact, than anyone in the world actually knows about the subject at hand.

An economic foundation once announced that it had determined that a working girl living with her family in a large city required an income of $40.13 a week to maintain a decent standard of living.

Karl Marx long ago calculated that a 10-hour working day in a mill breaks down to "necessary labour = 3-31/33 hours and surplus labour = 6-2/33."

How much of Marx's wonderfully precise figures are bluff becomes apparent only when their basis is examined. It turns out to include the loosest of approximations: "We assume the waste to be 6% . . . the wear and tear we put at 10%. . . ."

No one can tell you to the penny how much it costs a girl to live. Yet how much more impressive $40.13 is than the more realistic "about $40," which is all the precision th[e] data could possibly support.

You'll need equal skepticism when you present, or stud[y] statistical material in pictorial form.

Charts and pictographs are an invaluable aid to unde[r]standing quickly what might be very difficult to comprehe[nd] from figures alone. Equally easily, however, they can mi[s]lead the eye and the brain.

What might be called the moneybags fallacy is among th[e] most prevalent. Given two incomes of, say, $50 and $10[0] a week, how can you represent them pictorially? The logic[al] thing is to use moneybags, one twice as big as the othe[r.] But that is not as simple to do as it sounds.

If one bag is made twice as tall as the other, it will al[so] be twice as wide and it will occupy not twice but four tim[es] the area on the page. That's bad enough, but what t[he] beholder visualizes is even worse: A real, three-dimension[al] moneybag that is twice as high as its neighbor will have n[ot] twice or even four times the volume, but eight times.

The result is utter confusion — and a gross exaggeratio[n.]

When you see this kind of representation, judge by t[he] raw figures alone. And if you need to make such a repr[e]sentation, fall back on an alternative method. Show the $5[0] by one moneybag and the $100 by two of the same size. [Or] have two stacks of dollars drawn, one containing 50 uni[ts,] the other 100.

Tricky Line Graphs

Line graphs are no less tricky in another way. When y[ou] meet one of these, look first for the part that may not [be] there — the base line. To say to your eye what the figu[re] should say to your mind, a line graph must begin at ze[ro.] If it starts at some other point — which it often will do in [an] unfortunate attempt to save space — you must visualize [the] part that isn't there.

What it all boils down to is that statistics, like any oth[er] language, can be abused.

In the hands of the careless user, or of one who with [the] best will in the world simply doesn't know what he is doi[ng,] the results will be as false as mishandled words.

In business, in our reading, as students of civilization, [as] citizens, we are all consumers of statistics. It is up to all [of] us to read statistical material with skepticism and sophi[sti]cation. By applying some of the principles discussed he[re] we can avoid the condition that Artemus Ward once warn[ed] us against: It's not so much our ignorance that gets us i[n] trouble, he pointed out, as "the things we know that a[in't] so."

THE STANDARDIZATION OF EDUCATIONAL AND PSYCHOLOGICAL TESTS

WILLIAM H. ANGOFF
SCARVIA B. ANDERSON
Educational Testing Service, Princeton, New Jersey

THE DEVELOPMENT and application of standardized tests probably represent one of the major contributions to educational progress in the last fifty years. But its success has not come without criticism; indeed, some of the success would not have been possible without the constructive criticism which has spurred test makers into improving their procedures and seeking new methods of assessing human mental processes. Some of the least constructive of the criticisms have stemmed from a fundamental view that testing is motivated by a mechanistic philosophy by which all men are cast into one mold, without regard for their essential individuality. The test makers, on the other hand, take the view that not only do they *not* disregard the essential differences among individuals, but that these differences are precisely what they seek to understand. They also maintain that the pursuit of this understanding is best accomplished by adopting the methods of scientific inquiry, by which they imply that all aspects of measurement be held constant and uniform, except for the individual's own performance. Only then can the variability in performance from one person to another be taken as evidence of the *abilities* of the individuals, and of nothing else.

The test makers will also take the position that, because it provides uniform methods and uniform standards for everyone, standardized testing necessarily yields fair and equitable assessments of performance for everyone. Thus, the process of standardization permeates all aspects of a test: the construction, administration, scoring, reporting, and evaluation of test results.

Test Construction

Ordinarily a standardized test poses the same questions for all students. The test maker attempts to write questions that will be regarded in the same way by all students who take the test. He pretests his questions in an effort to weed out ambiguities that result in different meanings to different people. (Pretests are conducted for other reasons as well: to insure the proper degree of difficulty for the test and the highest degree of reliability.) In most cases, he writes a variety of test questions in order to sample as widely as possible the distribution of knowledge in the specified area of the test. In this way, he avoids giving special advantage to a student for whom the test is heavily weighted with questions in which he happens to have special competence or for which he did special in-

Reprinted from *Illinois Journal of Education*, February, 1963, with permission from Superintendent of Public Instruction, State of Illinois.

tensive preparation in an attempt to "beat the test". In order to achieve a test which gives uniform opportunity to all students, the test maker asks not one or three or five questions, but fifty or a hundred, because only with large numbers of questions can he be confident of achieving an adequate sampling of knowledge. He also writes questions which will test specifically what he intends to test, say knowledge and understanding of the events leading up to World War II—not "test wiseness," not general intelligence, not handwriting ability, nor neatness, nor English composition. This is not to say, of course, that some of these other characteristics are unimportant; but fair assessment demands that they must be measured separately.

Administration and Scoring

The test maker also prescribes that the test be administered under uniform conditions—the same directions for all, the same presentation of questions, the same time limits, and, insofar as possible, the same favorable environmental conditions: proper light, ventilation, and temperature; convenient working space; general quiet, with freedom from extraneous disturbances.

Uniformity is also achieved in the scoring process. By restricting the nature of the student's responses and by removing from the task any opportunity the student may seize upon to bias the grading of his paper, the test maker insures virtually perfect scoring reliability. On a subjectively scored test, the teacher's ratings can be influenced by such diverse factors as neatness and legibility, good or poor prose, his own fatigue or boredom with the scoring task, his general feeling of well-being, and, not of least importance, *his prior biases toward the student*. The standardized test, on the other hand, is scored only for the student's performance on the questions that are asked him. Again, this is not to say that such factors as prose style or legibility of handwriting should not be tested. But if they are considered important enough to be tested, they should be tested independently. They should not appear as unreliable riders to another purpose, to be considered as part of the score or not, depending on the particular mood and predilections of the person who happens to be scoring the paper at the time. As in the administration of the tests, what is sought here is a fair and equitable score, uncontaminated by factors that can only be considered as irrelevant or biasing in terms of the stated purpose of the test.

Of course, all standardized tests are not "multiple-choice" tests. There are numerous instances in which a student is asked an "open-ended" question, as in the Stanford-Binet, the Wechsler-Bellevue, and the Interlinear Section of the College Board English Composition Test. In such cases, the rules for scoring are agreed upon in advance by a group of experts and set down to be followed rigidly in the scoring process. Thus, even with tests that call for some subjectivity in scoring, attempts are made, in the standardized test, to reduce to a minimum the influence of extraneous factors and to set uniform standards to be applied to all examinees without bias.

Scaling

Standardization is also achieved in the development of an appropriate score scale system. Very frequently tests are constructed in more than one form—to discourage students from memorizing the questions either for their own benefit on retest or to help other students achieve higher scores, to avoid the effects of practice in studies of educational change, and to allow a second measurement when the validity of the first is open to question. Even when the various forms are constructed according to common specifications and precautions are taken to adopt an item-sampling scheme that will yield a similar "mix" of items in all forms, there are almost certain to be small differences between forms. Occasionally the differences are large, not only with respect to the general level of talent for which the forms are appropriate, but also with respect to the range of talent for which they are appropriate. In such cases it would be grossly unfair to compare the raw score earned by one student who is given an easier form with the raw score earned by another student who is given a more difficult form. Therefore, in order to correct for differences between forms and to provide scores that are independent of the particular form that happened to be administered in any instance, scores on the various forms of a test are equated—or "calibrated"—and converted to a common reporting scale. (In order to avoid confusion this scale is made independent and different from the raw-score system for any single form.) Then, within the limitations imposed by the reliability of the equating method, one can be confident that a student's score was unaffected by the difficulty of the particular form he took. Teachers, admissions officers, and counselors are relieved of the obligation of taking into consideration the difficulty characteristic of each test form.

There are other advantages to equating. If the reporting scale is maintained intact and without change over a period of time during which new forms are introduced, it is possible to trace the quality of successive groups of examinees, to make studies of trends, and to compare individuals and groups tested at different times, in different places, and for different purposes.

The methods by which a scale is established and the methods by which it is maintained in the face of multiple forms constitute a sizable field of study by themselves. Frequently, a representative group of individuals ("representative" in terms of the population for which the test is designed) is tested to become the "standard group" on whom the scale is based. In later uses of the test, the "standard group," whose average performance provides the focal point of the scale, is used as the basic reference or normative group for purposes of evaluating individual scores. This procedure expresses the view that the "standard group" gives normative meaning to the scale. Multiple forms of the test that are introduced at later times are equated, by procedures to be described below, to the scale defined by the original group, a process which allows scores on all of the forms to be reported in terms of this single standard scale.

There are other approaches to the problem of scale definition. One of these is based on the philosophy that because of changes in the population, it is not always possible to give the scale lasting normative meaning. Moreover, even in those instances when the characteristics of the group may be expected to remain fairly constant, there is some question whether the scale should have any normative meaning or whether it should be a purely arbitrary scale of measurement, like the commonly used scales of inches, pounds, and Fahrenheit. The proponents of this view maintain that a measurement should be just a measurement and no more; that the evaluation of that measurement, as in the measurement of physical objects should come from other sources: from continued experience and increased familiarity with the scale and from comparison with the performance of groups of individuals who are either known to the test user or easily characterized for him.

The methods of equating two forms of a test all presuppose that the conversion of scores from one form to another involves simply an adjustment of units to account for differences in difficulty of the forms. Ideally this adjustment would be determined by administering both forms to all members of a group and observing the differences in performance on the forms—after first removing the effect of practice or fatigue on the form administered second. Variations on this approach, necessitated by practical considerations, include a) dividing a large group of individuals into two random halves, administering one form to each half, and observing the differences in the statistics on the test form that each group took; and b) administering the same "equating" test to two groups, each of which has been tested with one of the major test forms. Here, too, the differences in performance on the two test forms are observed, but not until adjustments are made for any differences in the two groups on the equating test.

In general, all of the methods of equating are used for the same purpose: to build and maintain a rigid standard scale system which will allow the greatest degree of flexibility in making comparisons and evaluations—from individual to individual, from group to group, and from one time to another for both individuals and groups.

Norming

An essential characteristic of the test standardization process is the presentation of reference data for appropriate norms groups. In some cases, as was just noted, the characteristics of the norms sample are built directly into the test scale itself. Tests which yield I.Q. scores fall into this category. In other cases, an arbitrary scale is maintained, and the test is accompanied by norms appropriate for the principal uses for which the test is intended.

Tests designed for general surveys of ability, aptitude, and achievement are frequently related meaningfully to "national" norms collected by grade or age. But for these tests and for other tests in specific areas, other types of norms may be desirable—norms differentiated by sex, geography, type of curriculum, rural-urban-suburban, public-private-parochial, etc. It is then the task of the test user to choose the appropriate norms from those that are available, and apply them in evaluating the performance of the individuals he has tested.

The norms that are developed for a test may be as elaborate as the test demands or the test-maker can afford. The process of norms development, however, is fundamentally the same, regardless of the number and type of norms that are constructed. The test maker defines the characteristics of the population from which he decides to sample, and proceeds to select a sample from this population which will be as nearly representative of the population as possible. Ideally, this would mean selecting all individuals at random from the population; however, for practical reasons other procedures are ordinarily employed. Typically, the schools in the nation are grouped into categories or strata, homogeneous by type, size, socio-economic level, or location, or by combinations of these characteristics; and entire schools are chosen at random from these strata. Sometimes, multi-stage cluster sampling techniques are employed, involving several steps: random sampling of communities, random sampling of schools within those communities, random sampling of classes within those schools, and, occasionally, random sampling of students from those classes. When possible, the methods of stratified sampling and cluster sampling are combined to yield norms samples that are not only economical as to size, but also possess the desired levels of reliability and representativeness.

When any particular student is to be evaluated, the best comparison group is a group of students with whom he is in competition or with whom he aspires to compete (or a group as similar to one of these as possible). Thus, if a test is to be used for educational guidance, an appropriate norms group consists of those students with whom the student will be in competition if he undertakes a particular course of study. If the test is to be used for selection at a given college, the appropriate norms group is the group of candidates with whom the student is competing for a place. If a test is to be used for evaluation of achievement in a specific school course, then the ideal group is the rest of the class.

Increasingly, the major test publishers are coming around to the point of view that the most valuable norms group may be one that is locally assembled by the test user himself. This does not relieve the publisher of the responsibility of providing more general norms; however, his norms may be considered only supplementary to the data collected on the local group.

Other Test Characteristics

Finally, the producer of a standardized test will make available to the test user, for his information in selecting and using the instrument, a set of data describing the various characteristics of the test: the use to which it is intended or for which it is recommended; an outline of the test content; the item difficulties and discrimination indices; data on the speededness of the test; its reliability and standard error of measurement; its predictive validity for various pertinent criteria; the pattern of growth, if the test is designed for use at more than one level; relationships with other tests or forms; and, finally, an evaluation of the strengths and weaknesses of the test for various purposes to which it might be put. The makers of standardized test are committed to the methods of scientific inquiry; they must also assume the obligations of science—making the results of their inquiry available to the public.

The procedures involved in the process of standardizing tests, as they are discussed here, are not by any means intended to constitute a set of minimum criteria for a test to be considered "standardized." Some highly useful tests follow the procedures of standardization in somewhat different ways from those that are outlined here. However, aside from the details of procedure, it is certainly reasonable to say that, taken together, the characteristic features of a standardized test are what make it a scientific measuring instrument, capable of precision and predictive of future achievement. For both human and practical reasons, the standardized test is a necessary outcome of the philosophy of a modern democratic society, in which large masses of individuals, competing for educational awards, or simply seeking better self-understanding, assemble for an objective, unbiased evaluation of their abilities. No other method that we know of today can provide measurement for the tremendous numbers of individuals who demand objective consideration of their talents. Certainly no other method that we know of today can accomplish this measurement as equitably as the standardized test.

… 33

IS TESTING A MENACE TO EDUCATION?

HENRY S. DYER

Educational Testing Service, Princeton, New Jersey

The title of this talk is a question: "Is Testing a Menace to Education?" Knowing who I am and what I do for a living, you would have every reason to believe that I am going to answer the question with a resounding, "No!" But you would be dead wrong, for I am going to answer the question with a tentative, "Yes, but—". Yes, testing *is* a menace to education, *but* probably not for the reasons you think. It is a menace to education primarily because tests are misunderstood and test results are misused by too many educators. In his recent book called *The Schools*, Martin Mayer speaks of testing as a "necessary evil." I disagree. It is not *necessarily* evil. Tests *could* be a blessing to education if only teachers and counselors and educational administrators would divest themselves of a number of misconceptions about what tests can and cannot do and would learn to use test results more cautiously and creatively in the educational process.

There are nine principal misconceptions that seem to stand in the way of the appropriate use of tests. Let's look at them one by one.

The *first* misconception is the notion that aptitude or intelligence tests measure something called "native ability," something fixed and immutable within the person that determines his level of expectation for all time. I am not prepared to say that such an inherent entity does not exist. The chances are it does. Studies in genetics certainly support the idea, and so do many psychological studies, especially the studies of twins reared separately under different conditions. But intelligence or aptitude tests do not *measure* such an entity—at least not directly, and certainly not in any interpretable manner. What intelligence tests do measure is the individual's performance on certain types of mental tasks. They measure this performance a long time after the child has first entered the world. The kinds of mental tasks that appear in any intelligence or aptitude test are clearly the kinds that a student *learns* to perform from his experiences in the world around him—experiences in school, at home, and elsewhere. The amount of learning based on such experiences may depend on many things that can vary enormously from one child to another—the number and quality of books available in his home, the kind of talk he hears, the richness and variety of his surroundings, the vividness and emotional quality of the thousands of happenings in his life from day to day. It is absurd to suppose that a child's score on an intelligence test by-passes all these factors that facilitate or

---

This is a reprint of a paper presented to the National Association of Secretaries of State Teachers Association, Atlantic City, June 24, 1961, and which was published in *New York State Education*, the Journal of the New York State Teachers Association, Vol. 49, October, 1961.

impede his learning. It is absurd to suppose that such a score gets directly at the brains he was born with.

I prefer to think of an intelligence test as essentially indistinguishable from an achievement test—that is, as a measure of how well, at a given point in time, a student can perform certain well-defined tasks. The main difference between the tasks in a so-called achievement test and those in a so-called intelligence test is, generally speaking, that the tasks in an achievement test are usually learned over a relatively short period of time and those in an intelligence test are learned over a relatively long period of time.

The consequences of thinking of an aptitude test as measuring some immutable determiner of student performance can be pretty serious. In the first place, such thinking encourages the dangerous idea that one can, from an aptitude score, decide once and for all at a fairly early age what kind and level of educational or vocational activity a student is fitted for. It nurtures that hardy perennial, for instance, that if a student has an IQ of 115 or better he ought to prepare for college, and if his IQ is below 115 he ought to make other plans. This, despite all the studies which have shown over and over again that an IQ may be highly variable for a given student, that colleges vary enormously in the quality of students they enroll, and that some low scorers succeed in college while some high scorers fail. I have often wondered how many educational crimes are annually committed on the strength of the theory that intelligence tests measure something they cannot possibly measure.

A second consequence of thinking of an intelligence test as measuring something unaffected by learning is almost as serious. It is the conception that a student with a high aptitude score and low achievement scores (or low grades in school) is an "underachiever" who is "not working up to capacity." This is another hardy perennial. It was questioned thirty years ago, but it is back with us again, and it can lead to some rather distressing treatment of individual pupils. The diagnosis goes that a student with a high aptitude score and low achievement scores is "unmotivated," or "lazy," or suffering from some sort of emotional disturbance. Granted that there may be some grounds for such diagnoses, nevertheless, they are scarcely inferrable from the discrepancy in scores alone. And some new and possibly more useful insights about such students might be forthcoming if one frankly regarded the discrepancies simply as differences in performance on one kind of achievement test as compared to another. To ask why a student has learned to answer the questions on a mathematical aptitude test better than he has learned to answer those in an achievement test in algebra is likely to lead to a much more fruitful line of inquiry than will result from the global and rather fuzzy assumption that the student is simply "unmotivated" or "uninterested" in algebra.

Finally, the idea that aptitude tests are supposed to measure native ability leads to the persistent and embarrassing demand that they should be "culture free," that if they are, as they must be, affected by the student's background of experience in school and at home, then, *ipso facto*, they are *"unfair"* to the underprivileged. I wish we could get it *out* of people's heads that tests are unfair to the underprivileged and get it into their heads that it is the hard facts of social circumstance and inadequate education that are unfair to them. Tests inevitably reflect the opportunities a student has had for learning. If educational opportunities are unequal, the test results will also be unequal.

A *second* misconception about tests is the notion that a prediction made from a test score, or from a series of test scores, or from test scores plus other quantifiable data, are, or should be, perfectly accurate, and that if they are not, the tests must be regarded as no good. This fallacy arises from a confused conception of what constitutes prediction. There are some people, maybe most people, who think of prediction as simply an all-or-none, right-or-wrong business. If a test score predicts that Johnny will get B in American History, the score is right if he actually gets a B; it is wrong if he gets a B— or a C. I suppose this is a legitimate way of thinking about prediction in certain circumstances, but it is scarcely fair to the test and it may well be unfair to Johnny. A more meaningful and useful way of thinking about a prediction is to regard it as a statement of the odds. For instance, a given test score might predict that Johnny has 8 chances in ten of getting a grade of B or better in American History, or 3 chances in a hundred of flunking the course. This approach recognizes that in forecasting future events, especially human events, we never have sufficient information to be sure of being right every time, but we do have information, in the form of test scores and other data, which, if appropriately organized, can help us make better decisions than would be possible without them.

A *third* misconception I wish to deal with is that standardized test scores are infallible or perfectly reliable. Reliability, I remind you, has to do with the degree to which the score of an individual stands still on successive testings. It rarely occurs to the uninitiated that a test can never be more than a *sample* of a student's performance and that, in consequence, the score on any test is afflicted with sampling error. To the man-in-the-street, to many teachers, school administrators, and parents, who have never reflected on the problem, a score is a score is a score, and they are shocked to find that when a student takes one test today and an alternate form of the same test tomorrow, his score can change. Anyone who deals with a test score must always be conscious that such a score, like any sort of measurement whatever, is clouded with uncertainty, that it is never more than an estimate of the truth.

A *fourth* misconception about tests is the assumption that an achievement test measures all there is to measure in any given subject matter area—that an achievement test in history, for example, measures everything a high school student should know about the facts of history and how to deal with them. It never seems to occur to some people that the content of a standardized achievement test in any particular subject matter area may be only partially related to what a specific course of study in that area may call for.

Let me cite two instances. Some time back a study was made of the relative merits of teaching chemistry with and without laboratory practice. The findings of the study showed that there was no appreciable difference between students who had had laboratory practice and those who had not. Both groups performed equally well on the achievement test in chemistry which was used as the criterion. It apparently never occurred to the investigators that the chemistry achievement test they were using contained no material appropriate for assessing the kinds of learning peculiar to laboratory instruction. The outcome could have been forecast in advance, since the test measured only those matters that both groups could be expected to learn from the textbooks and classroom discussion to which they were both exposed.

The second instance has to do with a supervisor of French instruction who called our office one day to ask us to recommend a good French test. We told her what we always tell such inquirers, namely, that we could not possibly recommend a good French test *for her purposes* until we knew what the French instruction consisted of and what its objectives were. We suggested that she look at several such tests and study the content of each in order to decide which one came closest to what she was trying to accomplish with her students. This suggestion struck her as a thoroughly novel and brilliant idea!

If people will only take the trouble to look critically at the insides of achievement tests and not just at their covers, they will almost certainly find that even the test best suited to their purposes still fails to sample *all* the types of learning that are sought in a given subject, or even all the most important types of learning. And it may also often include matters that the student is not expected to know. The consequence is, of course, that on a particular standardized achievement test a student may look considerably better or considerably worse than he really is, and decisions based on his score may miss the boat by a considerable margin.

A *fifth* misconception is that an achievement test can measure only a pupil's memory for facts. This used to be true. But a good modern achievement test gets at far more than a command of facts alone; it usually measures in addition the pupil's skill in reasoning with the facts he remembers and also his skill in reasoning with facts newly presented to him. It is this introduction into achievement tests of the requirement to reason, to cope with problems, to think clearly, critically, and even creatively that helps to blur the distinction between aptitude and achievement tests. The modern achievement test recognizes that as students come up through the grades they are, or ought to be, learning to think as well as to know. It recognizes also that there may be many different kinds of thinking to measure, depending upon the subject matter in which the thinking is required. The result is that a well-conceived battery of achievement tests gives the same sort of information one would get from a general intelligence test plus a good deal more.

A *sixth* misconception has to do with profiles of achievement or aptitude scores. This misconception is that a profile of scores summarizes clearly and efficiently a considerable amount of reliable information about the relative strengths and weaknesses of an individual. Test technicians have been worrying about this problem for a long time. They have inveighed repeatedly against the use of profile charts on the grounds that they are often grossly misleading, that the differences they depict—even when they appear large—may be, and usually are, unreliable differences, that the score scales used for the several tests in the profile may not be comparable, that the several measures which show on the profile may have the appearance of being highly independent measures when, in fact, many of them may be highly correlated—in short, that the apparent clarity and efficiency of a test score profile is really an illusion covering up all sorts of traps and pitfalls in score interpretation which even the most wary can scarcely avoid. Yet the profile chart is still in much demand and is in wide use, primarily I suppose because it is extraordinarily convenient. Mere administrative convenience is hardly sufficient justification for hiding confusion under a false coat of simplicity. Good test interpretation takes mental effort, a bit of imagination and some willingness to cope with complexity.

A *seventh* misconception is that interest inventories measure some kind of basic orientation of a student irrespective of the kinds of experiences to which he has been or will be exposed. Let me cite just one example of where this sort of muddy thinking can lead. A presumably well-trained guidance counselor in a high school where the large majority of students go on to college was confronted by a girl with top-notch scholastic standing in all of the college preparatory subjects. Her parents were college trained people; they had always expected that their daughter would go to a liberal arts college; the daughter had always enthusiastically entertained the same idea. The counselor, however, was apparently bewitched by one of the girl's scores on an interest inventory which indicated that her major interest was in clerical work. Disregarding all other evidence in the situation, the counselor insisted that the girl was unfitted for the work of a liberal arts college and would be happy only in a secretarial school. Tears on the part of the child, anger on the part of the parents, and hell-to-pay all around. Certainly interest test scores are useful in promoting thought and self-analysis, but certainly also the tests are scarcely capable of probing deeply enough into an individual's past and future to warrant anything approaching the dogmatism which characterized the counselor I have described.

The *eighth* misconception is that on a personality test an individual reveals deep and permanent temperamental characteristics of which he himself may be unaware. I suppose there is nothing about the whole testing business that frightens me more than this one. Anyone close to the research in personality testing who has any critical sense at all knows that we have still barely scratched the surface of a field whose dimensions are still far from defined. To put it perhaps a little too strongly, personality tests—the inventories, the projective tests, all of them—are scarcely beyond the tea-leaf-reading stage. To be sure, there is some interesting—even exciting—research going on in the area, but none of it yet adds up to tests that can be trusted as evidence leading to important decisions about children.

There are four major weaknesses in personality tests. First, they purport to measure traits such as introversion-extraversion, neurotic tendency, gregariousness, tolerance for ambiguity, and the like—all of which are highly fuzzy concepts, to say the least, and for none of which there are any agreed upon definitions. There is not even any general agreement on what we mean by the word "personality" itself. How can you describe or classify a person meaningfully with a test whose scores do not themselves have any clear or rigorous meaning?

Secondly, it is characteristic of current personality tests that the behavior they sample is essentially superficial nonsignificant behavior. By this I mean when a subject answers such a question as "Do you often daydream?" his response of "Yes" or "No" may well be nothing more than a purely random phenomenon quite unconnected with any of his habitual behavior tendencies—and this, even though he may be trying as hard as he can to be honest and cooperative. The whole essence of the measurement problem is to secure reliable samples of human behavior under standardized conditions which will have strong correlates with the universe of behavior an individual habitually exhibits in his waking life. The personality tests currently available have yet to demonstrate that they can provide such samples of behavior.

Thirdly, even if we were able to establish some meaningful personality traits, we still know little or nothing about their stability. We still don't know whether an introvert at age fifteen may not turn into an extrovert by the time he is twenty-two.

Finally, of course, practically all personality tests can be faked. I proved to my own satisfaction how fakable such tests are when I gave one to a class I was once teaching. I asked the students to take a personality inventory twice—once to prove that they were thoroughly well-adjusted people, and once to prove that they were ready for a mental institution. The first set of scores showed that the whole class was a bunch of apple-cheeked extroverts; the second set showed that they were all nuts.

Please do not misunderstand me. I take a very dim view of current personality tests, and I think the general public is being much too frequently taken in by the mumbo-jumbo that goes with them. On the other hand, I am very much in favor of as much solid research as we can possibly get into the fundamental dynamics of human behavior, for we shall never be in full command of the educational process until we have far more understanding than we now have of what makes children tick. There are glimmerings of hope, but we are not out of the woods yet, and who can tell when we will be? In the meantime, let's not kid ourselves by putting our trust in gimmicks.

The *ninth* and final misconception is this; that a battery of tests can tell all one needs to know in making a judgment about a student's competence, present and potential, and about his effectiveness as a human being. The fact of the matter is that no test or series of tests now available is capable of giving the total picture of any child. Tests can illuminate many areas of his development; they can suggest something about his strengths and weaknesses, they can show in certain respects how he stands among his peers. But there are still many important aspects of learning and human development where we must still rely upon the observation and judgment of teachers if we are to get something that approaches a complete description of the child as a functioning individual. Any evaluation of the pupil that relies solely on test scores is bound to be incomplete and sometimes seriously misleading. There are subtle but supremely important human elements in the teaching-learning situation that no combination of tests yet devised is able to capture. Such elements are elusive, but if we ever lose sight of them, the educational process in all its ramifications will become something less than the exciting human enterprise it should always be.

Well, these are the nine misconceptions which I think most frequently lead to wide misuse of tests and test results. Some of our brasher critics have argued that, since tests are so widely misused, they do constitute a menace to sound education and, therefore, should be abolished. This argument is specious. It is the same as saying that automobiles should be abolished because they are a menace to human life when reckless drivers are at the wheel. Or it is the same as saying that the manufacture of soap should be prohibited because too many kids use it to mark up store windows on Hallowe'en. Or it is the same as saying that teachers should be abolished because too many of them make psychometric hash out of marks and test scores.

In any case, I think it is highly unlikely that tests will be abolished, anymore than that textbooks will be abolished. Too many schools have discovered that, menace or not, they cannot operate effectively without them. Over the last six years, according to the American Textbook Publishers Institute, the number of tests sold to the schools has risen from under 6 million to over 13.5 million. Clearly tests are here to stay. The problem is not one of doing away with tests and testing but of getting people to use tests intelligently. When this happens testing will cease to be a mere administrative convenience or, worse still, a burden on the souls of teachers and pupils; it will become an effective instrument for vitalizing the total educational process and for helping to insure that in these days of skyrocketing enrollments the individual pupil will not be lost in the shuffle.

BEHAVIOR GENETICS AND INDIVIDUALITY UNDERSTOOD

Behaviorism's counterfactual dogma blinded the behavioral sciences to the significance of meiosis.

JERRY HIRSCH
University of Illinois

Individual differences are no accident. They are generated by properties of organisms as fundamental to behavioral science and biology as thermodynamic properties are to physical science. Much research, however, fails to take them into account. The behavioral sciences have attempted to erect a superstructure without paying sufficient attention to its foundation. A uniformity of expression over individuals, and even across species, has too often been assumed for behaviors under study. The uniformity assumption is explicitly incorporated into a spate of mathematical models that have been developed to formalize the study of behavior: Bush and Mosteller (*1*), for example, built theirs for "organisms that can be considered 'identical' at the start of an experiment. . . ." Rosner (*2*) speaks of "a fundamental attitude" which keeps psychophysics (*3*) "oriented toward the sources of uniformity in behavior." In this article I consider some effects that such assumptions about heredity, individuality, and behavior have had on the behavioral sciences.

Three Approaches to Behavior

In the study of behavior, three points of view can be distinguished. (i) Only common properties of behavior are studied among individuals and species. (ii) Only common properties of behavior are studied among individuals, while both similarities and characteristic differences are studied among species. (iii) Similarities and differences are studied among individuals, populations, and species.

The first view prevails when an organism is used as a tool for studying behavioral correlates of stimulus conditions, reinforcement schedules, deprivation regimens, pharmacological agents, or physiological mechanisms. It is hopefully assumed that the form of any relation observed—for example, that between stimulus and response—will have universal generality. The organism's role is essentially that of an analyzer, like the role of the Geissler tube in physics. In their illuminating discussion "The misbehavior of organisms," the Brelands (*4*), drawing on over 14 years of faithful application of the methods and assumptions of behaviorism, show that behaviorism also assumes "that the animal comes to the laboratory as a virtual *tabula rasa,* that species differences are insignificant, and that all responses are about equally conditionable to all stimuli." They relate (*4*) a history of "egregious failures" which they feel "represent a clear and utter failure of conditioning theory."

From the second viewpoint the behavior of animals is as characteristic of their species as is their form. This view prevails in ethologically oriented studies—for example, studies of such instincts as reproductive, parental, or territorial behavior. All members of a species are assumed to manifest a given behavior pattern, in some typical way. In Mayr's cogent analysis (*5*) this represents typological thinking whose replacement "by population thinking is perhaps the greatest conceptual revolution . . . in biology."

The third approach characterizes behavior genetics: the study of the relations between the genetic architecture of a taxon and the distributions of its

---

Reprinted from *Science,* Vol. 142, No. 3598, December 13, 1963. Copyright 1963 by the American Association for the Advancement of Science.

behavioral phenotypes. It employs the methods of both the behavioral sciences and genetics. The growth of this field can be attributed to protest against the counterfactual uniformity postulate, combined with the realization that we can now have a description and analysis of behavior based on a deeper understanding of the materials on which the behavioral sciences make their observations.

The key to our present understanding of the structure of life came during the first half of this century, from investigations of transmission cytogenetics (6) and population cytogenetics (7). Through study of cell division and reproduction (mitosis, meiosis, and fertilization), together with statistical analysis of variations in the expression of traits among offspring of specified matings, transmission cytogenetics gave us our first picture of the fundamental units of life (genes and chromosomes) and of the variation-generating probability mechanism (meiosis) by which lawfully combined random samples of these units are passed on from parents to offspring. Through study of (i) the distributions of genes in populations, (ii) the mechanisms responsible for both stability and change in gene frequencies, and (iii) the role of such mechanisms in evolution, population cytogenetics has given us some understanding of ensembles of these units that comprise the gene pools of populations and species—the taxa that are natural units of evolution.

Understanding Individuality

The phenotype (appearance, structure, physiology, and behavior) of any organism is determined by the interaction of environment with its genotype (the complete genetic endowment). Each genotype is the end product of many mechanisms which promote genotypic diversity in populations.

Ordinarily members of a cross-fertilizing, sexually reproducing species possess a diploid, or paired, set of chromosomes. Most species whose behavior we study are sexually dimorphic. The genetic basis of this dimorphism resides in the distribution of the heterosomes, a homologous pair of sex chromosomes (XX) being present in the mammalian female and an unequal pair (XY) in the mammalian male. Sexual dimorphism guarantees that any population will be variable to the extent of at least two classes. Whether sex-chromosome or other genotypic differences are involved in any particular behavior remains an empirical question to be investigated separately for every population. It can no longer be settled by dogmatic attitudes and assumptions about uniformity.

Chromosomes other than sex chromosomes are called autosomes. Every autosome is normally represented by a homologous pair whose members have identical genetic loci. Alternative forms of a gene any of which may occupy a given locus are termed alleles. If an individual receives identical alleles from both parents at homologous loci, he is said to be homozygous for that gene. If he receives two alleles that differ, however, he is said to be heterozygous for that gene. The process by which a gene changes from one allelic form to another is called mutation.

When a gene is represented in the population gene pool by two allelic forms, the population will be genotypically polymorphic to the extent of at least three classes. That is, individuals may be homozygous for either of two alleles or heterozygous for their combination.

Study of populations has revealed that often extensive series of alleles exist for a locus. Well-known examples are the three (actually more) alleles at the ABO-blood locus in man and a dozen or more alleles at the white-eye locus in *Drosophila*. Benzer (8), in his study of the internal genetic architecture of *one* "gene" with a corresponding physical structure of probably less than 2000 nucleotide pairs, the rII region of the T₄ bacteriophage, found 339 distinguishable mutational sites, and he expects to eventually find some 428. There is no reason to believe that we shall find less complexity in cellular organisms as further refinement increases the resolving power of our techniques for analyzing them. In general, for each locus having n alleles in the gene pool, a population will contain $n(n + 1)/2$ genotypic classes. Mutation insures variety in the gene itself.

Sexual reproduction involves meiosis —a complex cellular process resulting in a meristic division of the nucleus and formation of gametes (reproductive cells) having single genomes (a haploid chromosome set). One homolog in every chromosome pair in our diploid complement is of paternal origin and the other is of maternal origin. In meiosis, the homologs of a pair segregate and a gamete receives one from each pair. The assortment to gametes of the segregating homologs occurs independently for each pair. This process insures diversity because it maximizes the likelihood that gametes will receive unique genomes. For example, gametogenesis in *Drosophila willistoni* produces eight alternative gametic genomes, which, if we represent the three chromosome pairs of this species by Aa, Bb, and Cc, we designate ABC, ABc, AbC, aBC, Abc, aBc, abC, abc. In general, n pairs of chromosomes produce 2^n genomes (if we ignore the recombination of gene linkages that actually occurs in crossover exchanges between chromosomes). Man, with 23 chromosome pairs, produces gametes with any of 2^{23} alternative genomes. This makes vanishingly small the chances that even siblings (other than monozygotes) will be genetically identical. Since the gamete contributed by *each* parent is chosen from 2^{23} alternatives, the probability that the second offspring born to parents will have exactly the same genotype as their firstborn is $(\frac{1}{2}^{23})^2$, or less than 1 chance in over 70 trillion! The probability that two unrelated individuals will have the same genotype, then, is effectively zero (9).

The argument for the genotypic uniqueness of members of populations is even more compelling, since other conditions also contribute to diversity. So, it is clear, the organisms which the behavioral sciences study are intrinsically variable before they undergo differentiating experiences. The mechanisms responsible for this variety are mutation, recombination, and meiosis. Add to these individual experience, and it becomes evident why individuals differ in behavior. In fact, the more reliable our methods of observation become, the more evident will this variety be.

The Abnormality of the Normal

For Watson, its founder, behaviorism was "a natural science . . . [whose] closest scientific companion is physiology. . . . It is different from physiology only in the grouping of its problems, not in fundamentals or in central viewpoint" (10). Assumptions about the uniformity and normality of material under investigation are often made in physiology, the science after which, more than any other, experimental psychology has attempted to pattern itself. We may, therefore, get a better grasp of the individuality-uniformity distinction by examining the differences between organisms whose behavior is studied by behavioral scientists and systems whose functioning is studied by physiologists.

Since the two disciplines are working at distinctly different levels of biological organization, the meaning of "normality" as operationally determined by them is quite different. Physiologists choose a normal organism to work with—one that looks healthy and does not appear unusual—and study one or more of its systems, such as the adrenals, gonads, or other endocrines, or regions of the nervous system. Either pre- or postexperimentally, anatomical, histological, or biochemical verification is made of the normality of the material under study, and sometimes of related or adjacent functions to boot. In the behavioral sciences we choose normal-appearing organisms to study too. We rarely perform biopsies unless there is a specific physiological interest, in which case we operate as the physiologist does.

Physiological systems are variable, not uniform. Williams (*11*) amply documents this and points out that implicit in our use of "normal" is reference to some region of a distribution arbitrarily designated as not extreme—for example, the median 50 percent, 95 percent, or 99 percent. We choose such a region for every trait. Among n mathematically independent traits—for example, traits dependent on n different chromosomes—the probability that a randomly selected individual will be normal for all n traits is the value for the size of that region raised to the nth power. Where "normal" is the median 50 percent and $n = 10$, on the average only 1 individual out of 1024 will be normal (for ten traits). When we consider at one time the distributions throughout a population of large numbers of physiological systems, we should expect negative deviates from some distributions to combine with positive deviates from others, both kinds of extreme deviates to combine with centrally located ones, and deviates of similar algebraic sign and magnitude to combine. Each individual's particular balance of physiological endowments will be the developmental result of the genotype he draws in the lotteries of meiosis and the mating ritual. Because of crossing over, most genes assort independently. Hence, we cannot expect high correlations among the systems they generate.

If, underlying every behavior, there were only a single such system—for example, if the male "sexual drive" were mainly dependent on the seminal vesicles (*12*) or if escape behavior were mainly dependent on the adrenals—then the same kind of distribution might be expected for both the behavior and the underlying system. Whatever uniformity might exist at one level would be reflected at the other. The last few decades of research on the biological correlates of behavior have made it increasingly clear that behavior is the integration of most of these systems rather than the expression of any one of them. Therefore, there is little reason to expect that the many possible combinations and integrations of those systems that go to make up the members of a population will yield a homogeneously normal distribution of responses for many behavioral measures. An organism richly endowed with the components of one subset of systems and poorly endowed with those of another is not to be expected to behave in the same manner as an organism with an entirely different balance of endowments. The obviousness of this fact is well illustrated by the differences in behavior among the various breeds of dogs and horses.

Reductionism

Another conviction, strongly held by some, is that *real* explanations must be reductionistic. Those who hold this view in its most extreme form assert that no behavior can be understood until its physical basis has been unraveled. And the search for the physical basis proceeds along physiological, biochemical, biophysical, or genetical lines, depending on the skills and predilections of the investigators.

In laboratory experiments, some rats learn mazes more readily on the basis of visual cues while others do better with predominantly kinesthetic cues (*13*). The kinds of differences in organization that can coexist as alternative forms within a species, as well as some relations between one behavior and the component subsystems that are alternative possibilities, have been further revealed in a series of studies of the effects of domestication. In some domesticated rats, activity in a revolving drum was controlled by the gonads: control rats had daily activity scores as high as 18,000 revolutions, while gonadectomized rats scored only a few hundred revolutions. Cortisone therapy restored a high activity level in the gonadectomized rats. When the same experiment was repeated on wild Norway rats, however, the presence or absence of gonads made no detectable difference in measured activity. Further study of differences between these domesticated and wild rats revealed larger adrenals in the wild rats and larger gonads in the domesticated (*14*). So it appears that activity may be under the control of adrenal output in one case and gonadal output in the other—that behavior is not a univocal index to an organism's balance of endowments. The fallacy of reductionism lies in assuming a one-one relation between different levels of organization. With degeneracy already demonstrated in the genetic code of messenger RNA base triplets for the amino acids of proteins, we should be surprised not to find it at the levels of complexity we are considering (*15*).

Behaviorism and Introspection

According to my naive picture, the pyramid of sciences forges links of knowledge "out" from the periodic table: on the one hand, "down" into atomic structure through advances in physics; on the other, "up" into life through the genetic code and organic structure by advances in biophysics and biochemistry. The place of the behavioral sciences in the outline of that pyramid has been clearly demarcated for some time (*16*). Our models and assumptions must be consistent with the knowledge that is burgeoning at other levels. This means doing our homework and learning (*17*) about developments in fields which may once have seemed remote from behavior, but which clearly are not. Unfortunately, we are still plagued by a legacy of pseudo-problems which, like MacArthur's old soldier, seem to be slowly fading away instead of discreetly dying.

Recently, in *Science* (*18*), immediately following Wilkin's exposition (*19*) of his magnificent work on nucleic acids that led to the Watson-Crick model, Skinner heeded a call to issue "a restatement of radical behaviorism. . . ." It may be recalled that behaviorism bears its title to call attention to the fact that it studies behavior objectively rather than mind subjectively. Under Watson, in 1913, it wished to distinguish itself from unreliable (?) introspectionist psychology, whose findings lacked intersubjective agreement. Under Skinner, 50 years after, it is still worried about "the dimensions of the things studied by psychology and the methods relevant to them."

Starting from the uniformity assumption, the introspectionists were attempting to study the generalized human mind by analyzing the contents of their own consciousness. Of course, the study of mind through analysis by different individuals of the contents of their consciousness inevitably revealed individual differences. Under a given set of stimulating conditions, different people reported different sensations. According to Boring (20) "there is always to be remembered that famous session of the Society of Experimental Psychologists in which Titchener, after hot debate with Holt, exclaimed: 'You can see that green is neither yellowish nor bluish!' and Holt replied: 'On the contrary, it is obvious that a green is that yellowish-blue which is just exactly as blue as it is yellow.' That impasse was an ominous portent. . . ."

In over 50 years no one has suggested that Titchener and Holt might *both* have been making reliable observations. The event Boring bemoans would not be looked upon as an "impasse" that represents "an ominous portent" by a behavioral science that understands the structure of the materials it studies. Until recently, some of our best information on the assignment of genes to human chromosomes came from introspective behavioral observation. We know that genes affecting red-green color discrimination are carried on the X chromosome. We know it because some people fail to report differences in sensation easily observed by others, and the determining factors are transmitted to sons by mothers but never by fathers. Furthermore, Graham (21) has made excellent use of the introspections of one individual whose two eyes receive different color sensations from the same stimulus. Wouldn't it have been of great interest to learn how colored stimuli appeared to other members of the Titchener and Holt families? How many more potentially fruitful leads have been lost in the behavioral sciences because of rigid adherence to the counterfactual uniformity assumption?

Now, what was really wrong with introspection? Is there any other method by which Penfield could have made the startling discovery that apparently long-forgotten experiences remain stored in specific regions of our brain? He succeeded in restoring "lost" memories to introspectively observed consciousness by electrical stimulation of appropriate regions of exposed human brains (22). If the behaviorists had scrutinized the assumptions, which they shared with introspective psychology, they might not have been so quick to condemn its method. Every method has limitations, which it behooves its users to understand.

Behavior Genetics

There now exists a substantial and rapidly growing literature on the behavior genetics of many organisms, from *Drosophila* to man—what Tryon (23) calls "the basic science of individual differences." It comes from research far less hampered by unsound premises. In Fuller and Thompson's useful summary (24) we can see "its documentation of the fact that two individuals of superficially similar phenotype may be quite different genotypically and respond in completely different fashion when treated alike." This field, like others, is passing through stages.

The goal of the early work was a genetics *of* behavior. It took a while to learn that heritability is a property of populations and never of behaviors: the relation between behavioral variation and relevant genetic variation is never constant. It must be measured in specific populations under specific conditions, because it varies with both. Tolman (24), Tryon (24), and Heron (24) each measured individual differences in rats' ability to learn and then, by selective breeding, produced strains of "maze-bright" and "maze-dull" rats. Hall (24) and Broadhurst (24) selected for differences in emotional responses. Analogous studies have been made of performance on an animal 'intelligence test" (25).

Many strains of small mammals (mice, hamsters, rats, guinea pigs, and rabbits) are maintained under varying inbreeding regimens for purposes of medical and other research. When different strains within a species are compared, it actually becomes a challenge *not* to find differences in one or more behaviors. When strain comparisons are followed by appropriate genetic crosses, genetic correlates of behavioral differences are demonstrated. Such experiments have been performed for a large variety of behaviors: alcohol preference (26), hoarding (24), mating competition (24), susceptibility to audiogenic seizure (24), exploratory tendency (24), and various learning measures (24).

Paralleling the animal research are studies of human pedigrees, studies of family resemblances, twin comparisons, population surveys, and studies of race differences. Again, heritabilities have been demonstrated for many behaviors; for example, nature-nurture ratios were computed for intelligence-test and personality-test performance. Kallmann and his associates have pioneered, and others have joined, in collecting an impressive body of evidence on genetic factors in schizophrenia and other psychopathologies (27).

In 1963, with the wisdom of hindsight, we can ask why so many demonstrations were necessary. Should it not have been common knowledge that within each population the variation pattern for most traits will be conditioned by the nature of the gene pool, and that this will differ among populations? The answer lies in one phrase: the heredity-environment controversy.

The "opinion leaders" (28) of two generations literally excommunicated heredity from the behavioral sciences. Understandably, they objected to amateurish labeling of behaviors as instincts without proper experimental analyses. Also, they were repelled by the pseudogenetics of Hitler and other purveyors of race prejudice (29). On the other hand, impressed with the power of conditioning *procedures*, they proclaimed their faith in analysis of experience as the starting point for behavioral science—as though experience, like the Cheshire Cat's grin, could exist without the organism. "Our conclusion . . . is that we have no real evidence for the inheritance of traits," said Watson (10). While acknowledging that there are heritable differences in form and structure, he claimed there is no evidence that those differences are related to function, because "hereditary structure lies ready to be shaped in a thousand different ways" (30). Behaviorism still makes the gratuitous uniformity assumption that all genetic combinations are equally plastic and respond in like fashion to environmental influences (31).

We are now in a more fruitful period. Experimental analysis is yielding information about genes and chromosomes and how they act. The way is open to understanding molecular— ultimately submolecular (32)—mechanisms and to following metabolic pathways between genes and phenotypes. In the honey bee, Rothenbuhler (24) found that resistance to foulbrood disease (a bacterial infection of the larvae) depends on homozygosity of the worker bees for recessive alleles of at least two genes: one which enables them to uncap compartments containing infected larvae and another which enables them to remove those larvae from the hive (33).

Médioni (34), in his studies of phototaxis (light-oriented locomotion) in *Drosophila*, employed genetic, physiological, and stimulus variables in an exquisitely detailed analysis articulating relations between components of behavior, components of the organism, and stimulus properties of the environment. Behaviorally, phototaxis is resolvable into five components: (i) a photopositive phase; (ii) a sensory adaptation factor [Viaud's *capacité photopathique* (35)]; (iii) an exploratory phase; (iv) a photokinetic factor; and (v) a photoinhibition phase. The interplay of the behavioral components depend on (i) the intensity and wavelength of light, (ii) the differential effects of stimulation through the ocelli and through the compound eyes, (iii) sex, and (iv) genetic background and geographical region of racial origin. Races in 17 regions of the Northern Hemisphere, from Japan across Eurasia to America, arrange themselves into two distinct North-South clines, an Eastern and a Western, in which light preference diminishes with latitude of origin.

Our laboratory has made the most detailed analysis, to date, of relations between the genome and a behavioral phenotype in studies of geotaxis (gravity-oriented locomotion) in *Drosophila*. Behavioral distributions for populations are obtained in the apparatus shown in Fig. 1. Selective breeding from a geotactically and genetically heterogeneous foundation population has produced the two strains shown in Fig. 2, which have diametrically opposite response tendencies. Other methods produced three populations differing with respect to both degree and kind of similarity in chromosome constitution among their members. Two parameters of their behavioral distributions were thus controlled. The least dispersion occurred in the population in which all members carried two of the three large chromosomes in identical form. The other two populations, differing from each other with respect to the single chromosome distributed in identical form to all their members, differed in central tendency but not in dispersion, which was twice that of the first population. Figure 3 shows, for this model situation, the kind of prediction and control that an understanding of population structure and its genetic basis may yield.

Erlenmeyer-Kimling's subsequent chromosome analysis shows that genes influencing the response to gravity are distributed throughout the genome. The first two chromosomes in the unselected foundation population contribute to positive geotaxis, and the third to negative. Selection pressure both enhances and reduces their effects, depending on the direction of selection (*36*).

At the molecular level, an exciting development is the measurement, by Hydén and Egyházi (*37*), of changes, with learning, in the RNA base ratios in nuclei of specific mammalian nerve cells and in their glia. This work, if confirmed, represents a major advance in our search for the physical basis of experience. Hydén's speculative, but interesting, suggestion is that the electrical disturbance of the nerve impulse releases, in some as yet unspecified way, a repressed region of chromosomal DNA. This DNA henceforth produces, on demand, its characteristic RNA to code the protein that facilitates forward transmission of the particular temporal pattern of electrical frequencies that first released the DNA. This suggestion is the first to be made that appears capable of reconciling the universal feature of improvement with practice with the idiosyncratic features of individual performance. In this schema the individuality encoded in the chromosomal DNA of each genotype at meiosis and fertilization is propagated directly into the learning and memory mechanism by means of the established sequence of DNA producing RNA producing protein. Such a schema could thus accommodate the distributions of individual differences invariably found in studies of learning and memory.

The study of man is also moving beyond the stage of wondering whether we can find a heritability for this or that behavior. Phenylpyruvic oligophrenia, a form of mental deficiency accompanied by a high concentration of phenylpyruvic acid in the urine, had early been traced to a gene-controlled enzymatic deficiency in phenylalanine metabolism (*27*). Now, Down's syndrome (mongolism) has been associated with the presence of extra chromosomal material (*24*).

Human populations are dimorphic for taste sensitivity to certain bitter compounds. Different races show different distributions with respect to this trait, as well as to almost every other

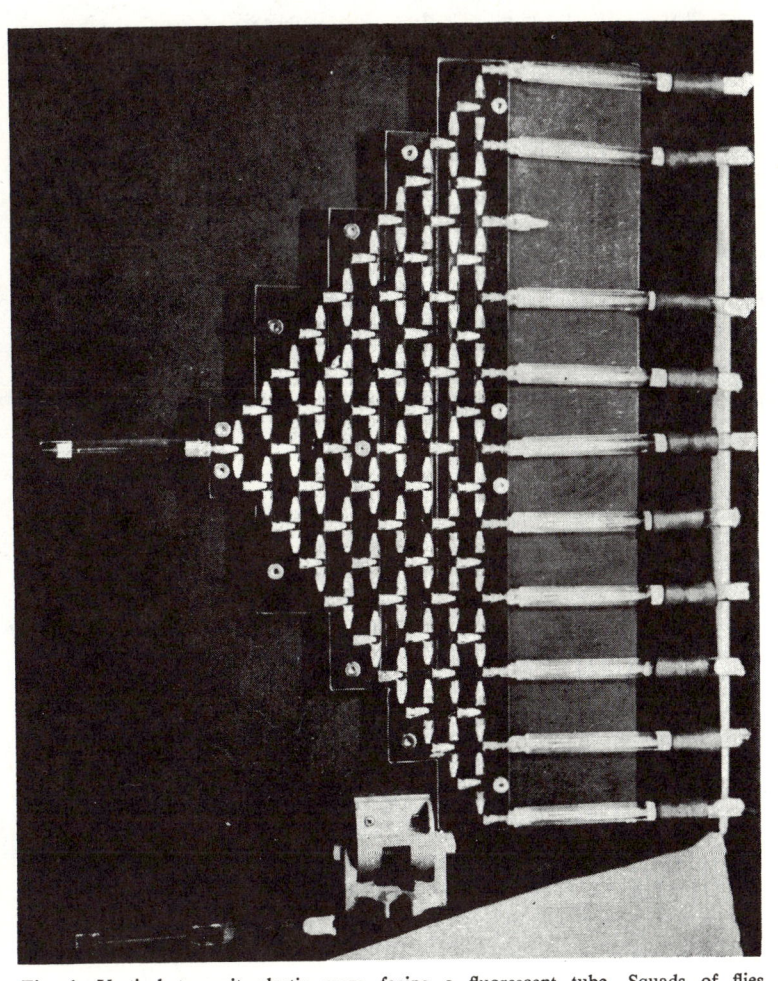

Fig. 1. Vertical ten-unit plastic maze facing a fluorescent tube. Squads of flies introduced in the vial at left are collected from the vials at right. They are attracted through the maze by the odor of food and by light. Small trap-like funnels, having a larger opening continuous with the alley surfaces and a small one debouching in midair, discourage backward movement in the maze. [Hirsch (*51*)]

trait that has been genetically analyzed. On the basis of behavioral observations indicating that an individual's ability to taste certain compounds depends upon the presence of his own saliva, Cohen and Ogdon (38) suggested that components of the saliva might play a critical role in tasting ability. Lately, Fischer and his co-workers (39) have shown in vitro that the bitter-tasting thioureas are oxidized faster by the saliva of nontasters than by that of tasters. Presumably, at low concentrations so much of the compound is oxidized in a nontaster's mouth that the few molecules which might reach their receptor sites remain undetectable. Furthermore, Fischer and his associates have now confirmed Cohen and Ogdon's finding that, in order to taste certain compounds at all, even a taster requires the presence of his own saliva. Superficially at least, it appears that saliva, like many body tissues, cannot be transplanted. A valuable observation here would involve an exchange of saliva between identical twins, who are presumably alike in body chemistry.

The ramifications of the taster phenomenon appear to be legion. There is a significantly higher incidence of non-tasting of the bitter compounds among persons with nodular goitre (40), among patients with congenital athyreotic cretinism, and among parents of the latter as well (41). In another study (42) it was found that, among 38 parents of children with Down's syndrome, none was able to taste quinine. Furthermore, all but one of the fathers in that sample were unable to taste a bitter thiourea. Finally, a correlation exists between taste sensitivity and dislike of foods: the more sensitive tasters find more foods objectionable (43).

Race Differences

A problem of continuing social importance, for an understanding of which most behavioral scientists have lacked a proper conceptual basis, is the question of race differences. To the liberals this question has been a continuing source of embarrassment (44). They have made little progress in answering it since the signing of our Constitution and Bill of Rights, when it was *asserted* that all men are created equal. To the prejudiced the question has presented no difficulties, because they *know* other races are inferior to their own; this seems as obvious to them as the flatness of the earth did to our ancestors.

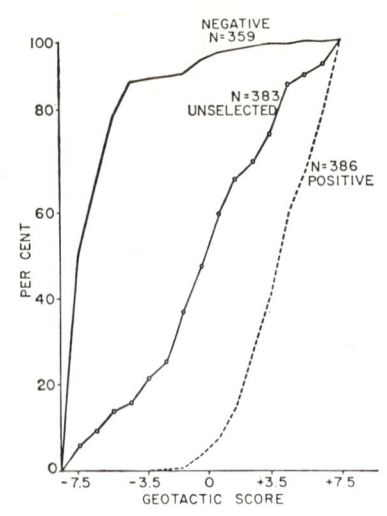

Fig. 2. Cumulated percentages of animals (males and females) that received geotactic scores in a 15-unit maze, from an unselected foundation population (middle curve) and from the two selected strains (outer curves). [Hirsch and Erlenmeyer-Kimling (52)]

This question appears in another perspective when it is examined in the light of current knowledge of population structure. Dobzhansky (45) has clearly called attention to the difference between equality and identity. Genotypic uniqueness creates biochemical individuality. Without enforcing conformity—irrespective of heredity, training, or ability—a democratic ethicosocial system offers to all equality of opportunity and equal treatment before the law. Genetics explains both individual and population uniqueness. Even though reproductively isolated populations belong to the same species and have the same genes, the relative frequencies of different alleles of genes in their gene pools are almost certain to differ. Mutations and recombinations will occur at different places, at different times, and with differing frequencies. Furthermore, selection pressures will also vary (46). In analyzing data from such populations we have learned to ask, not whether they are different, but, rather, in what ways they differ.

Races are populations that differ in gene frequencies. Observations on populations are summarized in distributions, so often assumed to be normal (47). When we add the assumption of common variance, or make transformations to obtain it, the data fit into the ever popular analysis-of-variance models. *The* difference between two populations must then be a difference between means, because the assumptions of normality and homogeneity of variance for the model leave no other property with respect to which the distributions can differ. The final step in this fantastic chain of reasoning has recently been taken in *Science* by Garrett (48). He ignores individual differences and claims that wherever two populations differ on some scale of measurement, no matter how vague, any individual from the population with *the* higher mean is better than any individual in the other population, and that intermarriage will "be not only dysgenic but socially disastrous"!

Distributions have other properties, such as dispersion, skewness, and kurtosis (peakedness), and no single one

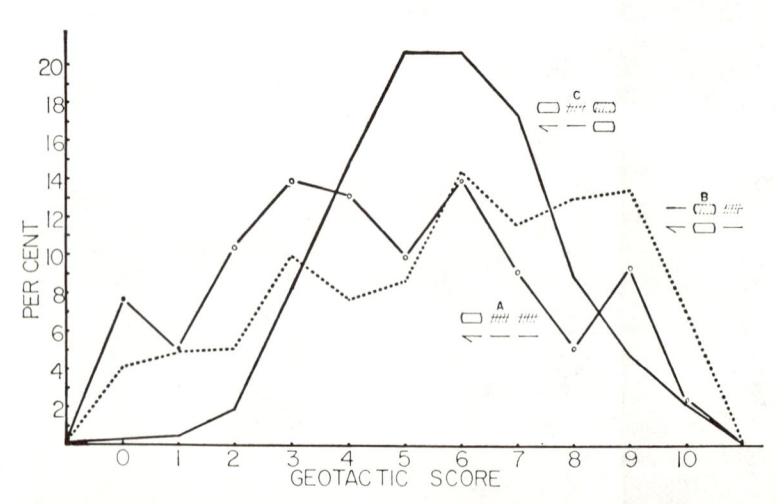

Fig. 3. Distributions of geotactic scores in a ten-unit maze for males of three populations (described in text). (Rectangles) Chromosomes carried in identical form by all members of a population; (dashes) chromosomes varying at random; (hatching) heterozygosity; (half-arrowhead) the Y chromosome of males. (In Fig. 2 the abscissa scale was reversed and the zero point was shifted to the center of the distribution.) [Hirsch (51)]

is exclusively important. Where these other properties have been examined, the inadequacy of a preoccupation with the central tendency and a hasty assumption of normality has been easy to document (49). There is no reason to expect two populations with different heredities and different environments to have precisely the same distribution for any trait. We can expect to find varying combinations of similarities and differences in the several properties of distributions when we compare different populations for a given trait, or any set of populations for different traits. Furthermore, the number of traits for which we could make comparisons is effectively unlimited, and many of the traits will be uncorrelated (11). Again, a lack of intrinsic correlation would come as no surprise to a behavioral science that understands its materials, because traits are the developmental result of thousands of genes, most of which, because of crossing over, sooner or later undergo independent assortment.

For ease of exposition, I have not considered environment in discussing race. Certainly, it is no less important than genetic endowment. The ontogeny of a responsible and effective citizen requires prolonged socialization, highly dependent upon the socializing agency. A genotype must have an environment in which to develop a phenotype. But the same genotype can produce quite different phenotypes, depending on the environments in which it may develop. Furthermore, a given environment can nurture quite different phenotypes, depending on the genotypes which may develop there. This fact is attested daily by parents and teachers who find that a method of tuition admirably successful with one child may be worthless with another, who nevertheless can learn by a different method. So, while environment makes an undeniably important contribution to the particular values obtained in phenotypic measurements, consideration of particular environments should not change our general picture of population structure. Without an appreciation of the genotypic structure of populations, the behavioral sciences have no basis for distinguishing individual differences that are attributable to differences in previous history from those that are not, and no basis for understanding any differences whatsoever where there is a common history.

Conclusions and Summary

Traditionally, many behavioral scientists have assumed that individuals start life uniformly alike, and that individual differences result only from differentiating experiences. To assume this is as contradictory to the established fact of uniqueness at conception as to assume that entropy is as likely to decrease as it is to increase. Recognition of the contradictory nature of this assumption does not make the role of experience in ontogeny any less important, but we now realize that the effects of experience are conditioned by the genotype. Therefore, a careful reconsideration of our statistical tools, experimental methods, theoretical models, and research goals is in order.

Many problems that have generated violent controversy now appear in totally different perspective. Introspection may provide a legitimate probe into subjective experience, without requiring intersubjective agreement. The concept of a normal individual has no generality. The outlook for understanding the physical basis of behavior has never been more promising. Awareness that a multiplicity of variable systems comprise its substrate, however, emphasizes the integrity and importance of the different levels of biosocial organization at which the several sciences work. In place of reductionism, we may now think of studying correlations between phenomena, reliably observed and analyzed at various levels, and of assessing the correlations over an ever-widening range of conditions. The controversial aspects of the heredity-environment question and of the race-differences question arise from failure to understand the genetics of individual and population differences and the rationale of their statistical analysis (50).

References and Notes

1. R. R. Bush and F. Mosteller, *Stochastic Models for Learning* (Wiley, New York, 1955).
2. B. S. Rosner, in *Psychology: A Study of a Science*, S. Koch, Ed. (McGraw-Hill, New York, 1962), vol. 4, p. 299.
3. Psychophysics is the study of changes in response associated with changes in physically specified stimuli.
4. K. Breland and M. Breland, *Am. Psychologist* 16, 681 (1961).
5. E. Mayr, *Animal Species and Evolution* (Harvard Univ. Press, Cambridge, 1963), p. 5.
6. T. H. Morgan, A. H. Sturtevant, H. J. Muller, C. B. Bridges, *The Mechanism of Mendelian Heredity* (Holt, New York, 1915).
7. T. Dobzhansky, *Genetics and the Origin of Species* (Columbia Univ. Press, New York, ed. 2, 1941).
8. S. Benzer, *Proc. Natl. Acad. Sci. U.S.* 47, 403 (1961); ———— and S. P. Champe, *ibid.* p. 1025; S. P. Champe and S. Benzer, *ibid.* 48, 532 (1962).
9. J. Hirsch, in *Roots of Behavior*, E. Bliss. Ed. (Hoeber, New York, 1962), p. 6. This calculation has provoked intense resistance. Its implications for well-encrusted modes of thinking in the "establishment" of the behavioral sciences are clearly most unwelcome. In an already legendary correspondence (part of which Mosteller circulated privately without informing me), F. Mosteller and J. Tukey independently attempted to disprove it. Both mathematicians overlooked the simple empirical fact that two sexes are required to produce children in the human species. Of course, my calculation is most conservative: assuming 10,000 human genes and an average of four alleles each gives ten combinations per locus and the astronomical number of $10^{10,000}$ potential human genotypes!
10. J. B. Watson, *Behaviorism* (Univ. of Chicago Press, Chicago, new ed., 1959), pp. 11, 103.
11. R. J. Williams, *Biochemical Individuality* (Wiley, New York, 1956); *Science* 126, 453 (1957); R. J. Williams, R. B. Pelton, F. L. Siegel, *Proc. Natl. Acad. Sci. U.S.* 48, 1461 (1962).
12. F. A. Beach and J. R. Wilson [*Proc. Natl. Acad. Sci. U.S.* 49, 624 (1963)] have demonstrated that this is not the case.
13. I. Krechevsky, *J. Comp. Psychol.* 16, 99 (1933).
14. C. P. Richter, *J. Natl. Cancer Inst.* 15, 727 (1954).
15. M. F. Perutz, *Proteins and Nucleic Acids Structure and Function* (Elsevier, Amsterdam, 1962); R. V. Eck, *Science* 140, 477 (1963).
16. R. J. Williams, *Science* 124, 276 (1956); R. W. Gerard, *Behavioral Sci.* 3, 137 (1958).
17. B. Glass, in *Expanding Goals of Genetics in Psychiatry*, F. J. Kallmann, Ed. (Grune and Stratton, New York, 1962), p. 259.
18. B. F. Skinner, *Science* 140, 951 (1963).
19. M. H. F. Wilkins, *ibid.*, p. 941.
20. E. G. Boring, *Am. J. Psychol.* 59, 173 (1946).
21. C. H. Graham and Y. Hsia, *Proc. Am. Phil. Soc.* 102, 168 (1958).
22. W. Penfield, *Proc. Natl. Acad. Sci. U.S.* 44, 59 (1958).
23. R. C. Tryon, *Am. Psychologist* 18, 134 (1963).
24. J. L. Fuller and W. R. Thompson, *Behavior Genetics* (Wiley, New York, 1960), p. 38.
25. W. R. Thompson and A. Kahn, *Can. J. Psychol.* 9, 173 (1955).
26. G. E. McClearn and D. A. Rodgers, *Quart. J. Studies Alc.* 20, 691 (1959).
27. F. J. Kallmann, Ed., *Expanding Goals of Genetics in Psychiatry* (Grune and Stratton, New York, 1962).
28. G. Lindzey's phrase (private communication).
29. J. H. Steward, *Science* 135, 964 (1962).
30. J. B. Watson, *Behaviorism* (People's Institute Publishing Co., New York, 1925), p. 77.
31. The irresistible attraction that these ideas have had in the behavioral sciences seems all the more appalling today when one reads the excellent systematic exposure of the "fallacies" of behaviorism published in 1930 by Jennings, a well-known and highly respected scientist of that period. [H. S. Jennings, *The Biological Basis of Human Nature* (Norton, New York, 1930); I thank Professor Donald D. Jensen of Indiana University for directing me to Jennings.] What is more, Watson had read Jennings. He cites those parts of the book that suit his purposes (see 10).
32. A. Szent-Györgyi, *Introduction to a Submolecular Biology* (Academic Press, New York, 1960); M. Kasha and B. Pullman, Eds., *Horizons in Biochemistry Albert Szent-Györgyi Dedicatory Volume* (Academic Press, New York, 1962).
33. To demonstrate the independence of the second gene, Rothenbuhler opens compartments for bees that cannot open them themselves.
34. J. Médioni, thesis, University of Strasbourg (1961), partially summarized in *Ergeb. Biol.* 26, 72 (1963).
35. G. Viaud, *J. Psychol. Normale et Pathologique* 42, 386 (1949).
36. L. Erlenmeyer-Kimling and J. Hirsch, *Science* 134, 1068 (1961); J. Hirsch and L. Erlenmeyer-Kimling, *J. Comp. Physiol. Psychol.* 55, 722 (1962).
37. H. Hydén and E. Egyházi, *Proc. Natl. Acad. Sci. U.S.* 48, 1366 (1962); 49, 618 (1963).
38. J. Cohen and D. P. Ogdon, *Science* 110, 532 (1949).
39. R. Fischer and F. Griffin, *Behavior Genetics Symposium, 17th International Congress of Psychology Washington, D.C.* (1963).
40. H. Harris, H. Kalmus, W. R. Trotter, *Lancet* 1963-II, 1038 (1949); F. D. Kitchen, W. Howel-Evans, C. A. Clarke, R. B. McConnell, *Brit. Med. J.* 1959, 1069 (1959).
41. T. H. Shepard, *J. Clin. Invest.* 40, 1751 (1961).
42. R. Fischer, A. R. Kaplan, F. Griffin, D. W. Sting, *Am. J. Mental Deficiency* 67, 849 (1963).
43. R. Fischer, F. Griffin, S. England, S. M. Garn, *Nature* 191, 1328 (1961).
44. *Science* 134, 1868 (1961).
45. T. Dobzhansky, *ibid.* 137, 112 (1962).
46. R. H. Post, *Eugenics Quart.* 9, 131 (1962).
47. L. S. Minckler, *Science* 133, 202 (1961).
48. H. E. Garrett, *ibid.* 135, 982 (1962); S. Genovés, *ibid.* p. 988.
49. H. G. Yamaguchi, C. L. Hull, J. M. Felsinger, A. I. Gladstone, *Psychol. Rev.* 55,

216 (1948); J. Hirsch, *Am. J. Orthopsychiat.* **31**, 478 (1961).
50. I am indebted to E. R. Hilgard for suggesting that I write this article and to the following for commenting on a draft of the manuscript: E. W. Caspari, J. Cohen, D. E. Dulaney, Nikki Erlenmeyer-Kimling, R. W. Frankmann, L. J. Goldsmith, D. A. Hamburg, R. C. Hostetter, C. L. Hulin, L. G. Humphreys, H. L. Jacobs, R. Kesner, G. Ksander, G. E. McClearn, J. E. McGrath, O. H. Mowrer, F. H. Palmer, D. Rosenthal, S. Ross, Leigh M. Triandis, P. Tyler, and M. W. Weir. This work is partially supported by a National Science Foundation grant (G-21238) to the Center for Advanced Study in the Behavioral Sciences, Stanford, Calif.
51. J. Hirsch, *J. Comp. Physiol. Psychol.* **52**, 304 (1959).
52. —— and L. Erlenmeyer-Kimling, *Science* **134**, 835 (1961).

Section Nine

Personality, Adjustment, and Mental Health

In the first paper of this section, Professor Holt discusses "idiographic" and "nomothetic" approaches to the study of personality. The idiographic approach stresses uniqueness, and holds that since all human personalities *are* unique, a meaningful study of personality cannot be accomplished by quantitative studies which make inter-individual comparisons. Conversely, the nomothetic approach, while recognizing uniqueness in personality, rules out intra-individual studies as unscientific. Holt takes to task advocates of both positions. He argues that the idiographic point of view is an artistic and non-scientific one, while at the same time, the nomothetic approach is simply a caricature of science.

In the second paper, Raymond J. McCall observes that even the most casual observer of one's fellow man realizes that human beings react differentially to stress. One person is able to undergo and withstand unbelievable physical and mental hardships while another seems to fall apart at the loss of a glove. All of us have experienced, and have had to deal with frustrations of one sort or another since our emergence into the world. Some of us develop characteristic patterns of behavior when our world seems to go awry. We try to find some balance and we attempt, effectively or not, to preserve ourselves. We do not always understand our own actions, words, or motives when we are faced with a stressful situation. Perhaps our reaction to such situations is to rationalize our behavior or to "forget" something unpleasant or even to flee. Such reactions, of course, have been termed "defense mechanisms."

McCall's paper "The Defense Mechanism Re-examined: A Logical and Phenomenal Analysis" enables us to take another look at twelve such mechanisms and he explains them somewhat differently than has been the case in the past. Repression, isolation, rationalization, reaction-formation, compensation, defensive devaluation, and six other mechanisms are analyzed. McCall acknowledges psychology's debt to Freud but departs from Freudian explanations of these mechanisms.

The next paper in the section, "Stress and Distress and Identity Formation in College and High School," is by Graham B. Blaine, Jr., a psychiatrist. He urges the academic world to be cognizant of the vulnerability of adolescents in our culture. We do not provide any one line of demarcation between the statuses of adulthood and childhood. We confer adult status at one age for one type of behavior (driving a car) and perhaps at another age for different activities (entering into binding legal agreements or marriage). And these differ widely across this country. A sense of competence, conscience, the development of personal identity and commitment must be fostered if adolescents are to develop in a healthy way. Blaine takes care to point out many of the stresses inherent in academia and acknowledges that faculty and students alike may not find the way to maturity easily.

In the fourth article in this section, Rachman observes that behavior therapy, scarcely a decade old, has developed out of experimental psychology's studies of the learning process in human beings. Neurotic behavior is viewed as acquired and therefore subject to "established laws of learning." This behavior is viewed as habitual, maladaptive, and learned. Consequently, these learned maladaptive responses should then be amenable to extinction and inhibition, as are other responses. Rachman strongly refutes criticisms of this approach and concludes that it not only works but has the advantages of being quantifiable, precise, and amenable to systematic planning for each individual.

In the final paper in this section, the well-known psychiatrist Karl Menninger discusses what he calls the "crime of punishment." Society, he says, wants crime, needs crime, and gains definite satisfaction from the present mishandling of it. We know that punishment is not the most effective way to alter behavior, yet society persists on a course of action that basically doesn't work. In its place, Menninger advocates a total transformation of prisons, if not their complete disappearance. Only through such a transformation, he says, can we truly protect the community from a repetition of offenses, while at the same time reclaiming offenders for social usefulness.

INDIVIDUALITY AND GENERALIZATION IN THE PSYCHOLOGY OF PERSONALITY[1]

R. R. HOLT

New York University

One of the hardiest perennial weeds in psychology's conceptual garden is the notion that there are nomothetic (generalizing) and idiographic (individualizing) branches, types, or emphases of science. Many respected and important contributors to psychology—especially to personology, the psychology of personality—have quoted these terms with respect and have used them as if they contributed something useful to methodology (cf. Allport, 1937a; Beck, 1953; Bellak, 1956; Bertalanffy, 1951; Colby, 1958; Dymond, 1953; Falk, 1956; Hoffman, 1960; Sarbin, 1944; Stephenson, 1953; the list could be considerably extended). It is the purpose of this essay to examine the historical origins of this cumbersome pair of concepts, their logical implications, the reasons psychologists espouse them, and alternative solution to the underlying problems. In so doing, I hope—no doubt fondly, but none the less ardently—to lay this Teutonic ghost which haunts and confounds much of modern psychology.

The principal exponent of the nomothetic–idiographic dichotomy in this country has been Gordon W. Allport (1937a, 1940, 1942, 1946, 1955), a pioneer in academic personology and a man who has brilliantly clarified many important issues in the field. On this par-

---

[1] This paper was completed during my year at the Center for Advanced Study in the Behavioral Sciences, to which I am grateful for the opportunity to do so. For constructively critical readings of an earlier draft, I am happy to thank Drs. Lawrence Z. Freedman, Jacob W. Getzels, Abraham Kaplan, George S. Klein, Harriet B. Linton, and Gardner Murphy.

Reprinted from *Journal of Personality*, Vol. 30, Pp. 377–404, 1962.

ticular point, I shall try to show, the artist in him has probably dimmed the vision of the scientist. The underlying problem with which Allport wrestles is vexing enough: the unusual nature of personality as a scientific subject matter. Allport readily concedes that everything in nature is unique, but maintains that natural sciences are not interested in the unique leaf, stone, or river. Only personology, the argument continues, takes as its very subject matter the unique personality as opposed to the generalized human mind or the behavior of organisms at large. The rest of psychology takes care of the general laws of behavior and experience and is thus nomothetic (literally, setting down laws);[2] what is left over is the impressive fact that every personality is different, and must be studied in such ways as respect and try to capture this uniqueness—in short, by an idiographic science (literally, portraying what is private or peculiar; i.e., individual). With these two curious words adopted from Windelband, then, Allport describes what he sees as two complementary branches of psychology, both of which are necessary for complete coverage.

On the other hand, many distinguished contributors to personology, from Freud to Murphy (1947), have found no need for such an approach to the scientific study of individuality, and the sharp voice of Eysenck (1954) has been heard rebutting Beck (1953) and proclaiming that psychology should be nomothetic throughout. Clearly, the issue is controversial.

Historical Background: The Romantic Movement in Science[3]

Kant, writing in the middle and late 1700's and reacting against reductionism, is one of the intellectual ancestors of this issue (which can, of course, be traced back to Plato and Aristotle—like any other problem in psychology; cf. Popper, 1957). Though he did not himself fall into the dualistic belief that mind and matter were so different that different methods had to be applied to their study, he wrote about these issues on too sophisticated a level for his followers. Thus, the analytic and generalizing methods of natural science were fine for the study of matter, but the mind, according to the post-

---

[2] This is the generally accepted meaning. Brunswik (1943), however, used it in a different sense, which occasionally causes confusion: as pertaining to a science of exact laws expressible as functions or equations, and opposed to statistical generalizations. Both are within the scope of the nomothetic, as understood here. Rickert used a slightly different term, nomological.

[3] In preparing this historical summary, I have relied principally on Roback (1927), Allport (1937a, 1937b), Boring (1929), Parsons (1937), Stein (1924), Tapper (1929), Friess (1929), Klüver (1929), and the *Encyclopedia of the Social Sciences*. I am aware of some oversimplification in speaking about *the* romantic movement in science; a variety of figures and currents of thought that could be characterized as romantic may be distinguished in the history of nineteenth-century science, some of them only loosely related to the movement described here.

Kantians, had to be studied also by an additional method, intuition of the whole. Being impressed with the concrete uniqueness and individuality of personality, they did not want to analyze it but to grasp it by a direct empathic act.[4]

Yet for the next century, no one developed such an intuitive approach to personality into anything; meanwhile, physics and chemistry, and even some branches of biology, grew rapidly and used the developing scientific methods with great success in the realm of matter. Mechanics developed early, and Newton's laws of motion were misunderstood as being foundation stones of mechanism and materialism. As Singer (1959) points out, Newton's laws were quite abstract and did not deal with physical bodies at all; but in their early great successes they were applied to the motions of the planets, and thus were thought of as the laws of material masses. It could hardly have been otherwise, because of the prevailing tenor of philosophical and scientific thought. The world was simply not ready for the field-theoretical implications of Newton's theories. Even so great a physicist as Lord Kelvin found "meagre and unsatisfactory" any physical knowledge that could not be expressed in a mechanical model.

Though the facts of their own disciplines did not require it, then, natural scientists—helped along by the overgeneralizations of contemporary philosophers—adopted a hard-headed, materialistic, and mechanistic positivism. It was assumed that all reality was orderly, observable, classifiable, and susceptible of mechanistic explanation; to the extent that it seemed not to be, the province of science ended. It was expected that the secrets of life itself would shortly be reduced to physico-chemical formulas. The resulting clash with religion and humanism seemed an inevitable consequence of being a good scientist. "What was not realized was that the success of science was due to the faithfulness of its practice, while its destructiveness [of humanistic, cultural values] arose from the error of its philosophy which saw that practice as though it were the outcome of a world-view with which it was in fact fundamentally incompatible." (Singer, 1959, p. 420.)

This was a classic atmosphere, ripe for the romantic revolt that started in poetry at the turn of the nineteenth century and swept through the arts. The humanities are accustomed to see the pendulum swing from classicism to romanticism and back again; from a time of reason, order, control, and clarity to one of passion, ambiguity, free expression, and revolt. To a degree, such movements are felt in the sciences as well, though usually more slowly. In science, we have a temperamental difference between the tough-minded and the tender-minded, as James put it, or in Boring's phrase, the

---

[4] For clarification of Kant's role in these matters, I am indebted to my friend Abraham Kaplan.

advocates of *nothing but* against those of *something more;* in the nineteenth century, it was objectivism and positivism vs. subjectivism and intuitionism. The hard-headed positivists had had their way for a long time; near the end of the century, however, there was something of a romantic revolt in science, tipping the balance toward the subjectivists. Independently, in two different parts of Germany, Wilhelm Dilthey in Berlin and the "southwesterners" Windelband and Rickert proclaimed the primacy of understanding (*Verstehen*) in certain kinds of science over quantification of elements, in the part of the general intellectual current with which we shall be concerned here.

They propounded the distinction between two kinds of science: the *Naturwissenschaften*, natural sciences, and *Geisteswissenschaften*, the German translation of J. S. Mill's "moral sciences." The latter term, often re-translated as "social sciences," meant actually a good deal more, for it included philosophy and the humanities as well as history, jurisprudence, and much else that is often excluded from social science today. In an attempt to develop separate methodologies for the *Naturwissenschaften* and *Geisteswissenschaften*, W. Windelband and H. Rickert took up, developed and popularized a distinction between two types of science that had been proposed by A. A. Cournot, the French founder of mathematical economics.[5] Cournot, who was also something of a philosopher of science, had a sophisticated concept of chance and examined the role it played in various fields of knowledge in the process of classifying them. In the exact sciences, precise laws were possible, he said, but in history, chance played such a large role that only a probabilistic discipline was possible. As a later philosopher of history, Eduard Meyer, put it: any particular event "depends on chance and on *the free will of which science knows nothing but with which history deals.*" (Quoted by Weber, 1949, p. 115, from Meyer's *Zur Theorie und Methodik der Geschichte*, Halle, 1900.)

It should be clear by now that we are dealing with not just a pair of isolated terms but a complex set of methodological concepts and viewpoints. The nomothetic–idiographic distinction can no more be understood out of the context of the *geisteswissenschaftliche* movement than can any isolated culture trait torn from its cultural embeddedness. For the sake of convenience, I shall refer to this complex of ideas as the romantic movement in science. There have been so many major and subtle shifts in our outlook that it is difficult for us to see the issues with the eyes of *ca.* 1900; recall, how-

---

[5] See the article on *Geisteswissenschaften* in the *Encyclopedia of the Social Sciences* and Cournot (1851). The reader who is interested in a richly detailed picture of the issues and their background will do well to read Popper (1957) and chapters 13 and 17 in Parsons (1937). An excellent briefer account is given by Klüver (1929), in which references to the principal relevant works of Windelband and Rickert may be found.

ever, that vitalism was a live doctrine then, and the ideas of chance and free will were closely-connected, respectable concepts. Many scholars conceived of history as having been shaped primarily by the acts of great men; as we shall see, the theme of the relation between personality and achievement is a recurrent preoccupation of the romantics.

It is factually true that history, biography, and literary criticism are primarily interested in increasing our understanding of particular events, persons, or works, rather than in treating these as incidental to the discovery of general laws. But men like Windelband and Rickert took the jump from this proposition to the sweeping declaration that all of the disciplines concerned with man and his works should not and by their very nature cannot generalize, but must devote themselves to the understanding of each particular, and its integration "as a real causal factor into a real, hence concrete *context.*" (Weber, 1949, p. 135) The repetition of the word "real" in this passage underscores the conception that only the concrete was real, hence abstractions could not be conceived of as causes of particular events. Moreover, abstract analysis of specific events or persons was thought to be fallacious, since it destroyed the unique unity that was the essence of any such particular. This essence was qualitative, not quantitative, and often consisted of verbal meanings (as opposed to objective facts as the subject matter of natural science), which cannot be measured but only interpreted. By identifying Cournot's methodological distinction with their own between the knowledge of Being (*Sein*), obtained in physical science, and the consciousness of and relatedness to norms (*Sollen*) in the cultural sciences, Windelband and Rickert started the great debate on the role of values in science.

For psychology, Dilthey was the most important figure in this movement. He was a philosopher, an admirer of Goethe and Schopenhauer, rebelling against Christianity and Hegel, though influenced by the Biblical hermeneutics of Schleiermacher. He wanted to respect the heart's reasons the head will never know, to understand life in its own terms, not to explain it. The anti-intellectual element in such a goal is perceptible, and indeed, he is part of the current in German thought that provided the philosophical background for Nazism. He wanted, not a reduction of data either to physical-material or to idealistic terms, but a direct insight into the vital nature of things as articulated wholes. His approach was empirical, but in a different sense from the atomistic English tradition, stressing the importance and primacy of the unbroken whole, the *Strukturzusammenhang*. Obviously, he helped prepare the seedbed for Gestalt psychology. He was optimistic, unlike some of his successors (e.g., Spengler), and very influential in Germany.

Basic to the development of the social and cultural sciences, he thought, was the development of a new psychology, which he called *verstehende* psychology—a descriptive discipline concerned with the systematic knowledge of the nature of consciousness and of the inner unity of the individual life, and with the understanding of its development. It did not analyze nor start with elements, but with experienced relationships. The most important unifying forces in a man were purpose and moral character. He saw the intimate relation of the person to his social setting, and insisted that individual human character was an outgrowth of institutions, not vice versa.

These are only fragments from Dilthey's large output of ideas, which lacked system and order; his work was brought together only after his death, by friends. Nevertheless, it stimulated many workers in diverse fields: jurisprudence, economics, sociology, philosophy, genetics, history, and psychology.

Dilthey's most important psychological follower was Spranger, who is known chiefly for his book *Lebensformen* (Spranger, 1922; translated as *Types of Men*). He too distinguished sharply between explanatory and descriptive psychology, favoring the latter, *verstehende,* type. *Verstehen,* he says, is the mental activity "that grasps events as fraught with meaning in relation to a totality." He was opposed to the analysis of personality into elements, but wanted to stay on the level of "intelligible wholes." As a focus for the study of individuality, he followed Dilthey again in proposing that the person's values, which determined the direction of his strivings, be considered of primary interest.

Dilthey had propounded three forms of Weltanschauung which underlie and pervade the personalities as well as the doctrines of the philosophers whom he studied. Spranger proposed his famous six ideal types of values, to which actual individual values more or less correspond: the theoretical, economic, aesthetic, social, political, and religious. He did not recognize the possible cultural determination of his choosing just these six, but traced them back to instincts. Each value type has its own ethics (economic: utilitarianism; aesthetic: harmony), and its own style of life in many other ways. The entire scheme was rather ingeniously worked out.

This theory followed the new ideas in stressing the unity of personality, the way in which many details of behavior become comprehensible when we know such key facts about the total structure as the principal values toward which a man is oriented; to underline the contrast between the prevailing atomistic psychology and his own, Spranger called it *Struktur* psychology. As a general theory of personality, it suffers from incompleteness, and its main influence today comes from its having stimulated the production of a widely-used paper and pencil test, the Allport-Vernon-Lindzey Study of Values, which is still in active use as a research instrument.

The history of the psychology of *Struktur* and *Verstehen* since Spranger is not yet finished; its influence is still felt in personology, and as a school it still has adherents in Germany. G. W. Allport has done the most to bring it to this country; there were a number of lesser figures, but they have not made significant contributions.

William Stern, a man of some influence in psychology, must be at least briefly mentioned even though he began in intelligence testing and his work converged only rather late with the main line of development traced above. The nomothetic–idiographic distinction played no part in his writings, though he was influenced by *verstehende* psychology. He had been a pioneer and an established figure in child psychology and the psychology of individual differences, when he became convinced that conventional psychology was wrongly conceived. As differential psychologists, he said, we are studying isolated mental functions, the ranges and correlates of their variations, but overlooking the important fact that all such functions are embedded in personal lives. As child psychologists, we talk about the growth of intelligence or the like, forgetting that only *persons* grow. Reasoning thus, and basing his psychology on his personalistic philosophy, he decided that a radical re-beginning was imperative; psychology had to be rebuilt with the indivisible, individual person as the focus of every psychological investigation. Even Gestalt psychology with its emphasis on totalities and its similar anti-elementarism was insufficient, for: "Keine Gestalt ohne Gestalter." Stern went into most of psychology's classical problems, such as perception, making the point that there are not separate problems of spatial perception in hearing, vision, touch, etc.—there is only one space, *personal* space, and it is perceived by whatever means is appropriate. Most of the facts that had been established in traditional general psychology were brought in, with this new twist.

Stern's theory of motivation was a complex one, including drives (directional tendencies), instincts (instrumental dispositions), needs, urges, will, pheno-motives and geno-motives, etc., in too subtle and highly elaborated a structure to be recounted here. He did not have a theory of personality as such; rather, the personalistic viewpoint pervaded all of his general psychology. There was a specific theory of character, however, conceived of as the person's total make-up considered from the standpoint of his acts of will, his conscious, purposive striving. Though stratified, character is a unified structure and may be described by a list of traits, but this is only the beginning; much stress was laid on the particular, concrete structure. Particular traits, said Stern, no matter how precisely described, have meaning only when you see what function they play in the structure of the whole personality.

These are the principal psychological figures in the stream of ideas that produced the distinction between nomothetic and idiographic *Wissenschaften* and then applied the latter approach to the problems of psychology. Perhaps the name of Jaspers, in psychopathology, should be added. He helps to establish the continuity between the romantic movement at the turn of the century and the contemporary existentialist-phenomenological movement in psychiatry. The *geisteswissenschaftliche* point of view made even more headway in the social sciences, from which some influence still comes to bear on psychology. Popper (1957) has applied the term *historicism* to one of the main streams in sociology, history, and economics that developed as part of the romantic reaction against positivist, natural-scientific methodology. Such potent names as Marx, Engels, Spencer, Bergson, Mannheim, and Toynbee are among the historicists, and the movement is by no means dead today, despite the vigor of attacks by logical positivists which have refuted the underlying logic of this position. I will not further consider this important group of theorists, who have been adequately routed (Popper, 1957; cf. also Popper, 1950).

How useful were the new ideas to the group of psychologists discussed above? What they took from the romantic revolt was its emphasis on and permission to study as legitimate objects of inquiry, personality, values, motivation, and the interrelation of such factors with cognition (e.g., ideology, perception). Starting with Dilthey's first disciples and going on through the solid contributions of Spranger and Stern, these men did not adhere to a strict distinction between idiographic and nomothetic approaches, and were disinclined to make any substantial change in their accustomed ways of scientific work. Any follower who wholly gave up general concepts and stuck closely to intuitive contemplation of indivisible Gestalten simply dropped out of the picture; the men who are remembered used the new battle cries to help shift their fields of activity slightly, and to develop new types of concepts—which as concepts were on no different level of abstractness from the ones Dilthey and the southwesterners attacked so vehemently.

Note, for example in the above summaries, the generalizing, abstract nature of the motivational concepts used by Spranger and Stern: both retained values and instincts, which were assumed to be found in all persons. As soon as they stopped their polemics and got down to work, the men of this romantic revolt strayed off the intuitive reservation and came up with conceptual tools methodologically indistinguishable from those of so-called nomothetic science. In a way, Stern was the most consistent in the attempt of his *Psychology from a Personalistic Standpoint* (1938) to reshape all of psychology from bottom to top; but on closer examination, the changes turn out to be largely verbal. It is all very well to talk about personal space, for example, but no idiographically personalistic research methods were developed. One could hardly say that there has been any further development of a personalistic psychology of perception, except in the sense that Stern has helped focus attention on new types of generalized variables derived from a study of individual differences in perceptual behavior (cf. Klein and Schlesinger, 1949).

Nevertheless, all of this work did represent an important groundswell in the history of ideas, and it had some useful influence on the behavioral sciences. It did not make them idiographic, but it directed their attention to new or neglected problems and novel kinds of variables, as well as to the issue of structure: the ways the variables are organized. Like many rebellions, it revolted against a tradition that was stultifying, only to produce an opposite extreme, which if taken literally would have been equally useless or more so. Fortunately, scientists only occasionally take their concepts quite that literally and with such logical consistency; especially at a time that old ideas are overthrown, the important content of the new movement is often emotional. Through the drama of overstatement, a prevailing but opposite overemphasis may be overthrown, and in calmer times other men may find a sensible position from which to move forward.

Certainly the psychology and social science that held the stage in Germany during the 1880's and 1890's were in many ways inadequate as scientific approaches to important human problems. It was a day when not only value judgments but even an interest in the psychology of values was banned from scientific concern. Fechner and Wundt had started with problems it is easy to dismiss as trivial, minute, or far removed from what the man on the street thinks of as psychology. Experimental psychology had to start that way, and it can now look back on an illustrious, slow development of methods and concepts, which today permit laboratory studies of personality and some of life's more pressing issues. But 70 years ago, is it any wonder that a person who was interested in man the striver, the sufferer, the spinner of ideologies—as Dilthey was— thought that the classical scientific approach itself might be at fault? Surely the world of inner knowledge, of passions and ideals, had been left out, and the *verstehende* movement was a revolt against this one-sidedness.

The Historical Role of Differential Psychology

In psychology, the romantic movement has been felt particularly in personology, the psychology of personality. And one reason that its impact was particularly great there is the fact that personology grew out of differential psychology, the psychology of individual differences.

The first efforts of the "new psychology" of the 1890's were devoted to finding empirical generalizations and abstract laws about such functions as sensation and perception (concepts which themselves were the heritage of faculty psychology). It was what Boring has called the science of the average, health, adult (and, one might add, male) mind, a subtly Aristotelian conception that relegated the study of women and children, and of abnormal and exceptional behavior generally, to a subordinate status. Even so, there remained embarrassing observations of exceptions to the general laws even when the subjects were "average, healthy adults"; and so the field of differential psychology was invented as a kind of wastebasket to take care of these annoying anomalies. From the standpoint of the highest type of psychology, which was concerned with laws in a way not expected of differential psychology, the unexplained residual variance continued to be considered error and to be treated as if it were random and unlawful.

The psychologists who were content to work with the miscellany of leavings from all the high-caste tables in psychology were further handicapped by the taint of practical application, for they were principally involved in applying psychology to mundane problems like educating children, treating the disturbed, and selecting employees. Such work called for the prediction of behavior, and it quickly became apparent that the general laws provided by "scientific psychology" left a great deal unpredicted; it was practically imperative to supplement them by some kind of lore that dealt with all the other important determinants.

As time went on, differential psychologists made a radical shift in approach. In the era when individual differences were thought of as error—as not lawful, really—they were catalogued and measured, and a few attempts were made to parcel out the variance in terms of sex, age, ethnic group, and other gross demographic categories. During the past couple of decades, however, personologists have increasingly begun to recognize that all the error-terms of standard psychological equations are their own happy hunting grounds. Individual differences in such hallowed perceptual phenomena as time-error, size-estimation, and shape-constancy proved to be not random at all but reliably related to other dimensions of individual differences in cognitive phenomena and in noncognitive realms, too (cf. Gardner, Holzman, Klein, Linton, & Spence, 1959).

The fallacy involved in treating individual differences as if they were random and unlawful resembles that of the nineteenth-century scientists who concretized Newton's laws as propositions concerning mechanical bodies. In both cases, the grasp of certain principles lagged behind what could have been expected. Objectively viewed, the laws that govern individual variation in the perception of apparent movement are just as abstract as the laws that cover the general case, and seem to have a different methodological status only because of the accident of history that brought about the discovery of the latter first. And, despite the implied promise in Klein and Schlesinger's title (1949), the study of such general principles does not bring the perceiver, the person in Stern's sense, back into perceptual psychology; it is merely a change in the axis of generalization, so to speak, not a way of becoming less abstract about perception.

The Logic of the Romantic Point of View in Personology

Let us now consider each of the main propositions that make up the romantic point of view, and state the logical objections to them systematically.

1. *The goal of personology must be understanding, not prediction and control.* The goal of those who profess an idiographic point of view is not anything so antiseptic and inhuman as a family of curves; it is *understanding*. In one sense, it is proper to say that we understand poliomyelitis when we have isolated the responsible viruses and have identified the conditions under which they attack and cripple a person, but this is not *Verstehen*. That conception is an empathic, intuitive *feeling* of knowing a phenomenon from the inside, as it were. To take a more congenial example, we do not understand why a particular boy becomes delinquent from knowing that he comes from a neighborhood that an ecological survey has determined to be economically deprived and socially disorganized; whereas after we have read Farrell's *Studs Lonigan* and have seen such conditions and the embeddedness of delinquency in them portrayed with artistic power and vividness, then we understand (in the sense of *Verstehen*) the relation between these phenomena.

From this example, it should be clear that the feeling of understanding is a subjective effect aimed at by artists, not scientists.[6] In science, when we say we understand something, we mean that we can predict and control it, but such aims are foreign to the romantic viewpoint. When Allport says (as of course Freud and many others have said also) that novelists and poets have been great intuitive psychologists, in some ways the greatest psychologists, the statement has two (not necessarily coexistent) meanings: that literary men have known many significant variables of and propositions about personality (e.g., the role of unconscious incestuous wishes in determining many kinds of behavior), or, that they have been able to create the most vivid, compelling portraits of people, which give us the sense of knowing and understanding them. The latter effect is achieved by judicious selection and artful distortion, not by exhaustive cataloguing and measurement of traits, motives, or structural relations. Indeed, the idea of a catalogue is the very antithesis of art, just as a painful realism that tries to copy nature slavishly is the death of an artistic endeavor.

Here we see the issues drawn clearly. Is personology to be an art, devoted to word portraits that seek to evoke in the reader the thrill of recognition, the gratifying (if perhaps illusory) feeling of understanding unique individuals? Or is it to be a science, which

---

[6] As Gardner Murphy points out (in a personal communication), there are many cases, "all the way from Leonardo da Vinci to Joseph Audubon and John Muir, of scientist-artists, in whom it is not conceptually very feasible to make the roles distinct." I agree that it would be difficult, and perhaps I exaggerate the differences, but they do exist as Weberian ideal types.

enables us to study these same persons in all their uniqueness and to derive from such study general propositions about the structure, development, and other significant aspects of personality? If we elect for a science, we must abandon art whenever it takes us in a different direction than the one demanded by the scientific method, and we must recognize that the ideal of an idiographic science is a will-o'-the-wisp, an artistic and not a scientific goal. Science may be supplemented by art, but not combined with it.

There is a legitimate art of personality, literary biography. An artist like André Maurois is not hindered by not being a scientist of any kind. We should recognize that an artist's quest for "truth" differs from a scientist's in being a striving not for strict verisimilitude but for allusive illumination; its criterion is the effect on some audience—something to which science must remain indifferent.

Since some personologists (notably Freud, Murphy, Allport, and Murray) have had much of the artist in them as well as the scientist and have been masters of prose writing, it is no wonder that at times the artistic side of their identities has come uppermost. If Allport had been less aesthetically sensitive, he might not have failed to distinguish between artistic and scientific goals. Often, too, poor scientists are at the same time poor writers, and an inferior case study may be poor either because its facts are wrong and its interpretations undiscerning, or because it is poorly put together and lacks the literary touch that can put the breath of life into even a routine case report. The more art a scientist possesses—so long as he does not let it run away with him—the more effective a scientist he can be, because he can use his aesthetic sense in constructing theory as well as in communicating his findings and ideas to others.

2. *The proper methods of personology are intuition and empathy, which have no place in natural science.* As has been indicated above, intuition and empathy were used by the romantics as ways of gaining direct and definitive understanding, and were considered to be complete scientific methods. The contemporary personologist has no quarrel with their use in the practical arts of clinical psychology and psychoanalysis, nor as ways of making discoveries and formulating hypotheses. Indeed, the more secure scientists are in their methodological position, the more respect they usually have for intuition (and in psychology for the closely related methods of empathy and recipathy). Thus, the claim that these operations have no place in natural science is false; they are used by all scientists in the most exciting and creative phase of scientific work: when they decide what to study, what variables to control, what empirical strategies to use, and when they make discoveries within the structure of empirical data. As to their sufficiency, I need only remind the reader that the methodology of verification, the hypothesis-testing phase of scientific work, involves well-developed rules and consensually established procedures, and that intuition and empathy have no place in it.

3. *Personology is a subjective discipline as contrasted to objective branches of psychology, being concerned with values and meanings, which cannot be subjected to quantification.* Elsewhere (Holt, 1961), I have dealt with the contention that there is a fundamental methodological difference between disciplines that deal with verbal meanings and values, and those that deal with objective facts. Briefly, the argument is the familiar one that objectivity is only intersubjectivity, and that meanings (including values) may be perceived and dealt with in essentially the same ways as the data of natural science, which must be discriminated and recognized also. Moreover, a logical analysis of the operations carried out in disciplines such as literature, concerned with the understanding of individual works and little (if at all) with generalization, shows that these workers outside of science use many of the *same* methods of analyzing texts as the quantitative content-analysts of social psychology, with their exclusive concern with generalization. Their work has shown that meanings may be quantified and in other ways treated as objectively as any other facts of nature. Other objections to quantification grow out of antipathy to abstract variables of analysis, and will be considered in the following section.

4. *The concepts of personology must be individualized, not generalized as are the concepts of natural science.* The belief that the concern of personology with unique individuals (see below) contrasts fundamentally with the exclusive concern of nomothetic science with generalities logically implies that the two types of discipline must have different types of concepts. As the chief spokesman for the romantic point of view in psychology, Allport calls for the use of individual traits, which are specific to the person being studied, not common traits, which are assumed to be present to some degree in all persons. But to describe an individual trait, we have to take one of two courses: either we create a unique word (a neologism) for each unique trait, or we use a unique configuration of existing words. The first approach is clearly impossible for communication, let alone science; personology would be a complete Babel. The second solution, however, turns out to be a concealed form of nomothesis, for what is a unique configuration of existing words but a "fallacious attempt to capture something ineffably individual by a complex net of general concepts"? Allport himself has explicitly ruled out this possibility:

...each psychologist tends to think of individuals as combinations of whatever abstractions he favors for psychological analysis. This procedure, common as it is, is wholly unsuitable for the psychology of personality. For one thing, such abstract units are not distinctively *personal*.[7] (1937a, p. 239)

---

[7] Allport wrote these words in the context of rejecting Murray's system of needs (1937a); yet elsewhere (Allport, 1937b) he praises as "strikingly personal" such concepts (or dimensions) of W. Stern (1938) as depth-surface, embeddedness-salience, nearness-remoteness, and expectancy-retrospect!

An idiographic discipline thus must be a dumb or an incomprehensible one, for intelligible words—even some of Allport's favorite, literary ones, like *Falstaffian,* which he does consider "personal"—abstract and generalize, proclaiming a general pattern of resemblance between at least two unique individuals, Falstaff and the case being described. Any such trait thus becomes common, not individual.

One of the great methodologists of social science, Max Weber (1949) developed an apposite analysis of scientific concepts and their development in reaction against the romantic movement in his country at the turn of the century (cf. Parsons, 1937). He had the insight to see that the exponents of *Geisteswissenschaft* were trying to do the impossible: to capture the full richness of reality. There are three identifiable stages in the scientific study of anything, Weber said. To begin with, one selects from nature the historical individual (or class thereof) one wishes to focus on; for example, the Boston Massacre, the personality of Einstein, the cathedral at Chartres. Even though limited, each of these is infinitely rich in potentially specifiable aspects and configurations. One could study one of these, or even a tiny "flower in a crannied wall," until doomsday and not exhaust everything that could be known about it. Without doing any more abstracting than focusing on a particular topic, one can only contemplate it; and this is where the idiographic approach logically must stop. The method of intuition or *Verstehen* is essentially a wordless act of identification with the object, or some other attempt to "live in it" without analyzing its Gestalt.

The second stage, that of the ideal type, is a rudimentary attempt to see similarities between historical individuals, while staying as close as possible to their concrete particularity. Ideal types are much used in psychology, especially in diagnosis, for any syndrome such as schizophrenia is a complex of identifiably separate but loosely covarying elements, never encountered in exact textbook form. The lure of ideal types is that they give the brief illusion of getting you close to the individual while still allowing a degree of generality. But this advantage is illusory, the apparent advantage of a compromise that denies satisfaction to either party. Concrete reality (fidelity to the unique individual) *is* forsworn, and the advantages of truly general concepts are not attained. An ideal type does not fit any particular case exactly, and the failure of fit is different in kind as well as degree from one case to another. For an ideal type "is a conceptual construct which is neither historical reality nor even the 'true' reality. It is even less fitted to serve as a schema under which a real situation or action is to be subsumed as one *instance*. It has the significance of a purely ideal *limiting* concept with which the real situation or action is compared and surveyed for the explication of certain of its significant components." (Weber, 1949, p. 93)

The final stage of scientific development, therefore, is the fractionation of ideal types into their constituent dimensions and elements, which Weber called abstract analytical variables. Paradoxically, only a truly abstract concept can give an exact fit to any particular individual! I cannot say exactly how Falstaffian or how schizophrenic or how big any particular subject may be, but I can name a particular value of an abstract analytical variable, height, that fits him as closely as his skin. The example would be less convincing if chosen from psychology because we do not have as well-established, unitary dimensions as the physical ones, and not as simple and unarguable operations for measuring them as the use of the meter stick; the principle, however, is the same.

The fit is exact, of course, only because an abstract analytical concept does not purport to do more than one thing. If I try to measure the breadth of a person's interests, I make no pretensions to have "captured the essence of his personality." Not having tried, I cannot properly be accused of failing. But I have chosen a variable that can be measured, and thus potentially its relations to other aspects of personality can be discovered and precisely stated. Curiously, Allport attacks general variables on the ground that they "merely *approximate* the unique cleavages which close scrutiny shows are characteristic of each separate personality" (Allport, 1946; his emphasis). His preferred *ad hoc* approach may seem less approximate because many of the general variables used in personology are ideal types, lacking true abstract generality. The solution, however, lies in a direction diametrically opposed to the one toward which Allport beckons. And it does not consist in escaping from approximation. Scientific models of reality can *never* fit perfectly; the attempt to force such identity between concept and referent sacrifices the flexibility and power of abstract concepts in a chimerical quest for the direct grasp of noumena.

Parenthetically, the recent vogue of existentialism and Zen Buddhism in psychology may be partly attributed to the promise they extend of providing a way of grasping the total richness of reality. Part of the lure of *satori* or any other mystical ecstasy of a direct contact with the world, unmediated by concepts, may stem from the necessary distance imposed by the scientific necessity to abstract. But despite their confusing jargons, which make them seem superficially quite different from the late nineteenth-century romantic movement we have been considering, both of these fashionable doctrines suffer from the same fallacies. Mystical experience, like aesthetic experience, offers nothing to the scientist qua scientist except an interesting phenomenon that may be subjected to scientific study.

5. *The only kind of analysis allowable in personology is structural, not abstract, while natural science is not concerned with structure.* It is true that the scientific psychology of Dilthey's heyday had no place for structural analysis in the sense introduced by the

romantics. Psychology dealt with a number of functions, which were treated implicitly or explicitly as quite independent of one another. It had no methods parallel to those of exegetic Biblical scholarship or literary criticism, which seek out the internal organization of ideas in a specific text. And the reductionistic enthusiasts for analyzing things were not interested in putting the pieces back together again, nor very clear themselves that analysis need not mean dismemberment. This state of affairs made it easy to think that analysis could be destructive, and that structural relations between the parts of the personality could be studied only in concrete, unique individuals, so that structure[8] seemed to be an exclusive concern of idiographic disciplines.

There are really two points here: the distrust of analysis, and the emphasis on structure. The first of these has been partly dealt with in the preceding section; it was based on a misunderstanding of the nature of astract concepts.

On the second point, structural concepts and structural analyses are commonplace in science at large today. Such structural disciplines as stereochemistry and circuit design were (at best) in their infancy at the time of the idiographic manifestoes. Today, natural science uses abstract, structural, and dispositional concepts simultaneously with a minimum of confusion. Presumably, the same may be true of personology someday, too.

One merit of the romantic tradition in personology is that it has consistently highlighted the problem of structure. At the time Allport was taking his position on these matters (in the late 1920's and early 1930's), the predominant American conceptions of personality were "and-summative" (the sum total of a person's habits, traits, etc.), and the problem of structure was ignored. The early academic personologists who concentrated their efforts on personality inventories, single variables, or factor analyses, all tended to disregard entirely the structuring of these elements or to assume simple, universal answers (e.g., orthogonal factor-structure).

At the same time, however, Freud (1923) was developing the structural point of view in psychoanalysis, and today psychoanalytic psychology is increasingly concerned with the problem and has developed a variety of variables to deal with it (cf. Rapaport & Gill, 1959; Holt, 1960; and see the recent work of G. S. Klein and his associates on cognitive controls as structural variables: Gardner *et al.*, 1959). Drawing on this tradition and that of psychopathology generally, psychodiagnosis concerns itself with structural variables

---

[8] Ironically, in psychology the adherents of structuralism were among those who carried atomistic, reductionistic analysis to its most absurd extreme: the Titchenerian introspectionists. The Gestalt psychologists, though appalled by the equally atomistic behaviorism and structuralism alike, concentrated their efforts on perceptual patterning, leaving untouched most of the structural problems that concern personology, particularly the enduring invariances of molar behavior.

and their constellation into a limited number of ideal types (e.g., the obsessive-compulsive type of ego-structure) which, in the best practice, are used not as pigeonholes but as reference-points in terms of which the clinician creates individualized analyses of personality structure.

6. *There can be no general laws of personality because of the role of chance and free will in human affairs.* There are hardly any contemporary personologists who openly espouse this argument. It played an important part in the development of the romantic point of view, as we have seen, and persists in Catholic psychology. It is generally admitted, however, that scientific work requires the basic assumption of strict determinism throughout. Closely examined, chance becomes ignorance; when we discover systematic effects where "error" existed before, the chance (at least in part) disappears. Theoretically, the exact path of a bolt of lightning and the exact events of a human life could be predicted rigorously, if we only had all of the necessary data at hand.

7. *General laws are not possible in personology because its subject matter is unique individuals, which have no place in natural science.* It is not difficult to dispose of this last, supposedly critical point of difference between *Naturwissenschaft* and *Geisteswissenschaft*.

The mechanistic, pre-field-theoretical science of Windelband's day contained a curious dictum that has been one of the principal sources of confusion on this whole issue: *Scientia non est individuorum*—science does not deal with individual cases. This hoary slogan dates back to the days when Aristotle was the last word on matters scientific, and the whole point of view it expresses is outdated in the physical sciences. According to this philosophy, the individual case was not lawful, since laws were conceived of as empirical regularities. This is the point of view (Plato's idealism or what Popper calls *essentialism*) that considers an average to be the only fact, and all deviation from it mere error.

Freud and Lewin have taught us that psychic determinism is thoroughgoing (see above), and the individual case is completely lawful. It is just difficult to know what the laws *are* from a study of one case, no matter how thorough. We can surmise (or, if you will, intuit) general laws from a single case in the hypothesis-forming phase of scientific endeavor, but we can verify them only by resorting to experimental or statistical inquiry or both.

There is truth in the old adage only in one sense, then: We cannot carry out the complete scientific process by the study of an individual. It is true that in certain of the disciplines concerned with man, from anatomy to sensory psychology, it has usually been assumed that the phenomena being studied are so universal that they can be located for study in any single person, and so autonomous from entanglement in idiosyncratically variable aspects of individuals that the findings of intensive investigation will have general applicability to people at large. Every so often, however, these assumptions turn out not to be tenable. For example, when Boring repeated Head's study (in one case, himself) of the return of sensation after the experimental section of a sensory nerve in his arm, he did not find the protopathic-epicritic sequential recovery, which had been so uncritically accepted as to be firmly embedded in the literature. No matter how intensively prolonged, objective, and well-controlled the study of a single case, one can never be sure to what extent the lawful regularities found can be generalized to other persons, or in what ways the findings will turn out to be contingent on some fortuitously present characteristic of the subject—until the investigation is repeated on an adequate sample of persons. As excellent a way as it is to make discoveries, the study of an individual cannot be used to establish laws; bills of attainder (that is, laws concerned with single individuals) are as unconstitutional in science as in jurisprudence. Note, however, that law of either kind, when promulgated, is still conceived as holding quite rigorously for the single individual.

Science is defined by its methods, not its subject matter; to maintain the opposite, as Skaggs (1945) did in an attack on Allport, is to perpetuate the confusion, not resolve it, and Allport (1946) was an easy victor in the exchange. There can be and is scientific study of all sorts of individuals. Particular hurricanes are individualized to the extent of being given personal names and are studied by all the scientific means at the meteorologist's command. A great deal part of the science of astronomy is given over to the study of a number of unique individuals: the sun, moon, and planets, and even individual stars and nebulae. There may not be another Saturn, with its strange set of rings, in all of creation,[9] yet it is studied by the most exact, quantitative and—if you must—nomothetic methods, and no one has ever considered suggesting that astronomy is for these reasons not a science nor that there should be two entirely different astronomical sciences, one to study individual heavenly bodies and the other to seek general laws. Further examples are easily available from geology, physics, and biology. Once we realize that individuals are easily within the realm of orthodox scientific study, and that science does not strive for artistic illusions of complete understanding, the issue is easily seen as a pseudo-problem. Psychology as a science remains methodologically the same, whether its focus be on individual cases or on general laws.

---

[9] After these words had been written, I was amused to find that Cournot used this same example, and even similar wording, in supporting his position that "it is no longer necessary to accept to the letter the aphorism of the ancients to the effect that the individual and particular have no place in science" (1851, p. 443).

Granted, then, that individual personalities may and must be studied by the scientific method in personology, with the use of general concepts, what is the role of general laws in such a science? Where does it get us to make scientific studies of personalities, if each is unique, and if that uniqueness is the heart of the matter?

Personalities *are* in many ways unique, but as Kluckhohn and Murray (1953) point out, every man is also like all men in some ways and like a limited number of others in still other ways, making generalization possible. If every personality structure were as much a law unto itself as Allport implies, it would be impossible to gain useful information in this field; there would be no transfer from one case study to another. As anyone knows who has tried it, there is a great deal.

It is a mistake to focus personology on just those aspects of a person that are unique, as Weber (1949) saw clearly half a century ago. "The attempt to understand 'Bismarck,' " he said for example, "by leaving out of account everything which he has in common with other men and keeping what is 'particular' to him would be an instructive and amusing exercise for beginners. One would in that case ... preserve, for example, as one of those 'finest flowers' [of such an analysis of uniqueness] his 'thumbprint,' that most specific indication of 'individuality.' " And some of the most critical points about him for predicting his behavior would have to be excluded because he shared them with other persons. Indeed, in contemporary psychodiagnosis, it is considered most useful to treat as a quantitative variable the degree to which a person's responses resemble those of the group as a whole.

The only kind of law that Allport could conceive for personology was one (like his principle of functional autonomy) that describes how uniqueness comes about. Personology has not been much restrained from seeking general relationships among its variables by this narrow view, however; the journals are full of investigations in which aspects of personality are studied genetically (that is, are related to the abstract variable of age) or are correlated, one with another. Once one treats uniqueness not with awe but with the casual familiarity due any other truistic fact of life, it ceases to pose any difficulty for personology.

Writing intensive case studies (on the genesis and structure of individual personalities) turns out not to be a particularly fruitful method, except for the generation of hypotheses. This is a very important exception, but the point is that personology does not proceed mainly by adding one exhaustive scientific biography to another, looking for generalizations afterwards. The Gestaltist taboo on studying any variable out of its context in the individual life is an overstatement. There is, of course, such a phenomenon as the interaction of variables, but it is not so far-reachingly prevalent as to make impossible any study of two variables at a time. As

Falk (1956) has shown, this condition of interactive nonsummativeness is found in many other kinds of subject matter besides personality and creates no major difficulties of method or procedure.

In summary, in this section we have looked at the major propositions of the romantic point of view as applied to personology, and have found that the "basic differences" between this field and natural science are completely illusory. No basis for a separate methodology exists, and the objections to applying the general methodology of science to personalities turn out to be based on misunderstandings or on a narrow conception of natural science that is an anachronism today.

It by no means follows, as Eysenck (1954) puts it, that the science of personality should therefore be considered nomothetic. The nomothetic conception of science must be rejected as a caricature of what any contemporary scientist does. The only way to justify the application of the term nomothetic to the natural science of the present is to change the definition of the term so much that it no longer resembles its original meaning, and becomes an unnecessary redundancy. It can only lead to confusion to introduce such (unacknowledged) changes of definition; the nomothetic is as dead a duck today as the idiographic, and neither term adds anything to contemporary philosophy of science.

Many psychologists have followed Allport in taking the apparently sensible "middle position" of trying to deal with the objections that have been raised to his extreme idiographic pronouncements by saying, let's have a personology that is *both* nomothetic and idiographic (e.g., McClelland, 1951; MacKinnon, 1951). Thus, whenever he approaches the realization that the idiographic discipline of which he dreams is unworkable, Allport says, in effect, "I am not an extremist; common traits have their uses, even though they are only approximations, and personology can use both nomothetic and idiographic contributions." In practice, what this amounts to is that whenever attention is focused on individual cases, the inquiry is called idiographic, and otherwise it is considered nomothetic.

My objection to this "solution," this apparently reasonable compromise between antithetical positions, is that it is achieved only by a perversion of the original definitions, and that it accomplishes nothing except the preservation of a pair of pedantic words for our jargon. If one really accepts the arguments for an idiographic *Geisteswissenschaft* he can logically have no truck with nomothetic methods. They exist no longer, anyway, except in the history books; scientific method, as understood and practiced today in natural science and personology alike, is not a combination nor blend of nomothetic and idiographic approaches, but something bigger and better than both of them. The original dichotomies were badly formulated and based on misconceptions. The accompanying terminology might best be forgotten along with them.

Is There an Idiographic Method?

The last stand of the proponents of the romantic dichotomy is the contention that there are distinct generalizing (nomothetic) and individualizing (idiographic) *methods* in personology. This is the point of departure for Stephenson (1953), and some others who are enchanted by the mystique of Q. Inflating his ingenious rating technique into a whole so-called methodology, Stephenson has argued that his device of rating on an ipsative instead of a normative scale creates a specifically idiographic method for personology. When one Q-sorts a group of items for a subject, he makes a set of ratings which are forced into a normal distribution and scaled according to each item's applicability to this particular person (which is ipsative scaling, as opposed to the usual normative ratings where the standard is the distribution in a population of comparable persons). The device is clever and often useful; it enables a judge to give quantitative ratings to a great number of variables for one person without any reference to any sort of standard population; the population is intrapersonal (cf. Block, 1962).

Here is a technique suited to individual cases; is it therefore idiographic, something fundamentally different from conventional scientific methods of rating personality? Hardly. Actually, Q-sorts are typically used in large studies in which the individual case is an anonymous statistic. Moreover, it is a kind of Procrustean bed, imposing a standard pattern of ratings on every personality: all must have the same mean, standard deviation, and near-normal distribution. What is even further from the spirit of Allport's crusade for individual traits, the "items" are common traits, applied to everyone with no allowance for their failure to fit certain cases. In summary, then, the Q-sort is quite unacceptable in the traditional meaning of the term idiographic, and the use of that term to signify the fact that it is applied to individuals is simply a grandiloquent pose.

Following Allport (1942), others (e.g., Dymond, 1953; Hoffman, 1960) have revived the tired old terms either in an attempt to bolster, or in an attack on, the contention that clinical predictions must be superior to statistical predictions, because the clinician uses idiographic methods which alone are appropriate to predictions about individual cases. Here is another badly formulated pseudo-issue (Holt, 1958). Whether a clinician or a formula does better in making a particular kind of prediction is an empirical question, and one of little general interest. Clinicians and statisticians have their own proper spheres of activity, which overlap but little, and the difference between their activities has nothing to do with methodological issues. The method of clinical judgment has a great deal in common with the hypothesis-forming and theory-building phases of work in all the sciences (Holt, 1961).

In the end, we see that there is no need for a special type of science to be applied to individual personalities, and that the attempt to promulgate such a science fell into hopeless contradictions and absurdities. Today, Windelband's terms continue to appear in psychological writing but largely as pretentious jargon, mouth-filling polysyllables to awe the uninitiated, but never as essential concepts to make any scientifically vital point. Let us simply drop them from our vocabularies and let them die quietly.[10]

Summary

The conception of two kinds of disciplines, a nomothetic science to study general principles and find abstract laws, and an idiographic science to study individuality, arose as a protest against a narrow conception of science in the nineteenth century. But the romantic movement of which it was a part started from fallacious premises, such as the conception that science is defined by its subject matter rather than its method, and its radical principles were never actually applied in pure form by any of its adherents. The idiographic point of view is an artistic one that strives for a nonscientific goal; the nomothetic, a caricature of science that bears little resemblance to anything that exists today. Since no useful purpose is served by retaining these mischievous and difficult terms, they had best disappear from our scientific vocabularies.

---

[10] Surely a trivial but none the less an annoying characteristic of the word idiographic furnishes a further argument for its consignment to oblivion: the strong tendency of printers to assimilate it to the more familiar but wholly different word *ideographic* (pertaining to ideographs or picture-writing). For example, Skaggs's paper (1945) contains *only* the misspelled version.

References

Allport, G. W. *Personality, a psychological interpretation.* New York: Holt, 1937(a).
Allport, G. W. The personalistic psychology of William Stern. *Char. & Pers.,* 1937, **5,** 231-246. (b).
Allport, G. W. Motivation in personality: Reply to Mr. Bertocci. *Psychol. Rev.,* 1940, **47,** 533-554.
Allport, G. W. The use of personal documents in psychological science. *Soc. Sci. Res. Council Bull.,* 1942, **49.**
Allport, G. W. Personalistic psychology as science: A reply. *Psychol. Rev.,* 1946, **53,** 132-135.
Allport, G. W. *Becoming: Basic considerations for a psychology of personality.* New Haven: Yale Univ. Press, 1955.
Beck, S. J. The science of personality: Nomothetic or idiographic? *Psychol. Rev.,* 1953, **60,** 353-359.
Bellak, L. Freud and projective techniques. *J. proj. Tech.,* 1956, **20,** 5-13.
Bertalanffy, L. von. Theoretical models in biology and psychology. *J. Pers.,* 1951, **20,** 24-38.
Boring, E. G. *A history of experimental psychology.* New York: Appleton-Century, 1929.
Brunswik, E. Organismic achievement and environmental probability. *Psychol. Rev.,* 1943, **50,** 255-272. Also in M. H. Marx (Ed.) *Psychological theory: Contemporary readings.* New York: Macmillan, 1951.
Colby, K. M. *A skeptical psychoanalyst.* New York: Wiley, 1958.

Cournot, A. A. (1851) *An essay on the foundations of our knowledge.* (Trans. M. H. Moore). New York: Liberal Arts Press, 1956.

Dymond, Rosalind. Can clinicians predict individual behavior? *J. Pers.,* 1953, **22,** 151-161.

Eysenck, H. J. The science of personality: Nomothetic! *Psychol. Rev.,* 1954, **61,** 339-342.

Falk, J. L. Issues distinguishing nomothetic from idiographic approaches to personality theory. *Psychol. Rev.,* 1956, **63,** 53-62.

Freud, S. (1923) *The ego and the id.* London: Hogarth, 1947.

Friess, H. L. Wilhelm Dilthey. *J. Philos.,* 1929, **26,** 5-25.

Gardner, R., Holzman, P. S., Klein, G. S., Linton, Harriet B., and Spence, D. P. Cognitive control: A study of individual consistencies in cognitive behavior. *Psychol. Issues,* 1959, **1,** No. 4.

Hoffman, P. J. The paramorphic representation of clinical judgment. *Psychol. Bull.,* 1960, **57,** 116-131.

Holt, R. R. Clinical *and* statistical prediction: A reformulation and some new data. *J. abnorm. soc. Psychol.,* 1958, **56,** 1-12.

Holt, R. R. Recent developments in psychoanalytic ego psychology and their implications for diagnostic testing. *J. proj. Tech.,* 1960, **24,** 254-266.

Holt, R. R. Clinical judgment as a disciplined inquiry. *J. nerv. ment. Dis.,* 1961, **133,** 369-382.

Jones, E. *The life and work of Sigmund Freud.* Vol. 1. New York: Basic Books, 1953.

Klein, G. S., & Schlesinger, H. J. Where is the perceiver in perceptual theory? *J. Pers.,* 1949, **18,** 32-47.

Kluckhohn, C., & Murray, H. A. Personality formation: The determinants. Chap. 2 in C. Kluckhohn & H. A. Murray (Eds.), *Personality in nature, society, and culture.* New York: Knopf, 1953.

Klüver, H. Contemporary German psychology as a "cultural science." In G. Murphy, *An historical introduction to modern psychology.* (1st ed.) New York: Harcourt, Brace, 1929.

McClelland, D. C. *Personality.* New York: Dryden Press, 1951.

MacKinnon, D. W. Personality. *Ann. Rev. Psychol.,* 1951, **2,** 113-136.

Murphy, G. *Personality: A biosocial approach to origins and structure.* New York: Harper, 1947.

Murray, H. A. *Explorations in personality.* New York: Oxford Univ. Press, 1938.

Parsons, T. (1937) *The structure of social action.* Glencoe, Ill.: Free Press, 1957.

Popper, K. R. *The open society and its enemies.* Princeton, N. J.: Princeton Univ. Press, 1950.

Popper, K. R. *The poverty of historicism.* Boston: Beacon, 1957.

Rapaport, D., & Gill, M. M. The points of view and assumptions of metapsychology. *Int. J. Psychoanal.,* 1959, **40,** 153-162.

Rapaport, D., Gill, M. M., & Schafer, R. *Diagnostic psychological testing.* 2 vols. Chicago: Yearbook Publishers, 1945-46.

Roback, A. A. *The psychology of character.* New York: Harcourt, Brace, 1927.

Sarbin, T. R. The logic of prediction in psychology. *Psychol. Rev.,* 1944, **51,** 210-228.

Schafer, R. Psychological tests in clinical research. *J. consult. Psychol.,* 1949, **13,** 328-334. Also in R. P. Knight & C. R. Friedman (Eds.), *Psychoanalytic psychiatry and psychology.* New York: International Universities Press, 1954.

Singer, C. *A short history of scientific ideas.* London: Oxford Univ. Press, 1959.

Skaggs, E. B. Personalistic psychology as science. *Psychol. Rev.,* 1945, **52,** 234-238.

Spranger, E. (1922) *Types of men.* (Trans. P. J. W. Pigors) Halle: Niemy, 1928.

Stein, L. Historical optimism: Wilhelm Dilthey. *Philos. Rev.,* 1924, **33,** 329-344.

Stephenson, W. *The study of behavior: Q-technique and its methodology.* Chicago: Univ. of Chicago Press, 1953.

Stern, W. *General psychology from a personalistic standpoint.* (Trans. H. D. Spoerl) New York: Macmillan, 1938.

Tapper, B. Dilthey's methodology of the *Geisteswissenschaften. Philos. Rev.,* 1925, **34,** 333-349.

Weber, M. *The methodology of the social sciences.* (Trans. & ed. by E. A. Shils and H. A. Finch) Glencoe, Ill.: Free Press, 1949. (The material collected here was originally published from 1904 to 1917.)

THE DEFENSE MECHANISMS RE-EXAMINED: A LOGICAL AND PHENOMENAL ANALYSIS

RAYMOND J. McCALL
Marquette University

COPING VERSUS DEFENSIVENESS

If we assume that a self-directed self-realization is the ideal by relation to which such concepts as "mental health" and "psychological adjustment" (or, as I would prefer to say, *psychological well-being*) take on meaning, then we should recognize that movement toward this ideal would depend upon a continuing attitude of self-concern and self-esteem, very like what William McDougall called the *master sentiment of self-regard.*

In a primitive sense, self-regard is not something which has to be learned. No one who has observed two-year olds carefully could doubt that a high valuation of the self and a deep-rooted set to seek one's advantage are natural and spontaneous, and generally resistive to the slightest effort toward modification in the direction of reciprocation, sharing, or other social values. Yet in later childhood and adulthood this primal self-regard is often offset by profound feelings of inadequacy and inferiority, even of self-condemnation and self-loathing. It would seem, then, that a well integrated and durable sense of self-worth is by no means an automatic and inevitable consequence of childish self-seeking.

In considering the influence of social forces upon personality, it is only recently that we have begun to appreciate that it is not only the qualities of the self which are socially influenced but the very self-concept and the evaluation of the self in relation to developmental and other standards. When we have grasped the fact that self-evaluation is socially mediated, it requires little further thought to realize that the direction of this evaluation is not always flattering. Beginning with the family, and no doubt most importantly and effectively therein, every social group evaluates its junior members with respect to its own norms, and, nearly always finding the individual in some respects wanting, seeks by disapproval and its derivatives to motivate him to alter his behavior and his inner dispositions appropriately. In so doing it is likely to convey to the individual a view of himself as something less than he should be.

It is precisely because the self-concept is made up largely, as Sullivan so beautifully phrases it, of the *reflected appraisals of significant others* in our social environment, that it is possible for that environment virtually to compel internalization of a largely disparaging estimate of the self—to drive home an image of the self as stupid, inept, uncontrolled, disorganized, inconsiderate, lazy, selfish, base, disgusting, or perverse—which will naturally conflict with that primitive self-regard and self-seeking which are apparently part of our native equipment. Thereby, conflict is introduced into the very heart of the self, a conflict which must be resolved if cognitive consistency and emotional integration are to be at all possible.

It is seldom, of course, that the "appraisals" by the "significant others" are entirely negative; hence the contradiction of one's self-esteem is not absolute and unconditioned. One is unlikely to be appraised as *simply inept*, but as *intelligent and well-meaning but inept*, or as a charming child *except for* that disgusting tinge of sexuality or inconsiderateness, or that evil temper. Such ambivalent evaluations complicate rather than remove the conflict. There is no doubt, in any case, that imputations contrary to our self-esteem set us at odds with ourselves, and that upon the manner of our handling the conflicting self-attitudes turns much that is pertinent to the psychology of abnormality.

It would seem that if self-regard is to be retained as the motor of self-enhancement and self-realization, the organism should have some means of safeguarding its primitive self-esteem against this kind of contradiction. If we sense in the attitude of "significant others" a judgment of us at odds with our own feelings of worth, or if we find ourselves strangely motivated to act in ways which contradict standards of behavior which we have already accepted for ourselves, then there are two possible attitudes which we may adopt, each of which has enormous consequences for the self-concept and the future adjustment of the person to the reality around him. The first of these we shall call *coping*, the second *defensiveness*.

Coping implies a realistic facing up to the difficulty by, for example, acknowledging the hitherto unrecognized deficiency or peculiarity (adjusting the self-image), and endeavoring to control or modify it appropriately, especially in its behavioral expression. This is the way of insight, reality-testing, and emotional control. It does not rest self-esteem upon the childishly idealistic image of the perfect self but values the self despite its imperfections and seeks to bolster self-esteem by accomplishment.

The second way of dealing with threat of this kind to self-esteem, the way of *defensiveness*, is far easier than coping because it evades the threat and nullifies it symbolically rather than facing up to it and endeavoring to overcome it directly. It is a kind of automatic and indeliberate psychic manipulation which sets defense above adjustment, and refusing to acknowledge the threat to self-esteem as a real threat, admits it like a Trojan horse into the citadel of the self. It is as though the adverse judgment of significant others or the detection of unacceptable qualities or dispositions in ourselves is so disruptive of self-esteem that it cannot be borne. We say to ourselves in effect "Oh, no! That can't be true," and proceed to act as though it were not. At the same time, of course, there is some recognition that this unacceptable element is or can be true, for otherwise it would constitute no threat. In substance, then, the contradiction is at once denied and accepted, an impossible position to hold openly, as Freud brilliantly and profoundly saw. The human person, said Freud, can live with this contradiction only by suppressing one of its terms (rendering it "unconscious"), by deceiving himself into thinking that what it glimpsed as true is not true. It is perhaps Freud's greatest contribution to abnormal psychology to have penetrated so deeply into the workings and implications of this defensively-determined initial self-deception. From this he went on to identify what he and his daughter, Anna, called the "ego defense mechanisms," the various unconscious maneuvers by which the inner self seeks to defend its integrity against the imputation of unacceptable qualities and tendencies, and to show the importance of these maneuvers in the development of abnormal or peculiar habits and attitudes.

The Phenomenology of Defense Mechanisms

No one who writes in this area can be unaware of the fact that we are all standing on Freud's shoulders, and there is good reason to commend Anna Freud as well for her attempt to present systematically the Freudian position. But in acknowledging our debts to the Freuds, *père et fille,* we may still be chary of subscribing to Freudian constructs and postulates which are far removed from simple phenomenological description and which constitute a kind of systematic mythology of the libido. In this mythology is included the highly dubious assumption that the "ego" is entirely the vassal of the "instinctual apparatus" (the "id"), that sexual and destructive impulses, the latter arising from the "death instinct," are the only sources of anxiety, and that the subject of the defense-mechanisms is always this same anxiety. Because we employ the generic term "defense mechanism" and in most instances the specific terms (such as *rationalization, compensation, displacement, projection*) for particular instances thereof, terms which were coined by Freud or his immediate followers, we perhaps commit ourselves to general concepts like "psychic conflict" and "unconscious motivation" but in no significant degree are we bound to the elaborate theoretical system which Freud and his followers have built up to account for these phenomena, or to specific aspects of this system which are supposedly related directly to "ego defense." We may, for example, accept the notion of hostility as frequently involved in the defense mechanism of *projection* without committing ourselves to the "death instinct" as its ultimate root, or to infantile "spitting out" as its prototype, or to homosexuality as its concomitant (Fenichel, 1945).

Adhering, then, as closely as possible to a phenomenological method, we may begin by describing defense mechanisms as *self-protective maneuvers, pertaining to perception and motivation, mental or psychic, yet largely unconscious, designed to soften or disguise what is unacceptable in or to the self.* Though not deliberately adopted, defense mechanisms have an apparent utility as disguises of our weaknesses and baser motives.

Not only Freud and the orthodox Freudians, but many others, have seen the defense mechanisms as essentially protection against *anxiety,* particularly of the sort deriving from aberrant sexual impulse. However important this particular kind of defense may be—and we should be careful not to underestimate it—there is little evidence in favor of regarding all defense mechanisms as deriving from it. We run less risk of over-generalization (or misplaced concreteness), therefore, if we maintain that *whatever* is threatening to our self-esteem is a fitting subject for cognitive-appetitive self-defense. Perhaps sexually derived anxiety has a special importance and intensity, but it would seem that the defense mechanisms may be evoked by anything that conflicts with our *minimum ideal* of what the self must be. This might include incompetence, stupidity, selfishness, indecisiveness, or any other self-devaluating experience or circumstance. It may be that the three interrelated conditions of the self—*anxiety, hostility,* and *sexuality*—are peculiarly suited to elicit the *habitual and exaggerated* employment of defenses which seems to characterize the neurotic, but our description and analysis of the defense mechanisms should take cognizance of the fact that they are employed by normal as well as by neurotic and other types of abnormal persons.

On this, as well as on other accounts, defense mechanisms should not be confused with *symptoms* of neurosis or other abnormal conditions.[1] The mechanisms are purely *endopsychic* or mental (cognitive-appetitive) devices, ways of perceiving and desiring, giving a protectively distorted registration of the self and its world, and connoting a matching wish to have them free of threats to our self-regard. Symptoms, on the other hand, are not limited to the psychic, to ways of thinking and wishing, but attach themselves to our behavior in any of a thousand ways as well as to our thoughts and feelings, and may disturb our physiological as well as our psychological functioning. Thus, *perceiving* your boss as though he were your tyrannical father connotes the defense-mechanism of *displacement*, while developing a severe *phobia* at the prospect of going out of the house on work days (without knowing why) would be a *neurotic symptom*, just as developing high blood pressure after a short time on the job might be designated a *psychosomatic* or *psychophysiologic symptom*. In many instances the defense mechanism and the symptom may be related as antecedent and consequent, but there is no justification for confusing relatively simple cause with its more heterogeneous and often distant effects.

To say that the defense mechanisms are largely *unconscious* is to stress by implication that they are always in corresponding degree *self-deceptive*. If, indeed, the individual were not taken in by them they would not serve to defend his self-esteem against the intimation of inadequacy or dereliction. That unconscious *defense* is less effectively adjustive than conscious *coping* is evident if we consider that, however variously the ideal of self-realization may be construed, the self-directively adjustive life is a *conscious* life; a never-ending task of modifying situations to suit the demands of the self, modifying the latter to suit the requirements of the former, or (most often) effecting some compromise between the two.[2] From any perspective, this involves insightful awareness in such matters as understanding the limitations of one's own powers and performance; recognizing our

---

[1] This confusion detracts from much of Anna Freud's analysis in her widely admired book, *The Ego and the Mechanisms of Defense* (1954).

[2] Recall the famous prayer: "O Lord, give me the courage to change what has to be changed, the patience to bear what cannot be changed, and the wisdom to tell the difference between the two."

social dependence and the need of acquiescing in the reasonable demands of others; acknowledging the irrational and imperfect elements in ourselves (not just in others or in the institutions of our society); admitting to oneself at least failure of adaptation when it occurs and the consequent need for self-correction, renewed effort, and variation in our approach. Not only, we should add, are these modes of coping different from defense; they are made difficult or impossible by the subjectively protective set of the defense mechanisms which in effect blinds us to our own real requirements other than those dictated by self-esteem.

It would appear, therefore, that the self which is defended by defense mechanisms is not the insightful, reality-oriented, and socialized self. Rather, it is the infantile self with its islands of self-ignorance, its imperfectly socialized dependency, its delusive overvaluation of itself ("narcissism"), and its defective reality-contact. However important it may be for self-realization that the individual retain his energizing self-regard, it seems that when subjectively oriented defense assumes primacy over objectively oriented coping, we have an immature and intrinsically maladaptive organization, perhaps indeed the very *Anlage* of the neurotic personality structure.

Descriptive Analysis of Defense Mechanisms

Lists of defense mechanisms are variable in length and in the intricacy of the logical and psychological considerations offered in their support. We shall consider an even dozen in what appears to be the most nearly logical order for an understanding of their pertinence to abnormal psychology. They are:

1) Repression
2) Isolation
3) Rationalization
4) Reaction-formation
5) Compensation
6) Defensive devaluation
7) Displacement
8) Projection
9) Withdrawal
10) Identification
11) Undoing
12) Autism

1. *Repression: the attempted exclusion from awareness of self-devaluating experiences* such as shameful memories and unacceptable motives whether hostile, fearful, sexual, pettily selfish, crude, dishonest, or contemptible.

Repression is said to be the most fundamental of defense mechanisms, since unless the self-devaluating memory or motive is somehow removed from the center of consciousness, it is difficult to see how we can be deceived into using other means to defend against it. All other mechanisms would thus seem to depend upon at least an initial repression. At the same time, the very existence of other mechanisms indicates that repression is not entirely successful in "warding off" the self-depreciating experience. If to rationalize or project or displace a hateful impulse or shortcoming I must be less than perfectly aware of that impulse or shortcoming, by the same token there would be no need for me to rationalize, or project, or displace if through repression

I had succeeded in putting the whole matter out of mind. It is for this reason that the term *"attempted* exclusion" has been incorporated in our definition of repression.

The Freudians speak of repression in quasi-topographical terms as a process by which "drives and memories" are "pushed down into the unconscious." Pursuing the metaphor, they hold that such repressed material continues to exist *unchanged* "in the unconscious," but being barred from direct expression, can return only in symbolic or disguised form as "symptoms," "sublimations," or other "derivatives." One possibility, however, which they acknowledge but to which they seem not to have devoted sufficient attention, is that repression may be *from the beginning* less than an all or none affair, and that what they are pleased to call "the return of the repressed" may sometimes signalize only its failure to depart.

There is a tendency, too, for them to regard conscious-unconscious as a simple dichotomy, and to speak of mental states as one *or* the other. It is more in accord, however, both with scientific usage and with everyday experience to think of conscious and unconscious as the opposite ends of a continuum rather than as dichotomous contraries, and to recognize that the departure from and approach to consciousness may be gradual. Of some experiences I may be quite unconscious, as of events taking place prior to my second birthday, and you may be utterly unaware of crassly selfish reasons for wanting to do someone a good turn. Frequently, on the other hand, we are able to bring past events to the margin of consciousness, if not to its center—as psychoanalysis has made very clear—and frequently, too, we dimly sense an element of self-seeking in our more "unselfish" attitudes.

There is thus much in our psychic life that is neither clearly conscious nor entirely unconscious. Perhaps if we imagine clear and focal consciousness as the center of a spiral, and unconsciousness as exemplified by increasing removal from that focal center but having its exact boundaries fluid and unspecified, we shall have a topographical analogy that limps a little less than the one implied by the sharply divided surface and subsurface of the Freudian iceberg. It would seem, at any rate, more descriptively accurate to think of repression as initially incomplete, and of the unconscious as a relative condition, than to assume a total repression into total unconsciousness of a totally unchangeable psychic content that can be re-admitted to awareness only by way of symbolization. Only the Freudian penchant for an over-simplified, two-valued logic and for a mechanical model of the human psyche requires thinking in such rigid categories.

In discussing repression and the unconscious it also seems worthwhile to keep in mind the difference between the psychic *process* of repression, and its *product*, the repressed experience. Even if we assume that the act of repression is totally unconscious, it does not follow that the self-devaluating experience is always rendered totally unconscious, or even rendered unconscious in all its self-devaluating aspects. Though I am not conscious of repressing, I may remain conscious of certain parts of an experience which has self-depreciating implications, and perhaps even vaguely conscious of the self-depreciating elements themselves. It is possible, in short, that at times repression is only partially successful because it is only partial. This does not rule out the possibility that some repressed material may return to awareness in symbolic form, but leaves open the additional possibility that in some instances only part of the original experience is repressed.

2. *Isolation.* Isolation may be defined as *the cutting off or blunting of unacceptable aspects of a total experience.* To accept isolation as a mechanism underscores the partial nature of at least some repression, since isolation seems to be nothing but a special kind of partial repression, one indeed whose partial nature is most evident. Thus in the most common manifestation of isolation the individual appears to be in possession of all the facts of a situation but not to recognize them for what they are, or not to register the whole situation in its most obvious implications of a derogatory sort. This is likely to impress the ordinary observer as peculiar or queer as when the mother of a severely retarded child regards her child's behavior as little different from that of other children despite its gross deficiencies; or when the long-suffering wife of the alcoholic sees her husband's trouble only in his being a little too sociable; or when the notably homely girl fails to appreciate the unmistakable implications of her unattractiveness. This kind of isolation seems to defend against deficiency in ourselves or in those close to us.[3]

We should note, however, that it is not so much the *existence* of the fact which is nullified by the partial repression as is its *motivational relevance* and *emotional implications,* from which its existence is isolated. In another kind of isolation—that found in certain types of obsessional neurosis and concerned with unacceptable impulses in the self—it is again not the fact which is denied to consciousness. In these cases the individual acknowledges the unacceptable desire but cannot recognize its relevance to his own motivational system. ("I love my wife. Why should I feel this crazy impulse to strangle her?") Perhaps, too, the homely girl *knows* that she is homely but fails to see this fact as relevant to her seldom being invited out by eligible males. Such "selective imperception" is very palpably defensive, not denying the experience but separating or isolating it from elements threatening to self-esteem.

3. *Rationalization.* Rationalization may be described as *pseudo-explanation of criticizable behavior or attitude which substitutes acceptable (often fancied) motives for its actual motives.* The rationalizer will view his idleness as needed relaxation, his cowardice as caution, his impatiently severe discipline as in the child's best interests.

In the classical view rationalization always involves repression of an unacceptable motive and its return in some disguise which is still close enough to the original to awaken defensive processes. Though it may in many instances be true, this smacks a little of cloak-and-dagger melodrama. Less mysterious and equally worth noting again is the palpable incompleteness or partial failure of the repression. It would seem, indeed, that *the sense of having an unacceptable purpose behind our action must be at least vaguely present in order for there to be any occasion to rationalize,* and this means that what is threatening to self-esteem has not been effectively repressed. Without recourse to the notions of banishment and return incognito, we might assume that in some instances a particular evil inclination has been repressed but that a residual, in the form of a vague or general feeling of guilt or unworthy disposition, abides with us and demands that somehow it be "explained away."

---

[3] Allport (1937) especially has noted the manner in which the self tends with maturity to broaden so as to include those closest to us. I am thus not only my physical and isolated self but, in a very real sense, those with whom I "identify."

The compulsory character of this demand for explanation is not hard to understand when we recall that from infancy on each of us is expected to be able to account for his conduct according to the standards of "reason" and "common sense" dictated by his culture and sub-cultures. The *fear of disapproval* by others for what is base and unworthy in one's conduct is one of the most powerful motives in human existence, and a plausible basis for that nameless but often unsettling apprehension which we call "anxiety" (McCall, 1962). In this sense there can be no reasonable doubt that rationalization operates as a defense against anxiety, reinforcing our efforts to escape disapproval by concocting allegedly laudable purposes for our behavior.

The task of rationalization is made somewhat easier by the fact that most of our actions are *multiply motivated* ("over-determined" is the Freudian barbarism), so that there may be "good" as well as "bad" reasons for our behaving as we do. The work of rationalization in this case is to point up, rather than invent, the good reasons for our action when repression has reduced, without quite eliminating, our awareness of the bad.

4. *Reaction-formation:* a singularly unhappy term for *defending self-esteem against one's partially repressed and unacceptable dispositions by over-desiring their opposite*. If rationalization is a kind of "refutation by argument" of implied unworthiness, reaction-formation is a "refutation by action." I lay the ghost of suspected meanness by behaving so very, very nobly that no one could possibly doubt the purity of my motives. Least of all, we should add, myself!

Though overworked in certain circles, reaction-formation ("antithetic counteraction" or "counteractive inversion" would be a more precisely descriptive term) is probably important in the genesis of certain moralistic compulsions and attitudes. It is fanciful to suppose that all perfectionism is motivated, as Freud thought, by the repressed desire for the exact opposite: that extreme neatness, for example, is simply "warding off" a powerful disposition to be disgustingly messy, that the ideal of perfect benevolence is motivated by an unacknowledged but uncompromising hostility and a savage cruelty, or that those who are most on the side of the angels are the biggest devils at heart. It is possible, nevertheless, to cite enough examples of "antithetically counteractive" motivation to give plausibility to such exaggerations; and where an individual's ethical attitudes are extreme and inflexible at the same time that he gives evidence of excessive preoccupation with the violation of ethical standards (especially by others), we may reasonably suspect something like reaction-formation to be at work.

To justify suspicion of reaction-formation, however, there should be indications of the persistence in some form (perhaps only symbolic) of the rejected motive while the reaction against it is truly immoderate, a "bending over backwards," a tendency to "protest too much" in action as well as in words, and an obsessive concern with morality and immorality in this particular area. Sexual irregularities may offer a special occasion for reaction-formation since sexual motivation is likely to be at once powerful and devious, yet subject to much restriction and criticism. Certainly those who spend a great deal of time investigating and exposing the sexual depravities of others are thereby afforded an opportunity to wallow in the shocking details thereof themselves. This may offer simultaneously a partial gratification of their own repressed sexual impulses (perhaps voyeuristic or Peeping Tom-like in nature) and the appearance of absolute virtuousness.

The Reverend Davidson in Somerset Maugham's classic "Rain" is close to an ideal embodiment of reaction-formation. His implacable hatred of sexual immorality, his relentless persecution of the loose woman, Sadie Thompson, his consuming joy at her "conversion," the aridity of his own married life, even his dreams of mountains which resemble a woman's breasts, point to the defensive and self-deceptive nature of his own rejection of sex. It is not then from an ideal morality that reaction-formation springs but from a rigid and uninsightful moralistic excess, through which symbolic glimpses of a very different sort of motivation appear. And, of course, it is not merely sexuality that may thus emerge. As Plato said of Antisthenes' contempt for worldly honors and other goods: "His vanity peeps out through the holes in his cloak."

Reaction-formation is not, however, to be confused with hypocritical pretense. The person employs this mechanism indeliberately rather than with full awareness, and there is usually little doubt of the sincerity of his desire for ethical righteousness. It is, in fact, the extremity of this desire which gives him away, making clear the defensive rather than adjustively coping nature of his love of virtue.

5. *Compensation.* If what remains threatening to self-esteem in the way of deficiency or dereliction cannot be "explained away" (rationalization) or "acted away" (reaction-formation), it can perhaps be *made up for.* This is the way of *compensation.* Compensation may then be described as a *defense mechanism which enables us to offset unacceptable tendencies or weaknesses by overvaluing and overstressing acceptable motives or strengths.* The interdependence of the two elements, "*over*valuation" and "weakness" is essential to the notion of compensation as a defense mechanism rather than as a mode of coping; and in defensive compensation there is always in all probability some repression, so that the deficiency or aberration is not consciously faced.

Alfred Adler, who invented the term "compensation," saw clearly that every style of life demands the stressing of certain values and the subordination or diminution of others. We have no warrant to speak of compensation as an unrealistic and uninsightful defense, however, unless the valuation of one goal is exaggerated as a means of defending self-esteem against an unacknowledged imperfection. So, to set great store by intellectual accomplishment is not compensation unless it is extreme and designed (unconsciously) to make up for physical or other defect; and striving for a successful career may well be nothing but adjustive coping unless it serves as a means of offsetting social unattractiveness or a comparable shortcoming.

Compensation is also to be distinguished from deliberate emphasis upon certain capacities and dispositions where these reflect natural endowment or general group expectation. Thus for the musically talented child in 18th century Germany to devote more of his energies to music than to any other interest, or for the athletically endowed American boy to work in and out of season to perfect his skills in fielding or foul-shooting, is by no accounting necessarily compensatory.

Nor should a direct attack on a weakness, designed to overcome whatever incapacity that weakness may connote, be confused with defensive compensation. The boy with polio who becomes a distance runner, the stutterer who will one day be a great orator, the frail child who develops into a partisan of the vigorous life are manifesting an actively coping rather than a defensive orientation. We should be chary of labeling as compensatory any behavior that does not imply unrealistic over-valuation and unadmitted defect.

A form of supposed compensation said to be common among modern women, due to their inferior status in our society and their resentment of male superiority and privilege, was designated by Adler "masculine protest." Whatever the merits of this notion (which has considerable currency among clinicians working with neurotic women), it too should not be overworked. In his later years Adler gave up the contention that one's entire style of life is determined by the mode of compensation for the sense of inferiority originating in childhood, and he relegated the famous "inferiority complex" to a secondary though still significant place in the development of personality. In any case, it would be a dangerous oversimplification to disregard the constructively adjustive aspect of much feminine striving, and to reduce all the efforts of women to overcome their dependent and subordinate status in our culture to a "masculine protest." Even to conjoin under this heading all instances of aggressive feminism, from the fastidiousness of the D.A.R. to the zealousness of the W.C.T.U., not excluding the manipulative proclivities of women executives, matriarchal dictators, and lady wrestlers, is to dilute the meaning of "masculine protest" to that of an anti-feminine expletive. Even following a more restrained usage, however, it is doubtful that much of what is called "masculine protest" has any bearing on compensation as a defense mechanism.

6. *Defensive devaluation.* If we cannot compensate for weaknesses and transgressions, we can divert our own and others' attention from them by concentrating on the faults of others. Though not included in the classical lists of defense-mechanisms, defensive devaluation appears to be an important self-protective maneuver, of a cognitive sort basically, *a focusing upon the weaknesses and aberrations of others as a means of calling attention away from one's own deficiencies.*

Behaviorally, defensive devaluation is likely to be expressed by endless and unwarranted "griping" at the bosses, the "brass," the government, or "people" generally. But the true defensive devaluator does not criticize in the hope of effecting reform but as a defense against his own sense of inadequacy and perhaps guilt. The presence of repression is indicated by his general insensitivity to faults in himself in the face of an extreme sensitivity to the inconsiderateness, stupidity, and similar faults of others. He sees the mote of his neighbor's eye but misses the splinter in his own, and with a vengeance. Yet he does not directly overemphasize his own assets as in compensation, nor does he attribute his own motives to others, as is supposed to take place in *projection*. Nor does defensive devaluation connote the profound lack of insight, characteristic of reaction-formation and, as we shall see, projection. It is thus perhaps the "least abnormal" of mechanisms, enabling us to say in effect "I know I have my weaknesses, but what do they amount to when you consider . . . ," followed by a litany of the foibles and iniquities of others, thereby mitigating the threat to self-esteem of our own failings without denying their existence.

7. *Displacement: Attaching an unacceptable motive and its accompanying affect to an alternative object which can provide partial (usually symbolic) release for the original motive without bringing the*

latter to awareness. Examples are numerous, as in the peculiar joy derived from beating a business rival at golf or bridge, satisfying a prying tendency by taking a job which involves conducting investigations into the lives of others (perhaps that of a psychologist!), carrying over a repressed hatred and fear of one's father to one's relations with his boss or with older authority figures generally.

Whether displacement plays as enormous a role in human motivation as postulated by Freud is open to considerable doubt, but there is no question that as a defense mechanism it has unusual importance in the genesis of neurotic symptoms and of neurotic "tendencies" found even in the normal person.

The symbolic and defensive nature of displacement is manifested by the presence of intense feeling quite disproportionate to the acknowledged importance of the current circumstance. When, for example, a man attaches a value to winning at bridge that the card game in itself could not by any reckoning warrant, when he is upset for days over a bad play or at losing to a neighbor, playing and replaying every trick in his mind, planning his strategy for the next game in great and anxious detail, we infer that beating his opponent at bridge is symbolic to him of something larger, that not the game itself but his self-regard is somehow at stake. So when a man is hatefully resentful of a superior where there is little or nothing in the behavior of the superior to justify this malevolent attitude, we may again look beyond the present situation to some other relation of which it may be symbolic and which, having been repressed, has been denied expression, such as resentment toward a domineering parent, rivalry with an older brother, and the like.

We may note in such cases a *reason to repress* the original motive and feeling. Thus the love and respect which we are supposed to feel, and often actually do feel, toward our parents or siblings, may make attitudes of dislike or resentment unacceptable and self-devaluating. This does not seem to be the case with all symbolic displacements, however, which therefore may not serve any special defensive purpose but take place simply as a result of the inevitable human disposition to symbolize. Thus my transfer of negative feeling from an earlier experience to a present one may be maladaptive without serving to protect self-esteem, as when I react to a new acquaintance on the basis of his (unrecognized) resemblance to an old rival. Though maladaptive, such displacements are unlikely to be productive of neurosis since the aberrant tendency is not reinforced by the continuing need to safeguard self-esteem and may be more readily modified by corrective experience.

In postulating that the defensive symbolism of displacement renders intelligible much peculiar feeling and behavior, and that phobias and compulsions and conversion symptoms often "make sense" in the light of their symbolically defensive purpose, Freud unquestionably contributed more than any other person to our understanding of neurotic and other abnormal phenomena. Freud also seems to have had reason on his side in arguing that sexual motives, because of their intrinsic urgency and the severe disapproval with which their manifestation in the young is likely to be greeted, are specially subject to symbolization and displacement, following inadequate repression.

It is something less than necessary, however, to concur in Freud's speculations regarding the unlimited displaceability of sexual motives and to conclude with him that not only many neurotic symptoms but many entirely normal activities of a higher order such as religious rituals, artistic endeavor, and intellectual interests equally represent symbolic fulfilments of sexual urges. To interpret prayer as satisfying the impulse to masturbate, painting as a displacement of the motive to smear excrement, and intellectual curiosity as a symbolic equivalent of the wish to play peeping Tom in the parental bedroom, requires a degree of credulity in the magical power of symbolism which is so far fortunately confined to some psychoanalysts and psychotics.

Some instances of apparent displacement involve little or no symbolism and most probably denote a rather obvious kind of "safety-valve" mechanism, as when the business man who has had to contain his ire all day takes it out on his wife and children in the evening; or when we, having put up with a series of frustrations or indignities, "blow up" at some trifling contretemps. These bear only a superficial resemblance to the systematically symbolic and elaborately self-deceptive displacements we find in many neurotics, and should not be considered to exemplify the defense-mechanism in any strict sense. Symbolism as well as self-defense is thus probably, as Freud thought, essential to the kind of displacement which contributes to neurosis.

8. *Projection.* Projection is one of the most important mechanisms for the understanding of psychological abnormality, but it is more pertinent to psychosis and the so-called personality pattern disturbances than it is to the relatively minor abnormalities or neuroses. To project is *to defend against unacceptable motives by attributing to others either the motives themselves or the criticism of oneself for having such motives.* The unacceptable is not explained away, counteracted, or made up for (as in rationalization, reaction-formation, and compensation); one gets rid of it projecting it onto others, by regarding it as the creation of others and not of oneself. Projection is instanced by interpreting neutral behavior in another as hostile, while not recognizing the reality and primacy of one's own hostility; by reacting to homosexual or other deviant sexual tendencies in oneself by first over-vigorously denying the possibility of any such tendencies, and thereupon ascribing to others unjust accusations against the self of having such tendencies. The two examples illustrate what may be distinguished as *primary projection* (direct attribution of our unacceptable motives to another); and *secondary projection* (attribution to others of critical attitudes toward the self for allegedly having unacceptable motives). What is projected in the latter case is *one's own* self-devaluating attitude which may well be a greater threat to self-esteem than the original (unacceptable) motive.

Since both kinds of projection ascribe to others what is actually our own motivational or attitudinal stance, the use of projection as a defense mechanism presupposes a profound lack of insight and a deep repression of our irrational and censurable dispositions. To project is thus not just to blame others for our problems; it is to blame others for our own baser motives and consequent self-critical attitudes. It would seem then that projection could be sustained only by a defensively "touchy" and uninsightful view of the self as irreproachable, combined with a basically suspicious and hostile view of others, a singularly unappealing combination but one whose existence is supported by the clinical impression that those with a high quota of hostility and low insight find projection relatively easy. It is worth noting, too, that when hostile motives are projected the inner need which they connote can still be satisfied by the counter-hostility we feel justified in manifesting after we have projected our original hostility to others. Projection may thereby be reinforced through rationalization, while a defensively devaluative attitude toward others may prepare the ground for it.

Since friction is an inevitable consequence of social closeness, and insight is achieved with difficulty, while the empathic understanding of others is rare indeed, it is not surprising that some tendencies toward hostile projection—sometimes called "paranoid trends"—are found everywhere. Extensive and elaborate use of projection is, however, rare in normal persons, probably because it involves so much distortion of the self-picture and so many uncritical suppositions regarding the motives of others. The deepening and stabilization of primary projection is characteristic of what is known as paranoid personality disorder, rather than of neurosis; and the elaboration of self-deceptive notions regarding the accusatory attitude of others toward oneself for sexual irregularities and the like (secondary projection) is generally symptomatic of paranoid psychosis. Perhaps the tendency to project is ubiquitous, but it is fortunately subject to limitation and correction where reality contact is good and insight at all present.

9. *Withdrawal.* This is a so-called minor mechanism, representing a defensive reaction to weakness or ineptitude which is at the opposite pole to compensation. It should not be confused with the symptomatic behavior of *social withdrawal,* though it may be antecedent thereto. In itself, defensive withdrawal is a purely mental mechanism, an *endopsychic retreat from what is desired but considered unattainable.* Like other defense mechanisms it presupposes the operation of repression, in this case at least to reduce the awareness of failure or incompetence. The complementary function of withdrawal is thus to reduce motivation or desire for the object whose attainment is thought to be beyond reach.

Coping or constructive adjustment demands, of course, that we learn our limitations and cease trying to reach the unattainable. Defensive withdrawal is something else: a subtle self-deception in which we convince (or all but convince) ourselves that we don't care about the loss of something we very much wanted. By relinquishing interest, by saying to myself "I don't care," I defend myself against the highly self-devaluating experience of failure, prospective or retrospective. "I didn't fail," I say in effect, "I just didn't try. And I didn't try because it doesn't really matter to me." What makes withdrawal essentially maladjustive is its prevention of further effort to attain the desired goal or even of the attempt to re-assess the situation. Perhaps what is needed in many cases is not a psychological "leaving the field" but the taking of a new tack, or a hard look at our past efforts in order to discover the reason for their failure. The stabilization of the withdrawal mechanism, however, so lowers the attraction of the goal—at least to consciousness—that re-appraisal and renewed effort are most unlikely to occur. If the habitual "withdrawer," then, "wards off" failure by giving up almost in advance, he effectively "wards off" success as well. Withdrawal-in-advance may thus be the mark of the inept or inadequate personality, while withdrawal after the event may be akin to the rationalization of failure. The fable of the fox and the sour grapes, though often interpreted quite differently, appears to exemplify this kind of withdrawal more than any other defense-mechanism.

10. *Identification.* Identification is *defending against the conviction of inadequacy and weakness by viewing oneself as somehow the same as or one with some figure of power or status.* It is probably less dependent on repression than most other mechanisms, though it may involve a diminished awareness of one's separate identity as a creature of weakness. In its original, childish form identification results in a detailed and intense imitation of a parent or other status person. It may be very thoroughgoing because it is a kind of natural extension of the process of learning by imitation, and because it may also involve a normal expression of affection. But behind this extreme imitation there is likely to be the primitive, magical thinking of identification which concludes in effect: "If I am like him in every act, I will take on his attributes of power and competence." Identification in this sense is undoubtedly important for the development of personality in childhood and early adolescence. It is to a great extent by "trying on" the attitudes and manners of acting suggested by others—most often through deeds rather than words—parents to begin with, but also older siblings, teachers, peer group leaders, and various other status figures, that we find for ourselves the style of life that (more or less) fits.

Despite the importance of identification for personality development, the persistence into adulthood of its childlike mode of thinking results in a neurotic immaturity. The individual may have to begin by identifying with a father or other mentor, but as he matures he must alter and adapt the model to the dimensions of circumstance and the substance of his own individuality. The ideal self must come closer to the capacities of the real self and to the possibilities determined by the actual and present life situation. To behave exactly like your father, for example, when your own capacities and temperament are quite different from your father's, and where the surroundings in which you find yourself are also quite different, is certainly maladjustive, however impressive your father's behavior may have been.

If identification does not disappear, it becomes radically altered in the normal adult, acquiring flexibility, becoming more broadly socialized, object-oriented, coping rather than defensive. The normal adult manifests a great deal of what is sometimes loosely called "group identification." He "identifies" with his profession or trade, his family, his country, his political party, his local community, his religion. If his identifications are thereby multiplied, they are also less total and involuntary and have only a limited resemblance to the defense mechanism found in the abnormal and the developmental contrivance employed by the immature. Adult identifications reflect what Allport has called the objectification and extension of the self: they manifest what through socialization the individual has become (Allport, 1937). Defensive identification, on the other hand, reflects what the individual is *not* but would become, as a means of escape from the self-devaluating reality of his own limitations.

In normal persons, too, identification (whether developmental or adult) seems closely related to affiliation and affection. The normal child loves and admires the parent with whom he identifies. The normal man "cathects" his family, his religion, his profession, his school. There is little affection manifested, however, in what the Freudians aptly call "identification with the aggressor," as when a child imitates to the letter in his actions toward a younger sibling the behavior of a brutal father whom he fears and hates; or when lighter-skinned Negroes exhibit prejudice toward their darker fellows; or when, as has been reported, concentration camp inmates outdo their guards in brutality toward their fellow prisoners, not stopping at murder and torture, and even sewing scraps of Gestapo uniform to their prison garb that they might resemble more closely their tormentors.

11. *Undoing.* Undoing is *symbolic restitution for a present impulse or past behavior considered unacceptable.* Distinction must again be made between restitution as a conscious and deliberate social act, designed to make up at least partially for a wrong done to another, and defensive undoing, a self-deluding kind of magical thinking by which we annul our delinquencies. The latter, like other defense-mechanisms, is based upon at least partial repression, while social reparation, which the psychoanalysts and others often confuse with undoing, presupposes a consciousness of wrong done and of a connection between the restitutional act and the original transgression. Nor is the thinking involved in the latter necessarily magical. When we apologize for an insult, for example, we do not ordinarily deceive ourselves or others into thinking that thereby the offending action is undone. Rather we express a wish, recognized as contrary-to-fact, that we had not committed the injury and we signify an intention not to repeat it. It is as an expression of present attitude and augury for the future that reparative behavior has social meaning. So the husband who brings flowers to his wife after he has treated her badly need not suppose that his past action is nullified, but simply that his present behavior gives some indication of his positive feeling toward her, which may serve to offset the earlier evidence of disregard. It is only when he is unaware of the relation between the two acts, or when he has displaced both actions to an entirely symbolic and unreal plane, that he gives evidence of employing undoing as a defense-mechanism in the strict sense.

Of course, there is some connection between defensive undoing and social reparation, especially developmentally. For the child who can see no connection between his behavior (which has been adjudged wrong) and the verbal formula, "I'm sorry," the latter may appear to be simply an incantation which prevents the evil consequences to him of the former. With the development of intelligence, however, he should acquire some understanding of the real, as opposed to the magical, effect of efforts to redress socially harmful actions. It is only when, as an adult, he reverts to a childishly magical use of symbolic restitution that we can regard his behavior as self-deceptively defensive and potentially neurotic.

12. *Autism:* a special kind of daydreaming by which *achievement in fantasy substitutes for achievement in fact and defends self-esteem against the sense of inadequacy and failure.* Autism goes farther than isolation and withdrawal since it substitutes a kind of activity for the deficiency or failure. It does not, however, go as far as compensation since the substituted activity is merely fantasy. This fantasy, moreover—and this is significant in differentiating autism as a defense-mechanism from ordinary fantasy—tends to prevent further effort toward real goals by consuming our time and attention in the effortless and empty satisfactions of reverie. Such fantasy neither prepares for nor relaxes from endeavor but substitutes therefor, and since its rewards are as faint as they are easy, it has a natural tendency to proliferate and expand.

James Thurber's short story "The Secret Life of Walter Mitty" remains the perfect literary expression of autism as a defense, but the mechanism does not require the elaborately inventive imagination manifested by Thurber's character. The tendency to use fantasy as an unconscious substitute for the motive and effort to achieve and as a means of disengagement from the self-devaluating experience of non-achievement suffices. And if, in this age of wonders, the personal fantasy-making mechanism falters, we have but to turn on the television set, make for the nearest movie house, or open the pages of any of the many unfunny "comic books" or apocryphal "true story" magazines, to have available a pre-packaged fantasy world in which even the effort of imagination has been minimized.

Where achievement in the direction of self-realization (*coping*) is prevented by reason of age (as in childhood, adolescence, and old age), or by reason of inability to accept the approved goals of one's culture or subculture—consider the man of integrity living in a dictatorship or the creative artist forced to live and work among Philistines—the autistic mechanism may prove a useful buffer against a too harsh reality. Where good adjustment is impossible, as it may be for the best of men in a bad society, or when caught in the web of adverse circumstance, fantasy may mitigate frustration and ward off despair. The self-depreciating but by no means ingenuous query "I can dream, can't I?" summarizes the understandably defensive posture of the normal man blocked by external factors over which he has little control, but not surrendering hope. What differentiates this from the autism found in the abnormal is that the adequate person will prefer coping to fantasy, where coping is possible; the inadequate may not.

Summary

This paper provides a phenomenological analysis of 12 major defense-mechanisms. The mechanisms are viewed as self-deceptive psychic strategies for protecting self-esteem against self-devaluating experiences. The debt to Freud is acknowledged, but the analysis is for the most part based on grounds other than the psychosexual.

Defense mechanisms are distinguished sharply from psychopathological symptoms, and while repression is admitted to be fundamental, its partial and unsuccessful nature is also stressed. Departing from classical views, isolation is defined in terms of motivational relevance; rationalization is related to "over-determination"; "antithetic counteraction" is regarded as a more precise term than "reaction-formation"; the coping types of compensation including masculine-protest are distinguished from the defensive variety; a new mechanism, somewhere between compensation and projection and labeled "defensive-devaluation" is introduced; the Freudian overuse of displacement is criticized; distinction is made between primary and secondary projection; the developmental is contrasted both with the mature and the defensive use of identification; undoing is differentiated from realistic social reparation; and the normality of some kinds of autism acknowledged.

REFERENCES

Allport, G. W. *Personality: A psychological interpretation.* New York: Holt, 1937.
Fenichel, O. *The psychoanalytic theory of neurosis.* New York: Norton, 1945.
Freud, Anna. *The ego and the mechanisms of defense.* London: Hogarth, 1954.
McCall, R. J., Invested Self-expression: Toward a Theory of Human Structural Dynamics. In A. A. Schneiders and P. J. Centi (Eds.), *Selected Papers from the ACPA Meetings of 1960-1961.* New York, Fordham Univer., 1962.

STRESS AND DISTRESS AND IDENTITY FORMATION IN COLLEGE AND HIGH SCHOOL

GRAHAM B. BLAINE, JR.
Harvard University

THE ADOLESCENT is more vulnerable to stress than either the child or the adult, and for a number of different reasons. In the first place he is at a stage of life in his physical development which makes him less facile and less graceful than at other times of his life. His natural physical clumsiness causes him to be self-conscious and uncertain of himself as he comes into new places and new situations, and is often further re-inforced by the presence of acne, buck teeth or other transient physical disfigurements which make him feel inadequate, self-conscious and ill-equipped to meet the various challenges presented by home, school and society.

In addition to these physical embarrassments adolescence also carries with it a confusing kind of cultural approach to responsibility. In many primitive societies the change from childhood to adulthood is a very abrupt one, the whole procedure often taking place as a result of a ritual which may occur in the period of a few hours. In our society, however, this borderline is a cloudy one. Responsibilities are given piecemeal. At one age the adolescent is expected to serve in the army, at another he may drive a car, at still another get married and still another he may drink alcohol. This contradictory way of allowing independence to young people causes confusion and makes them particularly susceptible to feelings of uncertainty and insecurity. There is also an internal vacillation between feelings of self-reliance and independence as opposed to childish feelings of dependency and need for encouragement and support from parents. The long period of time which it now takes to become fully educated and ready to take a place in our economic society also contributes to prolonged feelings of dependency and has contributed to a delay in the

---

Reprinted from the *Journal of the National Association of Women Deans and Counselors*, Vol. XXVII, No. 1, October, 1963.

achievement of maturity in many. The need for economic support from parents as well as the sheltering arms of a university in the form of living quarters and eating facilities and supervised instruction certainly do not contribute to self-reliance.

In addition to the physical and cultural factors which make the development of maturity more difficult there is also an added psychological factor which is not yet well understood. This is the fact that the barrier between the conscious and the unconscious seems to be far more permeable and less protective during this phase of development. Stresses which ordinarily might cause some mild neurotic symtoms at an earlier or later stage of life often result at adolescence in a complete breakdown of the defensive system and a flooding of primitive impulses into consciousness. We occasionally see dramatic psychotic episodes in high school and college students precipitated by rather ordinary events but these episodes are brief as a rule and once endured do not usually recur. The adolescent reacts dramatically and sometimes frighteningly to a variety of stresses but is very resilient and usually these reactions are only temporary.

If one is to experience adolescence successfully two important psychological qualities need to be carried over into adolescence from childhood. One of these is a sense of conscience and the other is a feeling of competence. Conscience is developed from examples set by parents, church and school. At one time "progressive" education insisted that it was important for a child to grow up unencumbered by parental standards and values. The theory was that the neuroses in later life were caused by inhibitions imposed by parents in early childhood. The child to grow up healthy should suffer no restrictions on his natural instincts according to these theorists. This way of bringing up children has since been proven to be a great mistake. Children need to have firm limits set for them as they grow, for only in this way can they learn to impose discipline upon themselves; without such limits they grow into irresponsible, selfish and conscienceless adults. Parents must use punishment and reward appropriately as a means of setting limits and encouraging good behavior.

The feeling of competence is encouraged in the child when encouragement is given for accomplishment appropriate to the level of the child's development. Parents need to be careful at all times not to expect more of a child than he is capable of producing. They also should leave no stone unturned in helping the child discover a particular area in which he can be competent. It is often hard to be as excited and as pleased about achievement in a third or fourth child as about one's first. However, for that late arrival it is even more important to feel appreciated than for his older brother or sister because he feels constantly in competition with these older siblings and often cannot understand that the reason he does not do as well is that he is younger or smaller. Younger children need extra praise and attention, to know that they are not expected to meet the same standards as the older children.

When children reach the age of 12 or 14 they enter the transitional period of adolescence. At this time the influence of parents upon the personality development of children becomes less; their word is no longer law; in fact quite the opposite is usually true. Whatever parents may advise is wrong just because it was they who said it. This is the time when the parents should remain generally in the background except when they are asked for help. They should try not to make much out of small issues but stand firm on certain significant and essential items such as late hours, drinking while driving, and so forth. For the most part, however, they must rely on the conscience which they have helped their children develop in earlier years to govern and control the behavior of their teen-age sons and daughters. It is at this time that school and church become important influences on the behavior and personality development of the individual. These institutions plus important lessons learned from experience determine the success which the child achieves and have a great influence on his future effectiveness as an adult later on in the world at large.

A most important task to be accomplished in the development of personality during adolescence is the establishment of identity. The achievement of a sense of identity as described by Erikson is "A feeling of being at home in one's body; a sense of knowing where one is going; and an inner assurance of anticipated recognition from those who count. We are most aware of our identity when we have just gained it, and we are somewhat surprised to make its acquaintance." In more detail he describes it as follows: "Man, to take his place in society, must acquire a conflict-free, habitual use of a dominant faculty to be elaborated in an occupation; a limitless resource, a feedback as it were, from the immediate exercise of this occupation from the companionship it provides; and finally, an intelligible theory of the process of life." On the surface, this does not sound very difficult or complicated. Actually all it means is that he gains a sense of inner security and enough self knowledge to feel like an individual who, though different in some ways from his fellow man, is nonetheless capable in certain areas, that he finds a job to do which is interesting and pays back something in the way of satisfaction or gratification, and lastly, that he have a religion or some theory about what life is all about which is thoroughly satisfying to him. This may seem routine, but adolescents find problems here and take these problems seriously. Much of their conflict centers around them.

The development of personal identity means that we incorporate into it various identifications or characteristics from people who have been important in one's life. These may be parents or teachers or even actors and movie stars. These limitations do not apply to the whole personality, as hero worship does, but simply to portions of the personalities of many people, which are modified and coalesced finally into one individual identity. In order to achieve a solidified personality, there must be no loss of an identity figure at a crucial stage of life, such as in the early teens. This loss may occur through death or through sudden disillusionment in a person who was formerly respected and admired. Neither must there be an overly intrusive parent, one who is constantly prodding, questioning, probing, in this way preventing his children from accomplishing anything on their own and by themselves. An overly dependent parent, one who cannot be independent either of his wife or of his own parents, also tends to have a weakening influence on the formation of identity in his child.

When a number of these adverse factors are present, two things may happen instead of the formation of a solid identity. One is "role diffusion," and the other "negative identity." In the first the person finds himself torn between a number of possible roles in life and unable to settle on any one for more than a short time.

A 24-year-old Radcliffe graduate in history came to the psychiatric clinic at the request of her husband because he felt that her wish to obtain a divorce after two years of marriage was a sign of emotional disturbance. Her mother was the headmistress of a girls' private school and her father dean of an engineering school. The girl felt that her husband was excessively demanding, cold and unappreciative. She said he was jealous of her career and wanted her to be at home all the time even though he spent most of his time at the laboratory working for his doctorate in physics. She contemptuously referred to her occupation as that of "mousewife" and spoke enviously of her unmarried colleagues. She professed to be in love with her thesis advisor who, she claimed, really understood her. Treatment revealed that she was caught in a role diffusion or identity crisis. She was unable to commit herself to a career or to marriage and unwilling to compromise. Her original identification had been with her headmistress mother but this had been shattered at the age of 14 when she saw behind the facade of marital happiness and discovered that her parents really hated each other. Later she learned that her mother was a failure as headmistress. She had no example of a woman who had achieved success as a wife or in a career and therefore could not thoroughly commit herself to either.

The second alternative, that of negative identity, is an identification on the part of the child with everything that his parents least want him to be. This does not spring simply from rebellion against parental standards but rather seems to come often as a result of feelings of envy which are unintentionally instilled in the child by parents who are constantly warning him against being a certain kind of person. Thus a mother with a brother who is an alcoholic may talk to her child of her concern about this brother and how little she wants her son to be like him. This results in a feeling on the part of the child that the uncle who is an alcoholic is getting more attention because of his alcoholism than the child may be for trying to be just what the family wants him to be. Also, if very high standards are set, a child may feel that it is impossible to achieve what the parents expect, and rather than be just halfway good it may be more satisfying to him to be all bad. After all one does receive more attention from parents if one is at the bottom of the class than in the middle. If one cannot get kudos for being the class leader, better to be the dunce than settle for the anonymity and the silent disapproval involved in barely passing.

Now let us turn to the effects upon the development of identity and the formation of personality structure which come from the influence of school and college. Study is the main job for the adolescent, his occupation and employment. Freud said that an individual could be deemed emotionally healthy if he could love and work. For the adolescent his studies are his work and those who cannot be successful students are almost always suffering from some kind of emotional difficulty. For an adolescent to be deemed healthy he must be successful in his studies at his approximate level of intelligence. Those who are not, the so-called under-achievers, usually are having difficulty for one of four reasons: they are working in a vacuum, have a feeling of basic inferiority, are being rebellious, or have a fear of success. It is important to realize that these various factors which seem to prevent success in studying, operate on an unconscious level. These students always profess to want to do well. In all cases they are struggling to fulfill their assignments and do indeed spend many hours in futile perusal of textbooks or gazing at a blank piece of paper attempting to begin a theme or an essay.

By working in a vacuum I mean that the adults who are important to the student are unable to express directly appreciation for what is accomplished. Too often in such cases the standards for success are pushed higher and higher as the student achieves better and better. He gets the feeling that there is no way of gaining the final reward and therefore loses his motivation entirely. Students need to know that teachers and parents are interested in the work they are doing and appreciate the result of conscientious work and study even though these efforts do not result in being first in the class.

Feelings of basic inferiority are caused by failure to attain a feeling of competence so important to the early development of the child. Although IQ scores may be high and the student may be constantly assured by those around him that he is intelligent he still may feel that he has an underlying inferiority and inadequacy which he does not dare find out about nor reveal to others. For this reason it is necessary for him never to make a total effort but always to be able to say that he could have done better if he had tried. He needs to have an excuse for failing because he is so afraid that if he does his best it will turn out to be far below the expectations of others as well as himself. Rebellion, of course, also plays an important part in underachievement. Many students have an unconscious need to retaliate against parents toward whom they feel antagonistic and resentful, by flunking out of school and thus bringing disgrace to the family. It must be remembered that this is an unconscious mechanism. Every student recognizes consciously that he hurts himself more than his parents by failing but in the area of the irrational unconscious, doing the opposite of what one is asked to do by authority represents a satisfying retaliation.

Fear of success would seem to be a paradoxical state of mind but for many the prospect of excelling is frightening indeed. They see those who are on top of the heap as being the object of envy and hatred. The more inconspicuous middle of the class seems less threatening. Also, for many shy individuals, being in the limelight and attracting the attention that outstanding scholars achieve today seems to be frightening and undesirable. Such students will often do exceedingly well until the very end of the semester when suddenly they will fall down in their work and bring their grades down to an average or below average level.

Studying may be a special stress in itself and it is therefore important for teachers and counselors to realize what lies behind underachievement. Therapeutic and preventive measures within the classroom and the counselor's office must sometimes reach a deeper level if a useful change in study habits is to be effected.

What are the specific stresses which college brings to the student arriving from the average school and home environment? The first and most obvious change is the greater freedom. The student is thrown on his own to plan his study time as he sees fit and to sleep, eat and use his leisure time in whatever way and to whatever degree he wishes. For many this kind of unrestricted freedom is too much of a temptation. Here the early training of conscience is important and has to be relied upon by the student. This conscience has been either reinforced or corrupted by examples of fellow students and teachers in high school. While the initial shock of unscheduled and unrestricted time cause a period of procrastination and libertine activity most students find within themselves self discipline enough to allow them to enjoy college and at the same time do the work that must be done.

A second stress which often comes into play in college is what we have come to term "major league shock." This is also known as "valedictorian syndrome" and is an anxiety, tension or depression which occurs in students with high achievement in their secondary schools who find that the greater competition of the college precludes their being at the top of the class. Many individuals who lead their class do not build this achievement into their character structure in such a way that they feel lost if they are not on top. However, there are many for whom being first is so important that it is an essential prop to their entire personality structure.

Another challenge or stress which comes with college is the demand to be creative. High school experience too often is simply a matter of memorizing and regurgitating what one has memorized in recitation and examinations. College usually demands creativity and original conceptualization, and some students find this new demand exceedingly hard to meet. Such students have trouble when it comes to writing papers. Writing examinations or reciting in class is often not too difficult for them but when asked to write a critical paper or come up with some new idea and put it in writing they panic or simply give up. The exposure and irrevocable commitment involved in putting words on paper is far more threatening to them than giving an oral recitation where one can watch the reaction of the listener.

Another stress which comes with college is an unexpected challenge to well established value systems. Students who come from religious schools or from small communities where people think much alike, are often shocked when they find their classmates have very different values from their own. Some educators believe that this kind of shock to basic principles is a healthy experience for the young adult. Others believe that since it is usually an unhappy experience and often unnecessary, it should be avoided.

The discovery that well respected and successful members of the college community can believe in a moral and ethical code directly opposite to one's own cannot help but be a shock when one first discovers it. Generally, however, this tends to be a broadening and enlightening experience. Most college students are flexible and liberal enough to re-evaluate their own value system in the light of others and make whatever adjustments turn out to feel right or seem logical. Some, on the other hand, are so shaken by this experience that they may suffer a major psychological breakdown or go through a period of extreme rebellion. We find, however, that students who have had firm but not excessively punitive upbringing do not act out their rebellion but only talk it out. There is an important difference. A non-militant Communist, an atheist who does not proselyte, or an advocate of free love who does not practice it is not doing the community around him any serious harm. The stress of encountering unfamiliar value systems in contemporaries whom one respects usually results in a strengthened internal ethical system which does not vary much from the originally formulated system set up by family and former school mates. After a transient period of confusion or rebellion the old standards re-emerge, and seem to come from within instead of being super-imposed from outside by others.

One source of distress in college which appears in the senior year is trouble with commitment and formation of career plans and goals. In the normal course of events most college students go through a period of experimentation. Erickson chooses to call this a psycho-social moratorium by which he means a time in which an individual has no commitments psychologically or socially but simply remains neutral observing and occasionally testing out various roles for himself. Hopefully this is accomplished during the course of junior and sophomore years and by senior year some kind of commitment for the future has been made. There are always a few students, however, who find themselves still unmotivated even at this late date and this becomes a source of great concern to them, particularly when they observe their classmates squared away towards some graduate school or business career. It is usually the students who have not been able to develop a feeling of competence in their childhood years or who have not been able to compete comfortably because of a feeling of inferiority or some fear of being hurt who have difficulty in this final phase of their college life.

It is important for college administrators, deans, and faculty to realize what kinds of stresses within the college and school environment cause distress to the students, and to try to moderate these stresses in such a way that they contribute to the healthy development of personality and not to its breakdown or destruction. Learning to tolerate and cope with stress is part of growing up. No school or college environment should be without it but understanding the basic problems involved in rebellion, identity formation, studying, and commitment is essential if the stress is to be held to a healthy level. The structure of the school and college as provided by its administrators and defined by its counselors must provide a force against which students can rebel without danger and with which they can identify to advantage. Providing and maintaining such an environment is your job and it is not an easy one.

INTRODUCTION TO BEHAVIOUR THERAPY*

S. RACHMAN

Institute of Psychiatry, Maudsley Hospital, London, England

Behaviour Therapy is a term used to describe a number of new psychotherapeutic methods which have been developed in recent years. Although the actual procedures vary from aversion conditioning to desensitization they all have a common theoretical basis (Wolpe, 1958; Eysenck, 1960 a, b; Jones, 1960; Metzner, 1961).

Behaviour therapy derives its impetus from experimental psychology and is essentially an attempt to apply the findings and methods of this discipline to disorders of human behaviour. The area of experimental psychology which has the most immediate and obvious value for psychotherapy is the study of learning processes. The early experience of behaviour therapy seems to vindicate these attempts and one can draw further encouragement from the very extensive information about learning processes which has yet to be tapped by therapists. The literature of experimental psychology provides a firm foundation for the development of scientific methods of psychotherapy.

A brief account of the rationale of behaviour therapy may be stated as follows. The position adapted by behaviour therapists is that neurotic behaviour is acquired. If neurotic behaviour is regarded as being acquired, then it must follow that such behaviour will be subject to the established laws of learning. Current knowledge about the learning process concerns not only the acquisition of new habit patterns, but also how habits are eliminated. The elimination of learned responses occurs either by a process of extinction, or by inhibition.

Wolpe (1961) has defined neurotic behaviour as "any persistent habit of unadaptive behaviour acquired by learning in a physiologically normal organism." Anxiety is "usually the central constituent of this behaviour, being invariably present in the causal situation." Similarly, Eysenck (1960a) postulates that "neurotic symptoms are learned patterns of behaviour which for some reason or another are unadaptive." It should be noted however, that neurotic symptoms may under certain circumstances result "not only from the learning of an unadaptive response, but from the failure to learn an adaptive response", (Eysenck, 1960a; Jones, 1960). A common example of this type is enuresis. The re-learning and un-learning techniques which have been used therapeutically include:

1. Desensitization based on relaxation (Wolpe, 1954, 1958 and 1961; Bond and Hutchison, 1960; Lazarus, 1963; Rachman, 1959; Hussain, 1963; Clarke, 1963; Walton, 1960 and 1963; Meyer, 1958).

---

*Reprinted from *Behavior Research Therapy*, Vol. 1, Pp. 3–15, 1963.

2. Operant conditioning (Ayllon, 1960 and 1963; Lindsley, 1956 and 1961: King *et al.*, 1960; Brady and Lind, 1961; Ferster and de Myer, 1961).
3. Aversion conditioning—chemical or electrical (Wolpe, 1958; Blakemore *et al.*, 1963; Freund, 1960; Raymond, 1956; Franks, 1960; Max, 1935).
4. Training in assertive behaviour (Salter, 1950; Wolpe, 1958; Lazarus, 1963).
5. Use of sexual responses (Wolpe, 1958; Lazarus, 1963).
6. Use of feeding responses (Jones, 1924a, b; Lazarus, 1960).
7. Extinction based on negative practice (Yates, 1960; Jones, 1960; Williams, 1959)
8. Anxiety-relief responses (Wolpe, 1958).
9. Avoidance learning (Lovibond, 1963; Jones, 1960).

Behaviour therapy has been successfully used in the treatment of a wide range of neurotic conditions including: *Phobias* (e.g. Wolpe, 1958; Lazarus, 1963; Meyer, 1958; Eysenck, 1960), *hysteria* (e.g. Brady and Lind, 1961; Sylvester and Liversedge, 1960; Wolpe, 1958), *enuresis* (e.g. Jones, 1960; Mowrer 1939; Lovibond, 1963), *sexual disorders* (e.g. Blakemore *et al.*, 1963; Rachman, 1961), *tics* (e.g. Yates, 1958; Walton, 1961; Barrett, 1962), *tension states* (e.g. Wolpe, 1958; Eysenck, 1960), *children's disorders* (e.g. Rachman, 1963). Recently, some limited improvements have been obtained even in psychotic illnesses (e.g. Cowden and Ford, 1962; King *et al.*, 1960; Ayllon, 1963).

ORIGINS

Modern psychology is dominated by what are known as "theories of learning". The two theories of learning which are of direct relevance to psychotherapy are those of Hull (reinforcement theory) and Skinner (operant conditioning). These theories are in a sense, modern versions of Behaviourism. Some of the most significant improvements are the insistence on quantitative studies, increasingly flexible methods and theorizing, and in the case of Hull, the use of the hypothetico-deductive method. In the past thirty years, psychologists have acquired a considerable amount of quantitative information concerning various human processes, particularly in the field of learning. The word 'learning' it should be noted is used in an extremely broad manner and includes any aspect of behaviour which is 'acquired' by experience. This excludes changes in behaviour which result from maturation or by direct intervention in the functioning of the nervous system.

Behaviour therapy has developed partly as a consequence of these advances in psychology and partly as a reaction to psycho-analysis and its derivatives (e.g. Wolpe and Rachman (1960) and Rachman and Costello (1961)). The need for a new approach to psychotherapy is emphasized by the disappointing results obtained with prevailing techniques (Eysenck, 1960c; Levitt, 1957; Bailey, 1956). Since 1948 systematic attempts have been made to apply the facts, theories, and methods of learning theory to the practice of psycho-therapy.

Before dealing with these more recent developments, two earlier investigations should be mentioned. The first is the case of Albert reported by Watson and Rayner (1920). They provided a classical demonstration of the development of a phobia in a young child. Having first ascertained that it was a neutral object, they presented an 11 month old boy, Albert, with a white rat to play with. Whenever he reached for the animal the experimenters made a loud noise behind the boy. After only five trials Albert began showing signs of fear in the presence of the white rat. This fear then generalized to similar stimuli such as furry objects, cotton wool, white rabbits. These phobic reactions were still present when Albert was tested 4 months later. The process involved in this demonstration provides a striking illustration of the way in which phobias can develop. The implications of this work are discussed in detail elsewhere (Wolpe and Rachman, 1960). It is sufficient for present purposes to note that this demonstration provided the first model of a human neurosis.

The second investigation of importance was that reported by Mary Cover Jones in 1924:

> A 3 year-old boy, Peter, showed fear of white rats, rabbits, fur, cotton wool and other similar objects. Jones treated Peter by de-conditioning methods. It was decided to start on the rabbit phobia as this seemed to be a focus of Peter's fears.
>
> Peter was gradually introduced to contacts with a rabbit during his daily play period. He was placed in a play group with 3 fearless children and the rabbit was brought into the room for short periods each day. Peter's toleration of the rabbit was gradually improved. The progressive steps observed in the process included: "rabbit in cage 12 feet away tolerated ... in cage 4 feet away tolerated ... close by in cage tolerated ... free in room tolerated ... eventually, fondling rabbit affectionately." Another measure employed by Jones involved the use of feeding responses. "Through the presence of the pleasant stimulus (food) whenever the rabbit was shown, the fear was eliminated gradually in favour of a positive response."

Using these techniques Jones overcame not only Peter's fear of rabbits but all his associated fears. The follow-up of this case showed no resurgence of the phobia.

The next important advance in behaviour therapy occurred in 1948. On the basis of the evidence accumulated on experimental neuroses in animals (dating back to Pavlov's work) and on his own experiments, Wolpe (1954, 1958 and 1962a) constructed a systematic theory of neurosis and psychotherapy. Merging the experimental evidence* with Hull's theory of learning, Wolpe elaborated the principle of reciprocal inhibition as the main basis of psychotherapeutic effects. Wolpe provided evidence that neurotic behaviour is acquired in anxiety-generating situations and that anxiety is always prominent in these conditions. Successful treatment of a neurosis, therefore, would depend on the reciprocal inhibition of neurotic anxiety responses, i.e. the suppression of the anxiety responses as a consequence of the simultaneous evocation of other responses which are physiologically antagonistic to anxiety. If a response which is incompatible with anxiety can be made to occur in the presence of anxiety-producing stimuli it will weaken the bond between these stimuli and the anxiety responses. Whereas most psychotherapists report cured or improved cases in the vicinity of 60 per cent, Wolpe claims a 90 per cent level of cures or 'marked improvements' with his methods. Wolpe compared his results with those obtained by other methods and by applying the x^2 test for significance, showed that it is highly improbable that his higher proportion of successes can be accounted for by chance.

Wolpe developed several therapeutic techniques on the basis of learning theory and the most prominent of these is 'systematic desensitization'. This method will be described and then illustrated by case histories.

An inquiry is first conducted in order to ascertain which stimulus situations provoke anxiety in the patient. The patient is told that he can add to or modify this list at any time. The stimuli are then categorized by the therapist and the patient is asked to rank the stimuli in order, from the most to the least disturbing. This ranked list of noxious stimulus conditions is referred to as the hierarchy. In the first case discussed below for example, one would refer to the 'ambulance hierarchy' and the 'hospital hierarchy'. Hierarchies can contain from 5 to 25 items. The hospital hierarchy mentioned above consisted of the following stimulus situations; a hospital in the distance, a hospital ten corners away, walking past the hospital, standing outside the gates, walking in the grounds, standing outside the foyer, in the foyer, walking in the corridors, standing in a small ward of 4 beds, in a larger ward and in a surgical ward with a few bandaged people in bed. The construction of the relevant hierarchies generally takes 1–3 interviews and the patient is concurrently given practice in hypnotic and relaxation procedures. Hypnosis is not an essential requirement, and in these cases where the patient refuses to be hypnotized or requires prolonged practice the procedure can be omitted and deep non-hypnotic relaxation employed instead.

---

* Papers dealing with the background evidence include those of Gantt (1944), Liddell (1944), Lazovik and Lang (1960), Metzner (1961), Bandura (1961), Eysenck (1960b, c), Bachrach (1961), and Broadhurst (1960).

When the hierarchies have been worked out, the subject is told which stimuli are to be presented in each session and is advised to signal with his hand if a stimulus presentation disturbs him unduly. This is an important instruction and should on no account be omitted, for the arousing of anxiety during the session can be damaging. In our experience it has been found that with most patients it is possible by observing his facial expressions, bodily tension, respiration and so forth, to perceive such disturbances before the patient actually signals. When such disturbances occur the therapist immediately 'withdraws' the stimulus and calms the patient. No session should be concluded when a disturbance occurs, but before rousing the patient the therapist should continue and present a further 'easy' stimulus which has already been successfully overcome. The reason for this is to be found in the commonly observed fact that the last item of any learning series is well retained. Anxiety which occurs at the end of a session is likely to require a longer period before dissipating.

When the preliminary instructions have been given, the patient is relaxed (hypnotically or otherwise) and then told to visualize the various stimuli, e.g. 'Picture a hospital in the distance... Now stop picturing that and go on relaxing.' Each stimulus is visualized for 5–10 seconds and 2–4 different items are presented each session. Each item is generally presented twice. When the requisite number of stimuli have been presented the patient is slowly roused and then asked for a report on his reactions. If the items were visualized vividly and without undue disturbance, the therapist then proceeds to the next items in the following session. The items lowest in the hierarchy (i.e. the least disturbing ones) are introduced first and the therapist proceeds slowly up the list depending on the progress achieved and the patient's reactions. In this way, it is possible for the patient to eventually picture formerly noxious stimuli without any anxiety whatever. This ability to imagine the noxious stimulus with tranquility then transfers to the real-life situation (see below).

ILLUSTRATIVE CASES

Case 1

A 14-year-old boy was referred for treatment of a phobia. He had suffered from a fear of ambulances and hospitals for a period of 4 years. He stated that he was frightened by the sight of ambulances and avoided them wherever and however possible, e.g. by planning his journeys in advance and changing direction when an ambulance was sighted. He reported having fainted on several occasions when an ambulance was nearby. He was also scared of hospitals and nursing homes and refused to visit these institutions. His social and scholastic adjustments were both satisfactory and systematic desensitization was commenced after an initial period of training in relaxation. Separate hierarchies of noxious situations were constructed for the ambulance and hospital phobias. The ambulance-hierarchy ranged from easy (non-disturbing) stimuli such as a parked ambulance in the distance and a derelict ambulance in a scrap-yard, to difficult ones like sitting in an ambulance (a) next to the driver or (b) in the back. In the hospital-hierarchy the first easy situation was a distant hospital which could be barely seen and the final one, a surgical ward. Three days after the third desensitization session the subject walked past a parked ambulance with its rear doors open and experienced no anxiety. Two further situations of a similar nature occurred during the course of therapy and neither of these evoked fear. After 10 interviews he was much improved and was able to visit the hospital and approach ambulances without difficulty. After a 3-month period there has been no recurrence of the earlier fears.

Case 2

A married woman of 34 was referred for treatment of an anxiety neurosis of 5 years' duration. She had received intermittent treatment during this period, including a brief spell of psycho-analysis, without apparent success. Two weeks before her first interview she had been advised to consider the possibility of undergoing a leucotomy.

She complained of attacks of fear with sweating, trembling and severe headaches. A wide variety of situations appeared to provoke these attacks, which tended to occur most severely and frequently in the late afternoon and in dull, overcast weather. The anxiety-producing situations included walking in the street, being outdoors in the afternoon, shopping, telephoning, crowds of people and places of public amenity. She also reported an inability to cope in social situations and disturbing feelings of inadequacy and inferiority. Her sexual activity had been disrupted in recent months as the anxiety had increased and was unsatisfactory. She had been taking 2-3 tranquillizing tablets per day for a short period with slight, variable results.

Application of the Thematic Apperception Test and the Willoughby neurotic-tendency inventory revealed neurotic trends such as guilt, hypersensitivity and a marked lack of confidence (the Willoughby score was extremely high, 87, indicating severe neurotic disturbance).

The patient was instructed in the use of assertive responses and deep (non-hypnotic) relaxation. The first anxiety hierarchy dealt with was that of dull weather. Starting from 'a bright sunny day' it was possible for the subject to visualize 'damp overcast weather' without anxiety after 21 desensitization sessions, and 10 days after the completion of this hierarchy she was able to report that, "The weather is much better, it doesn't even bother me to look at the weather when I wake up in the morning" (previously depressing). In addition to this improvement, she was also able to go out for short periods during the afternoon. The following hierarchies were then dealt with: telephoning, shopping, having guests at the house, walking in the street, going to places of public entertainment, sitting in the garden in the afternoon.

Two weeks after the completion of the last hierarchy, the patient was given the Willoughby test again. Her score had dropped 40 points to the slightly inflated score of 47. She also reported increased sexual responsiveness, a slight improvement in interpersonal relationships and increased self-confidence. The patient commenced a refresher course in stenography with the intention of obtaining employment. She had not worked for 7 years. She voluntarily reduced her dose of tranquillizers to one a day and dispensed with them completely 1 week later.

At this stage the patient's husband fell seriously ill and she was able to support him emotionally despite the considerable effort involved. As her husband's health improved, she suffered a minor relapse for 2 weeks and then returned to her improved state spontaneously.

After 8 months of treatment, comprising 65 interviews devoted largely to systematic desensitization, this patient was 'much improved' in terms of Knight's criteria (symptom improvement, increased productivity, improved sexual relations, improved interpersonal relations, increased stress tolerance).

During the course of therapy, part of the reason for the development of the anxiety state in this patient was unearthed. When she was 17 years old she had become involved in a love affair with a married man 12 years her senior. This affair had been conducted in an extremely secretive manner for 4 years, during which time she had suffered from recurrent guilt feelings and shame, so much so, that on one occasion she had attempted suicide by throwing herself into a river. It was her custom to meet her lover after work in the later afternoon. The dull weather can be accounted for, as this affair took place in London.

Case 3

Bond and Hutchison (1960) obtained marked improvement in a patient with a severe and long-standing case of exhibitionism by using the reciprocal inhibition technique. The patient was a 25-year-old married man of average intelligence. His first exposure occurred at age 13 following sex play with a younger girl. His exhibitionism continued throughout adolescence and had reached "bizarre proportions" by the time he reached adulthood. The attacks of exhibitionism were preceded by tension, dread and sexual excitement. Attacks were often provoked by the perception of attractive young women.

The antecedent tension was constant and the patient often exposed several times a day. He had been convicted for indecent exposure on 11 occasions and had as a result spent a considerable amount of time in detention. The severity of his condition is best illustrated by the author's account. "A frequent practice was to hide completely nude in a small wooded area in the centre of the town where he then lived and spring out and expose himself to the first woman who passed." Various types of therapy had failed to relieve his condition.

It was decided to attempt Wolpe's desensitization procedure and the patient was accordingly trained to relax. A hierarchy of exposure-provoking stimuli was constructed and the patient gradually desensitized over a period of 30 sessions. By the eighth interview the patient evidenced distinct improvements. He was less tense, less prone to expose himself and able to venture out unaccompanied. As the desensitizing therapy continued, further evidences of progress appeared. His exhibitionist urges declined in frequency and strength, his sexual fantasies diminished and he reported an improvement in his sexual relations with his wife.

Therapy had to be discontinued after 29 sessions but the patient reported in succeeding months that he was much improved. He then exposed himself in a feeble and uncharacteristic manner in a store. The patient was returned for treatment on a weekly basis and 2 months later no relapse had occurred.

A full description of these and other methods developed by Wolpe (1958) is given in his book "Psychotherapy by Reciprocal Inhibition." He also describes the treatment of a wide range of cases, including anxiety states, phobias, compulsions and sexual disorders. Additional case material is provided in "Behaviour Therapy and the Neuroses" edited by

Eysenck (1960b). This text also contains several important papers on theory and methodology.

Inhibition and extinction. Neurotic behaviour has been defined as "persistent unadaptive learned behaviour in which anxiety is almost always prominent and which is acquired in anxiety-generating situations." Behaviour which is learned can also be 'un-learned'. The processes by which responses are ordinarily diminished in magnitude and frequency of occurrence are 'extinction' and 'inhibition'

Similarly neurotic behaviour is open to modification and elimination by the process of inhibition and extinction. The numerous types of psychological inhibition which have been observed or postulated include proactive, retroactive, external, reciprocal, reactive and conditioned inhibition. For several reasons, mainly of a practical nature, conditioned inhibition has received the greatest amount of attention in psychotherapy. Conditioned inhibition is generated when stimuli are associated with the cessation of a response in the presence of reactive inhibition (a negative drive tending to cause cessation of activity). Conditioned inhibition is acquired in the same way as positive behaviour patterns are learnt. It increases progressively as a function of the number of rewarded or reinforced trials and like all habit patterns is relatively permanent. It does not dissipate spontaneously even over long periods of time. Because of these characteristics, conditioned inhibition has been widely employed by psychotherapists in their attempts to eradicate neurotic behaviour.

Wolpe's technique of psychotherapy is an attempt to produce a conditioned inhibition of neurotic behaviour by the repeated simultaneous presentation of incompatible response tendencies (reciprocal inhibition). In this way, the tendency to respond anxiously to the noxious stimulus (e.g. blood) is superseded by the stronger and incompatible relaxation response. Repeated doses of this reciprocal inhibition (which is by itself temporary in effect) in the consulting room will steadily build up a permanent 'conditioned' inhibition of the neurotic behaviour.

For every behaviour pattern there is another type of behaviour which is incompatible with the first. The task of the therapist is to find an acceptable response pattern which is antagonistic to the neurotic activity of the patient and to substitute this adaptive behaviour for the non-adaptive, neurotic behaviour. Wolpe has proposed relaxation or feeding or avoidance or sexual or assertive responses as possible substitutes for neurotic behaviour, according to the requirements of the case.

Operant conditioning. The work of Skinner on operant conditioning has recently been applied to problems of psychotherapy. Although Skinner's theoretical views differ from those of Hull, the practical application of his work to psychotherapy involves a similar rationale. Behaviour disturbances are regarded as problems in the acquisition and retention of complex responses. Consequently, these disturbances are open to manipulation and modification by the recognized processes of learning. Skinner (1953, 1959) argues that the use of appropriate learning techniques should enable the therapist to shape human behaviour in the desired direction of improved mental health. Operant conditioning has been the subject of intensive research and the information which has been collected can be fruitfully applied to the training and re-training of maladjusted behaviour.

From the therapeutic point of view, the four most significant concepts are reinforcement, intermittent reinforcement, selective reinforcement and successive approximation. In operant conditioning, the strengthening of the response (reinforcement) is dependent on the response itself. Reinforcement cannot follow unless the response appears. It is the response which causes the reward to arrive and this reinforces (strengthens) the responses. This process is of course different from that described by Pavlov (classical conditioning). It will be noticed that the subject in an operant conditioning situation, plays an active role in the learning process whereas the subject's part in classical conditioning is a relatively passive one.

Considerable research has been devoted to the analysis of rewards (reinforcers) in the operant conditioning situation. A highly significant finding is that if reinforcers are presented irregularly (in time or sequence) they are more effective. This intermittent reinforcement produces stronger responses than can be obtained by rewards presented on a regular basis. Apart from its value for the therapist, this observation is useful in the analysis of many aspects of human behaviour (Ferster, 1958). For example, it helps to account for the often surprising effects of inconsistent parental care on the behaviour of children.

Experimental work has led to the development of the technique known as selective reinforcement. The use of this method enables one to simultaneously strengthen a desirable response and extinguish an undesirable one. Briefly, this method involves rewarding the appearance of the selected response and withholding rewards when the undesired response appears. In this way, the person's behaviour can be shaped in the desired direction. The skilful use of this method coupled with 'successive approximation' brings a wide variety of human behaviour into the range of therapeutic manipulation. 'Successive approximation' refers to the gradual and graduated building up of a new response on the basis of the person's existing repertoire of responses. By careful planning it is possible to build up the person's simple responses (such as pressing a lever) into complex patterns of socially co-operative behaviour. This process is illustrated by the work of King *et al.* (1957, 1960) on schizophrenic patients.

To date, most of the research on operant conditioning has been concerned with the development of new techniques and the refinement of existing ones. Some examples from case material will, however, illustrate the therapeutic possibilities of operant conditioning.

Case 4

> Brady and Lind (1961) were able to cure a patient suffering from hysterical blindness with this method. The patient had lost his sight after being involved in an accident. No organic basis for this loss of vision could be found and he received various types of psychotherapy without success. Two years after the onset of the illness he was treated by a conditioning technique. He was conditioned to respond to the presence of a light in the following way. The patient was informed that he would be rewarded with tokens when he pressed a small lever. These tokens could be exchanged at the hospital canteen for various articles. The light was switched on at irregular intervals and when a lever-pressing response followed the presentation of the light, the patient was given a token. He gradually learnt to respond to the light. This conditioned response was accompanied by vague visual sensations until he eventually reported that he could see the light. After regaining this visual ability he progressed further and full vision was restored.

Numerous studies of the behaviour of psychotic patients raise the possibility of obtaining limited improvements in these cases by the methods of operant conditioning. King, Armitage and Tilton (1960) conditioned 12 schizophrenic patients to operate a lever using food, cigarettes and other items as rewards or reinforcers. When the patients reached a stable rate of responding, they were conditioned to more complex tasks involving verbal behaviour and even social co-operation. By comparison with 3 matched groups comprising 12 schizophrenics each, the conditioned group showed the greatest overall improvement. The patients in the conditioned group improved in "level of verbalization, motivation to leave the ward, more interest in occupational therapy, decreased enuresis."

Other investigations of psychotic patients include those of Lindsley (1956, 1960) and Ayllon and Michael (1959, 1963). Some promising work on the treatment of children has also been reported by Baer (1962) and Bijou and Orlando (1961) among others.

It would be unwise to offer dogmatic assertions until more research work has been conducted but the following assessments are proposed on the basis of the available information. Firstly, operant conditioning methods are likely to prove of particular value in the treatment of what may be called deficit behaviour disorders. This would encompass disorders which arise out of a failure to develop adequate behaviour, such as aphemia, alexia, anorexia and so forth. It could also be used in developing psychological functions which are only partially or improperly operative. Secondly, operant conditioning is likely to prove extremely valuable in the treatment of children's disorders. Many of these disorders are of the deficit variety discussed above and in addition, the technique itself seems to be admirably suited for use with children (Rachman, 1963). It is simple, the control of rewards is easier with children and it can be conducted with a minimum reliance on language.

SOME THEORETICAL CONSIDERATIONS

An objection which is frequently presented by critics of behaviour therapy is the concept of 'basic causes'. They argue that this therapy deals only with symptoms and leaves the basic cause or causes of the neurosis untouched; that this 'superficial approach' to the treatment of neurotic behaviour is destined to bring about only temporary alleviation of symptoms (at best) and may well aggravate the patient's condition. They claim that it is only when the 'inner forces of the psyche' have been restored to harmony by free association, transference and interpretation that the person is normal again. The major objections may be summarized as follows: Behaviour therapy (a) is superficial, (b) is symptom-orientated, (c) ignores the deep inner causes of the neuroses, (d) can effect only temporary improvements and (e) smothers certain symptoms only to provoke new ones.

Behaviour therapy is not superficial if this implies either that such treatment is 'not complete' or that it can be applied with success only in certain minor types of behaviour disorders. There is considerable clinical and experimental evidence which shows, on the contrary, that such therapy is both complete and capable of being applied in many types of disorder, including those which are regarded as 'deep-seated', e.g. phobic states and anxiety neuroses of longstanding. Examples of therapeutic successes with enuretics, hysterics, stutterers, drug-addicts, homosexuals, phobic states, alcoholics and tension-states, have been reported in which the 'superficial approach' has provided complete or near-complete recovery. In many of the cases referred to here, the improvement has been obtained without either therapist or patient knowing what the 'basic cause' of the illness was. A particularly striking example of such a case is provided by Wolpe (1958);

> A 37 year-old miner was seen in a state of intense anxiety. He had a very marked tremor and a total amnesia for the previous 4 days. He said that his wife, on whom he was greatly dependent, had cunningly got him to agree to "temporary divorce" 6 months before and was now going to marry a friend of his. No attempt was made at this juncture to recall the lost memories. The patient was made to realize how ineffectual his previous attitudes had been and how he had been deceived. As a result he angrily "had it out" with his wife and a few others. The anxiety rapidly decreased and he soon felt sufficiently motivated to organize his whole life differently. At his fifth interview (10 days after treatment began) he said that he felt "a hundred per cent" and was full of plans for the future. Yet he had still recalled nothing whatever of the forgotten 4 days. The patient later recalled the lost memories under hypnosis. No important consequences ensued. A few months later he married another woman and was apparently very well adjusted generally.

Other examples are provided by Lazarus and Rachman (1957), Lovibond (1963) and Salter (1950).

Can this evidence be taken to mean that a knowledge of the causative factors is unnecessary? The answer to this problem would appear to be a qualified affirmative. In some instances it seems unlikely that improvement in the patient's condition can be effected without such knowledge. On the other hand it would appear from the numerous therapeutic failures reported by analysts and other therapists, that in certain cases insight and interpretation do not assist. A very obvious example of such a state of affairs can be observed in the treatment of psychopathy. An appraisal of the data leads us to the conclusion that while a knowledge of the causative process and genesis of the individual neurosis can be of considerable value in therapy, improvement can nevertheless be obtained in many cases without such knowledge.

Too great a concern with 'underlying causes' may under certain circumstances even impede therapeutic progress. The case of the miner treated by Wolpe and quoted above is one such instance. The 'forward-looking approach' as opposed to the historical technique has much to recommend it. It is quite conceivable that a patient with some pressing, immediate problem (e.g. pending divorce) may receive a severe and unnecessary jolt from the apparent lack of concern of the non-directive therapist.

With regard to the observation that objective psychotherapy is symptom-orientated, this is generally true. The treatment of the symptom or symptoms is quite logically one of the first considerations of the psychotherapist. In numerous cases there is little else that is required as 'the deep inner causes', if they exist, cease to be relevant (Mowrer, 1950). The five cases reported by Lazarus and Rachman (1957) all bear this contention out. In Case 1 above, the precise reason or reasons for the ambulance-phobia developing in this 14 year-old boy were never discovered. The fear was inhibited and extinguished by systematic desensitization and this removal of the symptom was sufficient.

Does behaviour therapy effect only temporary improvement? There is some evidence that improvements obtained by these techniques are long-lasting or permanent, but it must be admitted that the design of research work in the field of therapy, both objective and psychoanalytic, has been inadequate in this respect.

Behaviour therapy has also been criticized on the grounds that it merely smothers the neurotic symptoms. Because the 'basic causes' of the maladaptive behaviour have not been treated, it is said that new symptoms will necessarily arise to replace the extinguished behaviour patterns. For example, training an enuretic to relieve himself in the lavatory or teaching a stutterer to speak fluently will merely result in the patient 'adopting' some new deviant response. While such 'transfer' of symptoms can occur, its frequency has probably been unduly exaggerated (Wolpe, 1958; Yates, 1958). In those cases where transferred symptoms arise the therapeutic procedure is quite uncomplicated. The therapist after having desensitized the patient to the original noxious stimulus situations, if confronted with a so-called 'substitute-symptom' would proceed to desensitize this new symptom in turn. When this treatment has been successfully completed, the probability of recurrence is slight. It will be agreed that all neurotic symptoms in the patient have some degree of interdependence and that the weakening or extinction of any one symptom is likely to affect all the others in like manner. The symptom which is treated first is usually the most resistant. Behaviour patterns treated subsequently are more easily modified. If a new symptom arises it can be expected to be of rather weaker strength and hence readily amenable to inhibition or extinction. This symptom-substitution phenomenon and its treatment has been described by Lazarus and Rachman (1957). One of their cases, a married woman of 29, had developed a phobic reaction to dogs as the result of a traumatic incident 5 years earlier. After 3 years of psychoanalysis, her fear of dogs had disappeared but instead she she had developed a chronic anxiety state with numerous, varied phobias (symptom-substitution). After 6 weeks of intensive psychotherapy (28 sessions) she was much improved, but her dog-phobia returned. After a further 28 sessions devoted mainly to the inhibition of this phobia, she was discharged as 'much improved'. A year later she was still healthy and the extinction of the dog-phobia had been maintained. This case-history illustrates the treatment of symptom-substitution by objective psychotherapy and also the development of a substitute symptom under psycho-analysis.

Reservations about the improvements obtained with behaviour therapy are sometimes based on the claim that the effective mechanism is not the re-learning process but rather, some aspect of the patient-therapist relationship, for example transference, insight, derepression. Such introductions are unnecessary and in a neat demonstration Wolpe (1962b) was able to isolate the effective agent in the treatment of a woman with a traffic phobia. The therapeutic sessions were restricted to conditioning practice only and it was shown that the time and amount of the patient's improvements were directly related to the conditioning sessions. Furthermore, a change of therapist failed to disturb the direct relationship between conditioning treatment and actual improvements.

PROSPECT

Behaviour therapy has now developed to the point where large scale field trials with adequate controls can be carried out. The evaluation studies which are presently available can at best, be regarded as highly suggestive and encouraging. Wolpe (1958) has reported that nearly 90 per cent of 210 patients had either been much improved or apparently recovered after a median number of 23 interviews. Lazarus (1963) states that 78 per cent of the 408 patients who consulted him derived marked benefit. Of these 408 patients, Lazarus classified 126 as suffering from severe disturbances and in this sub-group the improvement rate was 62 per cent. Hussain (1963) reported that 95 per cent of his 105 patients were much improved by behaviour therapy which generally lasted less than three months. In addition to these reports on the effects of behaviour therapy with large groups of patients, there are numerous accounts of successes claimed with small numbers of patients (e.g. Eysenck, 1960). On the other hand, a small retrospective survey conducted by Cooper (1962) suggested that some phobic cases treated by behaviour therapy tended to relapse. Clearly, the effectiveness of behaviour therapy needs to be determined by strict, highly controlled experiments.

As the recent developments in operant conditioning procedures demonstrate, there are many more therapeutic procedures which can be derived from experimental psychology. It is to be hoped that new clinical methods will continue to increase the scope and effectiveness of behaviour therapy. The high rate of spontaneous remissions in neurotic illnesses constitutes a problem of considerable theoretical and practical importance (Eysenck, 1962) and research in this area would also be most valuable.

CONCLUSIONS

Behaviour therapy offers substantial advantages as a method of treating disorders of behaviour. It has developed out of established psychological theories and has a large body of experimental evidence on which to proceed. The therapeutic process and its outcome are both open to quantification. It permits precision and a systematic planning of the treatment required in individual cases. Behaviour therapy has now reached the point where large-scale field tests are possible and indeed, necessary.

REFERENCES

AYLLON, T. (1960) Some behavioural problems associated with eating in chronic schizophrenic patients. Read at an APA meeting, Chicago.
AYLLON, T. (1963) Intensive treatment of psychotic behaviour by stimulus satiation and food reinforcement. *Behav. Res. Ther.* **1**, 53–61.
AYLLON, T. and MICHAEL, J. (1959) The psychiatric nurse as a behavioural engineer. *J. exp. Anal. Behav.* **2**, 323–334.
BACHRACH, A. L. (1962) *Experimental Foundations of Clinical Psychology.* Basic Books, New York.
BAER, D. M. (1962) Laboratory control of thumbsucking in three young children by withdrawal and representation of positive reinforcement. *J. exp. Anal. Behav.* In press.
BAILEY, P. B. (1956) The great psychiatric revolution. *Amer. J. Psychiat.* **113**, 147–168.
BANDURA, A. (1961) Psychotherapy as a learning process. *Psychol. Bull.* **58**, 144–159.
BARRETT, B. H. (1961) Reduction in rate of multiple tics by free-operant conditioning methods. Unpublished paper.
BLAKEMORE, C. *et al.* (1963) Application of faradic aversion conditioning in a case of transvestism. *Behav. Res. Ther.* **1**, 29–34.

Bond, J. and Hutchison, H. C. (1960) Application of reciprocal inhibition therapy to exhibitionism. *Canad. med. Ass. J.* **83**, 123–128.

Brady, J. and Lind, D. L. (1961) Experimental analysis of hysterical blindness. *Arch. Gen. Psychiat.* **4**, 331–339.

Broadhurst, P. (1960) Abnormal animal behaviour, in *Handbook of Abnormal Psychology*. Ed. H. J. Eysenck. Pitmans, London.

Clark, D. F. (1963) Treatment of a monosymptomatic phobia by systematic desensitization. *Behav. Res. Ther.* **1**, 63–68.

Cooper, J. E. (1961) Some aspects of the use of behaviour therapy in psychiatry. Dissertation, University of London.

Cowden, R. and Ford, L. (1962) Systematic desensitization with phobic schizophrenics. *Amer. J. Psychiat.* **119**, 241–245.

Eysenck, H. J. (1960a) Personality and behaviour therapy. *Proc. royal Soc. Med.* **53**, 504–508.

Eysenck, H. J. (1960b) *Behaviour Therapy and the Neuroses*. Pergamon Press, Oxford.

Eysenck, H. J. (1960c) *Handbook of Abnormal Psychology*. Pitmans, London.

Eysenck, H. J. (1962) Spontaneous remission. *Amer. J. Psychiat.* In press.

Ferster, C. B. (1958) Reinforcement and punishment in the control of human behaviour in social agencies. *Psychiat. Res. Rep. Amer. psychiat. Ass.* **10**, 101–118.

Ferster, C. B. and de Meyer, M. (1961) The development of performances in autistic children in an automatically controlled environment. *J. chron. Dis.* **13**, 312–345.

Franks, C. (1958) Alcohol, alcoholism and conditioning. *J. Ment. Sci.* **104**, 14–33.

Freund, K. (1960) Problems in the treatment of homosexuality, in *Behaviour Therapy and the Neuroses* Ed. H. J. Eysenck. Pergamon Press, Oxford.

Gantt, W. H. (1944) Experimental basis for neurotic behaviour. *Psychosom. Med. Monog. Suppl.* **3**, Nos. 3 and 4.

Hussain, A. (1962) Unpublished paper.

Jones, H. G. (1960a) The behavioural treatment of enuresis nocturna, in *Behaviour Therapy and the Neuroses*. Ed. H. J. Eysenck. Pergamon Press, Oxford.

Jones, M. C. (1924a) The elimination of children's fears. *J. exp. Psychol.* **7**, 383–390.

Jones, M. C. (1924b) A laboratory study of fear: The case of Peter. *Pedagog. Sem.* **31**, 308–315.

King, G. F., Armitage, S. and Tilton. J. (1960) A therapeutic approach to schizophrenics of extreme pathology. *J. abn. (soc.) Psychol.* **61**, 276–286.

King, G. F., Merrell, D., Lovinger, E. and Denny, M. (1957) Operant motor behaviour in acute schizophrenics. *J. Personality* **25**, 317–326.

Lazarus, A (1960) The elimination of children's phobias by deconditioning, in *Behaviour Therapy and the Neuroses*. Ed. H. J. Eysenck. Pergamon Press, Oxford.

Lazarus, A. (1963) The results of behaviour therapy in 126 cases of severe neuroses. *Behav. Res. Ther.* **1**, 69–79.

Lazarus, A. and Abramovitz, A. (1962) The use of "emotive imagery" in the treatment of children's phobias. *J. ment. Sci.* In press.

Lazarus, A. and Rachman, S. (1960) The use of systematic desensitization psychotherapy, in *Behaviour Therapy and Neuroses*. Ed. H. J. Eysenck. Pergamon Press, Oxford.

Lazovik, A. D. and Lang, P. J. (1960) A laboratory demonstration of systematic desensitization psychotherapy. *J. Psychol. Stud.* **11**, 238–242.

Levitt, E. E. (1957) The results of psychotherapy with children. *J. cons. Psychol.* **21**, 189–196.

Liddell, H. S. (1944) Conditioned reflex method and experimental neurosis, in *Personality and the Behaviour Disorders*. Ed. J. McV. Hunt. Ronald, New York.

Lindsley, O. R. (1956) Operant conditioning methods applied to research in chronic schizophrenia. *Psychiat. Res. Rep. Amer. psychiat. Ass.* **5**, 118–139.

Lindsley, O. R. (1960) Characteristics of the behaviour of chronic psychotics as revealed by free-operant conditioning methods. *Dis. nerv. Syst.* **21**, 66–78.

Lovibond, S. H. (1961) *Conditioning and Enuresis*. Thesis, University of Adelaide.

Lovibond, S. (1963) The mechanism of conditioning treatment of enuresis. *Behav. Res. Ther.* **1**, 17–21.

Max, L. (1935) Breaking a homosexual fixation by the conditioned reflex technique. *Psychol. Bull.* **32**, 734.

Metzner, R. (1961) Learning theory and the therapy of the neuroses. *Brit. J. Psychol.* Monogr. Suppl. 33.

Meyer, V. (1957) The treatment of two phobic patients on the basis of learning theory. *J. abn. (soc.) Psychol.* **55**, 261–265.

Mowrer, O. H. and Mowrer, W. (1938) Enuresis: A method for its study and treatment. *Amer. J. Orthopsychiat.* **8**, 436–459.

Orlando, R. and Bijou, S. W. (1960) Single and multiple schedules of reinforcement in developmentally retarded children. *J. exper. anal. Behav.* **3**, 339–348.

Rachman, S. (1959) Treatment of anxiety and phobic reactions by desensitization. *J. abn. (soc.) Psychol.* **102**, 421–427.

Rachman, S. (1961) Sexual disorders and behaviour therapy. *Amer. J. Psychiat.* **46**, 57–70.

Rachman, S. (1962) Child psychology and learning theory. *J. child Psychol. Psychiat.* **3**, 149–163.

Rachman, S. and Costello, C. G. (1961) The aetiology and treatment of children's phobias: A review. *Amer. J. Psychiat.* **118**, 97–105.

Raymond, M. J. (1956) Case of fetishism treated by aversion therapy. *Brit. Med. J.* **2**, 854–856.

SALTER, A. (1950) *Conditioned Reflex Therapy.* Creative Age Press, New York.
SKINNER, B. F. (1953) *Science and Human Behaviour.* Macmillan, New York.
SKINNER, B. F. (1959) *Cumulative Record.* Appleton-Century-Crofts, New York.
SYLVESTER, J. and LIVERSEDGE, L. A. (1960) Conditioning and the occupational cramps, in *Behaviour Therapy and the Neuroses.* Ed. H. J. Eysenck. Pergamon Press, Oxford.
WALTON, D. (1961) Experimental psychology and the treatment of a tiqueur. *J. child Psychol. Psychiat.* **2,** 148–155.
WALTON, D. (1963) The interaction effects of drive, reactive and conditioned inhibition. *Behav. Res. Ther.* **1,** 35–43.
WATSON, J. B. and RAYNER, R. (1920) Conditioned emotional reactions. *J. exp. Psychol.* **3,** 1–14.
WILLIAMS, C. D. (1959) The elimination of tautrum behaviour by extinction procedures. *J. abn. (soc.) Psychol.* **59,** 269–270.
WOLPE, J. (1958) *Psychotherapy by reciprocal inhibition.* Stanford University Press, Stanford.
WOLPE, J. (1961) The systematic desensitization treatment of neuroses. *J. nerv. ment. Dis.* **132,** 189–203.
WOLPE, J. and RACHMAN, S. (1960) Psychoanalytic evidence: A critique based on Freud's case of Little Hans. *J. nerv. ment. Dis.* **131,** 135–143.
WOLPE, J. (1962a) Experimental foundations of some new psychotherapeutic methods, in *Experimental Foundations of Clinical Psychology.* Ed. A. J. Bachrach. Basic Books, New York.
WOLPE, J. (1962b) Isolation of a conditioning procedure as the crucial psychotherapeutic factor: A case study. *J. nerv. ment. Dis.* **134,** 316–329.
YATES, A. J. (1958) The application of learning theory to the treatment of tics. *J. abn. (soc.) Psychol.* **56,** 175–182.

THE CRIME OF PUNISHMENT

KARL MENNINGER

Menninger Foundation, Topeka, Kansas

FEW words in our language arrest our attention as do "crime," "violence," "revenge," and "injustice." We abhor crime; we adore justice; we boast that we live by the rule of law. Violence and vengefulness we repudiate as unworthy of our civilization, and we assume this sentiment to be unanimous among all human beings.

Yet crime continues to be a national disgrace and a world-wide problem. It is threatening, alarming, wasteful, expensive, abundant, and apparently increasing! In actuality it is decreasing in frequency of occurrence, but it is certainly increasing in visibility and the reactions of the public to it.

Our system for controlling crime is ineffective, unjust, expensive. Prisons seem to operate with revolving doors—the same people going in and out and in and out. *Who cares?*

Our city jails and inhuman reformatories and wretched prisons are jammed. They are known to be unhealthy, dangerous, immoral, indecent, crime-breeding dens of iniquity. Not everyone has smelled them, as some of us have. Not many have heard the groans and the curses. Not everyone has seen the hate and despair in a thousand blank, hollow faces. But, in a way, we all know how miserable prisons are. *We want them to be that way.* And they are. *Who cares?*

Professional and big-time criminals prosper as never before. Gambling syndicates flourish. White-collar crime may even exceed all others, but goes undetected in the majority of cases. We are all being robbed and we know who the robbers are. They live nearby. *Who cares?*

The public filches millions of dollars worth of food and clothing from stores, towels and sheets from hotels, jewelry and knick-knacks from shops. The public steals, and the same public pays it back in higher prices. *Who cares?*

Time and time again somebody shouts about this state of affairs, just as I am shouting now. The magazines shout. The newspapers shout. The television and radio commentators shout (or at least they "deplore"). Psychologists, sociologists, leading jurists, wardens, and intelligent police chiefs join the chorus. Governors and mayors and Congressmen are sometimes heard. They shout that the situation is bad, bad, bad, and getting worse. Some suggest that we immediately replace obsolete procedures with scientific methods. A few shout contrary sentiments. Do the clear indications derived from scientific discovery for appropriate changes continue to fall on deaf ears? Why is the public so long-suffering, so apathetic and thereby so continuingly self-destructive? How many Presidents (and other citizens) do we have to lose before we do something?

THE public behaves as a sick patient does when a dreaded treatment is proposed for his ailment. We all know how the aching tooth may suddenly quiet down in the dentist's office, or the abdominal pain disappear in the surgeon's examining room. Why should a sufferer seek relief and shun it? Is it merely the fear of pain of the treatment? Is it the fear of unknown complications? Is it distrust of the doctor's ability? All of these, no doubt.

But, as Freud made so incontestably clear, the sufferer is always somewhat deterred by a kind of subversive, internal opposition to the work of cure. He suffers on the one hand from the pains of his affliction and yearns to get well. But he suffers at the same time from traitorous impulses that fight against the accomplishment of any change in himself, even recovery! Like Hamlet, he wonders whether it may be better after all to suffer the familiar pains and aches associated with the old method than to face the complications of a new and strange, even though possibly better way of handling things.

The inescapable conclusion is that society secretly *wants* crime, *needs* crime, and gains definite satisfactions from the present mishandling of it! We condemn crime; we punish offenders for it; but we need it. The crime and punishment ritual is a part of our lives. We need crimes to wonder at, to enjoy vicariously, to discuss and speculate about, and to publicly deplore. We need criminals to identify ourselves with, to envy secretly, and to punish stoutly. They do for us the forbidden, illegal things we *wish* to do and, like scapegoats of old, they bear the burdens of

---

Reprinted from *Saturday Review*, September 7, 1968.

our displaced guilt and punishment—"the iniquities of us all."

We have to confess that there is something fascinating for us all about violence. That most crime is not violent we know but we forget, because crime is a breaking, a rupturing, a tearing—even when it is quietly done. To all of us crime seems like violence.

The very word "violence" has a disturbing, menacing quality.... In meaning it implies something dreaded, powerful, destructive, or eruptive. It is something we abhor—or do we? Its first effect is to startle, frighten—even to horrify us. But we do not always run away from it. For violence also intrigues us. It is exciting. It is dramatic. Observing it and sometimes even participating in it gives us acute pleasure.

The newspapers constantly supply us with tidbits of violence going on in the world. They exploit its dramatic essence often to the neglect of conservative reporting of more extensive but less violent damage—the flood disaster in Florence, Italy, for example. Such words as crash, explosion, wreck, assault, raid, murder, avalanche, rape, and seizure evoke pictures of eruptive devastation from which we cannot turn away. The headlines often impute violence metaphorically even to peaceful activities. Relations are "ruptured," a tie is "broken," arbitration "collapses," a proposal is "killed."

Meanwhile on the television and movie screens there constantly appear for our amusement scenes of fighting, slugging, beating, torturing, clubbing, shooting, and the like which surpass in effect anything that the newspapers can describe. Much of this violence is portrayed dishonestly; the scenes are only semirealistic; they are "faked" and romanticized.

Pain cannot be photographed; grimaces indicate but do not convey its intensity. And wounds—unlike violence—are rarely shown. This phony quality of television violence in its mentally unhealthy aspect encourages irrationality by giving the impression to the observer that being beaten, kicked, cut, and stomped, while very unpleasant, are not very painful or serious. For after being slugged and beaten the hero rolls over, opens his eyes, hops up, rubs his cheek, grins, and staggers on. The *suffering* of violence is a part both the TV and movie producers *and* their audience tend to repress.

Although most of us *say* we deplore cruelty and destructiveness, we are partially deceiving ourselves. We disown violence, ascribing the love of it to other people. But the facts speak for themselves. We do love violence, all of us, and we all feel secretly guilty for it, which is another clue to public resistance to crime-control reform.

The great sin by which we all are tempted is the wish to hurt others, and this sin must be avoided if we are to live and let live. If our destructive energies can be mastered, directed, and sublimated, we can survive. If we can love, we can live. Our destructive energies, if they cannot be controlled, may destroy our best friends, as in the case of Alexander the Great, or they may destroy supposed "enemies" or innocent strangers. Worst of all—from the standpoint of the individual—they may destroy us.

Over the centuries of man's existence, many devices have been employed in the effort to control these innate suicidal and criminal propensities. The earliest of these undoubtedly depended upon fear—fear of the unknown, fear of magical retribution, fear of social retaliation. These external devices were replaced gradually with the law and all its machinery, religion and its rituals, and the conventions of the social order.

THE routine of life formerly required every individual to direct much of his aggressive energy against the environment. There were trees to cut down, wild animals to fend off, heavy obstacles to remove, great burdens to lift. But the machine has gradually changed all of this. Today, the routine of life, for most people, requires no violence, no fighting, no killing, no life-risking, no sudden supreme exertion; occasionally, perhaps, a hard pull or a strong push, but no tearing, crushing, breaking, forcing.

And because violence no longer has legitimate and useful vents or purposes, it must *all* be controlled today. In earlier times its expression was often a virtue; today its control is the virtue. The control involves symbolic, vicarious expressions of our violence—violence modified; "sublimated," as Freud called it; "neutralized," as Hartmann described it. Civilized substitutes for direct violence are the objects of daily search by all of us. The common law and the Ten Commandments, traffic signals and property deeds, fences and front doors, sermons and concerts, Christmas trees and jazz bands—these and a thousand other things exist today to help in the control of violence.

My colleague, Bruno Bettelheim, thinks we do not properly educate our youth to deal with their violent urges. He reminds us that nothing fascinated our forefathers more. The *Iliad* is a poem of violence. Much of the Bible is a record of violence. One penal system and many methods of child-rearing express violence—"violence to suppress violence." And, he concludes [in the article "Violence: A Neglected Mode of Behavior"]: "We shall not be able to deal intelligently with violence unless we are first ready to see it as a part of human nature, and then we shall come to realize the chances of discharging violent tendencies are now so severely curtailed that their regular and safe draining-off is not possible anymore."

Why aren't we all criminals? We all have the impulses; we all have the provocations. But becoming civilized, which is repeated ontologically in the process of social education, teaches us what we may do with impunity. What then evokes or permits the breakthrough? Why is it necessary for some to bribe their consciences and do what they do not approve of doing? Why does all sublimation sometimes fail and overt breakdown occur in the controlling and managing machinery of the personality? Why do we sometimes lose self-control? Why do we "go to pieces"? Why do we explode?

The Madhouse (Bedlam) by William Hogarth—"No one a hundred years ago believed mental illness to be curable. Today all people know [it is] in the great majority of instances...."

—Bettmann Archive.

The rack—"We need criminals . . . to envy secretly, and to punish stoutly. They do for us the forbidden things we wish to do and, like scapegoats of old, they bear the burdens of our displaced guilt. . . ."

These questions point up a central problem in psychiatry. Why do some people do things they do not want to do? Or things we do not want them to do? Sometimes crimes are motivated by a desperate need to act, to do *something* to break out of a state of passivity, frustration, and helplessness too long endured, like a child who shoots a parent or a teacher after some apparently reasonable act. Granting the universal presence of violence within us all, controlled by will power, conscience, fear of punishment, and other devices, granting the tensions and the temptations that are also common to us all, why do the mechanisms of self-control fail so completely in some individuals? Is there not some pre-existing defect, some moral or cerebral weakness, some gross deficiency of common sense that lets some people stumble or kick or strike or explode, while the rest of us just stagger or sway?

When a psychiatrist examines many prisoners, writes [Seymour] Halleck [in *Psychiatry and the Dilemmas of Crime*], he soon discovers how important in the genesis of the criminal outbreak is the offender's previous *sense of helplessness or hopelessness*. All of us suffer more or less from infringement of our personal freedom. We fuss about it all the time; we strive to correct it, extend it, and free ourselves from various oppressive or retentive forces. We do not want others to push us around, to control us, to dominate us. We realize this is bound to happen to some extent in an interlocking, interrelated society such as ours. No one truly has complete freedom. But restriction irks us.

The offender feels this way, too. He does not want to be pushed around, controlled, or dominated. And because he often feels that he is thus oppressed (and actually is) and because he does lack facility in improving his situation without violence, he suffers more intensely from feelings of helplessness.

Violence and crime are often attempts to escape from madness; and there can be no doubt that some mental illness is a flight from the wish to do the violence or commit the act. Is it hard for the reader to believe that suicides are sometimes committed to forestall the committing of murder? There is no doubt of it. Nor is there any doubt that murder is sometimes committed to avert suicide.

Strange as it may sound, many murderers do not realize whom they are killing, or, to put it another way, that they are killing the wrong people. To be sure, killing anybody is reprehensible enough, but the worst of it is that the person who the killer thinks should die (and he has reasons) is not the person he attacks. Sometimes the victim himself is partly responsible for the crime that is committed against him. It is this unconscious (perhaps sometimes conscious) participation in the crime by the victim that has long held up the very humanitarian and progressive-sounding program of giving compensation to victims. The public often judges the victim as well as the attacker.

Rape and other sexual offenses are acts of violence so repulsive to our sense of decency and order that it is easy to think of rapists in general as raging, oversexed, ruthless brutes (unless they are conquering heroes). Some rapists are. But most sex crimes are committed by undersexed rather than oversexed individuals, often undersized rather than oversized, and impelled less by lust than by a need for reassurance regarding an impaired masculinity. The unconscious fear of women goads some men with a compulsive urge to conquer, humiliate, hurt, or render powerless some available sample of womanhood. Men who are violently afraid of their repressed but nearly emergent homosexual desires, and men who are afraid of the humiliation of impotence, often try to overcome these fears by violent demonstrations.

The need to deny something in oneself is frequently an underlying motive for certain odd behavior—even up to and including crime. Bravado crimes, often done with particular brutality and ruthlessness, seem to prove *to the doer* that "I am no weakling! I am no sissy! I am no coward. I am no homosexual! I am a tough man who fears nothing." The Nazi storm troopers, many of them mere boys, were systematically trained to stifle all tender emotions and force themselves to be heartlessly brutal.

MAN perennially seeks to recover the magic of his childhood days—the control of the mighty by the meek. The flick of an electric light switch, the response of an automobile throttle, the click of a camera, the touch of a match to a skyrocket—these are keys to a sudden and magical display of great power induced by the merest gesture. Is anyone already so blasé that he is no longer thrilled at the opening of a door specially for him by a magic-eye signal? Yet for a few pennies one can purchase a far more deadly piece of magic—a stored explosive and missile encased within a shell which can be ejected from a machine at the touch of a finger so swiftly that no eye can follow. A thousand yards away something falls dead—a rabbit, a deer, a beautiful mountain sheep, a sleeping child, or the President of the United States. Magic! Magnified, projected power. "Look what I can do. I am the greatest!"

It must have come to every thoughtful person, at one time or another, in looking at the revolvers on the policemen's hips, or the guns soldiers and hunters carry so proudly, that these are instruments made for the express purpose of delivering death to someone. The easy availability of these engines of destruction, even to children, mentally disturbed people, professional criminals, gangsters, and even high school girls is something to give one pause. The National Rifle Association and its allies have been able to kill scores of bills that have been introduced into Congress and state legislatures for corrective gun control since the death of President Kennedy. Americans still spend about $2 billion on guns each year.

Fifty years ago, Winston Churchill declared that the mood and temper of the public in regard to crime and crimi-

Cell in Women's House of Detention, New York City—a public "blind and deaf to the expense, futility, and dangerousness of the resulting penal system."

nals is one of the unfailing tests of the civilization of any country. Judged by this standard, how civilized are we?

The chairman of the President's National Crime Commission, Nicholas de B. Katzenbach, declared recently that organized crime flourishes in America because enough of the public wants its services, and most citizens are apathetic about its impact. It will continue uncurbed as long as Americans accept it as inevitable and, in some instances, desirable.

ARE there steps that we can take which will reduce the aggressive stabs and self-destructive lurches of our less well-managing fellow men? Are there ways to prevent and control the grosser violations, other than the clumsy traditional maneuvers which we have inherited? These depend basically upon intimidation and slow-motion torture. We call it punishment, and justify it with our "feeling." We know it doesn't work.

Yes, there *are* better ways. There are steps that could be taken; some *are* taken. But we move too slowly. Much better use, it seems to me, could be made of the members of my profession and other behavioral scientists than having them deliver courtroom pronunciamentos. The consistent use of a diagnostic clinic would enable trained workers to lay what they can learn about an offender before the judge who would know best how to implement the recommendation.

This would no doubt lead to a transformation of prisons, if not to their total disappearance in their present form and function. Temporary and permanent detention will perhaps always be necessary for a few, especially the professionals, but this could be more effectively and economically performed with new types of "facility" (that strange, awkward word for institution).

I assume it to be a matter of common and general agreement that our object in all this is to protect the community from a repetition of the offense by the most economical method consonant with our other purposes. Our "other purposes" include the desire to prevent these offenses from occurring, to reclaim offenders for social usefulness, if possible, and to detain them in protective custody, if reclamation is *not* possible. But how?

The treatment of human failure or dereliction by the infliction of pain is still used and believed in by many non-medical people. "Spare the rod and spoil the child" is still considered wise counsel by many.

Whipping is still used by many secondary schoolmasters in England, I am informed, to stimulate study, attention, and the love of learning. Whipping was long a traditional treatment for the "crime" of disobedience on the part of children, pupils, servants, apprentices, employees. And slaves were treated for centuries by flogging for such offenses as weariness, confusion, stupidity, exhaustion, fear, grief, and even over-cheerfulness. It was assumed and stoutly defended that these "treatments" cured conditions for which they were administered.

Meanwhile, scientific medicine was acquiring many new healing methods and devices. Doctors can now transplant organs and limbs; they can remove brain tumors and cure incipient cancers; they can halt pneumonia, meningitis, and other infections; they can correct deformities and repair breaks and tears and scars. But these wonderful achievements are accomplished on *willing* subjects, people who voluntarily ask for help by even heroic measures. And the reader will be wondering, no doubt, whether doctors can do anything with or for people who *do not want* to be treated at all, in any way! Can doctors cure willful aberrant behavior? Are we to believe that crime is a *disease* that can be reached by scientific measures? Isn't it merely "natural meanness" that makes all of us do wrong things at times even when we "know better"? And are not self-control, moral stamina, and will power the things needed? Surely there is no medical treatment for the lack of those!

LET me answer this carefully, for much misunderstanding accumulates here. I would say that according to the prevalent understanding of the words, crime is *not* a disease. Neither is it an illness, although I think it *should* be! It *should* be treated, and it could be; but it mostly isn't.

These enigmatic statements are simply explained. Diseases are undesired states of being which have been described and defined by doctors, usually given Greek or Latin appellations, and treated by long-established physical and pharmacological formulae. Illness, on the other hand, is best defined as a state of impaired functioning of such a nature that the public expects the sufferer to repair to the physician for help. The illness may prove to be a disease; more often it is only vague and nameless misery, but something which doctors, not lawyers, teachers, or preachers, are supposed to be able and willing to help.

When the community begins to look upon the expression of aggressive violence as the symptom of an illness or as indicative of illness, it will be because it believes doctors can do something to correct such a condition. At present, some better-informed individuals do believe and expect this. However angry at or sorry for the offender, they want him "treated" in an effective way so that he will cease to be a danger to them. And they know that the traditional punishment, "treatment-punishment," will not effect this.

What *will*? What effective treatment **is there for such violence? It will surely have to begin with motivating or stimulating or arousing in a cornered individual the wish and hope and intention to change his methods of dealing with the realities of life. Can this be done by education, medication, counseling, training? I would answer** *yes***. It can be done successfully in a majority of cases, if undertaken in time.**

THE present penal system and the existing legal philosophy do not stimulate or even expect such a change to take place in the criminal. Yet change is what medical science always aims for. The prisoner, like the doctor's other patients, should emerge from his treatment experience a different person, differently equipped, differently functioning, and headed in a different direction than when he began the treatment.

It is natural for the public to doubt that this can be accomplished with criminals. But remember that the public *used* to doubt that change could be effected in the mentally ill. No one a hundred years ago believed mental illness to be curable. Today *all* people know (or should know) that *mental illness is curable* in the great majority of instances and that the prospects and rapidity of cure are directly related to the availability and intensity of proper treatment.

The forms and techniques of psychiatric treatment used today number in the hundreds. No one patient requires or receives all forms, but each patient is studied with respect to his particular needs, his basic assets, his interests, and his special difficulties. A therapeutic team may embrace a dozen workers—as in a hospital setting—or it may narrow down to the doctor and the spouse. Clergymen, teachers, relatives, friends, and even fellow patients often participate informally but helpfully in the process of readaptation.

All of the participants in this effort to bring about a favorable change in the patient—i.e., in his vital balance and life program—are imbued with what we may call a *therapeutic attitude*. This is one in direct antithesis to attitudes of avoidance, ridicule, scorn, or punitiveness. Hostile feelings toward the subject, however justified by his unpleasant and even destructive behavior, are not in the curriculum of therapy or in the therapist. This does not mean that therapists approve of the offensive and obnoxious behavior of the patient; they distinctly disapprove of it. But they recognize it as symptomatic of continued imbalance and disorganization, which is what they are seeking to change. They distinguish between disapproval, penalty, price, and punishment.

Doctors charge fees; they impose certain "penalties" or prices, but they have long since put aside primitive attitudes of retaliation toward offensive patients. A patient may cough in the doctor's face or may vomit on the office rug; a patient may curse or scream or even struggle in the extremity of his pain. But these acts are not "punished." Doctors and nurses have no time or thought for inflicting unnecessary pain even upon patients who may be difficult, disagreeable, provocative, and even dangerous. It is their duty to care for them, to try to make them well, and to prevent them from doing themselves or others harm. This requires love, not hate. This is the deepest meaning of the therapeutic attitude. Every doctor knows this; every worker in a hospital or clinic knows it (or should).

There is another element in the therapeutic attitude. It is the quality of hopefulness. If no one believes that the patient can get well, if no one—not even the doctor—has any hope, there probably won't be any recovery. Hope is just as important as love in the therapeutic attitude.

"But you were talking about the mentally ill," readers may interject, "those poor, confused, bereft, frightened individuals who yearn for help from you doctors and nurses. Do you mean to imply that willfully perverse individuals, our criminals, can be similarly reached and rehabilitated? Do you really believe that effective treatment of the sort you visualize can be applied to people *who do not want any help,* who are so willfully vicious, so well aware of the wrongs they are doing, so lacking in penitence or even common decency that punishment seems to be the only thing left?"

Do I believe there is effective treatment for offenders, and that they *can* be changed? *Most certainly and definitely I do.* Not all cases, to be sure; there are also some physical afflictions which we cannot cure at the moment. Some provision has to be made for incurables—pending new knowledge—and these will include some offenders. But I believe the majority of them would prove to be curable. The willfulness and the viciousness of offenders are part of the thing for which they have to be treated. These must not thwart the therapeutic attitude.

It is simply not true that most of them are "fully aware" of what they are doing, nor is it true that they want no help from anyone, although some of them say so. Prisoners are individuals: some want treatment, some do not. Some don't know what treatment is. Many are utterly despairing and hopeless. Where treatment is made available in institutions, many prisoners seek it even with the full knowledge that doing so will not lessen their sentences. In some prisons, seeking treatment by prisoners is frowned upon by the officials.

Various forms of treatment are even now being tried in some progressive courts and prisons over the country—educational, social, industrial, religious, recreational, and psychological treatments. Socially acceptable behavior, new work-play opportunities, new identity and companion patterns all help toward community reacceptance. Some parole officers and some wardens have been extremely ingenious in developing these modalities of rehabiliation and reconstruction—more than I could list here even if I knew them all. But some are trying. The secret of success in all programs, however, is the replacement of the punitive attitude with a therapeutic attitude.

Offenders with propensities for impulsive and predatory aggression should not be permitted to live among us unrestrained by some kind of social control. *But the great majority of offenders, even "criminals," should never become prisoners if we want to "cure" them.*

THERE are now throughout the country many citizens' action groups and programs for the prevention and control of crime and delinquency. With such attitudes of inquiry and concern, the public could acquire information (and incentive) leading to a change of feeling about crime and criminals. It will discover how unjust is much so-called "justice," how baffled and frustrated many judges are by the ossified rigidity of old-fashioned, obsolete laws and state constitutions which effectively prevent the introduction of sensible procedures to replace useless, harmful ones.

I want to proclaim to the public that things are not what it wishes them to be, and will only become so if it will take an interest in the matter and assume some responsibility for its own self-protection.

Will the public listen?

If the public does become interested, it will realize that we must have more facts, more trial projects, more checked results. It will share the dismay of the President's Commission in finding that

—UPI.

Family visits prisoner under new program, Tehachapi, California—". . . a transformation of prisons, if not their total disappearance in their present form and function."

no one knows much about even the incidence of crime with any definiteness or statistical accuracy.

The average citizen finds it difficult to see how any research would in any way change his mind about a man who brutally murders his children. But just such inconceivably awful acts most dramatically point up the need for research. Why should—how can—a man become so dreadful as that in our culture? How is such a man made? Is it comprehensible that he can be born to become so depraved?

There are thousands of questions regarding crime and public protection which deserve scientific study. What makes some individuals maintain their interior equilibrium by one kind of disturbance of the social structure rather than by another kind, one that would have landed him in a hospital? Why do some individuals specialize in certain types of crime? Why do so many young people reared in areas of delinquency and poverty and bad example never become habitual delinquents? (Perhaps this is a more important question than why some of them do.)

The public has a fascination for violence, and clings tenaciously to its yen for vengeance, blind and deaf to the expense, futility, and dangerousness of the resulting penal system. But we are bound to hope that this will yield in time to the persistent, penetrating light of intelligence and accumulating scientific knowledge. The public will grow increasingly ashamed of its cry for retaliation, its persistent demand to punish. This is its crime, *our* crime against criminals—and, incidentally, our crime against ourselves. For before we can diminish our sufferings from the ill-controlled aggressive assaults of fellow citizens, we must renounce the philosophy of punishment, the obsolete, vengeful penal attitude. In its place we would seek a comprehensive constructive social attitude—therapeutic in some instances, restraining in some instances, but preventive in its total social impact.

In the last analysis this becomes a question of personal morals and values. No matter how glorified or how piously disguised, vengeance as a human motive must be personally repudiated by each and every one of us. This is the message of old religions and new psychiatries. Unless this message is heard, unless we, the people—the man on the street, the housewife in the home—can give up our delicious satisfactions in opportunities for vengeful retaliation on scapegoats, we cannot expect to preserve our peace, our public safety, or our mental health.

Section Ten

Social Behavior

The first paper of this section deals with a review of studies of social facilitation. One of the oldest areas of investigation in social psychology, social facilitation refers to the effects of the behavior of one individual on the behavior of another. Do we work faster and more efficiently when others are watching? What effect on behavior is produced by the presence of others also working on the same tasks as we? Are animals other than human beings influenced by the presence of others? These are some of the questions investigated by social psychologists over the years and summarized by Zajonc in this paper.

In the second article of this section, Dr. Haggstrom makes the statement that one cannot use poverty as an explanation for the psychological characteristics that are often associated with poverty. The characteristics of the poor, he argues, stem not from a lack of money but from being unable to affect one's social situation. In order to change the social problems related to poverty, it is suggested that the "major community" (the "establishment") will have to change its relationship to the poor so that they have a greater stake in the broad society and can successfully participate in decision-making processes.

Tajfel, in his paper on "stereotypes," is concerned with a number of different questions related to prejudice. How do people process information that leads to the development of stereotypes? Are there different kinds of prejudice? Can prejudice be modified? The topic of prejudice is, of course, an old one, but Tajfel has some new insights into how prejudice may be altered. He looks particularly at educational campaigns—campaigns which in the past have not been particularly successful. Based on his research, Tajfel suggests that a content analysis aimed at specifying the characteristics used to differentiate specific groups might serve as a basis for effective educational campaigns. Such campaigns would be designed to counteract specific aspects of bias which are known to be particularly widespread or particularly intense.

The next paper, dealing with problems in research on psychological warfare, is the only one of its kind to be published since the beginning of the U.S. involvement in Viet Nam. Speaking in very general terms, the author highlights many of the major obstacles faced by the practitioner of perhaps the most humane kind of warfare. In addition to setting forth several of the still unresolved difficulties, the paper presents a number of examples of both American and Viet Cong psywar leaflets.

Richard Flacks, a sociologist, turns our attention to the legitimacy of national authority in the United States. He feels that such legitimacy is fast reaching a historical turning point. Traditionally, there have existed relatively high levels of trust regarding authority figures (scientists, members of the national government and armed services) which have included willingness to relegate judgmental processes from individuals to these people. This tradition, as Flack sees it, is rapidly eroding. Reviewing recent research, he tells us that: (1) if authority is perceived as beneficial to groups, institutions, or values to which an individual is committed, then legitimacy will be attributed to that authority; (2) the attribution of legitimacy is a function of trust; and (3) perception of a generalized consensus supporting legitimacy makes it easier for individuals to attribute legitimacy to authority.

A discussion of individual differences and the capacity to resist authority is presented, followed by a presentation of "cracks" in the support of authority. Flacks concludes that "militarism, racism, narrow rationalism and imperialism have become illegitimate" and that other values are ascending which will become the bases for legitimacy.

Morton Deutsch begins his paper, "Psychological Alternatives to War," with five basic assertions which he concludes necessitate mankind's seeking and finding alternatives to war if human beings are to remain on earth. Psychology may properly address itself to this, he feels, because psychological concepts are central to international relations. The author carefully examines the question of the inevitability of wars. In his view neither war nor peace are inevitable, but exaggerating the possibility of the former contributes to a "self-fulfilling prophecy."

Deutsch reminds us that our behavior is largely a function of our perception of our "world" and that this is subject to distortion. Several causes of misperception are presented along with a discussion about how these may operate in international relations in ways which make war more likely. He suggests that it is necessary to develop attitudes of mutual trust and interests, mutual acceptance, welfare, and full communication if a stable peace is to be achieved. Competition can flourish and work for mankind only if we are successful in the quest for alternatives to military conflict.

SOCIAL FACILITATION

ROBERT B. ZAJONC
University of Michigan

Most textbook definitions of social psychology involve considerations about the influence of man upon man, or, more generally, of individual upon individual. And most of them, explicitly or implicity, commit the main efforts of social psychology to the problem of how and why the *behavior* of one individual affects the behavior of another. The influences of individuals on each others' behavior which are of interest to social psychologists today take on very complex forms. Often they involve vast networks of interindividual effects, such as one finds in studying the process of group decision-making, competition, or conformity to a group norm. But the fundamental forms of interindividual influence are represented by the oldest experimental paradigm of social psychology: social facilitation. This paradigm, dating back to Triplett's original experiments on pacing and competition, carried out in 1897 (*1*), examines the consequences upon behavior which derive from the sheer presence of other individuals.

Until the late 1930's, interest in social facilitation was quite active, but with the outbreak of World War II it suddenly died. And it is truly regrettable that it died, because the basic questions about social facilitation—its dynamics and its causes—which are in effect the basic questions of social psychology, were never solved. It is with these questions that this article is concerned. I first examine past results in this nearly completely abandoned area of research and then suggest a general hypothesis which might explain them.

Research in the area of social facilitation may be classified in terms of two experimental paradigms: audience effects and co-action effects. The first experimental paradigm involves the observation of behavior when it occurs in the presence of passive spectators. The second examines behavior when it occurs in the presence of other individuals also engaged in the same activity. We shall consider past literature in these two areas separately.

Audience Effects

Simple motor responses are particularly sensitive to social facilitation effects. In 1925 Travis (*2*) obtained such effects in a study in which he used the pursuit-rotor task. In this task the subject is required to follow a small revolving target by means of a stylus which he holds in his hand. If the stylus is even momentarily off target during a revolution, the revolution counts as an error. First each subject was trained for several consecutive days until his performance reached a stable level. One day after the conclusion of the training the subject was called to the laboratory, given five trials alone, and then ten trials in the presence of from four to eight upperclassmen and graduate students. They had been asked by the experimenter to watch the subject quietly and attentively. Travis found a clear improvement in performance when his subjects were confronted with an audience. Their accuracy on the ten trials before an audience was greater than on any ten previous trials, including those on which they had scored highest.

A considerably greater improvement in performance was recently obtained in a somewhat different setting and on a different task (*3*). Each subject (all were National Guard trainees) was placed in a separate booth. He was seated in front of a panel outfitted with 20 red lamps in a circle. The lamps on this panel light in a clockwise sequence at 12 revolutions per minute. At random intervals one or another light fails to go on in its proper sequence. On the average there are 24 such failures per hour. The subject's task is to signal whenever a light fails to go on. After 20 minutes of intensive training, followed by a short rest, the National Guard trainees monitored the light panels for 135 minutes. Subjects in one group performed their task alone. Subjects in another group were told that from time to time a lieutenant colonel or a master sergeant would visit them in the booth to observe their performance. These visits actually took place about four times during the experimental session. There was no doubt about the results. The accuracy of the supervised subjects was on the average 34 percent higher than the accuracy of the trainees working in isolation, and toward the end of the experimental session the accuracy of the supervised subjects

---

Reprinted from *Science*, Vol. 149, July 16, 1965. Copyright 1965 by the American Association for the Advancement of Science.

was more than twice as high as that of the subjects working in isolation. Those expecting to be visited by a superior missed, during the last experimental period, 20 percent of the light failures, while those expecting no such visits missed 64 percent of the failures.

Dashiell, who, in the early 1930's, carried out an extensive program of research on social facilitation, also found considerable improvement in performance due to audience effects on such tasks as simple multiplication or word association (4). But, as is the case in many other areas, negative audience effects were also found. In 1933 Pessin asked college students to learn lists of nonsense syllables under two conditions, alone and in the presence of several spectators (5). When confronted with an audience, his subjects required an average of 11.27 trials to learn a seven-item list. When working alone they needed only 9.85 trials. The average number of errors made in the "audience" condition was considerably higher than the number in the "alone" condition. In 1931 Husband found that the presence of spectators interferes with the learning of a finger maze (6), and in 1933 Pessin and Husband (7) confirmed Husband's results. The number of trials which the isolated subjects required for learning the finger maze was 17.1. Subjects confronted with spectators, however, required 19.1 trials. The average number of errors for the isolated subjects was 33.7; the number for those working in the presence of an audience was 40.5.

The results thus far reviewed seem to contradict one another. On a pursuit-rotor task Travis found that the presence of an audience improves performance. The learning of nonsense syllables and maze learning, however, seem to be inhibited by the presence of an audience, as shown by Pessin's experiment. The picture is further complicated by the fact that when Pessin's subjects were asked, several days later, to recall the nonsense syllables they had learned, a reversal was found. The subjects who tried to recall the lists in the presence of spectators did considerably better than those who tried to recall them alone. Why are the learning of nonsense syllables and maze learning inhibited by the presence of spectators? And why, on the other hand, does performance on a pursuit-rotor, word-association, multiplication, or a vigilance task improve in the presence of others?

There is just one, rather subtle, consistency in the above results. It would appear that the emission of well-learned responses is facilitated by the presence of spectators, while the acquisition of new responses is impaired. To put the statement in conventional psychological language, performance is facilitated and learning is impaired by the presence of spectators.

This tentative generalization can be reformulated so that different features of the problem are placed into focus. During the early stages of learning, especially of the type involved in social facilitation studies, the subject's responses are mostly the wrong ones. A person learning a finger maze, or a person learning a list of nonsense syllables, emits more wrong responses than right ones in the early stages of training. Most learning experiments continue until he ceases to make mistakes —until his performance is perfect. It may be said, therefore, that during training it is primarily the wrong responses which are dominant and strong; they are the ones which have the highest probability of occurrence. But after the individual has mastered the task, correct responses necessarily gain ascendency in his task-relevant behavioral repertoire. Now they are the ones which are more probable—in other words, dominant. Our tentative generalization may now be simplified: audience enhances the emission of dominant responses. If the dominant responses are the correct ones, as is the case upon achieving mastery, the presence of an audience will be of benefit to the individual. But if they are mostly wrong, as is the case in the early stages of learning, then these wrong responses will be enhanced in the presence of an audience, and the emission of correct responses will be postponed or prevented.

There is a class of psychological processes which are known to enhance the emission of dominant responses. They are subsumed under the concepts of drive, arousal, and activation (8). If we could show that the presence of an audience has arousal consequences for the subject, we would be a step further along in trying to arrange the results of social-facilitation experiments into a neater package. But let us first consider another set of experimental findings.

Co-action Effects

The experimental paradigm of co-action is somewhat more complex than the paradigm involved in the study of audience effects. Here we observe individuals all simultaneously engaged in the same activity and in full view of each other. One of the clearest effects of such simultaneous action, or co-action, is found in eating behavior. It is well known that animals simply eat more in the presence of others. For instance, Bayer had chickens eat from a pile of wheat to their full satisfaction (9). He waited some time to be absolutely sure that his subject would eat no more, and then brought in a companion chicken who had not eaten for 24 hours. Upon the introduction of the hungry co-actor, the apparently sated chicken ate two-thirds again as much grain as it had already eaten. Recent work by Tolman and Wilson fully substantiates these results (10). In an extensive study of social-facilitation effects among albino rats, Harlow found dramatic increases in eating (11). In one of his experiments, for instance, the rats, shortly after weaning, were matched in pairs for weight. They were then fed alone and in pairs on alternate days. Figure 1 shows his results. It is clear that considerably more food was consumed by the animals when they were in pairs than when they were fed alone. James (12), too, found very clear evidence of increased eating among puppies fed in groups.

Perhaps the most dramatic effect of co-action is reported by Chen (13). Chen observed groups of ants working alone, in groups of two, and in groups of three. Each ant was observed under various conditions. In the first experimental session each ant was placed in a bottle half filled with sandy soil. The ant was observed for 6 hours. The time at which nest-building began was noted, and the earth excavated by the insect was carefully weighed. Two days afterward the same ants were placed in freshly filled bottles in pairs, and the same observations were made. A few days later the ants were placed in the bottles in groups of three, again for 6 hours. Finally, a few days after

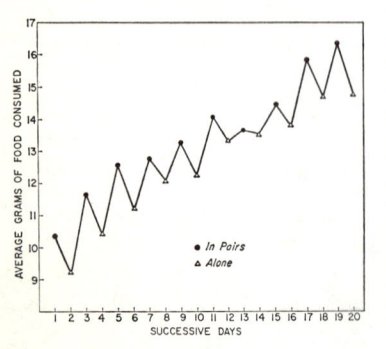

Fig. 1. Data on feeding of isolated and paired rats. [Harlow (11)]

the test in groups of three, nest-building of the ants in isolation was observed. Figure 2 shows some of Chen's data.

There is absolutely no question that the amount of work an ant accomplishes increases markedly in the presence of another ant. In all pairs except one, the presence of a companion increased output by a factor of at least 2. The effect of co-action on the latency of the nest-building behavior was equally dramatic. The solitary ants of session 1 and the final session began working on the nest in 192 minutes, on the average. The latency period for ants in groups of two was only 28 minutes. The effects observed by Chen were limited to the immediate situation and seemed to have no lasting consequences for the ants. There were no differences in the results of session 1, during which the ants worked in isolation, and of the last experimental session, where they again worked in solitude.

If one assumes that under the conditions of Chen's experiment nest-building *is* the dominant response, then there is no reason why his findings could not be embraced by the generalization just proposed. Nest-building is a response which Chen's ants have fully mastered. Certainly, it is something that a mature ant need not learn. And this is simply an instance where the generalization that the presence of others enhances the emission of dominant and well-developed responses holds.

If the process involved in audience effects is also involved in co-action effects, then learning should be inhibited in the presence of other learners. Let us examine some literature in this field. Klopfer (*14*) observed greenfinches—in isolation and in heterosexual pairs—which were learning to discriminate between sources of palatable and of unpalatable food. And, as one would by now expect, his birds learned this discrimination task considerably more efficiently when working alone. I hasten to add that the subjects' sexual interests cannot be held responsible for the inhibition of learning in the paired birds. Allee and Masure, using Australian parakeets, obtained the same result for homosexual pairs as well (*15*). The speed of learning was considerably greater for the isolated birds than for the paired birds, regardless of whether the birds were of the same sex or of the opposite sex.

Similar results are found with cockroaches. Gates and Allee (*16*) compared data for cockroaches learning a maze in isolation, in groups of two, and in groups of three. They used an E-shaped maze. Its three runways, made of galvanized sheet metal, were suspended in a pan of water. At the end of the center runway was a dark bottle into which the photophobic cockroaches could escape from the noxious light. The results, in terms of time required to reach the bottle, are shown in Fig. 3. It is clear from the data that the solitary cockroaches required considerably less time to learn the maze than the grouped animals. Gates and Allee believe that the group situation produced inhibition. They add, however (*16*, p. 357): "The nature of these inhibiting forces is speculative, but the fact of some sort of group interference is obvious. The presence of other roaches did not operate to change greatly the movements to different parts of the maze, but did result in increased time per trial. The roaches tended to go to the corner or end of the runway and remain there a longer time when another roach was present than when alone; the other roach was a distracting stimulus."

The experiments on social facilitation performed by Floyd Allport in 1920 and continued by Dashiell in 1930 (*4, 17*), both of whom used human subjects, are the ones best known. Allport's subjects worked either in separate cubicles or sitting around a common table. When working in isolation they did the various tasks at the same time and were monitored by common time signals. Allport did everything possible to reduce the tendency to compete. The subjects were told that the results of their tests would not be compared and would not be shown to other staff members, and that they themselves should refrain from making any such comparisons.

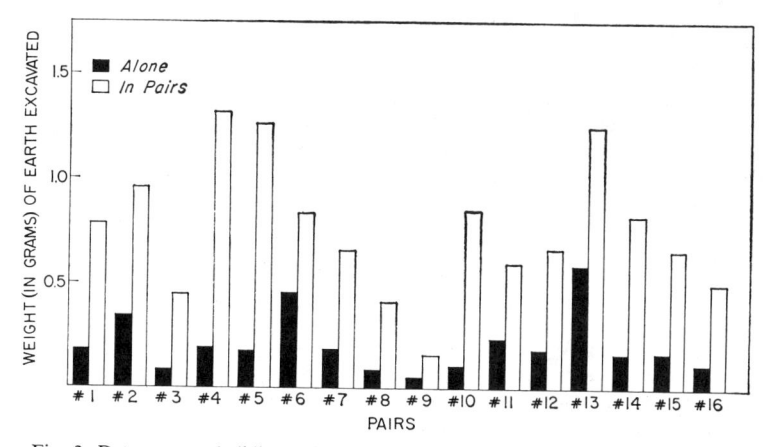

Fig. 2. Data on nest-building behavior of isolated and paired ants. [Chen (*13*)]

Among the tasks used were the following: chain word association, vowel cancellation, reversible perspective, multiplication, problem solving, and judgments of odors and weights. The results of Allport's experiments are well known: in all but the problem-solving and judgments test, performance was better in groups than in the "alone" condition. How do these results fit our generalization? Word association, multiplication, the cancellation of vowels, and the reversal of the perceived orientation of an ambiguous figure all involve responses which are well established. They are responses which are either very well learned or under a very strong influence of the stimulus, as in the word-association task or the reversible-perspective test. The problem-solving test consists of disproving arguments of ancient philosophers. In contrast to the other tests, it does not involve well-learned responses. On the contrary, the probability of wrong (that is, logically incorrect) responses on tasks of this sort is rather high; in other words, wrong responses are dominant. Of interest, however, is the finding that while intellectual work suffered in the group situation, sheer output of words was increased. When working together, Allport's subjects tended consistently to write more. Therefore, the generalization proposed in the previous section can again be applied: if the presence of others raises the probability of dominant responses, and if strong (and many) incorrect response tendencies prevail, then the presence of others can only be detrimental to performance. The results of the judgment tests have little bearing on the present argument, since Allport gives no accuracy figures for evaluating performance. The data reported only show that the presence of others was associated with the avoidance of extreme judgments.

In 1928 Travis (18), whose work on the pursuit rotor I have already noted, repeated Allport's chain-word-association experiment. In contrast to Allport's results, Travis found that the presence of others decreased performance. The number of associations given by his subjects was greater when they worked in isolation. It is very significant, however, that Travis used stutterers as his subjects. In a way, stuttering is a manifestation of a struggle between conflicting response tendencies, all of which are strong and all of which compete for expression. The stutterer, momentarily hung up in the middle of a sentence, waits for the correct response to reach full ascendancy. He stammers because other competing tendencies are dominant at that moment. It is reasonable to assume that, to the extent that the verbal habits of a stutterer are characterized by conflicting response tendencies, the presence of others, by enhancing each of these response tendencies, simply heightens his conflict. Performance is thus impaired.

Avoidance Learning

In two experiments on the learning of avoidance responses the performances of solitary and grouped subjects were compared. In one, rats were used; in the other, humans.

Let us first consider the results of the rat experiment, by Rasmussen (19). A number of albino rats, all litter mates, were deprived of water for 48 hours. The apparatus consisted of a box containing a dish of drinking water. The floor of the box was made of a metal grille wired to one pole of an electric circuit. A wire inserted in the water in the dish was connected to the other pole of the circuit. Thirsty rats were placed in the box alone and in groups of three. They were allowed to drink for 5 seconds with the circuit open. Following this period the shock circuit remained closed, and each time the rat touched the water he received a painful shock. Observations were made on the number of times the rats approached the water dish. The results of this experiment showed that the solitary rats learned to avoid the dish considerably sooner than the grouped animals did. The rats that were in groups of three attempted to drink twice as often as the solitary rats did, and suffered considerably more shock than the solitary subjects.

Let us examine Rasmussen's results somewhat more closely. For purposes of analysis let us assume that there are just two critical responses involved: drinking, and avoidance of contact with the water. They are clearly incompatible. But drinking, we may further assume, is the dominant response, and, like eating or any other dominant response, it is enhanced by the presence of others. The animal is therefore prevented, by the facilitation of drinking which derives from the presence of others, from acquiring the appropriate avoidance response.

The second of the two studies is quite recent and was carried out by Ader and Tatum (20). They devised the following situation with which they confronted their subjects, all medical students. Each subject is told on arrival that he will be taken to another room and seated in a chair, and that electrodes will be attached to his leg. He is instructed not to get up from the chair and not to touch the electrodes. He is also told not to smoke or vocalize, and is told that the experimenter will be in the next room. That is all he is told. The subjects are observed either alone or in pairs. In the former case the subject is brought to the room and seated at a table equipped with a red button which is connected to an electric circuit. Electrodes, by means of which electric shock can be administered, are attached to the calf of one leg. After the electrodes are attached, the experimenter leaves the room. From now on the subject will receive ½ second of electric shock every 10 seconds unless he presses the red button. Each press of the button delays the shock by 10 seconds. Thus, if he is to avoid shock, he must press the button at least once every 10 seconds. It should be noted that no information was given him about the function of the button, or about the purpose of the experiment. No essential differences are introduced when subjects are brought to the room in pairs. Both are seated at the table and both become part of the shock circuit. The response of either subject delays the shock for both.

The avoidance response is considered to have been acquired when the subject (or pair of subjects) receives less than six shocks in a period of 5 minutes. Ader and Tatum report that the isolated students required, on the average, 11 minutes, 35 seconds to reach this criterion of learning. Of the 12 pairs which participated in the experiment, only two reached this criterion. One of them required 46 minutes, 40 seconds; the other, 68 minutes, 40 seconds! Ader and Tatum offer no explanation for their curious results. But there is no reason why we should not treat them in terms of the generalization proposed above. We are dealing here with a learning task, and the fact that the subjects are learning to avoid shock by pressing a red button does not introduce particular problems. They are confronted with an ambiguous task, and told nothing about the button. Pressing the button is simply not the dominant response in this situation. However, escaping is. Ader and Tatum report that eight of the 36 subjects walked out in the middle of the experiment.

One aspect of Ader and Tatum's results is especially worth noting. Once having learned the appropriate avoidance response, the individual subjects responded at considerably lower rates than the paired subjects. When we consider only those subjects who achieved the learning criterion and only those responses which occurred *after* criterion had been reached, we find that the response rates of the individual subjects were in all but one case lower than the response rates of the grouped subjects. This result further confirms the generalization that, while learning is impaired by the presence of others, the performance of learned responses is enhanced.

There are experiments which show that learning is enhanced by the presence of other learners (21), but in all these experiments, as far as I can tell,

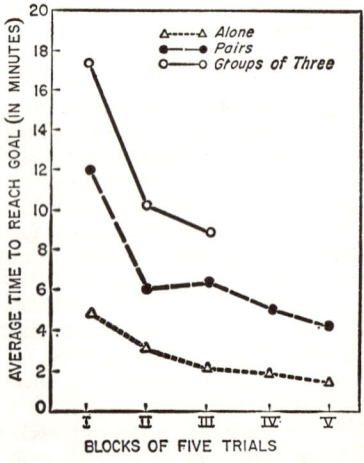

Fig. 3. Data on maze learning in isolated and grouped cockroaches. [Gates and Allee (16)]

it was possible for the subject to *observe* the critical responses of other subjects, and to determine when he was correct and when incorrect. In none, therefore, has the co-action paradigm been employed in its pure form. That paradigm involves the presence of others, and nothing else. It requires that these others not be able to provide the subject with cues or information as to appropriate behavior. If other learners can supply the critical individual with such cues, we are dealing not with the problem of co-action but with the problem of imitation or vicarious learning.

The Presence of Others as a Source of Arousal

The results I have discussed thus far lead to one generalization and to one hypothesis. The generalization which organizes these results is that the presence of others, as spectators or as co-actors, enhances the emission of dominant responses. We also know from extensive research literature that arousal, activation, or drive all have as a consequence the enhancement of dominant responses (22). We now need to examine the hypothesis that the presence of others increases the individual's general arousal or drive level.

The evidence which bears on the relationship between the presence of others and arousal is, unfortunately, only indirect. But there is some very suggestive evidence in one area of research. One of the more reliable indicators of arousal and drive is the activity of the endocrine systems in general, and of the adrenal cortex in particular. Adrenocortical functions are extremely sensitive to changes in emotional arousal, and it has been known for some time that organisms subjected to prolonged stress are likely to manifest substantial adrenocortical hypertrophy (23). Recent work (24) has shown that the main biochemical component of the adrenocortical output is hydrocortisone (17-hydroxycorticosterone). Psychiatric patients characterized by anxiety states, for instance, show elevated plasma levels of hydrocortisone (25). Mason, Brady, and Sidman (26) have recently trained monkeys to press a lever for food and have given these animals unavoidable electric shocks, all preceded by warning signals. This procedure led to elevated hydrocortisone levels; the levels returned to normal within 1 hour after the end of the experimental session.

Table 1. Basal plasma concentrations of 17-hydroxycorticosterone in monkeys housed alone (cages in separate rooms), then in a room with other monkeys (cages in same room). [Leiderman and Shapiro (35, p. 7)]

Subject	Time	In separate rooms	In same room
M-1	9 a.m.	23	34
M-1	3 p.m.	16	27
M-2	9 a.m.	28	34
M-2	3 p.m.	19	23
M-3	9 a.m.	32	38
M-3	3 p.m.	23	31
Mean	9 a.m.	28	35
Mean	3 p.m.	19	27

(Conc. of 17-hydroxycorticosterone in caged monkeys, μg per 100 ml of plasma)

This "anxiety" reaction can apparently be attenuated if the animal is given repeated doses of reserpine 1 day before the experimental session (27). Sidman's conditioned avoidance schedule also results in raising the hydrocortisone levels by a factor of 2 to 4 (26). In this schedule the animal receives an electric shock every 20 seconds without warning, unless he presses a lever. Each press delays the shock for 20 seconds.

While there is a fair amount of evidence that adrenocortical activity is a reliable symptom of arousal, similar endocrine manifestations were found to be associated with increased population density (28). Crowded mice, for instance, show increased amphetamine toxicity—that is, susceptibility to the excitatory effects of amphetamine—against which they can be protected by the administration of phenobarbital, chlorpromazine, or reserpine (29). Mason and Brady (30) have recently reported that monkeys caged together had considerably higher plasma levels of hydrocortisone than monkeys housed in individual cages. Thiessen (31) found increases in adrenal weights in mice housed in groups of 10 and 20 as compared with mice housed alone. The mere presence of other animals in the same room, but in separate cages, was also found to produce elevated levels of hydrocortisone. Table 1, taken from a report by Mason and Brady (30), shows plasma levels of hydrocortisone for three animals which lived at one time in cages that afforded them the possibility of visual and tactile contact and, at another time, in separate rooms.

Mason and Brady also report urinary levels of hydrocortisone, by days of the week, for five monkeys from their laboratory and for one human hospital patient. These very suggestive figures are reproduced in Table 2 (30). In the monkeys, the low weekend traffic and activity in the laboratory seem to be associated with a clear decrease in hydrocortisone. As for the hospital patient, Mason and Brady report (30, p. 8), "he was confined to a thoracic surgery ward that bustled with activity during the weekdays when surgery and admissions occurred. On the weekends the patient retired to the nearby Red Cross building, with its quieter and more pleasant environment."

Admittedly, the evidence that the mere presence of others raises the arousal level is indirect and scanty. And, as a matter of fact, some work seems to suggest that there are conditions, such as stress, under which the presence of others may lower the animal's arousal level. Bovard (32), for instance, hypothesized that the presence of another member of the same species may protect the individual under stress by inhibiting the activity of the posterior hypothalamic centers which trigger the pituitary adrenal cortical and sympathetico-adrenal medullary responses to stress. Evidence for Bovard's hypothesis, however, is as indirect as evidence for the one which predicts arousal as a consequence of the presence of others, and even more scanty.

Summary and Conclusion

If one were to draw one practical suggestion from the review of the social-facilitation effects which are summarized in this article he would advise the student to study all alone, pref-

Table 2. Variations in urinary concentration of hydrocortisone over a 9-day period for five laboratory monkeys and one human hospital patient. [Leiderman and Shapiro (35, p. 8)]

Subjects	Amounts excreted (mg/24 hr)								
	Mon.	Tues.	Wed.	Thurs.	Fri.	Sat.	Sun.	Mon.	Tues.
Monkeys	1.88	1.71	1.60	1.52	1.70	1.16	1.17	1.88	
Patient		5.9	6.5	4.5	5.7	3.3	3.9	6.0	5.2

erably in an isolated cubicle, and to arrange to take his examinations in the company of many other students, on stage, and in the presence of a large audience. The results of his examination would be beyond his wildest expectations, provided, of course, he had learned his material quite thoroughly.

I have tried in this article to pull together the early, almost forgotten work on social facilitation, and to explain the seemingly conflicting results. This explanation is, of course, tentative, and it has never been put to a direct experimental test. It is, moreover, not far removed from the one originally proposed by Allport. He theorized (*33*, p. 261) that "the sights and sounds of others doing the same thing" augment ongoing responses. Allport, however, proposed this effect only for *overt* motor responses, assuming (*33*, p. 274) that "*intellectual* or *implicit responses* of thought are hampered rather than facilitated" by the presence of others. This latter conclusion was probably suggested to him by the negative results he observed in his research on the effects of co-action on problem solving.

Needless to say, the presence of others may have effects considerably more complex than that of increasing the individual's arousal level. The presence of others may provide cues as to appropriate or inappropriate responses, as in the case of imitation or vicarious learning. Or it may supply the individual with cues as to the measure of danger in an ambiguous or stressful situation. Davitz and Mason (*34*), for instance, have shown that the presence of an unafraid rat reduces the fear of another rat in stress. Bovard (*32*) believes that the calming of the rat in stress which is in the presence of an unafraid companion is mediated by inhibition of activity of the posterior hypothalamus. But in their experimental situations (that is, the open field test) the possibility that cues for appropriate escape or avoidance responses are provided by the co-actor is not ruled out. We might therefore be dealing not with the effects of the mere presence of others but with the considerably more complex case of imitation. The animal may not be calming *because* of his companion's presence. He may be calming *after* having copied his companion's attempted escape responses. The paradigm which I have examined in this article pertains only to the effects of the mere presence of others, and to the consequences for the arousal level. The exact parameters involved in social facilitation still must be specified.

References and Notes

1. N. Triplett, *Amer. J. Psychol.* **9**, 507 (1897).
2. L. E. Travis, *J. Abnormal Soc. Psychol.* **20**, 142 (1925).
3. B. O. Bergum and D. J. Lehr, *J. Appl. Psychol.* **47**, 75 (1963).
4. J. F. Dashiell, *J. Abnormal Soc. Psychol.* **25**, 190 (1930).
5. J. Pessin, *Amer. J. Psychol.* **45**, 263 (1933).
6. R. W. Husband, *J. Genet. Psychol.* **39**, 258 (1931). In this task the blindfolded subject traces a maze with his finger.
7. J. Pessin and R. W. Husband, *J. Abnormal Soc. Psychol.* **28**, 148 (1933).
8. See, for instance, E. Dufy, *Activation and Behavior* (Wiley, New York, 1962); K. W. Spence, *Behavior Theory and Conditioning* (Yale Univ. Press, New Haven, 1956); R. B. Zajonc and B. Nieuwenhuyse, *J. Exp. Psychol.* **67**, 276 (1964).
9. E. Bayer, *Z. Psychol.* **112**, 1 (1929).
10. C. W. Tolman and G. T. Wilson, *Animal Behavior* **13**, 134 (1965).
11. H. F. Harlow, *J. Genet. Psychol.* **43**, 211 (1932).
12. W. T. James, *J. Comp. Physiol. Psychol.* **46**, 427 (1953); *J. Genet. Psychol.* **96**, 123 (1960); W. T. James and D. J. Cannon, *ibid.* **87**, 225 (1956).
13. S. C. Chen, *Physiol. Zool.* **10**, 420 (1937).
14. P. H. Klopfer, *Science* **128**, 903 (1958).
15. W. C. Allee and R. H. Masure, *Physiol. Zool.* **22**, 131 (1936).
16. M. J. Gates and W. C. Allee, *J. Comp. Psychol.* **15**, 331 (1933).
17. F. H. Allport, *J. Exp. Psychol.* **3**, 159 (1920).
18. L. E. Travis, *J. Abnormal Soc. Psychol.* **23**, 45 (1928).
19. E. Rasmussen, *Acta Psychol.* **4**, 275 (1939).
20. R. Ader and R. Tatum, *J. Exp. Anal. Behavior* **6**, 357 (1963).
21. H. Gurnee, *J. Abnormal Soc. Psychol.* **34**, 529 (1939); J. C. Welty, *Physiol. Zool.* **7**, 85 (1934).
22. See K. W. Spence, *Behavior Theory and Conditioning* (Yale Univ. Press, New Haven, 1956).
23. H. Selye, *J. Clin. Endocrin.* **6**, 117 (1946).
24. D. H. Nelson and L. T. Samuels, *ibid.* **12**, 519 (1952).
25. E. L. Bliss, A. A. Sandberg, D. H. Nelson, *J. Clin. Invest.* **32**, 9 (1953); F. Board, H. Persky, D. A. Hamburg, *Psychosom. Med.* **18**, 324 (1956).
26. J. W. Mason, J. V. Brady, M. Sidman, *Endocrinology* **60**, 741 (1957).
27. J. W. Mason and J. V. Brady, *Science* **124**, 983 (1956).
28. D. D. Thiessen, *Texas Rep. Biol. Med.* **22**, 266 (1964).
29. L. Lasagna and W. P. McCann, *Science* **125**, 1241 (1957).
30. J. W. Mason and J. V. Brady, in *Psychobiological Approaches to Social Behavior*, P. H. Leiderman and D. Shapiro, Eds. (Stanford Univ. Press, Stanford, Calif., 1964).
31. D. D. Thiessen, *J. Comp. Physiol. Psychol.* **57**, 412 (1964).
32. E. W. Bovard, *Psychol. Rev.* **66**, 267 (1959).
33. F. H. Allport, *Social Psychology* (Houghton-Mifflin, Boston, 1924).
34. J. R. Davitz and D. J. Mason, *J. Comp. Physiol. Psychol.* **48**, 149 (1955).
35. P. H. Leiderman and D. Shapiro, Eds., *Psychobiological Approaches to Social Behavior* (Stanford Univ. Press, Stanford, Calif., 1964).
36. The preparation of this article was supported in part by grants Nonr-1224(34) from the Office of Naval Research and GS-629 from the National Science Foundation.

THE PSYCHOLOGIST LOOKS AT POVERTY

WARREN C. HAGGSTROM
Syracuse University

On the average, the poor in the United States have bad reputations. They are regarded as responsible for much physical aggression and destruction of property; their support is alleged to be a heavy burden on the rest of the community; and they are said not even to try very hard to meet community standards of behavior or to be self-supporting. Poverty, it is said, is little enough punishment for people so inferior and so lacking in virtue.

Roughly speaking, these common opinions about the poor have some accuracy. Socially notorious varieties of deviancy and dependency do flourish in areas of poverty to a greater extent than in the remainder of our society. The middle classes, of course, have their own faults, which are sometimes perceptively observed and described by the poor. The relatively prosperous tend to use their verbal facility to conceal aspects of social reality from themselves and tend to use word-magic to make themselves comfortable about being in their generally undeserved positions of affluence, positions in which they manage to obtain the most pay and security for doing easy and interesting kinds of work.

Since the United States is a middle class society, those who emphasize the bad reputations of the poor are regarded as hard-headed realists, while those who stress the phoniness of the middle classes are considered rather extreme and overly suspicious. When a social worker reports that the lower classes tend in the direction of schizophrenia and character disorders, he is viewed as having made a sober report of the existing state of affairs. Or when a social scientist discovers that the poor are unsocialized, childlike, occupy an early category in *his* category system of degrees of socialization, his discovery is treated as an important basis for further scientific work. But suppose that a leader of the poor announces that social workers tend to be "phonies" and "half-queer" as well, or suggests in his own language that social scientists are usually fuzzy-minded and socially irrelevant. This invidious description is not seen as a suitable hypothesis for investigation and research; it is rather said (without benefit of evidence) to be a symptom of the

---

Reprinted with the permission of The Free Press of Glencoe from "The Power of the Poor" in *Mental Health of the Poor*, by F. Riessman, et al., eds., Pp. 202–221, 1964.

ignorance or of the personal or political needs of the person making the statement.

We cannot, of course, simply shed the presuppositions which attach to our social positions, and those of us who see the poor from above are likely not to have viewed them from the most flattering perspective. But let us, in the following discussion, attempt to be critical and scientific by orienting ourselves to reasons and evidence rather than to common sense conceptual refinements of our current prejudices. We will first analyze a popular contemporary account of the psychology of poverty, and then advance a different orientation as a more precise explanation for available data.

Psychological Characteristics of the Poor

Social scientists have arrived at a rough consensus about the modal personality in neighborhoods of poverty:

(1) The poor tend to have a keen sense of the personal and the concrete; their interest typically is restricted to the self, the family, and the neighborhood. There is a particular stress on the intimate, the sensory, the detailed, the personal. Not struggling to escape their circumstances, the poor often regard their ordinary lives as being of much intrinsic interest. This is related to their primary concern with the problem of survival rather than with the problem of moving up in society, and to the value which they attach to skills needed in coping with deprivation and uncertainty as distinguished from skills required to make progress. It has frequently been reported that persons in areas of poverty appear to be apathetic, to have little motivation, to be unable to cooperate with each other in the solution of problems which they regard as important, and to lack occupational and verbal skills and leadership traits; and are characterized by parochialism, nostalgic romanticism, and prescientific conceptions of the natural and social orders. Instead of having love for one another as fellow human beings, they achieve positive mutual attitudes through seeing themselves as all in the same boat together.

(2) Caught in the present, the poor do not plan very much. They meet their troubles and take their pleasures on a moment-to-moment basis; their schemes are short-term. Their time perspective is foreshortened by their belief that it is futile to think of the future. Thus, when the poor use conventional words to refer to the future, those words tend to be empty of real meaning. They have little sense of the past and they go forward, but not forward to any preconceived place. Their pleasures and rewards are sought in the present; they find it difficult to delay gratification, to postpone satisfaction.

(3) There is much egoism, envy, and hostility toward those who prosper. There is a feeling of being exploited. There are many negative attitudes and few positive ones. The unity of the poor comes about through suspicion of and resentment toward outsiders, through opposition to common enemies and hostility to powerful groups. Disillusion about the possibility of advancement stems from a victim complex in relation to the powerful. There is a sense of inability to affect what will happen, a lack of conviction that it is within their power to affect their circumstances. The outside world cannot be trusted; it must be defended against. Outsiders and the outside are seen as risky, likely to injure you when you least expect it. Pessimism and fatalism about

being able to affect one's own situation stems from a feeling of being victimized by superordinate, capricious, and malevolent natural and social forces. Their lives appear to them to be fixed by the immutable forces of fate, luck, and chance. While well-to-do people tend to attribute causality to inner forces, the poor tend to make external attributes of causality, seeing themselves as subject to external and arbitrary forces and pressures.

The Social Problem of Poverty and Its Natural Solution

The poor, in short, are commonly seen as apathetic, child-like, not very competent, and hostile-dependent. Other research, emphasized in the past few years, has pointed out the extent to which the poor tend to occupy specific social categories (minority racial and ethnic groups, the elderly, ADC families, and the like), as well as the continuing large proportion of the population who have low incomes even in such an affluent society as the United States. It has been natural to get concerned about a large proportion of the population, the members of which have behavior patterns and psychological characteristics that tend to place them in opposition to or dependence on the remainder of the community.

Poverty has therefore again become a publicly recognized social problem in the United States. The general perception of a social problem leads to a search for its solution. Since a lack of money is the most universal characteristic of poverty, and since a general increase of income for some social groups would automatically abolish poverty, it seems clear to many persons that certain known steps are suitable to end poverty in the United States. Their view is that public policies should be developed and implemented that emphasize provision of jobs, increased access to education that leads to jobs, and higher minimum wage levels and welfare payments. Scientists, according to this view, can contribute by learning how to measure poverty with greater accuracy and by studying its adverse psychological and other consequences, and they should seek to understand how these consequences might be controlled.

In this natural line of reasoning it is assumed rather than demonstrated that the major problem of the poor is poverty, a lack of money. But this assumption is essential to the associated recommendations for scientific work and social policy. It may be well, therefore, to inquire in a more searching fashion whether the problems of the poor primarily result from a lack of money.

There are a number of phenomena which one could hardly anticipate on the basis of such an assumption:

(1) A given level of real income has various consequences depending upon the circumstances in which a person receives the income.

Among the poor, there are many subgroups, the members of which do not display the presumed psychological consequences of poverty. These include most of that portion of the leadership of the poor which is itself poor, those low income families with high educational aspirations for their children, low income members of religious groups such as the Hutterites, university student families with little income, and the like. In the past, of course, members of the lower middle class have survived on real incomes below those received today by comparable public welfare families—and without losing their capacity to struggle in the pursuit of distant ends. Many from the intelligentsia today in such countries as India and Japan have incomes that, in the United States, would place them with the poor. They may differ from educated Americans in personality characteristics, but they do not have the alleged psychology of poverty either.

(2) Increases in income often do not lead to a diminution of the expected psychological consequences of poverty.

For example, the rise in real per capita public welfare expenditures in the United States have not had a demonstrated effect on the psychological functioning of welfare recipients.

(3) Differences in income between otherwise comparable groups of poor do not appear to be accompanied by differences in psychological functioning.

For example, states vary greatly in the size of their payments to comparable welfare recipient families. Comparable families appear to resemble one another in psychological orientation regardless of relatively major differences in their incomes.

(4) When income remains constant, but persons in a neighborhood of poverty become involved in successful social action on important issues, in their own behalf, their psychological orientation does extend over a greater period of time, their feeling of helplessness does lessen, their skills and activities do gradually change.

For example, no one could have predicted on the basis of articles in the relevant scholarly journals that lowly Negroes from areas of poverty would, with some help, begin to organize with such effect that they would carry timid and ultra-conventional members of the Negro middle classes along with them into a militant struggle for freedom. It has also been reported that many "lower class" Negroes who have become part of the Muslim movement have had their lives transformed in the direction of greater order and achievement.

During this past summer I gathered some data concerning The Woodlawn Organization (TWO), a primarily "lower class," predominantly Negro organization which was initiated about two years ago in Chicago with the assistance of Saul Alinsky and the Industrial Areas Foundation. The poor constitute the bulk of active members, and are an important segment of the leadership of this community organization, which has already demonstrated its effectiveness and power. For example, TWO has delivered a majority of the votes from a Negro area to elect a white alderman who takes a strong civil rights position; the unsuccessful opponent was a Negro from the regular political organization. It has been able to secure its own conditions for implementation of an urban renewal development proposed by the University of Chicago for part of the Woodlawn area. TWO has carried out rent strikes and has taken other successful actions against owners of dilapidated slum buildings; it has organized picketing of stores that sell merchandise to people who cannot afford the high interest on installments; it has organized successful city hall demonstrations of more than a thousand persons. Over this period of widespread involvement, the poor appear to have gradually acquired skills of organization, longer range planning, and other qualities contrary to those which reputedly characterize areas of poverty. I observed a similar process occurring in "lower class" white neighborhoods in Northwest Chicago, where the Northwest Community Organization, another Alinsky associated enterprise, has been in existence for less than two years.

(5) When members of some groups lose or give up their wealth, they do not thereby acquire the psychology of poverty.

One has only to consider the vows of poverty taken by members of some religious orders to illustrate this assertion.

Since the psychology of poverty obtains only under specific and describable circumstances, one cannot therefore use poverty as an explanation for these psychological characteristics which often are associated with poverty.

We might briefly mention other problems involved in the ready identification of poverty as the major problem of the poor. First, it is invalid reasoning to proceed without evidence from the fact that the poor have distinctive failings to the assumption that poverty is important in the etiology of these failings. It is incorrect simply to take the defining characteristics of a social category to which a group of people belong (the category "poverty" in this case) and use it without further evidence to account for the peculiar afflictions of that group of people. Second, even if *all* poor today were to exhibit the psychology of poverty, this may be merely an accidental connection, and the fact of having little money could remain only distantly related, for example, to feelings of being dominated by irrational external forces. One should not confuse an observed regularity with an inevitable regularity, a conventional law with a natural law. Third, when a scientist observes that a group of persons, the poor, have adopted their own patterns of behavior and system of beliefs, this does not mean that the behavior and belief patterns are cultural or subcultural or that these patterns represent durable characteristics of the people involved over a wide variety of social situations. The patterns and beliefs may be situational, not internalized, and may shift readily as the situation changes. Just when social scientists appear to be getting the poor firmly in mind, the poor are transformed. Thus, the "psychology of the poor" may be quite different from the psychology of a neurosis the basis of which *is* internalized.

It is therefore likely that the natural solution to the problem of poverty is naïve: it merely assumes the determinants of the psychology of poverty.

The Self-Help Doctrine and Its Consequences for Dependent Persons

In rapidly industrializing societies in which there are many opportunities for individual advancement there typically arises some form of the doctrine of self-help. The common core of self-help views can be stated as follows: A person is good to the extent to which he has assumed responsibility for and accomplished the realization of his potentialities for maximum use of his native capacities in a long, sustained, and arduous effort to reach a distant legitimate goal. With enough effort any normal person can attain such goals; no special ability is needed.

In the older Western industrial nations a growing appreciation of the limitations of opportunity has provided increasing support for modification of the traditional doctrine, with the qualification that ability as well as effort is necessary to success, and that some persons have been born with more ability than others. Also, since the nineteenth century, the common legitimate goal has changed from entrepreneurship of a prosperous independent business to a high position in a large work organization, and the struggle begins in the institutions of learning before the transfer to a work setting.

According to the doctrine of self-help, *anyone,* given enough time and enough effort, could achieve success. Thus, to be poor could have either of two meanings. On the one hand, poverty was regarded as the original accompaniment of the highest development of character, the struggling poor who were later to become successful were most worthy of respect. On the other hand, poverty indefinitely prolonged might mean a character defect, a lack of will power. Poverty, therefore, was ambiguous; from it alone one could reach no conclusion about virtue.

However, an economy with limited opportunities for success plus the belief in equal opportunity for success according to merit made inevitable an assault on the self-esteem of the permanently unsuccessful.

Officially defined dependency was not usually regarded as ambiguous. The person on Welfare has left the struggle altogether and has sat back to allow others to furnish his sustenance. It is true that some persons, the crippled, the very young, the seriously ill, and so forth, clearly could not have avoided dependency. But as for the rest, the presumption of their ability to work and succeed if they only tried hard enough led to the inevitable conclusion that those who have left off trying are bad. The intensity with which this conclusion was known was also related to the fact that dependent persons were seen to be living at the expense of the rest of the community. Not only did the scoundrels manage to exist without honest labor, but they actually made of the rest of the community a duped partner to their idleness. Inexcused dependency became a social symbol communicating defective character, toward which there was a feeling of superiority tinged with contempt. Even in the best of circumstances professional helpers were automatically considered morally as well as materially superior to those helped, and thus the helping relationship became a concrete carrier of the general meaning of dependency: the unworthiness of the dependent.

In affecting the psychology of dependency, the self-help doctrine has also, of course, affect the *behavior* of persons who are in need. One way to evade the unpleasantness of being dependent is to avoid getting help at all in a dependent situation. Families in trouble, as was discovered in various studies, often hide away when they need help the most. The stigma attached to receiving assistance prevents the use even of available resources.

Official dependency in modern society is a residual category of persons unable to enter into the normal types of income-producing relationships. Such persons are unable to relate to the normal avenues for gaining support, and the presence and location of such avenues is therefore the major immediate condition or cause of dependency in modern society. Inability to relate to normal avenues of support symbolizes failure, and perception by a dependent person of his own dependency is sufficient to produce shame and guilt and their complications. Official dependency is fundamentally the perception of the use of relative social power within a superordinate-subordinate relationship; the doctrine of self-help in a contractual economy made financial dependency the focal point for this definition in modern society. The official assumption is that all working adults are equal in that they have entered into work contracts on an equal basis, contracts which they could have chosen to enter or not to enter.

The financially self-responsible person is assumed to be responsible also in other areas of his life. For this reason dependency can concern any area of superordinate-subordinate relationship, and there is always some stigma associated with any dependency relationship, even though there is often pleasure in divesting oneself of the burden of self-responsibility. Even the relationship of citizen to expert can be distasteful since it makes the citizen intellectually dependent on the expert.

The sharpest psychological impact of dependency has occurred where it is officially defined and therefore clearly perceived and sanctioned by the community. However, most dependency is not so explicitly defined; most of the poor are not "on welfare." Even so, the poor are generally perceived, however unclearly, as having failed, and this perception has hardened the community against them. In the latter case, the doctrine of self-help has intensified the feelings of hopelessness among the poor.

The extent of self-support is only one measure of the extent of dependency, a measure stressed only in connection with the doctrine of self-help. More generally, dependency is the placement of one's destiny in other hands. It is therefore especially characteristic of the areas of poverty, but also characterizes many other aspects of society, including the low echelons of large organizations, organization men at any echelon, and so forth. In a general sense dependency is also destructive, but more subtly so. If extent of self-realization is a measure of personality development, then dependency, which erodes self-realization with the loss of self-responsibility, is a measure of personality inadequacy. If the human personality develops as a decision process through self-responsible choices, then the taking away of self-responsible choices through assuming the subordinate position in a dependency relationship necessarily destroys personality.

The Social Situation of the Poor

Most of the poor are heavily dependent on outside forces. In many places, a poor person is much more likely to be subject to police interrogation and search, or to public identification as the object of police activity, than is a member of a middle class family. Urban renewal programs periodically disrupt the neighborhoods of poverty, scattering the families in several directions in accordance with standards which the poor do not understand or support. Schools function impervious to the concerns of the low income families whose children attend, or else schools may seek themselves to "lead" in the areas of poverty in which they are located, that is, they seek to impose school standards and definitions on the neighborhoods. Settlement houses run recreation programs that meet their own traditional criteria, but neighborhood youth often do not understand these criteria, often cannot engage in accustomed and legal modes of behavior and still participate in settlement house activities, often, involuntarily and without understanding, have to disperse friendship groups in order to participate in a recreation program.

Many families, having bought more than they can afford, especially through high-interest installment financing, have no way to know whether or when their furniture will be repossessed or their check garnisheed. Medical and psychiatric care are inadequate, inadequately understood, and uncertainly available, especially to the poor who do not have connections through welfare. The securing of general relief or categorical assistance is a humiliating experience at best for people imbued with self-help ideas, but the deliberate rudeness intended to discourage as many applicants as possible, the complex agency rules which are not so much bases for action as after-the-fact rationales to provide support for decisions already made, and the subjective and unpredictable decisions of social workers representing agencies to the poor, all combine to place the economic foundation of many families at the mercy of completely incomprehensible forces.

The poor who seek employment must find it in a dwindling supply of jobs available to unskilled and semiskilled persons (including domestics), often seasonal or temporary work. In addition, the landlords of the poor are frequently discourteous, seldom inclined to make adequate repairs on their buildings, and likely to blame the tenants for the condition of the ancient and crumbling structures for which high rents are charged.

In other words the poor, by virtue of their situation, tend to be more dependent than other groups on a larger number of powerful persons and organizations, which are often very unclear about the bases for their actions and unpredictable in their decisions, and which further render the poor helpless by condescending or hostile attitudes, explicit verbal communications which state or imply the inferiority of the poor, and callousness or actual harassment. If we divide the powerful persons affecting the poor into two groups, the benevolent in intention on the one hand, and the callous or punitive on the other, we will find that the majority of both type of power figure treat the poor as inferior and reach down to relate to them.

The situation of poverty, then, is the situation of enforced dependency, giving the poor very little scope for *action*, in the sense of behavior under their own control which is central to their needs and values. This scope for action is supposed to be furnished by society to any person in either of two ways. First, confidence, hope, motivation, and skills for action may be provided through childhood socialization and continue as a relatively permanent aspect of the personality. Second, social positions are provided which make it easy for their occupants to act, which make it possible for decisions of their occupants to be implemented in their futures. Middle class socialization and middle class social positions customarily both provide bases for effective action; lower class socialization and lower class social positions usually both fail to make it possible for the poor to act.

Thus, the dependency of the poor is not primarily a neurotic need to occupy dependency positions in social relationships, but rather it results from a deprivation of those minimal social resources, at every period of their lives, which the poor need and therefore must seek. The poor are not victims of the social system in the sense that "organization men" are victims. They are rather, as Michael Harrington has emphasized, the *other* America, outsiders to the major society. In consequence, members of the majority society are usually outsiders to the poor.

The initial dependency and its consequences are reinforced by the hardening of a consensus in the majority community about the nature of the poor, stabilization of the patterns of behavior in areas of poverty, and partial internalization of ideas and patterns of behavior in the children who grow up in both communities. Thus, the positions of poor persons in relationship to superordinate forces are expressions of two communities, a superior and powerful community and an inferior and weaker community; two communities with institutionalized ways of living which prop up the superordinate position of the one in relation to the other.

People isolate and segregate those they fear and pity. The stronger of the two communities has traditionally acted to alleviate the results perceived to be undesirable without changing the relationship of the two communities or ending the division into two communities. Since persons designing and implementing such programs did not consider the consequences of the division for their aims, they were able to maintain an intention to bring the poor into their society. The recommendations have been for improved law enforcement; public welfare; public housing; social settlements; higher horizons educational programs; social work with "hard core" families; urban renewal, clean-up, paint-up, and fix-up programs; block and neighborhood organizations; and the like. All these plans and programs have usually shared two characteristics: (1) they are initiated and supported from outside the neighborhoods of poverty and imposed on the poor; and (2) they fail to make any lasting positive impact on neighborhoods of poverty. That is, although a few persons and families become affluent and leave the neighborhoods, the majority remain poor and continue in an atmosphere of apathy, disorganization, and hostility, toward the programs designed to rescue them. These programs, presupposing the inferiority of the people in the area, perpetuate and exacerbate the inequality. Definitions of the poor are carried by the institutionalized helping hands. Insofar as these agencies have any *social* impact, the definitions embedded in them become self-fulfilling. But, although the powerful external social agencies—powerful in relation to the poor—are not very effective in carrying out their official tasks in areas of poverty, they do enable the stronger community to believe that something is being done about the social problem of poverty, reducing guilt and shame to such an extent that there remains little motivation to develop some effective means to bring the poor into the larger society.

On the basis of this sketch of the dynamics of the situation of the poor, the following classification can be made of the sources of the "psychology of poverty."

(a) In any modern industrial society the overall amount of power of the society tends constantly to increase, although the rate of increase may vary. Although everyone in the society may secure ownership of additional *material* goods as a result of technological progress, the additional *power* tends to be secured only by those persons and social systems with preexistent power. The poor boy with strong internalized drives and skills for success and the large corporation with effective control over technological advances in its field both illustrate the tendency for socially created power to attract to itself additional power. But the poor most often have neither the power created through childhood socialization nor that to be secured through attachment to a strong social system in which they have influence. In some countries, the population is predominantly poor, and this populace may have some power through the political process. But, in the United States the poor are an unorganized or ineffectively organized minority, unable even to exert influence in the political sphere. Thus, increments in power tend to attach to those with power, and the balance of power in a country such as the United States tends naturally to tilt against the poor.

(b) The fact of being powerless, but with needs that must be met, leads the poor to be dependent on the organizations, persons, and institutions which can meet these needs. The situation of dependency and powerlessness through internal personality characteristics as well as through social position leads to apathy, hopelessness, conviction of the inability to act successfully, failure to develop skills, and so on.

(c) As a consequence of the self-help doctrine, this "psychology of poverty" arouses the anger of the affluent toward the poor. Thus, the affluent can avoid the necessity to alter the social situation of the poor by assuming that the poor are bad and deserve their situation. This additional meaning of poverty makes rigid the dependency aspects of the social situation of the poor, and, to some extent, the poor accept the prevalent view of themselves. However, since the poor are not together in an unambiguously clear social category, they, at the same time, may reject being placed in such a category subject to the assumption of their dependency and inferiority. For example, persons eligible to live in public housing are not affected only by the convenience, space, and other physical characteristics of their living quarters. A large proportion seem to prefer dilapidated private housing operated by an indifferent landlord to better maintained, less crowded, less expensive quarters in a public housing project in which the management is concerned with tenant needs. The meaning of living in such a project may offset the superiority of the physical living arrangements.

(d) Over time the dependency relationship of the poor becomes institutionalized and habits, traditions, and organizations arise in both the affluent community and in the neighborhoods of poverty, maintaining the relationship between them. The poor react in part to the institutionalization itself. For example, "lower class" delinquency does not only stem from the fact that the poor have few and drab job opportunities. There is also the perception that the conforming poor tend to remain indefinitely in low social positions as well as the angry rejection by the adolescent poor of attempts, through law enforcement and social agencies, to control and manipulate them without altering their situation.

Consequences of this social process for the poor have been indicated at several points in the preceding discussion; we will only briefly recapitulate some of them here.

First, people tend either to retreat from or to attack forces controlling their lives which they cannot affect and which are not inescapable. For this reason the poor typically stand aloof from settlement houses, get minimally involved with social workers, drop out of school. Only forces too omnipresent to be escaped may ensure normative affiliation through identification with aggressors. It is easy to see the poor as paranoid since they are so often hostile to and suspicious of powerful objects which they may perceive in a distorted fashion. However, paranoia presumably requires origins in early childhood, while the hostility and suspicion of the poor naturally arise from their social position and their necessarily over-simplified and naturally personified perceptions of it.

Second, with less of their selves bound up in their self-conceptions than is the case with other groups, the poor do not entirely accept these definitions of themselves, but protect themselves by various psychological strategies from fully accepting the implications of their situation. The impact of the definitions then is primarily indirect; the definitions have consequences by creating the situation of the poor through the meaning of poverty to those who possess power. The situation gives rise to the typical absence of that hope which is associated with action and which gives salience to intentions and attitudes. Thus, the poor frequently verbalize middle-class values without practicing them. Their verbalizations are useful in protecting their self-conceptions and in dealing with the affluent rather than in any pronounced relationship to non-verbal behavior. This does not imply deliberate falsification; a poor person may have the necessary sincerity, intention, and skill to embark on a course of action but there is so much unconscious uncertainty about achieving psychological returns through success that the action may never be seriously attempted. As has been discovered in social surveys, the poor may not only pay lip service to middle class notions, but may, for similar reasons, say to any powerful person what they believe he wants to hear. That is, much of the behavior of the poor does not relate primarily to their own basic values, beliefs and perceptions held by others about the poor. The poor are normally involved in partly involuntary self-diminution; their behavior may therefore be remarkably transformed when, as has happened through social action, they begin to acquire a sense of power, of ability to realize *their* aspirations. Thus, the so-called differential values of the poor, which are ill-defined at best, are more nearly comprehensible as the psychological consequences of a long continued situation of perceived powerlessness in contemporary industrial society. They become a subculture to the extent that the traditions, orientations, and habits of dependency become internalized.

Third, the situation of the poor, the inability of the poor to act in their own behalf, creates a less complex personality structure for them than is the case with affluent persons with more linguistic skills. This does not necessarily mean that the poor have less effective personalities, or are unsocialized in comparison, since the personalities of more highly educated persons are often partly constituted by social elaborated fantasies which conceal reality and rationalize avoidance of problem solving.

Fourth, awareness of their common fate typically leads the poor to engage in mutual aid activities, activities which, in spite of involving only very minor skills, are precursors to the joint social action which develops naturally as the poor acquire organizational skills and confidence in using them.

Fifth, because of the social situation of the poor and the fact that the majority society has relatively little normative basis for social control in areas of poverty, these areas are often characterized by high rates of publicly discernible types of deviance: juvenile delinquency, school dropouts, alcoholism, illegitimacy, mother-centered families, and the like.

Finally, there are differential consequences of institutionalized, uncompensated powerlessness for the poor who have various social positions within areas of poverty. For example, because of the greater expectation for men to be powerful and to be sources of power, the consequences of powerlessness for "lower class" men is usually greater than that for women.

All of this suggests that the problems of the poor are not so much of poverty as of a particularly difficult variety of situational dependency, a helplessness to affect many important social factors in their lives, the functioning or purpose of which they do not understand, and which are essentially unpredictable to them.

Not Enough Money Versus Situational Dependency

With increased money the poor could at least be better able to cope with such forces, could be less dependent on some. What, then, is the relationship between the poverty of the poor and their situational dependency?

Money is a generalized source of power over people through a right to control over goods and services. As such, money is one of many kinds of power. Poverty, therefore, is one of many kinds of powerlessness, of being subject to one's social situation instead of being able to affect it through action, that is, through behavior which flows from decisions and plans. Since there are several varieties of generalized power, an absence of money is often replaceable *insofar as the psychological reactions to powerlessness are concerned*. An American Indian who lives in poverty may have considerable influence through authority relationships traditional in his culture. Members of religious orders who have taken vows of poverty remain able to exercise influence through their order and through relationships of interdependence with colleagues. The college student with a very low income has influence through the expectations of his future social position. When the poor engage in successful social action they gain power, even when their incomes remain unchanged.

In other words, when social scientists have reported on the psychological consequences of poverty it seems reasonable to believe that they have described the psychological consequences of powerlessness. And many persons without money have, or get, other varieties of power, or else identify with powerful persons or groups and therefore fail to exhibit these consequences. Even the poor do not react entirely on the basis of the social definition of them. There are counter institutions and traditions (churches, unions, and clubs) which deflect the impact of the majority definition. Primary groups (family and peer) also mediate and modify the community definitions they transmit. The behavior of the poor may not, therefore, reflect their self-conceptions; we should not suppose that the poor feel as would middle class persons in their situations, or as their behavior suggests they feel. This very resistance of the poor makes it possible to attempt the otherwise herculean task of trying to get the major society to alter its relationship to poverty by helping the poor themselves to build a backfire, to become strong and effective enough to challenge the invidious definitions that have been made of them.

Human personality is a process of decisions and actions on the basis of decisions. One becomes fully human only through acting in important areas of one's life. All social arrangements which take responsibility out of the hands of the poor, which make decisions and action more difficult or operative over a more restricted area, feed the psychology of powerlessness which is so widely (and correctly) regarded as undesirable. For example, it is often noted that the poor lack a time perspective. But only through action (important decisions and behavior on their basis) does one acquire a history and, with the history, a practical concern with the future.

What consequences does the social situation of the poor have for programs to help the poor? We will next consider some general answers to this question.

Redefining the Social Situation of the Poor

We can reject two possible alternatives.

First, the solution most frequently suggested is to help the poor secure more money without otherwise changing present power relationships. This appears to implement the idea of equality while avoiding any necessary threat to established centers of power. But, since the consequences are related to *powerlessness,* not to the absolute supply of money available to the poor, and since *the amount of power purchasable with a given supply of money decreases as a society acquires a larger supply of goods and services,* the solution of raising the incomes of the poor is likely, unless accompanied by other measures, to be ineffective in an affluent society. Where the poor live in serious deprivation of goods and services, an increase in the supply of those goods and services would be an important source of power, that is, of access to resources which satisfy crucial needs. However, when the poor do not live in actual deprivation, increases in money make relatively little impact on the dependency relationships in which they are entangled. The opportunity to participate in *interdependent* relationships, as a *member* of the majority society, requires an increase in *power.*

Second, the *self-help* doctrine is normally related to conventional criteria of success, and persons who have not met these conventional criteria therefore are threatened with feelings of guilt and shame. One theoretically possible solution would seem to involve redefinition of success, allowing social support to lives which are now viewed as failures. This, however, presupposes an ability to meet some alternative criteria of success through action, a possible solution for philosophers, poets, or beatniks, but not now generally possible for the poor. It may, however, be that the meaning of the self-help doctrine could be adequately extended to reward the social action of the poor who can act successfully through their own organizations.

Along these lines the criteria for an effective solution are reasonably clear. In order to reduce poverty-related psychological and social problems in the United States, the major community will have to change its relationship to neighborhoods of poverty in such fashion that families in the neighborhoods have a greater stake in the broader society and can more successfully participate in the decision-making process of the surrounding community.

It is frequently said that we must provide opportunities for the poor. To render more than lip service to this objective demands more power and more skill and more knowledge than we now possess for the bureaucratic provision of such opportunities. For example, there are a finite number of jobs available, fewer than the number of people looking for work. There are severe limits to the extent to which the adult poor can be trained for existing openings. A large proportion of the poor have jobs which do not remove them from the ranks of the powerless. Any great shift in opportunities made available to the poor within the structure of the majority community will threaten more powerful groups with vested interests in those limited opportunities, and the proponents of creating opportunities for the poor cannot themselves affect the political or economic process enough to implement their good intentions.

It is important to develop opportunities in sensitive relation to the perception by the poor of their own needs. When this is not done, the poor are not likely to be able to use efficiently the opportunities created for them. And, most central of all, rather than to provide opportunities for the "lower class," the poor must as a group be helped to secure opportunities for themselves. Only then will motivation be released that is now locked in the silent and usually successful battle of the neighborhoods of poverty to maintain themselves is an alien social world. This motivation which will enable them to enter the majority society and make it as nurturant of them as it is at present of the more prosperous population.

The involvement of the poor in successful and significant social action provides both immediate and compelling psychological returns and also the possibility of initiative to help the bureaucratic organizations related to the poor to fulfill their officially stated purposes. The institutions of the major community can be forced to establish relationships of interdependence, not of dependence, with the poor; professionals can help by accepting professional roles as employees of the organizations of the poor.

In our society inner worth as expressed in action, striving, the struggle is held eventually to result in attainment of aspirations. If one is not successful, one is viewed as worthwhile so long, and only so long, as one struggles. The poor tend to be regarded as failures and not struggling, and hence as worthless. This perception of worthlessness is incorporated in the conception which others have of the poor and also, to some extent, in the conceptions which the poor have of themselves. One way in which the poor can remedy the psychological consequences of their powerlessness and of the image of the poor as worthless is for them to undertake social action that redefines them as potentially worthwhile and individually more powerful. To be effective, such social action should have the following characteristics:

1. the poor see themselves as the source of the action;
2. the action affects in major ways the preconceptions, values, or interests of institutions and persons defining the poor;
3. the action demands much in effort and skill or in other ways becomes salient to major areas of the personalities of the poor;
4. the action ends in success; and
5. the successful self-originated important action increases the force and number of symbolic or nonsymbolic communications of the potential worth or individual power of individuals who are poor.

The result of social action of this kind is a concurrent change in the view which the poor have of themselves and in the view of the poor by the outside world. There is a softening of the destructive social reality and immediate psychological returns to the poor, although not without hostile reactions from advantaged persons and organizations with known or hidden vested interests in maintenance of the areas of poverty.

The only initial additional resources which a community should provide to neighborhoods of poverty should be on a temporary basis: organizers who will enable the neighborhoods quickly to create powerful, independent, democratic organizations of the poor. These organizations will themselves then seek from the rest of the community resources necessary to the neighborhoods for the solution of the problems they perceive. Agencies for the provision of training and education and opportunities can be developed under the control of the neighborhoods of poverty, thereby ensuring that the poor are in interdependent rather than dependent positions in relation to the agencies. This would meet the professed objectives of most communities since it would effectively motivate the poor to maximum use of opportunities, since the requirements of professional practice will ensure the quality of services rendered, and since the communities state their intention not to allow their help to become an instrument of domination.

The comment that "We know the needs of the poor" is accurate in a very general sense. But there is a great distance between this observation and a knowledge of how, in practice, those needs can be met. If a community is not merely giving lip service to meeting them, if a community wants to be effective as well as to have good intentions, then the way of meeting needs must be appropriate to the personal and social characteristics of those being helped. In this case, effectiveness requires that the only *unilateral* additional help be given at the outset and in the form of temporary assistance in the creation of democratic and powerful organizations of the poor. Through such organizations, the poor will then negotiate with outsiders for resources and opportunities without having to submit to concurrent control from outside. The outcome will be maximal motivation to take advantage of resources and opportunities which are sensitively tailored to their needs.

STEREOTYPES

H. TAJFEL
University of Bristol, England

A few days before I began to write this article I was in Switzerland. The tourist season was not yet in full swing, but enough tourists were around to play the game of trying to guess their nationality. The guesses are often correct; but it is perhaps more interesting to see the effect of the change of label—when the guess is shown to be wrong—on the way in which postures, movements, dress, hundreds of little signs, subtle or not subtle, rearrange themselves to yield a complete reinterpretation of the stranger. Previous cues acquire a new meaning. Additional cues are sought and found. A new image emerges—a very different one from that achieved when the wrong label was used.

This new image may or may not be nearer to "reality" than the first one—it is often shattered again if we happen to exchange a few words with the stranger. But the changes which take place do not occur at random: first, the interpretation fits one stereotype; then it is made to fit another.

This is the "stereotype" game, the "what-goes-with-what" game. The second *what* is the label, the assignment to a group—national, ethnic, religious, racial, social, professional or any other. With this label are associated a number of characteristics which are assigned to the individual as a first approximation to the "sort of person he is." It is quite obvious that this is an eminently useful activity. It saves time, it helps in the ordering of the social environment, it may have its uses in the prediction of behaviour of complete strangers. But for all its usefulness it very often goes wrong, and through its ubiquity it contributes to one of our most intractable social problems.

Prejudice—racial or any other—tends to be discussed predominantly, for very good reasons, in terms of its emotional and social roots and correlates, in terms of the vested interests—psychological, economic, social and political—which it serves. There exists, however, in many such discussions an implicit assumption which could bear some scrutiny. For this purpose, a distinction must be made between those who manipulate prejudice for specific purposes and those who are genuinely and honestly prejudiced. In the first category would be a Nazi shopkeeper who discovered that anti-Semitism provided him with an excellent opportunity for getting rid of uncomfortable competition. This man need not have been "prejudiced"; he need not have subscribed to the racist doctrines; he did not necessarily believe that the Jews were the monsters of Nazi mythology; he need not have perceived individual Jews to be possessed of such and such foul characteristics. He found it useful, however, to take advantage of the general situation, to manipulate it for his own ends, and he may well have abandoned without trace all "prejudice" when, with the change of conditions, its usefulness had come to an end. A white South African, convinced that the African majority in the country presents a direct and concrete threat to his very existence, may adopt certain kinds of policies without necessarily sharing in the belief in the inherent inferiority of the African. One need not belabour the issue. There is abundance of large-scale examples of deliberate use of prejudice in this manner.

But a distinction must be made between such "dishonest" prejudice and the honest variety which is an inherent aspect of an individual's Weltanschauung. On seeing a West Indian bus conductor, an honestly prejudiced person does not engage in an internal monologue which might consist of the following sequence; (1) this is a West Indian; (2) I don't like West Indians; (3) it would suit my general ideas to discover that this particular West Indian is rude; (4) I shall now pretend to myself that this bus conductor *is* rude.

Discussions of prejudice which focus primarily or exclusively on its emotional and social determinants are in danger of minimising the importance of a well known psychological phenomenon: people who are prejudiced tend to perceive the relevant parts and aspects of their social environment in their own special way. I would not wish to enter here into elaborate discussions concerning the proper definition of prejudice. It will be sufficient for present purposes to characterise it as a set of hostile attitudes towards specified groups of people. With these attitudes goes a readiness to perceive their objects in certain ways, to select information in a manner which supports them, to distort or ignore information which is incongruent with them. The prejudiced people have learned a perceptual skill: to select and interpret what is relevant, and to ignore what is not relevant, perhaps very much like a motorist who notices a set of traffic lights but ignores a beautiful cathedral on his way. There are, however, some essential differences: when the motorist's selection and interpretation of signals do not tally with their purpose and meaning, he will come to grief. In our present social conditions, the prejudiced idiosyncratic selection of signals rarely results in any penalty; and also their meaning is by no means clear and invariant.

A very large amount of writing concerning "stereotypes," or sets of fixed ideas and beliefs held about human groups, is buried in technical psychological journals. It is not the purpose of this article to review this literature, but some generalisations which emerge quite clearly may be briefly stated: people show an extraordinary readiness to characterise vast human groups in terms of a few fairly crude "traits"; these characterisations tend to remain fairly stable within a population and for fairly long periods of time; they tend to change to some extent, but without always altering fundamentally, as functions of social, political or economic changes; they become much more pronounced and hostile when social tensions arise; they are learned early and used by children before the emergence of clear ideas defining the groups to which they apply; they do not present much of a problem when little hostility is involved, but are extremely difficult to modify in a social climate of tension and conflict.

No psychologist who has a sense of proportion about the possibilities and the limitations of his discipline would claim that prejudice can be "explained" and dealt with on the psychological level alone. This is an infinitely complex problem, and in its handling we need the cooperation of legislators, social workers, economists, historians, sociologists, psychologists and many others. It remains, however, that the honestly prejudiced person described above has his own image of the world, and that the analysis of the *general* determinants of such images, independent of their specific characteristics which vary as functions of local conditions, presents a problem which is primarily psychological. This is one of the problems within the framework of a much wider psychological question; "How do we come to perceive the world the way we do?"

The first point to be made is a trivial one: when we are uncertain about the identity or the features of something concerning us in our environment, physical or social, we try to guess. But what, if any, are the rules of guessing? There is very little doubt that guessing is not random; it is strongly influenced by past experience, motivation, interests, needs, purposes. In a more formal way, expectancies are developed through previous experience which lead us to extrapolate from uncertainty to relatively stable relationships previously encountered. There is nothing new in this statement; it is inherent in Hume's analysis of causality and quite explicitly shown to apply to perceived relationships of events in the physical environment in the well-known experiments of Michotte[1] and Brunswik.[2]

The "what-goes-with-what" principle has, however, one important property which is of particular relevance to the problem of stereotyping. Drawing inferences about characteristics of other people is a notoriously difficult task and the results are notoriously unreliable. It is a form of guessing from highly ambiguous and variable cues. In situations of this type, every bit of information gathered in the past is used for all it is worth, and much more, and therefore every relationship encountered in the past is exploited well beyond the limits that would be warranted by its stability and its reliability. For lack of other information, someone with a high forehead is likely to be judged as more intelligent than someone less fortunate in the distribution of his facial areas. Brunswik provided an excellent experimental example of this type of phenomenon. He asked a group of subjects to judge from photographs the intelligence, likeability, energy and "good looks" of 46 young men who were unknown to the "judges." He then analysed the results from the point of view of correlations between the judgments of the various traits. A few examples will suffice. Intelligence and good looks were correlated in the judgments at .59; intelligence and energy at .84; intelligence and likeability at .62; and so on. The group of young men (who knew each other well as they were all members of a sub-unit of the U.S. Army Specialized Training Program) subsequently judged each other on the same four traits. Of the few examples of correlations between judgments quoted above, the one between intelligence and good looks dropped to .03 (i.e., no relationship at all); between intelligence and energy to .28; between intelligence and likeability to .00. The wild guesses of the first group of subjects were not completely wild; presented with a situation in which their information about the objects of their judgments was practically nil, they extracted illusory order from chaos by inflating slight relationships or creating relationships where none existed.

This is a fundamental aspect of stereotyping. A label attached to a human being, the assignment of an individual to one or another category, whether racial, ethnic, social, religious or regional, has some degree of meaning. This meaning can be described in terms of the assumed possession by the person who is being so classified of certain characteristics which go with the label—the inference is from the label to these characteristics. These inferences display the inflation of weak or nonexistent relationships which Brunswik demonstrated in another context. It is immaterial whether these relationships have been learned through personal experience of the user of the stereotype, or through hearsay, literature, mass media of communication, history books, or linguistic habits. In cases of uncertainty and of little knowledge of the individual to whom they apply they determine the direction of search for "telling signs," a search which is likely to be successful. In other words, they determine what will be noticed and what ignored, what will become the center of attention and what will remain at its periphery.

The subjective definition of a category of human beings will thus form the basis of the initial search for features which are expected to be found when a specimen is encountered. It will help to focus attention on some things and to deflect it from others. This does not, however, tell us very much about the *direction* of bias, and bias is the essential feature of stereotyped judgments.

Such judgments cannot be considered in a vacuum; they are not in the nature of absolute assertions, they are all implicitly comparative. A man is not "tall" in an absolute sense. He is relatively taller than other people. Whether physical or personal characteristics are concerned, stereotypes lead us to minimise certain differences between people who are members of the same group, and to exaggerate the same differences between those people and others who belong to another group.

The point is, however, that not all and any differences are minimised within a group and exaggerated between groups. Even a strongly prejudiced person will not necessarily maintain that West Indian women are bad cooks, though good cooking may be to him an important quality—one of the shining signs of perfection in a good woman. Good or bad cooking is not a relevant aspect of the West Indian stereotype, of the differentiations between West Indians and other people. The content of a stereotype, however acquired, determines the dimensions along which the bias in judgment takes place, and these dimensions are not necessarily a crude duplication of a division into good and bad. This point is not unimportant; it is possible to predict the nature and the direction of bias from a detailed knowledge of the composition of a stereotype, of the features which are subjectively associated with the label. It is not possible to predict the sort of bias that will occur from the knowledge that someone has a hostile or a tolerant attitude towards a given group of people.

This type of bias, depending on the features which are subjectively associated with the division of objects, events or people into distinct classes, is by no means confined to situations in which prejudice is involved. In some laboratory experiments we conducted recently in Oxford[3] we were able to show its existence in such an unemotional task as the judgment of length of lines. There were eight lines, each of slightly different length. They were shown one by one to each subject, and the whole series was repeated in random order several times. The subjects were asked to estimate the length of each line in turn. The lines alone were presented to one group of subjects. For a second group, some lines were labelled A and some B; these labels were unrelated to length. The third group was crucial to our purpose: each of the four shorter lines was always accompanied by label A; each of the four longer lines by label B. Therefore, the classification into A's and B's was related here to the dimension that our subjects were judging. We predicted that the third group, compared with the first two, would exaggerate differences in length between the lines from the two classes, and minimise such differences within each of the classes. The results of the experiments confirmed these predictions quite strikingly. We were able to produce in simple judgments of length the sort of bias which is usually found in judgments of characteristics of people classified in certain ways. "Stereotypes" about length of lines can arise, it seems, at least as easily as stereotypes about groups of people in complex social situations.

Stereotyping can, therefore, be considered as an inescapable adjunct to the human activity of categorising. As such, it is neither "bad" nor "good"; it is there, and presumably it serves some purpose in our continuous efforts to simplify the world around us. But it is hardly necessary to say that there are some important differences between these innocent laboratory games and the grimly serious matter of persistent unfairness of which we are all capable, in one way or another, when we assume our favourite posture as self-appointed judges of other people's "nature," "character," "personality," or what-not. I once had a student who, during a tutorial on problems of racial prejudice, admitted a little sheepishly that she was by no means free of it. She then volunteered some information about the well known rudeness of West Indian bus conductors. Did she feel, I asked, that they were on the whole inclined to be rude? Yes. From her experience, did she find that the proportion of rude bus conductors amongst the West Indian ones was greater than amongst the others? She had never paid much attention to the rudeness or politeness of the white bus conductors.

The two principal psychological differences between the "neutral" categorising and the prejudiced stereotyping emerge quite clearly from this relatively mild example: they are in the pronounced sharpening of those differences between human groups which happen to fit the stereotype, and in the resilience of these clear-cut differentiations. Both these phenomena warrant a slightly more detailed discussion.

First, the sharpening of differences. There is one obvious distinction between "neutral" categorisations and those which are associated with prejudice: in the latter, the classification is not a matter of indifference to the individual. He has a vested emotional interest in preserving the comfortable and comforting segregation of people into sheep and goats. If one may be permitted a further brief excursion into the laboratory, the effects on certain types of judgment of "relevant" differences between objects have been known for some time and are quite predictable. A simplified case may serve as an example. The psychological literature of the late forties and early fifties was full of experiments pointing to the existence of a phenomenon which was referred to as "perceptual over-estimation." Avoiding technicalities which would be of no interest here, one can state a fairly well-documented generalisation yielded by these studies: when a series of objects is judged in terms of some physical magnitude such as size, and it so happens that there is a correlation between size of the objects and the extent of their value to the person making the judgment, the differences in size between the objects tend to be exaggerated. Series of coins in which such a relationship often exists (though it is not perfect) are one example. If one shows to a number of people two coins in succession—for example, 2s. and 2s. 6d.—asking them to estimate the diameter of each in turn, one finds that the differences in diameter are consistently exaggerated in comparison with similar judgments made by other people of a pair of unknown coins identical in size and as similar as possible to the first pair in other characteristics.[4] When one repeats the experiment in another country, taking care to choose subjects to whom both pairs of coins are unfamiliar, one finds no difference between the estimated relationships in the size of the two pairs of coins. The same sort of phenomenon can be shown with regard to estimates of weight, brightness, number, etc. This accentuation of differences is related to the fact that they are associated with another kind of difference which happens to be of immediate importance in the handling of the objects and which determines which type of error will be a "good" error and which a "bad" one.

Just as differences between objects can be exaggerated in this way, so can be the differences between classes of objects when the classification is of some special relevance to the person making the judgments. In some American experiments[5] it has been shown that when groups of subjects are presented with a series of photographs of Negroes and whites, those people who had been previously ascertained to show a fair amount of anti-Negro prejudice tend to judge differences in skin colour between the two racial groups as greater than people who were at the unprejudiced end of the distribution.

It seems, therefore, that two conditions must be fulfilled for this exaggeration of differences to take place: (1) the characteristic which is judged must stand in a direct relation to the classification; (2) the classification itself must be of some emotional relevance.

The previous examples were taken from judgments of physical properties of objects or people. It seems that the same tentative laws apply to judgments of "personal" characteristics. To all of us some personal attributes are more important than others: to one person "intelligence" may be a more important characteristic of other people than "honesty"; to another "kindness" than "strength of character." It has been shown[6] that there is a tendency to judge other people in more extreme terms with regard to the attributes which are of more impact to those making the judgments. This is a very close parallel to the accentuation of differences on "relevant" physical dimensions. Another parallel is provided by evidence summarised in a recent volume by Sherif and Hovland.[7] These authors were primarily concerned with studies of attitude formation and attitude change. They describe studies in which their subjects were asked to rate in prescribed terms a number of statements concerning a specific social issue, such as, for example, that of desegregation. It is quite clear from the results that people who are strongly involved in the issue (whether for or against desegregation) tend to assign the statements to more extreme positions within the prescribed "scale" than people who are less involved. Similar findings exist with regard to relatively less inflammatory and drastic problems, such as the existence of fraternities in American colleges.

To return to stereotypes, it is hardly necessary to quote examples of differentiating biases in the case of prejudice. It is, however, interesting to see that these sharp differentiations need not always work in favour of the group to which the person making the judgments belongs. Cases of "self-hate" amongst members of minorities which are an object of prejudice are well known, and discussion of the origins of this "self-hate" is beyond the scope of this article. But it may be worthwhile to summarise the results of a recent Canadian study[8] in which the use of a classification, and the high relevance to the subjects of *some* personal attributes related to that classification, led them to underrate in a fairly consistent manner the qualities of their own group in comparison with another, relatively dominant, group.

Before the studies described, a word should be said perhaps about the general methodology of the comparative research on stereotypes. One cannot, of course, use the term "bias" unless one has some general criteria which define bias as a departure from a norm which is known. It is equally patent that stable and easily measured norms of that type do not exist in the case of judgment or assessment of people, especially when large groups of people are concerned. However, these difficulties need not be insuperable. In the absence of absolute criteria, relative ones can be supplied. This can be done in one of two ways: either by eliciting from two different groups their reactions to members of a third group; or by having the same individuals labelled as one thing or as another, and finding out how reactions to them vary as a function of the label. In both cases, the criteria are not only relative but specific to the study. They can, nevertheless, serve to provide fairly clear-cut information—in the first case, about reactions of two or more different groups towards another group, in the second case, about the reactions of one specified group towards two or more other groups.

The Canadian study just mentioned combined both these methods. Its aim was not a general study of stereotypes, but an investigation of one specific aspect of the problem: the amount and nature of stereotyping that occurs when inferences about people are made from hearing the language they speak, without any other information being available. In order to do this, Lambert and his colleagues tape-recorded a French and an English version of a short text read by four bilingual speakers. There were two groups of subjects, one consisting of French-Canadian students from the University of Montreal, another of English-Canadian students from McGill University. The subjects were led to believe that there were eight different speakers, four English and four French, and were asked to rate each speaker in turn on a number of personality "traits."

The data were analysed in several ways. Of direct interest here is the comparison of assessments of the French and English incarnations of the same speakers when judged by the French and English groups of subjects.[9] There was one group of traits with regard to which the French subjects, as compared with the English, overrated the English speakers and underrated the French ones. These traits were: leadership, intelligence, self-confidence, dependability, sociability. They are all clearly related to socio-economic success, which is a drastic and competitive issue for the French group in Montreal — especially for a group of college students. *Some* assumed differences associated with the ethnic classification are to these students of greater impact than to their English counterparts; as a result, these particular differences are relatively exaggerated by them while other differences, not so preoccupying, are not subject to this type of accentuation.

Apart from the interesting finding that in some conditions the stereotyped sharpening of differences can be directed against one's own group, the Montreal study provides a convenient point of departure for some general statements about the various factors which can enhance or reduce the validity of inference from such artificial investigations to "real life."

The study has one feature in common with many other such bits of research conducted in the approximately controlled conditions of psychological experiments: in the frantic attempts to devise situations which will isolate the relevant variables and thus allow some possibility of generalising, the baby is in grave danger of being thrown out with the bath water. In the Canadian study, and any number of other such studies about stereotypes, the relative uniformity of responses is produced at the cost of providing the subjects with a minimum of information about the people they are supposed to be judging: sound of voices, still photographs, or sometimes even simply a request to list the predominant characteristics of a "Turk," a "Patagonian," or of any other group which suits the passing fancy of the experimenter. One may well ask whether the judgments so obtained have anything in common with judgments made of solid three-dimensional exemplars of such groups who talk, laugh, are happy or sad, kind or unkind, and altogether display the infinite variety of human behaviour so destructive of the attempts to formulate predictive laws which imply uniformity.

The question can be rephrased. What are the effects on these judgments of the balance of specific information about an individual and general information (valid or not) about about the group to which he belongs?

This is best answered in terms of a short series of related statements:

(1) The less specific information one has about an individual, the greater will be the tendency to assign to him the characteristics which are assumed to be those of his group. This means that, on the one hand, the prejudiced judgments obtained in the context of experiments using a minimum of information about individuals are of low predictive value with regard to judgments made of "real people." On the other hand, these artificially extorted judgments are fairly useful as a reflection of sets of stereotypes embedded in a cultural context.

(2) It follows that when there is no emotional involvement in the use of the stereotype, when it represents no more than a moderately useful classifying device for lack of anything better to rely on, it is flexible and capable of change if information is received which flatly contradicts it or generally does not fit in.

(3) All this does not apply to stereotypes which are associated with a high emotional charge. In such cases, as was mentioned above, information is selec-

tively filtered through the focussing of attention on one or another aspect of the situation, and then even more selectively remembered. A classical example of this has been provided quite a long time ago by Allport and Postman.[10] In some of their experiments on the spreading of rumour they used a drawing which was presented to the first in a chain of subjects; the drawing was then removed and the first subject described it to a second, who in turn described it to a third, etc. The drawing represented a carriage in the New York subway in the middle of which stand two men, one white and one Negro, who seem to be quarreling. The white man has an open razor tucked in at his belt. "Here is," write Allport and Postman, "a typical terminal report" (the last in a chain of reproductions): "This is a subway train in New York headed for Portland Street. There is a Jewish woman and a Negro who has a razor in his hand. The woman has a baby and a dog. The train is going to Dyer Street and nothing much happened."

It is this selectivity and this self-reinforcing nature of stereotypes which go with prejudice that present the main difficulty for attempts to change the "image" through various educational techniques. Most of them, however well-intentioned, do not present the public at which they are primarily addressed—people who harbour intense prejudices—with effective reasons for selecting and retaining the intended message. The fault does not necessarily lie in these various attempts; any form of propaganda must remain fairly ineffective as long as it remains unrelated to the existence or the creation of an emotional climate which makes its aims desirable and rewarding, or at least acceptable. The advertisers have learned this simple principle a long time ago, and have been using it only too efficiently in their blend of "giving the public what it wants" and helping it to want what they wish it to want.

Nevertheless, it is possible that educational programs may be of some limited use even when they are not implemented in the context of long-term social changes. The previous discussion would lead one to the conclusion that in order to be useful such programs would have to conform to certain specific criteria. Heart-breaking stories about "good" members of groups which are objects of prejudice are not likely to produce sizeable or permanent changes. If a problem can be defined, as it was above, in terms of abandoning perceptual habits which consist of selection, accentuation and omission of some features of events relevant to a prejudice, communication concerning this problem must attempt a series of specific jobs rather than consist of a sequence of general messages about such-and-such people being "nice" despite the general opinion to the contrary. This is not impossible. Most studies on stereotypes show that their content is fairly stable within a culture, that there is a general consensus about the characteristics distinguishing the group which is an object of discrimination from the group which does the discriminating. It is, therefore, quite feasible to undertake a content analysis which would aim at a specification of the most relevant aspects of this differentiating bias. There is no shortage of sources of material on which such an analysis could be made. It seems to me that such educational programs, carefully constructed so as to counteract specific aspects of bias known to be particularly widespread or particularly intense, may well have a better chance of success than those based on the idea of a more general frontal attack.

Educational programs directed at children present their special problems. Many studies have shown that evaluation of groups other than their own exists in children at a very early age. This has some important consequences. Whatever may be the precise stage of cognitive and affective development at which these value judgments begin to appear, it is clear that they can be observed well before the time when the child is capable of forming abstract concepts and categories relating to the human groups to which his evaluations apply. It is, therefore, obvious that if a child is not conceptually ready to use a category such as "West Indians" or "Jews" or "French" or "Italians," though any and each concrete Jew or West Indian may already be "a good thing" or "a bad thing," then no amount of nice and nicely read stories about nice children belonging to one or another of these groups will help. The child will not be capable of generalising to a category which in his mind either exists in a very rudimentary form or does not exist at all. Negative evaluations are learned and over-learned in a variety of concrete everyday contexts. Counter-evaluations must act with the same simplicity and within similar contexts, and apply to people who are real to the child. Stories about a brave Eskimo boy will not teach a child a general attitude of ethnic tolerance, nor will they change anything in his immediate evaluative reactions towards the "dirty niggers" round the corner.

At later stages, as more abstract conceptual schemes develop, so can the procedures of counter-evaluation be changed. The ultimate aim does not consist of attempting to prevent the categorisation of human beings into distinct groups—this would be impossible and not even desirable—but of helping to create "neutral" categories, within which each human being is evaluated in terms of specific information about him, and not in terms of a powerful evaluative frame of reference applying to the category of which he happens to be a member.

References

1. A. Michotte, *The Perception of Causality*, English translation by T. and V. Miles, Methuen, 1963.
2. E. Brunswik, *Perception and the Representative Design of Psychological Experiments*, University of California Press, 1956.
3. H. Tajfel and A. L. Wilkes, British Journal of Psychology, 1963, 54.
4. H. Tajfel and S. D. Cawasjee, Journal of Abnormal and Social Psychology, 1959, 59.
5. P. F. Secord, W. Bevan and B. Katz, Journal of Abnormal and Social Psychology, 1956, 53.
6. H. Tajfel and A. L. Wilkes, British Journal of Social and Clinical Psychology, 1964.
7. M. Sherif and C. I. Hovland, *Social Judgment: Assimilation and Contrast Effects in Communication and Attitude Change*, Yale University Press, 1961.
8. W. E. Lambert, R. C. Hodgson, R. C. Gardner and S. Fillenbaum, Journal of Abnormal and Social Psychology, 1960, 60.
9. H. Tajfel, Canadian Journal of Psychology, 1959, 13.
10. G. W. Allport and L. Postman, *The Psychology of Rumour*, Holt, 1947.

PROBLEMS IN RESEARCH ON PSYCHOLOGICAL WARFARE

James O. Whittaker

The Pennsylvania State University

PSYCHOLOGICAL warfare operations in Vietnam are conducted by three relatively autonomous organizations. First, the Vietnamese run their own programme through the Ministry of Information in Saigon. Second, the American programme is run mainly by the Joint US Public Affairs Office (JUSPAO) which consists primarily of USIA personnel and military specialists with a variety of backgrounds. And finally, there are a number of military psywar units which operate directly under the command of MACV (Military Assistance Command—Vietnam). Most of my remarks will be concerned with JUSPAO since I am more familiar with that organization than the others.

JUSPAOs major effort in psychological warfare has been in the preparation of propaganda leaflets which may be grouped into four major categories: (1) those directed toward the civilian population of North Vietnam; (2) those directed toward infiltrating North Vietnamese troops, and air-dropped along the Ho Chi Minh trail; (3) those directed toward North Vietnamese troops in both North and South Vietnam; and (4) those directed toward rank-and-file Viet Cong designed to induce them to 'rally' to the GVN (Government of South Vietnam) through the Chieu Hoi programme. The Chieu Hoi programme, I should note, is an amnesty programme for members of the Viet Cong.

Literally millions of psywar leaflets have been printed and dropped, and in fact, it is not at all unusual for as many as ten million leaflets to be air-dropped over South Vietnam in one brief campaign. Keep in mind here that there are only about seventeen million people in South Vietnam. Yet despite the fact that millions upon millions of leaflets have been disseminated in the war thus far, I would estimate that in the early stages of our effort less than five per cent of the cost of paper and printing was

---

This is a reprint from a paper presented as part of a symposium on "Research in Vietnam: Psychological Studies in a Crisis Environment," for the American Psychological Association, Washington, 1967. It appeared in the (Australian) *Army Journal*, No. 238, March, 1969.

being expended to discover whether or not these leaflets were at all effective. The research section of JUSPAO has recently been expanded, but in my judgment there still tends to be a lack of assets for a large and continuing evaluation programme.

Of course research in psychological warfare involves a number of other problems in addition to a frequent lack of assets for evaluation research. Many of these problems plagued us during the Korean War and are still either unsolved or in various stages of solution. For example, the nature and purpose of psychological warfare is often misunderstood. We find on the one hand, some civilian and military personnel who dismiss the whole effort as worthless, while on the other hand there are those who attribute a sort of mystic power to programmes designed to 'manipulate men's minds.' Psychological warfare of course, is neither worthless, providing it is conducted properly, nor is it omnipotent. It is most clearly a support weapon having little power in itself, but having considerable effectiveness when used in conjunction with other activities.

Another problem involves the lack of criteria which can be used to assess the results of combat propaganda. As Daugherty has pointed out: 'First it is necessary to determine whether the desired target is being reached with the intensity and consistency desired, and second, it is desirable to ascertain what effect the effort is having on the individuals and/or groups addressed'.[1] Unfortunately, as he notes, there is often a lack of understanding or agreement as to the objectives to be sought. But even when there is reasonable agreement regarding the mission of psychological warfare, there are problems in establishing acceptable criteria for assessing effects, A great deal of work still needs to be done in this difficult area. Continuous feedback of results to the programme operators is obviously essential to an effective effort, and some mix of both quantitative *and* qualitative data is desirable.

Still another problem related to research in this area pertains to the development of better techniques and methods for the preparation and pre-testing of materials. Pre-testing of course is as essential to an effective programme as evaluation and perhaps even more so since poor materials may damage the very cause one is attempting to promote. Here, for example, I am thinking of materials which may actually strengthen the will to fight when they are designed or intended to have the opposite effect.

In the early stages of the psywar effort in Vietnam and before the organization of JUSPAO in 1965 pre-testing of leaflets by the Vietnamese was infrequently accomplished because of the lack of Vietnamese assets, and an appreciation for its value. Materials were prepared on the basis of intelligence whose timeliness was sometimes questionable, and former VC were infrequently employed. At the present time however, we are using panels of former VC rather extensively for pre-testing.

To illustrate the hazards of inadequate or no pre-testing in psychological warfare I would like to discuss briefly one of the leaflets used earlier in the year. This particular leaflet (Figures 1 and 2) is wordless in order to circumvent the problem of illiteracy. Here it should be noted that we have only very inexact literacy estimates for the Vietnamese population.

---

[1] W. Daugherty, *A Psychological Warfare Casebook*, Baltimore, The Johns Hopkins Press (1958)

Figure 1

One of the difficulties with wordless leaflets however, is that they are subject to greater misinterpretation than those with a text. In this one the intent of the artist seems obvious. The GVN is attempting to help the people, while the VC are doing the opposite. Although this may appear obvious to us, one former VC gave the following interpretation to the leaflet. On side one the teacher is showing the men which bugs *not* to kill. On the other side the VC are shooting a man spraying poison on the crops.

There is also another problem with this leaflet. On side two (Figure 2) VC are depicted with helmets showing stars on the front. Such a helmet is never worn by members of the VC or at least none of the ex-VC I talked with ever wore a hat like that. Nor are uniforms of the type shown here worn by the VC. Consequently, for the VC themselves,

Figure 2

Figure 3

as well as for the civilian population which knows very well what Viet Cong look like, there may be confusion as to who the characters are supposed to be. Pre-testing of leaflets avoids errors of this type.

The typical dress of the VC can be easily established as shown in the photo (Figure 3) which we took in a Chieu Hoi Centre in Tay Ninh Province close to the Cambodian border. None of the ex-VC shown here had been in the camp more than two months, since that is the maximum time they may remain there. Some of them in fact had left the VC only a few days before this picture was taken. You will note that the outfit worn typically consists of a black pyjama-like peasant garb. It should also be added that while with the VC they wear the same type of conical straw hat worn by all Vietnamese peasants.

The second leaflet shown here (Figures 4 and 5) is representative of those I think are good. There is considerable evidence of feelings of loneliness among many VC and North Vietnamese Army personnel, and also there are very strong family ties among the Vietnamese in general. This leaflet capitalizes upon motivation related to these factors.

Figure 4

Nhắn Gởi Các Anh Chiến Binh Việt Cộng

Chúng tôi nhớ đến các anh, các anh có nhớ đến chúng tôi không? Có khi nào các anh nhớ tưởng đến gia đình? Các anh biết là lực lượng Chính Phủ Việt Nam Cộng Hoà đang chiến thắng khắp các nơi. Tôi lo nghĩ không biết hiện anh đang ở đâu và có gì xảy đến cho anh không Chính sách Chiêu hồi của Chính Phủ chờ đón các anh trở về. Tôi mong rằng thư này đến tận tay anh để anh sớm quyết định trở về với chúng tôi. Tôi chờ đợi và mong ước anh trở về bình yên.

SP-941

Figure 5

Translated, this reads:

> To the Soldiers in the Ranks of the Viet Cong
>
> We miss you. Do you remember us? Do you ever think of your family? You know the GVN forces are winning everywhere. I worry about you. Where are you? What has happened to you? The Open Arms Policy of the GVN will welcome your return to us. I hope that this letter reaches you in time and that you will make up your mind to return to us. I am waiting for you, hoping for your safe return.

Current Viet Cong propaganda directed against American troops leaves much to be desired, and it is apparent that they not only face many of the same problems we face, but some others as well. For example, I doubt that they pre-tested the leaflet shown in Figure 6, or that it was very effective in undermining the morale of American servicemen. However, realistically I think, they do not aim much of their material at an American target or even a military target. Their main strategy is to maintain and increase civilian Vietnamese support for the Viet Cong. Therefore, most of their psywar output is aimed at that target, and toward that target the output is extensive. As an illustration, Figure 7 is a leaflet showing American students demonstrating against the war. Note that the text is in Vietnamese, and also, contrast the quality of this leaflet with the one shown in Figure 6.

The final leaflet I wish to show is directed against coloured US troops. Here again, note the higher quality of this material in contrast to the leaflet shown in Figure 6. Where they believe their propaganda may yield the best results, they obviously concentrate time and effort.

AMERICAN SERVICEMEN IN SOUTH VIETNAM

Why are your bloods shed too much in South Vietnam:

It is due to the Johnson administration's war-seeking policy that you are involved in the aggressive war which aims at turning South Vietnam into a U.S. colony.
You are fighting not for America's interests and honour.
There is no grudge between Vietnamese and American people. The Vietnamese people are fighting for their independence, freedom and peace likewise the American people had in the past fought against British imperialism for similar ideals (1775-1783)

Figure 6

**Không được tái diễn cảnh Triều-tiên. Rút quân ngay ra khỏi Việt-nam !
Mỹ phải chấm dứt tàn sát ở Việt-nam.
Độc tài Diệm, bù nhìn của tòa năm góc.**
Đó là những khẩu hiệu đấu tranh của nhân dân Mỹ biểu tình trước cơ quan mộ lính Mỹ tại đại lộ số 5 ở Nữu-ước đòi chánh phủ Mỹ rút quân ra khỏi miền Nam Việt-nam

Figure 7

Viet Cong leaflet directed at the civilian population of South Vietnam. Reference to Diem in the photograph shows it was used some time ago.

In my opinion more of our psywar effort should be geared toward the civilian population in South Vietnam since this is, without question, the number one target in the war in terms of a sucessful conclusion for either side. Research certainly needs to be conducted in terms of how psywar operations could be employed to increase civilian support for the GVN. Here however, we get into a problem area unique to the Vietnam conflict.

One of the most serious and widespread misconceptions in the United States is that the GVN is a puppet regime. Many people in this country apparently have the impression that Americans are running the whole show out there. In fact however, I believe that any American who has been to Vietnam would strongly assert that this is not true. We are still operating very much as advisers in many operational areas, and more frequently than we would perhaps wish, our advice is ignored. What I am saying here is that while we may be able to see a number of research areas needing investigation, in certain instances these areas are too 'sensitive' in terms of American-Vietnamese relations.

Finally, I would like to comment briefly on one extremely difficult problem which relates to the remarks I made earlier in connection with evaluation of the efforts of psywar activities. This is the problem of isolating the psywar variables in military conflicts from other variables. As an illustration of the difficulty of culling out the efforts of psywar operations, I am reminded of a visit we made to one Chieu Hoi Centre about 130 miles north of Saigon along the South China Sea. In connection with this Centre, the American adviser in the area had plotted monthly figures

Colored American servicemen!

20 million fellow-countrymen of yours in the U.S.A. are being abused, oppressed, exploited, manhandled, murdered by Racist authorities. You don't forgot the bloody Alabama cases, don't you?

Now, they are misleading you, driving you to S.VN and using your hands to slaughter the South Viêtnamese people who are struggling for PEACE - INDEPENDENCE - FREEDOM - DEMOCRATY - NATIONAL - REUNIFICATION, for EQUALITY and FRIENDSHIP between the peoples all over the world!

Is it conceivable that you resign yourselves to help the US aggressors, the common enemies of Colored Americans and Viêtnamese people, in murdering your Viêtnamese brothers for US monopolist capitalists' sake?

Resolutely oppose to your being sent to the battlefront, as the men of the 3rd Brig. 1st US Inf. div. at Lai khê did on April 66.

If forced to join the battle:
— CROSS OVER TO THE FRONT'S SIDE!
— LET YOURSELVES BE CAPTURED BY THE LIBERATION ARMED FORCES!
— DON'T RESIST, THROW YOUR WEAPONS 5m FAR AWAY AND LIE STILL!
— HAND YOUR WEAPONS OVER TO THE LIBERATION COMBATANTS, QUICKLY FOLLOW THEM OUT TO SAFER AREAS!

Through the Front's lenient policy, you will be well treated and the SVNNFL will arrange your repatriation as it did with Claude Mc Clure RA. 14703075, a colored American prisoner on last Nov. 27, 1965.

PEACE FOR VIETNAM!

Figure 8

for the number of ex-VC in residence. These figures remained steadily between 50 and 60 for a period of several months when suddenly they jumped to a peak of between 200 and 250. They remained high for about six weeks and then dropped to the previous level. When asked what might account for this unusual fluctuation, he indicated that the movement of an American division into the area corresponded almost exactly with the increase in the number of men in the Centre. When the division moved out of the area about six weeks later, the number in the Centre dropped to its previous level.

Here we have what appears to be a high correlation between degree of military activity in an area with the number of defections from enemy ranks. But can we be sure that some other variable or variables were not also involved? This is one of the major problems in assessing the effects of psywar operations. There are always other variables involved simultaneously so that it is extremely difficult, if not impossible, to establish cause-and-effect relationships between psywar operations and a criteria such as number of defectors, intelligence information given by civilians, and so on.

There are of course, other problems that one faces in conducting research in psychological warfare, and particularly in Vietnam. One of these is the physical danger of being shot, kidnapped, or blown up by a mine while in the field. I think these dangers tend to be exaggerated however in the minds of those who have never been in a combat situation of this type. The risk is so slight that it should not discourage behavioral scientists with an interest in research in crisis situations from pursuing that interest.

Probably the most fundamental of all problems relating to research in this area is financial. In my opinion, behavioral science research in general in Vietnam is pitifully small in view of the need, and in comparison to hardware research. In view of all we hear about 'winning the hearts and minds of the people,' the 'other war,' the importance of the pacification programme, and the obvious significance of political and psychological factors in the current struggle, it is amazing to me that less than the price of one jet aircraft has been spent thus far on behavioral science research in Vietnam. Unless this problem is solved a large share of the other problems I mentioned in this paper will remain unsolved. ☐

While the horizon of strategy is bounded by war, grand strategy looks beyond the war to the subsequent peace. It should not only combine the various instruments but so regulate their use as to avoid damage to the future state of peacefulness, secure and prosperous. Unlike strategy, the realm of grand strategy is for the most part still awaiting exploration and understanding.
—Liddell Hart.

44

SOME PSYCHOLOGICAL PERSPECTIVES ON LEGITIMACY

RICHARD FLACKS
University of California at Santa Barbara

When John Kennedy received his discharge from the armed forces after World War II, he wrote in his notebook, "War will exist until that distant day when the conscientious objector enjoys the same reputation and prestige that the warrior does today."

In a certain sense, the "distant day" apparently hoped for by the young John Kennedy has arrived. On the American campus, the draft resister assuredly has more prestige than the willing conscript. Drs. Howard Levy and Benjamin Spock likely are more widely honored among many medical students than those in the medical profession who have dutifully served in Vietnam. National magazines have provided us with more sympathetic details concerning the exploits of Pvt. Andrew Stapp, the Fort Hood Three, the Reverend William Sloane Coffin, and David Harris than of Medal of Honor winners, ace bomber pilots, and even Green Berets. I have no doubt that a poll of attendees at this conference would show more respect for the actions of Captain Dale Noyd, a psychologist court-martialed for refusal to use his skills in support of the Vietnam war effort, than for those psychologists who continue to aid military training, psychological warfare, and counterinsurgency. In the ghetto high schools of the country, it seems likely that the great hero of this war is Muhammed Ali. At my own university, 49 per cent of the graduate students and graduating seniors responding to a student government poll declare that they would not serve in the armed forces if drafted; Louis Harris finds that 20-30 per cent of male students nationally say they will refuse to serve. If John

---

This is a reprint of a paper prepared for the Annual Meeting of the American Psychological Association, San Francisco, September, 1968.

Kennedy's "distant day" still seems far off, it is nevertheless already here on certain campuses and in certain neighborhoods of the country (Lauter & Howe, 1968).

Current discussion of legitimacy focuses on this situation and is concerned particularly with speculation that instances of defiance, resistance, and disruption by young people, directed against established authority, represent a trend leading to the erosion and destruction of the legitimacy of military and other authority. This concern is too recent to have produced very much in the way of systematic research; instead, one is struck by the fact that whatever empirical social psychological research we have which bears directly on the problem of authority tends to dramatize the extent to which people do what they are told to do by those with authority.

There is, for example, a small tradition of rather striking experimental studies which demonstrate that persons tend to do what they perceive to be clearly expected of them by others whom they regard as having the right to have such expectations. Among the earliest of such studies[1] were those by Jerome Frank (1944) in which subjects were asked to perform impossible or disagreeable tasks, such as balancing a marble on a steel ball or eating dry soda crackers. In Frank's studies, subjects would continue to carry out the experimenter's instructions without overt resistance, unless explicitly informed of their right to refuse.

There are even more dramatic demonstrations of willing obedience in the recent experimental literature. Pepitone and Wallace (Gamson, 1968) encountered little resistance from subjects who were asked by experimenters to sort garbage. Martin Orne and his associates (1962; Orne & Evans, 1965) attempted to design tasks which would be refused by normal subjects so that the effects of hypnosis on subjects' willingness to accept commands could be demonstrated. In general, he found that it was extremely difficult to design a task so boring or meaningless that an unhypnotized subject would refuse an experimenter's request to continue with it. In later experiments, Orne and his associates were able to get subjects to do extremely disagreeable and harmful things by asking them to pretend that they were hypnotized. Subjects who simulated hypnosis were as fully willing as hypnotized subjects to pick up a poisonous snake, put their hands in nitric acid, and throw acid in an assistant's face. Even subjects who were told they were "normal controls" tended to show compliance with these requests. It should be added, of course, that

---

1. This discussion of the literature on conforming is indebted to Gamson (1968, pp. 127-135).

steps were taken by the experimenters to prevent actual injury to the participants in the experiments.

There are, finally, the well-known experiments by Stanley Milgram (1965) which have demonstrated the capacity of the experimental situation to create what Milgram calls "destructive obedience." Subjects asked to deliver what they believed to be extremely dangerous electric shocks to another person, in a situation in which the administration of shocks was defined as necessary to the success of an experiment, tended to deliver the maximum voltage even when they heard or saw the victim in pain and pleading for mercy. Even though they gave a variety of indications of stress and dislike for the situation, the majority of subjects in Milgram's basic situation continued to perceive an obligation to the experimenter to follow his orders.

Milgram's studies suggest some limits on the tendency of subjects to do what they are told to do. For instance, when commands conflict with one's personal inclinations, the latter are more likely to prevail if there is a way to evade the command without being detected or if one observes others defying the command openly. There is also the suggestion in his work that individuals who accept orders they regard as legitimate tend to believe that the primary responsibility for the consequences of such orders rests with the experimenter rather than themselves.

This small literature of experimentation on obedience is not entirely easy to interpret. Most obviously, these studies show that, at least in our culture, persons tend to be highly trusting of scientists and tend, consequently, to accept the authority of a scientist once they have committed themselves to helping him in an experiment. Although one might not wish to go very far in generalizing responses to scientific authority to other power relationships, it does seem that these experiments do constitute rather pure demonstrations of the effects of legitimacy, with other sources of motivation largely removed. These studies suggest that under conditions where authority is defined by subjects as legitimate, they appear highly ready to do what is expected of them, highly likely to delegate processes of judgment to the authority figure—even when coercion and reward are virtually absent and the consequences of obedience are likely to be negative. One concludes from these studies that it would be perilous to treat forms of compliance with national authority—such as readiness to enter military service or to pay taxes or to otherwise support war—as merely instrumental acts designed to avoid the severe negative sanctions associated with noncompliance or evasion. By the same token, obedience to national authority cannot be explained solely as positively instrumental nor as positively expressive of sentiments like patriotism or ideological commitment to the regime. What makes the experiments we have cited so striking is that they illustrate behavior undertaken *in spite of personal motive and without positive emotional commitment.* It is for this reason that they appear to be valid microscopic replications of such mass instances of obedience as submission to conscription or participation in bureaucratically organized genocide.

It is clear that Milgram's subjects and draft resisters stand for opposing aspects of the same culture and social system. Milgram's subjects seem to typify what C. Wright Mills called the "cheerful robot"; the prevalence of compliance in his experiments seems to support critics of modern society who fear the rise of "mass conformity." Yet the emergence of youthful opponents of militarism and of forms of protest based on civil disobedience and confrontation suggests the possibility of an opposing trend. Indeed, one of the more pressing tasks for social analysis is to attempt to understand which figure—Milgram's subject or the conscientious resister—best symbolizes the central trends in individual-authority relations in American society.

SOME STRUCTURAL DETERMINANTS OF LEGITIMACY

Although no coherent framework is yet available which can provide us with such systematic understanding, two lines of investigation in social psychology may be relevant for constructing such a framework. The first derives from the experiments we have cited and focuses on the way in which perceived characteristics of the authority structure influence the likelihood of obedience. Milgram's findings provide a basis for extrapolating at least three general propositions concerning those features of the authority structure which are central to the maintenance of its legitimacy.

1. Individuals tend to attribute legitimacy to authority when the exercise of that authority is perceived as beneficial to groups, institutions, or values to which the individual is committed. We have argued that explanations of compliant behavior cannot rest on notions of reward and punishment; indeed, the very definition of legitimacy involves the assumption that individuals comply with authority in spite of their personal motives. In other words, we can measure the legitimacy of a particular authority structure by the degree in which it can obtain conformity without the use of positive or negative sanctions. Nevertheless, claims to legitimacy by authorities in modern society usually must include an argument that the exercise of this authority is instrumental to the achievement of benefits or values collectively desired by subordinates. Thus, subjects in the experiments we have cited tended to assume that the orders given them were designed to advance science; they acted against their personal inclinations, not because they were coerced or rewarded but because they perceived their actions as instrumental to the achievement of a collective goal and they perceived the experimenter as a valid representative of that goal.

All modern nation-states are "pluralist" in the sense that they govern societies consisting of diverse classes, ethnic groups, institutions, and subcultures. The legitimacy of national authority in such societies depends in part on the maintenance of the perception that common interests and values are shared by these diverse groups, transcending that which divides them, that the national authority is the authentic guarantor of those common interests, and that continued support for national authority is relatively beneficial for each such group. In such a society, legitimacy is in danger of erosion if, for example, there is a persistent pattern of inequity experienced by members of a particular class or stratum, if adherents of particular value systems or subcultures feel threatened, unrepresented, or disillusioned by the going system, if the established common values of the national culture are weakened by rapid social change and the national authorities are seen as incompetent to generate or support new values, or if members of particular institutions experience significant discontinuities between their collective goals and those of the authorities. The erosion of established authority under these conditions is probably hastened if alternative structures are perceived or envisioned by those who are disaffected.

2. *Attribution of legitimacy is a function of trust; that is, the perception that those in authority are not biased against one or that the working of the system does not result in special costs for oneself or one's group.* The importance of trust in the experiments we have cited is rather clear; in both the Orne and Milgram experiments, it seems likely that subjects were willing to obey commands to commit destructive acts in the belief that the experimenter knew what he was doing and was able to eliminate or control any real danger in the situation. For Orne's subjects, this perception was probably reinforced when they observed that they were prevented from actually picking up the poisonous snake by the sudden appearance of a glass screen between themselves and the snake.

At the level of national authority, trust depends on such matters as the objectivity of the authorities in mediating conflicts, the degree in which the police and the courts implement the principle of equality before the law, the openness of the political system and the media of opinion to emergent groups and dissenting views, the trustworthiness of statements made by national leaders, the degree in which officially espoused policies are actually implemented and actually have the results claimed for them, and so on.

It should be clear that trust, as we have defined it, constitutes a somewhat different basis for legitimacy than perceived benefit. Certainly, the perception that a regime or political system is biased in one's favor constitutes an important source of legitimacy; nevertheless, as Gamson (1968, p. 57) has suggested, such perceptions by some members are likely to be less stable supports for a system than a general perception of nonbias—for if one group feels particularly advantaged by the system, others are likely to feel disadvantaged and will tend to withdraw their support. Gamson argues that the optimal level of trust for maintaining legitimacy in situations of high conflict is one in which conflicting parties see the authorities as unbiased.

3. *Individuals tend to attribute legitimacy to authority if they perceive a generalized consensus supporting legitimacy.* This consensus may be manifested through expressions of popular opinion; it may also be manifested by the ease with which the authority in question can call upon the backing of other centers of power in the society. The Milgram experiments, in addition to suggesting the importance of trust and perceived benefit as supports for legitimacy, indicated that compliance was substantially reduced when subjects perceived others disobeying. This finding is, of course, congruent with those of other experiments in conformity to group pressure which have repeatedly shown that subjects tend not to conform if they have social support for nonconformity.

No principle in social psychology is better established than the idea that individual attitudes depend on the perceived attitudes of significant others. In the case of legitimacy, the usual psychological mechanisms which bind people to accept consensual attitudes are importantly supplemented by the principle of consent of the governed. In a political democracy, the existence of general consensus about the legitimacy of a regime or a policy is a very powerful support because majority support is defined as the ultimate basis for legitimacy in the system. Thus those who are inclined to challenge legitimacy confront moral as well as psychological difficulties when they do so. These difficulties can be reduced, it appears, by the example of individuals who refuse to comply. Acts of noncompliance can have the effect of undermining the "pluralistic ignorance" which often underlies popular consensus. Many with private doubts conform because they believe others lack doubts; examples of open disobedience serve to make private doubts public. Furthermore, they can provide models of effective resistance: often, as Milgram has argued, persons tend to obey because they believe they have no alternative or because they lack the skills necessary for resistance; the overt resistant may make alternatives visible and skills available. In situations where compliance to authority entails major individual sacrifice and where obedience is demanded primarily because the commands are legitimate, public acts of individual noncompliance can be precursors of large-scale popular disaffection. This was surely the faith of Thoreau and those who have followed him.

Arthur Stinchcombe has recently argued that "power based *only* on the shifting sands of public opinion and willing obedience is inherently unstable" (1968, p. 161). In his view, it is not popular consent or the willing obedience of subordinates which is decisive for legitimating a power; rather "a power is legitimate to the degree that, by virtue of the doctrines and norms by which it is justified, the power-holder can call upon sufficient other centers of power, as reserves in case of need, to make his power effective" (Stinchcombe, 1968, p. 162). From a psychological point of view, we may interpret this statement to predict that individuals will tend to perceive the action of an authority as legitimate if that action has or is likely to have the support of other centers of power. We can also draw from it the prediction that popular disaffection and weakening consensus about legitimacy are less clear-cut signs of eroding legitimacy than is the failure by role-players in key institutions adequately to support the power of national authority. Finally, although Stinchcombe in his brief exercise in conceptual analysis does not deal with this point, we can expect a reciprocal relationship between popular opinion and the responsiveness of institutional leaders to the needs of national authority. In situations of growing popular disaffection, institutional authority may be decisive as a conservative force in backing up the legitimacy of the national authority; but if cracks should appear in the institutional structure, then popular disaffection may be accelerated. At any rate, Stinchcombe's strictures against overemphasizing the importance of popular consent as a basis for legitimacy are quite suggestive; they lead us to consider measuring the stability of a political system by looking at the intactness of the institutional framework rather than simply at public opinion and the distribution of attitudes.

INDIVIDUAL CHARACTER AND THE CAPACITY TO RESIST

Drawing on the Milgram and other experiments concerning obedience, we have been able to suggest some variables which seem centrally useful in describing the conditions under which persons tend to attribute legitimacy to political regimes and national authority. These variables have to do with perceived characteristics of the authority structure and with perceptions about the social context in which the authorities operate.

Another social psychological perspective on legitimacy is possible. This involves emphasis on the characteristics of subordinates rather than on the characteristics of the situation. In the Milgram studies, individual differences in the degree of compliance, in reaction time, and in eagerness to administer shock were observed. It is important to note that Milgram found that these differences were correlated with such "personality" measures as the F scale. The existence of such individual differences and such correlations leads us quite directly to that long tradition of research on "character" which has been a distinctive contribution of psychology to political analysis.

Familial Influences

Starting at least with Freud, there has been the hypothesis that the family constitutes a miniature political system and that attitudes toward parental authority are generalized or projected onto other political figures. Freud's view of the matter was notoriously pessimistic: the family was inherently authoritarian; in it men learned habits of submission, learned to repress or deflect their anti-authoritarian impulses, and, if well-socialized, came to idealize forms of paternal domination. But the psychoanalytic perspective does not require a view of socialization which emphasizes the repressive outcome of early childhood experience; Wilhelm Reich was among the earliest to suggest that children raised in democratic, egalitarian, and nonrepressive social settings could become adults with the capacity to resist irrational or tyrannical authority.

Speculation and investigation about the political effects of early socialization reached an important culmination with the research on the Authoritarian Personality (Adorno, Frenkel-Brunswik, Levinson, & Sanford, 1950). Whatever its methodological flaws, this research made quite credible the idea that attitudes of submission may be based on enduring personality dispositions, and that such dispositions have their origins in families characterized by highly dominant fathers, strongly hierarchical structures, rigorously differentiated sexual and generational roles, and low tolerance for free expression of impulses. Subsequent experimental studies, including Milgram's as we have noted, show positive relationships between F scores and submissive or conforming behavior.

Democratic or anti-authoritarian "personalities" have been far less well studied. Research with which I am most familiar concerns characteristics of student protesters; our own studies (Flacks, 1967), those of Brewster Smith and his associates (Block, Haan, & Smith, in press), and of Kenneth Keniston (1968) all provide evidence that student activists tend to come from families which are more egalitarian and democratic and less repressive than the families of students who are uninvolved in protest movements. Finally, one might call attention to case studies by Wolfenstein (1967) of "revolutionary personalities." They suggest a pattern in which paternal authority has been weak or absent at crucial stages in the development of these future revolutionaries; there is the suggestion in Wolfenstein's work that an important experience for creating the capacity for revolutionary leadership is that of having replaced one's father in the family in early adolescence. The psychoanalytic perspective contains grave and notorious dangers of psychological reductionism; still, I am convinced that the central hypotheses—that the family is a political system; that one learns within it habits of response to authority and attitudes toward appropriate behavior by authorities which can carry over to the larger political system—remain viable and fruitful ones for those who want to understand the capacities of individuals for conformity and resistance and the tendencies within cultures to facilitate or inhibit such capacities. Since political radicals and dissenters have often borne the brunt of psychoanalytic scrutiny used for *ad hominem* attack on their position, there is legitimate concern that the psychoanalytic tradition is conservative when applied to political theory. (A provocative treatment of the general problem of psychoanalysis and politics appears in Sampson, 1968.) But ever since Reich, it has been clear that psychoanalytic hypotheses on the formative role of parental authority could have radical critical functions. At any rate, we may relate our discussion of authoritarianism to the problem of legitimacy by asking such questions as: Does the persistence of authoritarian institutions and practices depend in part on the ability of these institutions to recruit appropriate character types? Is the legitimacy of, say, military authority likely to be materially affected by the emergence in the society of significant numbers of youths who are characterologically indisposed to submit to it?

The psychoanalytic tradition emphasizes the relationship between character development and political behavior, and tends to ignore explicit learning about government and politics. There is, however, a growing body of research on the latter. Briefly stated, the mass of such studies can, I believe, be summarized by saying that children tend to adopt the political beliefs and preferences of their parents, and moreover, that white children tend to be highly supportive of the American political system. In the words of Easton and Dennis (1965), summarizing their findings on children's images of government, "The small child sees a vision of holiness when he chances to glance in the direction of government—a sanctity and rightness of the demigoddess who dispenses the milk of human kindness. The government protects us, helps us, is good, and cares for us when we are in need, answers the child." The authors believe that this early set of emotions and perceptions forms the basis for later adult attitudes toward the state. This pattern of socialization is undoubtedly crucial in maintaining the legitimacy of authority in American society.

Although no one has studied blacks or student protesters in quite the same way, we may suspect that among both groups a high proportion had somewhat different images of government in early childhood. Black respondents are far more suspicious of government authorities than whites; this undoubtedly reflects not only their actual experience but also the received experience of their parents (Marvick, 1965). Student activists' political attitudes are in large measure continuous with those of their parents; it is probable that from a very early age they were reared to be skeptical about the sanctity and benevolence of established authority (Flacks, 1967). If the white majority tends to socialize their children to support the legitimacy of the national government, it seems also to be the case that significant minority subcultures tend to rear their children rather explicitly to have doubts about that authority. If the majority of white children talk as if they were raised in the nurseries of *Brave New World*, this would seem to ensure the stability of national authority as we now know it—and this appears to be the assumption underlying much of the work on political socialization. But the existence of at least two counter-cultures, socializing their children quite differently, suggests a more dynamic, less predictable political scene.

Competence

In recent years, psychologists have displayed increasing interest in the ways in which individual conceptions of self influence the capacity for initiative, autonomy, and rationality.

In a recent review Brewster Smith (1968) suggests that "competence" is a useful summary term for a variety of traits and attitudes which have been defined and measured in recent studies. The competent person, as Smith defines him, perceives the self as "causally important, as effective in the world ... as likely to be able to bring about desired effects, and as accepting responsibility when effects do not correspond to desire. In near equivalent, the person has self-respect." Although competence is likely to be associated with favorable levels of general self-evaluation or esteem, general esteem is less important than the sense of efficacy or potency (Smith, 1968, pp. 281-282).

Although competence bears some relationship to authoritarianism, since both concepts address the capacity of individuals for independence and self-determination, it clearly is a different sort of concept. In particular, references to competence have to do with aspects of self-awareness rather than with unconscious determinants. Whereas authoritarianism as a concept asks us to focus on early socialization and enduring traits as influences on the capacity for self-determination, a focus on competence leads us to emphasize the continuing role of experience and social interaction in shaping this capacity.

If there is a generalized capacity for independence, a generalized tendency to perceive oneself as causally important and potent, then this has clear implications for political behavior and relations to authority. Indeed, there exist a considerable number of studies relating efficacy to aspects of political behavior such as voting, activism, and alienation.

With reference to legitimacy, we may hypothesize that competence is related to the individual's readiness to delegate processes of judgment and evaluation to superordinate authority, or to participate smoothly in situations where decisions which affect him are beyond his control. For persons with high competence, the legitimacy of authority depends on the degree to which they have access to the decision-making process or believe that their judgments are taken seriously by superiors, or, perhaps most importantly, have the freedom to shape their own situation without reference to higher authority. Persons with low sense of competence, on the other hand, tend to view authority as untrustworthy, but also lack trust in their own ability to affect those in authority. They are, consequently, likely to be politically apathetic, fatalistically enduring what is imposed upon them (while sometimes trying to evade the most severe consequences), unless some route to efficacy becomes manifest (as is sometimes the case).

In modern society, formal education is the socializing experience which is supposed to be most directly relevant to enhancing competence. In practice, of course, it very often has the opposite effect, particularly on children of impoverished or working class background (Kozol, 1967). Nevertheless, it seems clear that achieving high levels of education does increase the sense of competence of many individuals, particularly in the political sphere.

Alongside the rise of mass higher education in modern society has been the increasing dominance of bureaucratic forms of authority. Bureaucratic organization rewards competence, but at the same time bureaucratic hierarchy rests on the assumption that there are major differences among men in their capacity to exercise authority, and that competence in this regard ought to give a few men great legitimate power to coordinate the lives of many others who ought not to expect much voice in decisions which control them.

There is, then, a contradiction between two of the great shaping institutions of the contemporary period—mass higher education and bureaucratic authority—a contradiction which has to do with opposed definitions of competence embodied in each of these institutions. This contradiction was noted by Max Weber in his classic essay on bureaucracy. Weber felt that the tension between liberal education and bureaucracy would probably be resolved by the erosion of liberal education and its replacement by technical training. It is clear that his expectations were to a very great extent accurate. Narrow specialization, emphasis on technique, and value neutrality in higher education are widely seen as the central trend; critics continue to see these as reducing the likelihood that the highly educated person will feel himself to be competent to take part in general citizenly activity.

Still, liberal education has not been totally erased, and more and more young people are getting exposed to it. These same young people, unlike their predecessors in the educated middle class, are very likely to spend much of their lives, both in the educational system and beyond it, under bureaucratic authority if they follow conventional career lines.

The heightened sense of competence produced by mass higher education and by comfortable status constitutes, I believe, one of the more important sources of instability for the legitimacy of established authority, particularly those authority structures which assume little competence and provide little autonomy for those subordinate to it.

Risk Taking

There is one final personal characteristic which seems to deserve mention as relevant to understanding the stability of authority in American society. This is the capacity to take risks in order to defy authoritative orders. There are undoubtedly numerous determinants of this capacity, and one doubts whether there is, in fact, a generalized trait—call it courage—which predicts willingness to take risks in all spheres of life. I particularly want to emphasize the possibility that one's socioeconomic status is an important determinant of one's capacity to take risks involving disobedience. In particular, it seems likely that high status and material security, particularly if one is born into them, tend to weaken the impact of those incentives and sanctions which are usually utilized by authority to maintain conformity. Obviously, most people at the top do a great many things to stay there; still, it seems to be empirically true that they also have more objective and subjective freedom of action. This is, in part, because the status and income incentives of the society are less attractive; in part, because one has been raised to exercise rather than defer to authority; in part, because one may have a certain degree of guilt about being affluent in an egalitarian society; in part, because one discovers the limitations and psychological costs of a life-style organized around material consumption and preservation of social status. At any rate, on this analysis, one should not find it surprising that among those most willing to be defiant of the draft; among those most prepared to face prison with some degree of equanimity; among those ready to take risks with respect to their future careers, a disproportionate number of children of affluence will be represented. Furthermore, on this analysis, one predicts that rising levels of affluence will greatly increase the number of young who are prepared to take the risks of challenging established authority.

SPECULATIONS ON THE FUTURE
OF AMERICAN NATIONAL AUTHORITY

I have formulated the foregoing propositions and hypotheses in what appears to be a deductive style; actually, however, this discussion should be read as *post hoc* argument. On the one hand, much of the previous discussion was designed to try to identify some general principles which would explain some of the data which we and others have obtained concerning the characteristics of student protesters. Second, this discussion was in large part an attempt to provide some rational grounds for the feeling, which I am sure I share with others, that present student protest movements against university administrations, against the war and the draft, are not isolated or ephemeral outbursts, but that they have major historical implications, particularly for the legitimacy of national authority in advanced industrial societies like our own.

The burden of social research which has relevance to anticipating the future of legitimacy in this society strongly suggests that the prudent observer will place his bets on continued stability. That is the implication of Milgram's studies and other experiments demonstrating the willing obedience of subjects undergoing scientific manipulation. It is the burden of research on the effects of political socialization. It is the clear implication of studies of political behavior, of voting habits and patterns, and public opinion. The main body of theory and research from diverse fields seems to say that the legitimacy of national authority in the United States rests on a broad consensus among Americans about political rules, about common values, about the trustworthiness of the system in general and the current regime in particular; and that this consensus is powerfully supported by the process of socializing the young on the one hand and by the prosperous and progressive consequences of the system on the other.

This kind of reasoning did not help social scientists to predict either the black revolt or the mass disaffection and rebelliousness of educated youth. Given the emergence of these movements, conventional social analysis leads us to expect that their effects will be neither symptomatic of, nor productive of, fundamental changes in the nature of authority and its legitimation in American society.

Such reasoning seems increasingly less credible with each passing day. And we need not rely solely on our emotional reactions to immediate turmoil to provide grounds for thinking that the legitimacy of established authority in the United States is reaching an historical turning point.

The Black Revolt

The black revolt is, of course, a primary reason for expecting a transformation of authority. The shift in its terms, from a movement for integration to a movement for colonial liberation, means that, by definition, a major portion of the black community has already decided that established authority on national and local levels is illegitimate. Current proposals for dealing with the racial crisis fall roughly into three categories: they are either proposals for the institutionalization of new forms of authority or proposals to restore the legitimacy of the political system by efforts to rapidly meet the economic needs of the black population, or they are frank appeals to recognize the collapse of legitimacy by proposing to maintain power through force.

Some of our previous discussion is helpful in understanding why legitimacy of authority has so rapidly eroded for black people. Without attempting a detailed analysis, the following points are worth mentioning:

1. Negroes have of course never felt particularly rewarded by the system nor have they been given any opportunity to see it as trustworthy. As we have previously suggested, this disaffection and mistrust is a product of direct and graphic experience; it is also a feature of the political socialization of Negro children and youth in the family.
2. The past decade has been one of increased disillusionment. Although the postwar period was expected to be one of rapid progress for Negroes, matters did not turn out this way. The gap between black and white economic position has tended to widen. Laws and government enactments which promised change were not effectively implemented. The promise of migration to the city has turned to despair. Of particular importance in intensifying distrust of and disaffection with the political system is the situation of black youth. The rising generation experiences enormous rates of unemployment and the knowledge that future opportunity will be meager; it contributes disproportionately to the casualties in Vietnam, suffers almost universal harassment at the hands of the local police—and all this in the context of an endless stream of promises and seductions. To vast numbers of black youth, it is clear that the system is strongly biased against them and that nothing is to be gained from further adherence to it.
3. The integration movement was crucial in the development of new stances toward authority. Its failure, of course, intensified disaffection. But its success in creating organization had the effect of increasing the competence and risk-taking capacity of many black people. It also transformed the consensus of the black community from one organized around accommodation and acceptance of established authority to one favoring assertiveness and independent power.

Of course, no elaborate framework of theorizing is needed to account for the emergence of deepening revolutionary sentiment in the black community. On the other hand, one need not assume that the existence of such a sentiment is particularly threatening to the long-term legitimacy of the American political system. Partial incorporation of Negro demands, it may be argued, can offset the more threatening implications of the movement; anyway, it may be said, the blacks are a special case of disaffection, with little resonance among whites.

The General Erosion of Legitimacy

I believe, however, that the inability of the American polity to deal effectively with Negro grievances is not the only source of erosion of its legitimacy. Indeed, the so-called youth revolt indicates that more general problems are, in fact, emerging. These, I would argue, have to do with major shifts in aspects of American culture to which I have already briefly referred. Among these changes I would emphasize the following:

1. *There has been a general decline of commitment to traditional "middle class values" throughout the society.* Many observers have commented on the erosion of the "Protestant Ethic"—a process which probably began with the turn of the century and which has been due largely to the impact of bureaucratization and increasing economic surplus. These processes have virtually destroyed the traditional capitalist economy; the cultural and characterological patterns associated with it have likewise lost their vitality. On the other hand, it is important to emphasize that the existing political and institutional élites continue to represent themselves in traditional ways and that large sectors of the populace still adhere to some version of the classic virtues of entrepreneurial success, self-discipline, and individualism which derive from the Protestant Ethic.

2. *The rapid growth of a sector of the middle class whose status depends on high education rather than property.* This group tends to be most critical of traditional values and of traditional capitalism generally, in part because of the exposure of these people to humanist values, in part because their vocations are often not tied directly to the business sector of the economy. In addition, as we have suggested, high education is likely to increase the interest of individuals in having autonomy and a voice in decision making.

3. *Associated with these trends has been the transformation of the American family, especially the family of the educated middle class.* This transformation involves increased equality between husband and wife, declining distinctiveness of sex roles in the family, increased opportunity for self-expression on the part of children, fewer parental demands for self-discipline, and more parental support for autonomous behavior on the part of children. Evidence from studies of student protesters suggests the existence of an increasingly distinct "humanist" subculture in the middle class, consisting primarily of highly educated and urbanized families, based in professional occupations, who encourage humanist orientations in their offspring as well as questioning attitudes to traditional middle class values, to arbitrary authority, and conven-

tional politics (Flacks, 1967). Although this humanist subculture represents a small minority of the population, many of its attributes are more widely distributed; and the great increase in the number of college graduates suggests that the ranks of this subculture will rapidly grow.

4. *These cultural changes inevitably generate discontent with established authority.* As we have already suggested, persons raised in these "new" ways are likely to be resistant to authority which is hierarchical, bureaucratic, or symbolic of traditional capitalist and nationalist goals. On the other hand, one might imagine that authority on the national and institutional levels in America could be flexible enough to offset serious disaffection on the part of this emergent group. Change in the direction of providing greater personal autonomy and participation, élites who speak the language of modernity and change, and the adoption of public programs that fulfill the vocational and personal needs of the educated humanists might be sufficient to keep their unrest within the framework of legitimacy.

There is, however, an awesome barrier to the achievement of this kind of incorporation, namely, the commitment of American political and corporate élites to the maintenance of an international empire. This commitment has numerous internal consequences. The most central for our purposes is that it necessitates the militarization of the youth—the imposition of conscription on the one hand and the "channeling" of youth into "necessary" occupations on the other. It is this situation, more than anything else, which converts the restiveness of educated youth into direct opposition, which leads them to challenge the legitimacy of established authority, and which, incidentally, connects them to militant black youth. For both black and white humanist youth, the persistence and growth of militarism and empire building constitute a fundamental violation of central values and a severe threat to individual and collective fulfillment of central aspirations.

Militant black and humanist white youth are most directly affronted by conscription and other consequences of American imperialism, and the result is that they come into direct and continuing conflict with authority as they try to resist its imposition. But imperialism has other consequences for political stability. For instance, continued commitment to massive military expenditures forces the postponement of domestic reform, thereby alienating, rather than incorporating, deprived minority groups and the educated middle class. Imperialist foreign policy seems to require a steady deterioration in the perceived trustworthiness of national authority: for instance, it requires the elaboration of covert, paramilitary institutions, management of information, and other practices which signify a loss of democratic control over foreign policy and an increase in direct efforts by the state to manipulate the domestic political process. The massive defense budget greatly enhances the power of the military and defense corporations, who exert powerful influence over policy without responsibility to the electorate. Those who oppose the military or who want to change foreign policy become increasingly convinced that national authority is biased against them, and legitimacy is further eroded.

One could go on in elaborating the many ways in which dissent and opposition to the Johnson Administration and its policies, or more general grievances on the part of the disadvantaged, have systematically been converted into more fundamental challenges to the legitimacy of national authority, in large part as a consequence of its imperialist character.

One might accept the above analysis and still seriously doubt whether the increasingly revolutionary mood of some sectors of the population represents an unmanageable challenge to the legitimacy of the present authority structure. The challenge is serious; the widespread use of armed force to occupy cities and protect various public installations and functions is a demonstration of this, as is the steadily rising number of jailed draft resisters, and ultimately, Lyndon Johnson's decision not to seek re-election. But its unmanageability depends on whether and in what manner the present mood spreads to other parts of the population.

If there is a potential for growing delegitimization of national authority beyond the strata who are presently disaffected, it ought to become manifest in the ranks of the armed forces. For, as we have suggested, if widespread potential discontent with legitimate authority exists, it can be catalyzed by the example of a small number of active disobedients. That small number has now begun to appear—in the form of public deserters, men who refuse orders, servicemen who participate in peace marches and love-ins. Now, a miniscule but growing movement for a union of servicemen has emerged, as well as a number of underground newspapers which are passed around army bases. Do these events represent the early stages of general disaffection among conscripts? This seems far less unlikely today than it did even a few months ago.

Catalysts and Cracks

We have also suggested that legitimacy depends on the readiness of other centers of power to provide backing for the challenged authority. There have, it seems to me, already developed some minor, if interesting, cracks in the institutional support for American national authority. One illustration of this is the willingness of some university authorities to accede to student demands to withhold class rank information from Selective Service boards and to readmit students convicted of violating the draft laws.[2] These are rather trivial gestures; still they are symbolic of the fact that some institutional authorities—particularly university administrators and church officials—find it increasingly difficult to support the establishment in general. At the opposite pole, one observes the increasingly open hostility of the police to efforts by local authorities to moderate civil disorder, resulting in increasing tension within the authority structure at least at the municipal level. Whether these actions suggest a more fundamental series of splits in the institutional framework again remains to be seen.

In short, I have been trying to say that there appears to be a fundamental incompatibility between the commitment of American national authority to the maintenance of a world empire and the continued legitimacy of that authority. The commitment to empire prevents the authorities from adequately meeting the demands of the disadvantaged. It necessitates forms of domination and social control which are antidemocratic and which reduce the trustworthiness of the authorities. It perpetuates forms of organization which prevent the political system from reflecting the vast cultural changes which are sweeping the society. It requires the deployment of youth for military and related purposes while cultural changes have made many youths characterologically unsuitable for such purposes.

These are some of the reasons for feeling that the draft resister and the Black Panther rather than the cheerful robot or the black bourgeois are the authentic vanguard of an emerging social and political order, and that the example of the resistant few is likely to continue to be catalytic for the ambivalent and passive many. The danger of a repressive response by beleaguered authority is quite real, as is the mobilization of popular support for the imposition of order at the expense of freedom. Yet the emergent characterological and cultural trends, and the revolutionary movements they

---

2. Another illustration would be the decision of Yale University officials to strip the ROTC there of its academic status. As reported in *The News American* (Baltimore, Md.) Editorial. Feb. 3, 1969. Similar actions were taken by other universities in recent months.

have spawned, promise a new social system, in which militarism, racism, narrow nationalism, and imperialism have become illegitimate and where individual dignity, individual conscience, and collective participation become the primary bases for legitimate authority. This promise makes the risks worthwhile for many of us.

REFERENCES

Adorno, T. W., Frenkel-Brunswik, E., Levinson, D., & Sanford, N. *The authoritarian personality.* New York: Harper & Row, 1950.

Block, J., Haan, N., & Smith, M. B. Activism and apathy in contemporary adolescents. In J. F. Adams (Ed.), *Contributions to the understanding of adolescence.* New York: Allyn & Bacon, in press.

Easton, D., & Dennis, J. The child's image of government. *The Annals,* September 1965, 361, 40-57.

Flacks, R. The liberated generation. *J. soc. Issues,* 1967, 23, 52-75.

Frank, J. Experimental studies of personal pressure and resistance. *J. gen. Psychol.,* 1944, 30, 23-64.

Gamson, W. *Power and discontent.* Homewood, Ill.: Dorsey Press, 1968.

Keniston, K. *Young radicals.* New York: Houghton-Mifflin, 1968.

Kozol, J. *Death at an early age.* Boston: Houghton-Mifflin, 1967.

Lauter, P., & Howe, Florence. The draft and its opposition. *The New York Rev. of Books,* June 20, 1968, X (12), 25-31.

Marvick, D. The political socialization of the American Negro. *The Annals,* September 1965, 361, 112-127.

Milgram, S. Some conditions of obedience and disobedience to authority. In I. D. Steiner & M. Fishbein (Eds.), *Current studies in social psychology.* New York: Holt, Rinehart & Winston, 1965. Pp. 243-262.

Orne, M. T. On the social psychology of the psychological experiment. *Amer. Psychologist,* 1962, 17, 776-783.

Orne, M. T., & Evans, F. J. Social control in the psychological experiment. *J. Pers. soc. Psychol.,* 1965, 1, 189-200.

Sampson, R. V. *The psychology of power.* New York: Vintage, 1968.

Smith, M. B. Competence and socialization. In J. Clausen (Ed.), *Socialization and society.* Boston: Little, Brown, 1968. Pp. 270-320.

Stinchcombe, A. *Constructing social theories.* New York: Harcourt, Brace & World, 1968.

Wolfenstein, F. V. *The revolutionary personality.* Princeton, N.J.: Princeton Univer. Press, 1967.

PSYCHOLOGICAL ALTERNATIVES TO WAR

Morton Deutsch[*]

Columbia University

I shall assume the truth of the following propositions:

(1) A large-scale nuclear war would achieve a result that no sane man could desire.

(2) When a small war occurs, there is a risk that it may turn into a large war; this risk would be considerably enhanced by the use of nuclear weapons. In the course of many small wars, the probability of a great war would become almost a certainty.

(3) The knowledge and capacity to make nuclear and other weapons of mass destruction cannot be destroyed; they will exist as long as mankind exists.

(4) Any war in which a nuclear power is faced with the possibility of major defeat or a despairing outcome is likely to turn into a large-scale nuclear war even if nuclear disarmament had previously occurred.

(5) A hostile peace will not long endure. From these propositions it follows that, if mankind is to avoid utter disaster, we must see to it that irrational men are not in a position to initiate nuclear war, we must find alternatives to war for resolving international conflicts, and we must develop the conditions which will lead conflicting nations to select one or another of these alternatives rather than resort to war.

My discussion in this paper centers primarily on the question of: how do we take the hostility out of the hostile peace? This question proliferates into other, related questions: how do we prevent the misperceptions and misunderstandings in international relations which foster and perpetuate hostility? how do we move from a delicately balanced peace of mutual terror to a sturdy peace of mutual trust? how do we move in the direction of a world community in which law, institutions, obligations, and simple human decencies will enable

---

[*] The views expressed in this paper do not represent, nor are they necessarily similar to, the views of any organization with which the author is affiliated.

This paper will appear as a chapter in Q. Wright, W. M. Evan, and M. Deutsch (Eds.), *How to Prevent World War III* (tentative title). New York: Simon and Schuster, in press.

mankind to enjoy a more amiable life? These are the central questions which must be answered if the world is to avoid disaster. The world will never again be in a position where it cannot destroy itself.

It is well for me to emphasize that opposition to war as a means of conflict resolution does *not* connote an opposition to controversy among nations. Controversy is as desirable as it is inevitable. It prevents stagnation, it is the medium through which problems can be aired and solutions arrived at; it is the heart of social change. Our objective is not to create a world in which controversy is suppressed but rather a world in which controversy is civilized; in which it is lively rather than deadly.

I do not pretend to have answers to the difficult questions I have raised. I raise them because I have something relevant to say and because I believe it is important to confront the fundamental questions. Too often we are distracted from them by short-run urgencies. You may well ask what can a psychologist say that is relevant? A wide reading, however, of acknowledged authorities in the study of war and international relations has convinced me that the dominant conceptions of international relations are psychological in nature. Such psychological concepts as "perception," "intention," "value," "hostility," "confidence," "trust," and "suspicion" recur repeatedly in discussions of war and peace.[1]

I wish to make it clear that what I have to say in this paper is *not* based upon well-established, scientifically verified, psychological knowledge. As psychologists, we have only meager, fragmentary knowledge of how to prevent or overcome distortions in social perceptions, of how to move from a situation of mutual suspicion to a situation of mutual trust, of how to establish cooperative relationships despite intense competitive orientations, of how to prevent bargaining deadlocks. I take it for granted that we need more and better research before we may claim to speak authoritatively on these matters. However, my intent here is not to outline the research which is needed but rather to discuss these urgent matters as wisely as I can. In so doing, I shall necessarily go beyond the facts to draw upon the insights and orientations which I have developed in a research career devoted to the understanding of the conditions affecting cooperation and in a psychoanalytic practice devoted to helping people overcome their self-defeating attitudes and their interpersonal distortions. The proposals which I make in this paper flow from these personal insights and orientations. They are, I believe, consistent with the meager knowledge that we have; but it is apparent that much more research-grounded knowledge is necessary if we are ever to get beyond the stage of "informed hunches." Although my "informed hunches" are offered with personal conviction, I hope that you will understand that my research continues and that I do not plan to leave these hunches untested.

---

[1] Perhaps there has been too much psychologizing about these matters; there are, after all, critical differences between persons and nations. Not the least of these is the fact that in a deadly quarrel between people it is the quarrelers who are most apt to be killed while, in a deadly quarrel among nations, the decision-makers are rarely the ones who have the highest probability of dying. Be that as it may, I shall assume that there is some merit in viewing nations, like persons, as behaving units in an environment and to conceive of international relations in terms somewhat analogous to those of interpersonal relations.

Is War Inevitable?

Is it possible that war is inevitable, that the psychological nature of man is such that war is an indispensable outlet for his destructive urges? True, there have been wars throughout human history and men have found outlets for psychological drives of all kinds in war—sadistic, masochistic, creative, heroic, altruistic, adventurous, etc. Yet, as Jerome Frank (forthcoming) has pointed out, the historical prevalence of a behavior pattern is not proof of its inevitability. Human sacrifice in religious rites, slavery, sorcery, certain forms of child labor, etc., have largely disappeared in modern, industrialized nations although such practices have existed throughout human history.

William James, in his classic paper, "The Moral Equivalent of War" (1911), recognized that war and the military spirit produced certain virtues which are necessary to the survival of any society. However, he went on to point out that militarism and war is not the only means for achieving the virtues of self-discipline and social cohesiveness, that it is possible to find alternative means for achieving the same psychological ends. (It is of interest to note that James's suggestion for a moral equivalent to war was a "Peace Corps" of youth enlisted in an army against *Nature*.) The view that alternative means for satisfying psychological motives can always be found is, of course, a basic concept in modern psychology. Egon Brunswick (1952) went so far as to elevate "vicarious functioning" (i.e., the equivalence and mutual intersubstitutability of different behaviors in relation to goal achievement) to the defining criterion of the subject matter of psychology.

Man's makeup may always contain the psychological characteristics which have found an outlet in militarism and war. There is no reason, however, to doubt that these characteristics can find satisfactory outlets in peaceful pursuits. Aggressiveness, adventurousness, idealism, and bravery will take a peaceful or destructive outlet depending upon the social, cultural, and political conditioning of the individual and upon the behavioral possibilities which exist within his social environment. Some may assert that war provides a more natural, spontaneous, or direct outlet for hostility and aggressiveness than any peaceful alternatives. Such an assertion is based upon a fundamental misconception of war: war is a highly complex, organized social activity in which personal outlets for aggression and hostility are primarily vicarious, symbolic, indirect and infrequent for most of the participants. This is especially true for the highly mechanized warfare of modern times which largely eliminates the direct physical contact between the aggressor and his victim.[2] Moreover, it is evident that no matter what his psychological make-up, an individual, *per se*, cannot make war. War-making requires the existence of complex social institutions necessary to organize and maintain a "war machine." This is not to say that a war machine cannot be activated by the decision of strategically placed individuals. Obviously, one of the great dangers of

---

[2] War is vastly over-rated as an outlet for direct aggressiveness; it does not compare with the directness of reckless automobile driving, a boxing match, or a football game. War is defined to be such a good outlet *only* because of our cultural conditioning: the military toys children are given to play with, the identification of heroism and bravery with war in so many novels, TV dramas, and films that we all are exposed to; the definition of patriotism in military terms in so many of our public ceremonials and holidays, etc.

our era is that a small group of men have the power to create a nuclear holocaust. Even a strategically placed individual can only activate a war machine if it exists; the mass of people, not being strategically placed, cannot directly activate a war no matter what their psychological predispositions are. It is relevant to note here that research by T. Abel[3] indicates that warlike attitudes in the populace tend to follow rather than precede the outbreak of war.

The impersonal character of modern war, as Erich Fromm (1960) has pointed out, makes it difficult for an individual to comprehend fully the meaning of his actions as he kills. It is easier for most people to kill faceless symbols of human beings at a distance than to kill people with one's bare hands. Thus, if the airmen of our Strategic Air Command were suddenly ordered to fly to the Soviet Union or China (or if Soviet airmen were ordered to fly to the U.S.) to drop nuclear weapons, most of them would comply. They would, I assume, be distressed by the thought, but they would comply. Would they comply, if the killings were personal—if they had to burn, mutilate, or suffocate the victims one by one? The psychological danger of modern, impersonal war is not that it is a good outlet for aggression but rather, to the contrary, that it does not permit the button-pusher to appreciate fully the destructive nature of his actions. Were he to do so, his destructive actions might be inhibited rather than encouraged.

Misperceptions Which Lead to War

Neither war nor peace is psychologically inevitable. Exaggeration of the inevitability of war contributes to a self-fulfilling prophecy: it makes war more likely. Exaggeration of the inevitability of peace does not stimulate the intense effort necessary to create the conditions for a durable peace: a stable peace has to be invented and constructed. There is nothing inevitable about it.

A fundamental theorem of the psychological and social sciences is that man's behavior is determined by the world he perceives. Perception is not, however, always veridical to the world which is being perceived. There are a number of reasons why perceptions may be distorted. I would like to consider with you five common causes of misperception, to illustrate the operation of each in international relations, and to indicate how these misperceptions can be counteracted or prevented.

1. *The perception of any act is determined both by our perception of the act itself and by our perception of the context in which the act occurs.* Thus, the statement "You did that extremely well" will be perceived rather differently if a Captain is saying it to a Private than if a Private is saying it to a Captain. A common source of distorted social perception results from misconceptions or false perceptions of context. The contexts of socials acts are often not immediately given in perception and often they are not obvious. When the context is not obvious, we tend to assume a familar context—i.e., the context which is most likely in terms of our own experience. Since both the present situations and past experiences of the actor and the perceiver may be rather different, it is not surprising that they will supply different contexts and interpret the same act quite differently. Misunderstandings of this sort, of course, are very likely when the actor and the perceiver

---

[3] T. Abel is cited in Jessie Bernard (1957).

come from rather different cultural backgrounds and they are not fully aware of these differences. The stock conversation of returning tourists consists of amusing or embarrassing anecdotes based upon misunderstandings of this sort.

Urie Bronfenbrenner's first-hand observations (1961) lead him to conclude that the Soviets and Americans have a similar view of one another; each says more or less the same things about the other. For example, each states: "*They* are the aggressors"; *their* government exploits and deludes the people"; "the mass of *their* people is not really sympathetic to the regime"; "*they* cannot be trusted"; "*their* policy verges on madness"; etc.

It is my contention that mutual distortions such as those described above arise, in part, because of an inadequate understanding of the other's context. Take, for instance, the Soviet Union's reluctance to conclude any disarmament agreement which contains adequate provisions for international inspection and control. We view this as a device to prevent an agreement or to subvert any agreement on disarmament which might be worked out. However, as Joseph Nogee has pointed out in his monograph on "The Diplomacy of Disarmament" (1960, p. 275): "Under present circumstances, any international control group reflecting the realities of political power would inevitably include a majority of non-Communist nations. Decisions involving actual and potential interests vital to the USSR would have to be made continuously by a control board the majority of whose members would represent social and economic systems the USSR considers inherently hostile. Any conflicts would ultimately have to be resolved by representatives of governments, and it is assumed that on all major decisions the capitalist nations would vote as a bloc . . . . Thus, for the Soviet Union, representation on a control board along the lines proposed by the West would be inherently inequitable . . . ."

I may assert that one can subjectively test the creditability of the Soviet position by imagining our own reactions if the Soviet bloc could consistently out-vote us at the UN or on an international disarmament control board. Under such conditions, in the present world situation, would we conclude an agreement which did not give us the security of a veto? I doubt it. Similarly, one can test the creditability of the American position by imagining that the Soviet Union had experienced a Pearl Harbor in a recent war and that it had no open access to information concerning the military preparations of the United States. Under such circumstances, in the present world situation, would it be less concerned about inspection and control than we are? I doubt it.

The distorted view that "the mass of their people are not really sympathetic to the regime" is also based upon an inadequate view of each other's total situation. In effect, we ask ourselves if Soviet citizens had the choice between (a) living in Russia if it were like the United States with its high standard of living and its political system of civil liberties, and (b) living in the present day Soviet Union, which would they choose? We think the answer is obvious, but isn't it clear that the question is wrong? The relevant comparison for them is between their past and their present or future: their present and future is undoubtedly vastly superior to their past. Similarly, the Soviet view is that a comparison between (a) Soviet society with its full employment and expanding economy with (b) capitalism in a permanent depression crisis would favor the Soviet Union. Perhaps it would, but is this the relevant comparison?

How can we prevent and overcome distortions and misunderstandings of this sort? Obviously, more communication, a great increase in interchanges of scholars, artists, politicians, tourists, and the like might be helpful. However, I think we should take cognizance of the findings of the vast body of research on intergroup contact: casual contact of limited duration is more likely to support deeply rooted distortions than remove them. To have any important effect, contact must be prolonged, functional, and intimate.

I suggest that the most important principle to follow in international communication on issues where there is controversy is one suggested by Anatol Rapoport (forthcoming). He advocates that each side be required to state the position of the other side to the other side's complete satisfaction before either side advocates its own position. Certainly the precedure would not eliminate all conflict but it would eliminate those conflicts based upon misunderstanding. It forces one to place the other's action in a context which is acceptable to the other and, as a consequence, prevents one from arbitrarily rejecting the other's position as unreasonable or badly motivated. This is the strategy followed by the good psychotherapist. By communicating to the patient his full understanding of the patient's behavior and by demonstrating the appropriateness of the patient's assumptions to the patient's behavior and past experiences, he creates the conditions under which the current validity of the patient's assumptions can be examined. The attempt to challenge or change the patient's behavior without mutual understanding of its assumptions usually produces only a defensive adherence to the challenged behavior.

2. *Our perceptions of the external world are often determined indirectly by the information we receive from others rather than by our direct experiences.* Human communication, like perception itself, is always selective. The perception of an event is usually less detailed, more abstract, and less complex than the event which is perceived; the communication about an event is also likely to be less detailed and less complex than its perception. The more human links there are in the communication of information about any event, the more simplified and distorted will be the representation of the event. Distortion in communication tends to take characteristic form: on the one hand, there is a tendency to accentuate the unusual, bizarre, controversial, deviant, violent, and unexpected; on the other hand, there is a tendency for communicators who are communicating to their superiors to communicate only that information which fits in with the preconceptions of their superiors.

If we examine our sources of information about international affairs, we see that they are particularly vulnerable to distorting influences. There are only a small number of American reporters in any country; they do not necessarily work independently of one another. They are under subtle pressure to report items which will catch the reader's interest and conform to their publisher's viewpoint. In a period of hostility between nations, these conditions are not conducive to getting a clear understanding of how events are perceived by the other side or a clear understanding of the other's frame of reference.

I suggest that we should recognize the dangers inherent in not perceiving the other side's point of view regularly. Recognizing these dangers, shouldn't we offer to make arrangements with the Soviet Union whereby we would each be enabled to present our own point of view over the other's radio and TV and in their leading newspapers?

Suppose the Soviet leaders are afraid to participate on a reciprocating basis, should we make the offer anyway? My answer is in the form of a question: do we have anything to lose by understanding their viewpoint as well as we can; wouldn't "truth squads" adequately protect us from deliberate attempts to mislead us?

3. *Our perceptions of the world are often very much influenced by the need to conform to and agree with the perceptions of other people.* Thus, in some communities it would be difficult for an individual to survive if he perceived Negroes as his social equals or if he perceived Communist China as having legitimate grievances against the United States. If he acted upon his perceptions he would be ostracized socially; if he conformed to the perceptions of other people without changing his own perceptions, so that they were similar to those prevalent in his community, he might feel little self-respect.

It is my impression that most social and political scientists, most specialists in international relations, most intellectuals who have thought about it, and many of our political leaders personally favor the admission of Communist China into the UN and favor our taking the initiative in attempting to normalize our relations with Communist China. Yet, conformity pressures keep silent most of us who favor such a change in policy. The strength of these conformity pressures in the United States on this issue is so great that it is difficult to think of Communist China or to talk about it in any terms except those which connote absolute, incorrigible evil. I believe this is an extremely dangerous situation, because without a fundamental change in United States-Chinese relations the world may be blown up shortly after China has acquired a stockpile of hydrogen bombs; this may take less than a decade.

How can we break through the veil of conformity and its distorting influences? Asch's (1956) insightful studies of conformity pressures point the way. His studies reveal that when the monolithic social front of conformity is broken by even one dissenter, other potential dissenters feel freer to break with the majority. The lesson is clear: those who dissent must express their opinions so that they are heard by others. If they do so, they may find more agreement than they anticipate.

4. *A considerable body of psychological research*[4] *indicates that an individual attempts to perceive his environment in such a way that it is consistent with his self-perception.* If an indvidual feels afraid, he tends to perceive his world as frightening; if he feels hostile, he is likely to see it as frustrating or unjust; if he feels weak and vulnerable, he is apt to see it as exploitative and powerful; if he is torn by self-doubt and self-conflict, he will tend to see it as at odds with him. Not only does an individual tend to see the external world in such a way as to justify his feelings and beliefs but also so as to justify his behavior. If an individual is a heavy smoker, he is apt to perceive cigarette smoking as less injurious to health than a nonsmoker; if he drives a car and injures a pedestrian, he is likely to blame the pedestrian; if he invests in something (e.g., a munitions industry), he will attempt to justify and protect his investment. Moreover, there is much evidence that an individual tends to perceive the different parts of his world as consistent with one another. Thus, if somebody likes you, you expect him to dislike someone who dislikes you. If somebody disagrees with you, you

---

[4] Much of this research is summarized in various articles in Katz (1960).

are likely to expect him to agree with someone who disagrees with you.

The danger of the pressure for consistency is that it often leads to an oversimplified black-white view of the world. Take, for instance, the notions that since the interests of the United States and the Soviet Union are opposed in some respects, we must be opposed to or suspicious of anything that the Communists favor and must regard any nation that desires friendly relations with the Soviet Union as opposed to the United States. If the Soviet Union is against colonialism in Africa, must we be for it? If nations in Latin America wish to establish friendly, commercial relations with the Communist nations, must we feel threatened? If Canada helps Communist China by exporting food to it, must we suspect its loyalty to us? Are nations which are not for us necessarily for the Communists? The notions expressed in affirmative answers to these questions are consistent with the view that the conflict between the United States and the Soviet Union can only be ended by total defeat for one or the other. But is it not possible that the conflict can be resolved so that both sides are better off than they are now? Recognition of this latter possibility may suggest that what benefits the Soviet Union does not necessarily harm us, and that nations with amicable relations with both the United States and the Soviet Union may be an important asset in resolving the cold war before it turns into a hot one.

The pressure for self-consistency often leads to rigid, inflexible positions because it may be difficult to change a position that one has committed oneself to publicly without fear of loss of face. To some extent, I believe this is our situation vis-à-vis the admission of Communist China to the United Nations and with regard to our policies toward Cuba. We are frozen into positions which are unresponsive to changing circumstances because a change in our positions would seem to us to be admission of mistaken judgment which could lead to a loss of face.

What can we do to avoid the "consistency of little minds" and the rigidities of false pride? These dangers to accurate perception are most likely when an individual feels under threat, when his self-esteem is at stake. I think in such circumstances it is prudent to seek the advice and counsel of trusted friends who are not so emotionally involved in the issues. Thus, I think it would be wise to consult with such nations as Brazil, France, and Great Britain on our policy toward Cuba and Communist China precisely because they do not have as deep an involvement with these countries as we do. Similarly, consultation with more or less neutral nations such as India, Sweden, Austria, and Nigeria might prevent us from developing an oversimplified view of the nature of our relations with the Soviet Union.

5. Ichheiser (1949) has described a mechanism, similar to that of projection, which leads to misunderstandings in human relations: the *mote-beam mechanism*. It consists in perceiving certain characteristics in others which we do not perceive in ourselves. Thus, the characteristics are perceived as though they were peculiar traits of the others and, hence, the differences between the others and ourselves are accentuated. Since the traits we are unable or unwilling to recognize in others are usually traits we consider to be undesirable, the mote-beam mechanism results in a view of the other as peculiarly shameful or evil. Thus, although many of us who live here in the North easily recognize the shameful racial discrimination and segregation in the South,

we avoid a clear awareness of the pervasive racial discrimination in our own communities.

Similarly, in international relations it is easy to recognize the lack of political liberties in the Soviet Union, their domination of the nations in Eastern Europe, their obstructiveness in the United Nations, etc., but it is difficult for us to recognize similar defects in the United States: e.g., the disenfranchisement of most Negro voters in many states, our domination of Latin America, our unfair treatment of the American Indian, our stubbornness in the UN in pretending that the representative from Taiwan is the representative of Mainland China. Since the mote-beam mechanism, obviously, works on both sides, there is a tendency for each side to view the other as peculiarly immoral and for the views to mirror one another.

What can be done to make the mote-beam mechanism ineffective? The proposals I have made to counteract the effects of the other type of perceptual distortions are all relevant here. In addition, I would suggest that the mote-beam mechanism breeds on a moral-evaluative approach to behavior, on a readiness to condemn defects rather than to understand the circumstances which produced them. Psychoanalytic work suggests that the capacity to understand rather than to condemn is largely determined by the individual's sense of self-esteem, by his ability to cope with the external problem confronting him, and by his sense of resoluteness in overcoming his own defects. By analogy, I would suggest that we in the United States will have less need to overlook our own shortcomings or to be fascinated with the defects of others to the extent that we have a thriving society which is resolutely overcoming its own problems of racial prejudice, economic stagnation, and lack of dedication to common public purposes.

While distortions in perception are very common for the reasons I have outlined above, it is also true that, in many instances, everyday experience provides a corrective to the distortions. When reality is sufficiently compelling, and when the contact with reality occurs with sufficient frequency, the distortions will be challenged and may yield. However, there are circumstances which tend to perpetuate and rigidify distortions. Let me briefly describe three major reasons for the perpetuation of distortions:

1. *A major psychological investment has been made in the distortion.* As a consequence, the individual may anticipate that giving up the investment will require drastic personal reorganization which might result in personal instability and the loss of social face and might precipitate unknown dangers. Anyone who has done psychoanalytic therapy with neurotic patients knows that no matter how costly and painful it is, a distorted but familiar mode of adjustment is hard to give up until the patient has sufficient self-confidence or confidence in his analyst to venture into unfamiliar terrain.

With regard to international relations, I think we have to consider that a disarmed world, a world without external tensions to justify internal political policies, a world without violence as a means of bringing about changes in the status quo would be an unfamiliar world: a world in which some would feel that their vested interests might be destroyed. For example, I am sure that many military men, scientists, industrialists, workers, and investors fear a disarmed world because they anticipate that their skills and knowledge will become obsolete, or they will lose social status, or they will lose financially. These fears have to be dealt with constructively or else they may produce defensive adherence to the views which justify a hostile, armed world.

I suggest that we must carefully plan to anticipate the psychological difficulties in the transition to a peaceful, disarmed world. As a basic strategy to overcome some of these difficulties, I would recommend that we consider a policy of *overcompensating* those who might be adversely affected by the change: we want to change the nature of their psychological investment from an investment in military pursuits to one in peaceful pursuits.

2. *Certain distorted perceptions perpetuate themselves because they lead the individual to avoid contact or meaningful communication with the object or person being perceived.* This is especially true when the distortions lead to aversion or hostility toward the object being perceived. For example, for reasons which go back to my childhood and about which I am not clear, I have a strong aversion to coffee, becoming nauseated at the thought of drinking it. As a consequence, I avoid coffee and my aversion is perpetuated. Newcomb (1947) has described a similar process of *autistic hostility* in interpersonal relations in which a hostile impulse may give rise to barriers to communication behind which a persistent attitude is protected. Similarly, in international relations, hostile attitudes between the U.S. and Communist China produce barriers to communication which eliminate the possibility of a change in attitudes. Here, the best antidote would seem to be communication which followed the rules of procedure suggested by Anatol Rapoport.

3. Merton, in his classic paper on *The Self-fulfilling Prophecy* (1957), has pointed out that distortions are often perpetuated because they may evoke new behavior which makes the originally *false* conception come true. The specious validity of the self-fulfilling prophecy perpetuates a reign of error. The prophet will cite the actual course of events as proof that he was right from the very beginning. The dynamics of the self-fulfilling prophecy help to explain individual pathology—e.g., the anxious student who, afraid he might fail, worries so much that he cannot study, with the consequence that he does fail. It also contributes to our understanding of social pathology—e.g., how prejudice and discrimination against the Negro keeps him in a position which seems to justify the prejudice and discrimination. So too in international relations. If the representatives of East and West believe that war is likely and either side attempts to increase its military security vis-à-vis the other, the other side's response will justify the initial move. The dynamics of an arms race has the inherent quality of a "folie à deux," wherein the self-fulfilling prophecies mutually reinforce one another.

Psychological Alternatives to War

In the preceding section, I have attempted to indicate some of the sources of misperception in international relations and some of the conditions which tend to perpetuate the distortions or make them come true. Our present international situation suggests that the distortions have come true. The East and the West are in an arms race and in the throes of an ideological conflict in which each side, in reality, threatens and feels threatened by the other. How can we reverse this hostile spiral which is likely to result in mutual annihilation?

As I present some specific proposal, I will indicate the psychological assumptions underlying them: assumptions which come from theoretical and experimental research I have been doing on interpersonal trust and suspicion and interpersonal bargaining (Deutsch, 1949; 1958; 1960a; 1960b; 1961; Deutsch & Krauss, 1960).

1. *There are social situations which do not allow the possibility of "rational" behavior so long as the conditions for mutual trust do not exist.* Let me illustrate with a two-person game that I have used in my experimental work on trust and suspicion. In this game, each player has to choose between pressing a red button and a green button: if both players press the red button each loses $1.00; if both players press the green button, each wins $1.00; if Player A presses the green button and Player B presses the red button, A loses $2.00 and B gains $2.00; and if Player B presses the green button and Player A presses the red button, B loses $2.00 and A gains $2.00. A superficial rational calculation of self-interest would lead each player to press his red button since he either wins as much as he can or loses as little as he can this way. But, if both players consider only their self-interest and press their red buttons, each of them will lose. Players oriented toward defeating the other player or toward their self-interest only, when matched with similarly oriented players, do in fact choose the red button and do end up losing consistently.

I believe our current international situation is in some respects similar to the game I have described. A characteristic symptom of such "nonrational situations" is that any attempt on the part of any individual or nation to increase its own welfare or security (without regard to the security or welfare of the others) is self-defeating. In such situations the only way that an individual or nation can avoid being trapped in a mutually reinforcing, self-defeating cycle is to attempt to change the situation so that a basis of mutual trust can develop.

Comprehension of the basic nature of the situation we are in suggests that *mutual security* rather than national security should be our objective. The basic military axiom for both the East and West should be that *military actions should only be taken which increase the military security of both sides; military actions which give a military superiority to one side or the other should be avoided.* The military forces of both sides should be viewed as having the *common* primary aim of preventing either side (one's own or the other) from starting a deliberate or accidental war. Awareness of this common aim could be implemented by regular meetings of military leaders from East and West; the establishment of a continuing joint technical group of experts to work together to formulate disarmament and inspection plans; the establishment of mixed military units on each other's territory (see Kelman, forthcoming); etc. The key point we must recognize is that if military inferiority is dangerous, so is military "superiority"; it is dangerous for either side to feel *tempted* or *frightened* into military action.

2. *Our research indicates that mutual trust is most likely to occur when people are positively oriented to each other's welfare—i.e., when each has a stake in the other's doing well rather than poorly.* Unfortunately, the East and West, at present, appear to have a greater stake in each other's defects and difficulties than in each other's welfare. Thus, the Communists gloat over our racial problems and our unemployment and we do likewise over their agricultural failures and their lack of political liberties.

We should, I believe, do everything possible to reverse this unfortunate state of affairs. First of all, we might start by accepting each other's existence as *legitimate* and by rejecting the view that the existence of the other, *per se*, is a threat to our own existence. As Talcott Parsons (forthcoming) has pointed out, there is considerable merit in viewing the ideological battle between East and West in the world community as somewhat akin to our own two-party system at the national level. An ideological conflict presupposes a common frame of reference in terms of which the ideological differences make sense. The ideologies of East and West do share many values in common: technological advance, economic development, universal education, encouragement of science, cultural progress, health advances, peace, national autonomy, etc. We must accept the possibility that one side or the other will obtain an advantage on particular issues when there is a conflict about the procedures for attaining these objectives. But this is not catastrophic unless each side views the conflict as an all-or-none conflict of survival.

To establish a basis for mutual trust we, of course, have to go beyond the recognition of each other's legitimacy to a relationship which promotes cooperative bonds. This would be facilitated by recognition of the profound human similarities which link all mankind together. The human situation no longer makes it feasible to view the world in terms of "we" or "they"; in the modern era, our destinies are linked objectively; the realistic attitude is "we" *and* "they." More specifically, I think our situation would be improved rather than worsened if the people in the various Communist nations had a high standard of living, were well educated, and were reaping the fruits of the scientific revolution. Similarly, I think we would be better off rather than worse off if the political leaders of the Communist nations felt they were able to provide their citizenry with sufficient current gratifications and signs of progress to have their support; and if they were sufficiently confident of their own society not to fear intensive contacts with different points of view.

The implication of the above calls for a fundamental reorientation of our foreign policy toward the Communist nations. We must initiate cooperative trade policies, cooperative research programs, cooperative cultural exchanges, cooperative loan programs, cooperative agricultural programs, etc., and we must not be concerned if, at first, they appear to benefit more than we. We are, after all, more affluent than the Communist nations. Our objective should be simply to promote the values of economic well-being, educational attainment, scientific and industrial development which we share in common and which we believe are necessary to a stable, peaceful world. Let me emphasize here that I think this is especially important to do in our relations with Communist China. (It amazes me constantly that so little public attention is given to the extraordinary dangers involved in allowing our current relations with Communist China to continue in their present form.) The Communist nations (especially China) are likely to be suspicious of our motives, may even rebuff our initial attempts to establish cooperative relationships, and will undoubtedly not feel grateful for any assistance they may receive. These reactions are all to be expected because of the present context of international relations. Our policy of cooperation must be a *sustained* policy of *massive reconciliation* which does not reciprocate hostility and which always leaves open the possibility of mutual cooperation despite prior rebuff. In my view, we must sustain a cooperative initiative until it succeeds; in the long run, the alternative to mutual cooperation is mutual doom.

My rationale here is very simple. We have no realistic alternative but to coexist with the Soviet Union and Communist China. Coexistence among nations will be considerably less dangerous if we each recognize that poverty, illiteracy, economic difficulties, internal strain and crisis in a nation are likely to produce reckless, belligerent international policies rather than peaceful ones. After all, the delinquents and criminals in our local communities rarely come from those segments of our populace that are successfully dealing with their own internal problems or that are well integrated into and accepted by the broader community.

3. *To induce a cooperative orientation in another and to develop adherence to a set of rules or social norms for regulating interaction and for resolving disputes, it is necessary: (a) to demonstrate that one's own orientation to the other is cooperative; (b) to articulate fair rules which do not systematically disadvantage the other; (c) to demonstrate one's adherence to these rules; (d) to demonstrate to the other that he has more to gain (or less to lose) in the short and long run by adherence to the rules than by violation of them; and (e) to recognize that misunderstandings and disputes about compliance will inevitably occur and hence are not necessarily tokens of bad faith.*

The importance of a cooperative orientation to the development of mutual trust has been discussed above; it is reiterated here to emphasize the significance of a cooperative orientation in the development of any workable system of rules to regulate international relations. In discussion and negotiations concerning arms control and disarmament, there has been much emphasis on developing rules and procedures for inspection and control which do not rely upon cooperative orientations; surveillance of the other's actions is to replace trust in the other's intent. I think it is reasonable to assert that no social order can exist for long without a minimum basis in mutual trust; surveillance cannot do the trick by itself. This is not to deny the necessity of surveillance to buttress trust, to enable one's trustworthiness to be confirmed and one's suspicions to be rejected. However, I would question the view which seems to characterize our approach to arms control negotiations: namely, the less trust, the more surveillance. A more reasonable view might state that when there is little trust the only kinds of agreements which are feasible are ones which allow for simple, uncomplicated but highly reliable techniques of surveillance. Lack of trust between equals, paradoxically, calls for but also limits surveillance when the negotiations are not part of an effective community.

The inducing of adherence to rules to establish orderly relations among nations requires fair rules. It is easier to state the characteristics of an unfair than a fair rule: a rule is unfair if the party favoring it would be unwilling to accept it, were he in the situation of the other side. The history of disarmament negotiations suggests that neither the Soviet Union nor the United States has been interested in proposing fair rules. Nogee (1960) asserts (p. 282): "Every plan offered by either side has contained a set of proposals calculated to have wide popular appeal. Every set has included at least one feature that the other side could not possibly accept, thus forcing a rejection. Then the proposing side has been able to claim that the rejection is opposed to the idea of disarmament *in toto*. The objectionable feature may be thought of as the 'joker' in every series." He further points out (p. 281) "Disarmament negotiations themselves have become a weapon in the cold war. Speeches made in commission, committee, and Plenary Assembly have more often been designed to influence different segments of opinion than to reach an accommodation with the other nations represented at the conference table."

How can the formulation of fair rules be facilitated? A suggestion by Bertrand Russell (forthcoming) is pertinent here. He proposes the formation of a conciliation committee composed of the best minds from the East and West, with some of the leading thinkers from neutral nations also included. Such a committee, meeting together in quiet, unpublicized deliberation, might be given the responsibility of formulating rules which would be acceptable to both sides. The hope is that, with sufficient time, intelligent men of good will whose perspectives reach beyond the cold war may be able to formulate rules that are fair to all mankind.

Fair rules for certain matters, of course, do already exist. Some of these rules are written in the Charter of the United Nations, some in the decisions of the International Court of Justice at the Hague, some in the legal traditions which have governed various aspects of international relations through the centuries (e.g., the international postal system, international trade, "freedom of the seas," ambassadorial rights). As Arthur Larson (forthcoming) has pointed out, there is much need for legal research to make the existing body of international rules accessible and up-to-date and establish a legal machinery which is also accessible and adapted to settling the kinds of disputes that today's world produces. In addition, there is a need to induce acceptance of the body of law and legal machinery by the persons affected.

How to induce acceptance of such rules once they are formulated? It seems clear that if we wish to induce others to accept fair rules, our own course of conduct must exemplify supra-nationalistic or universalistic values; it must constantly indicate our willingness to live up to the values that we expect others to adhere to. We must give up the doctrine of "special privilege" and the "double standard" in judging our own conduct and that of the Communist nations. Can we really convince others that we are for international law when we reserve the right (in the so-called Connally amendment) unilaterally to declare a controversy to be a domestic matter and hence outside the World Court's jurisdiction? Can we really be persuasive when we reserve the right to intervene unilaterally against the establishment of a Communist nation in the Western hemisphere but deny a similar right to the Soviet Union and China? Do we promote international order when we use our power in the United Nations to prevent the admission of the most populous nation in the world and, thus, exclude it from discussion of matters which relate to its interests? We only undermine the possibility of establishing a world rule of law by declaring our sovereign interests to be above the law: the deepest legal traditions in all parts of the world rest upon the view that the sovereign is not above the law—he is under the law.

Would adherence to universalistic values and international law on our part allow a violator of fair rules of international conduct to profit and, thus, encourage his violation? Certainly, it makes no sense to encourage violations. However, an effective system of rules clearly defines what a violation is, specifies the procedure for ascertaining whether an act is a violation, prescribes the sanctions to be invoked against violations, and indicates the rights of self-defense or redress to the aggrieved party. Such a system presumably deters violation by making it unprofitable but it also limits and controls the response to violation so that it is appropriate and under law. We must, of course, be prepared to discourage violations of fair practices and to defend ourselves against them, but we cannot afford to do so in disregard of the universalistic values we espouse.

I suggest that our *attitude* toward violations should express, simultaneously, firm resistance to violations when they occur and clear receptivity to the possibility of renewing cooperative relations. Recriminations and a punitive, self-righteous attitude toward violations are unlikely to encourage the development of a desire for normal, civilized relations. Retaliation (counterthreat in response to threat, counteraggression in response to aggression) tends, rather, to nourish and intensify an existing or incipient hostile spiral. Policy guided by the need to demonstrate that one is "man enough" to be tough, that one isn't "chicken," tends to change situations where there is room for negotiation into competitive struggles for "face." Once this occurs, it becomes difficult indeed to yield without a severe loss of self-esteem.

4. *Mutual trust can occur even under circumstances where the parties involved are unconcerned with each other's welfare providing their relations to an outside, third party are such that this trust in him can substitute for their trust in one another.* This indirect or mediated trust is, of course, a most common form of trust in interpersonal relations. Since we exist in a community in which various types of third parties—the law, the police, public opinion, mutual friends, etc.—can be mobilized to buttress an agreement, we can afford to be trusting even with a stranger in most circumstances. Unfortunately, in a bipolar world community, which does not contain powerful "third parties," it is difficult to substitute mediated trust for direct trust.

There are two policy implications of this fact which I would like to stress. The first is the importance of encouraging the development of several strong, neutral groups of nations and the development of a strong, neutral United Nations that might mediate in conflicts between East and West. We have, of course, to be aware of the dangers of a *tertius gaudens*, in which a third party would attempt to play East and West off against one another to its own advantage. However, what I am suggesting is not a third bloc but rather a group of diverse, independent nations with criss-crossing interests that have the common objective of developing and maintaining an orderly world. In a neutral United Nations,[5] with a large group of independent voters, we would sometimes find ourselves on the losing side. But can we afford a United Nations in which the other side has little chance of ever winning a dispute with us?

The second implication follows from the realization that strong, responsible, independent nations and a strong, neutral United Nations do not yet exist and will take time to develop. Where no strong external community exists, it is important to recognize that bargaining—i.e., the attempt to find a mutually satisfactory agreement in circumstances where there is a conflict of interest—cannot afford to be guided by a Machiavellian or "outwitting the other" attitude. Where no external community exists to compel agreement, the critical problem in bargaining is to establish sufficient community between the bargainers that a mutually satisfactory agreement becomes possible: the question

---

[5] For a proposal to neutralize the United Nations, see Louis Sohn (forthcoming).

of who obtains the minor advantages or disadvantages in a negotiation is trivial in comparison to the question of whether an agreement can be reached which leaves both parties better off than a lack of agreement. I stress this point because some political scientists and economists, misled by the fact that bargaining within a strong community can often fruitfully be conducted with a Machiavellian attitude, unwittingly assume that the same would be true where no real community exists.

In concluding this section, let me quote from a monograph on the *Causes of Industrial Peace* (National Planning Association, 1953, p. 92) which lists the conditions that have led to peaceful settlement of disputes under collective bargaining:

1. There is full acceptance by management of the collective bargaining process and of unionism as an institution. The company considers a strong union an asset to management.
2. The union fully accepts private ownership and operation of the industry; it recognizes that the welfare of its members depends upon the successful operation of the business.
3. The union is strong, responsible, and democratic.
4. The company stays out of the union's internal affairs; it does not seek to alienate the workers' allegiance to their union.
5. Mutual trust and confidence exist between the parties. There have been no serious ideological incompatibilities.
6. Neither party to bargaining has adopted a legalistic approach to the solution of problems in the relationship.
7. Negotiations are "problem-centered"—more time is spent on day-to-day problems than on defining abstract principles.
8. There is widespread union-management consultation and highly developed information-sharing.
9. Grievances are settled promptly, in the local plant whenever possible. There is flexibility and informality within the procedure.

This is in accord with our discussion of the basic conditions for world peace: namely, the necessity of developing attitudes which consciously stress mutual acceptance, mutual welfare, mutual strength, mutual interest, and mutual trust and the necessity of developing approaches to disputes which consistently emphasize full communication, willingness to negotiate, and the specific issues in dispute rather than the ideological frame of reference of the parties in dispute.

The Conflict Between East and West

Underlying my discussion throughout this paper has been the thesis that the conflict between East and West can be resolved peacefully. This thesis grows out of the assumption that the only alternative to peace is mutual catastrophe. The conflict must be resolved peacefully, but can it be?

Public statements of the leaders of the two blocs define the conflict as a confrontation of two mutually irreconcilable ideologies; and we must acknowledge that basic ideological differences do exist. On the other hand, it must be borne in mind that neither the United States nor the USSR closely resembles its ideological "ideal type." Neither Karl Marx nor Adam Smith would recognize his offspring.

But the conflict of the Cold War has intensified our perception of ideological differences, while at the same time reducing our ability to perceive similarities. Thus, we in the West see a conflict between "free societies and a totalitarian system that is attempting to dominate the world." At the same time, our counterparts in the East see a conflict between "a system that represents the interests of the masses of the people and the imperialist, capitalist ruling cliques that wish to continue their exploitation of the people." Both descriptions are essentially mirror images of each other, each side claiming that their side stands for just, universalistic values which are opposed by the other side. We, in the West, however, see human justice as being threatened by the expansionist tendencies of the East while the leaders in the East see human justice being thwarted by the West's attempt to maintain the status-quo and to stem (what they consider to be) the natural tide of history.

The dominant theme of Freudian psychology is that the manifest life of the mind—i.e., what men know or pretend to know about the motives of their behavior—is often merely a socially acceptable rationalization of their unrecognized or latent motives. The difference between the manifest and latent content of behavior results from the need to present one's behavior to oneself, as well as to others, so as not to lose social or self-esteem. This need to "maintain face" can, of course, in turn be a determiner of behavior. I suggest that, although there are basic ideological differences between the East and West, the intensity of the ideological struggle primarily reflects an anachronistic power struggle between nations that have defined their prestige and security in terms of world leadership. The ideological differences within the West (e.g., between the U.S. and Portugal) or within the East (e.g., between Russia and China) are often as gross as those between East and West.

I suggest that if the United States and Russia were both capitalist or both communist nations, a similar struggle would have developed so long as each entertained some conception of itself as the leading world power. DeTocqueville anticipated this development in his book, *Democracy in America*, written in the 1830's before communism existed as a political ideology. Moreover, I suggest that similar power struggles can be expected with a somewhat altered cast as Western Europe re-emerges as a cohesive, powerful group, as Communist China develops, as some of the nations in Africa, Latin America, and Asia grow in strength. As more and more countries develop their economic potentials, it is likely that power will become more widely diffused and that the present conflict between the United States and the Soviet Union will be viewed as largely irrelevant by the rest of the world.

Traditionally, the quest for world power has been closely bound to strivings for national security, economic dominance, and/or international prestige or influence. The quest for power has commonly taken the form of the attempt to establish military supremacy. In previous sections of this paper, I have stressed the anachronism of the drive for military supremacy in the age of missiles and hydrogen bombs. Similarly, I believe the more powerful nations are beginning to recognize that the best opportunities for economic exploitation will arise from scientific research and development rather than from colonial domination, Eastern or Western style.

However, the quest for international prestige and influence is, I believe, a reasonable one for all societies. Hence we must find alternative social institutions and processes to militarism and war by which this quest can be pursued. Etzioni (forthcoming) has suggested a number of criteria which are relevant to the kinds of social institutions which should be created. Namely, the international competition for prestige should involve many different kinds of contests which are repeated at frequent intervals so that defeat is never *total* or irreversible. Moreover, he proposes that there be many different contestants in every contest so that competition is diffuse rather than sharply focussed. I further propose that competition be centered about achievements which represent genuine accomplishments of which all mankind can be proud.

Specifically, I suggest that the United Nations (or some other organization which includes Communist China) organize a series of periodic international contests which would enable the different nations of the world to reveal their achievements and progress in such fields as art, music, literature, the various sciences, space exploration, education, economic development, agriculture, sports, ballet, the theatre, cooking, architecture, medicine, women's fasions, the domestic arts, children's books, etc. The contests should be diverse enough to permit each national culture to display its unique attainments. The rules should require that the knowledge, skills, and techniques of the contest winners be made freely available to every nation. Awards might be granted on two separate bases: the relative level of absolute achievement and the relative amount of progress since the last contest. It is assumed that the societies who win many contests will be the ones who are effective in developing a culture that is richly creative and a populace who is educated, talented, and resourceful. There are, of course, difficulties in implementing such a proposal: in developing contests and rules which are not stacked for or against any nations. However, since the kinds of contests I am proposing already exist within many nations, there is a vast body of experience which can be drawn upon to develop workable rules.

I suggest that the United States, with the co-sponsorship of the Soviet Union, take the initiative in submitting such a proposal to the United Nations. If we are to engage in international competition for prestige and influence, let it be in peaceful rather than in militaristic pursuits, let it be in achievements from which all mankind can profit, let it be in activities which promote the recognition of the common values of mankind.

I conclude my paper with an Intellectual's Manifesto: Intellectuals, Scientists, Scholars, and Academicians of the world unite: we have nothing to lose but our ideological blinders. The problems besetting the world are too serious to permit our work to be beclouded by dogma or narrowly-conceived national interest. We cannot afford to let the slogans and categories of ideological conflict dominate our intellectual analysis. We must be free to view the great problems of our time—the nuclear arms race, the tremendous disparities in standards of living among the nations of the world, racial prejudice, ideological intolerance and the rapid increase in the world's population—in a way that allows us to take advantage of the explosion in knowledge now taking place. Let us begin to replace dogmatic, ideological assertion with an open-minded, objective, factual test of our theories and hypotheses about economic development, social change, and the development of creative, responsible people. Only by so doing will our common objectives of creating a saner, comelier, and more amicable life be achieved.

REFERENCES

Asch, S. E. Studies of independence and conformity: I. A minority of one against a unanimous majority. *Psychol. Monog.*, 1956, **70**, Whole No. 416.
Bernard, J. Parties and issues in conflict. *Conflict Resol.*, 1957, **1**, 111-121.

Bronfenbrenner, U. The mirror image in Soviet-American relations. *J. Soc. Issues*, 1961, **17**, No. 3, 45-56.

Brunswick, E. The conceptual framework of modern psychology. In *International Encyclopedia of Unified Science*, Chicago: Univ. of Chicago, 1952.

Deutsch, M. A theory of cooperation and competition. *Hum. Relat.*, 1949, **2**, 129-152.

Deutsch, M. Trust and suspicion. *Conflict Resol.*, 1958, **2**, 265-279.

Deutsch, M. The effect of motivational orientation upon trust and suspicion. *Hum. Relat.*, 1960a, **13**, 123-140.

Deutsch, M. Trust, trustworthiness, and the F scale. *J. Abn. Soc. Psychol.*, 1960b, **61**, 138-140.

Deutsch, M. The face of bargaining. *Operations Res.*, 1961, **9**, 866-897.

Deutsch, M. and Krauss, R. M. The effect of threat upon interpersonal bargaining. *J. Abn. Soc. Psychol.*, 1960, **61**, 181-189.

Etzioni, A. International prestige, competition and coexistence. *In* Q. Wright, W. M. Evan and M. Deutsch (Eds.), *How to Prevent World War III* (tentative title). New York: Simon & Shuster, forthcoming.

Frank, J. The motivational basis of a world without war. *In* Q. Wright, W. M. Evan and M. Deutsch (Eds.), *op. cit.*

Fromm, E. The case for unilateral disarmament. *Daedelus*, 1960, **89**, 1015-1028.

Icheiser, G. Misunderstandings in human relations. *Amer. J. Social.*, 1949, **55** (part 2), 1-70.

James, W. The moral equivalent of war. In *Memories and Studies*. New York: Longmans, Green, 1911.

Katz, D. (Ed.), Attitude change. *Pub. Opin. Quart.*, 1960, **24**, 163-365.

Kelman, H. C. A proposal for internationalizing military force. *In* Q. Wright, W. M. Evan and M. Deutsch, *op. cit.*

Larson, A. The role of law in building peace. *In* Q. Wright, W. M. Evan and M. Deutsch, *op. cit.*

Merton, R. K. The self-fulfilling prophecy. In *Social Theory and Social Structure*. Glencoe: Free Press, 1957 (rev. ed.).

National Planning Association, *Causes of Industrial Peace*. Washington, D.C.: Nat'l. Planning Assn., 1953.

Newcomb, T. M. Autistic hostility and social reality. *Hum. Relat.*, 1947, **1**, 69-86.

Nogee, J. The diplomacy of disarmament. *Internat. Conciliation*, 526, 1960, Carnegie Endowment for International Peace.

Parsons, T. Polarization and the problem of world order. *In* Q. Wright, W. M. Evan and M. Deutsch, *op. cit.*

Rapoport, A. Aggressiveness, gamesmanship and persuasion. *In* Q. Wright, W. M. Evan and M. Deutsch, *op. cit.*

Russell, B. Psychology and East-West tension. *In* Q. Wright, W. M. Evan and M. Deutsch, *op. cit.*

Sohn, L. B. Neo-neutralism and the neutralization of the United Nations. *In* Q. Wright, W. M. Evan and M. Deutsch, *op. cit.*